# PARADISE LOST, PARADISE REGAINED

# PARADISE LOST, PARADISE REGAINED

*The True Meaning of Democracy*

Arthur D. Robbins

ACROPOLIS BOOKS
*New York*

Copyright 2012 by Arthur D. Robbins
Acropolis Books
P.O. Box 2629
New York, NY 10009
www.acropolis-newyork.com

Publisher's Cataloging-in-Publication

Robbins, Arthur D.
    Paradise lost, paradise regained : the true meaning
of democracy / by Arthur D. Robbins.
    p. cm.
    Includes bibliographical references and index.
    LCCN 2011940038
    ISBN-13: 978-0-9676127-6-8
    ISBN-10: 0-9676127-6-4

    1. Democracy.  2. Political science--Philosophy--
History.   I. Title.

JC423.R63 2012                    321.8
                                  QBI11-600203

Interior design, Kate Nichols
Jacket design, Erika Fusari
Jacket image, *Eve* by Albrecht Dürer, courtesy of Museo del Prado, Madrid

This book is composed in 10.3 Sabon

Printed in the United States of America on permanent and durable acid-free paper

10 9 8 7 6 5 4 3 2 1

*For the children everywhere—*
*May they inherit a world that is free, just, and joyous*

*A lie can go half way around the world,*
*before the truth even gets its boots on.*
*—Mark Twain*

# CONTENTS

# PREFACE ❧

S OME TIME AGO, I read a book by Kenneth M. Dolbeare entitled *Political Change in the United States: A Framework of Analysis* (1974). At the end of the book, Dolbeare suggests to the reader that he design a new form of government. This new government, a government that never existed before, would suit the whims and fancies of the reader. Dolbeare imposed no constraints, no guides to work with. This was a most unusual proposition, at once both intimidating and empowering. How could one possibly presume to create a new government, if only in the imagination? On the other hand, wouldn't it be a wonderfully liberating experience to engage in such an exercise? New possibilities would open up. One would begin to see the current government through different eyes. The future would seem brighter, seen in the light of this new government.

Well, I took up Dolbeare's challenge. I did exactly as he suggested. I borrowed from Aristotle his use of the word "virtue" and proceeded to create a new form of government. For Aristotle, "virtue" meant the excellence of a thing. The virtue of a knife is its sharpness; the virtue of a workhorse is its ability to pull heavy loads. If I wanted to create a democracy, what would be its virtue? As I understood the word "democracy" then, and still do, the virtue of democracy as a form of government is its inclusion of the maximum number of citizens in the deliberative and legislative processes.

This then became my goal—to design a government that had this virtue. It would be a government that included hundreds of thousands or maybe even millions of citizens, not as passive observers but as actual governors. There would be no other considerations. I would not worry whether or not my new government was feasible or even desirable. I would not include any other constraints. I would simply proceed with my new government, heedless and free of any second-guessing.

For the past twenty years or so, I have been living with this imaginary government in my head. It has cast a warm glow of anticipation and optimism as I have lived out the harsh realities of how government has indeed been behaving in current reality. Though I took no steps to realize the new government I had created, it nonetheless existed for me as an alternate reality to the government that did exist.* I offer *Paradise Lost, Paradise Regained: The True Meaning of Democracy* in the hope that those who read it will join me in my journey to the land of imaginary government, where new possibilities exist as realities.

Rockport, Massachusetts
June 15, 2011

---

* The reader will learn something about this imagined government in Chapter 27, "Democracy Come True."

# ACKNOWLEDGMENTS

RALPH NADER TOOK time off from his busy schedule to read this book while it was still in manuscript form. He then spent three hours on the phone with me, offering detailed criticisms and suggestions. His moral support and editorial guidance have been invaluable.

I provided the raw material. Lynne Frost has shaped it. Her dedication to her craft, her attention to detail, her invaluable suggestions, many of which required yet more hard work from me, have made this a book that both of us can be proud of.

I personally value the interior design of a book. It welcomes me with its gentle grace or it alienates me with its hasty application and aesthetic indifference. I offer my warmest gratitude to Kate Nichols for her sensitive, lyrical design. I could spend hours just looking at the table of contents.

You can't tell a book by its cover, or so they say. I will be quite content if this book is only half as good as its cover. Erika Fusari has done an excellent job of taking Albrecht Dürer's magnificent painting and creating such an engaging cover. Thank you, Albrecht. Thank you, Erika.

Devesh Shah has been most enthusiastic in his appreciation and support for this project. It was he who referred to this book as "a democracy thriller," words I can't get out of my head. Devesh, thank you so much for everything.

S.H. is dedicated to creating a better world for all of us. Her passion and determination are catching. Thank you, Sandy, for never giving up.

Thank you, Deborah, for being my first reader and for being patient with me through difficult times. I promise to try and smile.

# Introduction

## The Specter of Government

*What in me is dark,*
*Illumine; what is low, raise and support.*\*

**M**ENTION THE WORD "government" in a conversation with a friend and you will probably get a roll of the eyes, perhaps a heavy-lidded look of contempt. Most likely your friend has never given much thought to the issue and has no wish to. "Government?" he might say, "war and taxes." He might have taken a course on government and found it incomprehensible or boring. If he were to try to focus on the concept he would have a sense of something big, overpowering, distant, potentially menacing. And there the conversation would end. It is my goal to create a different kind of conversation, one in which government as a concept, as a fundamental factor in everyone's existence, becomes alive with possibilities.

### New Eyes

We go away on vacation. We return home rested with "new eyes." We look at a favorite painting that has been hanging on the wall for years, so long that it had become wallpaper. Now it stands out with the freshness and immediacy that initially drew us to it. It is my hope that *Paradise Lost, Paradise Regained: The True Meaning of Democracy* will provide the reader with a new perspective, that it will serve as a catalyst and will supply the energy necessary for a reexamination of what we have, for too long, taken for granted about our government.

The new insight we seek is not to be found in the daily news. We need something akin to a philosophical understanding, a level of abstraction

---

\* John Milton (1608–1674) was an English poet best known for his epic poem "Paradise Lost." The quotations that begin each chapter are borrowed from this masterpiece. Milton has given some of his best lines to Satan, lines that I have redirected to fit the content of my chapters. I hope Satan won't mind.

that permits us to escape the effect of day-to-day occurrences. Once we have come to understand the purpose and function of government in general, we will be equipped to study a particular government and to measure its accomplishments against our understanding of what it is that government in general should be expected to achieve.

Government is a means for organizing ourselves into a cohesive unit with an identity. In the past the unit was the tribe. Presently it is the nation-state. But the functions have not changed. We expect our government to protect us, to provide for justice, and to make it easier for us to take care of the basic necessities in life, such as food, shelter, and some kind of useful work. Government also has another function, too frequently over-looked—that of providing us with the opportunity for participation, for an expansion of our intellect and sense of self as we partake in the process of making choices that affect our collective destiny.

Our current form of government is so much an ingrained part of our lives that we often forget there are alternatives. "The government we have is the government we should have, obviously." I think most people feel that way about their government, regardless of where they live. Yet it is instructive to look elsewhere and to see how similar problems are being solved under different forms of government. Maybe there are different answers, better answers.

Reading history serves the same purpose. We can look into the past and see that not all government is the same and that different societies choose different solutions to the same problems. Ancient Athens and the Roman Republic were contemporary societies faced with similar problems: grain supply, land use, indebtedness. Yet they chose significantly different solutions. The Italian city-states developed as small-scale separate and independent societies with an experimental approach to governance while simultaneously, to the north, large-scale autocratic empires were in the making.

I believe all history is selective. This book is no exception. I have certain biases, and they will be reflected in the selection of materials and the way in which they are presented. I will be choosing examples that illustrate my point.

So, what are some of my biases? I am in favor of political democracy. I am opposed to war. I believe that democracy as a form of government is a powerful integrating force that respects individual differences and encourages individual self-development while winning the allegiance of all to the common good. It creates unity in diversity. I believe that war is destructive of human and natural resources, and that it disrespects the ecosystem upon which we all depend. I believe that one can have war or one can have democracy, but one cannot have both.

I am going to present democracy in a positive light. I will be searching for hints of it anywhere I can find them, for my purpose is to make democracy comprehensible as a form of government. I will be arguing that, broadly speaking, government shapes character, that different governments produce different kinds of citizens, and that democracy produces a more enlightened citizenry than other forms of government.[†]

The narrative will unfold in four stages. Part I—"Paradise Lost: Democracy in Historical Context"—is a chronological investigation of democracy, starting in Athens and ending with the democratic experiments in the Italian city-states. Ancient Athens, by its example, provides us with the true meaning of the word "democracy"—government by the governed. The Italian city-states offer an unusual opportunity to study government in evolution. Though none of them were political democracies by inclusion, some of them came close. Especially instructive is the variety of formulas used to establish fairness and honesty in the selection of those who would govern. It is uplifting to see how government can have a positive effect on its citizenry and act responsibly in its attempt to provide for their needs.

In Part II—"Democracy in America: Opportunity Missed"—we will take a look at the critical years between 1776 (the signing of the Declaration of Independence) and 1788 (ratification of the Constitution). We will examine in some detail the evolution and ultimate demise of the Pennsylvania state constitution of 1776. In the course of our quest for the true meaning of the word "democracy," we will learn that this meaning has been perverted over the centuries and that what most of us consider to be democracy is in fact oligarchy. Some of the most interesting and original thinking on the subject of democracy can be found in the writings of the Anti-Federalists, those who were opposed to the signing of the Constitution. They understood the true meaning of democracy, and they recognized the risk involved in trusting government to those who lust for power.

In Part III—"The Quest for Unbridled Power: Democracy Crushed"—we will explore the contradiction between war and democracy by visiting periods of history when violent forces have crushed emergent self-governance. Warriors such as Alexander of Macedon, Genghis Khan, and Napoleon—iconic figures in world history—each trampled upon democratic movements in their march to power.

In addition to the highly visible actions of the warriors, we will scrutinize the machinations of invisible oligarchs operating behind the scenes to gain control of government in the service of special interests and in opposition to the needs of the broader populace. Special attention will be directed at bankers and speculators who, as a group, need a strong central, anti-democratic government as a means of gaining control of the flow of money and establishing financial policy favorable to

---

† Of course, government is not the only factor in play. The distribution of wealth, social structure, and religion are other powerful shaping forces. But my focus here will be on government alone.

their interests. These forces have been operating against the interests of democratic government for the past five hundred years, going all the way back to the reigns of Charles V and his son Philip II of Spain, and perhaps even farther.

Too often we see history as some distant, impersonal force that shapes events in a way that seems mysterious and beyond human control. However, one can argue just the opposite, that the unfolding of history is the work of particular individuals who lust for power. Who are they? What is their emotional makeup? Are those who seek power and abuse it like us? Or do they form a class apart? What about us, history's bystanders—does it matter if we are in the mix or out? We think our own choice as to whether or not we participate in government is a matter of indifference to our personal well-being. We might be mistaken.

Part IV—"Paradise Regained: Democracy in the Modern Age"—addresses government in its contemporary context, including consideration of the concept of change itself. I will offer some practical thoughts on how governmental institutions can be modified to make them more democratic. We will be visiting countries in Europe, Latin America, and Asia to examine some experiments in government in contemporary society. We will linger awhile in India. Though India is a constitutional oligarchy, there are democratic elements to be found in the structure and processes of its government, especially when compared with Western governments.

Our study of democracy concludes with a consideration of what it might be like to live in a true democracy. Economically, politically, ecologically, and sociologically, world society is in a state of transformation. Governments currently in place are not designed to meet emerging needs. Devising a form of government that is less highly centralized and that is more responsive to the common good is becoming imperative. If such a government is to achieve its desired ends, it will, in its formation, include all of us.

## Ancient Athens and Modern India

Ancient Athens is the fullest realization of democracy known to Western civilization. We call it a democracy for two reasons. One, all elements in society, from the poorest and most humble to the wealthiest and most exalted, participated in the affairs of government on equal footing. Two, Athenians governed on their own behalf. They didn't choose others to speak for them. They spoke for themselves. Between 30,000 and 60,000 Athenian citizens charted their own course. On a given day, as many as 6,000 people would attend a meeting of the assembly. If one wants to get a sense of a how democracy functions, ancient Athens provides an excellent example.

As a collective, did Athenians always act rationally and with concern for human welfare? Not always, but most of the time. In ancient

Athens there were slaves with no political rights. Women were denied access to the political process. Obviously, these institutionalized prejudices were exclusionary and undemocratic. Yet Athens was a democracy nonetheless. It would have been a more perfect democracy had slaves and women been included.

India is ripe for democracy for two fundamental reasons: its religion and its social structure. Democracy thrives on diversity and strong local communities. Hinduism as a religion is democratic in its lack of a strong centralizing, controlling force and in its emphasis on individual forms of belief and worship. Until relatively recently, the backbone of Indian society was the small local village, a self-contained economic and social entity. Such diversity and localization are ideal conditions for the growth of democracy. Homogenization and centralization lead to totalitarianism.‡

Although we will be studying government in its historical context, my primary goal is to shed light on current, existing forms of government and to provide a framework for a critical analysis of their effectiveness. It is my assumption that there are many who are not completely happy with the government they have but firmly believe that any alternative is both inconceivable and undesirable. Like many a bad marriage, the relationship between the citizen and his government endures not out of love, or necessarily even respect, but out of habit. The energy necessary to envision an alternative, to believe in it, and to work toward it has been dissipated in exchange for the security and familiarity of a long-standing relationship.

The first step in changing a relationship requires examining it from a new angle, looking below the surface. This may be the hardest part of all, to see things differently, perhaps more accurately. The effects of habit—the erosion of hope and energy—undermine our intellect and independence of judgment. We learn to believe that which serves to justify our continued allegiance to a relationship that has gradually lost its meaning and legitimacy. Things have changed progressively, by accretion. But we are so accustomed to what we "see" that we don't recognize the change. We see what used to be.

## Inverted Totalitarianism

Most Americans assume that they live in a democracy. They might see some disturbing trends they consider to be anti-democratic in nature, but they regard them as temporary, as surface phenomena that do not alter the form of government at its core. In *Democracy Incorporated: Managed Democracy and the Specter of Inverted Totalitarian-*

---

‡ By no means is India a perfect society. There is corruption and there is sectarian violence. But I will not be discussing those facets of Indian culture. They are not my subject matter and they do not affect the aspects of Indian civilization that are favorable to the emergence of democracy.

*ism* (2008), Sheldon S. Wolin offers a radically different perspective. He invokes the legacies of Hitler, Mussolini, and Stalin. These were men who used their personality and intellect to shape and dominate their countries. No aspect of life—civic, artistic, intellectual, religious, familial, or political—escaped their control. That control was total and crushing. Absolute, unquestioning submission was expected. Masses were organized and activated in support of the government. None of this is the case in the United States, of course, and yet ...

Wolin coined the term "inverted totalitarianism" to describe a form of government that in many ways achieves the goals of totalitarianism but by different, gentler means. Inverted totalitarianism is "driven by abstract totalizing powers, not by personal rule."[1]§ The leader is not the architect of the system. He is its product. He fulfills a pre-assigned role.

The system succeeds not by activating the masses but by doing just the opposite, "encouraging political disengagement."[2] "Democracy" is encouraged, touted, both domestically and overseas. To use Wolin's terminology, it is "managed democracy," "a political form in which governments are legitimated by elections that they have learned to control,"[3] a form of government that attempts to keep alive the appearance of democracy while simultaneously defeating democracy's primary purpose, self-government.

In managed democracy "free politics" are encouraged. Thus the populace is placated and pacified. Believing that in fact they have the government they want, people are lulled into a state of passivity and acquiescence, leaving the controlling powers to operate as they see fit to advance their particular interests. Democratic myths persist in the absence of true democratic practice.

Therefore, rather than dismantling the preexisting political system, as the twentieth-century totalitarians did, their modern-day brothers actually defend and support the system. Their "genius lies in wielding total power without appearing to."[4] What was once a citizenry has become an "electorate," the populace divided against itself in groups of competing interests whose opinions on circumscribed issues are constructed and manipulated to produce a desired outcome that is fed back into the hopper, resulting in the necessary pronouncements at election time.

Fear of violence is, for the most part (depending on race and ethnicity), absent in America's inverted totalitarianism. Yet fear is nonetheless employed as a means of control. It is a more subtle kind of fear, more insidious and more intractable. It is a fear that lingers indefinitely, though it is never fully identified as fear itself. Currently fear has two sources, one obvious, one less so.

---

§  Specific literature citations for quoted material appear in the Endnotes section at the back of the book. Additional comments related to the text discussion are presented as footnotes. Full publication details for all books and other works mentioned in the text and notes are provided in the Bibliography.

We are safe at home, we are told, but only if we succeed in protecting ourselves from the terrorists who want to take away our form of government, our lifestyle, even our lives. Terrorists are everywhere and nowhere, all the time. Because they are hidden, lacking in scruples, and tricky, we can never feel safe. We must depend on our government to protect us. We must surrender all control, even rights guaranteed by the Constitution, in the hope that our leaders will keep us safe.

In addition, there is a more deep-seated fear, a nagging fear, that is harder to combat—the fear generated by economic uncertainty—which constantly reminds us that our livelihood and everything we own could be taken from us and we could be left sleeping in tents, as many are in the state of California. Trillions of dollars were handed over to Wall Street speculators. Jobs are being outsourced to China. Unemployment is unchecked. Budgets are being cut at the Federal and local levels. What feels like a recession, perhaps even a depression, persists, and government seems to be doing very little to remedy the situation, largely because the uncertainty it creates generates the compliance the government seeks. "Unlike the Nazis," says Wolin, "the [George W. Bush] administration has done little to allay the recession's effects and much that exploits the accompanying insecurities."[5]

One could argue that the sidelining of the citizenry and the assumption of power by an all-powerful central government, unaccountable to its electorate, represents a radical departure from precedent and from the intentions of the founders. A closer look, however, reveals something quite different. Prior to ratification of the U.S. Constitution, there was open debate about its meaning, its benefits, and its liabilities. In the *Federalist Papers*, James Madison and Alexander Hamilton took up the cause of the Constitution. There was intense opposition to its adoption,[¶] and it never would have been ratified had it not been forced through by means of intimidation and deception.

Madison had made explicit his rejection of democracy and his wish to create a strong central government that marginalizes the citizenry. He would limit representation, create large electoral districts, and locate the government away from the local constituency.[**] Hamilton had openly advocated monarchy and hoped to mount a standing army, with himself at its head. He planned to march through the South and then on to establish American control in Latin America. The word "empire" was invoked no fewer than three times in the *Federalist Papers*.[††]

---

¶ Like the *Federalist Papers*, many of the expressions of opposition took the form of published letters and essays. *The Anti-Federalist: Writings by the Opponents of the Constitution* (edited by Herbert J. Storing) is an excellent collection of these writings.

** In Chapter 2, "False Friends," Madison's views on democracy are discussed in some detail.

†† It is also worth noting that the same financial interests that have taken control in recent years also fought for ratification of the Constitution, by which means they stood make considerable gains on their speculative investments.

## Civic Education

Americans have long looked upon their Constitution and their founders with pride and admiration. To discover that much of this is myth, to discover an alternate reality at odds with the one we have grown to accept as given, is a most disturbing experience. Yet if we are willing to take the journey we will end up on solid ground once again. We will feel empowered and optimistic about our future.

What is required is a massive reorientation of our society concerning governance. We are operating under a cloud of ambiguity, confusion, and lethargy. There is a general lack of appreciation of the degree to which government impinges upon our lives. We miss opportunities for self-governance because we don't know they exist.

We need to be reeducated and revived. This seems a daunting task. Yet several examples from the recent past demonstrate that such a large-scale reorientation is possible.

Not so long ago it was routine to go to a bar, drink too much, and drive home intoxicated, too frequently causing an accident, sometimes with loss of life. But the educational and lobbying efforts of MADD (Mothers Against Drunk Driving) have changed the attitude toward drinking and driving. There are legal consequences for driving while under the influence. Most of us now understand that driving while intoxicated is a bad idea. We have been educated.

The same applies to smoking. Smoking was once an integral part of social life for the vast majority of the population. No one ever thought that enjoying a cigarette could be harmful to himself or the person standing next to him. In recent years, however, the attitude toward smoking has changed radically. There are still many smokers, though their numbers are considerably reduced. Those of us who don't smoke are no longer at risk from the harmful effects of the next person's cigarette smoke. As a society we have been enlightened.

A similar process is under way concerning the food we eat. We are being educated as to the harmful effects of feeding cows corn instead of grass. We are growing worried about the effects of chemical fertilizers and chemical additives. We read labels with greater awareness and concern for the content of what we eat. There is a large-scale movement to eat food that is healthful and locally grown.

We are in the midst of addressing the most critical issue any society has yet had to face: global warming. Glaciers are melting. Temperatures are rising. Weather is becoming more severe and unpredictable. Rising sea levels could cause certain island societies to disappear altogether. Climate change will have widespread detrimental effects on animal and plant life. The entire ecosystem is in jeopardy. As recently as ten years ago, the general public knew little if anything about any of this. Now just about everyone is conversant on the subject to a greater or lesser degree.

It is now more important than ever to become educated on the subject of government, for only government can organize and direct the collective action necessary for addressing the issues that threaten our planet.

To orient ourselves with regard to government we need to ask some very simple questions, such as the following: What kind of government do we live under—a monarchy, an oligarchy, or a democracy? Is that government designed to serve the common good (e.g., the ecosystem)? Are there structural changes that could be made in the current government that would make it better able to fulfill its fundamental purpose? What are the different kinds of solutions to the problems of government that have been arrived at in the past and in other parts of the world?

These and other questions will be addressed as this book unfolds. If, by the end of our journey together, you find yourself thinking more critically and imaginatively about the nature of government and its purpose—perhaps even coming up with a few ideas of your own about what could be tried to create a government that better serves the common good—then I will have achieved my goal in writing *Paradise Lost, Paradise Regained: The True Meaning of Democracy.*

# PART I

# PARADISE LOST

*Democracy in
Historical Context*

# What Is History and
# Why Does It Matter?

*War wearied hath perform'd what war can do,*
*And to disorder'd rage let loose the reins.*

W E ARE ABOUT to begin our journey. We will be traveling across countries and continents, across centuries. Democracy has its friends, its enemies. It has false friends. We shall meet them all. We undertake this journey with the purpose of understanding democracy in its historical context, to isolate the conditions that favor its emergence and those that threaten its survival.

Our guides will be historians. Many of them are trustworthy; some of them are not. Thus, we will need to be vigilant and at times skeptical. For though we think of history as being something objective, fixed, and absolute, it is, in reality, something else.

One could say that history is everything that has ever happened, going back in time as far as one can go—every heartbeat, every ripple in every pond, every lover's sigh, every transmigration of every electron—from the Big Bang that created the universe to the economic crisis of 2008 that might undo it. In other words, history thus construed is without limit.

It becomes immediately obvious that conceiving of history in these terms is meaningless and ungraspable. We can't relive it. We can't learn anything from it. It is just there. If we are to make sense of this infinite stream of facts and events, we need to shape it. This is where the historian comes in. What a historian does is to cut a slice in time somewhere, pick a certain subject or theme, and then use the facts to paint a picture. There are many more facts than he can ever use. He must select what he includes. If we say that it is the job of the historian to both delight and instruct, then the ultimate rendering must be shaped in such a way that it will be of interest and have meaning and value to the reader.

We go to history to learn and understand. We want to learn where we came from so we can better understand where we might be heading. We want to learn how cultures and civilizations function so we can better understand what works and what doesn't work in our own society. Was democracy a good thing? Where did it succeed? Where did it fail? What were the strengths and weaknesses of a particular culture, and how did democracy fit into the picture? We read history to find out.*

What we learn is determined in part by the values we espouse and by the values and prejudices of the historian. What we learn will determine our ability to plot the future. Our reading of history will leave us feeling empowered or disempowered.

One or two things become clear: (1) Though the facts and events that make up the historical narrative exist independently of and prior to the writing of history, history itself—the narrative the historian creates— does not exist in any a priori sense. It does not predate the moment of its writing. (2) History is what historians say it is, and what they say it is will always be biased, by definition. That is, the way in which historians select and reject certain facts and events, the way in which this material is organized, affects how we perceive and respond to the narrative. Adjectives that are applied here and not there create a certain impression, favorable or unfavorable. In other words, history is a creative enterprise.†

History has a rhetorical function. It is trying to win us to a certain position. It reflects the values, beliefs, and prejudices of the historian. Is war a good thing or not? Is individual life a sacred matter? Was Alexander Hamilton a gentleman or a scoundrel? Was Socrates an innocent victim of Athenian "mobocracy," or was he a threat to the survival of Athenian democracy?‡ Are warriors noble, or are they self-serving egotists? We read history to find the answers to these questions. The answers we get will inevitably be shaped by the world outlook of those who provide them.

Modern "objective" history—history as a "scientific" academic discipline—is a relatively recent invention. The first Departments of History were established at the University of Berlin in 1810 and at the Sorbonne in 1812. The third quarter of the nineteenth century gave birth to academic journals in Germany, France, Italy, and England. And it is the academic imprimatur, the claim to scientific objectivity, that cows us into unthinkingly believing what we read without taking into account the message that is being delivered.

The academic historian seeks to achieve a position of apparent neutrality with regard to the material he is discussing. He avoids discussion

---

* The Swiss historian J. C. L. Simonde de Sismondi said that history should be "explored ... for instructions in the government of mankind." Quoted in Daniel Waley, *The Italian City-Republics*, p. 174.
† According to Friedrich Hegel, "It is incumbent upon him [the historian] to bring before our imaginative vision this motley content of events and characters, to create anew and to make vivid the same to our intelligence with his own genius." Quoted in Hayden White, *Metahistory: The Historical Imagination in Nineteenth Century Europe*, p. 107.
‡ See I. F. Stone, *The Trial of Socrates*.

of cause and effect, because that would entail taking sides. He has a tendency to depersonalize the historical narrative by taking individual human action out of the formula. He is more comfortable with abstractions and concepts. As a consequence, events just seem to happen, by themselves, in a manner that defies analysis and understanding.

Alexis de Tocqueville made the point that the way in which history is construed by the historian affects how we readers of history feel about our collective destiny. History founded in abstraction makes us feel powerless. History that identifies human action as its wellspring leaves us with a feeling of empowerment. "Historians who live in democratic ages [read U.S. oligarchy in the 1830s] then, not only deny that the few have any power of acting upon the destiny of a people, but deprive the people themselves of the power of modifying their own condition, and they subject them either to an inflexible Providence or to some blind necessity." He adds, "In perusing the historical volumes [of our age] ... it would seem that man is utterly powerless over himself and all around him. The historians of antiquity taught how to command; those of our time teach how to obey."[1]

Today we hear that globalization is the source of our misery. We are led to believe that concepts can act. We are made to feel powerless. Sentences like the following, found in just about all histories, have the same effect:

> In the early 1700s, the Russian Empire took the offensive against Poland using military force and bribery.
> France's invasion of Russia in 1812 was a turning point in the Napoleonic Wars.

Taken literally, such statements are mystifying. They create a white haze of ambiguity and mental distance. The statements are incomprehensible because they are nonrational. After all, what is the Russian Empire? Is it an amorphous form outlined on a map? Is it a certain physical land mass? Is it the people taken collectively? A form on a map cannot invade another country, nor can a land mass, nor could the entirety of the Russian population. If we substitute Peter the Great for "the Russian Empire" and Napoleon for "France," we enter the realm of rational discourse. Once our attention is directed to a particular individual and the actions he took, we can start thinking rationally about these events and their meaning for society. We can wonder what Peter was up to. Was he acting for personal reasons of power and glory, or did he have the best interests of his country at heart? Was violence the only solution? Should one man be given so much power?

Thus, in reading history, often we need to clear away the haze of ambiguity by translating abstractions into concrete realities, remembering that only live human beings can act and bring about change, for better or for worse.

Historians can go to the other extreme as well—hero worship. Rather than eliminate the human element from the equation, they may exalt a par-

ticular individual in a manner that is biased and misleading, while simultaneously claiming their own neutrality and objectivity. The effect on us
readers is the same as depersonalization. We feel powerless when faced with
these larger-than-life figures who have destroyed civilizations and taken
millions of lives.§ We are led to believe that the actions taken by these men
were glorious and hence desirable, that the good they achieved by their violence outweighs the harm. Thus, there is nothing to be done to stop such
excesses, nor should we want to stop them. These men are to be admired
and accepted on their own terms. They should not be judged. Once again
we are disempowered in our attempts to make sense out of history by applying our own judgment to the subject matter as a means of sorting things out
and drawing conclusions about what is desirable and possible.

Ultimately, in reading history, we are searching for answers to some
very basic questions. Is there a plan? Is it all inevitable? Is there a meaning? Is it possible for us to take charge of our collective destiny and set
it in a particular direction? But before we can begin to address these
fundamental questions, we must consider a question about the very
enterprise of reporting history: Is there a way of organizing history as
written that will help us grasp its deeper meaning?

For an answer to this final question, we can turn to writers like
Hegel and Marx. And to enhance our understanding of these writers,
let us first briefly consider the thoughts of Hayden White, a historian
who has examined the writing of history from a literary standpoint.
In *Metahistory: The Historical Imagination in Nineteenth Century
Europe* (1973), White organized historical writing by the shape and
tone of its narrative. According to White's schema, the historian can
retreat into cynicism (the satirical mode). He can ally himself with the
hero who rises above the fray (the romantic mode). He can step back
in philosophic detachment and analyze the forces at play (the comic
mode). Or he can experience the tragedy and try to elucidate a means
of understanding it that will lead us to a brighter day (the tragic mode).

## *The Comic Mode*¶

Friedrich Hegel** was a philosopher of history, rather than a historian. He
was perhaps the first, in the Western world, to think about universal history—the development of civilization around the world and across time.††
Hegel studied, analyzed, and critiqued the writings of historians. His

---

§ In chapters that follow, I will discuss Alexander the Great, Genghis Khan, and Napoleon.
¶ See Appendix for further discussion of Hegel's philosophy of history.
** Georg Wilhelm Friedrich Hegel (1770–1831) was one of the major German philosophers of
the nineteenth century. He was one of the first to attempt to arrive at a comprehensive under-
standing of change, and he had a profound influence on Karl Marx. With Johann Gottlieb Fichte
and Friedrich Wilhelm Joseph Schelling, Hegel was one of the creators of German idealism.
†† For an earlier and equally impressive study of universal history, see Arab philosopher
Ibn Khaldun's (1332–1406) *Prolegomena.*

struggle to come to terms with the misery that man has wrought is enlightening, as are his insights into what history is and how it redeems itself.

In the course of his writings, Hegel seems to have passed through all four modes mentioned by White and ended up in the comic mode. He shifted from irony and defeat to romantic optimism via Christianity and the triumph of good over evil. Seeing the tragic in the rise and decline of each individual civilization, he then found comic resolution by taking universal cultural history—as opposed to history in its discrete parts—as his subject matter. At this level of abstraction, he was able to find progress.

History, as Hegel saw it, was "made" by individual men, some of whom were heroes, some of whom were ordinary men, some of whom were criminals. The great men or heroes are those who show themselves to be "in cooperation with the common end which underlies the ideal notion of the conditions which confront them" but are in conflict with the existing social order.‡‡ The ordinary men are those "who fail to rise in stature to the demands made on their energy." The criminals, the depraved, are those who are content "to give free rein to an individual force which is ... foreign to all such common ends."[2]

Hegel was deeply saddened by the moral decay he saw across the various civilizations he studied, but was heartened by the fact that in declining and disappearing, these civilizations could be seen as a totality whose meaning for history could be gleaned only once they had completed their historical trajectory. Looking at ancient civilizations—Rome, Greece, Persia, India—that had run through their cycle of existence, he could see the formal whole as having passed through four phases: (1) birth and early growth, (2) maturity, (3) old age, and (4) dissolution and death.

These earlier civilizations were doomed to dissolve because in each civilization there was an internal contradiction that prevented it from living out the ideal of the notion that was the premise of its existence. The demise of the civilization resolves the contradiction by creating a synthesis, which is the basis for the next civilization.

The progress that Hegel found was not in the concrete world of "sin and suffering"[3] but in the abstract world of intellect. One can see that there is intellectual progress in the degree to which a given civilization gains cognizance of itself as a collective whole with a purpose. This self-awareness is expressed in the writings of its poets, playwrights, and philosophers, but most especially in the writings of its historians. It is the historians who, in their writing of history, convey or fail to convey a self-conscious awareness of historical occurrence as part of some meaningful whole.

Using this criterion, Hegel organized and ordered civilizations from less to more self-conscious. Where there is savagery, there is no sense of

---

‡‡ For example, Caesar, in his efforts to fulfill his own image of his importance in the world, and in conflict with the existing social forces, completely reconstituted Roman society, leading it in a direction that Hegel would have characterized as the ideal notion of Roman civilization, that is, its imperial destiny.

history. There is endless present. There is no sense that the culture taken as a whole is any different from nature. The Orient, which Hegel saw as exemplifying the "childhood" of history, represents progress over savagery. Man has differentiated himself from nature but has instead, in ancient China (a theocratic despotism), merged with the sovereign. There is still no real sense of history. Individuals have no self-consciousness of personality or of rights. Cultures operate in a cyclical process.

India, a theocratic aristocracy, represents progress over China. The political body, no longer monolithic, is broken up into parts, leading to political tension and awareness of difference. Persia represents progress over India in that, while still allowing for differences, the culture supplies an overarching spiritual unity. In Egypt there is a separation of spirit and matter, leading the way to the emergence of the individual in Greece. Thus, each civilization prepares the way for a higher level of development in the next.

The ethical life of the Greek polis allows for expression of personal individuality. However, the relationship of the individual to the state is not self-conscious. It is unreflective and based on obedience to custom and tradition, according to Hegel. This is the period of "adolescence." In ancient Rome, individual personality is recognized in the granting of formal rights, leading to a degree of personal self-awareness on the part of the individual, who feels separate and endowed. But freedom is limited. The state becomes an abstraction whose demands must be met by individual Romans. There is a tension between the principles of individuality and universality (the state), leading to political despotism and insurgency against it. This stage (ancient Rome) in the history of civilization gives expression to "manhood."§§

The Germanic realm was composed of Germany and the Nordic peoples, the major European nations (France, Italy, and Spain), and England. Here the principle of subjective freedom comes to the fore. This involves a gradual development that begins with the rise of Christianity and its spiritual reconciliation of inner and outer life and culminates in the appearance of the modern nation-state. Civilization has reached "old age."

For Hegel, the modern nation-state can be said to manifest a "personality" with self-consciousness of its inherent nature and goals. It is able to act rationally in accordance with its self-awareness. The modern nation-state is a "spiritual individual," the true historical individual, because of the level of realization of self-consciousness that it actualizes. The development of the perfected nation-state is the end or goal of history because it provides an optimal level of realization of self-consciousness, a more comprehensive level of realization of freedom than mere natural individuals, or other forms of human organization, can produce.

The history of civilization in the broad sense can be seen as a spiral that starts from a low point in the infancy of civilization, rising as it passes through

---

§§These sketches in no way do justice to Hegel's thinking. The goal here is to understand his outlook in the most general way and to see how it might have merit.

each new stage of maturity, ever growing and assimilating as it moves to each higher level of advancement, and then sinking into death. Exactly where is all this leading? Is there a final resting point? Hegel might argue there will be a resting point when and if there is a universal perception of the ideal notion of civilization, which is then realized in actual living. There are no internal contradictions. Universal civilization is conceived as being at one with itself. There is a unity of consciousness and being. History is over.

By envisioning history in broad global terms, across time, Hegel enables us to grasp civilization in its entirety as a first step in understanding its evolution. If civilization is to remedy itself, it must first become cognizant of itself as an object of thought and analysis. This is what Hegel has done. I think he is mistaken, however, in making universal self-consciousness his final destination. He has escaped into a world of subjectivity. In so doing he has left the world of living beings. He has marginalized issues of the common good and social justice, as well as issues of war and peace. His celebrating the nation-state—especially the German nation-state—is an expression of a personal preference. This belief in the nation-state is neither a universal truth nor a universally shared value. The subjection of the individual to, and the individual's absorption by, the nation-state is the formula for fascism. Individual existence disappears as a value.

But, in addition and perhaps more importantly, I think Hegel failed to properly apply his own theory. If he had applied it consistently, he might have come up with a different end point. This becomes clear in his treatment of ancient Athens in comparison with ancient Rome. Many would argue, by making reference to Athenian culture—its historians, philosophers, playwrights, orators, and statesmen (such as Pericles)—that Athens was many times ahead of Rome in its consciousness of itself. How can one possibly argue that Rome, having produced very little in the way of theatre, literature, philosophy, or history, is more mature than Athens? I believe one cannot, yet Hegel must if he is to reach his end point of the modern nation-state as the goal of historical development. He must ignore the possibility that it was democracy in Athens—a citizen-state—that produced such a high level of self-awareness, a degree of historical self-consciousness that probably has not been achieved since. To accurately appraise Athens would entail, as well, consideration of the notion that it is government itself that is a chief factor in determining societal development.

## The Romantic Mode

Hegel took culture and its evolution as his subject matter and ended up in the clouds. Karl Marx[¶¶] did just the opposite. With both feet planted

---

¶¶Karl Heinrich Marx (1818–1883), German philosopher, political economist, historian, and political theorist, is the author of *The Communist Manifesto* (with Friedrich Engels, 1848) and *Das Kapital* (1867).

firmly on solid ground he attempted, like Hegel, to come up with a broad understanding of universal history. As his subject matter, he chose the mode of production that characterizes a particular society.

Marx saw civilization as having passed through four phases: (1) primitive communist, (2) slave, (3) feudal, and (4) capitalist. He hypothesized an early civilization (primitive communist) in which man is at one with nature and cooperates with his fellow man in producing what he needs to live. All of this changes when division of labor appears, an occurrence Marx attributed to physical differences between men and women, between the strong and the weak. With this division there is alienation of man from nature, from his fellow man, and from himself.

Once labor is divided, "each man has a particular, exclusive sphere of activity, which is forced upon him and from which he cannot escape. He is a hunter, a fisherman, a shepherd, or a critical critic, and he must remain so if he does not want to lose his livelihood."[4] People are torn between being whole men and the necessity of functioning as specialized instruments of production. The social force that produces this schism is perceived as natural and hence ineluctable, generating a feeling of powerlessness and quiet despair.

The division of labor results in a class conflict that endures over time and produces the events we call history. This is what Marx meant when he spoke of "the materialist conception of history," history being determined by the modes of production, which in turn generate class conflict. From the serfs of the Middle Ages come the burghers of the earliest towns, and from the burghers come the earliest elements of the bourgeoisie. As population expands, needs grow. The feudal system is replaced by a system of manufacturing. Division of labor among guilds is replaced by division of labor within the guild.

The relationships of production—slave–master, nobleman-serf, bourgeoisie–proletariat—are the foundation or base of society. Everything else is superstructure: religion, government, law, ideology, art, literature, history, social consciousness. The superstructure is determined by the base. Our government, our religion, our self-expression as a culture, and our social consciousness are all consequences of the mode of production.

The relationship between base and superstructure is a one-way relationship. The base determines the superstructure and never the other way round. When the mode of production changes, there will be a change in the superstructure. Changes in the mode of production occur when there is a change in material conditions. Soil erosion, the introduction of a new form of technology, increase or decrease in population—these are all material conditions that bring about a change in the mode of production and hence the relationships of production, which in turn affect the superstructure.

In the South of the early United States, conditions were favorable for the growth of cotton and tobacco. Wealthy landowners imported slaves to do the work. In New England, the land was difficult. There developed a mercantile class devoted to trade and banking. In each case arose a superstructure—religion, government, and a level of social consciousness—that corresponded to and was determined by the mode of production.

Marx did his writing as capitalism was developing into the dominant form of production, pitting the captains of industry against the working class. He believed that the proletariat—including disaffected members of the bourgeoisie—would ultimately prevail and set up a new society based on a new mode of production in which the proletariat would rule. But this could not occur until the proletariat had become conscious of itself as a class, a class with a destiny and the will to realize it. Here Marx borrowed from Hegel the concept of consciousness and its dialectical evolution.

Marx introduced cause-effect analysis into the study of universal history. A change in the material conditions of production causes a change in the mode of production, which causes a change in the relations of production, which causes a change in social consciousness, and so forth. Although this is a mechanistic, deterministic outlook on how society evolves, Marx nonetheless believed that by understanding the mechanics of social existence one would be in a position to take action and bring about change. Hegel, who showed little concern for the material conditions of human existence, was unable to explain what creates the change in consciousness that he described. Marx saw the evolving social consciousness as an instrument in man's liberation from the conditions of his oppression.

Marx's description of capitalism, its evolution, and its effects on those who live through it is as valid today as when it was written 150 years ago: the profit motive, the need for new markets, the need for cheap labor, the movement toward monopoly, the psychological alienation and physical isolation of one man from the next, and the alienation of man from nature. Marx's wish to understand the source of man's suffering and to remedy it was a noble one. By applying cause-effect analysis to universal history, Marx held out the possibility of fundamental change. And he saw the importance of development in consciousness as a prelude to that change. Yet, as with Hegel, there are some internal contradictions.

Marx's chief concept is the division of labor, leading to exploitation and class struggle. Division of labor comes about because of biological differences between man and woman: one is stronger than the other. This kind of argument poses a problem, however. Marx has framed his general theory of history in terms of society. His concepts are sociological or societal. To have his primary causal factor rooted in biology is reductionistic. He is employing one conceptual framework, biology, to explain phenomena in another more abstract conceptual framework, that of sociology or economics. For his theory to be valid he would have to explain division of labor in sociological or economic terms.

Further, is it always the case that where there is division of labor, there is dominance and exploitation? If so, why? These are questions for which Marx has no answer. It is Marx's position that the proletariat will be the savior of mankind. Once this class becomes conscious of

itself as an instrument of change and accumulates the necessary foresight and will to act, it will take charge, rule in its own name, and
transform the base of society from a capitalist to a communist mode of
production. Pre-history will come to an end. History will begin.

However, Marx believed that there is one-way causality between
base and superstructure. This, it seems to me, would preclude the superstructure (i.e., social consciousness) from being a causal agent in bringing about change at the base. If he were to allow social consciousness
to have this kind of effectiveness, then he would open up the possibility
that other elements in the superstructure might affect the base as well.

It is Marx's position that the mode of production (the base) determines the form of the superstructure (i.e., government). Is it conceivable
that the opposite is true—that the form of government determines the
mode of production?

One could argue that monarchy/tyranny, where all of the power is
concentrated in one person, produces a slave/serf economy and that oligarchy, where there are several potentially conflicting sources of power,
produces capitalism. What kind of economy might a democracy produce? One can imagine certain general characteristics. If national government were directed by a multitude of local councils, power would be
dispersed, in all likelihood favoring the development of small businesses,
small farms, and small-scale industry that would be responsive to local
demands. Oligarchy, by virtue of its centralized power, favors the ever-
increasing concentration of wealth. In a democracy, where power is dispersed, there would be a more equal distribution of wealth, a greater
degree of social justice, and more attention to the common good.

Marx offers some guidance in understanding universal history, but
I believe he falls victim to a certain kind of reasoning that serves to
mystify and confuse, rather than enlighten. He speaks of capitalism as
being the source of man's misery. He speaks of class conflict as being
the material cause behind the unfolding of history. "Capitalism" and
"class conflict" are concepts, abstractions. Concepts can't act. They
can't cause things to happen. Only people can. The fog is lifted once
one begins to understand history as being composed of the acts of consequence undertaken by specific human beings.

In contrasting the writings of Hegel and Marx, one gets the sense that
deciding on the content of history determines a great deal about one's
understanding of the course of societal development. Hegel decided that
a society's consciousness of itself is the content of history, leading him
to draw certain conclusions about the overall meaning and direction of
history. Marx chose the mode of production as his content and was led
in a radically different direction. What then should one choose as one's
content if the goal is to stay rooted in concrete reality and arrive at an
understanding of history that is empowering to those of us who read
history with the goal of bringing about change for the better?

## Tolstoy's Battlefield

Leo Tolstoy*** was a member of the Russian aristocracy. Leading a rather aimless existence in his early adulthood, in 1857 he left Russia and had his first encounter with European culture and politics. During his 1857 visit to Paris, Tolstoy witnessed a public execution, a traumatic experience that would mark the rest of his life. He expressed feelings of revulsion toward the state for its acts of violence and exploitation, and became an ardent advocate of social progress based in simple human values, the enemy of violent solutions of any kind.

Tolstoy's *War and Peace* is thought to be one of the greatest novels ever written, but the author saw his book more as a work of history than a work of fiction. One of his primary interests was to investigate the causes of the Decembrist revolt,††† and the result was a massive novel with 580 characters, many historical, others fictional. *War and Peace* tells the story of five aristocratic families and the entanglements of their personal lives with the history of 1805–1813, principally Napoleon's invasion of Russia in 1812. The story moves from family life to the headquarters of Napoleon, from the court of Alexander I of Russia to the battlefields of Austerlitz and Borodino.

Count Pyotr Kirillovich Bezukhov, Pierre, is the central character and often a voice for Tolstoy's own beliefs and struggles. Pierre decides to leave Moscow and go to watch the Battle of Borodino from a vantage point next to a Russian artillery crew. There he experiences firsthand the death and destruction of war. The battle becomes a hideous slaughter for both armies and ends in a standoff. This is Tolstoy's commentary on the gratuitous viciousness of war.

Tolstoy wrote two epilogues to the novel in which he discussed his theory of history. He began the second epilogue as follows: "The subject of history is the life of peoples and of humanity."[5] The fundamental question to answer is "What force moves nations?"[6] The modern historian might respond "powerful men," like Napoleon. But, for Tolstoy, that was not good enough, because by what means could it occur that vast numbers of people would do Napoleon's bidding? What is the causal connection between Napoleon's issuing a command and the movements of an army of half a million men? In the past, one could make the connection via the guiding hand of the Deity. In the absence of such an overarching force, historians are at a loss to explain cause and effect. Tolstoy went on to get

---

*** Leo Tolstoy (1828–1910) was a Russian writer and novelist, and his *Anna Karenina* (1877) and *War and Peace* (1869) are considered to be among the great pieces of fiction in any era.
††† When Czar Alexander died in November 1825, it was assumed that his brother Constantine would succeed him. However, Constantine removed himself from the line of succession and his younger brother Nicholas assumed the throne. On December 14, 1825, in an action that came to be known as the Decembrist revolt, Russian army officers leading about 3,000 soldiers refused to declare allegiance to the new czar. Their goal, instead, was to establish a form of constitutional monarchy, along European lines. With the support of 9,000 troops who remained loyal to him, Nicholas I quickly suppressed the revolt.

involved in a tangle of abstract questions and answers, along the way dismissing, without argument, the possibility that power can "be that direct power of the physical ascendancy of a strong creature over a weak one."[7]

I believe that Tolstoy, like Hegel and Marx, has been led astray by his definition of the content of history. In Tolstoy's case, the definition is much too vast and abstract. To say that history is the "life of peoples and of humanity" is to say a great deal while saying not much at all. It is not much different from saying that history is everything that has ever happened. Such a definition of the content of history can take one down a path of reasoning leading to abstract final causes and divine intervention.

Yet I think Tolstoy has something important to teach us on the subject of history. One simply has to consider the title of his novel: *War and Peace*. Is that not, indeed, what history is about—war and peace—mostly war, very little in the way of peace? Is history anything other than a vast battlefield, after the battle is over—a mountain of corpses watered with oceans of blood, made up of men, women, and children from around the world and across time who were slaughtered to satisfy the warrior in his quest for blood and glory?[‡‡‡]

There are the ancient bones, reduced to piles of dust, commingled with the earth. There are bones and skulls, still recognizable shapes. There are the mangled bodies, crushed skulls, spilled guts, and pools of blood, the putrefying odor of the more recently dead. There are the silent gasps, the desperate waiting, the whimpers, groans, and cries of agony of those expiring as these words are being written. This, I believe, is history. It is the history excised from the books and broadcasts. It is the history we don't want to know about.[§§§] But it is history nonetheless. And it will determine our destiny, if we allow it.

"Well, that is a really bleak picture," you might say. "What about advances in medicine and technology, for instance?" Granted, there is the history of medicine, the history of technology, and many other "histories of" one could cite—the history of photography, the history of art, the history of farming, the history of golf, to mention a few. There are many more. And in each of these areas one could quite convincingly make the case for progress. Yet none of these is history, per se, the history that fills textbooks, the history that was taught by my high school teacher.

History, per se, has as its domain everything that is left after all the "histories of" have been accounted for. It describes the war and pillage and leaves the historian with the challenge of making sense of this "panorama of sin and suffering," in Hegel's words.

---

[‡‡‡] The numbers add up to something like 390 million. See "Selected Death Tolls for Wars, Massacres and Atrocities before the 20th Century" (http://necrometrics.com/pre1700a.htm) for some of the details. Of course, this does not account for the wounded and maimed, whose number is easily twice as large, nor the destructive impact on the economy, civic life, and psychic existence of those who survive "intact."

[§§§]   Said C. Wright Mills, "We study history ... to rid ourselves of it." *The Power Elite*, p. 274.

It is no mere coincidence that the first two histories written in the Western world are about war: Herodotus' story of the fifth-century B.C. Greco-Persian Wars and Thucydides' history of the Peloponnesian War, which occurred later in the same century.¶¶¶ These important works simply document the fact that the subject matter of history is war.

As we acknowledge war and its aftermath as the ultimate subject of history, we can begin to understand that warriors have ruled the world for the past five thousand years. And consequently, though true democracy has made a few relatively brief appearances, for the most part it has repeatedly dissolved into a cloud of empty rhetoric. Warriors don't want to have to ask for permission to make war.****

Considered in this light, one might argue that democracy is a bulwark against war. Where democracy and democratic values prevail, where power is widely dispersed, there is no opportunity for warriors to take charge of government. Further, one can argue that democracy offers a twofold benefit: (1) individual and culture reach their highest level of development,†††† and (2) the worth of each human life is at a premium; state-organized killing is at a minimum.

Continuing this line of reasoning, one is led to conclude that war is neither incidental nor accidental, but rather that it is a direct consequence of the form of government,‡‡‡‡ an integral and sustaining element in the oligarchic governing process, "the inseparable ally of political institution."[8] According to libertarian Sheldon Richman, "War is a government program." Why? "Because power-seekers and privilege-seekers [seek] outlets for their ambitions." In the 1950s, C. Wright Mills put it even more simply: "Warfare is the only reality." Early in the twentieth century, sociologist Max Weber declared that the modern state is "that human community which (successfully) lays claim to the *monopoly of legitimate physical violence* within a certain territory" (italics added).[9]

Randolph Bourne (1886–1918) was a progressive writer and public intellectual best known for his unfinished work "The State," which was discovered after his death. Bourne was steadfastly opposed to America's entering into World War I. According to Bourne, "The State is inti-

---

¶¶¶ See M. I. Finley's *The Portable Greek Historians: The Essence of Herodotus, Thucydides, Xenophon, Polybius*, for excerpts from both works.
**** It is interesting to contemplate what would happen if we simply changed the vocabulary. Suppose instead of declaring "war" on a country, we declared "death" on a country. Suppose we called the "Department of Defense" the "Department of Death and Devastation." Would it still be as easy to mobilize the citizenry?
†††† John Dewey (1859–1952), American philosopher, psychologist, and educational reformer, said, "The keynote of democracy as a way of life may be expressed … as the necessity for the participation of every mature human being in the formation of values that regulate the living of men together; which is necessary from the standpoint of both the general social welfare and the full development of human beings as individuals." Quoted in Benjamin Barber, *Strong Democracy*, p. 139.
‡‡‡‡ Said Thomas Paine, "to establish any mode to abolish war … would be to take from such government the most lucrative of its branches." *The Complete Writings of Thomas Paine*, p. 343.

mately connected with war, for it is the organization of the collective community when it acts in a political manner, and to act in a political manner towards a rival group has meant, throughout all history—war." Thus, war is the basic organizing principle of oligarchic government. "War is the health of the State," said Bourne. "Only when the State is at war does the modern society function with that unity of sentiment, simple uncritical patriotic devotion, cooperation of services, which have always been the ideal of the State lover."[10]§§§§ War brings us all together, as we seek shelter and protection under the same umbrella.

In his *Enquiry Concerning Political Justice and Its Influence on Morals and Happiness*, written at the end of the eighteenth century, English political philosopher William Godwin made this impassioned statement on the subject of war:

> Man is of all other beings the most formidable enemy to man. Among the most various schemes that he has formed to destroy and plague his kind, war is the most terrible. Satiated with petty mischief and retail of insulated crimes, he rises in this instance to a project that lays nation waste, and thins the population of the world. Man directs the murderous engine against the life of his brother; he invents with indefatigable care refinements in destruction; he proceeds in the midst of gaiety and pomp to the execution of his horrid purpose; whole ranks of sensitive beings, endowed with the most admirable faculties, are mowed down in an instant; they perish by inches in the midst of agony and neglect, lacerated with every variety of method that can give torture to the frame.[11]¶¶¶¶

Where power is concentrated and centralized, it is easy for a single individual or relative handful to mobilize the engines of war.***** Where power is dispersed throughout the citizen population and the citizen population itself is directly involved in making life and death decisions, war is a less likely outcome. Thus, the goal is to bring an abrupt halt to history by creating a form of government in which the lust for violence is contained. In the words of Anaïs Nin, "Our real objective is to create a human being who will not go to war."[12]

---

§§§§ See Christopher Hedges, *War Is a Force that Gives Us Meaning.*

¶¶¶¶ See also Major General Smedley D. Butler, USMC Retired, "War Is a Racket," available at http://lexrex.com, which begins, "WAR is a racket. It always has been. It is possibly the oldest, easily the most profitable, surely the most vicious. It is the only one international in scope. It is the only one in which the profits are reckoned in dollars and the losses in lives."

***** Hermann Goering, founder of the Gestapo, explains: "Why of course the people don't want war. Why should some poor slob on a farm want to risk his life in a war when the best he can get out of it is to come back to his farm in one piece? Naturally the common people don't want war; neither in Russia, nor in England, nor in America, nor in Germany. That is understood. But after all, it is the leaders of the country who determine policy, and it is always a simple matter to drag the people along, whether it is a democracy, or a fascist dictatorship, or a parliament, or a communist dictatorship. Voice or no voice the people can always be brought to the bidding of the leaders. That is easy. All you have to do is to tell them they are being attacked, and denounce the pacifists for lack of patriotism and exposing the country to danger. It works the same in any country." Quoted in G. M. Gilbert, *Nuremburg Diary*, from an interview with Goering conducted April 18, 1946.

# 2

# False Friends

*By falsities and lies the greatest part*
*Of mankind they corrupted.*

THOUGH CLOUDED IN its meaning, and most often misconstrued, there is little doubt that the word "democracy" has great appeal across vast swaths of mankind. It is a word that glows with warmth and inner brightness, beckoning to those who long for freedom, safety, and a wholesome, uplifting way of life. It is a word that resonates with an unspoken longing to live in a community of like-minded men and women, where the ultimate goal is the fullest realization of the individual potential of each and every member.

One would think that an idea with so much intrinsic appeal would attract advocates of passion and integrity. Unfortunately, this is not always the case. Some of democracy's most ardent advocates in word are often its most dedicated opponents in deed. The last thing you want to hear is that some Western leader plans on bringing democracy to your country. Likewise, some of those who write about democracy—political philosophers, academics, and the like—cringe at the thought that the common man might actually pull himself up by his own bootstraps. I refer to those writers and thinkers who appear to align themselves with the democratic cause while simultaneously undermining its foundation as "false friends." It is better to have no friends at all.[*]

Nicholas Murray Butler (1862–1947) was an educator and President of Columbia University. He was an adviser to seven presidents and a friend of statesmen in foreign nations. In 1931, he received the Nobel Peace Prize. A building on the Columbia campus—Butler Library—bears his name. In his time he was seen as an educator and a humanitarian. Yet it was he who said, in a moment of candor, "an educated proletariat is a

---

[*] In 1984, Benjamin R. Barber put it this way: "A people has as much reason to suspect its philosophical counselors as the counselors have to suspect the people." *Strong Democracy: Participatory Politics for a New Age*, pp. 95–96.

constant source of disturbance and danger to any nation."[1]

Such undemocratic thoughts are nothing new in America. Butler was simply echoing a sentiment that goes back to the early colonial days. It was Gouverneur Morris, lawyer and merchant, one of the leading minds of the Revolution, who offered one of the harshest assessments. Upon seeing around him men of modest means becoming politicized, Morris lamented the fact that "the mob begin to think and reason. Poor reptiles! ... They bask in the sun, and ere noon they will bite, depend upon it."[2]

Eighteenth-century philosophers in France and England—writers like Rousseau, Montesquieu, and Locke—were often cited by those involved in writing the U.S. Constitution. None of them were true friends of democracy.

Jean-Jacques Rousseau (1712–1778) was a Swiss-born political philosopher whose most important work was *Du Contrat Social* (*The Social Contract*), published in 1762. He was of the belief that political society was based on an implicit social contract in which citizens collectively sacrifice certain rights in exchange for others. It is this contract and our agreement to live by it that require our obedience to the laws that govern. As far as Rousseau was concerned, "a true democracy never existed and never will exist." Why? Because "it is against the natural order of things that the greater number should govern and the smaller number be governed."[3]†

James Madison has been hailed by many as the father of the American Constitution. Certainly he will offer support for democracy. Unfortunately, not.‡ In *Federalist* No. 10,§ Madison begins by lamenting the fact that factions divide and that there would appear to be irreconcilable opposing interests in any society. For example, there are people who own property (i.e., land) and people who don't. There are creditors and there are debtors. There are mercantile interests, farming interests, manufacturing interests, and moneyed interests. How can these diverse interests be united under one government to serve the common good? Democracy, according to Madison, is not the answer:

It may be concluded that a pure democracy, by which I mean a society

---

† When Rousseau says that democracy is "against the natural order of things," we can assume that what he means is that he personally is opposed to the idea. In discussions of political ideas, abstractions are often used as camouflage for personal preference.

‡ "The American political system was not born a democracy, but born with a bias against democracy." Sheldon S. Wolin, *Democracy Incorporated: Managed Democracy and the Specter of Inverted Totalitarianism*, p. 228.

§ The *Federalist Papers* are a collection of eighty-five letters first published in several New York newspapers between October 1787 and May 1788. The letters were originally published anonymously under the pseudonym "Publius" and were authored by Alexander Hamilton, James Madison, and John Jay. Their purpose was to rally support for ratification of the U.S. Constitution. There were letters opposing ratification as well; these have been gathered and published under the title *The Anti-Federalist: Writings by the Opponents of the Constitution* (edited by Herbert J. Storing).

consisting of a small number of citizens, who assemble and administer the government in person, can admit of no cure for the mischiefs of faction. A common passion or interest will in almost every case, be felt by a majority of the whole; ... and there is nothing to check the inducements to sacrifice the weaker party.¶ ... Hence it is that such democracies have ever been found incompatible with personal security or the rights of property; and have in general been as short in their lives as they have been violent in their deaths.[4]

Madison goes on to argue that

Theoretic politicians, who have patronized this species of government, have erroneously supposed that by reducing mankind to a perfect equality in their political rights, they would at the same time be perfectly equalized and assimilated in their possessions, their opinions, and their passions.[5]

In other words, it is not Madison's goal to "reduc[e] mankind to a perfect equality in their political rights." What, then, is his solution to the problem? A republic, in which government is delegated to "a small number of citizens ... elected by the rest."[6]

Here is a another example of disdain for true democratic practice. This time it is James Madison, speaking in *Federalist* No. 55: "Had every Athenian citizen been a Socrates, every Athenian assembly would still have been a mob."[7] I hope this isn't political science at its best.** It sounds more like Madison's sputtering contempt for democracy and the lower classes. To characterize an assembly filled with some of the most reasonable men in history as a "mob" is to twist the meaning of the word beyond recognition, for purposes of propaganda.†† It is to show gross disrespect for the Athenian assembly. These are the words of an oligarch, not a democrat.

---

¶ The aversion to majority rule is a theme that repeats itself many times in discussions of democracy. Implied are the assumptions that the majority will legislate to the detriment of some minority and that that is a bad thing. That the minority should legislate on its own behalf to the detriment of the majority seems to be a matter of little concern.

** Clinton Rossiter, the editor of what many regard as the definitive edition of the *Federalist Papers*, referred to the letters as "the most important work in political science that has ever been written ... in the United States" (1961 edition, p. vii).

†† George Rudé has written two excellent books on the subject of "the mob," which he deliberately refers to as "the crowd." Using police records and other archival resources from the 18th and 19th centuries in England and France, Rudé brings alive the people and their cause. For the most part we are dealing with workers seeking justice and some bread in their belly. There were food riots in Paris in the spring 1775. In July 1791, fifty thousand unemployed workers demonstrated at the Champ de Mars in Paris. The National Guard appeared. Stones were hurled. Fifty demonstrators were shot down. In 1812, in Nottingham, England, hosier workers protesting work conditions broke into shops and destroyed hundreds of frames used to manufacture stockings. In most cases, the actions were preceded by petitions and remonstrances that failed to produce a result. Where there was violence it was directed against property, not persons. See Rudé's *The Crowd in History: A Study of Popular Disturbances in France and England 1730–1748* and *The Crowd in the French Revolution*. See also Richard D. Parker, *Here, the People Rule: A Constitutional Populist Manifesto*. This is a slight volume, originally delivered as a lecture, in which Parker explores the sensibility of those who would construe ordinary people taking political action as "the mob."

## De Tocqueville's Confusion

Alexis-Charles-Henri Clérel de Tocqueville (1805–1859) was born into the landed aristocracy of Normandy, France. His father was a royalist prefect who supported the Bourbon monarchy. His great-grandfather was a liberal aristocrat killed in the French Revolution. De Tocqueville studied law and received a position as apprentice magistrate at the Versailles court of law. During this period he began to develop increasingly liberal sympathies as a result of his belief that the decline of the aristocracy was inevitable. Under the pretext of studying the American prison system, he persuaded his government to send him to America. In 1833, he published his report on American prisons. In 1835, he published the first volume of *Democracy in America*, observations on American political culture and political institutions.

De Tocqueville is learned and humane. He writes with grace and depth of insight. He has an eye for the telling detail. His overall generalizations are usually on the mark. One can learn a lot about the American mentality and political system by reading de Tocqueville's work. Yet, he was no friend of democracy. He cannot escape the prejudices of his class.

He was overwhelmed and offended by the chaos and hubbub of a new society, by the unrefined manners of a people unfettered by the constraints of a preexisting medieval culture and the social constraints of a rigid class structure. "No sooner do you set foot upon American ground than you are stunned by a kind of tumult; a confused clamor is heard on every side, and a thousand simultaneous voices demand the satisfaction of their social wants."[8‡‡] Though sympathetic to American efforts to establish an open society, supported by a broad base of popular involvement, de Tocqueville clearly prefers a well-functioning monarchy based in the devotion of a thoughtful and loyal aristocracy.[§§]

De Tocqueville's greatest concern is what he sees as the lack of talent in government, a dearth he attributes to the typical American's belief in equality and his suspicion of anyone who would place himself above the common man by virtue of learning or intellect. "The natural instincts of democracy induce the people to reject distinguished citizens as their rulers."[9] Americans, he fears, are destined to be governed by people just like themselves. "On entering the House of Representatives at Washington," he observes, "one is struck by the vulgar demeanor of that great assembly. Often there is not a distinguished man in the whole number." They are mostly "village lawyers, men in trade, or even persons

---

‡‡     Bear in mind that when de Tocqueville visited America there were not fifty but only twenty-four states. Most of the power and political tumult were on the state and local levels. Only gradually did a central, national government gather the power it enjoys in the year 2012. Today he would experience a level of political quiescence that would contrast sharply with what he observed more than 170 years ago.

§§ Of the aristocracy, de Tocqueville says, "An aristocratic body is too numerous to be led astray by intrigue, and yet not numerous enough to yield readily to the intoxication of unreflecting passion. An aristocracy is a firm and enlightened body that never dies." *Democracy in America*, Vol. 1, p. 245.

belonging to the lower classes of society." At least in New England, "the common people are accustomed to respect intellectual and moral superiority and to submit to it without complaint."[10]

Mediocrity of leadership and corruption in government are, as de Tocqueville sees it, a defining characteristic of democratic government. "The men who are entrusted with the direction of public affairs in the United States are frequently inferior, in both capacity and morality, to those whom an aristocracy would raise to power."[11] Corrupt governors lead to corruption of the governed,[¶¶] for "they in some measure lend the authority of the government to the base practices of which they are accused."[12]

Here is de Tocqueville at his best, damning with faint praise:

> If you hold it expedient to divert the moral and intellectual activity of man to the production of comfort and the promotion of the general well-being; if a clear understanding be more profitable to man than genius; if your object is not to stimulate the virtues of heroism, but the habits of peace; if you had rather witness vices than crimes, and are content to meet with fewer noble deeds, provided offenses be diminished in the same proportion; if, instead of living in the midst of a brilliant society, you are contented to have prosperity around you; if, in short, you are of the opinion that the principal object of government is not to confer the greatest possible power and glory upon the body of the nation, but to ensure the greatest enjoyment and to avoid the most misery to each of the individuals who compose it—if such be your desire, then equalize the conditions of men and establish democratic institutions.[13]

In *Democracy in America*, de Tocqueville has a chapter entitled, "Unlimited Power of the Majority in the United States, and Its Consequences." He speaks of the "absolute sovereignty of the majority"[14] and the excessive sway this majority holds over the legislature and the entire system of government.[***] He bemoans the fact that constituents impose certain expectations upon their representatives, which they are expected to fulfill.[†††] He draws parallels between the tyranny of a king and "the tyranny of the majority," which he sees as no less dangerous. For "a majority taken collectively is only an individual, whose opinions, and frequently whose interests, are opposed to those of another individual, who is styled a minority."[15‡‡‡]

Tyranny has been defined as "a government in which a single ruler is vested with absolute power"[16] and as "very cruel and unjust use of power or authority."[17] Has not de Tocqueville violated the true meaning of the word by overextending its use? The majority are not driven by a

---

¶¶   In a similar vein, the American author Henry George, writing in 1879, observed that "national character must gradually assimilate to the qualities that win power." *Progress and Poverty*, p. 532.

***   Once again, it is important to remember that he is speaking of state governments, not the federal government.

†††   In the next section, I discuss a similar concern raised by John Stuart Mill.

‡‡‡   In *The Public and Its Problems*, John Dewey observes, "The world has suffered more from leaders and authorities than from the masses" (p. 208).

single overriding, selfish, self-serving passion. Members of a majority one day can become members of a minority the following day when the issue changes. I don't know of any examples of the majority acting cruelly and despotically in its legislative capacity. De Tocqueville offers none. "I do not say that there is a frequent use of tyranny in America in the present day."[18]§§§ It would appear that class interest and personal apprehension have gotten the better of our writer.

De Tocqueville identifies a contradiction in his thinking that he never fully resolves. "I hold it to be an impious and detestable maxim," he declares, "that, politically speaking, the people have a right to do anything; and yet I have asserted that all authority originates in the will of the majority. Am I, then, in contradiction with myself?"[19] I believe he is. While he speaks of the "tyranny of the majority," implying an iron-willed, persistent, and immutable cast of mind, he laments "democratic instability" and "the mutability of the laws" consequent to the frequent rotation in office and the formation of new majorities. As de Tocqueville points out, even state constitutions are ever-changing; almost all had been amended within the thirty years prior to his arrival.[20] Thus, with de Tocqueville, as with many other writers on democracy, what is nobly proclaimed in the abstract in the first half of an essay is systematically undermined when issues are addressed in concrete terms in the second half.¶¶¶

The lack of precision in de Tocqueville's use of the word "democracy" is the cause of some confusion. I believe that what he is reacting against are not acts of government but the role of the majority in forming and enforcing public opinion. Here, I think his points are valid and apply as much today as they did in the first half of the nineteenth century. "It is in the examination of the exercise of thought in the United States," says De Tocqueville, "that we clearly perceive how far the power of the majority surpasses all the powers with which we are acquainted in Europe." In Europe there is dissent even where there is tyranny. Not so in America. As long as an issue is under debate, there is free discussion. Once a decision is made, "every one is silent, and the friends as well as the opponents of the measure unite in assenting to its propriety."[21]

A king can control the actions of his subjects but not their will. But in America, as de Tocqueville tells it, "the majority possess a power that is physical and moral at the same time, which acts upon the will as much as upon the actions and represses not only all contest, but all controversy." Already, in the 1830s, he claimed, "I know of no country in which there is so little independence of mind and real freedom of discussion as in

---

§§§  History abounds with examples of the minority governing at the expense of the majority. Rome, during the period of the republic, certainly qualifies. The needs of the majority were consistently ignored, begrudgingly and briefly acknowledged, and then ignored again. In the United States today, in the year 2012, a small minority once again ignores the well-being of the vast majority.

¶¶¶  Mill, discussed in the next section, is another excellent example of such a commentator.

America."[22] He could find "very few men who displayed that manly candor and masculine independence of opinion which frequently distinguished the Americans in former times, and which constitutes the leading feature in distinguished characters wheresoever they may be found."[23]

How is this loss of thoughtfulness and will to be explained? Representative government had been in place for less than fifty years. Had it already left its imprint on the American way of thinking? Is it the electoral process itself and the division along party lines that stifle thought? Is the citizen left to believe, "You had your chance. You cast your vote for the representative of your choice. Now you must remain silent until the next election. To speak out after an election is to be a poor sport and to question the system itself. Are you sure that is what you want to do? You, the people, are sovereign, the ultimate source of all power. How can you complain or criticize the outcome when you yourself are the source of power that created it?" In the name of democracy, freedom of thought is squelched.

## John Stuart Mill, Democrat or Elitist?

John Stuart Mill (1806–1873) was a British philosopher, political economist, and member of Parliament. He is best known for his essay "On Liberty," published in 1859, in which he doggedly defends the right of each individual to express his views, no matter how unpopular. Like de Tocqueville, Mill is concerned about the leveling effect of public opinion. "Whatever crushes individuality," he says, "is despotism, by whatever name it be called."[24]

Mill was educated at home by his father, the Scottish philosopher and historian James Mill. He was shielded from the influence of other children and was held to a strict regime, with the goal of establishing a genius intellect. At the age of three, Mill was taught the Greek alphabet. By the age of eight, he had read, in Greek, all of Herodotus and six of Plato's dialogues. At the age of twenty-one, he had a nervous breakdown.

Gradually, Mill recovered his equilibrium. Following in his father's footsteps, he went to work for the British East India Company and remained there until 1858. From 1865 to 1868, he was an independent member of Parliament, representing the City and Westminster constituency. During his time as an MP, Mill advocated easing the burdens on Ireland. He became the first person in Parliament to call for women to be given the right to vote. He was a strong advocate of women's rights and such political and social reforms as proportional representation, labor unions, and farm cooperatives.

In 1860, Mill's essay "Considerations on Representative Government" was published. This is an interesting document because it clearly reveals the ambiguous and often contradictory sentiments many writers display on the subject of democracy. In the abstract, Mill is an enthusi-

astic supporter of democracy. When he gets down to cases and begins
to deal with real possibilities in the real world, however, he reveals himself to be an unrepentant oligarchic elitist.

Initially, Mill offers himself as the voice of "representative democracy." He proclaims that "the ideally best form of government is that in
which the sovereignty,**** or supreme controlling power in the last resort,
is vested in the entire aggregate of the community;†††† every citizen not
only having a voice in the exercise of that ultimate sovereignty, but being,
at least occasionally, called on to take an actual part in the government
by the personal discharge of some public function, local or general."[25]

It sounds pretty good to be the "sovereign." There is a lot of power in
that. Then we learn that we, the people, are the controlling power, "in
the last resort." So, I guess we are not in power on a day-to-day basis,
only on a "last resort" basis. We not only have "a voice," but we are
actually "occasionally" called upon "to take an actual part in the government by the personal discharge of some public function, local or general." Notice how the second half of that statement vitiates the meaning
of the first half. The word "actual" in the second part makes clear that
the first part is little more than empty rhetoric. What do we actually do
with all this power we have, we the people? We discharge, "some public
function, local or general." Occasionally. Doesn't sound like a lot.

At the end of this lengthy chapter entitled "That the Ideally Best
Form of Government Is Representative Government," Mill reiterates
his position that "the only government which can fully satisfy all the
exigencies of the social states is one in which the whole people participate." All are to "share in the sovereign power of the state." Once
again, I am on my throne. And once again I am knocked off, for "since
all cannot ... participate personally in any but some very minor portions of the public business, it follows that the ideal type of a perfect
government must be representative."[26]

The deeper he gets into his subject matter, the more pronounced
Mill's anti-democratic, elitist sentiments become. One would think that
a representative would speak for his constituency. That is to say, on
key issues, in his votes and policy initiatives, he would reflect, as accurately as he could, the true sentiments of those he allegedly represents.
Not so, says Mill. He gives the example of the Dutch United Provinces,
where the members of the States General "were mere delegates ["mere
mouthpieces"].... When any important question arose which had not
been provided for in their instructions, they had to refer back to their
constituents, exactly as an ambassador does to the government from
which he is accredited."[27] To me this sounds like a good thing. After all,

---

**** The oxymoronic implications of the phrase "representative democracy," as well as the
concept of popular sovereignty, will be critically examined in Chapter 13.
†††† The community as an "aggregate" is an abstraction. To invest power in an abstraction is meaningless.

would I knowingly vote for someone whom I knew, in advance, would not accurately reflect my views?

Mill's position is that we the people, taken individually, one at a time, are for the most part too dull-witted to make intelligent choices and that we will be naturally prone to choose our superiors to represent us and that, naturally, we would want them to think for us. Because we are being represented by men of "superior intellect" and "superior powers of mind," they should then be free from the constraints imposed upon them by "the average elector," since "his opinion [the representative's, he of superior intellect] will be the oftenest right of the two."[28]

"It is so important," Mill insists, "that the electors should choose as their representatives wiser men than themselves, and should consent to be governed according to that superior wisdom."[29]‡‡‡‡ Once electors acknowledge "the extraordinary difference in value between one person and another,"[30] they will have no problem in finding ways to single out those people and select them as their representatives. They will understand that it would be an "affront to require that they [the ones of superior judgment] give up that judgment at the behest of their inferiors in knowledge."[31]

Mill is asking a lot of us, the dull-witted ones. One, we are to have enough wisdom and humility to recognize that we are dull-witted. Two, we are to accept our dull-wittedness and willingly defer to our superiors. Three, though dull-witted, we should be clever enough to recognize our superiors and mature enough to defer to them.

But, of course, Mill, genuinely of superior intellect and in many ways worthy of representing us lesser beings, is missing an important point and begging the most important question. Exactly what are the critical matters that are to be decided upon by our government, and who is best qualified to make those decisions? For example, let us talk war and peace for a moment. Is Mr. Mill prepared to argue that he of superior intellect legitimately has the judgment and moral prerogative to decide that I, a humble artisan, should risk my life in a war that he happens to think is a good idea? Does his superior intellect endow him with the knowledge of exactly what my best interests are? Is he really in the best position to know how to spend my money, the money I worked hard for and hand over to the government as taxes? I think these are self-answering questions and that Mill's learned disquisition on representative government is little more than a plea for his own class interest.

Mill defines as false democracy that "which is really the exclusive rule of the operative classes,"§§§§ in which all others are "unrepresented and unheard"¶¶¶¶ and from which the only escape from "class legisla-

---

‡‡‡‡  This is not much different from Plato's view in his *Republic*. See Chapter 15, "Democracy as Myth," herein.

§§§§ I assume Mill means the working class—artisans, laborers, and the like, perhaps even small shopkeepers.

¶¶¶¶  Mill offers no historical examples of such a form of democracy.

tion in its narrowest form" is hoping that the uneducated "operatives" will choose representatives better educated than they, to whom they will defer.***** His greatest fear is that "manual laborers," "the great majority of voters, in most countries," would rule. His solution is to assign more votes to "the higher intellectual or moral being."[32]†††††

According to Mill's weighted voting scheme, an employer is more intelligent than the laborer he hires. "A banker, merchant or manufacturer is likely to be more intelligent than a tradesman."[33] Assuming a time test of three years for these superior occupations, they should be awarded two or more votes, as opposed to the laborer's one. The "liberal professions" and those requiring higher degrees of education would be granted multiple votes as well, thereby "preserving the educated from the class legislation of the uneducated."[34]

Mill is openly concerned about unfettered democracy and believes that therefore in any democratic constitution there should be "a nucleus of resistance to the democracy."[35] He applauds the achievements of the Roman Senate, "the most prudent and sagacious body that ever administered public affairs,"‡‡‡‡‡ in "moderat[ing] and regulat[ing] democratic ascendancy," of exercising "the power of holding the people back," "of rectifying the people's mistakes."[36] How distant are the echoes of the people as sovereign, the "supreme controlling power."

Matters have not changed greatly with the passing of the years. Twentieth-century writers are equally as prone to anti-democratic sentiment as their antecedents in earlier centuries. There is a steady beat of anti-democratic thought from writers and public figures.

## Two Cheers for Democracy

Bertrand Russell, Third Earl Russell (1872–1970), was a British philosopher and logician who lived to celebrate his ninety-seventh birthday. Russell was a socialist and a pacifist. He was a prominent anti-war activist, and he was imprisoned for his pacifist activism during World War I. He campaigned against Adolf Hitler. He was actively opposed to nuclear arms and was famously photographed during a sit-down demonstration opposing the United States' involvement in the Vietnam War. In 1950, Russell was awarded the Nobel Prize in Literature, "in recognition of his varied and significant writings in which he champions humanitarian ideals and freedom of thought."

---

***** Notice how class legislation on the part of the majority (i.e., the "operatives") is to be feared. No mention is made of class legislation on the part of an elite minority, which, in fact, describes most of what has occurred over the course of history.

††††† It is not necessarily the case that a college professor is more moral or in possession of better judgment than a shopkeeper or craftsman. For all we know, it's just the other way around.

‡‡‡‡‡ The Roman Senate was the exclusive provenance of the Republic's most elite and powerful families. They took care of themselves and only reluctantly paid any attention to the *hoi polloi*. Surely Mill does not mean to imply that one should "hold the people back" by assassinating those who speak for them. That is what took place in ancient Rome.

Russell wrote *A History of Western Philosophy* (originally published in 1945), which is a classic in its field. In a chapter on Aristotle's "Politics," Russell has this to say about ancient Athenian democracy:

> The Greek conception of democracy was in many ways more extreme than ours; for instance, Aristotle says that to elect magistrates is oligarchic, while it is democratic to appoint them by lot. In extreme democracies, the assembly of the citizens was above the law, and decided each question independently. The Athenian law courts were composed of a large number of citizens chosen by lot, unaided by any jurist; they were, of course, liable to be swayed by eloquence or party passion. When democracy is criticized, it must be understood that this sort of thing is what is meant.[37]

How disappointing it is to see someone of Russell's caliber, an intellect and a humanitarian, write so sloppily on such an important subject. When he says, "ours," in the first sentence, "The Greek conception of democracy was in many ways more extreme than ours," I assume he is speaking of the British government, which, on a good day, was an oligarchy. It never was, nor was it intended to be, a democracy. It is oligarchic to elect magistrates, not because Aristotle says so, but because when the many choose the few, the outcome is oligarchy.

Russell uses the phrase "extreme democracies" when he means democracy *tout simple*. In other words, for Russell, a scion of a prominent aristocratic family, democracy was an extreme. Says Russell, "the assembly of the citizens was above the law, and decided each question independently." The assembly of the citizens wasn't "above the law." It *was* the law.

The Athenian law courts were indeed composed of a large number of citizens chosen by lot. This is what made them democratic. It is true that they were "unaided by any jurist." That was one of their greatest strengths. There were no hefty fees to be paid and lengthy legal battles that could last for years. Justice was swift and cheap. And it was as just if not more so than the version Russell had in mind.§§§§§

When Russell says that the Athenians "were, of course, liable to be swayed by eloquence or party passion," he is implying that in the British system of justice, in which jurists prevail, there is an absence of "eloquence or party passion." Surely he can't be serious. And then there is the final dismissive comment, giving clear expression to Russell's class prejudice, "When democracy is criticized, it must be understood that *this sort of thing* is what is meant" (italics added).

In America, the alleged home of modern democracy, the story is much the same. In representative government, we are told, electors are

---

§§§§§ See Charles Dickens' *Bleak House* for a biting satire of the British legal system. The book describes the case of *Jarndyce and Jarndyce*, a generations-long battle over a large inheritance. By the time the case is resolved, legal fees have consumed the entire estate. The case has become emblematic of an endless legal proceeding.

to choose their leaders every so often and then retire from the public domain, allowing those in charge to do their job without interference. In essence, the role of the citizen living in a "democracy" would be to vote once every few years and then mind his own business.

Let us listen to Edward Bernays on the subject. Bernays (1891–1995), born in Vienna, nephew of Sigmund Freud, is considered to be the founder of the field known as public relations. Bernays' clients included President Calvin Coolidge, Procter & Gamble, CBS, the United Fruit Company, the American Tobacco Company, General Electric, and Dodge Motors. He was an active promoter of Freud's psychoanalysis in America and, in a characteristic manner, used Freud's enhanced reputation as a means of furthering his own interests.

Bernays pioneered the use of psychology and sociology in the manipulation of public opinion. His best known book is *Propaganda* (originally published in 1928). In this book, he poses the rhetorical question, "If we understand the mechanism and motives of the group mind, is it not possible to control and regiment the masses according to our will without their knowing about it?"[38] He answers it as follows:

> The conscious and intelligent manipulation of the organized habits and opinions of the masses is an important element in democratic society.... Those who manipulate this unseen mechanism of society constitute an invisible government which is the true ruling power of our country.... We are governed, our minds are molded, our tastes formed, our ideas suggested, largely by men we have never heard of. This is a logical result of the way in which our democratic society is organized. Vast numbers of human beings must cooperate in this manner if they are to live together as a smoothly functioning society.... In almost every act of our daily lives, whether in the sphere of politics or business, in our social conduct or our ethical thinking, we are dominated by the relatively small number of persons ... who understand the mental processes and social patterns of the masses. It is they who pull the wires which control the public mind.[39]

Certainly this is not the notion of democracy understood by most of us who think we are actually living in a democracy. But Bernays is not the only cynic who has appropriated the word "democracy" and turned it into its opposite as a means to self-empowerment.

Some may recall the words of former New York City Mayor Rudolph Giuliani on the subject of freedom, a concept many of us associate with democracy. "Freedom," he said, "is about the willingness of every single human being to cede to lawful authority a great deal of discretion about what you [sic] do and how you [sic] do it."[40] In other words, do as you are told. This was Plato's idea as well. It was Plato who argued that the commonwealth prospers when there is "harmonious agreement between the naturally superior and inferior elements on the question which of the two should govern" and that justice is "the observance by everyone, child or woman, slave or freeman or artisan, ruler or ruled, of this principle that each one should do his own proper work without interfering with others."[41] Mind your own business, says Plato. Leave it to us, the politicians, philosopher kings, to see that things get done right.

It is in this spirit that some writers have openly advocated political apathy. If it is the job of the experts (i.e., professional politicians and bureaucrats) to govern, then the less interference from the rest of us, the better. The fact that fewer and fewer Americans are voting in national elections is seen as a good thing. W. H. Morris Jones believes that to create an atmosphere in which one is obligated to vote smacks of totalitarianism. In his article "In Defence of Apathy," he argues that "many of the ideas connected with the general theme of a Duty to Vote belong properly to the totalitarian camp and are out of place in the vocabulary of liberal democracy." Political apathy "is a sign of understanding and tolerance of human variety." It has a "beneficial effect on the tone of life." It acts as an "effective counter-force to the fanatics who constitute the real danger to liberal democracy."[42]

Here we see the fear-based theory of government, a mode of thinking that seems to characterize most writing on the subject of democracy. The "horde," the "herd," the "mob," the "fanatics" are first hypothesized and then must be contained by any means possible, even if it be by their own apathy. Impassioned belief, political commitment, the struggle to have one's voice heard, one's needs addressed, these are all anathema in a democracy, according to the authorities on the subject.

H. L. Mencken (1880–1956) was born in Baltimore, Maryland. He also died there. He became known as the "Sage of Baltimore." He started out as a reporter for the *Baltimore Morning Herald* and then moved to *The Baltimore Sun*. He co-founded *The American Mercury*, a literary magazine that soon gained national recognition. He became known as a wit, a wag, and a pundit. He was widely quoted.

Mencken had little but contempt for the average Joe, which he did little to hide. He had nothing but scorn for democracy. He said that "The doctrine that the cure for the evils of democracy is more democracy is like saying that the cure of crime is more crime."[43] He also said that "Democracy is the art and science of running the circus from the monkey cage."[44] Here, I believe, the common man is being likened to a monkey. According to Mencken, "Democracy is the theory that the common people know what they want, and deserve to get it good and hard."[45] In other words, the average Joe is too stupid to know what he wants or what is good for him, contentions which may or may not be true.

In *Notes on Democracy* (originally published in 1926), Mencken repeatedly uses the word "mob" and phrases like "the sovereign mob" and "the mob man" in places one would expect to see the words "people" or "citizenry." Democracy, as Mencken sees it, is a process of "false pretences and ignoble concealments." There is "the mob, theoretically and in fact the ultimate judge of all ideas and the source of all power." There is the demagogue, "the one who preaches doctrines he knows to be untrue to men he knows to be idiots," and the "demaslave," the one who listens and believes. The common man's love of liberty, "like his love of sense, justice and truth, is almost wholly imaginary." When he is free, he is lonely. What the common man really wants is just to feel safe, hence his veneration for the policeman and his longing for "the warm reassuring smell of the herd." He lives with an inflated sense that he "is really important to the world—that he is genuinely running things," "that his views are taken seriously by his betters," thus empowering the rogues and mountebanks who really run the show.

Mencken is no kinder to the "camorra of self-seeking" elected representatives, the typical American lawmakers who rise out "of the muck of their own swinishness," men who have "lied and dissembled," men who have crawled and know "the taste of boot-polish," men who are willing to embrace any issue, "however idiotic," that will get them votes and "sacrifice any principle, however sound," that will lose them votes.

Mencken certainly wanted to outrage, irritate, and provoke. Yet, regrettably, one must acknowledge that there is more than a grain of truth in his comments on the American political scene, both then and now. However, there is a legitimate question to ask as well. Is the government Mencken is satirizing, American government, a true democracy or is it some other form of government? Mencken himself raises the issue. Is there a distinction to be made between "representative democracy and direct democracy?" he asks. No, he says. Such distinctions are simply the ranting of "political sentimentalists" who don't know what they are talking about. Here, I think, Mencken's wit gets the better of him. I hope to demonstrate in the pages that follow there is nothing sentimental about the distinction between representative and direct democracy and that in fact much of what is said to be true about democracy, based on observation, is inaccurate because democracy is not what is being observed.

There have been mobs—riots and violence—but there has never been a "mobocracy," a form of government in which the mob rules. "Mobocracy" is a hypothesized form of government, a rhetorical device used by the opponents of democracy as a means of slander and intimidation. "Watch out or you'll end up with a mobocracy. Is that what you want?"

Joseph A. Schumpeter (1883–1950) was born in what is now the Czech Republic and was then a part of the Austro-Hungarian empire. Though not a Marxist, Schumpeter was an economist who believed that capitalism would eventually collapse due to a lack of entrepreneurship and that it would be replaced by some form of socialism. From 1932 to 1950, he taught at Harvard. His best known work in English is *Capitalism, Socialism, and Democracy* (originally published in 1942), in which he expressed the belief that the electorate was ignorant and superficial and ultimately would end up being manipulated by the politicians. Hence, it was both unlikely and undesirable that the people could or would rule themselves. Rather, he saw democracy as a competition among leaders for ascendancy. Once elected to office, political action would be the provenance of the politician, not the voter. Although periodic votes by the general public legitimize governments and keep them accountable, the policy program is very much seen as their own and not that of the people, and the participatory role for individuals is usually severely limited. The theme that people living in a democracy should not participate in government seems to be a pretty steady one.

Considering the contradictory and often deprecating attitudes of those who opine on the subject of democracy, it is not surprising that just about everyone has difficulty taking the word seriously. Democracy has anonymously been referred to as "a ship of state whose officers try to steer a straight course in all directions," "a form of government whose citizens have complete freedom to choose which candidate they prefer to mess things up for them," "a form of government in which the people often vote for someone different but seldom get something different," and "a form of government where you can say what you think even if you don't think."[46]

Well, if we can't get three cheers for democracy, can we at least get two? E. M. Forster (1879–1970), essayist, novelist, and short story writer, had this to say in 1939: "So Two Cheers for Democracy: one because it admits variety and two because it permits criticism. Two cheers are quite enough: there is no occasion to give three."[47] George Bernard Shaw (1856–1950), Irish-born playwright, essayist, and music critic once said, "Democracy is a word all public men use and none understand."[48] Perhaps he was closest to the truth.

3

# Ancient Athens

## *Wellspring of Democracy*

*All things invite*
*To peaceful counsels, and the settled state*
*Of order.*

T HE TRUEST FORM of democracy the world has ever known did not appear all at once, full blown from the head of Zeus, as Athena is alleged to have done. Instead, Athenian democracy emerged in phases over a period of hundreds of years, and it continued to evolve even as it reached its apogee under the leadership of Pericles.*
Gradually it disappeared, not due to any weakness in its democratic processes but as result of the wars of attrition with Sparta. Ultimately, a debilitated citizenry lacked the commitment necessary to sustain a form of government that required so much in devotion and personal energy.

Initially, there were many small communities in Attica, the area sur-

---

* Many excellent resources might be consulted as part of an in-depth study of democracy in ancient Athens. Among the best are these. Charles Freeman's *The Greek Achievement* offers a comprehensive and readable overview of Greek civilization, with a chapter devoted to Athenian democracy. *The Greeks*, by H. D. F. Kitto, is a classic in the field. Kitto's is a more personal interpretation. He focuses on the uniqueness of the Greek way of thinking and its expression in the political life of the Athenian citizen. As its title implies, R. K. Sinclair's *Democracy and Participation in Athens* has for its subject matter the day-to-day functioning of Athenian democracy, with special emphasis on the direct participation of the average citizen. In *Democracy Ancient and Modern*, M. I. Finley offers a thoughtful overview of democracy by comparing and contrasting Athenian democracy with what is considered to be democracy in the twentieth century. Werner Jaeger's *Paideia: The Ideals of Greek Culture* is a three-volume study of Greek character and personality as revealed in the classical literary and philosophic works. Jaeger offers a rich appreciation of Greek culture, especially its poetry. However, when he addresses issues of governance and the influence of class, he makes unwarranted claims. In discussing Athenian democracy, he speaks of "mass-rule" and "extreme democracy." His insistence on the necessity of a "governing class" in all instances simply does not apply in the case of ancient Athens.

rounding and including Athens. There were weak monarchs and rival clans or noble families. At the time of the Trojan War, which took place in the thirteenth or twelfth century B.C., if it took place at all, there emerged a monarch of legendary proportions whose name was Theseus, who reputedly unified Attica, with Athens as its center. Whether this is a true version of events or not, it is true that Attica did become a unified whole, a necessary precursor to Athens emerging as the dominant force in the region.

The time from 1100 B.C. to 800 B.C. is known as the Greek Dark Ages. This period begins with the presumed Dorian invasion and the end of the Mycenaean civilization in the eleventh century B.C. and continues up until establishment of the first Greek city-states in the ninth century B.C. The archaeological evidence shows a collapse of civilization in the eastern Mediterranean world during this period, as the great palaces and cities of the Mycenaeans were destroyed or abandoned.

The Dark Ages were followed by what is known as the Archaic period in Greek history, 750 B.C.–480 B.C. During this interval, while Sparta was asserting ascendancy, Athens was still a second- or third-rate power. A growing population and a shortage of land seem to have created internal strife between the poor and the rich in many city-states.

The *archon* (chief magistrate) Draco made several important reforms to the Athenian law code in 621 B.C. The laws he laid down formed the first written constitution of Athens. Penalties under Draco's code were severe, giving rise to the modern sense of the word "draconian." For example, any debtor whose status was lower than that of his creditor was forced into slavery. Minor infractions could result in death. Nonetheless, this code represented progress over the oral tradition, which could be exploited to the advantage of the wealthy classes. Now all were subject to the same verifiable code of law.

The lower classes continued to be exploited by the upper classes. The small farmer could mortgage his land to a wealthy noble and then, if unable to make his mortgage payments, would lose the land and be enslaved by the noble and perhaps even sold abroad. Thus, indebtedness was a major factor in civil strife between the classes, which parallels the situation in the contemporaneous Roman Republic. It is interesting to contrast the solutions provided by these two parallel Mediterranean civilizations. Rome responded with violence and repression. Athens responded with democracy.

Sometime toward the beginning of the sixth century B.C., Solon, an Athenian statesman, lawmaker, and lyric poet, introduced legal reform that replaced Draco's code with a more humane system of justice. Solon put an end to enslavement for debt, reduced debts, put a limit on the size of estates, restored lands that had been lost by debtors, and restored to Attica those who had been sold abroad. Solon encouraged an agriculture based on olive and wine production. He favored the immigration of craftsmen from abroad, and he encouraged Athenians to teach their sons a trade. The Council (*boule*), under Solon, remained an oligarchic stronghold (something like the Roman Senate), whereas the Assembly (*ekklesia*) was opened to all citizens.

Solon departed and civil strife broke out all over again, leading to the rule of the tyrants.[†] Pisistratus, who reigned from 546 B.C. to 527 B.C., is an example. He was an educated aristocrat who took steps to preserve the forms of Solon's moderately democratic constitution and to alleviate the plight of the poor. He sought to make drama and epic poetry available to the people at large. In addition, he established a brilliant court and engaged in a building program that would elevate Athens from a local agrarian community to a city of international importance.

## The Classical Period

The fall of the last of the tyrants in 510 B.C. began what is known as the Classical period in Greek history, a period that includes most of the fifth and fourth centuries B.C. and ends with the death of Alexander the Great in 323 B.C. In 508 B.C., an aristocrat by the name of Cleisthenes took Athens yet further down the road to democracy. He understood that an imbalance in leadership was created by the tribal system, resulting in a leader of one of the prominent families assuming the powerful position of *archon*. What Cleisthenes did was not to eliminate tribes but to redefine them. He dismantled the original four tribes and replaced them with ten brand new tribes constituted of roughly equal numbers of *demes* (parishes). However, the *demes* making up each tribe were spread out and not contiguous.

Having divided Attica into three broad subdivisions—city, inland, and coast—Cleisthenes proceeded to construct the tribes out of the inhabitants of these noncontiguous land masses, with Athens as the natural meeting place for the disparate elements. A given tribe would contain men from the hills, seamen, and small farmers. Family loyalties and class provided little advantage. Cleisthenes built on the work of Solon by further limiting the power of the Council and enhancing the power of the Assembly. All that remained to do to bring about true democracy was to eliminate the last of property qualifications and to introduce sortition as the means of selecting magistrates, Council members, and jurors.

The next defining moment in the rise of a unified Greek city-state[‡] was war with Persia, beginning in 499 B.C. and lasting until 448 B.C., when the Greeks were victorious over the invading Persian armies. These victories enabled Athens to bring most of the Aegean and many other parts of

---

† The word "tyrant" in ancient Greece, like the word "dictator" during the period of the Roman Republic, did not carry with it the measure of odium it currently bears.

‡ Charles Freeman, in *The Greek Achievement*, speaks of a "democratic coup" occurring in 461 B.C. that resulted in shift of greater power to the Assembly (p. 223).

Greece together in the Delian League, an Athenian-dominated alliance.

In 445 B.C., Pericles was elected *strategos* (general), solidifying his position as first among equals. His oratorical skills and his vision as a leader had been defining elements in the Assembly going back to 461 B.C. The period between 461 B.C. and 429 B.C., the year of Pericles' death, is what has come to be known as the Golden Age or the Age of Pericles, a period in which Athenian democracy and culture achieved their greatest fulfillment.

The year 431 B.C. saw the beginning of a long and debilitating war with Sparta, which ended in Athenian defeat in 404 B.C. Neither Athens nor Athenian democracy would ever be quite the same after that. Yet Plato and Aristotle were still to come.

Even while democracy prevailed, aristocratic elements were always in the background looking to replace democracy with oligarchy. In 411 B.C., there was a coup precipitated by dissatisfaction over the handling of the war with Sparta. Democracy was restored four months later but was overthrown again in 404 B.C. Democratic government was replaced by an oligarchy of thirty individuals, who have come to be known as the "Thirty Tyrants." The Thirty began a purge of important leaders of the popular party during the Peloponnesian War. Hundreds were condemned to execution by drinking hemlock, and thousands more were exiled from Athens. The Thirty Tyrants were overthrown by the exiled general Thrasybulus and his allies from Thebes in 401 B.C., ending their eighteen months' reign.

Finally, in the first half of the fourth century B.C., Sparta was defeated in war and no longer represented a menace to Athens. Invaders from the north, however, dealt the final blow to Athenian independence. In 338 B.C., the armies of Philip II of Macedon defeated the combined forces of Athens and Thebes and initiated Macedonian hegemony in Greece. Further, the conquests of Philip's son, Alexander the Great, made the traditional Greek city-state obsolete. Athens remained a wealthy city with a brilliant cultural life, but it ceased to be an independent power. In the second century B.C., after two hundred years of Macedonian supremacy, Greece was absorbed into the Roman Republic.

If we use the reforms of Cleisthenes in 510 B.C. as the start date and 338 B.C. as the end date, we can say that democracy flourished in Athens for close to two hundred years, with lapses brought on by war with Sparta and political coups in 411 B.C. and 404 B.C. In each instance, however, there was a return to democracy, which is testimony to the resiliency of the political institutions.

Using his powers as a statesman and orator, Pericles was able to bring democracy to its fullest expression while simultaneously presiding over a blossoming of artistic and intellectual expression that was one of the richest the Western world has ever known. One of Pericles' most popular reforms was to allow *thetes* (Athenians without wealth) to occupy public office, while diminishing the power of the *archons* (the wealthy magistrates). Another was to authorize a special salary for the citizens who attended the Assembly, thus encouraging participation among those of modest means.

Pericles oversaw the reconstruction of the Acropolis, which had been severely damaged by Persian invaders. The sculptor Phidias created a colossal gold-plated marble statue of Athena that was situated in the interior of the Parthenon, where its splendor could reach the faithful through the open doors, and another of Zeus that was placed in the Sanctuary of Olympia and was considered in its time and in later ages to be one of the marvels of the world.

Athens became the center of Greek theater, where performances of works by Aeschylus, Sophocles, Euripides, and Aristophanes were open to the public. This period saw the emergence of some of the most important philosophers in Western thought, including Socrates, Anaxagoras, Democritus, Empedocles, and Protagoras. Western history saw its beginnings in the writings of Herodotus and Thucydides.

Athenian culture continued to thrive, even under Roman domination, yet the richness of Athenian political life dwindled after reaching its zenith in the time of Pericles. There are several reasons for this decline. In 430 B.C., plague swept through Athens, killing perhaps a quarter of the population. In addition, war with Sparta and the Macedonian invasions played a large role in sapping the collective political will.

The Delian League had been formed around 477 B.C., at the time of war with Persia. The League started as a voluntary association of about one hundred fifty city-states under Athenian leadership. Gradually, this defensive association became a source of Athenian wealth and power. Secession was not tolerated. Rebellion could be brutally repressed. Monies were siphoned off to pay for some of the major building programs under Pericles. Maintaining the polis§ at this level of grandeur became a drain on the treasury and served to erode political cohesion.

## Democracy at Work

Ancient Athens was the first and only citizen-state. As such, its democratic institutions deserve to be known and understood. I believe that these institutions have never been fully appreciated, and that their true value has still not been exhausted. Might they not serve as an inspiration and source of guidance for us in the twenty-first century, as we look for new forms of government to replace older institutions that have outlived their usefulness?

---

§  The word "empire" does not apply to this situation. The Delian League should not be equated with Roman dominance in Italy. As Kitto points out in *The Greeks*, the Athenians had a genius for statesmanship, whereas "the achievement of the [Roman] Republic was to fill Rome with a pauperized rabble, to ruin Italy and provoke slave-revolts and to govern the empire ... with an open personal rapacity that an Oriental monarch would not have tolerated" (p. 97).

In Athens, the people—not their representatives—about six thousand of them, gathered in the Assembly at least once a month and more frequently as required. There citizens debated and voted on the issues that affected their community and their nation as a whole. By a show of hands and sometimes by casting a black (no) or white (yes) ball into a clay jar, they voted to go to war or not, to receive ambassadors or not, to grant a certain individual citizenship or not. They voted on what projects to fund and what not to fund.¶ They voted on laws regulating the exportation of grain, which was in short supply. They decided how much should be charged for leasing a temple's land. They decided how many and who should be the envoys representing Athens in foreign lands. "The week-by-week conduct of a war ... had to go before the Assembly week by week."[1]

The Assembly met at least forty times a year, and approximately nine decrees were passed at each meeting. Anyone in the Assembly had the right to speak and propose legislation.** The meetings took place at a site known as the Pnyx, located less than one kilometer west of the Acropolis. The Pnyx is a small, rocky hill surrounded by steps carved on its slope. There is a large flat platform of eroded stone set into its side, known as the *bema*, the "stepping stone," or speakers' platform. The Pnyx was used for popular assemblies in Athens as early as 507 B.C., when the reforms of Cleisthenes transferred political power to the citizenry. It was then outside the city proper but close enough to be convenient. The Pnyx looks down on the ancient *agora*, the commercial and social center of the city. It was here that the citizenry debated and decreed for some two hundred years.

In addition to participating in the debates occurring in the Assembly (the *ekklesia*), the Athenian citizen could be called upon to serve as a juror in one of the many legal actions involving private or public suits, to serve in an administrative capacity as magistrate overseeing some government function (such as water or grain supply, building projects, or trade), or to serve on the Council (the *boule*). The *boule* was a body of five hundred members and was responsible for drafting preparatory legislation for consideration by the Assembly, overseeing the meetings of the Assembly, and in certain cases executing legislation as directed by the Assembly.

The members of the *boule* were selected by a lottery held each year

---

¶ The ancient Greeks systematically avoided direct taxation, whether on property or income, as a means of raising revenues. Taxation, they believed, was tyrannical. As an alternative, they derived income from state property, farms, mines, and houses that were let; from court fees and fines; and from such indirect taxes as harbor dues.

**Aristotle was of the opinion that if one had to choose between the decision made by a select few or a large number, "the many, though not individually good men, yet when they come together may be better, not individually, but collectively, than those who are good men" (quoted in Sinclair, *Democracy and Participation in Athens*, p. 215). Despite his unveiled contempt for the multitude, Aristotle nonetheless believed that their decisions might well be superior to those of a select elite.

among male citizens over thirty years of age. Fifty men would be chosen from each of the ten Athenian tribes, with service limited to twice in a lifetime. There were ten months in the Athenian calendar, and one of the ten tribes was in ascendancy each month. The fifty citizen councilors (*prytanies*) of the dominant tribe each month served in an executive function over the *boule* and the *ekklesia*. From that group of fifty, one individual (the *epistates*) would be selected each day to preside over the *boule* and, if it met in session that day, the *ekklesia*. The *epistates* held the keys to the treasury and the seal to the city, and he welcomed foreign ambassadors. It has been calculated that one-quarter of all citizens must at one time in their lives have held the post, which could be held only once in a lifetime. Meetings of the *boule* might occur on as many as 260 days in the course of a year.

The third element of the Athenian democracy was the system of jury courts known as the *dikasteria*. Jurors were selected by lot from an annual pool of 6,000 citizens (600 from each of the ten tribes) over the age of thirty. There were both private suits and public suits. For private suits the minimum jury size was 201; it was increased to 401 if a sum of more than 1,000 drachmas was at issue. For public suits there was a jury of 501. On occasion a jury of 1,001 or 1,501 would be selected. Rarely, the entire pool of 6,000 would be put on a case. No Athenian juror was ever subjected to compulsory empanelment, voir dire, or sequestration, nor was any magistrate empowered to decide what evidence the jury could or could not be allowed to see.

Jurors could not be penalized for their vote—unless it could be shown that they had accepted bribes. But the practice of selecting juries randomly on the morning of the trial and the sheer size of the juries served to limit the effectiveness of bribery. The Athenian court system did not operate according to precedent. No jury was bound by the decisions of previous juries in previous cases. This is a striking difference between Athenian law and more familiar systems such as Roman law or English common law. Such a system of justice was consistent with the Athenian opposition to elitism and the oppressive effects of received wisdom in matters of justice. Each citizen used his own common sense to make judgments based on personal belief and prevailing mores.

Some crimes had penalties predetermined by law, but in most cases the choice was left up to the jury. The most common penalty was a fine, and the loser paid the winner's court costs. The severest penalties were enslavement and capital punishment. Milder penalties included exile and "dishonor," which meant exclusion from the political, economic, and religious life of Athenian society. Imprisonment was unknown as a penalty. Any criminal too dangerous to be allowed on the streets was either executed or exiled. There was no police force. Victims had to rely on friends and relatives to enforce judicial decisions. If these lacked sufficient force, it might be necessary to appeal to a powerful patron.

Jury courts had the power of judicial review over legislation and the acts of magistrates and politicians. A citizen could challenge in court a law that was being proposed in the Assembly. A trial would then ensue, which could result in the law's being withdrawn. A citizen could challenge the competency of a serving magistrate. A trial would ensue, and the officeholder could remain in office or could be removed. A politician could be prosecuted for having proposed an unconstitutional law or decree in the Assembly, whether his proposal had passed or not. If the disputed measure had already been enacted into law, and the proposer was found guilty, the law was automatically repealed. Juries made frequent use of this power. A few hundred ordinary citizens could strike down, as unconstitutional, legislation enacted by an Assembly of six thousand people.

Cases were put forward by the litigants themselves, and single speeches on each side were timed by water clock. In a public suit the litigants each had three hours to speak. Much less time was allotted in private suits, the time proportional to the amount of money at stake. Justice was rapid, because a case could last no longer than one day. There were no lawyers. There were no judges, only juries of the litigants' peers. This was amateur justice—perhaps the best kind.

Most disputes were settled through arbitration, either public or private. In private arbitration, the two parties to the dispute would select a mutually agreeable third person or persons to decide the case. The results of private arbitration were recognized in the law as binding and final, and no appeal was permitted (unless malfeasance could be shown on the part of the arbitrator). Alternatively, contending parties could bring their dispute to a state-appointed public arbitrator drawn from the board of public arbitrators, which consisted of all male citizens in their sixtieth year.

There were about eleven hundred officeholders or administrators in Athens whose job it was to oversee the day-to-day responsibilities of a complex communal life. Of those eleven hundred, all but one hundred were chosen by allotment. An individual would put his name forward to hold a certain office in the year prior to his desired tenure. He had to be at least thirty years of age, or in some cases forty. His name was chosen at random from the pool of nominees, and he held office for a year. It was assumed that officeholders had no special expertise. The lack of expertise was mitigated by the fact that magistrates served as part of a panel overseeing a certain function, and that what one lacked in knowledge another might have.

A magistrate could hold his position only once in a lifetime, another way of minimizing the amount of harm any individual could cause. As a further precaution, all magistrates were subject to a review beforehand that might disqualify them for office. Any citizen could challenge a magistrate for his conduct, leading to a trial that could result in his being removed from office and possibly penalized. Thus, accountability to the citizenry was built into the system at the most fundamental level. Even Pericles, the most esteemed figure in Athenian life, could be chastised and fined for his conduct of the war with Sparta. Just about every important politician had to face trial at some point in his career. Convicted, the public official might be removed from office, fined, or, in extreme cases, ostracized†† or executed.

About one hundred officeholders were chosen by election, as opposed to lottery or allotment. Ten of these elected officials were the *strategoi* (generals), who were the exception to the rule that an individual could hold a particular office only once. The others were magistrates required to handle large sums of money. Elected officials too were subject to review before holding office, as well as scrutiny while they were in office. And they too could be removed from office anytime the Assembly met. In one case from the fifth century B.C., the ten treasurers of the Delian League were accused of misappropriation of funds. Put on trial, they were condemned and executed one by one until—before the trial of the tenth and last—an error of accounting was discovered, allowing him to go free. Any officeholder, chosen by allotment or election, from the lowest level functionary to the most powerful general, could be challenged by any citizen at any time.

## Citizenship

It has been estimated that in the fourth century B.C., Attica, the larger land mass of which Athens was the capital, had a population of 300,000–350,000 people,‡‡ including men, women, children, slaves, and foreigners (*metics*). Of this 350,000, there were some 30,000 males who were citizens entitled to vote in the Assembly. In the previous century, there might have been as many as 60,000. The Peloponnesian War, the plague, and a stricter definition of "citizen" account for some of the difference.

Only adult male Athenians, eighteen years and older, who had completed their military training had the right to citizenship in Athens. This excluded a majority of the population, namely women, children, slaves,§§

---

†† Ostracism was a formalized and severe course of action in ancient Athens. Details are provided later in this chapter.

‡‡ Of those, about half (approximately 150,000) lived in Athens itself.

§§In the fifth and sixth centuries B.C., there were as many as 80,000 slaves in Attica, on average three or four slaves per household. Aristotle is alleged to have had thirteen, Plato six. Critics should remember that at its inception, the alleged democracy in the United States harbored some 200,000 slaves out of a population of about three million. Obviously these slaves in America had no voting rights. Nor did women, who were denied the franchise until the passage of the Nineteenth Amendment to the Constitution in 1920. Detractors often argue that Athens was a slave society and that without slaves its citizens would not have had the opportunity to participate in a democracy. It is important to remember that 90 percent of the Athenian economy rested on the shoulders of the small farmers, most of whom worked their own farms and could not even afford to feed a slave. For the most part, slaves were used for domestic purposes by the aristocracy. Observers of the Athenian scene noted that slaves moved about freely in society and that walking in the streets one wouldn't know the difference between a slave running an errand and a citizen. A major exception to this use of slaves was the silver mines, where slaves were brutally exploited.

and resident foreigners. Citizenship was limited to those males who were legitimately descended from citizens on both sides of the family. Despite the obvious exclusions, one must remember that there were no property qualifications for citizenship and that the humblest cobbler, the smallest farmer, and the landless rower of a trireme were on equal footing with the wealthiest of aristocrats when it came to speaking in the Assembly and proposing legislation, holding office, or impeaching an officeholder for malfeasance.

If we consider broadly the form of government in ancient Athens and its system of justice, one overriding dynamic becomes evident: fear of power, fear of the concentration of power, fear of the abuse of power. This was reflected in the use of large juries (thus making bribery and manipulation more difficult), the absence of lawyers, the absence of a police force, the wide use of arbitration, reliance on current values and common sense for passing judgment (rather than the intricacies of common law), the use of a citizen army rather than a standing professional army controlled by the state, and the use of sortition rather than election as a means of choosing magistrates and members of the *boule*.¶¶ Specific procedures were instituted to prevent the kinds of snap votes in the Assembly that enabled the aristocracy to overthrow the democracy in 411 B.C. and 404 B.C.

At the first meeting of each year, the Assembly was asked to vote whether the laws, grouped into four categories, were adequate or not. Laws judged to be inadequate would be discussed at a subsequent meeting. In the interim, citizens could propose changes, which would be written on a white board and displayed in public. Thus, urgency could not be used as an argument to force through a law that ultimately would be at odds with the common good. The Athenian system operated on the principle of *Ho boulomenos* (he who wishes), meaning that any citizen could propose a law, bring suit against a magistrate, or speak to the Assembly, thus establishing political equality among the citizenry. The primary concerns were to maximize citizen participation in government and to minimize corruption and the consolidation of power.

Rotation in office in this governmental system merits special mention. As R. K. Sinclair points out, "The related notions of limited tenure and rotation and the principle of collegiality*** severely curtailed the opportunities for individuals ... to use office to acquire a position of leadership."[2] Aristotle makes repeated reference to tenure in office. "Where there is natural equality of the citizens," he says, "and it would be unjust that anyone should be excluded from the government ... then it is better, instead of all holding power, they adopt a principle of rota-

---

See Kitto, *The Greeks*, p. 132.

¶¶  Though chosen by lot, most officials underwent preliminary scrutiny before a jury court. The questions raised sought to establish that the person in question was actually an Athenian citizen and that he had fulfilled his financial and military responsibilities. See Sinclair, *Democracy and Participation*, pp. 77–78, for the details.

***  In this context, Sinclair defines collegiality as "the sharing of power among colleagues within the field of their competence." *Democracy and Participation*, p. 80.

tion."[3] In other words, where there is political equality, justice requires that everyone be given a chance to serve. If someone monopolizes the office, then others are being denied that opportunity.

Later, Aristotle lists as one of the democratic institutions "restriction of the tenure of office to six months, that all of those that are of equal rank may share in them." But, in addition to the principle of serving and sharing in office, rotation serves to put a limit to the concentration of power. "The short tenure of office prevents oligarchies and aristocracies from falling into the hands of families." And further, "it is not easy for a person to do any great harm when his tenure of office is short, whereas long possession begets tyranny in oligarchies and democracies."[4] Again, Aristotle says "that no one should hold the same office twice, or not often, except in the case of military offices; that the tenure of all offices ... should be brief."[5] The more people who rotate through a given office, the less likely it is someone wishing to extend an offer of bribery will find a willing recipient. It is more difficult to corrupt the many than the few.[†††]

This obsession with the abuse of power was reflected in yet another tradition that to the modern way of thinking might seem frivolous or arbitrary: ostracism. When it was suspected that someone was getting too big for his britches, he might be ostracized. The Athenian people as a whole could vote for the expulsion from the city of any citizen they chose. Unlike exile, ostracism was not a penalty for a crime. Also unlike exile, it was applied only to the prominent and powerful—those whom the people feared might be positioning themselves for a coup.

The procedure was straightforward. Someone would propose to hold an ostracism, and the Assembly would vote on the proposal. If it won, then an ostracism would be scheduled. On the day of the ostracism, every adult male citizen could turn in a ticket (*ostrakon*) inscribed with the name of the person he thought Athens could best do without, and the person who got the most votes had to leave the city for ten years.

It has been argued that this procedure could be used arbitrarily for vindictive means. One commonly told anecdote supports such a thesis. There was an Athenian statesman by the name of Aristeides, popularly known as "Aristeides the Just." One day when Athens was holding an ostracism, an illiterate farmer came up to Aristeides, not knowing who he was, and asked him for help in inscribing his *ostrakon*. Aristeides agreed to help, and asked whose name the farmer wanted to inscribe. "Aristeides!" the farmer said. When asked what he had against Aristeides, the farmer replied that he was sick of hearing Aristeides called "Aristeides the Just" all the time. So Aristeides duly inscribed his own name on the ticket, and ultimately he was the one who was ostracized. True or not, this story certainly illustrates the role of ostracism in Athenian society and the power

---

††† Despite all these precautions, *demagogoi* would emerge. Using glib rhetoric, false promises, and the formation of cabals, they would create disorder and manipulate the discussion to lead to wished-for outcomes.

of a humble farmer in helping to check the power of a wealthy aristocrat.

Nonetheless, there are examples of a prominent individual using his power to advance a personal cause. There could be reasoned debate, at the highest level, in which opposing views would be expressed, leading to a vote in which one side or the other would carry the day. On other occasions, however, the Assembly would be whipped up into an emotional frenzy and make decisions the members would later regret. The story of the debate over the fate of Mytilene combines all of these factors.

In 428 B.C., three years into the war with Sparta, the island of Lesbos revolted against Athens, declaring its independence from the Delian League and thus depriving Athens of an important ally. Mytilene was its chief city. The Athenian Assembly, roused into an angry, vengeful state by a leather manufacturer named Cleon, ordered the execution of the entire male population of Mytilene. The following day, in a calmer state, the Athenians were having second thoughts. The debate was renewed. Cleon, who was satirized by Aristophanes as a violent and illiterate buffoon, spoke first. Democracy, he said, is inconsistent with empire. If you wish to rule you will use power to subdue those who rebel. Your failure to act will be seen as a sign of weakness. The Lesbians acted recklessly and should be punished. Failure to punish them will result in other rebellions. As reported by Thucydides, Diodotus replied, as follows:

> Haste goes with folly, passion with coarseness and meanness of mind; both are the enemies of wise counsel....
>
> Cleon asserts that to put them [the Mytilenes] to death will best serve us, by discouraging others from revolting: I explicitly contradict this....
>
> Men are naturally disposed to do wrong, in public and private matters, and increasingly severe penalties have failed to check this.... Moreover, each individual, when acting with others, carries his own ideas to the extremes. Let us not therefore do something foolish by trusting to the death penalty, and allowing no possibility to those who have revolted of changing their minds.... In [Mytilene], the common people did not assist the rebellion, and, when they got arms, surrendered the city to you: if you now kill them, you will play into the hands of the aristocrats....
>
> This is the advantageous policy and the strong policy, because the party which deliberates wisely against his enemy is more formidable than the one which acts with a violence born of recklessness.[6]

The vote was close, but Diodotus won. Another boat was sent out to stop the execution of the Mytilenes and scarcely arrived in time. But the lives were saved.

The people of Melos—who were sympathetic to the cause of Sparta— were not so fortunate. In 416 B.C., in the midst of the ongoing war with Sparta and after a winter of starvation, the Athenians, under the leadership of Alcibiades, took the island of Melos. All of the men capable of bearing arms were killed, and the women and children were enslaved.

## Losing Paradise

Certainly, the rashest action taken by the Assembly was the invasion of Sicily in 415 B.C. Alcibiades, who had led the Athenians in their brutal treatment of the people of Melos, was a student of Socrates. He was an aristocrat noted for his arrogance, good looks, and courage. He was a prominent orator, a general, and (ultimately) a turncoat. Even as the war with Sparta continued, Alcibiades made an impassioned plea to the Assembly for an invasion of Sicily, arguing that victory in Sicily would expand the Athenian empire and bring in great riches. Counter-arguments from Nicias[‡‡‡] and others were ignored, though Sicily clearly had little if any strategic value in the war with Sparta. Diverting forces from the struggle with Sparta was ill advised, yet Alcibiades prevailed. The adventure was a complete rout. Something like forty thousand lives were lost, as well as half of the Athenian fleet. Based on an event that took place in Athens just prior to the departure for Sicily, Alcibiades was brought up on charges of sacrilege. He fled to Sparta, where he served as military advisor in several campaigns against his native Athens. He made enemies in Sparta as well and eventually fled to Persia, where he appears to have been assassinated.

Actions like the invasion of Sicily can be (and have been) used to argue that government cannot be entrusted to a democracy.[§§§] A cross section of the population gathering in large numbers will make rash decisions, the argument goes. We need a select few who know what they are doing to run things properly. The trial of Socrates in 399 B.C. is likewise pointed to as an example of irrational and vindictive behavior on the part of a class of people who are unfit to govern.

In Western civilization, Socrates has been raised to the position of "secular saint."[7] His person, his name, his ideas are surrounded by a haze of myth and worship that for the most part conceals the true nature of his character and teachings. I. F. Stone in his excellent *The Trial of Socrates*[¶¶¶] studies the verdict against Socrates in the context of Socrates' teachings, his attitude toward his accusers during the trial, and the political climate in Athens at the beginning of the fourth century B.C.

Stone sees the verdict against Socrates as an exception to a proud tradition of free speech that characterized Athenian democracy and found its fullest expression in the dramatic festivals, which were quintessential examples of Greek tolerance for outspoken political criticism and satire.

---

‡‡‡ Nicias, a member of the aristocracy, was an Athenian politician and general during the period of the Peloponnesian War. Following the death of Pericles in 429 B.C., he became the principal rival of Cleon in the struggle for the political leadership of the Athenian state.

§§§ It is important to remember that such actions were usually taken when the people abandoned their collective wisdom and trusted to the judgment of an aristocratic leader.

¶¶¶ Stone was a dedicated journalist and writer, a persistent prodder of the establishment and received truth. Late in life he took a decade to master ancient Greek so as to be able to grapple with original sources for his book on Socrates.

As Stone points out, "The Athenian equivalent of a free press was the theater."[8] The Greeks were a religious people and revered their gods. Yet in his play "Clouds," Aristophanes (writing in 423 B.C.) could with impunity make lewd comments about Zeus. Even in the midst of war with Sparta, dramatists would ridicule key political figures.

Stone lists four words in ancient Greece that were synonymous with the right to free speech: *isegoria, isologia, eleutherostomou,* and *parrhesia.* Peitho, or "persuasion," was an Athenian goddess commemorated in sculpture by Praxiteles and Pheidias. Athens in the fifth century B.C. was an open city. Philosophers, writers, thinkers, and lecturers flocked from other areas to be a part of the intellectual excitement.

Why, if there was such a strong tradition favoring outspokenness, was Socrates singled out for condemnation? Further, if his teachings were such a threat, why did Athenians wait until Socrates' seventieth year—after he had been practicing as an itinerant philosopher for decades—to prosecute him? Socrates was accused of corrupting the youth. What could he have said that was so threatening to the Athenians who voted for his death?

According to Xenophon, Socrates was accused of teaching his companions to look down upon the laws of Athens, of despising the established constitution, and of inciting his followers to violence.[9] He taught them that "the one who knows should rule, and the others obey."[10] In other words, he taught his followers to despise democracy and overthrow it.

Socrates had nothing but contempt for the smith, shoemaker, merchant, or sea captain who spoke in the Assembly and made the laws. What was their qualification?, he would ask rhetorically. When there was a need to expand the navy or build a building, did Athenians not consult the experts? Well, should they not consult experts when it came to governing?[****] Members of the Assembly were nothing but "dunces and weaklings."[11]

Socrates, who saw himself as the wisest of Athenians, was famous for his negative dialectic. He would question his interlocutor, often one of the men who played key roles in the Assembly, until that person was cornered and unable to deliver a convincing argument in favor of a cherished conviction. Most of the questioning hinged on the meaning of a certain word. Unable to come up with a satisfactory definition, the hapless victim of Socrates' interrogation, irritated and humiliated, would have to accept defeat. Was this perhaps Socrates' intention, to demonstrate that the common man, the bedrock of Athenian democracy, was too foolish to govern and that only "the one who knows," the single wise man, should rule?

The trial of Socrates took place in 399 B.C. By that time, the moral and political fiber of Athens was less than it was at the peak of Athenian glory under Pericles. The combination of plague and war had

---

**** Aristotle, on the other hand, believed that each citizen was endowed with civic virtue, the ability to distinguish right from wrong and administer justice. For him the issue was not knowledge, as it was with Socrates, but rather character and judgment.

diminished both the numbers of the population and the resiliency of the citizenry. War with Sparta had extended from 431 B.C. to 404 B.C., a span of twenty-seven long years, and had ended in defeat for Athens. But of equal importance were continuing threats to democracy during this same period. Repeatedly—in 411 B.C., 404 B.C., and 401 B.C.—Sparta was able to draw disenchanted members of the Athenian aristocracy to foment rebellion against Athenian democracy.

The aristocrats had secret clubs known as "synomosiai." Prominent members of the aristocracy met in secret and used meetings of these groups to plot their political and military strategies. Key leaders involved in the coups in 411 B.C. and 404 B.C. were close associates and students of Socrates. His anti-democratic teachings supplied these restless, egotistical, and violent aristocrats with the intellectual ammunition they needed to turn against democratic society. In 411 B.C., Alcibiades, Socrates' favorite—the same one who had presided over the massacre in Melos and led the fateful expedition to Sicily—was the leader in bringing about the Dictatorship of the Four Hundred. In 404 B.C., it was another of Socrates' protégés, Critias, who organized the coup that brought in the Dictatorship of the Thirty and the deaths of fifteen hundred Athenians. In typical Athenian fashion, there was complete amnesty for the conspirators, perhaps preparing the way for yet another coup attempt in 401 B.C., which was successfully squelched.

The unbridled contempt for Athenian democracy demonstrated by men like Alcibiades and Critias is a direct expression of the beliefs and teachings of Socrates, which is why, just two years after the latest in a string of threats to democracy, Socrates was charged with corrupting the youth, or, more accurately, preaching the overthrow of democracy.

One could argue that Socrates was merely exercising his right to free speech. Had he taken such a position, he might well have been acquitted. Out of a jury of five hundred, two hundred eighty voted to convict. Two hundred twenty voted to acquit. It is certainly conceivable that a conciliatory attitude on the part of Socrates could have won over an additional thirty votes or so. Instead, his sneering attitude and determination not to offer a proper defense suggest that he himself might have brought on his conviction and death. Further, it is likely, based on other examples, that had he pleaded for exile, it would have been granted. Thus, though the conviction of Socrates leaves a blemish on our memories of Athenian democracy at its height, it is nonetheless true that Socrates was a direct threat to the survival of Athenian democracy. It is also true that he was given a trial, a fair trial.

Ancient Athens was not a perfect society, but it was a functioning political democracy. Overseeing an area of some nine hundred square miles (roughly the size of the state of Rhode Island) the people of Attica governed themselves. The wealthiest aristocrat and the humblest artisan stood on equal footing in meetings of the Assembly, as participants in the Council, as jurors, and as magistrates. There were no representatives. There was no monarch. There were no oligarchs. Repeatedly, writers such as James Madison have claimed that divergent class interests make democracy impossible. Democracy in Athens gives the lie to that argument. Does political democracy require social democracy? The answer is no. Athens proves the case.[††††]

But not only did Athens succeed in governing itself, it did so from a position of *eunomia,* or harmony. In contrast to the immutability of fixed institutions imposed from without that Madison repeatedly advocated, Athens achieved its stability by virtue of the processes and interactions that characterized its political life. This kind of stability, as described by the Greek philosopher Heraclitus (535 B.C.–475 B.C.), has its basis in strife and tension. In fact, the word "stasis" in its origins does not mean quiescence or lack of movement, but rather its opposite—the presence of dynamic, opposing forces that balance themselves out.

Athenians of all classes *were* the state. They debated on equal footing the issues of the day, passed laws, ran the city on a day-to-day basis, filled the juries, and held all magistrates and even generals accountable for their conduct. There was no privileged class safe from public scrutiny and accountability.

These were a dynamic and self-confident people. Their intellectual and artistic achievements provide the foundation for Western civilization. Basically, they invented democracy. They were our first and remain our enduring philosophers, many of whose ideas are as valid today as when they were uttered some twenty-five hundred years ago. Greek architecture inspires us still. The vibrancy and richness of Greek dramatic writing from this era have yet to be equaled.

It is highly unlikely that a different form of government could ever have produced such riches, certainly not the one proposed by Plato in his *Republic* or the one that existed in Sparta.[‡‡‡‡] It was the democratic governing process itself—the pride it inspired, the intellectual and oratorical skills it required—that produced a public capable of creating and appreciating such a rich cultural life.

---

[††††]   As Finley observes, "There is little open pandering to the poor against the rich, to the farmers against the town, or to the town against the farmers." On many issues, "the division over policy did not closely follow class or sectional lines." *Democracy Ancient and Modern,* p. 67.

[‡‡‡‡]   Beginning about 650 B.C., Sparta rose to become the dominant military power in the region that is now southern Greece. It was a highly militarized society co-ruled by two hereditary kings. A serf class, the helots (who were neither free nor slave), made up more than 80 percent of the population, according to Herodotus. The helots were ritually humiliated and could be legally killed by Spartan citizens. Every autumn, according to Plutarch, Spartan leaders would declare pro forma war on the helot population, allowing any Spartan citizen to kill a helot without fear of consequences. These periods provided young Spartan men with the opportunity to complete a rite of passage or manhood test and experience their first kill. Through such brutal oppression of the helots, the Spartans were able to control the agrarian population and devote themselves to military matters.

# Government and Character

## *Lessons from Athens*

*And now his heart*
*Distends with pride, and, hardening in his strength,*
*Glories.*

THERE ALWAYS HAS been, and always will be, government. It provides the skeletal structure by means of which society organizes itself. When the Indians roamed North America before the Europeans arrived, they were organized into tribal units. The tribe provided for the distribution of food, settlement of disputes, protection from the enemy without. It was the primary form of communal organization and interaction. This was the Indians' version of government.

Government can be big. It can be small. It can be exclusive or inclusive. It can be friendly or hostile. In today's Western world, government seems like a distant, elusive but overpowering behemoth, whose heavy tread we seek to escape, especially when it comes to paying taxes. Allegedly, government operates on our behalf. Our wish to have it do so blinds us to the fact that it rarely does. Like small children, we believe what we are told by government and its minions—a handful of academics and the media. Father would not betray us, they tell us. To even consider that he might would leave us frightened and alone in the world.

Secretly, we resent government for never listening to us, for disappointing us so often. But what we can do? We are powerless when faced with its determined might. In moments of despair we blame government for all of our woes and wish we could do away with it altogether, thus confounding bad government with any kind of government at all.

Government is not going to go away. So the question is not whether or not we need government but, rather, what version of government is the best and why. Is there such a thing as good government? Is there such a thing as inherently bad government? How can we tell them apart?

Ambrogio Lorenzetti was a fourteenth-century Italian painter. Between 1338 and 1340, he painted a series of frescoes on three walls of the Palazzo Pubblico in Siena. The panels are commonly known as "Allegory of Good Government," "Effects of Good Government on Town and Country," and "Allegory of Bad Government and Its Effects on Town and Country." These frescoes are masterfully executed, vast, and all-encompassing.* What appeals to me most about these paintings is the mere fact that such subject matter would be chosen by the artist or his patrons. The paintings grace the walls of the room where the chief magistrates of Siena held their meetings. Their dominance of the space serves as an inescapable reminder to all who gather there that government does matter, that it can have both good and bad effects.†

One can well imagine how the effects of good government are portrayed. The buildings are solid. People in the square are dancing, plying their trades. Similarly, the rolling hills of the Tuscan countryside are lovingly depicted. The fields are verdant. Workers are tilling the land. An allegorical figure of security hovers above the landscape. Under bad government, the buildings are in disrepair, the fields are barren. Symbolic representations of evil prevail. The mood is dark and somber. Such is the contrast between good and bad government, a contrast that prevails as much today as when these paintings were executed.

Remembering that the Renaissance was a time of political turmoil and experimentation in government, it is not surprising that such subject matter would be viewed with interest and appreciation. People of the time, including artists like Lorenzetti, were very much aware of government good and bad, and understood how critical government was in the everyday lives of the populace. Treatises were written. Government, as a subject, was very much alive. Its workings had to be understood if there was to be any chance that it could be modified to suit the needs of the people.

Exactly what are those needs? We could say that the role of government is to set up a nationwide postal system so we can send letters to each other, to provide a national currency so we can do business with each other, to set up a system of highways that allows as to travel in cars and trucks from one end of the country to the other, to set up a military to protect us from foreign enemies. These indeed are functions that national government exercises. But are there other functions perhaps more profound and critical that we have failed to address? Let us consider what John Stuart Mill has to say on the subject.

One of the primary functions of government, according to Mill, is

---

* Excellent images of the frescoes can be found at the Web Gallery of Art, http://www.wga.hu/frames-e.html?/html/l/lorenzet/ambrogio/governme/.

† Says Alexis de Tocqueville, "to my mind, the end of good government is to ensure the welfare of the people, and not merely to establish order in the midst of its misery." *Democracy in America*, Vol. I (1945 [1840]), p. 95fn.

to shape the character of its denizens. The merit of political institutions, he says, consists in part "of the degree in which they promote the general mental advancement of the community, including under that phrase advancement in intellect, in virtue, and in practical activity and efficiency." Mill's thoughts hearken back to Lorenzetti's frescoes, where one sees the direct effect of government on the well-being of those who are governed. "A government is to be judged," says Mill, "by its action upon men, ... by what it makes of the citizens, and what it does with them; its tendency to improve or deteriorate the people themselves." In other words, government acts upon us. It shapes our character, values, and intellect. It can affect us positively or negatively. When political institutions are ill constructed, "the effect is felt in a thousand ways in lowering the morality and deadening the intelligence and activity of the people."[1]

Mill describes what it is like to live under a good despotism. The citizenry has handed its destiny over to the government, which ministers to its needs without consultation or involvement. This would seem to be a desirable state of affairs. But as Mill sees it, there are negative consequences. "Leaving things to the Government, like leaving them to Providence, is synonymous with caring nothing about them, and accepting their results, when disagreeable, as visitations of nature." People become mentally passive. Their intellect declines. Purpose in life is reduced to "the material interests ... to the amusement and ornamentation, of private life.... The era of national decline has arrived."[2] Thus, the moral fiber of the individual citizens and of the nation taken as a collective are a consequence of the degree of honest involvement in government by those who are governed. According to Mill, the logical conclusion is that a "completely popular government ... promotes a better and higher form of national character, than any other polity whatsoever."[3]

If government helps to shape character, then we need to decide what kind of character we prefer, "that which struggles against evils, or that which endures them; that which bends to circumstances, or that which endeavours to make circumstances bend to itself." As Mill points out, there is a general appeal to the passive type. The passive citizen is less a menace to those who govern and less a menace to his neighbor, who feels content to be surrounded by passive souls who offer no threat of competition or agitation. Contentment is the goal. However, if our intention is the improvement of mankind, active, "uncontented characters" are our only allies.[4]

William Godwin,‡ writing more than a half century earlier, at the time of the French Revolution, expressed similar sentiments. We need

---

‡ William Godwin (1756–1836) was an English political philosopher whose most enduring work bears the title *Enquiry Concerning Political Justice and Its Influence on Morals and Happiness.* Godwin was married to the pioneering feminist writer Mary Wollstonecraft, who died giving birth to a daughter named Mary, who went on to marry the poet Percy Bysshe Shelley. Mary Shelley became a novelist and is best known for her novel *Frankenstein.*

to consider, he said, that "politics and modes of government will educate and infect us all."[5] We need to understand that indeed government
conduct[§] has intellectual, moral, psychological, and emotional consequences for its citizens—that it, in effect, shapes us and "perhaps it
insinuates itself into our personal dispositions, and insensibly commu-
nicates its own spirit to our private transactions."[6] What we consider
to be our political education is, in effect, "the modification our ideas
received from the form of government under which we live."[7¶]

Max Weber, writing more than a century later, at the time of the
German defeat in World War I, makes the same point. It was the politicians who failed the public. They were lacking in "character," he says,
character "in the purely political sense of the word, which has nothing
to do with private morality. Nor was it by chance that they lacked it; it
was the result, rather, of *the structure of the state*" (italics in the original).[8] Government creates character. Different governments produce
different characters, some better, some worse.

In his introduction to Aristotle's *Politics*, Richard McKeon states,
"There is no simple relation between ethics, which is part of political
science, and political science conceived as the study of the state, for
the state influences the education and formation of its citizens and the
character of its citizens determines the constitution of the state."[9] Says
Aristotle, himself, it is the job of the legislator to see to it that citizens
"become good men.... The citizen should be molded to suit the form of
government under which he lives.... The character of democracy creates democracy, and the character of oligarchy creates oligarchy; and
always the better the character, the better the government."[10] Or, in the
words of Jean-Jacques Rousseau, "I had come to see that everything
was radically connected with politics, and that however one proceeded,
no people would be other than the nature of its government."[11]

## Plato's Theory of Character

Plato took up the same theme. He was keenly aware that government
shapes the character of the governed. His republic was set up with a few
active, intellectually alive rulers at the top and all the rest passive characters who knew their role in society, never veered from it, never questioned,
never sought to become actively involved in the process of governing.
That was Plato's ideal. He speculated on what kind of characters would

§ Just a reminder that the word "government" represents a concept. Concepts cannot act.
Only people can. The word "government" is thus shorthand for "person or persons in power."
¶ The French philosopher Claude Adrien Helvétius (1715–1771) was similarly concerned
about the effects on government on the mentality of the governed. He believed that we
were all equally endowed with intelligence and that differences could be explained by
circumstances. He makes special reference to the role of government: "The inequality of
intelligence that exists among men is a consequence of the government they live under"
(author's translation). Helvétius, *De l'Esprit*, p. 180.

prevail if this ideal were not reached or if the ideal were attained and then deteriorated to a less-than-ideal form. The governments he mentioned are characterized by a dominant value, or motive, each of which is considered to be a constitutive element in human nature. Plato reasoned that in these less-than-ideal forms of government, it is the preponderance of a certain kind of individual that produces a certain government, rather than the other way round. Nonetheless, there is a direct correlation between a certain form of government and a certain kind of character.**

In the republic, the ideal government, the dominant value is love of reason. The first phase of decline leads to timocracy. In this form of government, love of honor replaces love of reason as the dominant motive. In timocracy, active characters prevail. The men are ambitious and competitive. There is a hunger for war and glory. Sparta offers the obvious example.

Next in line is the oligarchy, or plutocracy—government of the few. Under this government, men are driven by a need for wealth. The rich become competitive with each other in the acquisition and consumption of wealth. Reason and ambition are harnessed to the pursuit of wealth. As materialism spreads through the society and the rich rise in social esteem, there is a decline in virtue. The unity of the state is compromised. The rich are in conflict with the poor, each plotting against the other. As they age and continue to spend and consume, these plutocrats either spend what they have and become beggars or else they become criminals.

The oligarch, as Plato describes him,

> values wealth above everything else.... He is a worker who satisfies only his necessary wants.... There is something squalid about him, with his way of always expecting to make a profit and add to his hoard—the sort of person who is much admired by the vulgar. [Where he can, he will be] dishonest without risk.... The base desires are there, not tamed by a reasonable conviction that it is wrong to gratify them, but only held down under stress of fear, which makes him tremble for the safety of his whole fortune.[12]

The next form of government is democracy. Here there is also a correlation between the character of the government and the character of its citizens. "Now what is the character of the new regime?" Plato asks. "Obviously the way they govern themselves will throw light on the democratic type of man."[13]

Recall that Plato had nothing but contempt for democracy. His revulsion was no doubt a consequence of the fact that democracy was not the outcome of abstract speculation but in fact was the government he lived under in Athens. His daily encounters with people he considered to be beneath him could only reinforce his theoretical objection to this form of government.

---

** Says Plato, speaking of the oligarchic type, "The type from which he has developed corresponded to the constitution from which oligarchy arose." *The Republic of Plato*, p. 277.

In a democracy, says Plato, "there is contempt for all the fine principles we laid down in founding our commonwealth.... With a magnificent indifference to the sort of life a man has led before he enters politics, it will promote to honour anyone who merely calls himself the people's friend." Broadly speaking, democracy "is an agreeable form of anarchy with plenty of variety and an equality of a peculiar kind for equals and unequals."[14]

As government falls into decline from the ideal of the republic, first to timocracy, then to oligarchy, then to democracy, there is a corresponding internal struggle within the spirit or soul of the citizen that leads to the defeat of certain virtues or appetites and the ascendancy of others, less desirable. "Knowledge, right principles, true thoughts, are not at their post; and the place lies open to the assault of false and presumptuous notions." In the case of the democrat, modesty and self-control "are thrust out into exile," to be replaced by "Insolence, Anarchy, Waste and Impudence."[15]

Plato shows a fair amount of psychological insight in describing the role of family life in shaping the character of he who will become a democrat. The father is parsimonious and only respects business-like desires. Other desires he dismisses as "frivolous embellishment." The son's hatred for his father's miserliness drives him to every kind of excess. However, as he matures and is exposed to other influences, the son chooses a middle course of moderation and thus a democrat is born.

Generally speaking, in a democracy, "the young copy their elders, argue with them, and will not do as they are told; while the old, anxious not to be thought disagreeable tyrants, imitate the young and condescend to enter into their jokes and amusements."[16] Even the animals enjoy a freedom they could not find under another form of government.

In Plato's scheme of things, as matters deteriorate in a democracy, three classes emerge and enter into conflict: (1) the drones, political leaders, wealthy, and aggressive; (2) a middle class devoted to making money; and (3) the small farmers who work their own farms. This third class, the farmers, the most numerous, will often look for a leader to represent their interests. They live out of town, at a distance from the Assembly, and they are not always able to leave their farms to speak for themselves. They might not be as articulate as the wealthy, who are better educated. And so they will choose someone who is visible and outspoken to speak for them, thus paving the way for despotism.

Whether or not one agrees with Plato's description of the various forms of government, how they come about, and the kinds of different characters they produce, I find his way of thinking to be instructive. In essence, Plato is uniting political philosophy and psychology into a new discipline that can be called "political psychology." Government, he is saying, is neither arbitrary nor irrelevant in one's consideration of the emotional makeup, character, and motivations of the governed. Quite the contrary, he says.

If we want to truly understand the individual, we need to understand the government he lives under. This, in essence, was Mill's point as well.

My primary interest is democracy. What kind of character and personality does it produce in its citizens? According to Plato, the democratic man was insolent, unruly, wasteful, and impudent. Since the character of government determines the character of the governed, by implication, it was the Athenian form of government that was flawed. Based on freedom and equality, it produced citizens who were unworthy of esteem in Plato's eyes.

Plato's observations might be accurate, though biased. Perhaps we can take his characterization of the Athenian citizen and reinterpret it to mean something more desirable than he intended. Words like "insolent" or "impudent," for example, could mean "proud," the kind of man who would not bow low to someone of pretension, such as Plato. Recall that Pericles—an aristocrat, a general, one of the most esteemed men in Athens—was himself brought to trial for his conduct during the Peloponnesian Wars. He was deprived of his post, fined, and then reinstated. That is the true meaning of political equality.

"Unruly" could mean independent and outspoken, not easily cowed or subjugated. "Wasteful" could describe someone who, in Plato's view, was self-indulgent, but it could also apply to someone who, perhaps, was not self-denying, someone who knew how to enjoy his life. Thus, using Plato's own words, one could argue that the Athenian was neither passive nor docile, but instead that he was outspoken, self-assured, and independent.

On two occasions during the wars with Sparta, once in 411 B.C. and again in 404 B.C., a clique of Athenian aristocrats conspired with Sparta to overthrow Athenian democracy. On each occasion, the Athenians fought back and regained their democracy. They showed great courage. They showed loyalty to their ideals and the form of government they cherished. It is a noteworthy element in the character of these loyal Athenians that they did not seek vengeance against the conspirators. There was a general amnesty. The dictators were even allowed to retain the properties they had illegally seized. Aristotle observed, some thirty years after these events, that the Athenians "appear both in private and in public to have behaved towards the past disasters in the most completely honorable and statesmanlike manner of any people in history."[17]

Thus, the Athenians were neither petty nor vengeful, nor were they avaricious. Anti-democrats repeatedly allege that, given the opportunity, the large numbers of poorer elements in society will organize to seize the property of the wealthy. History proves otherwise. Athens was a society with at least two classes, rich and poor, and it had an emerging middle class. The land of the aristocracy was never seized.†† Over

††   Athenian magistrates, upon entering office, had to take a vow that no Athenian citizen's land would be confiscated or redistributed.

a period of two hundred years the different classes lived side by side in relative harmony. Athens was a political democracy but it was not a social democracy, certain proof that you can have one without the other.

Athenians were open-minded and tolerant. They were quite comfortable seeing their leaders and their gods satirized. No one was too important or too powerful to be poked fun at. Nothing was sacred. Athenians obviously had a sense of humor. Even in times of war, freedom of speech was tolerated, as can be seen in the plays of Aristophanes. "At major public religious festivals, managed and financed by the state, the playwrights were expected to ridicule and abuse ordinary Athenians and their leaders, the war effort and any piece of legislation that came to mind, as well as to treat the gods with an irreverence that few Sophists would have risked."[18]

The average Athenian citizen was probably a good deal more articulate than the average American of today. Athenians attended the Assembly and debated among themselves the various laws and policies, which they were then to vote on. Anyone at the Assembly could rise to speak. Some who did so were among the prominent aristocrats. Others were drawn from among the common folk. A citizen would have to speak on his own behalf whether defending himself or charging someone else in court. There were no lawyers. There were no prosecutors. Socrates was brought up on charges by a wealthy tanner named Anytus. It was an unknown man by the name of Dioditus who challenged Pericles' successor, Cleon, on the subject of Mytilene. Should the people be massacred? Should they be shown clemency? It was Dioditus who most eloquently argued for clemency, and he won.

## Democratic Living as a Form of Education

In ancient Athens, there was no compulsory, state formulated education. There was no need for it. Education was a part of daily living. It was in the conversations in the public spaces. It was in the poetry. It was in the philosophy. It was in the theatrical and religious festivals. It was in the meetings of the Assembly, where everyone in attendance learned about their community, its needs, and its achievements.

For Werner Jaeger, who wrote *Paideia: The Ideals of Greek Culture* (1939–1944), Greek culture itself, in its most comprehensive and dynamic sense, was a form of education, or *paideia*. As Jaeger observes, speaking of the Greeks, "The greatest work of art they had to create was Man."[19] This is what makes ancient Athens unique. This is what is meant by a "humanist" society—one that has as its focus human life itself, a society that seeks to help the individual realize his potential to the fullest.

Thus, the average Athenian, even one of the most humble origins, achieved an unusually high level of intellectual sophistication. For although it is true that a good deal of the culture was produced by the aristocracy, it is also true that the theater, staged for the masses, nonetheless required considerable verbal and intellectual sophistication to grasp its deepest meanings and refined subtleties.‡‡ There was a strong oral tradition based in Homer's two epic poems, *The Iliad* and *The Odyssey*, and Hesiod's *Works and Days*,§§ which were as fundamental to Greek education as the Bible used to be in most early American homes.

Education, as the Greeks saw it, meant character development, for it was the individual's character that was his most important attribute. "How could the individual's claim to value and importance be justified, without the Greek recognition of the value of human character?"[20] The Greeks were the first to recognize that "education means deliberately molding human character in accordance with an ideal."[21] And that ideal is the political man (*zoon politikon*), he who participates in the life of the community, or polis. As Jaeger points out, in "the best period of Greece, mind without state was as impossible as a state without minds."[22] The state, itself, cannot be understood "unless viewed as the force which shaped man and man's life."[23] The individual contains within him the state, in the same way that the oak tree exists in the acorn. As each individual grows into maturity, his participation in the life of the polis brings the state into being. His realization of his essence as a human being takes its form by his participation in the communal state, the polis.

Thus, education is a communal project. It is "the process by which a community preserves and transmits its physical and intellectual character."[24] It is the community itself, not some special branch of government, that provides the model and structure for the educational process. The communal achievement—what it stands for and what it seeks to achieve—is transmitted by its culture. The process by which communal values are transmitted via the individual is what Jaeger calls "*paideia*." It is this broader meaning that gives the word "education" its special meaning in the context of ancient Athens.¶¶

Because they were filled with the spirit of community and all the richness that Greek culture had to offer, it is not surprising to learn

---

‡‡Observes one writer, "Tragedy was performed with religious solemnity ... before a vast, critical, amazingly intelligent audience." Quoted in I. F. Stone, *The Trial of Socrates*, p. 206.
§§Hesiod was a peasant and gives the peasant's perspective on life's struggles. Hard work is a virtue. Justice is the ideal to strive for. Homer's work gives us the perspective of the aristocracy. Valor in battle is the highest good. These two threads, that of the aristocrat and that of the peasant, evolving over hundreds of years, combined to create what came to be Greek character in ancient Athens.
¶¶ It wasn't until the fourth century B.C., as Athens was in decline, that traveling educators, known as Sophists, began playing an increasingly important role in Greek education. Sophists taught philosophy and rhetoric—the art of persuasion—for a fee. The most famous Sophist of all went by the name of Protagoras (ca. 490 B.C.–420 B.C.). He was a strong believer in democracy and the virtue of civic life. He was an agnostic who believed that man was the measure of all things.

that Athenians were optimistic, energetic, and enterprising. As Thucydides reports, the Corinthians, who were allies to Sparta and enemies of Athens, had this to say about their enemy:

> The Athenians are addicted to innovation, and their designs are characterized by swiftness alike in conception and execution.... They are adventurous beyond their power, and daring beyond their judgment, and in danger they are sanguine.... They are swift to follow up a success, and slow to recoil from a reverse. Their bodies they spend ungrudgingly in their country's cause; their intellect they jealously husband to be employed in her service.... The deficiency created by the miscarriage of an undertaking is soon filled up by fresh hopes, for they alone are enabled to call a thing hoped for a thing got, by the speed with which they act upon their resolution.... Their only idea of a holiday is to do what the occasion demands, and to them laborious occupation is less of a misfortune than the peace of a quiet life. To describe their character in a word, one might truly say that they were born into the world to take no rest themselves and to give none to others.[25]

Herodotus contrasts the character of the Persians under despotism with that of the Athenians living in a democracy. His subject matter is the war between Greece and Persia, which began in 499 B.C. and continued off and on until 448 B.C. The Persians were driven into battle with whips. The Greeks fought as free men. The Greeks defeated the invading enemy. Observes Herodotus, "equality is a good thing; seeing that while they were under despotic rulers the Athenians were no better in war than any of their neighbors, yet once they got quit of despots they were far and away the first of all."[26] Under despotism, the Greeks were cowardly. Living in a democracy, they were courageous. Thus does government shape character.

Aristotle makes a similar observation. He contrasts a professional army with a citizen army. The professional is better trained, knows better how to use his arms. When the odds are in their favor, the professionals will vanquish. However, when the odds are against them, they are the first to flee the battlefield for safety. "Citizen troops stand their ground and die fighting," says Aristotle. Citizens "think it is a disgrace to run away, and prefer death to safety."[27] Aristotle notes that Persian commanders had trenches dug *behind* their troops to prevent them from running away.

The issue of character is important to Greek culture and political life. For example, Plato would argue that virtue has its basis in knowledge. He thought that only those who are highly educated and carefully selected are fit to govern. Aristotle had a different viewpoint. He believed that civic virtue, a sense of fair play, and respect for the truth were evenly distributed among the population at large and that character, not knowledge, is what qualified the Athenian citizenship to govern itself.***

There are three known "Apologies," or dramatized versions of the trial of Socrates. The most famous is by Plato. There is also one by Xenophon, and least known is the one by Libanius. Libanius puts words in Socrates' mouth that Socrates never would have uttered, but in so doing he gives us a feel for what is unique about Athenian political culture.

Whoever visits Athens does not want to leave. "It is talk, sheer talk, and the joy of talking that is the prime attraction of Athens," says Socrates in Libanius' version of the "Apology." In Athens, "those who revere wisdom are held in higher esteem than those who are dreaded in battle. This is what makes the great difference between us and the non-Greek peoples."[28] Thus, Athens under a democracy is famous for its freedom of speech and the day-to-day exchanges that constitute its civic and political life—in the *boule* (i.e., the Council), in the Assembly, and in the marketplace.

In his dialogue entitled "Protagoras," Plato allows Protagoras to speak for himself. Although he acknowledges that when Athenians need special advice they go to experts, Protagoras continues, "but when they meet for a consultation on political art," that is, on questions of government, "where they should be guided throughout by justice and good sense they naturally allow advice from everybody, since it is held that everyone should partake of this excellence or else that states [the city-state, such as Athens] cannot be."[29]

It is through their participation that Athenian citizens learn what they need to know about participating in government. It is through participation that they consider the ideas and ideals that will guide them in their political decisions. As Charles Freeman observes, "the very act of being involved in politics ... forced men to think about abstract ideals, justice, goodness, the purpose of life, the ultimate nature of things and so hand in hand with political activity came the emergence of political thought."[30] This is Mill's view as well. He says:

> It is not sufficiently considered how little there is in most men's ordinary life to give any largess either to their conceptions or to their sentiments. Giving [the individual] something to do for the public supplies, in a measure, all these deficiencies. If circumstances allow the amount of public duty assigned to him to be considerable, it makes him an educated man. Notwithstanding the defects of the social system and

---

*** Alcibiades (whose transgressions are outlined in Chapter 3) was probably Plato's most brilliant student. He serves as a shining example of a bright and educated man who, lacking in character (i.e., virtue), was not fit to govern in a democracy. One could point to many a humble citizen, of modest formal education, but with strong character and civic virtue, who were fit to govern. Stone describes Alcibiades thusly: "Alcibiades flashes across the skies of Athenian history like a meteor. He was not only brilliant and handsome, a man of many talents, a military general of genius, dazzlingly proficient in political and philosophical discourse, an aristocrat who was idolized by the *demos*, erotically irresistible—in the bisexual world of antiquity—to women and men alike." Stone, *The Trial of Socrates*, p. 65.

moral ideas of antiquity, the practice of the dicastery [jury system] and the ecclesia [Assembly] raised the intellectual standard of an average Athenian citizen beyond anything of which there is yet an example in any other mass of men, ancient or modern.[31]

Says Kitto, "the Greeks thought of the Polis, as an active, formative thing, training the minds and characters of the citizens."[32] Kitto thought the Greeks had an unusual capacity for self-expression that is clear, precise, and subtle. He attributes this capacity in part to the Greek language itself. He speaks of the Greeks' "firm grasp of the idea and its expression in clear and economical form."[33] He also observes that the typical Greek was energetic and long-lived. He does a comparison of cultural figures from the eighteenth and nineteenth centuries versus their counterparts in fifth-century B.C. Athens and discovers that, on average, the latter outlived the former by decades. It is interesting to speculate that the active community life fostered by democratic living might have been a significant factor in the difference.[†††]

Kitto contrasts the concept of Roman law (which we in the United States have inherited) with the notion of law that prevailed in ancient Athens. Roman law regulated the relations between people and their affairs. It was the codification of practice. It had a static quality to it. For the Greeks, the laws were a "creative and moral power. They were designed not merely to secure justice in an individual case, but to inculcate Justice."[34]

The Athenians also had a genius for statesmanship, which the Romans lacked. In Athens, there was a pervading sense of the common good, the capacity to deal with social issues in a rational manner. Never did the Roman state "transfigure the life of its members as the Athenian polis did."[35]

The Athenian mind seemed to have a unique capacity for grasping the specific, immediate occurrence and to be able to generalize from it as a means of generating abstract thought that could lead to new solutions. This capacity for abstract thought as demonstrated in ancient Athenian philosophy and theater is probably what distinguishes this Greek culture from any that came before or has come since. Undoubtedly the multitude, complexity, and weightiness of the matters the average Athenian confronted on a daily basis were instrumental in developing this unusual gift.

In 431 B.C., at the end of the first year of Athens' war with Sparta, the Athenian general and statesman Pericles delivered a funeral oration, which was recorded by Thucydides[‡‡‡] in his *History of the Pelopon-*

---

††† In his *Outliers* (published in 2008), Malcolm Gladwell talks about a group of Italians who, in the 1880s and 1890s, migrated to a small town in Pennsylvania that they named Roseto after the town they had come from in the Old World. The new Roseto looked very much like their old town. Everyone in it spoke Italian, and in the early 1900s it was a little island unto itself. In the 1950s, a researcher discovered that men from Roseto rarely suffered from heart disease. It turned out their health was positively affected by their commitment to community.

‡‡‡ The fact that this is not a verbatim record, but rather that the oration has been assembled and in part created by Thucydides himself, in no way detracts from its usefulness in understanding the Athenian character.

*nesian War.* This is an eloquent and uplifting address in which the war dead themselves are given only brief mention. The focus is on what they fought for, why they fought so hard, and what is unique about Athenian society that would produce such courage and loyalty in its citizens.

Pericles gives special mention to "the form of government under which our greatness grew," a government that "favours the many instead of the few." This, Pericles reminds us, is "why it is called a democracy." The laws "afford equal justice to all." Social advancement is determined by merit rather than class considerations. "Nor ... does poverty bar the way."[36] The freedom enjoyed in political life extends to private life, where people are free to enjoy their private pursuits without interference.

Here is a government that is as proud of the responsibilities of political life as it is of the enjoyment it fosters. Says Pericles, "Further, we provide plenty of means for the mind to refresh itself from business." Quality of life is as much of a concern as civic responsibility and courage in battle. And citizens do not become fearful of foreigners when at war. "We throw open our city to the world and never by alien acts exclude foreigners." In contrast to the Spartans, who "from their very cradles ... seek after manliness, we live exactly as we please, and yet are just as ready to encounter every legitimate danger."[37] The Athenian is strong, independent, and proud. The society of which he is a part is solidly integrated. The humblest citizen is as empowered as the wealthiest. There is poverty but probably little in the way of crime because no one is left out. No one is on the fringes. There is no police force, in the modern sense. There probably is no need for one.

Despite the demands of livelihood and private life, "we are still fair judges of public matters ... regarding him who takes no part in these duties not as unambitious but useless." Discussion is seen not as a waste of time but as "an indispensable preliminary to any wise action."[38]

Referring to those who have died for Athens, Pericles observes that they chose to die resisting rather than live submitting. Gaze upon all that is wondrous about Athens, he says, and realize that "it was by courage, sense of duty, and a keen feeling of honour in action that men were enabled to win all this."[39] It is honor, not gain, "that rejoices the heart of age and helplessness."[40]

There is neither bitterness nor anger in Pericles' oration. Nor is he rattling the saber and calling for vengeance and retribution. There is no talk about glory in battle. In fact, the entire oration, though uttered at the time of war, is a paean to peace and the joys of civilized living.

## Athenian Democracy (and Character) in Decline

It was war, however, that was ultimately the undoing of Athenian democracy. In 401 B.C., Sparta was victorious. There was once again a threat to democracy. The people were worn out from battle and demoralized by defeat. The polis began its decline. The most visible sign that the times had changed was the trial and conviction of Socrates in 399 B.C. The free speech and tolerance that characterized Athenian culture at the height of democracy had become eroded. The citizen army was gradually replaced with an army of mercenaries. And the change in government was reflected in the character of the citizen and the way of life.

Says Kitto, "What we meet in the fourth century [B.C.] is a permanent change in the temper of the people."[41] There is more individualism. In the fifth century B.C., sculpture depicted the general or ideal type, the universal. In the fourth century B.C., sculpture pays attention to individual traits and passing moods. In drama, there is a shift from universal themes to the particular, the abnormal, the romantic. Philosophy shifts from themes of honor and virtue to discussions of following nature and seeking pleasure, which have nothing to do with the life of the citizen, living in the polis. Private life replaces public life as the primary concern. In the day of Pericles, homes built by the wealthy were relatively modest. In the time of Demosthenes, the wealthy build homes with splendor, designed to impress.

The cultural shift shows itself in theater as well. In the fifth century B.C., the comedies satirized political life and caricatured its leading figures. In the fourth century B.C., comedy makes jokes about cooks and the price of fish. In the fifth century B.C., the people who spoke in the Assembly were either leaders like Pericles or concerned citizens. In the fourth, the speakers tend to be people like Demosthenes, professional orators.

Education, likewise, becomes professionalized. In the day of Pericles, the life of the polis was a universal education for all citizens. In the time of Demosthenes, professional instructors such as the Sophists, who expect to be paid for what they teach, emerge as a dominant force. People who can pay for it get a special education. Others are left to fend for themselves. The expert replaces the amateur, and that is the end of democracy. The Greeks of the fifth century B.C. understood that governing was about value judgments and that in the field of value judgments there are no experts.

As the polis declines, the citizen is less aware, less involved, less committed. In 357 B.C., Demosthenes is trying to rouse Athenians to the menace coming from the north in the person of Philip II of Macedon. He is ignored and ridiculed. Athenians are lulled into quiescence by rumors of the death of Philip.

Kitto speaks of the "wholeness of mind."[42] Living in the age of Pericles, when life in the polis reached its apogee, living at a time when everyone was involved in everything, people thought in wholes, not in parts. The citizen was called upon to see the whole picture, the long view, in order to make decisions that affected the political entity in its entirety. It is not until the fourth century B.C. and the thinking of Socrates and Plato, as the polis itself begins to fragment, that the philosopher thinks of the individual as broken down into parts, a body and a soul. The Athenian thinker of the fifth century B.C. had a tendency to ask abstract questions, to deal in broad universal issues. He was neither practical nor pragmatic. In their dramas and histories, writers were more concerned with inner meaning than with the events themselves. The world of philosophy had to wait for the fourth century B.C., when thinkers like Aristotle would start to examine the concrete, natural world in some detail.

It is reasonably clear, in the case of ancient Athens, that in order for democracy to thrive there needed to be peace. In times of peace, power was equally dispersed throughout a self-governing citizen body. The individual had the opportunity to evolve into a full, emotional adult. Culture and community flourished, enhancing the sense of well-being, strengthening character and intellect. There was nothing to distract the government from its primary purpose, the common good.

With the onset of war, power became more centralized and concentrated. Individual and collective resources were redirected to survival. As Kitto observes, in contrasting fifth-century B.C. Athens with fourth-century B.C. Athens, "it is not merely that Athens had been exhausted by the long Peloponnesian War," it is that there had been "a permanent change in the temper of the people."[43] In a similar vein, R. K. Sinclair observes, "lack of success in the Peloponnesian War was the crucial factor which led to the overthrow of democracy."[44]

As a consequence of war, the values that had sustained the democracy became clouded and tenuous. The individual retreated from the community, which had become depleted of the resources that initially had sustained him, and instead sought solace in a private existence. The strength and integrity of character, indicative of Athens at its height, were worn down with the stress of constant war. There was nothing left to fend off the likes of Philip II of Macedon. Athens as a unique form of government, founded in citizen participation at all levels, disappeared.

# The Roman Republic

## *Oligarchy with a hint of Democracy*

*Round he throws his baleful eyes,*
*That witness'd huge affliction and dismay,*
*Mix'd with obdurate pride, and steadfast hate*

THE ROMAN REPUBLIC—APPROXIMATELY 509 B.C. to 44 B.C.—and the democratic government of ancient Athens— approximately 508 B.C. to 261 B.C.—were contemporaneous. They were Mediterranean neighbors and they faced similar problems: distribution of grain, indebtedness, class differences, land use. Due to its form of government, none of these problems was divisive in Athens. The same cannot be said of the Roman Republic, where there was constant strife and bloodshed, largely due to an oligarchic government that yielded nothing except under overwhelming pressure from the lower classes or from within its own ranks.

The word "republic" is derived from the Latin expression "*res publica*," which translates as "public thing" or "public affair." The term goes back to a period in Roman history that began in 509 B.C., when the Etruscan kings were expelled from Rome. For almost five hundred years, Rome was free from the tyranny of one-man rule. This freedom ended in 44 B.C., when Julius Caesar was declared dictator for life. Thus, the word "republic" was applied to the period before 44 B.C. because there was no monarch. The government in this era was not the populace-oriented system the name might suggest, however. It was instead an oligarchy of powerful Roman families who, initially, ruled exclusively for their own personal benefit.*

---

* See Andrew Linott's *The Roman Republic* for a brief, easy-to-read overview. For a dynamic and detailed portrayal of the political conflict ensuing toward the end of the Republic, see

Was there anything democratic about the Roman Republic? Certainly not in the early years. It was only reluctantly, and often temporarily, that the oligarchy would cede some power to the common folk and address their needs in the form of legislation and policy.

Before and during the period of the Republic, the ultimate and enduring power lay with the Senate, which was composed principally of wealthy families and former magistrates (i.e., former elected officials).[†] The Senate was Rome's only forum for free political discussion, and most legislation originated in the course of Senate debate.[‡] For the most part, it was the senators—that is, the leading men of the most prominent families—who established foreign policy, extended imperial reach, and maintained control of finance and state religion.[§] From among their numbers were chosen two consuls, the highest elected officials in the Republic. The two consuls jointly served a one-year term as head of state, commanding the army and administering domestic affairs.[¶] The consuls alternated dominance of power month to month, but either consul could veto the decisions of the other at any time.

The domestic conflict that was the ultimate undoing of the Republic—the Conflict of the Orders—began early on. The plebeians (the population at large), whose interests were being ignored by the patricians (the wealthy aristocracy, who controlled the Senate), made their voices heard for the first time in 494 B.C. The issues of the day—allocation of public lands won in war and the repayment of debt—were to remain the determining issues for the duration of the Republic. The plebeians wanted relief from exorbitant interest rates imposed on them by the aristocracy. They wanted to see an end to "debt slavery," which resulted when they were unable to repay a debt.[**] Their pleas ignored,

---

Michael Parenti, *The Assassination of Julius Caesar*. Harriet I. Flower edited *The Cambridge Companion to the Roman Republic*, which offers a comprehensive overview of culture, society, and government during this period.

† The Roman historian Sallust, writing in the first century B.C., as the Republic was coming to an end, himself a senator, complained that a small faction was in control, "giving and taking away as they please; oppressing the innocent and raising their partisans to honor; while no wickedness, no dishonesty or disgrace, is a bar to the attainment of office. Whatever appears desirable, they seize and render their own, and transform their will and pleasure into their law, as arbitrarily as victors in a conquered city." Quoted in Michael Parenti, *The Assassination of Julius Caesar*, p. 54.

‡ From the beginning of the Republic to its end, the number of senators increased from three hundred to nine hundred.

§ For an outline and description of the various governmental institutions during the Republic, see Flower, *The Cambridge Companion*, pp. 61–65.

¶ Individual magistrates, starting with the two consuls, had a great deal of power over daily affairs. It is worth noting, however, that there were two consuls (not one) and that they were elected for a one-year term, a relatively brief period when measured against terms typically served by politicians in twenty-first-century America. Frequent rotation in office is a democratic feature. The more people who serve in government, the more democratic is that government.

** A debtor could become a slave to his creditor for failure of payment.

the plebeians, who constituted the core fighting force of the Roman army, "seceded." They left town. As a result, the patricians decided to negotiate with representatives of the people. The first negotiators for the plebeians were known as "tribunes." What began as a temporary form of representation went on to become a fixture of the Roman Republic.

Tribunes were empowered to come to the defense of any debtor who was threatened by a creditor. The person of the tribune was considered to be inviolate. Immediate vengeance was justified if one of them came to harm. In time, the ranks of the tribunes grew to ten individuals.

The tribunes presided over the *Concilium Plebis* (Assembly of the Plebeians), which met and passed on resolutions promulgated by the Senate. The Assembly of the Plebeians could meet only if summoned by a magistrate. Patricians were not admitted. The plebeians attended standing, not seated, and they could listen but not enter into the debate. They could vote to accept or reject a particular proposal. Resolutions passed by the body were known as "plebiscites."

Initially, plebiscites applied only to plebeians. In 449 B.C., however, a law was passed that made plebiscites binding on all Romans. This law had to be passed again in 287 B.C., because the wealthy and powerful had a tendency to ignore those laws that threatened their interests. The same applies to issues of debt and land use, which had to be addressed again and again. For example, some twenty-seven measures were aimed at limiting the rate of interest on loans.

Eventually tribunes were allowed to become consuls. Although this was progress of a kind, in fact, plebeian tribunes were usually wealthy in their own right—*nouveau riche*, one might say—and so the ranks of rulers were still open to only a very small percentage of Roman citizens.

## Bloody Deeds

Addressing the needs of the small peasant farmer was an uphill battle and ultimately a risk to one's life. Initially, small peasant landholders were the core of Roman farming. But as Rome became more and more ambitious and fought wars of conquest farther and farther away from home, peasant foot soldiers were less available to farm and protect their land. A member of the aristocracy might take over a peasant's land in the peasant's absence and have it worked by slaves. A peasant foot soldier could return from war and find himself landless.

Subsistence farming gradually evolved into farming and animal husbandry for a larger market. Conquest of foreign lands brought tens of thousands of slaves to Roman territory.[††] These slaves began replacing the small peasant farmers as a source of labor. The land acquired by conquest was supposed to be fairly distributed among the peasant foot soldiers. Instead, members of the aristocracy simply took it and used it

---

†† There was an estimated influx of some 150,000 slaves in the year 167 B.C.

for their own purposes. Public lands that were supposed to be available for public use were seized by the aristocracy.

In 133 B.C., the tribune Tiberius Gracchus, a noble of plebeian origins, proposed a bill enforcing the limits on holdings of public lands and the grazing of animals, a direct challenge to the practices of members of the aristocracy. Using aggressive political strategies and bypassing the influence of the Senate, he managed to get the bill passed. Tiberius was considered by his opponents to be a tyrant and a demagogue.‡‡ On the day of his election for a second term as tribune, he was murdered by a mob of senators and their henchmen. His supporters were hunted down and killed.

Tiberius' younger brother Gaius was elected tribune in 123 B.C. and then reelected in 122 B.C. He sought to reinforce and expand upon his brother's efforts. Gaius strengthened the laws forbidding arbitrary prosecution of Roman citizens by unruly magistrates. He saw to the passage of a new agrarian law involving colonial settlements. By this time, Rome was no longer able to supply its own grain, and grain had to be imported. Gaius provided for the building of granaries and the sale of grain throughout the year at subsidized prices. Gaius sought to reorganize the collection of taxes and the prosecution of those who improperly collected tax monies. In so doing, he sought to set limits on the powers of senators and to hold them accountable for their misconduct—like his brother had done a decade earlier. He met a similar fate. In 121 B.C., Gaius and two hundred fifty of his supporters were murdered by senate assassins. Another three thousand alleged sympathizers were rounded up and executed.§§

The blood of those who sought to attend to the basic needs of the general population during the Roman Republic could fill a river. These men were routinely slaughtered by their adversaries in the Senate.¶¶ In 100 B.C., a Senate death squad murdered Lucius Appuleius Saturninus, tribune, and Gaius Servilius Glaucia, a reform-minded senator who proposed a law to distribute affordable grain to the plebeians and another involving court reform, which had as its purpose the setting

---

‡‡  "Demagogue," like other words involving government and politics, can be confusing and is often misapplied. Literally, it means "leader of the people." The ruling oligarchy does not want to see the people empowered, and so "demagogue" has come to be a term of opprobrium. It refers to someone who recklessly and for self-serving purposes stirs up the masses with impassioned rhetoric. But suppose the demagogue actually delivers on his promises, as Tiberius Gracchus did, or as Pericles did. Is he still a "demagogue" in the bad sense of the word? And what about the politician who appeals to the masses with false promises and uses his office to enrich himself and his friends? What do we call him? A shrewd politician? For a discussion of the word, see Sinclair, *Democracy and Participation in Athens*, p. 37.

§§  For a sustained discussion of the constant struggle to address the needs of the Roman population at large, see Parenti, *The Assassination of Julius Caesar*, especially chapter 4, "Demagogues and Death Squads."

¶¶  By the time of the late Republic, somewhere toward the end of the second century B.C., the Senate itself was divided between the *optimates* (who favored the interests of the wealthiest families) and the *populares* (who promoted measures for the benefit of the people at large).

of limits on the arbitrary use of Senate power. Marcus Livius Drusus, a tribune and a reformer, like Saturninus and Glaucia, was stabbed to death in 91 B.C. His assassin was never sought out. Around 88 B.C., a friend of Drusus, Sulpicius Rufus, a tribune and reformer, was also hunted down and killed. Publius Clodius Pulcher, known to history as Clodius, a tribune allied with Julius Caesar, got a law passed allowing for the organizing of craft guilds and unions. He proposed a law giving full political rights to freedmen and many slaves. He fought to have free grain distributed to the plebeians. He was murdered in 52 B.C. Rome gradually descended into civil war as various powerful personalities sought to assert their political power through the use of force.

In 59 B.C., Julius Caesar became consul and formed a triumvirate with Pompey and Crassus. Crassus met with a disastrous military defeat and was killed by the enemy as he attempted to negotiate a peace. There resulted a civil war, pitting Pompey and his forces against Caesar and his. On January 10, 49 B.C., Caesar led his troops across the Rubicon River and onto Italian territory, thus committing an act of treason. He prevailed for a time, ruled briefly as dictator,*** and then served as consul. Under Caesar's leadership there was once again land reform amid violent opposition. During his last years, he founded new settlements for veterans of his army and for eighty thousand of Rome's plebeians. Elsewhere he took similar steps to benefit twenty thousand poor families with three or more children. He mandated that large landholders make up their workforce of at least one-third free men, as opposed to slaves. He took steps to reduce the burden of debtors, erasing one-fourth of all outstanding debt. He updated and streamlined voter roles and had the proceedings of the Senate and the Assemblies posted on a daily basis. And on the morning of March 15 (the Ides of March), 44 B.C.—just a month after he had been declared dictator for life—as a Senate session was about to begin, sixty conspirators, among them some of the leading citizens of Rome, slashed at Caesar with daggers, felling him with twenty-three stabs, thus ending the life of another *popularis*.†††

As this event—and others like it—demonstrates, the Roman Republic was an oligarchy. At any moment in its history the ultimate power resided with a relative handful of powerful men from wealthy families who would stop at nothing to defend their prerogatives. Containment of individual power was a constant challenge to maintenance of stable government.

---

*** Dictator was an official Roman title. In times of political turbulence and instability, the Senate would authorize the consuls to appoint a dictator, who would have complete authority over the Roman people and would serve for a fixed period, usually not more than six months.

††† This is not the whole story. Caesar was born into a patrician family. He was known for his sexual exploits—both hetero- and homosexual—and for extravagant expenditures of borrowed money. He stole three thousand pounds of gold from the Capitol itself. His military exploits resulted in hundreds of thousands of deaths, not including the uncountable numbers of Roman soldiers who lost their lives to Caesar's ambition.

## A Culture of Power

The arbitrary exercise of authority was deeply rooted in Roman society. The power dynamics of public life reflected the power dynamics of family life. In Rome, "the ideal household also served as the paradigm of authority and of social order in society and in the state as a whole."[1]

At the head of the family was the *pater familias*, the patriarch, who could be at times arbitrary and tyrannical, at times righteous and just. His rule dominated the lives of all of his living descendants, his wife, his slaves, and his servants. His legal power—a typically Roman concept— was virtually unlimited. It was the father who would recognize a child as legitimate at birth by raising it from the ground. His failure to do so would result in the child's being exposed to die or sold into slavery. He could put his children, even his adult children, to death with impunity. He could punish all members of his family, including his wife. He could sell his children into slavery. Household slaves were regularly beaten and exploited sexually. Female slaves as young as seven were given to older male slaves as a reward.

The absolute power of the father in the household mimics a "political culture in which power and obedience always and everywhere take precedence over individual liberties and each person's freedom of choice."[2] The continuing spread of Roman authority over a larger and larger land mass, the brutal suppression of opposition, the imposing personalities of consuls and military commanders—motivated by greed and the need for self-glorification—are consistent with a family structure in which a single male head of household governs with absolute and at times ruthless authority, in which the household is his empire, in which his home is resplendent with artifacts commemorating his achievements.

In contrast to ancient Athens, where sculpture tends to deal with the universal and political figures are for the most part anonymous, in Rome we see the glorification of individual conquerors and political leaders in the bust style of sculpture. The penetrating and defiant gaze of Roman leaders revealed in these busts is emblematic of a culture that prizes individual power over community well-being. The *res publica*, or community, provides the opportunity for the powerful to make grand appearances before a passively admiring public. "Spectacle and public self-representation were as important to the Roman office holder as to any modern politician."[3] The magistrate, holding high office, would move through the streets, attired in his toga with its purple border, accompanied by an entourage, to the cheers of an admiring public. The return of a triumphant general was an opportunity for the greatest spectacle of all.

Fittingly, the early American oligarchs turned for a model not to Athens, characterized by its democratic processes and individual liberty, but to

Rome,‡‡‡ a government in which a relative handful of oligarchs ruled and dominated the political, social, and domestic culture with their lust for power and self-glorification. By invoking the Roman Republic, which, in Hamilton's eyes, "attained to the pinnacle of human greatness,"[4] Madison, Hamilton, and Jay are, in fact, advocating oligarchy, as Madison himself says, through the election of a small number of "proper guardians."[5]

Borrowing selectively from Rome, the framers of the U.S. Constitution carefully left behind the Republic's most democratic features. Two stand out. The first concerns war. In the days of the Roman Republic, going to war was decided by those who were going to risk their lives in fighting it, through a vote in the Centuriate Assembly.§§§

A second important democratic feature of the Roman Republic concerns legislation. Although most legislative initiatives came from the Senate, where formal debate took place, a law did not become official until the people voiced their acceptance. If they voted it down, the law was rejected. The only proposals that became law were those the people had agreed to accept.

Significant democratic features of Roman government—the right of soldiers to vote on whether or not to go to war, the right of the people at large to veto legislation proposed by the Senate, agrarian laws that set limits to the amount of public land the aristocracy could appropriate, the right of the people to try the nobility for crimes against the state, dividing executive power between two consuls who were replaced on an annual basis—are summarily rejected by Madison. He is explicit on this point when he explains that the difference between ancient governments and American government lies *"in the total exclusion of the people in their collective capacity* from any share in the [American government]"[6] (italics in the original).

In the Roman assemblies, the people themselves were present and they spoke for themselves. In the American House of Representatives, the people do not speak directly. They are spoken for by a small number of men and women. In Rome, freed slaves had the right to vote. At the end of his term, a consul was obliged to give the people an accounting of his conduct. He was liable to criminal prosecution by the people for his misdeeds. In Rome, the people, gathered in the Forum, were called upon to ratify peace terms and treaties. Regardless of economic status, no male was excluded from the vote. At the time of the Declaration of Independence, this was true in none of the thirteen future states.

---

‡‡‡ In *The Federalist Papers*, Madison, Hamilton, and Jay signed their essays, "Publius." Publius Valerius Poplicola was the founder and first consul of the Roman Republic.

§§§ Although it is true that the voting structure in this assembly favored the wealthier elements, and that often these individuals would vote for war and not enter into battle themselves, it is also true that the small landholding peasants—the foot soldiers, who constituted the bulk of the army—had a say in the matter. More often than not, when the issue arose, they appear to have voted in favor of war. An even more just procedure would compel those who voted for war to fight and allow the others to do as they chose.

Thus, we see how the early American oligarchs read their history selectively. The military glory of Rome and its legislative achievements—that is, its gathering of power and wealth unto itself—are extolled. The Roman Senate's brutal elimination of political adversaries who spoke on behalf of those whose needs and rights were being trampled upon is ignored, as are the democratic elements that evolved over the course of the Republic.

Nor is it by accident that ancient Athens and its extraordinary achievements in government, philosophy, and literature should be ignored, dismissed, or disparaged. The last thing the budding American oligarchy wanted to do was to win sympathy for a society in which government included all elements of that society on equal footing. Remember, it was Madison who famously said, "Had every Athenian citizen been a Socrates, every Athenian assembly would still have been a mob."[7]

# Experiments in Government

## *The Italian City-States*

*Darkness fled,*
*Light shone, and order from disorder sprung.*

THERE ARE MOMENTS in history when societies are organizing themselves for the first time. In such periods, political
culture unfolds independently of outside control and precedent. There is much discussion about what government should be
like. There is experimentation and innovation. Government is experienced as evolutionary. It assumes different forms as different elements in society seek to establish means to ensure that their interests
will be represented.

Examined in retrospect, these episodes provide an unusual opportunity to study and think about the various forms that government
might assume. One such formative period occurred in America during the twelve-year interval between 1776 (the year the Declaration
of Independence was signed) and 1788 (the year the U.S. Constitution was ratified by nine out of the thirteen original states). Another
example of the birth and evolution of governmental structures can
be found in the city-states of northern Italy during the early phase
of their development at the end of the Middle Ages and beginning
of the Renaissance. In both instances, we can see the emergence of
democratic ideas and institutions, which were eventually overcome by
powerful, vested minority interests.

## Laboratories of Government

Beginning about the year 1000, in a period that has come to be known
as the High Middle Ages, there was, in northern Italy, an explosion

in population and an increase in economic activity that resulted in a renaissance of urban life not seen since the days of the Roman Empire. Nominally under the control of the German kings, these northern Italian city-states in fact operated independently of any external authority. In the absence of a strong German presence, there resulted a political vacuum that pulled in a number of rival political forces. Both the Catholic Church and the Italian nobility sought to assert their authority. The Guelphs (supporting the Papacy) and the Ghibellines (fighting on behalf of the Holy Roman Empire) were in a state of perpetual warfare. There were violent struggles for dominance within the nobility itself, pitting one family against another.

The expansion of commerce saw the emergence of yet another political force, a growing commercial class whose interests were at odds with both the nobility and the Church. This commercial class—principally notaries, money lenders, coin makers, merchants, and landed proprietors, as well as some small tradesmen and artisans—needed protection from the unreasonable taxation of the nobility and its arbitrary use of violence. The combination of these interests led to the development of a form of local political organization known as the commune, a sworn association of freemen collectively holding some public authority.*

Over a period of about fifty years, communes were formed in places such as Pisa, Lucca, Milan, Parma, Rome, Pavia, Genoa, Bologna, Siena, and Florence.† Initially, these communes were established by the nobility themselves as a means of holding on to acquired territory and expanding into the surrounding countryside, often at the expense of the Church. Gradually, upper elements in the commercial class were given a share of power. Fleetingly and minimally, the interests of the lower elements in society were also given voice.

An experimental approach to government was characteristic of the Italian city-states. Practices and institutions were constantly changing, which can create some confusion in the mind of anyone trying to make sense of it all. Three variables dominate: (1) Each of the early communes, a dozen or more, had a different form of government. (2) Each of the communes developed at a different rate and in a somewhat different direction. (3) Considerable evolution of government forms took place over a

---

* An excellent reference for this period in Italian history is Lauro Martines' *Power and Imagination: City-States in Renaissance Italy*. See also Daniel Waley, *The Italian City-Republics*.

† Venice has a different history. She never fully escaped the clutch of empire and absolute rule. Venice was ruled by a doge, who was the civilian, religious, and military leader. Like the popes, doges were elected for life. The first doge was chosen, under the aegis of the Byzantine Empire, sometime in the eighth century. In the thirteenth century, limits were set on the doge's power, and authority was shared with various councils. Membership in these councils was limited to a select group of powerful and wealthy Venetian families. Loyalty to the state was expected and ruthlessly enforced. There was not even a nod in the direction of democracy. Dissent was crushed brutally. Denunciations were encouraged, secrecy guaranteed. Torture was not uncommon.

relatively compressed period. Broadly speaking, the Italian city-states started out as communes in the twelfth century, evolved into oligarchies in the thirteenth century, and ended up (in many cases) as one-man tyrannies in the fourteenth century—moving from quasi-democracy to oligarchy to monarchy, from a plural executive to a single executive.

Commune membership, as the system evolved, was based on the *consorteri*, an association of anywhere from ten to forty sworn and armed families. The governing body of the commune was the general assembly (or greater council), which consisted of the founding members and their descendants. Leadership was drawn from among men privileged and well born, largely urban knights, and the upper tier of the successful commercial class. As the commune's population grew, the general assembly was replaced with a legislative council.

Wealthy and powerful families built enormous towers measuring two hundred feet or more from ground level. These towers, each with its own *piazza*, and the immediately surrounding area determined a neighborhood and a pocket of power. The region of the Italian city-states was a checkerboard of such towered enclaves. Street violence was common. Membership in and loyalty to these family enclaves was often necessary for survival.

The communes, though highly selective as to legal membership, were nonetheless exercises in self-government. Citizenship was confined to those who owned a home and had resided in the commune for a considerable period. Citizenship was active. It entailed "undertak[ing] the burdens and services" of the commune.[1]

The general assembly elected between four and twenty consuls, usually for a term of six months to one year. The consulate wielded executive and judicial authority on a day-to-day basis. As a check on their authority, the consuls were answerable to the general assembly on critical matters. For example, in 1219, the consuls of Piacenza were forced to abandon a truce with Parma and Cremona because the truce had been made "without the consent of the people and of many nobles."[2]

Numerically speaking, the extent of citizen involvement was considerable. The size of the greater councils could run to a thousand or more. In Genoa, in 1292, a council of six hundred members debated for seven days on the subject of war between France and Sicily. One hundred five councilors made speeches. In the communes, there were many posts to be filled. In Pisa, in 1162, there were ninety-one. In Siena, in 1257, there were eight hundred sixty offices. Thus, a high proportion of the male population had some form of direct participation in government. It has been estimated that in ancient Athens, in a given year, one-third of the citizenry served in government in some capacity. A similar level of participation is said to have occurred in the Italian city-states.

Several different terms are used to refer to components of the social structure in this period of history, and these terms assume different meanings in different settings. The early struggle for power was between the church and the nobility. As commerce and manufacture developed, a third force entered the fray, *il popolo*. In some communes, "*popolo*" referred to the upper middle class. In Genoa, the term was applied to the lower middle class of artisans and small shopkeepers. In Bologna, the *popolo* excluded the *lanaioli* (wool manufacturers) but took in other guilds.‡

Initially, class differences were vague and fluid. The *popolo* was all-inclusive. It was a force for social and political change. However, once the *popolo* had achieved its political goals, it became ossified and fragmented. There were rich and there were poor. At this point, another term appeared: "*il popolino*," the commoners, or the lower class, collectively speaking. Referring to a single individual commoner, one would use the term "*popolano*"; two or three individual commoners were "*popolani*."

The number of consuls (magistrates) could vary from year to year, as could the size of the councils, or assemblies. There are examples of councils ranging from two hundred up to four thousand members. Not only did the number of consuls and the size of the council vary, but the means for electing councilors and high officials was also continually being experimented with.

A meeting of the major guilds held in Florence in 1292 considered as many as twenty-four different methods for electing high officials. There were indirect election schemes whereby electors were chosen first; these individuals then made the final choice. Another means was to have outgoing councilors select their successors. There was also selection by lottery, or sortition. Some election methods employed a combination of these procedures. For example, in selecting the *podestà* of Vincenza, twenty electors were chosen by lot. Of these, twelve were eliminated by voting. The remaining eight then proposed three names, from which the final selection was made by a further vote of the full council. One can agree or disagree with such elaborate procedures. The important point is that they were instituted as a means of establishing impartiality and preventing the concentration of power. Such experimentation is based in a robust attitude toward government and strong sense of personal independence. These are attitudes one would hope to find in a democracy.

The same attitudes can be observed in the procedures governing the assemblies themselves. Usually a simple majority was necessary for a measure to pass. However, where critical issues were at stake, in an attempt to combat rashness, a larger quorum could be required, as well as a larger majority, varying from 75% or 80% of those present to even as high as 91% or 94%. Parma had four different categories of business requiring four different quorums and majority votes.

---

‡ Here is one definition: "merchants and men halfway between wealth and poverty." Quoted in Waley, *The Italian City-Republics*, p. 131.

There were also attempts to limit verbosity. Pistoia determined in 1294 that no councilor should speak more than once a week. In Parma, an attempt was made to prevent any speaker from mentioning what any previous speaker might have said.

By the end of the twelfth century and the beginning of the thirteenth, as particular families rose to positions of prominence by means of wealth, property, and political clout, the communal form of government had weakened. Internal disputes involving rival families made governing the commune a challenging and at times impossible affair. It ultimately became clear that a strong man, with limited powers, might at times be required to maintain order and provide for the common good.§ This figure was known as the *podestà*. He was imported from outside the commune as a way of ensuring his impartiality. His term was limited to six months, or at most a year.

In Medina, as a means of maintaining neutrality in civic affairs, it was required that neither the *podestà* nor any of his family members have relatives in Medina. He was not to leave the commune during his tenure without the permission of the general council, nor was he to eat or drink in the company of any citizen.¶ He was forbidden from engaging in trade of any kind. Another stipulation aimed at guaranteeing neutrality was to require that the *podestà* reside in three different regions of the city during his tenure.

In Pistoia, the *podestà* was prohibited from opening any official mail except in the presence of town elders. At the end of his term of office, the *podestà* was required to undergo a *sindicatus*, or investigation of his conduct in office.** He had to pledge to return any funds or property illicitly obtained.†† Typically, the *podestà* was ineligible for reelection. In Padua, the penalty for even proposing reelection was death.

Communes alternated between periods of consular and podestral government, as different factions sought to assert their authority. Sometimes different forms of government coexisted and overlapped. In Piacenza, in 1220, the *popolo* chose its own *podestà*. In 1222, it was agreed that half of the offices of the commune should be allotted to the *popolo*. In Pistoia, the *popolo* was able to pass legislation of such force that the inscription on one statue declares that "Statutes of the *Popolo* are to prevail over statutes of the commune."[3]

The independent city-states could become armed camps, the object of strong allegiance and often violent patriotism. They battled each other for control of roads, riverways, tolls, and customs, and for the

---

§ As you may recall, a similar solution was adopted in the Roman Republic, where a dictator could be named to serve for a period of six months in times of extraordinary challenge.
¶ Compare this policy with what goes on in Washington, D.C., today.
** This is similar to the procedures in place in ancient Athens. Officeholders were held accountable for their conduct.
†† Once again, how starkly such concerns contrast with the conduct permitted government officials in modern times.

right to monopolize commerce in certain goods. Pavia went to war with Milan over its claims to territory. Pisa and Genoa were at war almost continuously between 1067 and 1085. Florence conquered Fiesole in 1125 and afterward went to war with Lucca.

However, for several generations, before being torn apart by homicidal rivalry within the nobility itself, these communes were relatively harmonious internally, drawn into a strong unifying bond against common external enemies. Communes freely elected their own consuls, governed their own local counties, and made their own laws.

The communes were initially formed as unions of noble families. Gradually, however, the *popolo* and even the *popolino* won political and social respect. In an unusual attempt at social justice that contrasts dramatically with the modern mentality, crimes committed by a magnate (wealthy leader with executive power) against a *popolano* (commoner) were to be punished by a penalty four times the normal for the same offense against another magnate. In addition, again in contradiction to current practice, the word of a magnate was ipso facto considered to be of less juridical worth than that of a *popolano*. In the event that a magnate would kill a *popolano*, his house was to be destroyed at once, his property confiscated, and he himself sentenced to death.

## Government Instability

The peaceful evolution of government was interrupted by the arrival of Frederick II of Hohenstaufen (1194–1250), who was also known as the Holy Roman Emperor. Part genius—he was alleged to have been fluent in six languages—part poet, part savage, Frederick made up his mind that it was time for his presence to be felt in northern Italy, along with that of his infamously cruel son-in-law Ezzelino da Romano. In 1237, Frederick prevailed over the Lombard League.‡‡ His fortunes were reversed a year later, as the Italian city-states once again asserted their independence.

However, there was a price to be paid for the communes. The violent, militarized victory brought more power to certain prominent leaders at the expense of the more broad-based governments that had been evolving. A new form of government appeared—the *signoria*—a form of one man rule that in many instances produced violent dictatorship. In Milan, the wealthiest of the city-states, the Visconti family ruled for more than seventy years, starting in 1277. Bernabo Visconti, who held sway from 1349 to 1389, was as ruthless and self-indulgent as the worst of the *signori* (rulers, or lords). Bernabo enjoyed boar hunting, and anyone who interfered with this pleasure, inadvertently or otherwise, was put to death by torture. Terrified Milanese were forced to maintain five

---

‡‡   The Lombard League was an alliance that had formed against Frederick I Barbarossa, around 1167, and included most of the city-states of northern Italy.

thousand boar hounds, with strict responsibility for their health and safety. Such excesses became common in lesser communes, as well, as group leadership ceded to the rule of individuals, by brute force.

Thus, the progress the communes had made in establishing self-government and in addressing a range of interests broader than those of the nobility met with reversals as the nobility in league with the wealthiest members of the merchant class reasserted authority. The result was an oligarchy of moneyed interests, or tyrannical one-man rule, with (in some instances) intermittent returns to more representative forms of government.

Conflicts between powerful factions resulted in mass expulsions, confiscation of enemy property, razing of houses, and formation of armies in exile. As the dominant position of the upper classes became more and more solidified, the lower class had a greater and greater burden to bear. In the second half of the fourteenth century, there were revolts of craftsmen and skilled workers in Lucca, Siena, Perugia, Florence, and Bologna.

On July 20, 1378, workers in Florence stormed the government palace, took over, and held power for five and a half weeks. Taxes were eliminated or drastically reduced. Measures were taken against grain hoarding. There were efforts to recover communal property appropriated by influential citizens and to implement direct personal taxes. The most radical group was the *ciompi*, or wool workers, who called for a suspension of interest payments on the public debt and a two-year moratorium on all personal debt. Ultimately, the workers were defeated in a bloody street battle. Interestingly—and at variance with the fears James Madison would express four centuries later—the "mob" (i.e., the propertyless workers), when in power, did nothing to oppress the rich or confiscate the property of the wealthy landowners. All they sought was relief from overwhelming taxation and debt and equal access to grain, at a fair price.

Although the signorial (one-man rule) form of government prevailed during the fourteenth, fifteenth, and sixteenth centuries, the spirit of the communes never fully died out. Their legislative bodies remained in place in many *signorie*. Usually employed as a rubber stamp to give an air of legitimacy to the prince's arbitrary wish, sometimes legislators were honestly consulted for necessary direction. In Milan, after the Visconti failed to provide for their own succession upon the death of Filippo Maria in 1447, the self-governing city-state reemerged as the Ambrosian Republic (so named in honor of the city's patron saint) and thrived for two and a half years before it was crushed by an army under the leadership of Francesco Sforza.

Of all the Italian city-states, Florence, the seat of much of the creative and intellectual energy that came to be known as the Renaissance, remained faithful to its tradition of self-government longer than any other. Even when under the ostensible control of the Medici family, Florence was closest to what, today, we might call a democracy—though, in fact, it was a representative oligarchy with democratic elements.

In the year 1400, Florence was governed by a council of eight *priori* known as the *signoria* and had a head of state known as the *gonfaloniere*. All positions were rotated at two-month intervals, with those who would serve chosen by lot from predetermined pools of candidates whose names were placed in eight leather pouches known as *borse*. Between selections, the *borse* were stored in the Santa Croce church.

Candidates were nominated and selected such that each of the city's four quarters would be represented by two *priori*. Six of the selected *priori* came from the major guilds (lawyers, cloth merchants, wool makers, bankers), and two came from the minor guilds (butchers, bakers, carpenters, innkeepers, etc.). Having served, a candidate had to wait two years before he was eligible to serve again. This system benefitted democratic interests by opening up offices to new candidates. It made the anti-democratic consolidation of power more difficult. In principle, if not always in practice, there was political equality. Just about anyone, regardless of his station in life, could serve in government.

Once elected, the *gonfaloniere* and the eight *priori* moved into the *Palazzo della Signoria*, where they resided for their two months' tenure. They received a modest stipend to cover their expenses and were provided with servants. In theory, anyone from a lawyer to a butcher could be in charge. In practice, however, the position of *gonfaloniere* was usually held by a senior member of a major family. In 1402, as a member of the wool merchants guild, Giovanni de' Medici was selected for the *priori*. In 1421, he was elected *gonfaloniere*, preparing the way for generations of Medici, whose influence prevailed, on and off, well into the seventeenth century.

The rule of the Medici was twice interrupted when Florentines rose up against their control and returned to self-government, once for a period of eighteen years, beginning in 1494, and again in 1527, for a period of three years. Thus, the spirit of self-government was percolating in the background, even as the forces in support of one-man rule were strongest. Changeability and experimentation were Florence's greatest assets. As the Swiss historian Jacob Burckhardt observed in *The Civilization of the Renaissance in Italy*, the Florentine spirit "was incessantly transforming the social and political condition of the state, and as incessantly describing and judging the change."[4] Dante expressed a similar sentiment: Florentines, "what you weave in October doesn't last to mid-November. How often you have changed laws, coinage, offices, usage, and renovated every part!"[5]

## Civic Pride

Despite the turbulence of life in the commune, there developed a strong sense of unity, civic involvement, and loyalty. There was a lively awareness of the issues of the day, and these issues were energetically debated in the streets and the squares. Even in the larger communes, everyone knew everyone else. Speaking of Pavia, with a population of fifty thousand, one observer comments, "They know each other so well that if anybody enquires for an address he will be told at once, even if the person he asks lives in a quite distant part of the city; this is because they all gather twice a day, either in the 'court' of the commune or in the (adjoining) cathedral piazza."[6] These are the kinds of conditions one would expect to prevail in a democracy.

The commune governments exercised an unusually high degree of responsibility with regard to the economy and living conditions of their citizens. Prices for building materials were fixed. Interest rates were fixed. In Siena, as a means of ensuring the supply of bread, the commune itself assumed a monopoly for the sale of flour. In Modena, the commune decreed that bakers should always have water and brushes in front of their ovens, in case of fire. There was considerable legislation concerning cleanliness of streets and public places. It was forbidden to throw rubbish into the streets. The fouling of rivers with sewage or the industrial waste of dyers, tanners, and others was prohibited.

The commune saw that there were doctors in residence. There was a strong emphasis on education. There was competition among communes for the allegiance of students and faculty. There were prescribed limits as to the size of classes. In Parma, the maximum class size was sixty. By the late thirteenth century, the literacy rate was probably quite high. In Florence, in the fourteenth century, it was estimated that between eight thousand and ten throusand children were receiving an elementary education.

Civic pride resulted in the emergence of a literary genre in which the author sings the praises of his commune. One such work written in the early twelfth century lovingly describes the commune of Bergamo, with its strong walls, gates, piazzas, excellent water supply, and virtuous citizens, living in peace, with dignity and respect for the law:[7]

> Fighting and disturbances are rare amongst them,
> Golden Peace ties the citizens with a firm knot.
> Both poor and rich live a peaceful existence.
> The place is no common one, for observance of the laws,
> For its dignity, its piety, the purity of its concord.[8]

Great pride also was taken in the commune's architecture and natural beauty. The goal was to outshine one's neighbors. Siena incorporated a meadow within its city walls. The city undertook the construction of its *Palazzo Pubblico* with the same goal in mind. In designing their piazza, the *Campo*, the leaders of Siena made sure to require that all houses facing onto the piazza had the same type of window. Parma took equal pride in its piazza, which the citizens saw as a place of dignity. Certain activities were forbidden there, including spinning, suckling children, and eating figs. The city government undertook to design public buildings and public spaces with regard to beauty and overall unity. The authorities were town planners. The city's fountains, even those in the walls that surrounded the commune, were all constructed with this larger aesthetic in mind.

Although the Italian city-states of the early and middle Renaissance were not literal democracies,§§ their governing structures incorporated democratic elements and are instructive in understanding what democracy is and how it comes about. The significance of these hybrid governments lies in the fact that the people chose their rulers and were free from outside intervention, hereditary authority, and the tyranny of one-man rule. The democratic components came about in response to the need for a government that was responsive to common concerns and evolved as new requirements appeared and new dynamics of power became dominant. These democratic features thrived in a climate of thoughtfulness about government—about what works and what doesn't work. Such democratic institutions, though not all-inclusive as governments, did give voice to the people.

Examples of democratic processes in the Italian city-states abound, and several have already been discussed in this chapter. In some cases, a general assembly elected consuls, or executives, who served only for a year. In Florence, governing officials were chosen by lot and were rotated out of office every two months; these individuals then had to wait two years before they could serve again. Rotation in office and selection by sortition¶¶ are features of a democratic government. Further, especially in places like Florence, there was a gradual movement to greater and greater inclusiveness. Initially, the communes were the province of the nobility. Gradually, members of the wider moneyed classes were included. To a lesser degree, elements of the lower classes—farmers and artisans (i.e., the *popolino*)—were given a say in governmental affairs. The *ciompi*, or wool workers, of Florence—the "mob"—governed for a period of five weeks and showed themselves to be responsible and appropriate in their actions.

The writers of the time understood something about the importance of their form of government and their role in history. Thomas Aquinas (1225–1294), Italian-born philosopher and theologian, points with pride to the fact that "a single city administered by elected magistrates who are changed every year is often able to achieve far more than a king who rules over three or four cities."9***

---

§§ Martines (*Power and Imagination*) refers to them as "constitutional oligarchies."

¶¶    Sortition, also known as allotment, is an equal-chance method of selection by some form of lottery, such as drawing colored pebbles from a bag. It is the most democratic form of selecting individuals to govern because it establishes absolute political equality among those in the pool of potential officers.

*** Yet Aquinas is no friend of democracy, which he characterizes as an "iniquitous" form of government, "a form of popular power in which the common people, by sheer force of numbers, oppress the rich, with the result that the whole populace becomes a kind of tyrant." *On Princely Government*, quoted in John Dunn, editor, *Democracy: The Unfinished Journey, 508 B.C. to A.D. 1993*, p. 60.

Brunetto Latini, another thirteenth-century writer, contrasts governments in countries such as France, where the people are obliged to submit to the rule of kings and hereditary princes, with the Italian system of "governing cities by the year," where "citizens ... are able to elect their own *podestà* or *signore*."[10] In a similar vein, Marsilius of Padua, in his treatise "The Defender of Peace," written in 1324, at the very moment when Padua was about to fall under the sway of hereditary rule by the Carraresi family, eloquently argues in favor of elective as opposed to hereditary rule.

Thus, the Italian city-states did succeed in providing a modicum of stability for civic life in a time of social, economic, and political turbulence. They provided a setting for some of the richest unfolding of individuality known to civilization at that time and since. Despite the cruelty and exploitation of the worst of the tyrants, there was freedom from the overarching, monolithic state, which so effectively squelches individual development.

As Burckhardt points out, it was in the Italian republics and especially in places like Florence that the modern individual first emerges, conscious of himself as separate and different, reflecting upon himself and his collective existence. Burckhardt refers to the increasing numbers of "complete men," or "many-sided men," which he attributes to the "political circumstances" of the time, that is to say, the Italian city-states themselves.[11] By the thirteenth century, northern and central Italy had become the most literate society in the world. Fifty percent of the male population could read in the vernacular. This did not happen by accident.

The Italian city-states have much to teach those of us whose goal is a deep understanding of government, its functions, and its possibilities. It is uplifting to hear of civic pride and to learn of a government that shows genuine concern for the well-being of its citizens, a government that is open and experimental in its procedures and institutions. It is too easy now, living in the twenty-first century, to be cynical about government. We need to be reminded that it wasn't always this way. Here is Burckhardt again, writing in the early nineteenth century on the subject of the Italian city-states:

> From the moment they formed their own governments, and formed them for the common good, they prospered: while every other nation suffered, they rose in intelligence as well as virtue.... Their experience directed the meditations of some superior minds formed in the government of the Italian republics, who rose from the practice to the theory of civil society, and showed, not only to their own country, but to future nations and ages, the object to which all human associations should tend, and the best means by which to attain it.[12]

# PART II

# DEMOCRACY IN AMERICA

*Opportunity Missed*

# Early Voices in America

*But other powers as great*
*Fell not, but stand unshaken, from within*
*Or from without, to all temptations arm'd.*

ON MAY 10, 1773, the British Parliament passed the Tea Act, allowing the British East India Company to export tea to the colonies without paying customs duties, infuriating wealthy importers like John Hancock, who was faced with hundreds of indictments for refusing to pay these taxes. When British ships arrived in Boston harbor loaded with tax-free tea, conflict ensued as to whether or not colonial authorities should allow the tea to be unloaded. Under the leadership of Samuel Adams, a protest meeting was held on the night of December 16. An estimated eight thousand people were said to have attended. Disguised as Indians, protesters left the meeting and headed to the wharf, where the *Dartmouth* lay at anchor. Working through the night, they managed to dump 342 casks (45 tons) of tea worth an estimated £10,000 (equivalent to more than a million dollars today) into the waters of Boston harbor, an event that has come to be known as the Boston Tea Party.

The British Parliament responded with several laws that infuriated the colonists even more. The Massachusetts Government Act in essence did away with that colony's existing government and replaced it with a government appointed by the king. Town meetings were severely limited. Fearing that similar actions were to be taken throughout the colonies, delegates from twelve of the thirteen colonies gathered at Carpenters' Hall in Philadelphia on September 5, 1774. This meeting of the First Continental Congress established a compact among the colonists known as the Articles of Association. Delegates organized a boycott of British imports, hoping to influence British policy by nonviolent means. Tensions continued to rise. On April 19, 1775, the first shot in the war for independence was fired. The Declaration of Independence was signed on July 4, 1776. What were once thirteen colonies were now thirteen independent states. In January 1776, six months before the signing of the Declaration of Independence, New Hampshire had already ratified the first state constitution of the new nation.

Starting in May of 1775 and continuing until March of 1781, the Second Continental Congress acted as the national government of the newly liberated colonies, raising armies, directing strategy, appointing diplomats, and making formal treaties. It was this body that adopted the Declaration of Independence. After more than a year of debate, on November 15, 1777, the Congress passed and sent to the states for ratification the Articles of Confederation, the country's first written constitution.

The Articles of Confederation provided for a unicameral legislature. Each state had one vote but was entitled to a delegation of between two and seven members. Delegates were appointed annually by state legislatures and could not serve for more than three out of any six years. A committee of the Congress was authorized to appoint one of its members to preside as president. No person was allowed to serve in the office of president for more than one out of any three years.

Article III of the Articles of Confederation read, "The said States hereby severally enter into a firm league of friendship with each other, for their common defense, the security of their liberties, and their mutual and general welfare." Note the casual, informal nature of the agreement. It is a "league" based in friendship. The theme is repeated in Article IV, where it is provided that "the better to secure and perpetuate mutual friendship and intercourse among the people of the different States in this Union," the inhabitants of the States "shall be entitled to all privileges and immunities of free citizens in the several States."

Article VIII stipulates that the costs of war shall be defrayed from a common treasury to which each state contributes in proportion to the value of all the land within that state. Congress sets the time frame, but each state is responsible for raising the necessary revenues from its citizenry. Congress itself has no central taxing authority but "has the sole and exclusive right and power of regulating the alloy and value of coin struck by their own authority" (Article IX). The Congress is authorized to borrow money, to "emit bills on the credit of the United States," and to lay out sums to "cover public expenses," every six months passing on to the states an accounting of monies borrowed and spent. Congress is authorized to build and equip a navy, to establish the number of land forces required, and to call upon the states to fulfill their quotas.

Basically, Congress acted as a coordinator of national affairs among a loose confederation of states, assuming the authority necessary for running the war of independence against Britain. It is important to remember that when the first shot was fired, there was no Declaration of Independence. There were no state constitutions. The final draft of the Articles of Confederation was established in November 1777. The Articles were not fully ratified until March 1781, the same year the British surrendered.

The Treaty of Paris, signed in 1783, officially brought an end to the war and recognized the sovereignty of the United States. By this time, the new American government was saddled with debts. It owed money to France and Holland. States had raised monies to fund the war by selling securities, which they now had to pay off. Where was all of this money to come from? Officers in the army had been promised pensions. How were the pensions to be paid?

There was a general consensus that the Articles of Confederation needed to be revised. But there was little agreement as to what new powers should be granted. The colonies had enjoyed decades of independence and a relatively free way of life. They were loath to compromise their separate powers now that they had become states in a sovereign nation.

In September of 1786, a committee of five states—under the chairmanship of Alexander Hamilton—met in Annapolis to discuss ways Congress could be empowered to exercise some control over foreign and domestic commerce and to find the means to raise the money it needed to pay its debts. The committee members concluded that they were unable to reach any conclusions without wider representation from the thirteen states, and so a decision was made to call another meeting. This gathering was to meet in Philadelphia, where delegates from each of the states were to discuss measures to improve the government of the new country. Although the states' representatives to what has come to be known as the Constitutional Convention were only authorized to amend the Articles of Confederation,* the representatives held secret, closed-door sessions and wrote an entirely new constitution.

There are two important groups to consider in discussing the critical years between May 1775, when the Second Continental Congress met, and May 1790, the year the last state (Rhode Island) ratified the U.S. Constitution: the Federalists (supporters of the new Constitution) and the Anti-Federalists (opponents of the Constitution and supporters of the Articles of Confederation). Like many key terms used in the discussion of American government and politics, these two—Federalists and Anti-Federalists—are applied in a manner that is at variance with the true meaning of the words themselves. What the names actually mean is the opposite of what they would appear to mean.

Under the Articles of Confederation, thirteen autonomous states were united into a loosely structured league of mutual defense and support. Modern equivalents might be the League of Nations, the United Nations, or the European Union. The clique of wealthy merchants, land-

---

* The Massachusetts state legislature was very specific in stating that its delegates were being sent to the convention "for the sole and express purpose of revising the Articles of Confederation" (quoted in Jackson Turner Main, *The Anti-Federalists*, p. 115). The New York delegation had been given similar instructions. Two of the delegates left the convention in protest when they saw what was happening.

owners, and ambitious politicos who touted themselves as "Federalists" in fact wanted to do away with the federation of thirteen independent governments and replace it with a single, strong central government. In a shrewd move of Orwellian guile, these individuals (supporters of the new Constitution) called themselves "Federalists"—a term that would be congenial to a populace that did not want a change in government—when in fact they were nationalists who actually wanted to undo the confederation. Their true position, however, was not federalist but instead was actually anti-federalist. This left those who opposed the new Constitution with a bit of a dilemma. Because the more popular word (i.e., "Federalist") had already been taken, those who were in opposition to the Constitution and in favor of maintaining the confederation under the Articles of Confederation—the true federalists (in the proper sense of the word)—had to accept the label "Anti-Federalist," though in fact they were and knew they were the true federalists.

The Federalists were in favor of a strong, centralized oligarchic form of government and were opposed to true democracy. The Anti-Federalists favored decentralized, local governments, which provided for the maximum participation of the largest number of citizens. They spoke the language of democracy. In an effort to restore the true meaning to these important words, when I use the word "Federalist" I will attach the word "oligarchs" in parentheses. When I use the word "Anti-Federalist" I will attach the word "democrats" in parentheses.

The Anti-Federalists (democrats) had a deep understanding of the structure of government (person or persons in power)[†] and the workings of the political process. They were prescient in many ways. Just about all of their concerns about what could go wrong and why it would go wrong were realized. They suspected that the Constitution would lead to a takeover by a powerful oligarchy beyond the reach of the people. They were right.

To appreciate the legitimacy of the Anti-Federalist position, it is necessary to recall that the Constitution that was being offered for ratification contained no Bill of Rights and none of the later amendments that give the Constitution a populist veneer. As the Anti-Federalists saw the Constitution, only the opening rhetoric—"We, the People"—smacked of democracy. The rest of the language was aristocratic and monarchic. The Anti-Federalists objected to the elitist Senate, a single executive (the president) who was both chief executive officer and commander in chief of the army and who had veto power over congressional legislation, a Supreme Court given life tenure and performing beyond the control of the people, unlimited power of taxation in combination with a standing army, and underrepresentation in the House of Representatives. More

---

† Every so often, when I use the word "government" I will put the words "person or persons in power" alongside, in parentheses. Thus will I guard against the error of reifying and anthropomorphizing the word "government." Government is an abstract concept. It neither acts, nor thinks, nor feels. Only people do.

fundamentally, the Anti-Federalists objected to the unfettered transfer of power to a strong, central government.

The colonists, though separated from Britain by an ocean, had lived under the thumb of British rule, and they had grown to resent it more and more. Thus, they had received an important lesson in power and its abuse, and this knowledge was to be applied to their own situation once independence was declared. In addition, many had been inspired by writings such as *Cato's Letters*, a series of essays jointly published by British writers Thomas Gordon and John Trenchard between 1720 and 1723, and James Burgh's *Political Disquisitions*, which was published in Philadelphia in 1775. Both of these works address the evil workings of power and the cautions that must be taken in granting it.

"The love of power is natural," writes Burgh, "it is insatiable; it is whetted, not cloyed, by possession."[1] In a similar vein, Gordon and Trenchard observe, "All history affords but few Instances of Men trusted with great Power without abusing it, when with Security they could."[2] The people must hold on to power for themselves and grant it sparingly, under strict supervision. "Political jealousy ... in the People, is a necessary and laudable Passion," says "Cato" (i.e., Gordon and Trenchard). Rulers must be "narrowly watched, and checked with Restraints stronger than their Temptation to break them."[3]

## Government and the Public Trust

Thus was the climate in the years prior to ratification of the Constitution. Mistrust of government was a recurring theme in the political dialogue. In fact, this one issue—that of trust or mistrust of government—differentiates Federalists (oligarchs) from Anti-Federalists (democrats) as well as any other. Trust us with power, say the Federalists (oligarchs) of themselves. We are virtuous. We wish you no harm. Why would we want to betray you? Anyway, you, the people, have all the power.

The *theoretical* and rhetorical granting of power to the people was one of the chief means the Federalists (oligarchs) used in their efforts to manipulate the doubters into adopting a position that was fundamentally at odds with their true interests. The entire fate of America and to a large degree the world hung on that one word, "trust." To their credit, the Anti-Federalists (democrats) did not trust their would-be rulers. They saw the theorizing and the rhetoric for what they were, a bid for power that was self-serving and without limit.

In the *Federalist Papers*, Alexander Hamilton exuberantly promotes the Constitution. I'm going to be straight with you, he says. "The consciousness of good intentions disdains ambiguity."[4] In other words, my straight talk is a sign of my good intentions, says Hamilton of himself. Trust me.

Madison cannot imagine that government would betray the trust of the people. "I am equally unable to conceive," he declares, "that there are at this time, or can be in short time, in United States, any sixty-five or a hundred men capable of recommending themselves to the choice of the people at large, who would either desire or dare, within the short space of two years, to betray the solemn trust committed to them."[5]

John Jay, also in the *Federalist Papers*, takes a similar tack: Corruption? How could you even think such a thought? "He must either have been very unfortunate in his intercourse with the world, or possess a heart very susceptible of such impressions, who can think it probable that the President and two thirds of the Senate will ever be capable of such conduct. The idea is too gross and too invidious to be entertained."[6]

The Anti-Federalists (democrats) disagree. Concerning the possibility of corruption in the distribution of offices, says Anti-Federalist (democrat) Melancton Smith of New York, "The constitution appears to be a restraint, when in fact it is none at all. I presume, sir, that there is not a government in the world in which there is greater scope for influence and corruption in the disposal of offices. Sir, I will not declaim, and say all men are dishonest; but I think that, in forming a constitution, if we presume this, we shall be on the safest side."[7] Speaking of the House of Representatives, which he considers too small in numbers to adequately represent its constituency, "Brutus" of New York argues, "This branch of the legislature will not only be an imperfect representation, but there will be no security in so small a body, against bribery, and corruption."[8] "The Impartial Examiner" from Virginia agrees. When

> prosperity, voluptuousness, excessive fondness for riches, and luxury gain admission and establish themselves,—these produce venality and corruption of every kind, which open a fatal avenue to bribery. Hence it follows, that in the midst of this general contageon [sic] a few men—or one—more powerful than all others, industriously endeavor to obtain all authority; and by means of great wealth—or embezzling the public money,—perhaps totally subvert the government, and erect a system of aristocratical [sic] or monarchic tyranny in its room. [We must guard against such eventualities or] the liberties of this country will be lost—perhaps forever.[9]

Thus, we do not create an honest government (persons in power) by trusting to the integrity of those who govern, say the Anti-Federalists (democrats). We create an honest government by distrusting those who would govern, "by continually guard[ing] against Power; for when once Bodies of Men, in authority, get Possession of, or become invested with, Property or Prerogative, whether it be by Intrigue, Mistake or Chance, they scarcely ever relinquish the Claim, even if founded in Iniquity itself."[10]

Anti-Federalist "Brutus" points out, "Many instances can be produced, in which the people have voluntarily increased the powers of their rulers; but few, if any, in which rulers have willingly abridged their authority. This is sufficient reason to induce you to be careful, in the first instance, how you deposit the powers of government."[11] He goes on to warn that "power, lodged in the hands of rulers to be used at discretion, is almost always exercised to the oppression of the people, and the aggrandizement of themselves."[12] Even more strongly, "Can the annals of mankind exhibit one single example," asks Patrick Henry of Virginia, "where rulers overcharged with power, willingly let go the oppressed, though solicited and requested most earnestly?"[13]

The Federalist (oligarch) Madison, on the other hand, repeatedly seeks to assure his readers that they have nothing to fear from a strong, central government because all power is derived from the people.[14] He also maintains that the "ultimate authority ... resides in the people alone,"[15] that the people are "the only legitimate fountain of power,"[16] that they are "the fountain of authority."[17] The greatest defense against oppression and abuse of power is "the vigilant and manly spirit which actuates the American people."[18]

In response to concerns about abuse of power within the new governmental structure, Thomas Jefferson‡ came up with a good answer, a means of having the people exercise their powers of vigilance over government to which Madison makes repeated reference. Jefferson was of the opinion that whenever two of the three branches of government, each by a two-thirds majority, agreed that the constitution had been breached or was in need of modification, a convention should be called. Madison responds first by complimenting Jefferson for his "fervent attachment to republican government."[19] He agrees with Jefferson's line of reasoning and acknowledges (as quoted earlier) that since power is derived from the people, they should be turned to as means of ensuring that the letter and spirit of the constitution are being adhered to. However, he then proceeds, for the rest of *Federalist* No. 49 and all of No. 50, to offer many "insuperable objections against the proposed recurrence to the people."[20]

According to Madison, too many appeals to the people concerning the structure and functioning of government would imply "some defect in the government" and would "deprive the government of that veneration which time bestows on everything," as well as the "requisite stability."[21]§ A further and more serious objection "against a frequent reference of constitutional questions to a decision of the whole society" is "the danger of disturbing the public tranquility by interesting too strongly the public passions."[22]

In addition, there is a tendency, Madison continues, among republican governments, for the legislature to expand its influence "at the

---

‡ Jefferson, who had been principal author of the Declaration of Independence, did not participate in the Constitutional Convention because he was out of the country at the time, serving as America's Minister to France. He did, however, receive a copy of the Constitution and offered comments, including advocacy for a Bill of Rights.

§ Elsewhere, Madison speaks of "the mischievous effects of a mutable government." *Federalist Papers*, No. 62, p. 380.

expense of the other branches,"[23] a tendency that would be realized if such conventions were called, probably under impetus from the legislative branch. If in fact the people are that fountain of authority mentioned earlier, why indeed should not their voice be heard loud and clear? Remember that the legislature is the closest thing that the people—the source of all authority, power, and so forth—have to a voice in representative government. They have no control over the behavior of members of the federal judiciary or the executive or the Senate, whom they do not even directly elect.¶

The Anti-Federalists (democrats) understood that the form of government had broad consequences for society as a whole. The strong, centralized government sought by men like Madison and Hamilton would produce a certain kind of economy, a certain culture, a certain way of life. It would lead to a strong military establishment and a yearning for empire.**

## War or Peace?

In his *Federalist Papers* writings, Hamilton, of course, is arguing for the very conditions the Anti-Federalists (democrats) seek to avert. He speaks of Europe, whose "superiority ... has tempted her to plume herself as the mistress of the world." It is up to the United States to respond to her "arrogant pretensions.... to vindicate the honor of the human race, and to teach that assuming brother, moderation."[24] Here we see Hamilton breathing the flames of hubris and brandishing the sword of conquest in defense of American honor.

We need to be strong, powerful, and in control to defend ourselves against foreign enemies, says Hamilton. The powers necessary for common defense, "ought to exist without limitation, *because it is impossible to foresee or define the extent and variety of national emergencies, and the correspondent extent and variety of the means which may be necessary to satisfy them*"[25] (italics added). This is the rationale for the warrior state, in words that could have been uttered by the current president, in the year 2012. It was the warrior mentality that shaped the form of government from its inception and has defined its course ever since.

The Anti-Federalists (democrats) were of a different mentality. They

---

¶ As the Constitution was originally written, senators were chosen by state legislatures. Only after ratification of the Seventeenth Amendment in 1913 were the people given the right to elect their senators directly.

** In what may or may not come as a surprise, the word "empire" occurs no fewer than three times in the *Federalist Papers*. Hamilton refers to "The fabric of American empire" (*Federalist* No. 22, p. 152). He also argues in favor of an "energetic government," for how else can one "preserve the Union of so large an empire" (No. 24, p. 157). In discussing the popular reaction to the results of the Constitutional Convention, Madison refers to the United States as "this great empire" (No. 40, p. 252). According to Sheldon S. Wolin, "Virtually from the beginnings of the nation the making of the American citizen was influenced, even shaped by, the making of an American imperium" (*Democracy Incorporated*, p. 189).

wanted a peaceful, harmonious, unassuming government that would leave the citizenry free to pursue lives of quiet productivity and domestic tranquility. Patrick Henry exhorts the reader to go among the common men, where "you will find the same tranquil ease and contentment; you will find no alarms of disturbances: Why then tell us of dangers to terrify us into an adoption of this new Government?"[26] "Fear is the passion of slaves," he warns. "Let not our minds be led away by unfair misrepresentations and uncandid [sic] suggestions."[27]

Concerning Hamilton's militaristic stance, "Brutus" maintains that the first business of government is "The preservation of internal peace and good order, and the due administration of law and justice. The happiness of a people depends infinitely more on this than it does upon all that glory and respect which nations acquire by the most brilliant martial achievement." European governments are "administered with a view to arms, and war." Their leaders fail to understand that the purpose of government is "to save lives, not to destroy them.... Let the monarchs in Europe, share among them the glory of depopulating countries, and butchering thousands of their innocent citizens." Let us set a different example, says "Brutus." Let us give the world "an example of a great people, who in their civil institutions hold chiefly in view, the attainment of virtue, and happiness among ourselves." Defense against external enemies is "not the most important, much less the only object" of government.[28]

"The Federal Farmer" says, "The greatest blessings we can wish for, are peace, union, and industry, under a mild, free, and steady government."[29] We need a simple government that trusts to local assemblies that jealously guard their powers. "The strength of the government, and the confidence of the people, must be collected principally in the local assemblies; every part or branch of the federal head must be feeble, and unsafely trusted with large powers."[30] Do we want a simple government (people in power) or a splendid government? asks Patrick Henry. Do we want empire and glory, do we want to "make nations tremble," or do we want liberty?[31]

The Anti-Federalists (democrats) believed that the more concentrated power became, the easier it would be for a cabal of self-interested oligarchs to take over. Thus, the more people in government—specifically in the House of Representatives, the alleged representative, democratic branch of government—the more difficult it would be for a minority to subvert the wishes of the majority. Anti-Federalists even went so far as to question the principle of representation itself.

"A Farmer," from Maryland, commends the Swiss confederacy, a union of independent cantons, where "every farmer is by birth a legislator." He warns us that we should "never ... trust power to representatives, or a national government."[32] Where representation has been tried, we learn, "it has always proved defective, if not destructive." Writing in 1788, he aptly describes conditions that still prevail, more than two hundred twenty years later:

One candidate to recommend his pretensions, discloses and descants on the errors of the preceding administration—The people believe him and are deceived—they change men, but measures are still the same.... the next candidate ... is again believed, and his constituents again deceived; a general disgust and sullen silence ensue; elections are deserted; government is first despised and then cordially hated.[33]

What solution does "A Farmer" offer? In essence, what he proposes is democracy, though he doesn't use that word. He would entrust the power to govern to the people themselves—"the yeomanry," or "free-holders"—that is to say, the small landowners, working their own farms. How would it work?

The laws which pass the legislature before they become binding, should be referred to the different counties and cities—printed reasons drawn by committees, might if necessary, accompany each, together with an annual estimate of public wants and a detail of the expenditures of the former sums granted. Let these laws then be submitted to the free deliberation of the *freeholders* of the counties and cities—the numbers of yeas and nays be taken on each by the presiding magistrate, and transmitted to the executive, who may then upon comparing the returns from the several counties and corporations, declare what laws are the will of the people.[34] (italics in the original)

In other words, the people themselves—not their representatives—legislate. They vote for or against expenditures and laws. This is the true meaning of the word "democracy."

And suppose we opt for representation instead. On what basis should representatives be chosen? Whom should they represent? How many should there be? Should all levels in society be proportionally represented?

From Federalist (oligarch) Alexander Hamilton we learn that it is "visionary" to expect that there will be "representation of all classes of the people by persons of each class." Mechanics and manufacturers[††] will understand that "their habits in life have not been such as to give them those acquired endowments, without which in a deliberative assembly the greatest natural abilities are for the most part useless."[35] In other words, Hamilton, like John Stuart Mill,[‡‡] believes that these humbler folk are too dull witted and unsophisticated to govern. They will naturally want their "natural patron and friend," the merchant, to speak for them.

There are undoubtedly many who would agree that government is too complicated and debate too sophisticated for the working class. This may or may not be true. But are mechanics and artisans too simple minded to understand what it means to risk their lives in war? Are

†† Manufacturing at the end of the eighteenth century was a much more humble calling than it is today.
‡‡ Recall from Chapter 2 that Mill, in his 1860 essay "Considerations on Representative Government," expressed the very same thoughts.

they not able to think reasonably about how much they want to be taxed and how those tax receipts are to be spent? Are they incapable of determining what an acceptable rate of interest on a loan is, and what policies concerning repayment of debt are fair and reasonable? And are they really so lame brained as to believe that the merchant who charges usurious interest and hires them at substandard wages is qualified to speak for them? Apparently Hamilton thinks so. For what he argues we should end up with is a "representative" body of "landholders, merchants and men of the learned professions"[36] who will "truly represent" the "interests and views of the various classes of the community."[37] Hamilton acknowledges that "the people commonly *intend* the PUBLIC GOOD" (italics and capital letters in the original) but agrees with Madison that they must be saved "from very fatal consequences of their own mistakes."[38]

The defeated minority of the Pennsylvania State Convention—those Anti-Federalists (democrats) who opposed the Constitution—had different concerns. They wanted to ensure that choosing a representative to speak for a set of people would be no different from having those people collectively present. In other words, they believed that representatives had to be knowledgeable of and sympathetic to the views of those they were standing in for. "Representation ought to be fair, equal and sufficiently numerous, to possess the same interests, feelings, opinions and views, which the people themselves would possess, were they all assembled."[39] Melancton Smith of New York put it this way: "When we speak of representatives," we think of individuals who "resemble those they represent; they should be a true picture of the people; possess the knowledge of their circumstances and their wants; sympathize in all their distresses, and be disposed to seek their true interests."[40]

## Aristocracy or Democracy?

When speaking of government (person or persons in power), the key issue is numbers. The more people who govern, the more democratic the government. The fewer people who govern, the less democratic the government. It was Madison's view that, at the outset, there would be sixty-five representatives in the House, about one per fifty thousand, and that at a maximum, there would be one representative per thirty thousand. The Anti-Federalists (democrats) were appalled. As "Lycurgus" of Pennsylvania saw it, the House of Representatives was nothing but a "pretended concession to democracy."[41] It was "a mere shadow of representation," according to Melancton Smith,[42] and "a mere burlesque," according to "Brutus."[43]

There was all but universal agreement among the Anti-Federalists that the Constitution would create an aristocracy of power with minimal concern for the common good, and would put into power "those

harpies of power, that prey upon the very vitals; that riot on the miser-
ies of the community."[44] The Pennsylvania minority worked through
the numbers and came up with the following. In the House, made up of
sixty-five members, thirty-three individuals would constitute a quorum.
Of these, seventeen would constitute a majority, the sense of the House.
There were to be twenty-six members of the Senate, two for each state,
of which fourteen would constitute a quorum, eight of whom would
make a majority, or the sense of the Senate. Seventeen in the House plus
eight in the Senate equals twenty-five.

> Thus it appears that the liberties, happiness, interests, and great con-
> cerns of the whole United States, may be dependent upon the integrity,
> virtue, wisdom, and knowledge of 25 or 26 men—How inadequate and
> unsafe a representation: Inadequate, because the sense and views of 3
> or 4 millions of people diffused over so extensive a territory comprising
> such various climates, products, habits, interests, and opinions, cannot
> be collected in so small a body; ... from the nature of the thing, men of
> the most elevated rank in life, will alone be chosen. The other orders in
> society, such as farmers, traders, and mechanics, who all ought to have
> a competent number of their best informed men in the legislature, will
> be totally unrepresented.[45]

Of course, to James Madison and Alexander Hamilton, this is
exactly as it should be. By creating a large, strong, centralized government under the control of a wealthy elite, it would be difficult, if not
impossible, for the majority to realize their goals. This, then, is the ultimate reason for representative government, separation of powers, and
a bicameral legislature wherein the Senate, the more elite body of men,
can protect the people against "their own temporary errors and delusions."[46] Thus, a small group of men with similar financial and propertied interests will be in a position to thwart the "improper and wicked"
projects of the majority. Tyranny of a minority is advanced as a happy
alternative to the oft-referenced "tyranny of the majority."§§ The Federalists (oligarchs) wanted to erect barriers against the ruled to protect the
rulers. The Anti-Federalists (democrats) wanted to "fix barriers against
the encroachments of [the] rulers"[47] in order to protect the ruled.

Madison argues against the House of Representatives having too
many members as a means to "avoid the confusion and intemperance
of a multitude," when "passion never fails to wrest the scepter from
reason." "Had every Athenian citizen been a Socrates," we learn from
Madison, "every Athenian assembly would still have been a mob."[48]
Here we get the impression that the people are out of control and
must be protected against themselves, which is why we need a select,

§§ Cicero, writing to a friend in 59 B.C., could have been speaking for Madison when he
said, "the safety of the state is to the advantage of all good men, but most clearly benefits
men of fortune." Quoted in Michael Parenti, *The Assassination of Julius Caesar*, p. 88.

stable body, "a temperate and respectable body of citizens," such as the Senate, "as a defense to the people against their own temporary errors and delusions" and as a check against "the blow mediated by the people against themselves."[49] According to this argument, it seems that the people—that same "fountain" of power and authority Madison extolled when it suited him—are more like a volcano that must be capped or perhaps a wild beast that must be caged.[¶¶]

Appearances, stability, and good behavior seem to be Madison's primary concerns. Justice—"the end of government"[50]—comes in a distant fourth. He doesn't deny that a constitution might have defects or that representatives might violate the constitution. What matters most, however, is that government be venerated and therefore stable, beyond the reach of challenge from the people.

When Madison argues in favor of reason over passion, we might all agree, but we might also ask, Whose reason? Whose passion? It is also quite reasonable to argue for constitutional review, as Jefferson has. Pennsylvania had built such a provision into its constitutional process. That Madison speaks in measured tones certainly does not make him the voice of reason or justice. It does not make his reason more reasonable. His "reason" is opinion, just as is everyone else's. His devotion to protecting his property interests is no less passionate than the devotion of other elements of society to their own causes.[***]

The Anti-Federalists (democrats) believed that any power granted should be carefully outlined and specifically delimited. In other words, "The power we grant you is this. It is exactly this and nothing more. Any power not specifically granted is reserved for us, the people." Thus, they were troubled by the broad, ambiguous phrasing of the Constitution, which was open to interpretation and the acquisition of further unspecified powers by Congress, the president, and the courts.

For "Agrippa," the Constitution is "insidious in its form, and ruinous in its tendency."[51] "Brutus" finds that most of the articles in the Constitution "are conceived in general and indefinite terms, which are either equivocal, ambiguous, or which require long definitions to unfold

---

¶¶   Hamilton is alleged to have said in a debate with Jefferson, "Your *people*, sir, is nothing but a great beast." Quoted in David S. Muzzey, *An American History*, p. 192.

***   Madison—probably the most highly regarded and most often quoted of the Federalists (oligarchs)—is the perfect hypocrite. His words and actions are in complete contradiction. The people are in power, in theory. In practice, they must be fenced in and controlled. The people must be vigilant against abuse of power. Yet he specifically refuses to allow such vigilance via constitutional review. Passion and self-interest are to be guarded against, except if they happen to be James Madison's passion and self-interest, harnessed to the pursuit of power and the preservation of property, his property. Mutability in government—that is, changeability, lack of stability—is a grave danger. It "forfeits the respect and confidence of other nations." "It poisons the blessings of liberty." It undermines economic enterprise, and so forth. These noble, if specious, thoughts are being uttered by a man who is part of a cabal involved in overthrowing the existing government as enshrined in the Articles of Confederation and replacing it with another.

the extent of their meaning."[52] He is concerned that the new government "has a specious resemblance of a free government." "The gilded pill," he warns, "is often found to contain the most deadly poison."[53]

The Anti-Federalists (democrats) didn't have to wait long to find out just how right they were. In February 1791, barely halfway through his first term as President, George Washington was confronted with a significant constitutional question: Does the Constitution grant Congress the right to create corporations, in this instance, a national bank, as proposed by Hamilton and legislated by Congress? Such power is not spelled out in the Constitution. How then can the government legally create a national bank? After enumerating the many specific powers granted to Congress, Article I, Section 8, of the Constitution ends as follows: "To make all Laws which shall be necessary and proper for carrying into Execution the foregoing Powers." Well, there you have it, says Hamilton, "necessary and proper." The bank is necessary and proper and therefore within the purview of Congress. Innumerable powers have been acquired by Congress, the president, and the courts in the two centuries or so that have passed since the first "interpretation" of the Constitution was made. Volumes have been devoted to "constitutional law," interpreting what the Constitution "means." In essence, the Constitution "means" what those in power say it means, just as the Anti-Federalists (democrats) feared.

Not only were the Anti-Federalists (democrats) concerned about the small number of representatives and senators, they were concerned as well about the fact that there was no limit on the amount of time that members of Congress could serve. The Articles of Confederation had specified that (1) "delegates shall be annually appointed;[†††] (2) "no person shall be capable of being a delegate for more than three years in any term of six years"; and (3) there is "a power reserved to each State to recall its delegates, or any of them, at any time within the year, and to send others in their stead for the remainder of the year." Frequent elections, rotation in office, and the right of recall are three key elements in any representational government that can honestly lay claim to democratic intentions. None of these is provided for in the U.S. Constitution.

Watch out, says the Anti-Federalist "Centinel" of Philadelphia, or you will end up with a *permanent* ARISTOCRACY"[54] (italics and capital letters in the original). As "The Federal Farmer" points out, most of the states had annual elections for their representative body. He also makes it clear that the federated government under the Articles of Confederation, where the states were the primary locus of power, was the more democratic form of government. About fifteen hundred representatives from all states combined spoke for the people under the

†††  Madison quotes the adage circulating at the time, "where annual elections end, tyranny begins," and then dismisses it. *Federalist Papers*, No. 53, p. 330.

Articles of Confederation versus sixty-five for the national government under the U.S. Constitution. Says "Brutus" on the same subject,

> It is probable that senators once chosen for a state will ... continue in office for life. The office will be honorable if not lucrative. The persons who occupy it will probably wish to continue in it, and therefore use all their influence and that of their friends to continue in office. Their friends will be numerous and powerful, for they will have it in their power to confer great favors; besides it will before long be considered as disgraceful not to be re-elected. It will therefore be considered as a matter of delicacy to the character to the senator not to return him again.[55]

In 2010, there were twelve senators who had served without interruption for between thirty-six and forty-nine years. In the House, there were thirty-seven members who had served continuously for between thirty-six and fifty-three years. There are many more in both houses who have served continuously for substantial periods. So we have our "permanent aristocracy," just as was predicted.

## Concentration of Power

Long before Dwight D. Eisenhower spoke of the dangers of a military-industrial complex, the Anti-Federalists (democrats) were opposed to granting Congress open-ended authority to maintain standing armies—"those baneful engines of ambition"[56]—for reasons that were obvious to them almost two hundred years prior to Eisenhower. Standing armies are "inconvenient and expensive,"[57] says "The Impartial Examiner" from Virginia. "Brutus" declares, "The power in the federal legislative, to raise and support armies at pleasure, as well in peace as in war, and their control over the militia, tend, not only to a consolidation of the government, but the destruction of liberty."[58] To protect against such an outcome, "Brutus" offers a stipulation to the Constitution, which reads as follows:

> No standing army, or troops of any description whatsoever, shall be raised or kept up by the legislature, except so many as shall be necessary for guards to arsenals of the United States, or for garrisons to such post on the frontiers, as it shall be deemed absolutely necessary to hold, to secure the inhabitants, and facilitate the trade with the Indians; unless when the United States are threatened with an attack or invasion from some foreign power, in which case the legislature shall be authorized to raise an army to be prepared to repel the attack; provided that no troops whatsoever shall be raised in time of peace, without the assent of two thirds of the members, composing both houses of the legislature.[59]

Rationally speaking, the likelihood of the United States of today being invaded by another army is not very great under any circumstances. Yet most Americans would probably not agree to such a provision in the Constitution. We have become so accustomed to the presence of enormous military might that we would feel insecure and diminished without it, despite the fact that the army is frequently used not for defense but for aggressive purposes, for America's greater glory, in keeping with the vision of men like Alexander Hamilton.

According to the U.S. Constitution, "The President shall be commander in chief of the Army and Navy of the United States."[‡‡‡] This is just the kind of vague, open-ended wording that concerned the Anti-Federalists (democrats). Based on these words, and with no stipulated limitations, the president can order the army to shoot anyone, anywhere, in America and around the world. There is no stipulation that says he may not command his troops against his own people. There is no stipulation preventing the president from mobilizing the army without prior authorization from Congress.[§§§] Observes Patrick Henry,

> The president, in the field, at the head of the army, can prescribe the terms on which he shall reign master, so far that it will puzzle any American ever to get his neck from under the galling yoke.... Where is the existing force to punish him? Can he not at the head of his army beat down every opposition?

The U.S. Constitution grants Congress the power to declare war. But there is no link connecting *making* war and *declaring* war. Thus, Congress can offer financial support for a war anywhere around the world without actually declaring war. In fact, war has been officially declared only five times: the War of 1812, the Mexican American War, the Spanish American War, World War I, and World War II. But the United States has made war countless times. Millions of lives have been taken, cultures destroyed. And troops have been used on American soil as well.

In 1794, Federalist Alexander Hamilton, then Secretary of the Treasury, placed excise taxes on the manufacture of whiskey, snuff, refined sugar, and carriages. The excise tax was especially burdensome for many in western Pennsylvania, where just about everybody owned a still and where whiskey distilled from grain was an important source of income. Transportation was inadequate. Grains were difficult to get to market. Whiskey was much easier to transport. And hadn't these same people just fought in a revolution to free themselves from arbitrary taxation? The people resisted.

What resulted has come to be known as the "Whiskey Rebellion."

---

[‡‡‡] By contrast, a constitutional crisis was precipitated in Pakistan in 2001, when President General Pervez Musharraf chose to remain as chief of army staff and head of state at the same time. In the United States, a similar arrangement is actually written into the Constitution.

[§§§] In 1973, over President Richard Nixon's veto, Congress passed the War Powers Act, a resolution of Congress stating that the president can send troops into action abroad only by authorization of Congress or if American troops are already under attack or serious threat.

Armed groups spontaneously rose up along the western frontier of Pennsylvania, all told numbering around seven thousand men, some of whom threatened to take the federal arsenal in Pittsburgh. The mail was robbed. Court proceedings were interrupted. One group—disguised as women—assaulted a tax collector, cropped his hair, coated him with tar and feathers, and stole his horse. President George Washington, who at the time owned thousands of acres in western Pennsylvania, took this as an opportunity to demonstrate resolve and power on the part of the new federal government. He mounted an armed militia of thirteen thousand men, who succeeded in quelling the dissent. Jefferson found this whole display to be quite offensive, and labeled the effort to crush the tax rebellion as nothing more than making "war on our own citizens."[60] This marked the first time under the new U.S. Constitution that the federal government had used military force to exert authority on American soil. There would be other occasions as well.

In 1861, President Abraham Lincoln used his power as commander in chief to organize northern armies against a secessionist south, resulting in 610,000 deaths. Three hundred Lakota Indians were massacred by federal troops at Wounded Knee, in South Dakota, in 1890. In 1892, the army suppressed a silver miners' strike in Idaho. Army troops were used to quell a Chicago rail strike in 1894. Thirty-four strikers were killed. The Ludlow Massacre refers to the violent deaths of twenty people, eleven of them children, during an attack by the Colorado National Guard on a tent colony of twelve hundred striking coal miners and their families at Ludlow, Colorado, on April 20, 1914. Army troops were used to subdue rioting blacks in 1967. Forty-three blacks were killed. On Monday, May 4, 1970, four students were killed and nine wounded by national guard troops during an anti-war demonstration at Kent State University. Ten days later, at Jackson State College, two students were killed and twelve injured when police opened fire on protesters. All of these actions were perfectly legal. In no way did they violate the Constitution as originally ratified. All of these military excesses—both at home and abroad—would come as no surprise to the Anti-Federalists (democrats), who were uniformly opposed to the blanket powers transferred to a central government by virtue of the American Constitution.

The Anti-Federalists (democrats) had monetary concerns as well. They were worried about the unrestricted power—"general and unlimited"—granted to Congress to borrow money. "By this means, they may create a national debt, so large, as to exceed the ability of the country ever to sink it. I can scarcely contemplate a greater calamity," says "Brutus."[61] As of January 12, 2012, the national debt was $15,240,197,784,647.14 and increasing at the rate of $3.9 billion per day.¶¶¶

---

¶¶¶ In fiscal year 2011, the U.S. Government spent $454 billion of taxpayer money on interest payments to the holders of the national debt. http://www.federalbudget.com/.

Directly related to the power to borrow money is the issue of taxation. How is the government going to pay the interest on its debt if not by means of taxes levied on its citizenry? The Anti-Federalists (democrats) were opposed to blanket authority to raise revenues by internal taxation, without limit or purpose. "Brutus" comments, "It is proper here to remark, that the authority to lay and collect taxes is the most important of any power that can be granted."[62] "I can scarcely believe we are serious in proposing to vest the powers of laying and collecting taxes in a government so imperfectly organized for such purposes," says "The Federal Farmer."[63] The unlimited authority to raise money and make war should not be vested in the same body. "The purse and the sword ought not to be placed in the same hands in a free government."[64] Direct taxes, such as excise taxes and land taxes, "are often so oppressive, as to grind the face of the poor, and render the lives of the common people a burden to them."[65] As Melancton Smith wisely observes, "It is a general maxim, that all governments find a use for as much money as they can raise."[66]

The Anti-Federalists also had some strong opinions on the subject of the judiciary as prescribed in the Constitution. It is "unprecedented," says "Brutus," that a court "be rendered totally independent, both of the people and of the legislature."[67] "The supreme court under this constitution," he says, "would be exalted above all other power in the government, and subject to no controul [sic]."[68] This totally independent body is, in effect, a legislative body because it can rule in favor of or against acts of Congress. In the 2000 presidential election, it used its power to subvert the electoral process by preventing a recount.

It is our great misfortune that these early voices for the common good—the Anti-Federalists—speaking the language of democracy, were drowned out by a vocal and energetic minority—the Federalists—with nothing in mind but their own personal advancement. This vocal and energetic minority succeeded in eliminating democracy as a political possibility by putting in place a constitution whose primary purpose was the establishment of an aristocracy of financial and mercantile interests.

Thus, the evils of modern government (person or persons in power) are not accidental. They are not brought on anew by one regime or another. They are inherent in the government put in place by its anti-democratic, oligarchic founders. The U.S. Constitution was framed with an eye toward empire. It was in direct violation of the prevailing ethos of the time, which is why its promoters had to resort to lying, manipulation, and violence to see their wishes fulfilled.

8

# Democracy Denied

*But far within ...*
*The great seraphic lords and cherubim,*
*In close recess and secret conclave, sat;*
*A thousand demi-gods on golden seats*
*Frequent and full.*

LONG BEFORE THE American Revolution and the political turmoil that followed, there had been social unrest at home.[*] In
the period between 1776 and 1790, the agitation continued and
became more intense, fueled by the gross inequality of wealth and by
the democratic ideals that had motivated many small farmers to take up
arms against Britain. But there was also another factor. The war with
Britain had produced a burdensome debt, both foreign and domestic.
War bonds had been sold to raise money to supply the troops. Returning soldiers, who had purchased the bonds and were now desperate for
cash, sold them at a fraction of their face value to raise money to survive.
Speculators eagerly scooped up the bonds and then demanded that they
be paid interest on the face value. The only way the speculators could
be paid was for state governments to raise taxes, which is just what they
did. The result was that the small farmers were faced with a tax burden
that was even greater than what they had previously paid under British
rule. They were defaulting on their mortgages. Their lands and livestock
were being confiscated and sold off. They were being dispossessed.

In response, protests sprang up around the country. Some were violent, but most were peaceful. In 1787, the Delaware legislature agreed to
pay two years of interest to holders of state bonds.[†] During the election

---

[*] Howard Zinn's *A People's History of the United States: 1492–Present*, first published
in 1980, provides an honest look at the economic, social, and political conditions in early
America (see especially pp. 47–52).
[†] For a close look at this issue during the years leading up to ratification of the U.S. Constitution, see Woody Holton, *Unruly Americans and the Origins of the Constitution*.

that followed, voters were urged "not to chuse [*sic*] any man as representative, who had purchased certificates, or advocated the payment of
them."[1] This campaign was successful. Representatives in New Castle
County were replaced by men more favorable to the debtors' cause.
The assembly passed legislation denying interest to anyone who had
acquired their securities through speculation.

Rhode Islanders also took matters into their own hands. The public
supported the emission of paper money, which would provide relief for
debtors. The political establishment, however, opposed paper money
and proposed a statewide list of delegates who favored this position.
Voters in East Greenwich held conventions and put up their own list.
These candidates campaigned vigorously under the slogan "To Relieve
the Distressed," and they prevailed. The first order of business for the
newly elected legislature was to issue £100,000 in paper money and
delay the due date for taxes that had been requisitioned by Congress in
September of 1785.

In March of 1786, the Massachusetts state legislature imposed heavy
taxes, with more than half of the revenue allocated to pay bondholders.
Insurgents took to arms in protest of the taxes and were defeated. They
then went to the polls, where they were victorious. With the resulting
seventy-four percent turnover in the state House of Representatives, the
farmers got the tax relief they sought. For the year 1787, the state government imposed no taxes at all.[‡]

Citizens of Massachusetts and New Hampshire came up with
another strategy as well. Several townships resolved to send no representatives to their state's legislature. Since the decisions being made
were unfavorable to their cause, why send anyone? It was both a political strategy and a means of protesting a system they found inequitable.
In Massachusetts, farmers refused to pay their taxes and took the additional step of closing many of the state's courts.

There was growing discontent with the state of affairs that prevailed
in the newly liberated country. Maybe things had actually been better
under British rule. Petitioners in Brunswick County, Virginia, declared,
"the honest labourour who tills the ground by the sweat of his brow
Seams hitertoo to be the only sufferors by a revolution which ought to
be glorious but which the undeserving only reap the benefits off."[2]

With growing frequency, debtors were taking refuge within the
sanctuary of their homes. Other actions were taken that were less
benign and more openly hostile. In September of 1784, a South Carolina deputy sheriff tried to hand Hezekiah Maham[§] a summons to
appear in court to answer a creditor's complaint. Not only did he not

---

‡ Compare this result to matters in 2012, when congressmen are oblivious to the wishes
of their constituents, yet are reelected repeatedly, with terms often extending for decades.
The federal system is working just as Madison had hoped.
§ Maham had served as a colonel in the cavalry during the Revolutionary War.

accept the summons, Maham had the sheriff eat it, graciously supplying a beverage with which the sheriff could wash it down. In Virginia, there were one hundred fifty-five cases of delinquent farmers taking up arms against sheriffs who came to claim their property. Outraged debtors began nailing shut courthouses where decisions had been made depriving them of their property. Another strategy was for residents of a given community to agree that no one would bid on property put up for auction. Anyone who did bid, risked retaliation. Heavy taxation was producing vigorous opposition in just about every state. And in many cases, overburdened taxpayers were getting from their state legislatures the tax relief they sought.

It was not chiefly the social unrest but rather the good results that the farmers were getting from their legislatures that were most troubling to men like James Madison and Alexander Hamilton. In the *Federalist Papers*, they make repeated reference to social unrest and government instability, which (they maintained) could be overcome only by means of a powerful central authority. What they meant to say was that the local legislatures were too democratic, that is, they were responding to the wishes of their constituencies. That needed to be stopped. The only way to do so was to de-democratize government by replacing thirteen responsive state legislatures with one central government, with large election districts and minimal representation. With such a governmental structure, disgruntled farmers would have difficulty uniting and enforcing their will.

## Social Unrest and Counterrevolution

In the 1780s, eighty percent of the citizenry were small farmers. Obviously, by virtue of their numbers, in any open debate on critical issues, the farmers would prevail. To succeed, the relative handful of speculators needed to move their brethren—those with visibility—into positions of power and national recognition, where they could unite behind an alternate form of government that would squelch the burgeoning democracy.

What was needed was a single dramatic event that would demonize the lower classes and rally the citizenry—against its own self-interest—around a new Constitution. Students of American history will, no doubt, recognize the scenario. A group of powerful oligarchs wishes to take the nation down a path for which there is no popular support. There is a violent event that both instills fear and piques the national pride, thus justifying the preplanned endeavor.¶ Is it possible that, in the days leading up to the Constitutional Convention of 1787, there was a precipitating event such as this that was used to mobilize Ameri-

---

¶ Pearl Harbor was a catalytic event leading to U.S. involvement in World War II, as was the Gulf of Tonkin episode in the lead-up to war in Vietnam.

cans into choosing a form of centralized government with a standing army and powers of taxation, the very European formula against which Americans had just fought a long and bloody revolution?

Though there was discontent around the country, the citizens of the state of Massachusetts had an especially important role to play in fanning the flames of rebellion in the new nation just prior to the Constitutional Convention in Philadelphia. The Massachusetts state constitution of 1780 had raised the property qualifications for voting and ensured that only the wealthy could hold state office. The legislature was unsympathetic to the many debt-ridden small farmers who were losing their farms to the merchants who had lent them money. Meetings were held in the western part of the state in an effort to organize an opposition. Said one beleaguered citizen:

> I have been greatly abused, have been obliged to do more than my part in the war; been loaded with class rates, town rates, province rates, Continental rates ... been pulled and hauled by sheriffs, constables and collectors, and had my cattle sold for less than they were worth.... The great men are going to get all we have and I think it is time for us to rise and put a stop to it, and have no more courts, nor sheriffs, nor collectors nor lawyers.[3]

The riots and uprisings that followed were not a consequence of too much democracy but rather its lack. The citizenry was driven to desperation when its basic needs were not being addressed. One uprising was of particular importance in mobilizing support for a change in government. Small farmers in western Massachusetts, many of them veterans of the Revolution, watched as their cattle and lands were taken away and as their neighbors were imprisoned, all as a consequence of their inability to pay taxes and debt obligations. Daniel Shays had been a captain in the Continental Army. Having fought at Lexington, Bunker Hill, and Saratoga, Shays resigned once it became clear that he was not going to be paid for his efforts. Soon thereafter, he found himself in court for nonpayment of debts. He was one of many. At one point, he witnessed a sick woman who was unable to pay her debt have the bed taken out from under her.

The farmers of Massachusetts began organizing under the leadership of Continental Army veterans. They appeared at courthouse steps, demanding fair treatment; they used guns to prevent the courts from taking their property. Many of the state's militia—whose job it was to safeguard the courts—sided with the farmers instead. In the fall of 1786, Shays and a group of seven hundred armed farmers appeared in Springfield, Massachusetts. As they marched past the courthouse their ranks grew. Proceedings were cancelled. When Shays began a march of a thousand men to Boston, where the state legislature would be holding its next meeting, a blizzard forced them back. One of his men froze to death.

A militia sponsored by wealthy Boston merchants offered stiff opposition to Shays' rebels. A few shots were fired. There were several deaths. Finally, the outnumbered rebels dispersed. Shays took refuge in Vermont, and his followers began to surrender. About a dozen rebels were tried and condemned to death. Some were pardoned, but others were hanged.

The men under Shays' leadership were all patriots. Many had fought in the Revolution and had risked their lives to escape the burden of excessive debt and taxation. Now, under the new government, they found themselves caught in a new web of merchants and bankers who were no more reasonable or fair-minded than their predecessors had been. The rebels were well disciplined. They were not out to take other people's land. Their sole purpose was to hold on to what little they had so they could continue their sustenance farming.

All of this was still going on in September of 1786, when a handful of state delegations met in Annapolis, Maryland—under the leadership of nationalists like Hamilton and Madison—to discuss issues concerning commerce and trade among the states. Only five states were actually represented. Hamilton was one of two delegates from the state of New York. The small assembly decided they lacked sufficient numbers to take any action and agreed to reassemble in May of 1787 to address broader issues than those that had originally brought them together.

The period between these two conclaves was critical. Without the support of key figures like George Washington, the Constitutional Convention might never have taken place or else would have accomplished little of what men like Hamilton had in mind. In the space of eight months, energies had to be galvanized, and convincing arguments had to be mounted, in support of a program that would do away with one government and replace it with another. Washington was the key figure in this enterprise. He was the symbol of the new America. He was, to the public eye, beyond reproach, a figure of integrity whose judgment the nation would follow. In other words, he was the essential symbol for plotters like Robert Morris, Gouverneur Morris, and Alexander Hamilton. Shays' Rebellion came at just the right moment. It was the perfect source of necessary propaganda: "Men of property and wealth, watch out. We need a new powerful, central government to put the lid on such dangerous uprisings."

In a letter to Washington appealing to his wish for stability, hoping he could be persuaded into coming out of retirement to play a role in the Constitutional Convention, General Henry Knox refers to the "insurgents" (i.e., loyal Americans such as Daniel Shays and his followers) as people who have paid little or no taxes, who see wealth around them that they covet and a weak government in no position to offer serious opposition. Hence, claims Knox, they will take what they want. By common effort, the property of the United States has been wrenched from British hands and therefore, they believe, it belongs to everyone. And, says Knox, speaking for the Shayites, anyone who would put himself in opposition to this program for equity and justice will be "swept from off the face of the earth."[4] In essence, reality had been stood on its head. It was powerful bankers and propertied interests who were taking land from small farmers, not the other way round.

Although the Shayites might have argued that they had equal claim to any and all land, they never did. All they wanted was to stay out of jail and to retain their meager holdings. Knox had distorted the reality behind the rebellion and chosen inflammatory language as a means of stirring up a sentiment of fear for purposes of mobilizing the wealthy and powerful against a relative handful of farmers in need of debt relief. Men like Washington, with vast land holdings on the western frontier, became convinced that the country was on the verge of anarchy and that only a vigorous government could maintain order. The propaganda had worked. Without Shays' Rebellion and the propaganda that fed off it, it is doubtful that the nationalists would have succeeded. For George Washington, the case was convincing, and it factored into his decision to attend the Philadelphia convention. In a letter to James Madison, he wrote, "What stronger evidence can be given of the want of energy in our governments than these disorders?"[5]

Considering the circumstances that prevailed at the time of the Constitutional Convention, it is certainly not surprising that the gathering enjoyed little popular support. For one thing, it seemed to be the doing of a cabal operating in secret. For another, it represented a radical change in direction. Some might say a coup had taken place. Prior to the convention, it was the general understanding that the Articles of Confederation were to remain in force. There had been no groundswell for abandoning one form of government in favor of another. Yet that is what happened.**

What was under way was a struggle between those of modest means and a wealthy elite. "Appius," of South Carolina, speaking of two different sections of his state, described the differences as follows:

> One is accustomed to expence [sic], the other to frugality. One will be inclined to numerous offices, large salaries, and an expensive government; the other, from the modest fortunes of the inhabitants, and their simple way of life will prefer low taxes, small salaries, and a very frugal civil establishment.... One will favor commerce, the other manufactures; one wishes slaves, the other will be better without them.[6]

Wrote "Cornelius," of Massachusetts, in December of 1787, "I conceive a foundation is laid for throwing the whole power of the federal government into the hands of those who are in the mercantile interest;

---

** It is important to remember that the document that would replace the Articles of Confederation represented a step backward from rights citizens of many states already enjoyed. For example, many state constitutions had a bill of rights, but the U.S. Constitution, at its writing, did not. Blacks did not have their right to vote guaranteed on the national level until the Fifteenth Amendment was ratified in 1870. Women had to wait for ratification of the Nineteenth Amendment in 1920 to gain a similar right.

and for the landed [i.e., the small farmers], which is the great interest of this country, to lie unrepresented, forlorn, and without hope."[7] Similar sentiments were expressed by "Appius." The rich can take care of themselves. Government should attend to those of modest means. "A rich citizen ought to have fewer votes than his poor neighbor;[††] ... Wealth should be stripped of as many advantages as possible and it will then have more than enough.... And finally, ... in giving property the power of protecting itself, government becomes an aristocracy."[8]

The author of an essay that appeared in the *Boston Gazette* on November 26, 1787, argued eloquently against a rush to judgment on the Constitution:

> The deceptive mists cast before the eyes of the people by the delusive machinations of its INTERESTED advocates begins to dissipate.... Those furious zealots who are for cramming it down the throats of the people without allowing them either time or opportunity to scan or weight it in the balance of the intelligences, bear the same marks in their features as those who have been long wishing to erect an aristocracy in this COM-MONWEALTH—their menacing cry is for a RIGID government, it matters little to them of what kind, provided it answers THAT description.... These violent partisans are for having the people gulp down the gilded pill blindfolded, whole, and without any qualification whatever, these consist generally, of the NOBLE order of [Cincinnatus], holders of public securities, men of great wealth and expectations of public office, ... these with their train of dependents [form] the arisotcratick [*sic*] combination.[9]
> (capital letters in the original)

Rhode Island refused to send any delegates to the Philadelphia convention, suspecting that the organizers were up to no good. New Hampshire chose delegates but neglected to supply them with the funds they needed to attend. Patrick Henry of Virginia refused to attend. He "smelt a rat in Philadelphia, tending toward the monarchy."[10] Once the Constitution had been drafted, Mason and Randolph of Virginia, as well as Gerry of Massachusetts, refused to sign. Lansing and Yates of New York, Martin of North Carolina, and Mercer of Maryland had previously withdrawn from the convention.

In *An Economic Interpretation of the Constitution*, first published in 1913, Charles Beard argues that the Constitution was a counterrevolution, set up by rich bondholders for whom bonds were "personal property," in opposition to the farmers and planters for whom land was property, "real property." According to Beard, the Constitution was designed to reverse the radical democratic tendencies that had been unleashed by the Revolution among the common people, especially farmers and debtors. As he points out, the delegates to the Constitutional Convention were wealthy lawyers, merchants, and speculators. "Not one member repre-

---

†† This position makes an interesting contrast with John Stuart Mill's position, which is just the opposite. The elite, he believed, should be granted more votes.

sented in his immediate personal economic interests the small farming or mechanic classes."[11] Bear in mind that, at the time, small farmers made up eighty to ninety percent of the country's population.

The new government was carefully constructed with two goals in mind, both of them anti-democratic: (1) to circumscribe the power of the state legislatures, which were sympathetic to the plight of debtors and small farmers, and (2) to create a central power structure in which the majority (eighty to ninety percent of the population) could be dominated by a minority of wealthy oligarchs. The government's first goal (to circumscribe the power of the states) was achieved by (1) taking unto itself the power to raise taxes,[‡‡] (2) denying states the right to issue paper money, and (3) insisting that contracts (i.e., public securities) were sacrosanct.[§§]

The second goal (to create a central power structure) was achieved by means of "checks and balances." In fact, there were no balances, only checks—that is, checks on the House of Representatives, the popularly elected branch of government. The Senate, the presidency, and the judiciary[¶¶] were all aligned against grassroots interests. This was understood and intended from the outset.[***] Suppose the House of Representatives, the body with the larger number of members and the only one elected directly by the people,[†††] were to be sympathetic to the cause of debtors. Under the system of checks and balances, the Senate, the president (with his veto), or the Supreme Court could override them. Edmund Randolph, a delegate to the Constitutional Convention from Virginia, declared that the origin of "the evils under which the U.S. laboured" was "the turbulence and follies of democracy." Some check was needed against this tendency. A "good Senate seemed most likely to answer the purpose," since it would "restrain, if possible, the fury of democracy."[12] Beard described the plan thusly: "Property interests may through their superior weight in power and intelligence, secure advantageous legislation whenever necessary, and they may at the same time obtain immunity from control by parliamentary majorities."[13]

---

‡‡  By taxing consumer goods, the poor paid as heavily as the wealthy. The elite thus protected their own interests, installing the same kind of tax system that had so burdened the small farmer under British rule.

§§ As a means to lighten the tax burden, state legislatures had been paying interest on bonds at less than face value. The new Constitution would put a stop to this practice, providing a particular benefit to wealthy men with large bond holdings.

¶¶  Beard refers to "the peculiar position assigned to the judiciary, and the use of the sanctity and mystery of the law as a foil to democratic attacks" (*An Economic Interpretation of the Constitution*, p. 161). Says Hamilton, in *Federalist* No. 78, "In a republic [the judiciary] is ... an excellent barrier to the encroachments and oppressions of the representative body" (p. 465).

***  Recall that, initially, members of the Senate were elected by state legislatures, not directly by the people. Likewise, the president was indirectly elected, by an electoral college. And, of course, justices of the Supreme Court were *appointed* for life.

†††  At least this was the case until 1913, when ratification of the Seventeenth Amendment to the Constitution established direct election of members of the Senate as well.

But many saw right through the strategy of a divided government and, if fact, had been warning against it for years. In this statement from 1776, the "Centinel," of Pennsylvania, advocates for a government of simple structure, similar to that in his home state:

> The highest responsibility is to be attained in a simple structure of government.... If you complicate the plan by various orders, the people will be perplexed and divided in their sentiment about the sources of abuses or misconduct.[‡‡‡] ... By imitating the constitution of Pennsylvania, you vest all legislative power in one body of men ..., elected for a short period, and necessarily excluded by rotation from permanency and guarded from precipitancy and surprise by delays imposed on its proceedings, you will create the most perfect responsibility; for then, whenever the people feel a grievance, they cannot mistake the authors and will apply the remedy with certainty and effect, discarding them at the next election.[14]

Anti-democratic sentiments were on display like a leitmotif throughout the speeches and writings of Convention delegates. Said Massachusetts delegate Eldridge Gerry, "The evils we experience flow from an excess of democracy."[15] Nathaniel Gorham, of the same state, concurred: "All agree that a check on the legislature is necessary."[16] And, of course, there is the voice of Alexander Hamilton: "The people are turbulent and changing; they seldom judge or determine right.... Can a democratic assembly who annually revolve in the mass of the people," he asks rhetorically, "be supposed steadily to pursue the public good? Nothing but a permanent body can check the imprudence of democracy."[17][§§§] The bottom line, according to William Livingston of New Jersey, was this: "The people have been and ever will be unfit to retain the exercise of power in their own hands."[18]

## Victory at Any Cost

After the Constitution had been signed by the delegates in Philadelphia, each state needed to elect delegates to a state ratification convention. These delegates to the state conventions were then to debate and vote their preference for or against the Constitution. At the outset of their respective state conventions, seven states, that is, a majority— Massachusetts, New Hampshire, Maryland, Virginia, Rhode Island, New York, and North Carolina—were against ratification. In New Hampshire, where the Federalists could tell the numbers were against them, they adjourned the convention so they could change some minds in favor of the Constitution. Tactics like these were used around the country to defeat the will of the people in favor of a small minority positioned to benefit from the new form of government.

---

‡‡‡  This, of course, was the express intention of the designers of the Constitution.
§§§  Hamilton's solution was a president and a Senate that would serve for life.

Writing from Massachusetts in November of 1787, "Agrippa" noted
that New York showed no interest in even holding a convention, that
Virginia had put off its convention until May, and that Pennsylvania
seemed unlikely to accept the Constitution as written. "The same objects
are made in all the states," he said, "that the civil government which they
have adopted and which secures their rights will be subverted."[19] In other
words, Americans were happy with the government they had under the
Articles of Confederation and did not want to abandon it for another.

Aware that the Constitution as written would probably not be
adopted without extensive debate and amendments, the organizers of
the Philadelphia convention did their best to force it through quickly,
insisting that it must be accepted *in toto* or not at all. As testimony to
the weakness of their position and in violation of the thirteenth article of
the Articles of Confederation,¶¶¶ they required that only nine of thirteen
states ratify the document for it to become the law of the land, despite
the pleas of Benjamin Franklin for unanimity. Under the Articles of Confederation, amendments were to be ratified by state legislatures. Fearing
rejection by these bodies, the oligarchs decided to set up independent
conventions instead, where they felt they could exercise more control.

"Well," you might say, "it was ratified after all. Surely that is testimony to its popularity."

A close examination of the conditions under which the various votes
were taken reveals just the opposite.**** Pennsylvania was the second
state to ratify.†††† One might take that as a sign of enthusiasm on the
part of the Pennsylvanians. Not necessarily. In fact, nothing could be
more anomalous than to have the state with the most democratic constitution in the new nation and a strong tradition of outspoken opposition
to the forces of oligarchic oppression approve a form of government
that was clearly anti-democratic.

The overall strategy of the Federalists was haste. The logistics were
as follows. Only about three percent of the population lived in towns of
more than eight thousand. The Federalist strongholds were in cities like
Philadelphia (population twenty-eight thousand), New York, and Boston. These were the places where wealthy merchants, lawyers, and bankers lived and fraternized. In the span of a day they could gather and plot
their actions. The opposition, the small farmers (at least eighty percent

---

¶¶¶ "And the Articles of this Confederation shall be inviolably observed by every State,
and the Union shall be perpetual; nor shall any alteration at any time hereafter be made in
any of them; unless such alteration be agreed to in a Congress of the United States, and be
afterwards confirmed by the legislatures of every State."
**** For a county-by-county analysis of the vote for and against ratification, as well as
a clear exposition of the views of those opposed to the Constitution, see Jackson Turner
Main, *The Anti-Federalists: Critics of the Constitution, 1781–1788.*
†††† Pennsylvania ratified the Constitution on December 12, 1787. Delaware's positive
vote preceded Pennsylvania's by five days, occurring December 7, a scant twelve weeks
after the Constitutional Convention had approved the document.

of the population), were spread out over vast distances. In mid-winter the roads could be muddy or icy. Mails were slow. There was little opportunity for the opposition to gather in one spot for an exchange of ideas.

It is not surprising, therefore, to learn that only about twenty percent of the adult white male population turned out to elect delegates to the state conventions that would debate the Constitution. The opponents of democracy used this low turnout as evidence that the populace was too ignorant and indifferent to take charge of common affairs. A more obvious and less damaging explanation is the simple and obvious fact that majority of the citizens were deliberately kept in the dark by the Federalists (oligarchs).

Sensing that if they were given the opportunity to gather all the evidence and fully debate the issues, the Pennsylvania delegates to their state convention would reject the Constitution, the Federalists (oligarchs) moved quickly. The Constitution was sent to the Pennsylvania State Convention *before* the Constitutional Convention itself had even fully completed its work. The Federalists (oligarchs) marshaled their supporters and forced an early vote.‡‡‡‡

In September 1787, in a letter to General William Irvine, David Redick describes the frantic efforts of supporters of the Constitution to get immediate ratification in Pennsylvania:

> gentlemen runing into the Country and neibouring towns haranguering the rabble. I say were you to see and hear these things as I do you would say with me that the verry Soul of confidence itself ought to change into distrust.... I think the measures pursued here is a strong evidence that these people know it will not bear an examination and therefor wishes to adopt it first and consider it afterward.[20]

Several members of the minority (those in opposition to the U.S. Constitution) at the Pennsylvania State Convention, feeling they needed more time to deliberate before being forced into a decision, left the convention, denying the majority a quorum. Officers "broke into their lodgings, seized them, dragged them through the streets to the State house, and thrust them into the assembly room, with clothes torn and faces white with rage."[21] The Federalists (oligarchs) had control of the press and saw that very little news spread about the views of the opposition. When the vote in Pennsylvania was taken, forty-six voted in favor of ratification and twenty-three were opposed.

Beard, commenting on the Pennsylvania convention, put it very simply: "Everything was done that could be done to keep the public out

‡‡‡‡ After the vote, the delegates to the Pennsylvania convention who had stood in opposition to the Constitution wrote that "The election for members of the convention was held at so early a period and the want of information was so great, that some of us did not know of it until after it was over." Quoted in *The Anti-Federalist: Writings by the Opponents of the Constitution*, edited by Herbert J. Storing, p. 205.

of the affair."[22] A fellow named Lloyd Thomas, noted for his skill in shorthand, had volunteered his services for the Pennsylvania State Convention. When he was turned down, he decided to proceed on his own. He placed an advertisement guaranteeing a full and accurate report of the debates, at the rate of $1 per hundred pages. His promise was never fulfilled. He was bought out. All that he produced was one slender volume containing the speeches of two prominent Federalists (oligarchs).[23]

On December 18, 1787, in a report published in *The Pennsylvania Packet and Daily Advertiser*, the defeated delegates to the Pennsylvania State Convention described their plight. Speaking of the framers of the Constitution, they described "some men of excellent characters" and others "who were more remarkable for their ambition and cunning, than their patriotism." They made note of the fact that the framers deliberated for four months "under the most solemn engagements of secrecy." Their comments are eloquent and merit quoting at length:

> Whilst the gilded chains were forging in the secret conclave, the meaner instruments of despotism, without, were busily employed in alarming the fears of the people, with dangers which did not exist, and exciting their hopes of greater advantages from the expected plan than even the best government on earth could produce.
>
> The proposed plan had not many hours issued forth from the womb of suspicious secrecy, until such as were prepared for the purpose, were carrying about petitions for people to sign, signifying their approbation of the system, and requesting the legislature to call a convention.... The public papers teemed with the most violent threats against those who should dare to think for themselves, and *tar and feathers* were liberally promised to all those who would not immediately join in supporting the proposed government be it what it would. Under such circumstances petitions in favor of calling a convention were signed by great numbers in and about the city, before they had leisure to read and examine the system, many of whom, now they are better acquainted with it, and have had time to investigate its principles, are heartily opposed to it. The petitions were speedily handed in to the legislature.[24]

The delegates continued with a description of conditions on the night of the election of delegates to the Pennsylvania State Convention:

> several of the subscribers ... were grossly abused, ill-treated and insulted while they were quiet in their lodgings, though they did not interfere, nor had any thing to do with the said election, but, as they apprehend, because they were supposed to be adverse to the proposed constitution, and would not tamely surrender those sacred rights, which you had committed to their charge.[25]

The Pennsylvania dissenters went on to point out that, according to its own state constitution, for the state of Pennsylvania to change its form of government there must be a majority of the people in favor of such a change. At least seventy thousand citizens were entitled to vote, but only about thirteen thousand actually voted to select delegates. Though two-thirds of the convention delegates voted in favor of the constitution, they were speaking for only eighty-seven hundred Pennsylvanians. Thus, the state of Pennsylvania, by its own constitution, never legally ratified the Constitution.

Matters were not much better elsewhere. In Massachusetts, George Richards Minot noted in his journal that the Federalists (oligarchs) were obliged "to *pack* a Convention whose sense would be different from that of the people"[26] (italics in the original). The Federalists (oligarchs) published a report that the popular leader from Stockbridge, Massachusetts, John Bacon, was in favor of ratification. In fact, he was opposed. Similar falsehoods were published in other states, all to the same purpose—to claim there was no opposition to the Constitution and to demonstrate that prominent men supported it. There is evidence that Federalist (oligarch) delegates in Sheffield and Great Barrington, Massachusetts, were elected illegally.

In Connecticut, the newspapers were under the control of the Federalists (oligarchs), and delegates were threatened with exclusion from government office if they voted against the Constitution. In New Hampshire, the Federalists (oligarchs) also had control of the press. Anti-Federalist (democratic) literature was effectively suppressed. Commenting on the outcome, one citizen observed, "I believe it will be conceded by all, that they did not carry their Point by Force of argument and Discussion; but by other Means, which were it not for the Depravity of the humane Heart, would be viewed with the warmest Sentiments of Disapprobation."[27] In New York, there was evidence of election tampering. Federalists (oligarchs) were told to fold their ballots in a certain manner as a means of distinguishing them from those of the opposition. Learning of this ruse, Anti-Federalists (democrats) imitated the method of folding, thus defeating the attempts at disenfranchisement. In Dobbs County, North Carolina, the Anti-Federalists (democrats) had a clear lead. Federalists caused a riot and destroyed the ballots.

Not only did the Federalists (oligarchs) tamper with elections, print falsehoods, and use intimidation and manipulation to win votes, they also exercised control over the mails, thereby delaying the arrival of critical news and sometimes not delivering the mail at all, always selectively handicapping their opponents. George Clinton, governor of New York and future vice president, lamented that "while the new Constitution was in agitation, I have discovered that many letters written to me, have never been delivered, and that others especially those which came by private conveyances appeared to have been opened on their passage."[28]

Clearly there was nothing democratic about the tactics used by the oligarchy to put its Constitution in place. But even more important is the document itself. It set up a government in which the popular voice was reduced to an inaudible whisper. To understand why this is true, one needs to think for a moment in broad terms about politics and the structure of government.

## Government as a Numbers Game

As Max Weber[§§§§] points out, "Anyone engaged in politics is striving for power." If one says that "a question is a 'political' question, ... what is meant in each case is that interests in the distribution, preservation, or transfer of power play a decisive role in answering that question."[29] Thus, in the most fundamental sense, government is a means for organizing the distribution of power. When all of the power is located in one person, that government is called a monarchy or autocracy. When power is held by a relative handful, the government is known as an oligarchy or aristocracy. When political power is equally distributed among the citizen population, the government is known as a democracy. Thus, the nature and form of government are determined by the number of people who hold power. Government is a numbers game.

Ancient Athens was a democracy. Power was equally distributed among the citizen population. The general population (including men, women, children, foreigners, and slaves) was about 300,000. The number of citizens was about 30,000. Among these citizens, everyone had the same political power. The lowest in the social hierarchy was probably the trireme oarsman.[¶¶¶¶] He owned no land and had nothing but the strength of his back to recommend him for consideration. Yet he had equal standing with powerful members of the aristocracy, such as Pericles and Alcibiades.

Let us imagine for a moment that Athens, in the fifth century B.C., was a representative oligarchy and that the 30,000 citizens were actually speaking for the 300,000, rather than for themselves alone. Under these circumstances, there would be one voice for every ten Athenians. It would be an easy matter for the representative to invite to dinner the nine other Athenians he spoke for and discuss with them various policies, foreign and domestic. He would be left with a solid connection to his constituency and a clear sense of their preferences.

Now let's jump ahead more than two thousand years to the United States in the period between 1776 and 1787. At that time, there were thirteen separate constitutional oligarchies. Taken collectively, around 1,500 representatives served in state legislatures. The population was about 3 million. Thus, one voice would speak for 2,000 Americans,

---

§§§§ Maximilian Carl Emil Weber (1864–1920) was a German lawyer, politician, historian, political economist, and sociologist best known for *The Protestant Ethic and the Spirit of Capitalism* (published in 1905).

¶¶¶¶   The trireme was the warship used by the Greeks in defense of its shores. Thus, the oarsman played a key part in Greek survival, as demonstrated in the Athenian victory over the Persians in the battle of Salamis in 480 B.C., where 380 triremes, 170 oarsmen each, outlasted and outmaneuvered some 800 Persian warships.

clearly too many to invite over for dinner. However, most of that number could fit into a venue something like Town Hall, a theater in New York City with a seating capacity of 1,495. In such a setting, the represented could gather with their representative as a forum to discuss issues of general public concern.

In 1787, when the Constitution was ratified, the numbers changed significantly. The local state legislatures with their 1,500 representatives were replaced with one central assembly of 65, known as the House of Representatives. Now, one voice would speak for about 46,000 citizens, a number too large to fit into any town hall. To participate in a full citizens' forum, one would need a sports stadium and a pair of binoculars.

Currently, in the United States, the population is over 300 million. There are 435 members of the House of Representatives. Thus, one voice speaks for about 700,000 citizens. There is no sports stadium with such a capacity. Nor can one conceive of any physical venue where those who are spoken for can collectively meet with and discuss with their representative the issues that concern them most. This, of course, is the truest meaning of "oligarchy." Those who govern are inaccessible to those who are governed. The small number of those governing is the source of their power. As Gore Vidal observes, "The government has been from the beginning the *cosa nostra* of the few and the people at large have always been excluded from the exercise of power."[30]

Not only are oligarchic rulers inaccessible to the people at large, for the most part they think alike and get along quite well amongst themselves. As Gaetano Mosca points out, "A hundred men acting uniformly in concert, with a common understanding, will triumph over a thousand men who are not in accord and can therefore be dealt with one by one."***** In other words, a hundred men can sit down in a room and agree on a course of action. For a thousand men to find a room large enough and to find common ground is a lot harder.

As Madison understood, under the Constitution of 1787, which mandated large election districts, diverse interests would be harder to unite than in the smaller districts of state legislatures, where the population was more homogeneous. In a letter to Jefferson, he commented, "Divide et impera, the reprobated axiom of tyranny, is under certain qualifications, the only policy, by which a republic can be administered on just principles."[31]††††††

---

***** Gaetano Mosca (1858–1941) was an Italian political philosopher whose primary belief was that there always has been, will be, and should be a ruling class. This prejudice aside, Mosca has a broad understanding of the evolution of various forms of government in various cultures and in various historical epochs. He is a thoughtful and tasteful writer. He loses his equilibrium, however, when discussing certain subjects, such as socialism. The quoted passage comes from Mosca's *The Ruling Class* (*Elimenti di Scienza Politica*), p. 53.
†††††† Notice here, again, how Madison tries to cover his tracks by introducing the word "just" when he is simply plotting by any method available to set up a government that would bend to his interests.

Charles Cotesworth Pinckney, delegate to the Constitutional Convention from South Carolina, made a similar observation. He reasoned that because the new central government would cover a vaster territory than any single state, the sheer "number of citizens will not permit them all to be assembled at one time, and in one place." Deprived of this ability to spontaneously gather and discuss their grievances, the "multitude will be less imperious."[32]

At the state level, most legislators and most governors had to run for election every year. This meant that they were forced to answer to their constituency again and again. This rotation in office was a mechanism for accountability and responsibility. The Federal Constitution was designed with an eye to limiting accountability by keeping House members in office for two years, senators for six years, and the president for four. Federal judges could serve for life. Under the Articles of Confederation, there were limits imposed on the numbers of terms a member could serve. Similar limits applied in many state governments. No such limits applied in the Federal government, guaranteeing extended office holding by a small, entrenched minority who could acquire more and more power at the expense of the governed.

In contrast to men like Madison and Pinckney, there were others who had different ideas. Herman Husband was a wealthy landowner from North Carolina who moved to Pennsylvania, where his democratic trend of mind met with a more friendly reception. His answer to the tyranny of the speculators was a constantly depreciating paper currency.[33] Paper money was a more democratic means of exchange than gold and silver, which were in short supply. Depreciating the currency was a essentially a self-collecting tax, a progressive tax, because those with more money would lose more, and depreciation served as a means of curbing inflation.‡‡‡‡‡ Husband made various other proposals as well, including a series of taxes, among them a land tax,§§§§§ which would reduce the burden on farmers. Husband was of the belief that all legislation should be submitted to a plebiscite.

Husband believed that just about any solid citizen was fit to rule. There was no need for a cultivated, wealthy elite to take charge. In fact, there would be domestic peace if those whose needs were most desperate were allowed to speak for themselves in the assemblies. A "man who will make a good Mechanick, or a good Farmer ... is also capable, with a few Years Practice ... to make a good Assembly-man to rule the state."[34] Speculators, of course, would point out that putting farmers in the state legislatures would give them the opportunity to come to the

---

‡‡‡‡‡ In his understanding of economics, Husband was far ahead of his time. For a more recent take on the subject, see Margrit Kennedy, *Interest and Inflation Free Money: Creating an Exchange Medium That Works for Everybody and Protects the Earth.*
§§§§§ Henry George's *Progress and Poverty* (originally published in 1879) offers a comprehensive study of an economy supported exclusively by a land tax.

assistance of their brethren at the expense of the speculators, which, as Husband saw it, was the way it should be.

Regarding representation on the state level, Husband believed that every election district should be small enough that voters could converse with their representative. He felt that districts were too large and intimidating for the small farmer or artisan. His solution was to set up legislatures on the county level made up of representatives from each town in the county. Training at this level would give the humbler folk the confidence they needed to compete on the state level. Echoing sentiments described earlier¶¶¶¶¶ on the relationship between government and character, Husband observed that where the districts were large, "the Body of the Governors" would be able to "combine," whereas "the Body of the Governed" was "cut off from the Benefit of the Circulation of Life and Knowledge, and so become dead and ignorant."[35]

Husband understood matters as well as Madison. But unlike Madison, Husband wanted to set up a government in which the needs of the vast majority of the population would be attended to. Madison wanted a government structured to stifle the popular voice and leave the power in the hands of a small oligarchy who could use government to service its own personal needs. It was Madison's notion of government that prevailed in Philadelphia in 1787, permanently closing the doors to democracy in America.

The period between the Declaration of Independence, 1776, and the ratification of the Constitution, 1788, was a period of experimentation in government. It was a unique opportunity for citizens of the new nation to try different forms of government and see what worked best. It was during this period that some of the most spirited and intelligent discussions on the subject of government took place. It was during this period, when the citizenry had direct access to the government that controlled its destiny, that democracy was given its strongest voice.

Rather than a single government, there were thirteen different governments with thirteen different constitutions. Such circumstances bring home to individual citizens the true meaning of government as they observe how different governments, in close proximity, function and are modified based on circumstances. Some constitutions had a bill of rights; some didn't. Constitutions had various qualifications for voting and holding office. Nothing was fixed and absolute. A citizen could observe different solutions to the same problem and could develop intelligent and informed opinions about which he preferred and why. Healthy skepticism, suspicion, and mistrust are the basis for a thoughtful, honest political dialogue. These qualities were amply displayed during the years prior to the ratification of the Constitution and all but disappeared once it was ratified.

---

¶¶¶¶¶ See Chapter 5, "Government and Character: Lessons from Athens."

One can imagine that had the Anti-Federalists (democrats) prevailed, America might be a very different nation. War might not have become its primary occupation. The government might have provided the basis for a peaceful, productive life, with an actively involved citizenry. It was "Brutus," from the state of New York, who said that the first business of government is "The preservation of internal peace and good order, and the due administration of law and justice. The happiness of a people depends infinitely more on this than it does upon all that glory and respect which nations acquire by the most brilliant martial achievement." Let us give the world, he said, "an example of a great people, who in their civil institutions hold chiefly in view, the attainment of virtue, and happiness among ourselves."[36] "The Federal Farmer" expressed similar sentiments. "The greatest blessings we can wish for," he said, "are peace, union, and industry, under a mild, free, and steady government."[37]

Unfortunately, the men who took charge in the United States at the end of the eighteenth century had dreams of their own, and they weren't of "peace, union," and a "mild, free" government.

# America's Early Oligarchy

*And thou, sly hypocrite, who now wouldst seem*
*Patron of liberty.*

FOR MORE THAN two hundred years, the key figures in early American history have been looked up to as benign, selfless men of virtue and good intentions. It is based on our understanding of these early Americans that we believe we have a government that serves the loftiest needs of the vast majority of us who live under its protection. A closer look, however, reveals that there was nothing in the world outlook, character, or social standing of these men that can in any way be construed as democratic. They were, to a man, powerful elitists. And they set up a government they knew they could bend to their wishes at the expense of the common good.

George Mason of Virginia was a delegate to the Constitutional Convention and a principal mover of the Bill of Rights. In September 1787, he spelled out his objections to the government that had just been created, concluding: "This Government will commence in a moderate Aristocracy; it is at prese[nt] impossible to foresee whether it will, in it's [sic] Operation, produce a Monarchy, or a corrupt oppressive Aristocracy; it will most probably vibrate some years between the two, and then terminate in the one or the other."[1]

Oligarchs who lust for power—those who wear powdered wigs and waistcoats, as well as their modern counterparts in pinstripe suits—will do whatever it takes to get it and hold on to it. Is it fair to say that the imposition of the new Constitution in September of 1787 represented a *coup d'état*?* There was a government in place under the Articles of Confederation. A committee had been authorized to modify the Articles, not to create an entirely new government under a new constitution.

---

* Professor John W. Burgess thought so: "Had Julius or Napoleon committed these acts they would have been pronounced *coups d'états*." Quoted in Beard, *An Economic Interpretation of the Constitution*, p. 218.

The Constitutional Convention met under a dark veil of secrecy; something was being hidden from the public. Great pressure was exerted to have the Constitution adopted without the benefit of free, honest, open debate. Supporters resorted to lying, manipulation, violence, trickery, and treachery to get the document ratified.

The true meaning of what was being done by a powerful cabal, operating in secret, was not lost on those who were about to live out the consequences. One contemporary, by the name of Cornelius, writing in December of 1787, expressed his outrage:

> Will not the adoption of this constitution in the manner here prescribed be justly considered as a perfidious violation of that fundamental and solemn compact by which the United States hold an existence and claim to be a people? If a nation may so easily discharge itself from obligations to abide by its most solemn and fundamental compacts, may it not with still greater ease do the same in matters of less importance? And if nations may set the example, may not particular states, citizens, and subjects follow? What then will become of public and private faith? Where is the ground of allegiance that is due to a government? Are not the bonds of civil society dissolved? Or is allegiance founded only in power? Has moral obligation no place in civil government? In mutual compacts can one party be bound while the other is free? Or, can one party disannul such compact, without the consent of the other? If so, constitutions and national compacts are, I conceive, of no avail; and oaths of allegiance must be preposterous things.[2]

In a similar vein, another writer from Massachusetts observed:

> A system of consolidation has been formed with the most profound secrecy and without the least authority: And has been suddenly and without any previous notice transmitted by the federal convention for ratification.... The people of this state, unassisted by Congress or their legislature, have not had time to investigate the subject ... and under such circumstances have elected members for the state convention—and these members are to consider whether they will accept the plan of the federal convention, with all its imperfections and bind the people by a system of government, of the nature and principles of which they have not at present a clearer idea than they have of the Copernican system.[3]

"The Federal Farmer" spoke of "the tyranny of the one" and "the licentiousness of the multitude." They are "but small evils, compared with the factions of the few."[4] He made reference to a "junto of unprincipled men, often distinguished for their wealth or abilities, who combine together and make their object private interests and aggrandizement."[5] Another writer, "Agrippa" of Massachusetts, wondered whether Americans should "trust persons, who have from their cradles, been incapable of comprehending any other principles of government, than those of absolute power, and who have, in this very affair, tried to deprive them of their liberty, by a pitiful trick."[6] Warned "The Impartial Examiner" of Virginia, "No pomp of character, no sound of names, no distinction of birth,—no preeminence of any kind, should dispose you to hood-wink your own understanding; and in that state suffer yourselves to be led at the will of any order of men whatsoever."[7]

When the Revolution ended, there was a suggestion within the officers' corps that they not abandon their arms until they had been properly paid and recognized. This was an armed coup in the making. "Brutus" declared, "It remains a secret, yet to be revealed, whether this measure was not suggested, or at least countenanced, by some who have had a great influence in producing the present system [i.e., the Constitution]."[8] In other words, those who were involved in shaping the Constitution might have been open to the use of armed violence as a means of securing their own ends. In discussing the Philadelphia convention, the Pennsylvania minority spoke of men "who more were remarkable for their ambition and cunning, than their patriotism." Some "had been opponents to the independence of the United States."[9] This is an important revelation. What it means is that there were loyalists involved in drafting the U.S. Constitution who might have used their influence to satisfy the wishes of the defeated enemy, Great Britain. Were this so, it indeed would have been grounds for secrecy.

## The Early Triumvirate

If there were a coup, who might have been involved? Alexander Hamilton (1755–1804) would certainly head the list. Hamilton was a bastard child of uncertain lineage. He was born on the island of Nevis in the British West Indies, one of two illegitimate sons. His mother, Rachel, was sent to prison on charges of adultery by her first husband, who referred to her as "a whore." When Alexander was ten years old, Rachel's second husband, a merchant, abandoned his wife and her two sons to their own devices. The family found themselves at the bottom rung of a highly stratified society, where they probably had to endure the scorn of their betters. When Rachel died of yellow fever, her husband sued for her belongings, thus depriving her sons of even a meager inheritance.

Hamilton spent the rest of his life trying to hide and live down his inglorious past. He quickly worked his way to the top of the social ladder in America and became the center of political power in the days preceding the Constitutional Convention. Hamilton was hot-headed and ambitious. He was a shrewd political organizer who knew the game of power politics and played it well. He wanted to establish a government that could be used as an instrument of financial growth and allow the United States to become an economic power on the world stage, with himself as one of the principal players. This would require a strong central government. As Secretary of the Treasury under George Washington, Hamilton was able to implement his policies. Probably more than any other single figure, he helped shape America's economic and political future. The country Hamilton wanted is the country we have today.

Hamilton's admiration for Britain—its power, its glory, its form of government, and its financial system—resulted in his doing everything he could to see that the United States imitated its mother country in all respects. He wanted a president for life (that is, a monarch) and a Senate for life (that is, a House of Lords). There was even talk of referring to the president as "His Excellency." Establishing such a government would entail abolition of the state governments.[†]

By involving himself in a strong central government, Hamilton would raise himself in his own eyes and in the eyes of those around him. A weak, decentralized government, under the Articles of Confederation, provided no such opportunity. In July of 1779, a friend warned him that there was a rumor about that he was fomenting an army uprising to overthrow Congress and install Washington as dictator. Hamilton vigorously denied the accusation, and the matter gradually subsided. Similar charges were leveled against Hamilton throughout his career. Based on his devotion to the military, his avowed monarchical wishes, and his unbridled ambition, one can reasonably wonder if such rumors didn't have some basis in fact.

One of Hamilton's closest collaborators in overthrowing the existing government under the Articles of Confederation was Gouverneur Morris (1752–1816).[‡] Morris was born into one of New York's wealthiest landed families. It was he who said, "The rich will strive to establish their dominion and enslave the rest. They always did. They always will."[10] Certainly this observation applies to Morris himself.

During the Revolution, his mother, a loyalist, gave the family estate to the British for military use. Morris was active in New York politics and was largely responsible for the writing of the state constitution. He was a delegate to the Continental Congress and a signer of the Articles of Confederation. He was one of those, like Hamilton, who favored a strong central government, a view that had little support in the state of New York. Eventually Morris moved to Philadelphia, where he set up shop as a lawyer and merchant. He was appointed Assistant Superintendent of Finance for Pennsylvania and represented the state at the Constitutional Convention, where he was one of the most active participants. He spoke one hundred seventy-three times at the convention and was responsible for most of the final draft of the Constitution.

It was Morris who gave us the Constitution's preamble, ringing with democratic fervor: "We the People of the United States." Like the aspiring aristocrat Hamilton, Morris had nothing but scorn for the people.

---

† In the *Federalist Papers*, Hamilton had taken the opposite tack, reassuring the states that "It will always be far more easy for the State governments to encroach upon the national authorities than for the national government to encroach upon the State authorities" (No. 17, p. 119), thus demonstrating that in the service of his own ambition Hamilton was certainly capable of speaking first from one side of his mouth and then from the other.
‡ "Gouverneur" is a first name, not a title.

He regarded himself as a blueblood, and seeing around him men of modest means becoming politicized, he lamented the fact that "the mob began to think and reason."[11] An aristocrat to the core, Morris believed that "there never was, nor ever will be a civilized Society without an Aristocracy."[12] He envisioned a Senate made up solely of great property owners. It is highly unlikely that such a person, holding such views, would be speaking for anyone other than those of his own class. It is easy to imagine that he, along with Hamilton, had a plan for putting in a place a government that was congenial to their interests, an oligarchy of money and landed gentry who spoke for "We the People."

Gouverneur Morris was eventually rewarded for his service with an appointment as America's Minister to France, a post he held from 1792 to 1794. Comments from Thomas Paine, who was living in France at the time Morris served there, provide a window into the personality of Morris. Paine wrote, "His prating, insignificant pomposity rendered him at once offensive, suspected and ridiculous; and his total neglect of all business had so disgusted the Americans that they proposed drawing up a protest against him.... [He] is so fond of profit and voluptuousness that he cares nothing about character."[§]

The third member of the triumvirate was Robert Morris (1734–1806).[¶] Morris was born in Liverpool, England, and at the age of thirteen moved to Maryland to join his father, a tobacco exporter. At age sixteen, Morris was apprenticed to the shipping and banking firm of a wealthy Philadelphia merchant. When the merchant died four years later, Morris joined with the man's son in a partnership that would last for twenty-five years. The firm's import/export and banking pursuits made it one of the most prosperous businesses in Pennsylvania, and as a result Morris became both wealthy and influential in Philadelphia.

Though he had resented the British Stamp Act of 1765, Morris nonetheless wanted to remain a loyal British subject. He was a reluctant signer of the Declaration of Independence. Ultimately, this loyalist's name would be affixed, as well, to the Articles of Confederation and the U.S. Constitution.

Morris managed to increase his great wealth during the Revolution. In 1775, the Continental Congress contracted with his company to import arms and ammunition for the war effort. In addition, he profited handsomely through the activities of the many privateer ships he owned. These ships seized the cargo of English ships and then sold off the spoils in port. After the war, Thomas Paine and others criticized Morris for war profiteering. Morris lived in a sumptuous mansion, was tended by liveried servants, and was reputed to be the wealthiest man in Philadelphia.

---

§ Paine's criticisms appear in an open letter he wrote to George Washington in 1796. He had equally harsh words for Washington himself. Additional excerpts from the letter appear in the last few pages of this chapter. The full letter is available at http://www.cooperativeindividualism.org/paine_letter_to_washington_01.html.

¶ Robert Morris was in no way related to Gouverneur Morris.

Although his detractors worried that Morris was gaining "dictatorial powers," Congress, under the Articles of Confederation, unanimously voted to appoint him as Superintendent of Finance of the United States, a post he held from 1781 to 1784. Morris prevailed in his demands that Congress allow him to continue his business pursuits, even though they overlapped his duties as Superintendent of Finance. Just three days after assuming office, Morris proposed the establishment of a national bank. The Bank of North America, the first financial institution chartered by the government of the United States, was established in 1782.

Morris was elected to serve as one of Pennsylvania's delegates to the 1787 Constitutional Convention, and he succeeded in getting his friend Gouverneur Morris onto the committee as well. Robert Morris was active behind the scenes at the Philadelphia convention, but his most important public action there was to nominate his friend George Washington as the convention's president.

Later in life, Morris was involved in a wide array of business pursuits. A land speculation scheme involving millions of acres failed when a loan from Holland fell through. The new mansion he was constructing in Philadelphia remained incomplete. Morris had to flee his creditors, and eventually he ended up in debtors' prison. Congress passed a bankruptcy law to help him get out.

Alexander Hamilton and Robert Morris were close allies, and both were extremely ambitious. When Morris became Superintendent of Finance under the Articles of Confederation (a position Hamilton had coveted) in 1781, Hamilton sent Morris a thirty-page letter outlining his position on "Public Credit," expressing views that closely paralleled those of Morris. President George Washington tried to appoint Morris Secretary of the Treasury in 1789, but Morris declined and suggested Hamilton instead. Both men understood that he who would control the country would first have to control its finances. Both believed in a strong central government and a national bank. Both also understood the advantages of wealth and social position. Morris at his peak was one of the wealthiest men in the country. As a young man, after a short romance, Hamilton had married into the Schuyler family, one of New York's wealthiest and most powerful.

All three—Gouverneur Morris, Robert Morris, and Alexander Hamilton—were men of aristocratic leanings who had nothing but contempt for the people, "the mob." All three men had great admiration for Britain and its form of government. Both Robert Morris and Gouverneur Morris enjoyed friendly relations with George Washington, soon to become the first President of the United States. Alexander Hamilton had served as Washington's aide-de-camp during the Revolution.

These three men, taken together, probably had more influence than any other in seeing to it that the Articles of Confederation was scrapped. Together they succeeded in shaping the new government to suit their personal ambitions. Hamilton had represented New York at the Annapolis convention of 1786, which had ultimately determined that a constitutional convention should meet to set up a new government. During that convention in Philadelphia, Washington had appointed Hamilton to the committee of three that drafted the very restrictive rules that would make it easier for men like Hamilton, Gouverneur Morris, and Robert Morris to guide and control the debate.

Two other key figures were instrumental in the political movement that undid a standing government and a way of life in the name of personal ambition. One, of course, was George Washington, and we shall return to him in a few pages. The other key player was James Madison (1751–1836).

## Strange Bedfellows

Madison and Hamilton made strange bedfellows. Hamilton was flamboyant, a northerner, a banker, a warrior, and a militarist. Madison was none of these. He was taciturn and self-absorbed, a member of the southern landed aristocracy, and he saw a standing army as a permanent threat to personal liberty.**

Most historians argue that Madison changed radically from a nationally oriented ally of Hamilton in 1787–1788 to a states' rights–oriented opponent of a strong national government by 1795. Initially he worked in close partnership with Hamilton, authoring nearly a third of the articles of the *Federalist Papers*. At this point in his life, many of the views he articulated were consistent with those of Hamilton, particularly regarding the need for a strong central oligarchy and a general contempt for the mob and for democratic sentiments. However, it was Madison who drafted and became an ardent advocate of the first ten amendments to the Constitution—the Bill of Rights—one of the many contradictions of his career.

Madison was not ambitious in the way Hamilton was. He had no need to be. He was born into a slave-owning family in possession of ten thousand acres of land in Orange County, Virginia. Hamilton was out to get what he didn't have: status and wealth. Madison had a different motivation. He wanted to hold on to what he had and what he might lose in the absence of strong central oligarchy.

In *Federalist* No. 10, Madison expresses regrets "that our governments are too unstable, that the public good is disregarded in the

---

** In 1795, when he was no longer Hamilton's ally, Madison declared: "Of all the enemies to public liberty war is, perhaps, the most to be dreaded, because it comprises and develops the germ of every other. War is the parent of armies; from these proceed debts and taxes; and armies, and debts, and taxes are the known instruments for bringing the many under the domination of the few. In war, too, the discretionary power of the Executive is extended; its influence in dealing out offices, honors, and emoluments is multiplied; and all the means of seducing the minds, are added to those of subduing the force, of the people. The same malignant aspect in republicanism may be traced in the inequality of fortunes, and the opportunities of fraud, growing out of a state of war, and in the degeneracy of manners and of morals engendered by both. No nation could preserve its freedom in the midst of continual warfare." Quoted in Garry Wills, *James Madison*, p. 62.

conflicts of rival parties, and that measures are too often decided, not according to the rules of justice and the rights of the minor party, but by the superior force of an interested and overbearing majority."[13] Madison here seems to be objecting to majority rule and seems to be seeking a form of government in which the wish of the majority is mitigated or obstructed. His concerns are twofold: (1) "the rules of justice" and (2) "the rights of the minor party." Implied, though not stated, is that "justice" and "the rights of the minor party" are one and the same. Well, just who is this minor party and what are its special interests?

Madison's fundamental concern in organizing a government is the issue of divided interests.[††] How does government reconcile the differences between the propertied and the nonpropertied; between mercantile, banking, agricultural, and manufacturing interests; between debtors and creditors? Apparently Madison is not as neutral in this debate as his rhetoric would suggest. In fact, he has a very specific, personal interest, a minority interest, which he would like to see safeguarded:

> The diversity in the faculties of men, from which the rights of property originate, is not less an insuperable obstacle to a uniformity of interests. The protection of these faculties is the first object of government. From the protection of different and unequal faculties of acquiring property, the possession of different degrees and kinds of property immediately results; and from the influence of these on the sentiments and views of the respective proprietors ensures a division of the society into different interests and parties.[14]

So here we have it. The minor party to which Madison makes reference—and for which he seeks special consideration—is made up of those whose special faculties enable them to acquire property, in the form of land.[‡‡] It is assumed, not argued, that the rights of property originate from the "diversity of faculties" in obtaining it. Madison here makes no mention of the common good or of justice.

It is also assumed, not proven, that "the first object of government" is "the protection of these faculties." Differently stated, there is an elite minority residing in the thirteen states whose special faculties for acquiring property need to be protected, according to James Madison, who coincidentally just happens to be one of those gifted in acquiring property. And what are these "faculties" that are so precious? If one looks at the origins of the property held among the aristocracy in just about any society at any time, the origins seem to be of two kinds: either the government gives land or land is taken. The special faculties referred to, then, seem principally to be those of being either well connected or well armed.

---

†† These views, as reflected in Madison's *Federalist* writings, are discussed also in Chapter 2.

‡‡ Thomas Paine was of the opinion that "No better reasons can be given why the house of legislature should be composed entirely of men whose occupations is [sic] in letting landed property than why it should be composed of those who hire, or brewers, or bakers, or of any other separate class of men." *The Complete Writings of Thomas Paine*, edited by Philip S. Foner, p. xxix.

In Madison's case, the land owned was acquired by his great-great-grandfather and passed on to him by his parents. The great-great-grandfather apparently was the recipient of two "headrights"[§§] granted to him by the government as an early colonizer. He was able to expand his holdings by obtaining further government grants each time he paid for the passage of an indentured servant, whose labor was then his, free of charge. Thus, the special "faculty" in question here seems to be the willingness to accept land granted by the government.[¶¶]

In the period that concerns us here—the years leading up to ratification of the new Constitution—Madison was an indispensable ally of Hamilton in betraying the standing government under the Articles of Confederation and lobbying for a new central government under the control of a relative handful of men. He was joined in these efforts by another prominent, wealthy, landholding, slaveholding member of the southern aristocracy: George Washington.

## His Excellency

Washington had a key role to play in setting up the oligarchy under the new U.S. Constitution. He was the icon, the symbol the population would unite behind, serving to conceal from the public the machinations of the cabal under Hamilton's leadership. Hamilton knew this better than anyone and might never have given his energies to forming the new government if he had thought he would not be able to count on Washington as the front man. As his aide-de-camp, Hamilton composed the letters Washington would sign. Hamilton supplied the words, and Washington would open and close his mouth. Once Washington was president, Hamilton was able to continue as his ventriloquist from his office as Secretary of the Treasury.

Washington was a fourth-generation Virginian whose lineage in the New World began when John Washington migrated to the American shores in 1657. John was known to the Indians as "town-taker." He earned this moniker by successfully manipulating the law to swindle the Indians out of their land. George seems to have inherited John's appetite for land, as well as his wily tactics.

---

§§   The headright system was introduced in 1618 in the Jamestown colony in Virginia. The objective was to resolve labor shortages created with the advent of the tobacco economy, which required many workers and large plots of land. A headright is a legal grant of land usually given to a settler moving into an uninhabited area. Virginia colonists were each given two headrights of fifty acres apiece. Individuals would then receive one additional headright each time they paid for the passage of another individual, often an indentured servant.

¶¶   The popular Caribbean destination of Barbados began as a proprietary colony *given* to the Earl of Carlisle by King Charles I. What is today North Carolina, South Carolina, and Georgia was originally called simply Carolina. Carolina was given to eight powerful aristocratic allies of King Charles II. Lord Baltimore ended up with Maryland. Examples abound, both large and small, of land simply given away. By what manner or means a king can legally grant to his friends large tracts of land from which he is separated by thousands of miles of water, land upon which he has never set foot, to me remains a mystery.

Washington inherited an estate of some 2,000 acres, known as Mt. Vernon. He increased his holdings dramatically by marrying Martha Custis, one of the richest widows in North America. When Washington married Martha, by law everything that was hers became his: a hundred slaves and another 6,000 acres of land.

Washington wanted to be seen in the same light that shone upon the cream of the British aristocracy. Once he had married Martha and established his ascendancy in wealth and prestige, he pursued a life that was consistent with the image he chose to project. Fox hunting became something of an obsession. In 1768, according to his own notes, he spent forty-nine days—two to five hours each day—chasing down fox on horseback. Washington would travel to horse races in an expensive carriage, made in London, with leather interior and his personal crest emblazoned on the side. He purchased his Madeira in quantities of one hundred fifty gallons. His coats, shirts, pants, and shoes were all ordered from London. In attendance were two manservants. One was white and the other was a mulatto slave known as Bill Lee, who every morning would comb and tie his master's hair.

In 1767, after eight years of marriage, Washington went after land that had been expressly set aside by the Crown for the Indians, instructing his surveyor, if queried, to lie about what he was up to. In addition, Washington acquired 20,000 acres as a consequence of his military service. As a colonel in the Virginia militia, he was required by the Crown to distribute 200,000 acres of land to the soldiers under his command. Washington kept some of the best land for himself. His will, executed in 1800, lists 52,194 acres to be sold or distributed in Virginia, Pennsylvania, Maryland, New York, Kentucky, and the Ohio Valley. In addition to these properties, Washington also held title to lots in the Virginia cities of Winchester, Bath (now Berkeley Springs, West Virginia), and Alexandria, and in the newly formed City of Washington.[15]

Of George Washington, it has been said, by no lesser person than his biographer, Joseph J. Ellis, that "Benjamin Franklin was wiser than Washington; Alexander Hamilton was more brilliant; John Adams was better read; Thomas Jefferson was more intellectually sophisticated; James Madison was more politically astute."[16] Ellis might also have said, but didn't, that George Washington was the first in a long line of mediocrities to become President of the United States.*** Why then all the fuss? There are two principal reasons. The first is that Washington was a self-made icon. He deliberately cultivated a certain image based on physical appearance and demeanor designed to impress and gain admiration. The

***  Aaron Burr—in many ways as bright and prepossessing as Alexander Hamilton, whom Burr ultimately killed in a duel—described Washington as "a man of no talents and one who could not spell a sentence of common English" (quoted in Ron Chernow, *Alexander Hamilton*, p. 562). John Adams was of a similar opinion and dubbed Washington "Old Muttonhead" (Chernow, p. 520).

second is that he appeared on the scene at a time when the new country, without a history or iconography, was in desperate need of an icon.

Myths sprouted up around Washington almost from the outset. The most famous was that as a child he cut down a cherry tree and then admitted doing so to his parents. We owe this myth to Mason Locke Weems, an Anglican minister who decided he could make money by writing and then selling door to door his own books. He wrote the first biographies of George Washington, Benjamin Franklin, and William Penn. His creation of the story of George Washington and the cherry tree was consistent with Weems' moralizing tendencies.

One of Weems' best known stories of Washington's piety comes from Weems' account of Washington praying at Valley Forge. Weems tells of a man named Isaac Potts, who silently witnessed an unsuspecting Washington kneeling humbly in the snow, praying for God's blessing on his troops. Pure fiction.

Washington's teeth were not made of wood. They were carved from the finest hippopotamus ivory and gold. The upper and lower gold plates were connected by springs that pushed the plates against the upper and lower ridges of his mouth to hold them in place. Washington actually had to actively close his jaws to make his teeth bite together. If he relaxed, his mouth would pop open. There is speculation that this is the reason why he always looked so stern in his portraits. He was just trying to keep his teeth in.

As a young man, Washington had red hair. A popular myth is that he wore a wig, as was the fashion among some at the time. Washington did not wear a wig; instead he powdered his hair.

Washington gained his place in American history for his valor during the Revolutionary War. It is true that he could sit a horse probably better than any other American at the time, that he was doggedly persistent during the eight-year war, and that he never backed down in battle. He was blessed with good luck. He had two horses shot out from under him; felt bullets rip through his clothes and hat; lived through hard winters and a case of smallpox; and survived attacks by Indians, French and English troops, and cunning political opponents. Another time, it was related, an Indian guide turned on him and fired a pistol at point-blank range—but missed.

Washington was cold-blooded and cruel. Early in his career, when he was in charge of the Virginia militia, his discipline of his troops was unrelenting. Those found guilty of drunkenness or lewd behavior could receive up to a thousand lashes. Deserters, even those who returned voluntarily, faced hanging. With pride, Washington had erected a gallows forty feet high. Without hesitation, he saw to it that several deserters were hung as examples for the others. These were extreme steps to take, especially since his troops were not at war. They were simply patrolling the Virginia borders. Such was the man who is known to history as the "Father of His Country."

With the Revolution under way, Washington was the general in charge. But he was no military strategist. He made more than one blunder and succeeded in the Revolution in large measure due to the men around him, whose good advice he reluctantly and belatedly would follow. In July of 1776, some three hundred English ships and thirty-two thousand men gathered off Sandy Hook, New Jersey. New York City had to be evacuated. Hamilton doubted Brooklyn Heights could be defended against such an overwhelming force, but Washington would not be dissuaded. The battle of Brooklyn, in late August, was a full-blown fiasco. About twelve hundred Americans were killed or captured. Later, in October, a similar disaster occurred in White Plains, New York. In November, the British overran Fort Washington, at the northern end of Manhattan Island. Washington was roundly chastised for failing to properly safeguard his men, supplies, and armaments.

Years later, as the war was drawing to a close with the invaluable aid of the French, Washington—ignoring pleas for assistance in Virginia and the Carolinas—was determined to fight a grand battle in New York, where the British had established a powerful presence. This would be the dramatic victory Washington was looking for. Tactical retreats, the kind of hit-and-run so successfully employed by Nathanael Greene, were not in Washington's repertoire. He needed a grand display to burnish his image. Had Washington prevailed in his determination to stage a battle in New York, the outcome of the Revolution might have been quite different. However, the French general Count Rochambeau refused to cooperate and so Yorktown (in Virginia) became the site of the decisive battle. Subsequently, honest George would do his best to distort the record and make it appear as if Yorktown had been his idea all along.[†††]

Once the war was out of the way, Washington could return to his preferred pursuits, for a time, at least. He was unrepentant and unrelenting in his commitment to slave ownership. By the 1780s, he owned a little more than two hundred men, women, and children. He spoke of slaves as "a Species of Property" and posted notices for their recapture when they ran away. He had one difficult slave named Tom shipped off to the Caribbean with instructions to the ship's captain that he would fetch a decent price "if kept clean & trim'd up a little when offered to Sale."[17] After the decisive victory at the battle of Yorktown, there were slaves to be dealt with. Hundreds had sought refuge with the British.

---

[†††] Though militiamen made up about a sixth of the fighting force on the American side at Yorktown, both Washington and Hamilton had no respect, in principle, for local militias as a national defense, arguing that they were undisciplined, unmotivated, and unprepared. John Adams offered contradictory testimony, however. On June 10, 1775, he wrote, "Two days ago we saw a wonderful phenomenon in this city [Philadelphia]: a field day on which three battalions of soldiers were reviewed, making full two thousand men ... all in uniforms, going through the military exercise, and the manoeuvres with remarkable dexterity. All this has been accomplished in this city since the 19th of April; so sudden a formation of any army never took place anywhere." Quoted in J. Paul Selsam, *The Pennsylvania Constitution of 1776*, p. 78.

Though Washington had accepted freed black slaves into the Continental Army, he insisted that the slaves captured at Yorktown—many dying of smallpox—be rounded up and returned to their masters.

Washington spared no expense in trying to recapture two of his most valued slaves—his cook Hercules and Martha's servant Ona Judge—both of whom had served in the presidential household and escaped just before Washington's retirement from the presidency. After three years of searching, he tracked Ona down in New Hampshire and tried to get her to return. She agreed, provided she would be freed upon Washington's death. Washington adamantly refused, arguing, "it would neither be politic or just to reward unfaithfulness with a premature preference."[18] When the nation's capital was moved from New York to Philadelphia in 1790, there were practical issues to resolve concerning Washington's slaves. According to the law of the state of Pennsylvania, any slave living in the state for six months or more could demand emancipation. It was honest George's intention to defeat this law by removing his slaves from Philadelphia temporarily before six months had elapsed and thereafter have them return.

Unlike Hamilton, Washington never really wanted power for the sake of power. Washington wanted glory, military achievement, and a personal presence that would inspire awe and reverence—and that is just what he got. It was Hamilton, as his aide-de-camp early in the Revolution, who was one of the first to refer to him as "Excellency," a title Washington did nothing to discourage.

None other than Thomas Paine published a fierce open letter to George Washington dated July 30, 1796, while Washington still served as president. Paine's enmity can be explained, in part, by the fact that he had been arrested in Paris in December 1793, during the height of The Terror, and had been allowed to languish in prison for seven months, plagued by ill health and threats of the guillotine.‡‡‡ Washington did not lift a finger to come to his assistance. After all Paine had done for America, certainly he had reason to expect that the Executive Department would at least enquire after his well-being. Paine writes:

> Mr. Washington owed it to me on every score of private acquaintance, I will not now say, friendship; for it has some time been known by those who know him, that he has no friendships; that he is incapable of forming any; he can serve or desert a man, or a cause, with constitutional indifference; and it is this cold, hermaphrodite faculty that imposed itself upon the world and was credited for a while, by enemies as by friends, for prudence, moderation and impartiality.

Elsewhere in the letter Paine observes, "The character which Mr. Washington has attempted to act in the world is a sort of nondescribable, cha-

---

‡‡‡ Paine's full letter, which includes a detailed account of the incident in Paris, can be found at http://www.cooperativeindividualism.org/paine_letter_to_washington_01.html. The quoted passages from the letter that follow all come from this site.

meleon-colored thing called prudence. It is, in many cases, a substitute for principle, and is so nearly allied to hypocrisy that it easily slides into it."

He proceeds to indict Washington as a general and leader of his country in times of war:

> The part I acted in the American Revolution is well known; I shall not here repeat it. I know also that had it not been for the aid received from France, in men, money and ships, that your cold and unmilitary conduct … would in all probability have lost America; at least she would not have been the independent nation she now is. You slept away your time in the field, till the finances of the country were completely exhausted, and you have but little share in the glory of the final event. It is time, Sir, to speak the undisguised language of historical truth.§§§

Paine speaks also of an administration tainted by corruption, with Washington at its center:

> Monopolies of every kind marked your administration almost in the moment of its commencement. The lands obtained by the Revolution were lavished upon partisans; the interest of the disbanded soldier was sold to the speculator; injustice was acted under the pretence of faith; and the chief of the army [i.e., George Washington himself] became the patron of the fraud.

Washington had royal pretensions and did nothing to hide them. Paine decries Washington's attitude:

> Elevated to the chair of the Presidency, you assumed the merit of every-thing to yourself, and the natural ingratitude of your constitution began to appear. You commenced your Presidential career by encouraging and swallowing the grossest adulation, and you traveled America from one end to the other to put yourself in the way of receiving it.

Indeed, when Washington was unanimously elected first President of the United States, one supporter observed, "You are now a king, under a different name."[19] Had it been the day of his coronation rather than the day of his inauguration as president, the public reverence would have been no different. And Washington played his part to the hilt. Outside Philadelphia he mounted a white horse so thousands of spectators could witness him as he crossed the Schuylkill River. Early in his presidency, Washington made a tour of different parts of the country. For his journey south there was an entourage of eleven horses, including his favorite white parade steed, Prescott, whom he mounted at the edge of each town so as to make a glorious entrance. Prescott's hooves were polished and painted. He was fitted with a leopard-skin cloth and gold-trimmed saddle. So much for democracy.

---

§§§  There were rumors that Washington had in fact conspired with the British during the Revolution. See Ron Chernow, *Alexander Hamilton*, p. 507.

# Alexander Hamilton
# and the British Connection

*He seem'd*
*For dignity composed, and high exploit:*
*But all was false and hollow.*

AS WE CONTEMPLATE the possibility that there was indeed a conspiracy to overthrow the legitimate government of the United States under the Articles of Confederation and replace it with a powerful, centralized oligarchy under the Constitution, we must look for the purpose behind such an action. We have already considered the main actors, a cabal of men with the same financial interests—men like Robert Morris and Gouverneur Morris, operating under the leadership of Alexander Hamilton. We have looked at their actions, taken in secret, and the way they played upon a precipitating event—Shays' Rebellion—using it as a potent galvanizing force against the Articles of Confederation. Still, why would these men, supposed pillars of their communities, pursue such a course? One way to answer that question is to look at the outcome.

The key figure to study in this context is Hamilton. He was George Washington's Secretary of the Treasury from September 11, 1789, until his resignation on January 31, 1795. During his tenure in office, and even after, it was Hamilton, not Washington, who was the most powerful man in the country. Most of the important achievements of these early years of the American government were initiated and orchestrated by Hamilton. Washington was a figurehead. He lacked Hamilton's intelligence and his lust for power. Washington trusted Hamilton fully and rarely questioned his judgment.

If Hamilton had a fetish, it was banking. In 1781, at the age of twenty-six, he sent a thirty-page letter to Robert Morris—then Superintendent of Finance under the Articles of Confederation—outlining his plan for a national bank and a national debt to go with it. It was Hamilton's goal, via a national bank, to wed the "interest of the monied [sic] men with the resources of government."[1] A national debt, he maintained, would be a "national blessing. It will be powerful cement of our union."[2]* Three years later, in 1784, Hamilton founded the Bank of New York.

In 1780, when Hamilton married into the Schuyler family, one of the most prosperous and politically influential families in the state of New York, he acquired a brother-in-law by the name of John Barker Church. Church was a British subject who had left Britain under suspicious circumstances, probably in flight from the consequences of a bankruptcy brought on by gambling and stock speculation.[†] Church became influential in American affairs and amassed a fortune as a profiteer during the Revolutionary War. With his newfound wealth, Church returned to England in 1782, restored his reputation, and rose to the center of high society in London. Eventually, he was elected to Parliament. Upon leaving for England, Church designated Hamilton as his American business agent. When Hamilton founded the Bank of New York, Church was one of the principal shareholders. Church later returned to America.[‡]

In 1790, Hamilton delivered a report to Congress outlining his proposal for dealing with public debt. It was Hamilton's decision to redeem all war bonds at full face value, providing speculators with a windfall. The issue of redemption of war bonds had been brewing since the end of the war, when farmers and men of modest means returned home desperate for money. Speculators had swooped in and bought up the bonds from these individuals at steep discounts. Under the Articles of Confederation, some jurisdictions had taken measures to protect the interests of individual bondholders. Under the new Constitution, however, with Hamilton in the lead at Treasury, that all changed. The people who, with little wealth, had given what they could to support the patriotic effort ended up with fifteen cents on the dollar, while speculators who had sacrificed nothing reaped a generous reward. It should come as no great surprise that the Schuyler family and Church were among the chief beneficiaries of the new policy.[§]

---

* Whether or not a national debt is indeed a "powerful cement of our union" is open to debate. There is no question, however, that it is a boon to bankers.

† Church operated under the pseudonym John B. Carter after coming to America, presumably in an attempt to cast off past difficulties and obstruct those in Britain who might want to track his activities. Throughout the discussions in this volume, I will refer to him by his proper name, John Barker Church.

‡ In 1799, Church fought a duel with Aaron Burr and survived. In a twist of fate, it was Church's own pistols that brought about his brother-in-law's death, when they were used in Hamilton's 1804 duel with Burr, in which Hamilton was mortally wounded. A brief biography of Church can be found at http://www.historyofparliamentonline.org/volume/1790-1820/member/church-john-barker-1748-1818.

§ The correspondence between Hamilton and his father-in-law, Philip Schuyler, from the period when the Constitution was being formulated was destroyed by the son of one of Schuyler's executors. Beard, *An Economic Interpretation of the Constitution*, p. 109.

James Madison had advocated tracking the original bondholders and giving *them* the full benefit of their investment. Hamilton thought this was impractical. Clearly, the U.S. government, in debt to both national and foreign creditors, was in no position to make good on face value redemption of its bonds to any of the bondholders. Hamilton's decision to do so nonetheless simply meant that more money would have to be borrowed from the bank, a loan whose interest and principal would be paid through taxes on the very same people who got only fifteen cents on the dollar for their wartime investments. Hamilton was suspected at the time of leaking advance information on the redemption plan to speculators—both in Congress and among his business associates—before the report was made public.

Hamilton was an Anglophilomaniac. He was passionately—nay, compulsively—devoted to England and all things English. Basically, he wanted the new country—the United States of America—to imitate in all ways possible the setup that had allowed Britain to flourish as a colonial empire. Therefore, it was predictable that when, less than a year and a half into Washington's first term, Hamilton proposed a central bank to be known as the "Bank of the United States," he used the Bank of England as his model.

The Bank of England had been established in 1694, at a time when King William III needed money to wage war against France.¶ The government granted a charter to William Paterson to set up a private bank that would service the government's financial needs. The bank would lend money to the government, issue currency, and set interest rates. England's finances were in such a dire condition that the government was obliged to accept whatever terms Paterson offered. The terms most definitely were not favorable to the borrower. The government was charged an interest rate of eight percent per annum. In addition, the bank levied an annual service fee of £4,000 for management of the loan.

## Hamilton's Bank

Hamilton's bank, like the Bank of England, was to be a private, not public, institution. Like the Bank of England, the names of its shareholders were to remain secret. The bank was to issue currency and establish interest rates—that is, control the supply of money, increasing it or decreasing it as the bank saw fit, based on the interests of its stockholders. The bank was open to foreign as well as domestic investors, though foreign investors did not have voting rights. The bank was to be funded at $10 million, of which a $2 million share was to be purchased by the U.S. government (person or persons in power). Because the government didn't have the money to buy its share outright, the bank would in effect lend the money to the government, a loan that would be

---

¶ As Cicero put it, "The sinews of war are infinite money."

paid back in ten equal installments. The bank would serve as a depository for collected taxes, make short-term loans to the government, and function as a holding site for incoming and outgoing monies. The bank was to be granted a twenty-year charter, which would expire in 1811.**

Here, in microcosm, is the political economy of the United States from its inception up to this very moment in the year 2012: The government sets up a private institution, using public money, of which there is a ready and unremitting influx in the form of payments of interest on debt and monetary deposits. In order to make these interest payments on its debt, this same central government must impose federal taxes. And thus the cycle is complete for the private banking interests. Government has served its primary purpose. Under the Articles of Confederation, no such system would have been tolerated.

The Scottish philosopher, economist, and historian David Hume (1711–1776) had warned against a credit-based economy with a funded debt. He maintained that such a system necessitates imposition of oppressive taxes to pay the interest, creates dangerous disparities in wealth, indebts the nation to foreign powers, and renders the stockholders largely idle and useless for anything but playing the market. Hume felt that these evils greatly outweighed any advantages.

Hamilton ignored the warnings and proceeded to erect his banking system. He was intentionally setting up a moneyed oligarchy who would ultimately preside over America's government, directing it to serve their own private interests. Hamilton had his way, and things turned out exactly as David Hume had predicted.

William Duer (1743–1799) was a wealthy and well-connected New York developer and speculator when Alexander Hamilton appointed him to the Board of the Treasury in 1789. Duer had been helpful to Hamilton when he set up the Bank of New York, and this new position would give Duer a significant insider vantage point on American finance. After leaving his Treasury post in 1791, Duer began to speculate on rumors that the Bank of New York would be bought by the new Bank of the United States.

Relying heavily on funds from a partner and other investors—and making stock purchases on credit—Duer made investments that would benefit from rising Bank of New York stock prices (which would be a

---

** There are those who maintain that the failure of the United States to renew the bank charter in 1811 was a precipitating factor in America's decision to declare war in what has come to be known as the War of 1812. By the time the war ended in 1814, both sides had made some marginal gains, but both had also taken significant financial losses. A national bank in America was resurrected when the Second Bank of the United States was chartered in 1816. It has also been argued that the United States invaded Iraq in 2003 in part because Saddam Hussein had signaled that he intended to switch his reserve currency from the dollar to the Euro. And now, in 2012, some believe an invasion of Iran is made more likely by that nation's movement away from the dollar and into other currencies. The power of economic imperialism is not to be underestimated.

consequence of the rumored merger). What he hadn't counted on were competing interests working to drive the bank's stock prices down. The actions of Duer's competitors resulted in a run on the bank, setting off a contraction of the local money supply. In what is now known as the Panic of 1792, banks began to call in loans, and a wave of bank failures swept through New York's financial community. The availability of credit plummeted, and interest rates shot up to as high as one percent per day. Securities lost a quarter of their value in the space of two weeks. Duer was unable to cover his credit obligations and was ruined, ending up in debtors' prison.††

The market crash severely devalued government securites as well, and Hamilton had to step in to avert disaster. Drawing on the national Sinking Fund,‡‡ Treasury provided support for the market through the purchase of several hundred thousand dollars' worth of federal securities. In addition, Hamilton urged banks not to call in loans.

If all of this sounds familiar to readers in the twenty-first century, it should. In March of 2008, speculation and bad credit led to a collapse in the U.S. market. Hundreds of billions of dollars were subsequently pumped into the market by the Working Group on Financial Markets (a.k.a. the Plunge Protection Team), the latter-day counterpart to Hamilton's Sinking Fund. One could say, "Oh, how quaint it is to see history repeat itself thus." This is not history repeating itself. This is an example of America's government (person or persons in power) functioning exactly as it was meant to. The Anti-Federalists had predicted this result. So had David Hume. Have the government create a powerful central bank—operating as a private enterprise but with heavy public investments, issuing credit whose value fluctuates—and there will be speculation inevitably leading to cycles of boom and bust.

With his bank in place, Hamilton moved on to his second task—he needed to convince Congress to enact tax legislation. In 1791, he succeeded in getting a tax package passed. The most controversial element was a tax on whiskey, leading to what has come to be known as the Whiskey Rebellion.§§ Hamilton, who had earlier earned money as a tax collector under the Articles of Confederation, insisted on joining George Washington and his military force in bringing down the opposition in western Pennsylvania. Having levied the tax, he was determined to collect it—by brute force, if necessary. Washington and Hamilton set out on

---

†† An account of Duer's activities can be found in an article by John Steele Gordon, "The Great Crash (of 1792)," in *American Heritage* magazine. The affair, along with some personal insights on Duer, is also described in Charles R. Geisst's *Wall Street: A History, from Its Beginning to the Fall of Enron.*

‡‡ Hamilton had established this fund, modeled on a similar British mechanism, as a repository for excess customs revenues. In theory, the purpose of the fund was to facilitate retirement of public debt. In times of need, however, the fund could also purchase government securities to support their market price.

§§ The Whiskey Rebellion is discussed in more detail in Chapter 7.

their mission together. At the time, Washington was sixty-two years old and Hamilton thirty-nine.

Hamilton wanted to make an example of some of the perpetrators by having them hanged. Washington, in this instance, urged clemency. There was considerable distress over the use of such force against citizens legitimately aggrieved. Madison was concerned that the use of troops would lead to the establishment of a standing army and an ongoing threat to individual liberties. Jefferson saw the mission as another example of Hamilton's lust for unlimited power and his insidious involvement in Washington's decisions.

A national bank, an excise tax, and the use of military force to maintain order among the people—these were some of the outcomes of the installation of a powerful central government with Alexander Hamilton at the helm (in practice, if not officially). And there was another significant outcome. It concerns the relationship between the new nation, the United States, and her former colonial master, Great Britain.

## Breach of Faith: The Jay Treaty

The Paris Treaty of 1783 ended the Revolutionary War. In the following years, both signatories were lax in living up to their half of the bargain. Britain continued to occupy military posts on American territory. Britain denied American vessels trading rights in the British West Indies. A number of American states—mostly in the South—tarried in paying debts to their British creditors. By 1794, matters had been made worse by international conditions. France and Britain were at war. Americans found themselves forbidden to trade with Britain's enemy (i.e., France), which had been their ally in the Revolutionary War. More than two hundred fifty American ships engaged in trade with the French were seized by the British. In addition, the British were apparently inciting the Indians on America's northwestern border.

Matters grew increasingly tense between the two countries. Something had to be done. Washington, in his second term, decided to send John Jay, Chief Justice of the Supreme Court, to negotiate a treaty. The deal Jay got (which had largely been designed by Alexander Hamilton) had very little to recommend it. Basically, it was an insult to the new nation's pride and independence because it went some distance in reestablishing America's colonial dependency. Britain was given favored nation trading status. America acquiesced to British anti-French maritime policies. America's wish to remain neutral in the war and thus choose her trading partners was denied. Nor did Jay succeed in getting Britain to remove her ships from the Great Lakes or to desist in aiding the Indians in times of war. Jay was unsuccessful in negotiating an end to the impressment of American sailors into the Royal Navy. American vessels under seventy tons would be allowed to trade in the West Indies, but they could only carry cargoes allowed by the British. In exchange, America agreed to limit its export of cotton.¶¶

Opposition to the Jay Treaty was intense and widespread. Thomas Jefferson described it as "nothing more than a treaty of alliance with the Anglomen of this country against the legislature and people of the United States."[3] Republicans—men like Jefferson and James Madison***—saw Britain as the center of aristocracy and the main threat to America's civic values. There was considerable support for the French and the French Revolution throughout the country. Jefferson was of the belief that two important treaties between the United States and France were still in effect. Signed in 1778, in the midst of the war with Britain, the Treaty of Amity and Commerce and the Treaty of Alliance combined granted France preferred nation trading status and committed each country to come to the defense of the other. The Jay Treaty, in effect, substituted Britain for France.

Hamilton and Jay (and even Washington) were denounced as monarchists who had betrayed American values. Public protests were organized against Jay and his treaty. One of the rallying cries went, "Damn John Jay! Damn everyone that won't damn John Jay! Damn every one that won't put lights in his window and sit up all night damning John Jay!" His image was burned in effigy throughout the country. There were angry meetings of opposition in New York City, with Hamilton— a passionate proponent of the treaty—in the middle, repeatedly threatening to settle differences with his fists. Hamilton, who had resigned his position as Secretary of the Treasury at the end of January 1795, was the dominant figure in helping secure the treaty's approval by the required two-thirds vote in the Senate.

Why would the new nation, which had just freed itself from British dominance, submit to Britain all over again? Washington argued that another war with Britain had to be avoided at all costs. Madison, on the other hand, believed that Britain was in a weakened state and that America would have the upper hand in a trade war with Britain. Although retaliation by Britain was a threat to be considered, America was likely to prevail. Such a conflict would allow Americans to finally assert their independence fully. With the Jay Treaty, said Madison, Britain "has bound us in commercial manacles, and very nearly defeated the object of our independence."[4] America could make do

---

¶¶   The war with Britain that the Jay Treaty had been designed to avert in fact took place some seventeen years later. This was the War of 1812, and it was fought over some of the same issues that had eluded Jay in his 1794 negotiations: neutral trading rights, Britain's presence on the Great Lakes, seizure of American ships, and impressment of American sailors into the service of British forces.

***   Madison, at the start of his career, was an ardent Federalist and supporter of Hamilton. He then switched sides to join in the opposition against Hamilton, only to change colors again, back to where he started, once he became president.

without British manufactures. But the British West Indies would not long survive without American foodstuffs.[†††]

## Secret Agent Number Seven

In *Inventing a Nation: Washington, Adams, Jefferson* (published in 2003), Gore Vidal refers to Hamilton as "English Secret Agent Number Seven."[‡‡‡] In 1790, according to Vidal, Hamilton met with Major George Beckwith, aide to the governor-general of Canada and also a British agent, warning him of Jefferson's pro-French, anti-British sympathies. By 1791, Jefferson—then Secretary of State—realized that Hamilton was leaking the content of cabinet meetings to the British. According to Vidal, in July of 1794, while Jay was in England negotiating the treaty that bears his name, Hamilton met secretly in Philadelphia with George Hammond, the British Minister to the United States. In a series of private meetings with Hammond, Hamilton revealed much that would work to the advantage of the British and against American interests.[§§§] Under no circumstances, Hamilton assured Hammond, would America establish an alliance with any European power against Britain, thus allowing the British to play their cards without having to worry about the consequences. This certainly seems plausible, given the lopsided treaty arrangements. Jay's bargaining position had been effectively undermined.

If one considers the implications of the Jay Treaty in the light of what had occurred in the prior decade, one is struck by the fact that matters improved dramatically for the British once the Articles of Confederation were out of the way and the Constitution was in place. With the Jay Treaty, the strong relationship with France, codified by treaties signed in 1778 (under the Articles of Confederation), was undermined. Britain had thus succeeded in marginalizing the French and, in many ways, reversing the Treaty of Paris of 1783, which Britain had signed as the defeated enemy. The new Constitution, forged under the leadership of Alexander Hamilton, had established a centralized government with the levers of power in the hands of a small number of men. It was this concentration of power that allowed the British to gain on paper—the Jay Treaty— what they had lost on the ground at the end of the Revolutionary War.

The Bank of the United States, first established by Hamilton in

---

[†††] Madison's objections to the Jay Treaty can be found in a letter among the James Madison Papers, Library of Congress American Memory Collection: http://memory.loc. gov/cgi-bin/query/r?ammem/mjmtext:@field%28DOCID+@lit%28jm060034%29%29.

[‡‡‡] Ron Chernow, Hamilton's biographer, dismisses assertions that Hamilton was a British agent as "preposterous" (*Alexander Hamilton*, p. 294).

[§§§] Eugene Perry Link, in *Democratic-Republican Societies, 1790–1800*, supplies source details for letters from George Hammond, in which "in secret code Hamilton is named as Hammond's informer" (footnote, pp. 48–49). Considering his unrelenting helpfulness to the British cause, some have asserted that, in fact, it was Hamilton, not Hammond, who was Britain's real Minister to the United States.

1791,¶¶¶ was probably of even greater long-term benefit to Britain than the Jay Treaty. To get a clear sense of the degree to which this bank represented a threat not only to national solvency but to national sovereignty, one has but to read President Andrew Jackson's July 10, 1832, veto message delivered to the Senate regarding the renewal of its charter.[6]****

From Jackson's remarks, we learn that of the $28 million of private stock in the bank corporation in 1832, $8.4 million, more than a quarter, was held by foreigners, mostly in Great Britain. Jackson tells the senators that "By this act the American Republic proposes virtually to make them a present of some millions of dollars."[7] Jackson is concerned that the bank "will make the American people debtors to aliens in nearly the whole amount due to this bank, and send across the Atlantic from two to five millions of specie every year to pay the bank dividends."[8] Jackson's further warning of almost two hundred years ago is as relevant today as it was then:

> Should the stock of the bank principally pass into the hands of the subjects of a foreign country, and we should unfortunately become involved in a war with that country, what would be our condition? Of the course which would be pursued by a bank almost wholly owned by the subjects of a foreign power, and managed by those whose interests, if not affections, would run in the same direction there can be no doubt. All its operations within would be in aid of the hostile fleets and armies without. Controlling our currency, receiving our public moneys, and holding thousands of our citizens in dependence, it would be more formidable and dangerous than the naval and military power of the enemy.[9]

Is it possible that, with Hamilton as their agent, the British could orchestrate a conspiracy in which the old American government was replaced with a new one under the Constitution, permitting the British to reestablish their hegemony via the Bank of the United States and the Jay Treaty? Was there a conspiracy? Was Hamilton capable of such conduct? Was the Bank of United States simply a scheme to enrich a handful of American speculators, or were there international implications of consequence, in particular regarding England? Was there a means of executing such a reversal on an international scale?

Recall that Hamilton's brother-in-law, John Barker Church, was a Revolutionary War profiteer who returned to London a very wealthy man. There he became well connected in high society and got him-

---

¶¶¶ As discussed earlier, the twenty-year charter for the first Bank of the United States expired in 1811, under President James Madison. In 1816, however, Madison revived the national bank in the form of the Second Bank of the United States, granting another twenty-year charter. Andrew Jackson dealt that bank its death blow in 1832, when he vetoed the act of Congress that would renew the charter. Over the next four years, the bank was dismantled, and the charter expired in 1836. In 1913, the national bank rose from the ashes yet again, this time with a new name: the Federal Reserve Bank.
**** To get a comprehensive history of money and the various institutions through which its power is consolidated go to http://www.xat.org/moneyhistory.html.

self elected to Parliament in 1790. It was Church who left Hamilton in charge of his finances in New York when Church left for England. With these monies, in part, Hamilton set up his Bank of New York. Here in the person of his brother-in law was Hamilton's direct connection to the inner workings of British finance and government, a connection that could have worked in both directions.[††††]

Is there other evidence of an international conspiracy? Consider the involvement of the Freemasons. The Freemasons are an international secret society whose origins are somewhat hazy. The group's earliest activities can be traced to Scotland and England in the first quarter of the eighteenth century. Freemasonry's critics have described it as a business cult, a satanic religion, and a political conspiracy. It is a pervasive, hidden presence that has insinuated itself into government chambers in both England and the United States. Many people in America have long feared the Freemasons, believing they are a powerful force that is secretly trying to rule the country. The Anti-Masonic Party was founded in 1827, in part, in response to the Morgan Incident, which took place in upstate New York. After stating his intention to write a book exposing Freemasonry's secrets, William Morgan (1774–1826) was arrested, kidnapped, and then apparently killed. The Anti-Masonics were convinced that the Masons were murdering their opponents. But to involve Freemasonry in a conspiracy to overthrow the Articles of Confederation, we must look back several decades before the Morgan Incident.

Twenty-eight of forty signers of the Constitution were Freemasons or possible Freemasons. Most of George Washington's generals were Freemasons. Washington was sworn in as the first President of the United States by Robert Livingston, Grand Master of New York's Masonic Lodge. The Bible on which Washington took his oath was from his own Masonic lodge. The cornerstone of the Capitol building was laid by the Grand Lodge of Maryland. Washington became a Master Mason in 1753 in Fredericksburg, Virginia. The Grand Lodge of Pennsylvania nominated him as "Grand Master General for the Thirteen United American States," which he declined. He did serve as the Charter Master of Alexandria Lodge No. 39, Alexandria, Virginia, in 1788 and was reelected in 1789. Was there an international conspiracy, originating in England, the home of Freemasonry, with the intention of regaining control of the separated colonies via their financial institutions?

Amschel Rothschild (1744–1812), founder of the Rothschild international banking dynasty, is reported to have said, "Give me control of the economics of a country; and I care not who makes her laws." Operating in that tradition, the Bank of England had pressured Parliament to pass the Currency Act of 1764. The act made it illegal for the colonies to print

---

†††† The Treasury records for Hamilton's tenure have disappeared. See Beard, *An Economic Interpretation of the Constitution*, p. 74.

their own money, and it required that they pay future taxes to Britain in silver or gold. Up to this point, the colonies had been issuing their own money (called Colonial Scrip) and living in prosperity. All that changed after the Currency Act of 1764. Benjamin Franklin said, "In one year, the conditions were so reversed that the era of prosperity ended, and a depression set in, to such an extent that the streets of the Colonies were filled with unemployed."[10] There are those who believe the Revolution was ignited as much by the Currency Act as by the tax on tea.

Undoubtedly, there was conspiracy of some kind afoot in the writing and ratification of the Constitution. An oath of secrecy was required of all participants. Concern was so great about revealing what was going on during the Constitutional Convention that Benjamin Franklin, in his declining years, was supplied with a chaperone, lest he babble indiscreetly.[11] The American public did not have access to convention notes until 1840, when Madison's notes were published—*after* his death.[‡‡‡‡] Add to the secrecy the pressure tactics, lying, manipulation, control of the press, destruction of ballots, and mail tampering that went on during the ratification process and one is left with the impression that there was an organized effort to achieve a goal that violated the general will at the time.

Was Hamilton capable of such perfidy? Perhaps. He repeatedly took positions that seemed to place the interests of Great Britain over those of the United States. During the convention in Philadelphia, he delivered a six-hour speech in which he advocated a presidency and a senate for life, that is, essentially, a king and a house of lords. In his private writings, he revealed preference for a *hereditary* president for life. If that isn't a monarch, I don't know what is. A story surfaced that delegates at the Constitutional Convention were colluding to bring the Duke of York, George III's second son, from Britain to head an American monarchy.[12] It is believed that Hamilton was involved in the Newburgh Conspiracy of 1783, in which his friend Robert Morris and others were involved with military officers considering action against the government in pursuit of pensions due them after the war.

New York City was vacated during the Revolution and occupied by the British. There were those who stayed behind, however, loyalists who collaborated with the enemy. At the end of the war, those who had supported the Revolution wanted to return to their homes and businesses, which had been occupied by the loyalists. In a boon to his legal practice, Hamilton defended the interests of the British sympathizers over those of American patriots who had been forced to flee. His commitment to those who were loyal to Britain in a time of war, men who took what wasn't theirs from men who supported the cause of American independence, can be construed as seditious. In Paris at the end of World War II,

‡‡‡‡   A history of Madison's minutes is available at http://oll.libertyfund. org/?option=com_staticxt&staticfile=show.php%3Ftitle=1935&chapter=118618&layout =html&Itemid=27.

collaborators, like those Hamilton was defending, were executed.

In 1792, as Washington's first term was nearing its conclusion, Jefferson expressed concern that Hamilton planned to commandeer the government once Washington was gone, installing his banker friends as an aristocracy and himself as monarch. Preposterous, you say? Consider this. In 1798 (Washington's second term had ended and John Adams was president), Napoleon was on the rise and threatening all of Europe. In response to the Jay Treaty of 1795, the French had commandeered some American ships. Hamilton—out of office but using his considerable influence to direct affairs in the White House under Adams, as well as to get his way with Congress—used these events as a pretext to get Congress to authorize a "provisional army" (the phrase "standing army" was anathema to most Americans at the time). Considerable pressure was applied by Hamilton to get Washington to accept the leadership. The key part of Hamilton's plan was to have himself—America's answer to Napoleon Bonaparte—as second in command, with full knowledge that Washington, at the age of sixty-six and infirm, was in no position to actively participate in military affairs.

Hamilton's dream of becoming a general was realized. As Inspector General of the provisional army, he was second in command and devoted himself to the most minute details of military life: uniforms, equipment, and training. At the command "head right," he ordered, the soldier "turns his head to the right, briskly but without violence, bringing his left eye in a line with the buttons of his waistcoat and with the right eye looking along the breasts of the men upon his right."[13]

And Hamilton had a grand plan for his new army. In secret correspondence with Venezuelan-born Francisco de Miranda, Hamilton—having his six-year-old son write the letter so it could not be traced back to him—laid out a plan in which his army would march through the South, just to let the southern Republicans know who was in charge. Then, in preemptive attacks, he would take Florida from the Spanish and Louisiana from the French, and then continue his march through Mexico and Central America. At that point, joining forces with the British, Hamilton would liberate all of Latin America from Spain. But the French menace diminished and General Hamilton was denied the opportunity to undertake his fantastic adventure at the head of the U.S. Army.§§§§

John Adams referred to Hamilton as "the most restless, impatient, artful, indefatigable and unprincipled intriguer in the United States, if not in the world."[14] He was of the opinion that "Hamilton and party were endeavoring to get an army on foot to give Hamilton the command of it and then to proclaim a regal government, place Hamilton at the head of it, and prepare the way for a province of Great Britain."[15] Adams' wife, Abigail, referred to Hamilton as "a second Bonaparty."[16]

A large, strong standing army was an obsession with "Bonaparty." He

§§§§   See Ron Chernow, *Alexander Hamilton*, pp. 566-568.

wanted to boost taxes, take out a large loan, and establish military and naval academies. But there were few leaders at the time who shared this view. For Adams, a large military establishment was a "many bellied monster."[17] Jefferson had wanted to ban standing armies in the Bill of Rights. Madison believed that "War is the parent of armies; from these proceed debts and taxes; and armies and debts and taxes are the known instruments for bringing the many under the domination of the few."[18] Hamilton would undoubtedly and enthusiastically agree. These were his intentions, to set up a government and an economic system on the British model, in which a financial elite would rule.

Remember that the Bank of England came into being when the government was at war and needed to refill its coffers. From Hamilton's perspective, this was the role of government—to feed the banks. The system works as follows. The government's first task is to charter a central bank and hand it over to private interests. Its next job is to build an army and make war. To raise funds for its war, the government must go to the private central bank and borrow. Next comes the ongoing payment of interest on the money, assuming the principal is never paid back. To pay the interest, the government needs to raise taxes—that is, take money out of the pockets of the citizens and pass it along to the private bankers.

Thus, government (person or persons in power) plays a critical role in the lives of bankers. Governments are their best customers. No other entity is in a position to borrow such enormous sums and then be able to raise the funds to pay the interest on the debt. Said Thomas Jefferson, "I sincerely believe ... that banking establishments are more dangerous than standing armies, and that the principle of spending money to be paid by posterity, under the name of funding, is but swindling futurity on a large scale."¶¶¶¶ A century later, New York City mayor John F. Hylan expressed his concerns more dramatically:

> The real menace of our Republic is the invisible government, which like a giant octopus sprawls its slimy legs over our cities, states and nation. ... At the head of this octopus are [business] interests and a small group of powerful banking houses.... The little coterie ... virtually run our government for their own selfish purposes.... It operates under cover of a self-created screen [and] seizes our executive officers, legislative bodies, schools, courts, newspapers and every agency created for the public protection.*****

War is a key ingredient in the political economy established by Alexander Hamilton. War consumes enormous resources. As of late 2011, estimates of the direct and indirect costs of the current wars in Afghan-

---

¶¶¶¶   Jefferson expressed this sentiment in an 1816 letter to his long-time ally John Taylor of Caroline, who had served in the Virginia state legislature and the U.S. Senate. Thomas Jefferson Papers, Library of Congress American Memory Collection: http://memory.loc.gov/cgi-bin/query/r?ammem/mtj:@field(DOCID+@lit(tj110172)).

*****   These comments come from a 1922 speech by Hylan, who served as New York City's mayor from 1918 to 1925. He was speaking out against Rockefeller–Standard Oil and international bankers. http://en.wikipedia.org/wiki/John_Francis_Hylan.

istan, Iraq, and Pakistan are in the range of $3.2–4 trillion dollars.††††† That's good business for bankers. They thrive on war and will gladly finance any warrior nation that seeks funding. They funded both sides in World War II. They funded both sides in the Cold War (i.e., they financed the purchase of armaments for both the United States and the Soviet Union). And they must be quite happy with the current War on Terrorism being waged by the United States. "Perpetual War for Perpetual Peace" is their slogan.

All of this war-making and maneuvering by the banks comes at the expense of democracy. For the most part, true democracy as a form of government has little interest in war. It is a peaceful mode of existence. Its power is decentralized and widely dispersed, making it difficult to create the powerful central government essential to a warrior nation intent on waging war and then raising taxes to pay off the banks. To see how the government of the United States could have evolved otherwise, we need only study what early democrats came up with in the state of Pennsylvania.

---

††††† These estimates come from the Watson Institute for International Studies of Brown University. Their "Costs of War" website offers a good overview of the economic, human, and social costs of the wars. http://costsofwar.org/.

# Democracy Affirmed

## The People of Pennsylvania Write a Constitution

*And with preamble sweet*
*Of charming symphony they introduce*
*Their sacred song.*

I
N 1680, THE king of England granted to William Penn (1644–1718) forty-five thousand square miles of land west of the Delaware River. This colony became known as Penn's Woods, or Pennsylvania. The land was granted to William Penn as a means of canceling a debt of £16,000 owed to Penn's late father, Admiral William Penn.[1] Penn the younger was also heir to large landed estates in Ireland and England. He enjoyed a university education and ate, drank, and dressed in a manner consistent with his status as a member of the gentry. As a young man and against his father's wishes, he had converted to Quakerism.

Quakers believed that everyone was equal before God and that all manner of social distinction and hierarchy should be dispensed with. They refused the conventional gestures of deference toward royalty and aristocracy. They refused to bear arms. They dressed plainly and spoke plainly. Women were considered the equals of men.

The young Penn was outspoken in his Quaker views and was repeatedly sent to jail during the years 1667–1671. He crusaded for religious tolerance, defended Quakers in court, and traveled widely as a preacher in Germany, Holland, and Great Britain. He held devotional meetings on his estate and published more than fifty polemical and devotional tracts. It was Penn's intention to bring to his colony in the new world the Quaker values he had defended in Europe. However, unlike the Puritans, he would establish no church. He would encourage immigrants of all stripes. He spoke of "a Free Colony for all Mankind."[2]

Penn needed money to embark on his new enterprise, and he was able to raise £9,000 from six hundred subscribers, half of whom actually migrated to the new colony. Penn systematically arranged for the transfer of thousands of individuals to his colony. He established his capital city of Philadelphia (the City of Brotherly Love) with a grid of broad streets and spacious parks.

Like the majority of those who went to New England, most of the immigrants to Penn's colony were families of middling means. Only one-third were indentured. Most settled as farmers in rural townships. Some craftsmen and merchants stayed in Philadelphia, which became the wealthiest merchant community in the thirteen colonies.

Penn's policy of tolerance extended even to the Indians. He showed respect for their culture and assumed ownership of Indian land only after paying for it at fairer and higher prices than most other colonists. As a consequence, Penn's colony prospered in peace. Overall, the colony was egalitarian. Few were landless. Few were rich.[*]

What characterized Pennsylvania more than anything was its religious and ethnic diversity, its egalitarianism, and its fractiousness. Pennsylvanians were opinionated and outspoken. Politics were contentious and at times raucous. Penn bemoaned the fact that his colonists needed "to be humbled and made more pliable; for what with the distance and the scarcity of mankind there, they opine too much."[3] What he was in the middle of, without fully realizing it, was the beginning of a democratic society. There was little in the way of class difference. There was no dominant political force. There were conflicting opinions, forcefully— but for the most part, peacefully—expressed. This is some of what democracy is about, equality of condition, noisy disagreement.

Although diverse in their views on local issues, Pennsylvanians, broadly speaking, were united under the banner of Jeffersonianism and opposed what they saw as the power politics and elitist views of the Federalists under the leadership of Alexander Hamilton.[†] These views are illustrated in Pennsylvania's resistance to the idea of a national bank. When the Bank of North America was chartered in 1781 by the Continental Congress, it became the first national bank in America. In 1786, there was a debate between William Findlay (1768–1846)[‡] and Robert Morris,[§] Superintendent of Finance, as to whether or not the state of Pennsylvania should vote to recharter the bank.

---

[*] Despite his generally progressive policies, William Penn was resented for his patronizing authority. He was charged with speculating in land and holding aside large tracts for his favorites. He was inattentive in business matters and lost large sums through embezzlement by his business manager, leaving his finances in disarray and the ownership of his colony in question. Yet he donated generously to the Quaker cause. In 1707, he landed briefly in debtors' prison in England.

[†] Andrew Shankman's *Crucible of American Democracy: The Struggle to Fuse Egalitarianism and Capitalism in Jeffersonian Pennsylvania* is an invaluable guide to Pennsylvania's political history toward the end of the eighteenth and beginning of the nineteenth centuries.

[‡] Member, Pennsylvania state House of Representatives, 1797, 1804–1807; state treasurer, 1807–1817; governor of Pennsylvania, 1817–1820; member, U.S. Senate, 1821–1827.

[§] The background of Robert Morris is discussed in Chapter 9.

Findlay believed that permitting the Bank of North America—an immense concentration of wealth—to stay in business would undermine democracy in Pennsylvania and violate the state's Declaration of Rights, which explicitly prohibited the government from being used for "the emolument of any man, family, or set of men."[4] It was Findlay's position that though there was not perfect equality in Pennsylvania, conditions were favorable for democracy so long as nothing further was done to upset the happy balance, such as permitting great wealth to gather in the hands of a few powerful men via institutions like the Bank of North America. He was concerned with the anti-democratic use of political power that would ensue from this concentration of wealth. Citizens of modest wealth were most likely to actively promote the common good.

When elitist revolutionary leaders had spurred on those of lesser means to resist British tyranny, they had made the mistake of using such words as "liberty" and "equality," words that had special meaning for the Pennsylvania artisans, mechanics, dockworkers, and small farmers had who actively participated in overthrowing the crown. Couldn't these humbler citizens honestly lay claim to active participation in governmental affairs? The spirit that had animated the popular committees that oversaw much of the day-to-day revolutionary activity still informed the thoughts of many ordinary citizens as they sought a role for themselves in the new country.

These sentiments of independence and political entitlement seemed to have been endemic to Pennsylvania even before the Revolution. In 1765, England passed the Stamp Act, which required that a tax stamp be affixed to all newspapers and legal documents. On October 5, when the citizens of Philadelphia saw the *Royal Charlotte* sail into port bearing the stamps, an assembly was called. Thousands gathered at the state-house to discuss the means for preventing distribution of the stamps. Their first step was to ensure that the agent responsible for distributing the stamps would either resign his position or refuse to fulfill his function. He chose the latter course. Newspapers ceased publication rather than purchase the required stamps. As a further protest, more than four hundred merchants agreed to suspend British imports. Public offices were closed from the first of November 1765 until May 1766, when the Stamp Act was repealed, providing an excellent example of democracy at work. There was no secrecy. There was no cabal. There were no top-down orders to be followed. Large numbers of people organized themselves for purposes of eliminating an injustice. And they succeeded.¶

The Stamp Act was replaced with the Townshend Revenue Act of 1767. Parliament believed that the colonists, while in opposition to a domestic tax, would accept a tax on products such as paper, paint,

---

¶ See J. Paul Selsam, *The Pennsylvania Constitution of 1776*, for a close look at events in Pennsylvania prior to the adoption of the state constitution.

glass, and tea that were imported into the colonies. In Pennsylvania, there was organized opposition to these taxes as well. Committees were set up throughout the colony and maintained regular communication. As the crisis mounted, resulting ultimately in the conflict with Britain, the necessary structures for organization and communication were already in place. These committees, all the way down to the local township level, were instrumental in mounting the revolutionary response.

This organized opposition to British taxation and the political infrastructure that accompanied it had another function as well. The energy and idealism stimulated by Britain's actions against the colonies were, in Pennsylvania, simultaneously directed against the government of the state itself. The charter William Penn had set up had outlived its usefulness, largely because the state's government was under the control of an elite corps of Philadelphia Quakers** who persisted in ignoring the petitions of the many farmers in the west and the large numbers of disenfranchised mechanics and artisans living and working in Philadelphia.

The British Parliament finally responded to the protests in the colonies by repealing the Townshend taxes in 1770, except for the duty on tea. After the Boston Tea Party of 1773, the British government in 1774 offered its response:

1. The Boston Port Act ordered that the port of Boston remain closed until the East India Company was reimbursed for its loss.
2. The Massachusetts Government Act virtually ended self-government in the state of Massachusetts and returned control to the crown.
3. The Administration of Justice Act decreed that accused British officials were no longer to be tried in Massachusetts.
4. The Quartering Act required all colonies to properly house British troops.

The people of Boston sent out a letter describing their plight and seeking the support of the other colonies. On May 19, 1774, Paul Revere arrived in Philadelphia with the letter from Boston.

The wealthy Quaker elite who controlled the Pennsylvania Assembly had no interest in taking on the crown. They were content to do little or nothing in response to the Boston appeal. But there were large numbers of people in Pennsylvania who felt otherwise. A group of concerned citizens organized a reading of the letter from Boston at a gathering at the City Tavern in Philadelphia. About three hundred people were present. The outcome was a letter to the people of Boston expressing support for their cause and promising to forward the Boston letter to the southern colonies, as requested. On May 30, the day the Boston Port Act was to go into effect, Philadelphia suspended all business activity. The bells of Christ Church "were muffled and rung a solemn peal at intervals, from morning till night."[5]

---

** To qualify to vote in elections under Penn's charter, a citizen needed either to be in possession of fifty acres of land or to be worth £50. The humble citizens of Philadelphia met neither qualification. Western farmers could vote but were denied representation in the Assembly.

## Taking Matters into Their Own Hands

On June 8, 1774, a petition was presented to Governor John Penn asking that he convene the Assembly to consider the actions that England had taken toward the colonies. The Governor declined. On June 18, some eight thousand people gathered in the State House Yard. It was agreed that the British act was unconstitutional and that the colonies should call a Continental Congress to decide on a response. A committee of forty-three was selected to conduct further business. Committees were established in every county. All of this was orderly, extralegal activity, with large numbers of people taking matters into their own hands when government (person or persons in power), in this case the governor, was unresponsive.[††]

On July 15, another meeting took place, with representatives from Philadelphia and all the counties present. This meeting, which had no authority other than its numbers and the power of its convictions, passed sixteen resolutions and instructed the Pennsylvania Assembly to summon its members and choose delegates for the Continental Congress. Bear in mind that it was the Assembly, the constituted legal body, being given orders from the extralegal gathering. Reluctantly, the Assembly met and chose delegates for the First Continental Congress.

The local militia themselves—known as "Associations," their members as "Associators"—were units of political organization drawn from the humbler elements in society. They demanded a voice in their own affairs.[‡‡] The Assembly had appointed two brigadier generals to command the Associators. The foot soldiers, who lacked a voice in the Assembly, would not abide by a choice in which they were denied a vote. Thus, they ignored the Assembly's selections and chose their own generals. As J. Paul Selsam observes,

---

[††]   Sometimes, the quiet stubbornness of a large number of ordinary folk can have a significant political effect. The early phase of the French Revolution offers a similar example. On May 5, 1789, king Louis XVI opened the first Estates-General—General Assembly— that had been held since 1614. The Estates-General was made up of three separate bodies: the clergy, the nobility, and the commons. Traditionally, the three estates had met separately. The commons, however, insisted that all three meet together and invited the clergy and the nobility to join them. The nobility and the clergy declined, and so the commons met on their own and debated. They continued to meet on their own and by June 17 had given themselves the title "National Assembly" and had begun to draft a constitution. Shut out of their regular meeting place by the king, they met at a new location and took an oath not to adjourn until they had completed their constitution. The king ordered them to abandon the project. "With relatively few histrionics, they refused. On the next day, they met again, and were joined by a majority of the clergy. On the day after, forty-seven nobles and some more of the clergy came over. On June 27, Louis himself wrote formally requesting the two upper houses to merge with the lower to form a National Assembly." Crane Brinton, *A Decade of Revolution, 1789–1799*, p. 5.

[‡‡]   The important role of small farmer foot soldiers in establishing democracy in Pennsylvania in the eighteenth century echoes the role played by the same set of people in the formation of a democratic society in fifth-century B.C. Athens.

It is now evident that the war with England was affording the elements long disfranchised by the old regime an opportunity to assert their claims to a participation in the government. Through their various committees and military associations they were gradually usurping power which legitimately belonged to the constituted authorities.... Separation would undoubtedly mean the end of the Charter and the end of the rule of that class which had held sway from the very beginning of the colony.[6]

Under pressure from the growing movement to displace the Assembly and install a different form of government, the Assembly acquiesced to hold an election in which representation would be expanded and more fairly distributed. The election was held on May 1, 1776. The Declaration of Independence had not yet been issued. Though the colonies were at war with England, the ultimate meaning of the war had not yet become apparent to the colonists. There were many who wanted to retain their attachment to the mother country. Thus, the days leading up to the election in Pennsylvania were heated.

Nor did things cool down after the representatives were chosen. Two key issues were still being debated at once: separation from England and formation of a new government for Pennsylvania. There was a flurry of newspaper articles, pamphlets, and handbills. Meetings were held, and animated conversations buzzed in taverns and coffeehouses. The war of words continued. On June 4, 1776, the *Pennsylvania Evening Post* was so filled with news, letters, and articles pro and con that, with apologies, the editor declared that there was no room for advertisements. What is noteworthy about these events is the active involvement of large numbers of impassioned, informed citizens and the degree to which opposing views were able to find a home in the local newspapers.[§§] This openness and freedom disappeared a decade later when similar debates were going on concerning ratification of the U.S. Constitution.

As the fighting continued, as the casualties mounted, as word spread of the suffering at the hands of the Hessian mercenaries hired by the British to fight their war, it became more and more apparent that all of the thirteen colonies would have to establish new and independent governments. Thus, even before the Declaration of Independence was signed, governments were being organized. In its recommendation "to the respective Assemblies and Conventions of the United Colonies," the Continental Congress urged that

where no government sufficient to the exigencies of their affairs hath been hitherto established, to adopt such government as shall, in the opinion of the representatives of the people, best conduct to the happiness and safety of their constituents in particular, and America in general.[7]

---

§§ Can one imagine, in the year 2012, the *New York Times* suspending its editorial control and its advertisements so as to make space for an assortment of conflicting political ideas, many of which it does not support?

Members of the Continental Congress recognized that much of the resistance to fighting for independence from Britain came from the old, entrenched elite. They understood that this was especially true in Pennsylvania, one of the last holdouts against separation from England. New governments would bring fresh blood and a new spirit. Thus, pressure was being applied from without, especially from New England, as well as from within, to form a new government in Pennsylvania.¶¶ In response, James Wilson, speaking for the entrenched Pennsylvania oligarchy, warned that if the old government were to be dissolved, "there will be an immediate dissolution of every kind of authority: the people will be instantly in a state of nature."[8]

On May 20, 1776,*** a meeting was held in the State House Yard in Philadelphia. Despite the rain that was falling, between four and five thousand attended. Rather than the "state of nature" predicted by Wilson, this was was an orderly meeting in which various resolutions were enthusiastically endorsed. It was proclaimed that the current Pennsylvania Assembly was unfit to follow the instructions of the Continental Congress to create a new government. It was resolved that the people ought to bypass the Pennsylvania Assembly, call a state convention, and construct their own government.

There was a strong reaction against the May 20 meeting from various elements in the establishment. One of the most obvious objections was that the sitting Assembly could undertake to comply with the recommendations of Congress and draft a new constitution within several weeks. It was estimated that it would take the popular, extralegal convention perhaps three months to achieve the same goal. During that period, there would be no government whatsoever. Concern was also expressed that a new government was to be formed in the midst of war, leading to further instability and unpredictability.

There was confusion on all sides. James Wilson lamented that affairs in Pennsylvania "have been in such a fluctuating and disordered Situation that it has been almost impossible to form any Accurate Judgment concerning the Transactions as they were passing, and still more nearly impossible to make any probable Conjectures concerning the Turn that Things would take."[9] As another observer commented, "the Convention Scheme has turned Everything up side down."[10] This unsettled state is characteristic of democracy as it takes shape and goes through various transformations. Stasis and immobility are characteristics of monarchy and oligarchy.

On June 18, 1776, there was an ad hoc meeting of the Pennsylvania

---

¶¶   At this critical point in Pennsylvania history, there were three political forces at work. There was the entrenched Quaker oligarchy that wished to continue with Pennsylvania's existing form of government. There was the opposition from within the state that was moving ahead with setting up a new government. There was the opposition from without, the Continental Congress, that also wanted to see a new government in Pennsylvania, but for its own reasons. It needed support in breaking away from Britain. Pennsylvania's old government was resisting.
***   On this same day, as thousands met outside, the Assembly held a meeting but lacked a quorum. Thus did this legally constituted body pass steadily into the shadows of irrelevancy as it ignored the demands of its constituents.

citizen body with representation from all the counties and Philadelphia in attendance. Officers were elected and committees were set up. This body (the "Conference"), completely ignoring the existence of the legally constituted Assembly, now assumed complete responsibility for drafting a new constitution for Pennsylvania. One of the first acts of the Conference was to abolish property qualifications in setting up the election of delegates to the convention. Delegates were to take an oath to "establish and support a government in this province on the authority of the people only."[11]

The Continental Congress had requested that Pennsylvania provide a contingent of six thousand troops. The Assembly took no action. The Conference itself, with no official legal authority, responded instead and became actively involved in mustering and organizing the militia. The Conference established a *"Council of Safety*, to exercise the whole of the executive powers of government, so far as relates to the military defence and safety of the province."[12] In an address to the people, the members of the Conference stated that not only were they fighting for "permanent freedom, to be supported by a government which will be derived from yourselves, and which will have for its object not the enrollment of one man, or class of men only, but the safety, liberty and happiness of every individual in the community."[13]

## Democracy at Work[†††]

The extralegal Pennsylvania Constitutional Convention held its first meeting on July 15, 1776. Benjamin Franklin was unanimously elected

---

††† Early U.S. history offers another example of democracy, one that predates Pennsylvania by more than a hundred years. Roger Williams (1603–1684) was a man of the cloth who was a free thinker, a humanist, and one of the few early democrats. He was primarily a political philosopher rather than a theologian. He was banished from the Massachusetts Bay Colony for his tolerant and forward-looking ideas. He migrated to what is now Rhode Island and set up a working democracy, something likes Pennsylvania's.

Williams understood the political state "as the sovereign repository of the social will, and the government ... as the practical instrument of society to effect its desired end" (Parrington, *The Colonial Mind, 1620–1800*, p. 67). For Williams, government has its basis in political equality and the consent of the governed. Government in his eyes is flexible, responsive, and continually changing. Said Williams, "a People may erect and establish what *forme* of *Government* seems to them most meete for their *civill condition*. It is evident that such *Governments* as are by them erected and established, have no more *power*, nor for no longer time, then the *civill power* or people consenting and agreeing shall betrust them with" (quoted in Parrington, p.70; italics in the original).

Citizens express their will and government is held accountable by means of initiative, referendum, recall, and appeal to arbitration. In the government set up by Williams in Providence, Rhode Island—conceived as "nothing so much as a great public-service corporation" (Parrington, p. 73)—there were frequent elections, a single-chambered legislature, and the right of recall of all laws, including the constitution. Williams was governor from 1654 to 1658.

In words that recall ancient Athens, Parrington describes the political experience in Rhode Island as follows: "In spite of many difficulties that grew out of the sharp individualism of vigorous characters, the colony proved to be a good place to dwell for those who were content to share the common rights and privileges" (p. 74). Parrington remembers Williams as "the most generous, the most open-minded, most lovable of the Puritan emigrants" (p. 74). His religious tolerance and his democratic ideas made him an enemy of his peers. As of 1927, the commonwealth of Massachusetts had yet to rescind the decree banishment issued against him.

convention president. Simple rules of procedure were written. When the debate got tedious, any four members could call the question, and the president would so abide. No member could interrupt another when speaking. No member was to willfully pervert the meaning of what another had said. There was to be no indecent language. It was requested that motions be printed rather than written in longhand because "several [members] could read *print* better than writing"[14] (italics in the original).

The members of the Pennsylvania Constitutional Convention were obviously men of humble origins. These were not "great" men. With few exceptions, none had read widely on government. Most were farmers and merchants; the majority were militiamen (Associators). Detractors referred to the members as "numsculs." Franklin was erratic in his attendance due to his responsibilities to the Continental Congress, and he seems not to have been a principal contributor. However, there were important contributions from two nonmembers of the Convention: George Bryan, a jurist from Philadelphia, and a schoolmaster known as Mr. Cannon.

During the course of its deliberations, the ad hoc Pennsylvania Convention assumed the legislative and executive responsibilities of government, thus superseding the Assembly in its functions. One of the first acts had been to vest the executive authority of the province (i.e., the Pennsylvania colony) in a Council of Safety, with Thomas Warton Jr. its president. This executive role was to continue until March 4, 1777, when the new government, under a new constitution, would be installed. Debtors and imprisoned criminals were to be released from prison. Continental bills were made legal tender in the state. The Convention undertook to revise the judiciary as well. On September 3, it inducted justices of the peace throughout the counties, "under the authority of the people only, deriving no power whatever from their late constitution."[15]

By September 5, 1776, the new Pennsylvania state constitution was nearing its final draft. The Convention ordered four hundred copies be printed for public review. Copies of the constitution appeared in the local papers on September 10 and then again on September 18. On September 28, the constitution was adopted by the Convention. Of the ninety-six members, twenty-three did not sign. The constitution was never submitted to a popular referendum. This was also the practice with other state constitutions being written at the time.

Overall, the original constitution of the colony of Pennsylvania, under Penn's leadership, had been as democratic as any of the thirteen. But the revised version was in a class by itself, making it probably the most democratic form of government ever experienced in North America, if not beyond.‡‡‡ Not to be ignored is the influence of Thomas Paine's pamphlet *Common Sense*, which was a rich source of democratic ideas

---

‡‡‡ In 1790, the state constitution of Pennsylvania was modified to conform to the less democratic and more conservative tastes that informed the federal constitution of 1787, which had been framed by the ruling elite.

men like John Adams (of Massachusetts) did their best to combat.

The Pennsylvania Constitution of 1776 provided for near-universal manhood suffrage; a weak, plural executive; and a unicameral, annually elected legislature. Unlike the U.S. Constitution, which would be drafted little more than a decade later, the Pennsylvania state constitution had a Declaration of Rights, modeled on that of Virginia, which had been published the preceding May.

The Declaration guaranteed the rights of free assembly, free press, free speech, and redress of grievances, as well as the right of emigration and the right to refuse to bear arms, based in conscientious objection. Religious freedom was guaranteed to all—save the members of the Assembly, who were required to take an oath professing faith in God—thus lifting the ban on Catholic officeholders that had previously existed in Pennsylvania.

All proceedings were to be published and open to public inspection. The chambers, when the legislature was in session, were to remain open to all persons who chose to pay a visit. In further homage to the constituency, all bills of a public nature were to be printed for public review before final debate, amendment, and passage. Except in cases of emergency, these bills had to await the following session of the Assembly to actually become law.§§§

Representation was to be proportional to the number of taxable citizens in each county, thus eliminating the gross inequalities that characterized representation under the old charter, in which the Quaker elite had dominated. There were no property qualifications for holding office.¶¶¶ Elections were to occur annually. A representative could serve no more than four years out of any seven.

Rotation in office and annual elections are key elements of government if one is to prevent the monopoly of power that usually occurs when there are no such provisions. Such rotation is consistent with the notion that any inhabitant is worthy and capable of serving in government. Said one convention member in a letter to a friend, "Our principle seems to be this: that any man, even the most illiterate, is as capable of any office as a person who has had the benefit of education."[16]

As a safeguard against corruption in office, the constitution provided that "any elector, who shall receive any gift or reward for his vote, in meat, drink, monies, or otherwise, shall forfeit his right to elect [i.e., vote] for that time, and suffer such other penalties as future laws shall direct." So much for selling one's vote. "Any person who shall directly

---

§§§ This provision was an important start but only a half measure, because there was no means for registering and including in the final law an actual response from the public. A truly democratic procedure would have had the citizens themselves legislating for themselves by voting for or against the laws. This is what happened during the Roman Republic.
¶¶¶ Only one other state, Delaware, had eliminated property qualifications for holding office at this time.

or indirectly give, promise, or bestow any such rewards to be elected, shall be thereby rendered incapable to serve for the ensuing year."[17] So much for buying one's vote. Representatives were to serve without pay, except in those instances where a man was called into service "to the prejudice of his private affairs." However, should an office become so profitable as to "occasion many to apply for it, the profits ought to be lessened by the legislature."[18]

The democratically minded Pennsylvanians had no room for a single, powerful executive with veto power over Assembly legislation. Instead, the new constitution established a plural executive with powers limited to executing the law. Representatives chose one member from Philadelphia and one from each of the counties to serve on the Executive Council for three years. Any councilor who served for three consecutive years was required to wait four years before he could serve again. The president and vice-president were chosen annually through election by the Executive Council and the Assembly. The president was commander-in-chief of the state forces but could do nothing without prior approval of the Council. The Council was to conduct routine state business, communicate with other states on matters of mutual concern, and outline issues to be debated by the Assembly. The president and the Council together had the power to appoint and commission judges for a term of seven years, with the possibility of reappointment. The power of impeachment was vested in the Assembly. All state officers were impeachable.

As a further safeguard against corruption and abuses of power, the Pennsylvania Constitution instituted a Council of Censors consisting of two representatives from each city and county, to be elected once every seven years. Its responsibility was to preserve the integrity of the constitution and the rights of the citizens. In essence, the Council of Censors was to serve as an ombudsman to ensure that the constitution was honored in letter and in spirit and that the citizenry was not suffering due to arbitrary governance. The Council had the power to subpoena people, papers, and records; to publicly censure state officers; to order impeachments; and to recommend the repeal of laws in violation of the constitution. The power of amending resided in the Council of Censors, which could call a convention to meet to revise the constitution based on the Council's recommendations. Any proposed amendments were to be published six months prior to being voted upon, thereby allowing constituents to instruct their delegates as to their wishes.

The publication of the new Pennsylvania Constitution produced a strong, angry, derisive responsive from the Quaker oligarchy, whose power had been undermined. The very element in society whom they had deliberately excluded from government was now in charge. At a time when British troops were on the march and headed toward Pennsylvania, the internal divisions engendered by the conflict over the new constitution rendered the state almost defenseless, as the conflicting parties could not unite themselves against the common enemy. Many who had fought hard for the new constitution were savoring their victory. Many were indifferent to the war with England. Could these common soldiers march off to war confident that their hard-won victory wouldn't be undermined by their adversaries in their absence?

Indeed every effort was made by the conservative forces to undermine the new constitution and prevent installation of the new government. To a degree they succeeded, and thus participated in creating the very anarchy they had warned against. However, gradually the adherents of the new constitution were able to win over important elements to their side, and the new government took its seat. Noteworthy is the fact that despite these chaotic conditions, there was no random violence or bloodshed.

# The Struggle Continues

## *Democracy vs. Republicanism*

*So spake the false dissembler unperceived;*
*For neither man nor angel can discern*
*Hypocrisy, the only evil that walks*
*Invisible.*

PENNSYLVANIA'S CONSTITUTION OF 1776 had become a reality. In a most remarkable accomplishment, ordinary folk in the state of Pennsylvania—without recourse to secrecy, conspiracy, or violence—had been able to supersede an existing government, write a constitution that was consistent with their fundamental needs, and establish a new government in the midst of war. Their achievement should be an inspiration to anyone who believes that change is impossible.

Unfortunately, it could not last. A powerful oligarchy had taken charge of the American government with the express purpose of undermining the very democracy that the Pennsylvanians had struggled to realize. In 1790, under pressure from the U.S. Congress, organized under the new national oligarchy, Pennsylvania produced yet another constitution—one that mimicked in many ways the federal example and undid just about everything that had been democratic about the state's government. There was to be a Senate, an Assembly, a governor, and a judiciary serving for life. The oligarchs had won. But the democratic spirit lived on for about another decade in Pennsylvania.

By 1790, the people of the young nation had already begun to realize that they had been hoodwinked by the Federalists into ratifying a constitution they never should have accepted. Discussion groups were cropping up, organized by commoners who wanted to give voice to their democratic yearnings. By 1800, forty-two democratic societies had been established across America. The first society was organized by citizens of German origin living in Philadelphia. It was called the German Republican Society. The goals of society members were to oversee the conduct of government officers, educate themselves politically through group discussion, and enter into correspondence with other similar societies from around the country.*

## Philadelphia Democrats Speak Out

The democratic cause was taken up in Philadelphia by a newspaper known as the *Aurora*. The paper was edited by a grandson of Benjamin Franklin, Benjamin Franklin Bache, who became more and more outspoken as the U.S. government abandoned its alliance with France in favor of the Jay Treaty with Britain. War with France seemed imminent, and President John Adams set about imposing taxes and building a U.S. Army, Navy, and Marine Corps.

The exchange of rhetoric between those who favored and those who opposed such policies was heightened by the arrival in Philadelphia of the many Irish and English immigrants who were fleeing oppression in Britain, especially radical Irishmen like William Duane (1760–1835),† who became assistant editor at Bache's *Aurora*. The Federalist response, in 1798, under the leadership of President Adams, was passage of the Alien and Sedition Acts, whose primary purpose was to silence the *Aurora*. The president was given the power to punish or deport disorderly aliens and to incarcerate all subjects of nations at war with the United States.

German petitioners from York County, Pennsylvania, expressed their opposition to these policies as follows:

> while we are warmly attached to the union, we cannot but express our concern at several acts passed in the two last sessions of congress: the law for erecting a standing army, the Sedition and Alien laws, the stamp act, the direct tax on land, and the great increase in revenue officers.[1]

In January and February of 1799, armed German militia from western Pennsylvania prevented tax collectors from doing their job. The militiamen were arrested and held in a tavern in Bethlehem, Pennsylvania. In March, John Fries and one hundred forty armed men surrounded the tavern and freed the prisoners. Fries and his men believed they had behaved lawfully. Nonetheless, they were found guilty of an assortment of crimes, including treason for some, and Fries and others

---

* Remember that the word "republican" at this period in history refers to an agrarian party under the leadership of Thomas Jefferson. During the same period, there were *sociétiés de pensée* serving the same function in France. See Eugene Perry Link, *Democratic-Republican Societies, 1790–1800*; and Crane Brinton, *A Decade of Revolution, 1789–1799*, pp. 18–19.
† Duane was born in the colonies. Before the Revolution, and while he was still in infancy, his family moved back to Ireland, where Duane grew up.

were sentenced to death. A mistrial was declared. Ultimately Fries was pardoned by Adams, who referred to the state of Pennsylvania as "the most villainous compound of heterogeneous matter conceivable."[2]

In 1798, *Aurora* editor Benjamin Franklin Bache died of yellow fever. William Duane, his assistant editor, married Bache's widow and assumed full responsibility for the *Aurora*. He was even more outspoken than Bache had been. It became the goal of the Federalists to silence him. Several times between 1798 and 1800 he was arrested for sedition and successfully defended by Alexander J. Dallas, an outspoken anti-Federalist. Eventually, Duane was convicted and had to go into hiding. President Thomas Jefferson allowed the Alien and Sedition Acts to expire and cleared Duane of all charges. Duane and those around him became ardent in their promotion of democracy. For the first time, this important word was introduced into the American political dialogue.

Duane, as editor of the *Aurora*, spoke for those who opposed the European condition wherein the masses labored to supply the needs of a small, empowered elite. He spoke for those who wanted a different kind of society—one in which social, economic, and political equality were the determining values, a society in which the many governed, not the aristocratic few. The people whose combined efforts had made the Revolution should be the ones who controlled the destiny of the new nation. In essence, Duane was campaigning to institute on the national level the kind of government that had prevailed under Pennsylvania's state constitution of 1776.

In its editorials, the *Aurora* encouraged sustained involvement in public affairs by the citizenry, leading to "a new science [that] would occasion so much communication of sentiment through the neighborhood, that in another generation it would change the condition of society [and] bring men nearer on a level." Constant engagement in public debate and democratic decision making in which the majority ruled would "preserve and promote [a] happy mediocrity of condition,"[3] thus preventing the concentration of property and political power in the hands of a select few. One need not fear such majority rule. America was starting from a position of near equality of condition. There would be no politics of vengeance. There was land and wealth enough for all, so long as the near equality of condition was preserved by means of democratic politics. Such a society was a just society and inherently would safeguard the rights of the many, because the many were governing themselves.

Philadelphia democrats like Bache and Duane were especially opposed to certain elements in the federal constitution. They believed in change, innovation, experimentation. They thought that separation of powers was a bad idea. Separation of powers would allow a judiciary, unaccountable to the people, or a single individual, the executive, with veto power, to defeat the will of the people. For a similar reason, bicameral legislatures—in which one house, the "upper" house, composed of a more select and smaller number of representatives, could obstruct the wishes of the "lower" or more popularly elected body—were anti-democratic. They believed a judge should be impeached not solely for violating rules of good conduct (i.e., actually committing crimes) but also, and more importantly, for rendering decisions or behaving from the bench in such a way as to render himself an enemy of democratic government.

Judge Samuel Chase heard the case against John Fries, who had helped free the militiamen who had interfered with collection of taxes. "True liberty," Chase argued, "did not ... consist in the possession of equal rights, but in the protection by the law of the person and property of every member of society." One could therefore argue that a monarchy could preserve property as well as a democracy, observed his democratic opponents. With universal suffrage, Chase proclaimed, "instead of being ruled by a respectable government, we shall be governed by an ignorant mobocracy."[4] Such words, in the view of Philadelphia democrats, constituted an impeachable offense. When judges exhibited such dangerous tendencies, they should be removed from the bench.

According to the Philadelphia democrats, laws should be simply written, comprehensible to the ordinary man, and frequently repealed if contrary to the popular voice. Laws should be written and interpreted to protect the common good, not to advance the commercial interests of the powerful and ambitious. The role of judges and lawyers in legal disputes should be minimized. Judges should not be in a position to interpret law and therefore, potentially, contradict and override the intentions of the legislature, in essence becoming lawmakers.

The Pennsylvania Constitution of 1790 had enabled the higher courts to use their interpretation of the law as a means to further economic development, leading to the greater concentration of land holdings in the hands of fewer and fewer owners. By 1800, in Chester County, Pennsylvania, the top ten percent of the population controlled thirty-eight percent of the wealth, while the bottom sixty percent controlled only seventeen percent. This is exactly what the democrats had feared. Why not settle property disputes in another manner? Instead of a judge, why not rely on the office of arbitrator? An arbitrator is less concerned with law and more concerned with an equitable adjustment. The law can be a means of ensnarement for the ordinary citizen, leading to time-consuming and costly lawsuits beyond the means of most of those who most require the protection of law. Arbitrators, on the other hand, would be chosen from within the community and hence would be sensitive to community values and the sense of fair play that prevailed. Their tenure in office would be contingent upon the community's goodwill.

The Philadelphia democrats—speaking for Philadelphia workers, small merchants, and small farmers—were a powerful voice at the turn of the nineteenth century. They were strident, outspoken, impassioned. They had introduced the word "democracy" into the political dialogue. And they had made it stick. They believed that government should be directly accountable to the people, meaning everyone. In response, another political voice emerged in Pennsylvania, a voice more moderate, less aroused, and less impassioned but no less determined. This voice spoke for a different set of interests and had its own journal— *The Freeman's Journal*—just as the Philadelphia democrats had their *Aurora*. This opposition party was known as the Quids.‡

## The Oligarchs Reply

The Quids were in a tight spot. Their interests were primarily economic and middle class. But post-Revolutionary society was bursting with a new way of thinking that threatened those interests. Independence had given many people the hope for a different kind of society, with different values, based on a different kind of government. Thus, those who favored unfettered economic development, such as the Quids, could not openly oppose democratic beliefs at a time when these ideals were so alive for large numbers of people who had just risked everything for independence. They had to speak the language of democracy while advancing a program that would erode the very conditions necessary for it to thrive.

What the pro-development forces did was to take the word "democracy" and link it with the word "republic," by which they meant representative government, an aristocracy of "the wise and virtuous,"§ essentially substituting one word for the other without actually appearing to do so. With the word "republic," all discussion of the common good, accountability, impeachment of the judiciary, proper legislation, and the nature of the legal system disappears from the conversation. In essence, the content is excised from the political dialogue. In its place is the rhetoric of well-being, rooted in economic development and freedom of opportunity. Democracy becomes a "cultural style"[5] instead of a political program.

The Quids did not want change, agitation, or experimentation—that is, the democratic process. They wanted a predictable political structure in which power was divided among the legislature, the executive, and the judiciary, allowing for either the executive or the judiciary to override the legislature. They were less concerned with justice and the common good, and more concerned with property rights and private energy.

---

‡ For the origin of the name "Quid," see Andrew Shankman, *Crucible of American Democracy*, p. 96.

§ In 1810, John Jay argued that "those who own the country are the most fit persons to participate in the government of it." In 1813, in a letter to John Adams, Thomas Jefferson expressed a similar sentiment. He too spoke of rule by a select aristocracy. He distinguished, however, between a "natural" aristocracy—that is, those who are born with "virtue and talents," those "who have been provided virtue and wisdom enough to manage the concerns of society"—and an artificial aristocracy "founded on wealth and birth, without either virtue or talents." As Jefferson saw it, the best form of government would be the one that provides "most effectually for a pure selection of these natural *aristoi*." John Jay quoted in Shankman, *Crucible of American Democracy*, p. 16; Thomas Jefferson quoted in Merrill D. Peterson, *The Portable Jefferson*, pp. 534–535.

For them, democracy meant equality—not equality of condition, but equality of opportunity. In an open economy, with unlimited economic development, everyone would have the opportunity to prosper. Like Jefferson, but with a different kind of wisdom in mind, their political goal was to place the "right men" in office, men who would oversee the economic development that would bring unlimited benefit to everyone.

In the Pennsylvania gubernatorial election of 1808, the Quids supported Simon Snyder. Snyder was a man of humble origins, a "clodhopper," who gave a certain flavor to the democratic "cultural style." With men like Snyder running for office, democracy came to mean not a set of ideas, but a down-to-earth, folksy demeanor and delivery—anti-intellectual, anti-elite—in style, that is. A cult of "democratic personality" emerged, along with a "democratic cultural ethos,"[6] neither of which had concrete consequences for democracy as a form of government.

Democracy was celebrated but not embraced. In an 1824 letter to Jefferson, William Duane, son of the long-time editor of the *Aurora*, declared that the nation had undergone a "revolution in speech."[7] In other words, the *word* "democracy" was in common use. But, programmatically, nothing significant had changed. Democracy had come to mean what the aristocracy—both natural and artificial—had wanted it to mean: getting the "right man" into office. It had come to mean its opposite, abstinence from genuine political involvement, the relinquishment of the opportunity for direct participation in government.

Words like "democracy," "liberty," and "prosperity" were woven into a mantra of belief and hope, a faith-based message that was closer to religion than it was to politics. There were no declared ideas, issues, or programs. Nothing was offered up for debate or discussion. The goal was to arrange for a transfer of power without appearing to do so. "Listen to us," said the Quids, "the wise and trustworthy. Believe what we say. We know what is good for you. We will take care of you. Everyone will live in prosperity." The citizenry should relinquish its right to self-government and surrender the control of affairs to those who are most convincing in asking for it.

The Quids were not trying to seize political power outright. They wanted to convince the electorate to grant them the power they needed so that they could lead. Their principal tactic was to discredit their rivals, whom they characterized as destructive, unprincipled, demagogues, anarchists. In many ways, manner and style of debate became the topic of debate, not the issues themselves. Discrediting one's adversaries became the preferred means of political exchange, leaving aside the issues in question. Form became more important than substance. Political dialogue was to occur in a routine, businesslike tone. It was the impassioned, agitated tone of the *Aurora*'s editorials the Quids objected to. Such impassioned argument had no place in a free society.

Both the Quids and the democrats wanted to see the land developed, roads and canals built. They both opposed the Bank of the United States because it was large and monopolistic. Instead, they favored local and state banks, many of them, which would be responsive to local needs. Where they differed was on the issue of control and power. Who, in fact, would oversee economic development? Who, what set of people, would control these constructions and institutions once they came into being? The democrats were concerned about inequality and believed that the origin of inequality was the unequal distribution of political power. People could accumulate dangerous amounts of wealth only when they were able to use public power for private purposes. Democracy wielded power for the many.

In 1805, Philadelphia journeyman cordwainers[¶] went on strike against their masters, leading to the first labor conspiracy trial in the nation's history. In addressing the jury, the presiding judge, speaking for the Quids, declared that "The acts of the legislature form but a small part from which the citizen is to learn his duties, or the magistrate his power and rule of action."[8] The law is complex and difficult to understand. It is thoroughly understood only by judges and lawyers. Thus, it is the law, according to the judge, that will determine right action, not some ephemeral and fluctuating legislature. In light of the judge's expression of support for the prosecution, the jury quickly decided against the laborers and in favor of their masters, underscoring the Philadelphia democrats' concerns about an independent judiciary acting in opposition to the will of the people and in favor of an elite minority.

The Quids placed their confidence in a document, the U.S. Constitution, as the source of political power. The democrats saw constitutions (that is, the new federal constitution) as a means for the aristocracy to assert its will at the expense of the will of the majority. To be ruled by a constitution is to be ruled by the dead. It is the living—those serving in the legislature at a given time—who should hold the reins of government, not a document, crafted by men, dead for decades or centuries. "If the people of this year discover a bad law, or wish a good one, they have as much right to it as the people of last year or those who made the constitution."[9]

Thoughts like these became rarer and rarer as a small oligarchy of vested interests took a firm hold of the political dialogue. The word "democracy" had been deliberately distorted to suit the needs of a group of men who wished to assume power on behalf of their own interests without appearing to do so. It is by no means accidental that the word "democracy" entered the political debate after the constitution had been adopted, at a time when the majority, whose interests had been sacrificed, yet still energized and empowered by the Revolution, began to realize that they had been passed over.

---

¶  A cordwainer (or cordovan) is somebody who makes shoes and other articles from fine, soft leather. The word is derived from "cordwain" or "cordovan," the leather produced in Córdoba, Spain.

# Democracy Defined

*Alone I pass'd through ways*
*That brought me on a sudden to the tree*
*Of interdicted knowledge; fair it seem'd.*

I F ONE WANTED to define the word "democracy" by example, one would have to look no further than the process leading up to the creation and implementation of the Pennsylvania state constitution in 1776. Yet it is not that version of "democracy" that has been handed down from generation to generation since that time. Instead, it is the version that emerged after the federal Constitution was in place and partisans like the Quids had set out to implement their program of economic expansion without revealing their true intentions. They succeeded in adapting the word to their purposes by sapping it of any real meaning or value. It is that version of "democracy" that we have inherited.

Since then, additional meanings have been attached to the word, a word that is often used and rarely understood. People with wildly contrasting political views will all agree: "Yes, democracy is a fine thing." What exactly do they mean?

Let us start by addressing the even broader issue of government itself. What exactly is the purpose of government? According to political scientist John G. Gunnell, who wrote *Political Philosophy and Time*, the purpose of government is "the creation of a home for man in the world."[1] That is to say, government is the most fundamental means of organizing a society. The home that man builds for himself will have a certain structure—a means for establishing the relationships between the various elements in society. How will the citizens be connected to each other and to their government? As Gunnell points out, there can be "an order based on power and one based on justice."[2] Monarchy and oligarchy are based on power. Democracy is based on justice. Justice, in this context, would be a form of government that establishes political equality and addresses the needs of everyone, that is, addresses the common good.

Well, just what kind of home does democracy create for those who dwell within? It is a home with room for everyone, a home where everyone has equal privileges. It is not the kind of home where a few people are in charge and are allowed to determine how matters will be set up and run for everyone else. Yet this is what existence has been like under the American oligarchy. For example, in the early years of the U.S. Constitution, sixty-five representatives spoke for three million Americans. That is, close to fifty thousand Americans had but one voice to express their many, varied, and often conflicting views.

Since then, population has increased a hundredfold while representation has increased only sevenfold. Today, in the year 2012, in the United States, matters are more than ten times worse as far as representation goes than they were when the constitution was ratified. Four hundred thirty-five people in the House of Representatives speak for a population in excess of three hundred million. The wishes of approximately seven hundred thousand citizens are channeled through one voice. Basically, the home that government is supposed to create for us is really *two* homes in America today—one where the government meets and another for the rest of us. Whatever democracy is, such an arrangement certainly does not offer an example.

In a true democracy, we all live under one roof. It is a form of government (person or persons in power) in which everyone governs all the time. Although there are few pure examples in history, governance under the Pennsylvania Constitution of 1776 was the closest the United States ever got to living out the true meaning of democracy. It is instructive to compare this Pennsylvania state constitution and the events leading up to its enactment with the events leading up to the creation of the U.S. Constitution of 1787.

By definition, an oligarchy starts with a small number of people. Alexander Hamilton, Robert Morris, and Gouverneur Morris, it seems to me, orchestrated the events leading up to the ratification of the Constitution and manipulated the content of the document itself, as well. Their true motivations remained hidden. Those who attended the Constitutional Convention were sworn to secrecy. Remember how the aging Benjamin Franklin was supplied with a chaperone to make sure he didn't blabber? Where there is secrecy, there is something to hide. Oligarchs will always need secrecy for one simple and obvious reason. What they are up to suits them and them alone. Were their intentions open to public inspection, their scheming would be brought to an abrupt halt. Thus, it is not surprising to learn that to have their way the early American oligarchs had to gain control of the press and the mails, suppress free and open debate, plant false stories, use physical force, destroy ballots, and cheat on the vote counts.

## Democratic Process in the State of Pennsylvania

When one looks at the situation in Pennsylvania leading up to the publication of the new state constitution in 1776, one is at a loss to say, "Oh, this is the work of so and so." In fact, it takes some arduous research to come up with even a few names. And what is found? Apparently a judge from Philadelphia named George Bryan and a schoolmaster known as Mr. Cannon are two of the principal authors of Pennsylvania's Constitution of 1776. "Well, who are they? Not terribly impressive," you say. And you are right. That is the point. Democracy is relatively anonymous. Just about anybody can do its work. There are no experts. Its intentions are open. Its positions are clear. Since democracy speaks for the vast majority, it does not need to resort to manipulation, deception, and intimidation to succeed. Thousands met in the courtyard of the Pennsylvania state house to express their views and organize their efforts. There was a network of committees starting in Philadelphia and going out to the smallest locality, involving all manner of citizenry in an active chain of communication on matters of import.

Here are some of the rules of debate devised for the U.S. Constitutional Convention, principally the work of Alexander Hamilton. I quote at length (and with apologies) from James Madison's notes to the Convention:

Immediately after the President shall have taken the chair, and the members their seats, the minutes of the preceding day shall be read by the Secretary. Every member, rising to speak, shall address the President; and whilst he shall be speaking, none shall pass between them, or hold discourse with another, or read a book, pamphlet or paper, printed or manuscript—and of two members rising at the same time, the President shall name him who shall be first heard.

A member shall not speak oftener than twice, without special leave, upon the same question; and not the second time, before every other, who had been silent, shall have been heard, if he choose to speak upon the subject. A motion made and seconded, shall be repeated, and if written, as it shall be when any member shall so require, read aloud by the Secretary, before it shall be debated; and may be withdrawn at any time, before the vote upon it shall have been declared.

Orders of the day shall be read next after the minutes, and either discussed or postponed, before any other business shall be introduced. When a debate shall arise upon a question, no motion, other than to amend the question, to commit it, or to postpone the debate shall be received.

A question which is complicated, shall, at the request of any member, be divided, and put separately on the propositions, of which it is compounded. The determination of a question, altho' fully debated, shall be postponed, if the deputies of any State desire it until the next day. A writing which contains any matter brought on to be considered, shall be read once throughout for information, then by paragraphs to be debated, and again, with the amendments, if any, made on the second reading; and afterwards, the question shall be put on the whole, amended, or approved in its original form, as the case shall be.

Committees shall be appointed by ballot; and the members who have the greatest number of ballots, altho' not a majority of the votes present, shall be the Committee. When two or more members have an equal number of votes, the member standing first on the list in the order of taking down the ballots, shall be preferred. A member may be called to order

by any other member, as well as by the President; and may be allowed
to explain his conduct or expressions supposed to be reprehensible. And
all questions of order shall be decided by the President without appeal or
debate. Upon a question to adjourn for the day, which may be made at
any time, if it be seconded, the question shall be put without a debate.
*When the House shall adjourn, every member shall stand in his place,
until the President pass him.*

Additional rules. That no member be absent from the House, so as to
interrupt the representation of the State, without leave.

That Committees do not sit whilst the House shall be or ought to be,
sitting.

*That no copy be taken of any entry on the journal during the sitting
of the House without leave of the House.*

*That members only be permitted to inspect the journal.*

*That nothing spoken in the House be printed, or otherwise published
or communicated without leave.*

That a motion to reconsider a matter which had been determined by
a majority, may be made, with leave unanimously given, on the same day
on which the vote passed; but otherwise not without one day's previous notice: in which last case, if the House agree to the reconsideration,
some future day shall be assigned for the purpose.* (italics added)


I think nothing is more telling than the stentorian, rigid, authoritarian, controlling tone of these rules. The verbosity and detail betray Hamilton's role. What ever happened to free and open debate? This meeting
was attended by fifty-five intelligent, discreet, well-behaved men. Why
the secrecy, why the verbiage restricting their behavior, if not for Hamilton's fear that he might lose control, that the public might get wind of
what was going on, and that all his scheming would come to naught?

At the Pennsylvania State Convention of 1776, one hundred eight
members participated. There were just fifty-five delegates to the U.S.
Constitutional Convention—at which not one state but thirteen states
were to be represented. The rules prevailing at the Pennsylvania State
Convention offer a dramatic contrast to those established by Hamilton.
At the Pennsylvania State Convention, there was no secrecy. The only
restriction was against cursing. The goal was to encourage spontaneous
discussion, free and open debate. When does debate come to an end?
There is no fixed formula. It comes to an end when it gets so "tedious"
that four delegates are motivated to call the question. It's that simple. I
am not so sure how Hamilton would have fared had he been prevented
from "willfully pervert[ing] the sense of what another member has said,"
another one of the rules prevailing at the Pennsylvania State Convention.[3]

Benjamin Franklin, the president of the Pennsylvania State Convention,

---

* This material can be found at the National Heritage Center for Constitutional Studies,
http://www.nhccs.org/Mnotes.html. The rules of debate were noted by Madison on May
28, 1787. It is not clear if the original, official notes for the Convention have ever been
established. The standard archival resource on the subject is the four-volume work edited
by Max Farrand, *The Records of the Federal Convention of 1787*, published in 1911. The
first three volumes are available at http://memory.loc.gov/ammem/amlaw/lwfr.html.

was absent most of the time. The Pennsylvania delegates needed no author-itarian figure to keep them in line, intimidate them, or discourage their exercise of free speech. Compare this atmosphere with George Washing-ton's cold, enduring presence as president of the U.S. Constitutional Con-vention. And then note the most telling of details: "When the House shall adjourn, every member shall stand in his place, until the President pass him." If these be not the trappings of monarchy, I know not what they are.

It is certainly not surprising—based on the processes and procedures leading up to and including the composition of these two disparate documents—that the Pennsylvania state constitution was rather demo-cratic and the U.S. Constitution was unreservedly oligarchic. All of the precautions that were taken by the authors of the Pennsylvania state constitution to prevent the concentration and abuse of power were scru-pulously avoided by the authors of the U.S. Constitution.

The Pennsylvania state constitution had a Declaration of Rights. The U.S. Constitution did not. The Pennsylvania legislature was made up of one house with broad-based representation. This single democratic house was to reign supreme. There was no second house or governor's veto to obstruct its wishes. The U.S. Constitution, on the other hand, introduced a second, oligarchic element, the Senate, with the express purpose of putting limits on the democratic impulse. Under the Penn-sylvania state constitution, all legislation written was to be made avail-able to the public for a period of six months prior to being passed into law. There is no such provision under the U.S. Constitution.

Representatives were to be elected annually under the Pennsylvania Constitution of 1776, biannually under the U.S. Constitution. In Penn-sylvania, a representative could serve no more than four years out of any seven. There are no such restrictions in the U.S. Constitution, leading to an oligarchy of representatives and senators who have served (as of 2012) anywhere from twenty to fifty years in many cases. Rather than deny that corruption existed, rather than trust to the virtuousness of their candidates for office, as James Madison and Alexander Hamilton in the *Federalist Papers* had exhorted their readers to do, under the Pennsylva-nia Constitution of 1776, anyone caught giving or taking bribes forfeited his office for a year and would "suffer such other penalties as future laws shall direct." There is no such provision in the U.S. Constitution.

Rather than vest unlimited power in a single executive, the president, give him veto power over acts of the legislature and a free hand in military matters, as U.S. Constitution did, in Pennsylvania, the power was vested in a plural executive, a council of members chosen from Philadelphia and each of the counties. After three consecutive years in the Pennsylva-nia Executive Council, a person was required to wait four years before standing for election to the Council again. The Assembly and Council chose one of the Council members to serve as president, for but *one year.* Despite this brief period of service, serious limits were placed upon the president's conduct in office. No military actions could be taken without the Council's involvement. Compare this with the arbitrary use of military power by the executive in the national government today.

Democracy is a process rather than a state of being. In a democratic form of government, the founding document, the structure of government, processes, and procedures are in a steady state of evolution, responding to new conditions, new demands, from one moment to the next, from one generation to the next. If democracy is an organic process, growing new roots, branches, and leaves as it moves through time, oligarchy more closely resembles a statue carved in marble. It is one and the same for always. This is true because the needs of the oligarchy never change: power for the few. Oligarchy trembles at the thought of change. Madison repeatedly argued in favor of "immutability."

To illustrate this point, consider the following. The Pennsylvania state constitution provided for a Council of Censors, with two members elected from each city and county. It was the job of this council to serve as ombudsman. Have some provisions of the constitution become outdated? Has legislation been passed that violates the spirit or letter of the constitution? Should amendments be offered? Are state officers behaving themselves and properly fulfilling their duties? These and like matters were the business of the Council of Censors. The U.S. Constitution has no such provision. The reader may recall Madison's strenuous objection to a similar proposal offered by Jefferson.[†] After complimenting Jefferson on his loyalty to republican principles, Madison proceeded, at length to offer various incontrovertible and "insuperable objections against the proposed recurrence to the people."[4]

I think it can reasonably be argued that the U.S. Constitution has very little that is democratic about it, either in its content or in its coming into being. It was carefully constructed to ensure concentration of power in the hands of a few, and it has succeeded in achieving that end without interruption since it was put in place. The United States is an oligarchy by intent. Those early Americans fondly referred to as the "Founding Fathers"[‡] represented an elite of wealthy property holders, merchants, and banking interests. They were determined to set up a government that they could control to their benefit while yielding as little power as possible to those of more modest means. They repeatedly and specifically spurned any attempts to establish a true democracy.

By contrast, the Pennsylvania Constitution of 1776, both in its content and in its coming into being, does its best to speak for the common man and the common good. Its authors did everything they could to prevent the concentration and abuse of power. We will never know how it would have fared over time because, in 1790, under pressure from

---

† The debate is discussed in Chapter 7.
‡ Warren G. Harding—twenty-ninth President of the United States—is credited with coining the phrase "Founding Fathers" in his keynote address to the 1916 Republican National Convention.

the constitutional oligarchy in charge of the new nation, Pennsylvania adopted a new constitution that did away with everything that was original and democratic about its predecessor.

## What Democracy Means

The first and most obvious thing to note about the word "democracy" is that it is, in its Greek origin, a political word. "*Demos*" refers to the people, "*kratos*" to power or rule. So, democracy is a form of government in which the people rule. The people, meaning all citizens living under a particular government, exercise power on their own behalf. Thus, the people and the government are one and the same.

Sometime in the eighteenth century, in reaction to the abuses of power exercised by the church and hereditary monarchs, democracy took on a second meaning. It became equated with freedom—freedom from arbitrary constraint. Citizens wished to be able to move about without fear of being imprisoned for expressing their opposition to their government. They wanted to be able to choose their own religion without fear of prosecution for their beliefs. They wanted to be able to publish their thoughts, free of censorship. The wanted to own property without having to worry about its being confiscated.

These and like concerns have imbued the word "democracy" with a great deal of passion and allegiance for many different people from around the world over the past two hundred years. But this meaning is not the meaning of the word in its origins. This kind of democracy is not a form of government. It is a negative concept in that it incorporates the wish to be free from something, to be left alone, to not be bothered. I refer to such democracy as civic democracy (C.D.). It is quite different from political democracy (P.D.). It does not describe a form of government. However, it might well be argued that political democracy without civic democracy will not long endure.

In the nineteenth century, probably largely as a consequence of the exploitation and economic inequalities brought on by the Industrial Revolution, the word "democracy" took on yet another meaning. If we are, all of us, to be free from want, to be able to lead comfortable and fulfilling lives, we need to live in a society where there is a relatively equal distribution of wealth, a society that for the most part does not know the meaning of the word "class," where neither wealth nor power is concentrated in the hands of the few. Such concerns usually fall under the heading of social democracy (S.D.). Social democracy concerns itself with the distribution of wealth, political democracy with the distribution of power.

Social democracy has various shades of meaning depending on the context. In America, it means "equality" in a very general, social sense. "You are no better than I. You are not my superior. I am as good as you. We are all equals." This kind of sentiment is in direct response to the European tradition of class differences, which Americans were determined to eliminate from their culture. In fact, there were economic and social differences in many sections of early America, differences that have become only more pronounced with the passing of the years. However, the *belief*, not the fact, of social equality prevails as a founding and sustaining myth and in many ways is a key belief in holding American society together.

In Europe, social democracy has more a explicit meaning. It means some form of government, not necessarily democratic, in which the government makes fundamental economic decisions and has direct control of some of the primary resources, with the ultimate purpose of establishing, in fact, the very social and economic equality that exists only as belief in the United States. This meaning of the word "democracy" is inconsistent with the original meaning of the word for two reasons. In its original meaning, democracy pertains to a form of government in which the people govern, not an economic program. And, secondly, any form of government in which a small number of governors dictate economic and social policy is clearly not a democracy. There are those who would argue that political democracy (P.D.) is impossible without social democracy (S.D.). I would argue the contrary—that, based on examples drawn from history and from political theory, political democracy (P.D.) cannot exist *with* social democracy (S.D.),§ where there is an oligarchic elite determining what is best for everyone else.

Early American colonial history provides an interesting example of social democracy. In 1732, a royal charter was awarded to a group of wealthy London philanthropists and social reformers who became known as the Georgia Trustees. For twenty-one years, they were to be in charge of a colony north of the Carolinas. The colony was named Georgia, in honor of King George II. It was the goal of the Trustees to ship the poor and downtrodden to this new colony with the hope of rehabilitating them through hard work with the reward of their own farms. Ninety percent of the funding was to come from Parliament. At the end of the twenty-one years, the colony would come under the direct control of the crown.

About eighteen hundred charity cases were shipped, at no charge to them, to their new homes on fifty-acre tracts in Georgia. Others paid their own way and were given similar land grants. In contrast to the Carolinas, where large plantations were worked by slaves, the Georgia Trustees wanted to set up small family farms worked by whites. The importation or possession of slaves was forbidden. The Trustees tried to create a morally uplifting environment by curtailing the consumption of rum. They wanted to limit litigation and agitation, as well, and decided therefore to ban lawyers from residing in their new colony. Instead of rice and indigo—the typical Carolina plantation crops—the Georgia farms would raise hemp, flax, mulberry (to feed silkworms),

---

§ See, for example, Chapter 15's discussion of Plato's *Republic* and its resemblance to the USSR.

and grapes. There was no elected assembly. The colony was governed by four officials (oligarchs) appointed by the Trustees.

Here we see the key elements of social democracy. There is a mandated equality in land ownership (S.D.+) and an attempt to establish a controlled environment (C.D.–) favorable to an uplifting way of life, under the control of preselected governors (P.D.–). For the times, it was a noble endeavor, though short-lived. The colonists looked south to Carolina, where the whites enjoyed a life of leisure and the black slaves did the work. Gradually they whittled away at the restrictions placed on them by the Trustees and eventually imported their own slaves and lawyers, drank rum, and created a colony that virtually replicated Carolina.

There is yet a fourth meaning that adheres to this most sticky of words, "democracy." It is the meaning that prevails in the United States as of this writing. It is a meaning that I believe emerged during those early years of political debate in Pennsylvania in the decade after the writing of the U.S. Constitution, when many Americans began to realize that they had been duped and that their true interests had been sacrificed to those of a wealthy aristocracy.

It was only after the drafting of the U.S. Constitution that the word "democracy" entered the political dialogue. Once it came, it would not leave. And for two centuries since, anyone who wishes to be elected to higher office in America must proclaim himself a friend of democracy. This particular kind of democracy, however, has no form, has no program, has no content. It stands for nothing. It is a sentiment, akin to a belief in God. It is like a potion or incantation that when uttered will magically cure what is ill. And it seems to have been invented by those clever Quids back around 1800, when they were seeking to promote a program of economic development but could not do so without winning over those who were agitating in favor of democracy.

Their sleight of hand was to make it appear as if the words "republic" and "democracy" were one and the same and that a "republican" form of government, in which a relative handful of men determine economic policy on the state and national level, is, in fact, democratic. They established a political tradition in which personal appearance and manner are all that matters, in which programmatic content is explicitly eliminated from the debate, and in which attacks on one's opponent are the most efficient way of making oneself visible and electable. What they were "offering" was "equal opportunity" to succeed, which is about as good an offer as saying that anyone in the United States has an "equal opportunity" to run a four-minute mile—true but meaningless, since most of us lack the means for doing so.

As discussed in Chapter 12, democracy became a "cultural style." A "true" democratic leader will talk and act in a folksy, anti-elitist way, creating an atmosphere of wellbeing but standing for nothing in particular that he is willing to openly advocate that is truly democratic. He will speak of "prosperity" and "liberty" but will offer no concrete proposals. This is what rhetorical democracy (R.D.) is all about—appearance, sleight of hand, empty promises.¶ It is one of the reasons democracy has such bad standing and is so often the object of ridicule.

The Founding Fathers were ambitious men and perhaps vain enough to believe in their own noble intentions, but they were not foolish. They realized that their true motives had to be concealed behind democratic rhetoric. Their ploy worked extremely well. Over the past two hundred years, one generation of oligarchs has passed on to the next a form of government enshrined in a mystique of beneficence that even the founders could not have conceived. In the process, the true meaning of the word "democracy" has been concealed and misapplied in so many different ways by writers and statesmen of all political stripes that it requires a conscious effort to reclaim the word for its true purposes. Believing, erroneously, they we live in a democracy, that we the people are indeed the government, we are deprived of the opportunity of setting up a government in which we truly are.

Vandana Shiva** has created an interesting variation on the theme of political democracy. She calls it "earth democracy." Where there is earth democracy, there is self-governance organized around issues of access to and distribution of natural resources. The local community controls its supply of water. It controls its seeds. It chooses the crops it plants and the means of fertilization.

Earth democracy has emerged as a response to globalization and its effects on the sustenance farmers of India, where sixteen thousand farmers committed suicide in the year 2004 alone.†† Government policies in the service of corporations like Cargill and Monsanto have forced farmers to buy seeds and fertilizers they can't afford. The result is reduced yield per hectare and increased indebtedness, with no end in sight. In despair, the small sustenance farmer—whose knowledge of the land and farming skills have been the backbone of Indian agriculture for thousands of years—sees no way out other than to take his own life. Says Shiva,

> Earth Democracy allows us to reclaim our common humanity and our unity with all life.... It protects the ecological processes that maintain life and the fundamental human rights that are the basis of the right to life, including the right to water, the right to food, the right to health, the right to education, and the right to jobs and livelihoods. Earth Democracy is based on the recognition of and respect for the life of all species and all people.[5]

---

¶ "Is deference to democracy popular among politicos of all shades because its dynamic is spent and its force is mainly rhetorical?" Sheldon S. Wolin, *Democracy Incorporated*, p. 218.
** Vandana Shiva is an environmentalist and philosopher who has written more than 20 books, including *Earth Democracy: Justice, Sustainability, and Peace* (published in 2005).
†† As Shiva points out, "Agriculture accounts for 70 percent of land use, 70 percent of water use, and 70 percent of the livelihoods on the planet." *Earth Democracy*, p. 129.

Earth democracy is a form of self-governance. It provides an opportunity for small local communities to meet, debate, and legislate on key issues that affect their wellbeing. Navdanya is a network of more than a half million small farmers in India who have organized themselves around the principles of sustainable agriculture. Instead of the monoculture imposed upon them by their government, they have returned to an approach of preserving biodiversity, which nourishes the soil and defends against pests without the introduction of chemical fertilizers. These farmers have reduced their costs by ninety percent. Their incomes are three times higher than those of farmers using Western industrial methods.

Shiva speaks of "water democracy," "food democracy," and "seed democracy." We are "earth citizens" and "earth children." She emphasizes the small and the local. The seed becomes a symbol. "The seed," she says, "is starting to take shape as the site and symbol of freedom in the age of manipulation and monopoly of life.... In smallness lies power."[6] Localization becomes the answer to globalization. "It treats every place as the center of the world, placing every person, every being at the center of ever widening circles of compassion and care."[7] Diversity is the answer to uniformity and centralization—diversity of species, of crops, of peoples, and of cultures.

## Some Telling Comparisons

What, then, *is* political democracy? Let us start with what it is not. It is not representative. It does not offer up some subset of people to speak on the behalf of the rest. It assumes that each individual member is qualified to pronounce on critical issues. It is not government by an elite. It does not seek some charismatic leader to guide it. It is not a form of government in which the citizen dutifully votes in an election every few years and then withdraws to the privacy of his chambers while the "experts" govern. It does not cultivate the apathy of its denizens. It is not "mobocracy," and it is also not "tyranny of the majority." It is a thoughtful and integrated expression of the entirety of its membership. It is not, as Edward Bernays would have us believe, "The conscious and intelligent manipulation of the organized habits and opinions of the masses" by "some unseen controllers" with "some pre-established outcome ... in mind."[8] It is none of these things. Nor is it, unfortunately, the much-beloved U.S. Constitution.

Well, then, what is political democracy? Is it a dream or a reality? Someone might say, "What about ancient Athens? That was a democracy." And someone else might counter, "Not so fast. What is democratic about a society where 30,000 men, out of a population of about 300,000, are in charge? Isn't that an oligarchy, like any other?"

In reply to both of these hypothetical respondents, I offer a comparison of three different societies and their governments so we can see if there really is something that sets Athens apart. Thus, let us consider ancient Athens and its contemporary, the Roman Republic, both thriving in the fifth century B.C., and bring into the discussion also the United States of America, some twenty-three hundred years later, at the end of the eighteenth century.

As noted, in Athens, out of a population of about 300,000 (including men, women, children, foreigners, and slaves), 30,000 were citizens. Women and slaves were not citizens, and the slave population alone was perhaps as large as 100,000.

For the Roman Republic, at roughly the same time, population estimates are less reliable. The total population might have been as high as one or two million. As in Athens, full citizenship was open to free men only (not women, not slaves). Women were not allowed to vote or to stand for civil or public office. Slaves numbered about twenty-five percent of the total population.

In the United States, at the end of the eighteenth century, at the time the Constitution was adopted and ratified, there was a population of about three million. Of these, about 645,000 (roughly twenty percent) were slaves. As in Rome and Athens, in the United States, at its founding, women could not vote. Due to property and or religious qualifications, significant numbers of white males also were unable to vote. Thus, in the United States, at its inception, full citizenship was restricted to a certain class of men.

Thus, some broad parallels apply to ancient Athens, the Roman Republic, and the United States in the year 1800. In all three societies, women and slaves were denied the rights of citizenship.

There are also some important differences. During the days of the Roman Republic, government was under the control of the Senate, which was composed of three hundred of the wealthiest and most prominent members of the Roman aristocracy, serving for life. In the early days of the United States, the government was in the hands of ninety-one congressmen (sixty-five Representatives and twenty-six Senators), speaking for propertied and mercantile interests. One notices the small number of official members of the governing elite in the United States, ninety-one, versus three hundred in the Roman Republic. In both cases, the number governing is small, and the people governing speak for a small minority of wealthy men. In other words, both governments were oligarchies.

Athens provides a significant contrast. Yes, it is true that Athens had a sizable population of slaves and that neither slaves nor women had political rights, just as was the case in Rome and the United States. However, in Athens, out of a population of 300,000, there were at least 30,000 who governed on their own behalf, from the poorest to the wealthiest. They spoke for the common good, for the population at large. The oligarchies in the United States and Rome spoke for probably five percent or less of the population (the wealthy) and consistently failed to address the common good.

As discussed in Chapter 5, living under the Roman oligarchy was a perilous existence for the vast majority of the population, who were subsistence farmers. When they became indebted, their land was seized by their aristocratic creditors and they were enslaved. These peasant farmers were also soldiers. When they returned from war, they often found themselves landless. Their farms had been taken over by the aristocracy. More and more they were at the mercy of the state for their grain, which was in short supply.

In this environment, men like the Gracchus brothers stepped forward to aid those without power to procure the basic necessities. Tribune Tiberius Gracchus pushed for reforms in land holdings and grazing rights. He and his followers were hunted down and killed. His younger brother Gaius trod a similar path. He brought about the passage of agrarian laws and the building of granaries. And Gaius and his followers were also rounded up and executed.

The American Revolutionary War was fought by farmer soldiers who returned from war to find themselves in much the same position as their Roman brothers. Their land and livestock were seized by their creditors. Shays' Rebellion and other protests like it were the consequence. The Whiskey Rebellion was another example of subsistence farmers trying to protect their livelihood. When the farmers refused to pay a newly imposed tax, Washington and Hamilton gathered any army, got on their horses, and rode out to settle the matter by force.

It is no accident that one reads of such incidents in the history of the Roman Republic and the United States. In both cases, there was government by and for the oligarchy, at the expense of the basic needs of the vast majority of the population. One finds no such crises in the history of ancient Athens. All classes were in charge, including the vast majority of small farmers. Certainly, they would address the basic needs of everyone, themselves included. If there were issues of grain supply, they would see to it the problem was resolved to serve the needs of everyone. That is how democracy works.

Democracy is inclusive. It addresses the needs of all. Oligarchy is exclusive. It addresses the needs of a few. In Pennsylvania, during the early days of the Revolutionary War, there were large gatherings of citizens, numbering in the thousands, who were dissatisfied with the state government. They spoke for the vast majority of the population in their state. They persisted, organized themselves, set up a shadow government,[‡‡] and soon became the new government authority. That is democracy is at work.

Let us not forget the first Pilgrims. Exactly one hundred lower-middle-class English men, women, and children aboard the Mayflower—who thought they were headed for Virginia—ended up on Cape Cod on November 10, 1620, and eventually settled in Plymouth six weeks later. There was friction and hostility as various members of this ad hoc com-

---

‡‡  Shadow governments have arisen thoughout history. In thirteenth-century Italy, in the time of the city-states, the *popolo*, or common folk, would organize themselves on the periphery of the communes controlled by the nobility, where they would establish a "fictitious commune." Martines, *Power and Imagination*, p. 56.

munity declared their right to have their voice heard. The only solution was to establish a government based on majority rule, leading to the formulation of the Mayflower Compact, which was signed by forty-one men. The Compact reads, in part:

> Haveing undertaken, for the glorie of god, and advancemente of the Christian faith and honour of our king & countrie, a voyage to plant the first colonie in the Northerne parts of Virginia, doe by these presents solemnly & mutualy in the presence of God, and one of another, covenant & combine our selves togeather into a civill body politick, for our better ordering & preservation & furtherance of the ends aforesaid; and by vertue hearof to enacte, constitute, and frame such just & equall lawes, ordinances, Acts, constitutions, & offices, from time to time, as shall be thought most meete & convenient for the generall good of the Colonie, unto which we promise all due submission and obedience.

This is democracy at work, everyone speaking for everyone, "combining ourselves together into a civil body politick." I doubt democracy has ever been more succinctly or better defined.§§

Looking back beyond even ancient Athens, we find that some of the earliest civilizations seem to have been democratic in nature. In the third millennium B.C., in southern Mesopotamia (what today is Iraq), in that area known as "The Cradle of Civilization," the Sumerians established the world's first cities. As Samuel Noah Kramer tells us, in *Cradle of Civilization*, these cities were self-governing towns and villages in their early stages. "Members of the ruling bodies were appointed not by a single omnipotent individual, as one might expect, but by an assembly made up of the community's free citizens." In the absence of want, rivalry, and violence, this was probably the natural way to set things up. There was no need for a "strong man." However, as these towns and villages prospered and expanded, "limited economic rivalries turned into bitter political struggles for power, prestige and territory,"[9] leading to warfare. It became necessary to choose someone capable and courageous, a single leader, the king, to organize and protect the society against violent threats. Thus it is that, in all phases of civilization, violence eliminates democracy.

---

§§However, a document even older than the Mayflower Compact also describes democracy very well. Marsiglio da Padova (ca. 1275–ca. 1342) was an Italian scholar trained in medicine who practiced a variety of professions. He was also an important fourteenth-century political thinker. In 1324, he wrote *Defensor Pacis*, which argues for the separation of church and state. He certainly sounds like something of a democrat. "We declare," he said, "according to truth and the opinion of Aristotle, the legislator, or the prime and proper effective cause of law, to be the people or the whole body of citizens or its weightier part, commanding or deciding by its own choice or will, expressed verbally in a general assemblage of the citizens, that something be done or omitted concerning the civil actions of men, under a temporal punishment or penalty." Quoted at http://www.shadowcouncil.org/wilson/archives/005523.html.

# American Government

## *The Shaping of American Character*

*For e'en in heaven his looks and thoughts*
*Were always downward bent, admiring more*
*The riches of heaven's pavement, trodden gold.*

I
N AN EARLIER chapter,* we explored the relationship between the form of government and the character of its citizens. We saw how the democratic form of government had a direct effect on the culture, character, and intellectual and emotional makeup of the Athenian citizen of the fifth century B.C. We saw how, as the structure of government underwent fundamental changes from fifth-century B.C. Athens to fourth-century B.C. Athens, there was a corresponding change in the intellect, culture, and character of its citizens. As the democratic government weakened, the individual retreated, citizenship weakened. Private life began to take precedence over public life. Commitment to the common good diminished.

Writing of Germany in the late nineteenth century, under the powerful autocrat Otto von Bismarck, Max Weber shows how a nation loses its political will when the citizenry lacks the opportunity to share responsibility for its own political fate. Weber describes the awkwardness of the average German traveling to other countries:

> Deprived of the accustomed carapace of bureaucratic regimentation, [they] lose all sense of direction and security—a consequence of being accustomed to regard themselves at home merely as the object of the way their lives are ordered rather than as responsible for it themselves. This is the reason for that insecure, self-conscious way of presenting themselves in public which is definitely the source of the Germans' much criticized

---

* See Chapter 4, "Government and Character: Lessons from Athens."

over-familiarity. In as much as it exists, their political "immaturity" results from the uncontrolled rule of officialdom, and from the fact that the ruled are accustomed to submit to that rule without themselves sharing responsibility.[1]

Such generalizations could apply to any culture at any time. One's sense of self and level of self-confidence are determined, in part, by the government one lives under. This becomes much harder to grasp as we change our focus to our own culture and our own time. Yet it is as true today as it was twenty-five hundred years ago in Athens, or more than a century ago in Germany.

The United States offers an interesting case study in government and its effects,[†] largely because this country started from scratch with a particular form of government—a constitutional oligarchy (P.D.–, that is, absence of political democracy) with strong emphasis on rhetorical democracy (R.D.+). And further, in early American history, there was a change in government that parallels the change in Athens from the fifth to the fourth centuries. Between 1776, when the thirteen colonies became thirteen states, each with its own form of government, and 1788, when the U.S. Constitution was ratified, there was a period of experimentation in government. Democratic values were on the rise. Citizens were actively involved in shaping their own political destinies. Then the Constitution put in place a centralized government with power concentrated in the hands of a few. The result was a notable change in the culture, character, and intellect of the citizenry.

## The Paltry American

If we would like to know something about the character and intellect of the average American in the early 1800s, Alexis de Tocqueville's *Democracy in America* is one of our best resources. It is important to remember that de Tocqueville was an aristocrat and that his bias is reflected in his attitude toward American culture. Nonetheless, I believe that his descriptions and insights are uncanny and startling in their validity more than one hundred fifty years later, all the more so when one takes into account that he was twenty-seven years old at the time of his American visit.

However, de Tocqueville is confused on the subject of democracy. He repeatedly makes broad generalizations about "democracy" based on his observations in the United States. But the country he visited was not a political democracy. It was an oligarchy. If we substitute the word "oligarchy" for "democracy," we can gain a clear sense of why the typi-

† David M. Potter devotes a full chapter to a discussion of American character. Is the American an individualist or a conformist? See "The Quest for National Character," in *The Reconstruction of American History*, edited by John Higham, pp. 197–220 and the related bibliography, pp. 234–235.

cal American has ended up the way de Tocqueville describes him.

De Tocqueville ascribes what is wrong with America to "equality." The equality he has in mind, however, is not the political equality that would prevail in a democracy, but "equality of condition," that is, social equality.‡

As de Tocqueville sees it, the leveling effect of social equality has a deleterious effect on individual and social development. Everyone is like everyone else. Character and culture settle into a condition of mediocrity. If only there were an aristocracy, says de Tocqueville, American culture would be qualitatively richer, the typical American more profound in his thought and emotion.

While de Tocqueville's observations are accurate, I believe his attribution of causality is in error. The Americans he observed were the way they were not because they were socially equal but because they lived in an oligarchy, which afforded them little or no opportunity to develop their capacity for abstract thought the way the Athenians did.

The typical American, as observed by de Tocqueville in the 1830s, is weak and isolated, plagued with feelings of insignificance. "Everyone shuts himself up tightly within himself and insists upon judging the world from there."[2] As an American in the twenty-first century, one might cringe at the following observation: "Nothing conceivable is so petty, so insipid, so crowded with paltry interests—in one word, so anti-poetic—as the life of a man in the United States."[3] I'm afraid the word "anti-poetic" truly does apply.

Because Americans are so focused on their own comforts and material success, they lack breadth of vision and depth of insight. Everyone is frenetically in pursuit of power, wealth, status. There is a whirlwind of activity and competition. De Tocqueville wonders, "Where is that calm to be found which is necessary for the deeper combinations of the intellect? How can the mind dwell on any single point when everything whirls around it ...?"[4] In the hustle and bustle of this vigorous economic life, "men are generally led to attach an excessive value to the rapid bursts and superficial conceptions of the intellect and on the other hand to undervalue unduly its slower and deeper labors."[5] As de Tocqueville points out, "A man cannot gradually enlarge his mind as he does his house."[6]

The literature produced under such circumstances will be geared more toward dazzling than toward developing a deeper appreciation for its aesthetic qualities.§ "The object of authors will be to astonish rather than to please, and to stir their passions more than to charm their taste."[7] Readers treat their authors as do kings their courtiers: "They enrich and despise them."[8]

Under such circumstances, independent thought will be at a mini-

‡ Here de Tocqueville gets it right: "The principle of equality may be established in civil society without prevailing in the political world." *Democracy in America*, Vol. 2, p. 100.
§ Morris Berman makes a similar point in *Dark Ages America: The Final Phase of Empire*, pp. 296–297.

mum. Not only is there a lack of time and peace of mind, as well as lack of an interested public, there is also the enormous weight of a multitude in agreement with each other on what is and is not an acceptable idea. Says de Tocqueville, "the power exercised by the mass upon the mind of each individual is extremely great." One does not need oppressive laws and censorship to discourage new ideas and critical thinking. "Public disapprobation is enough; a sense of their loneliness [that of independent thinkers] and impotence overtakes them and drives them to despair."[9]

De Tocqueville draws a contrast between life under a monarch and life under the kind of government he sees in the United States. Under a monarch, oppression was material, directed against the body itself: "The body was attacked to subdue the soul; but the soul escaped the blows which were directed against it and rose proudly superior." Such, he says, is not the case under a "democracy" (oligarchy, in fact). There the body is left free and the soul is enslaved. The master no longer says, "You shall think as I do or you shall die." Instead, he says:

> You are free to think differently from me and retain your life, your property and all that you possess; but you are henceforth a stranger among your people. You may maintain your civil rights, but they will be useless to you, for you will never be chosen by your fellow citizens if you solicit their votes; and they will affect to scorn you if you ask for their esteem. You will remain among men, but you will be deprived of the rights of mankind. Your fellow creatures will shun you like an impure being; and even those who believe in your innocence will abandon you, lest they should be shunned in their turn. Go in peace! I have given you your life, but it is an existence worse than death.[10]¶

The collective repression of intellect and critical thinking** leads to a weakening and debasement of character. There is a lack of courage, a lack of independent thought that contrasts with what had been the case in an earlier time. De Tocqueville notes, "I found very few men who displayed that manly candor and masculine independence of opinion which frequently distinguished the Americans in former times, and which constitutes the leading feature in distinguished characters wherever they may be found."[11]††

De Tocqueville finds Americans to be practical, small minded, and

---

¶ Danish philosopher Søren Kierkegaard (1813–1855) put it this way: "The most dangerous revolutions are not those which tear everything down, and cause the streets to run with blood, but those which leave everything standing, while cunningly emptying it of any significance." Aldous Huxley (1894–1963) said, in the Foreword to *Brave New World*, "A really efficient totalitarian state would be one in which the all-powerful executive of political bosses and their army of managers control a population of slaves who do not have to be coerced, because they love their servitude."

** See Richard Hofstadter, *Anti-Intellectualism in American Life.*

†† With the installation of a strong central government—an oligarchy, under the Constitution—American character and intellect declined. One has only to dip into the writings of the Anti-Federalists to see the difference. Almost immediately after the government shifted to Washington, all discussion of government, its meaning and purpose, its various forms and consequence, was replaced with the nasty vindictiveness of the struggle for personal power.

lacking in self-awareness and awareness of the sensitivities and needs of their fellow citizens.‡‡ This is so, he says, because in a democratic (i.e., oligarchic) community, "each citizen is habitually engaged in the contemplation of a very puny subject: namely, himself."[12] Needless to say, the American who thinks little of his fellow citizen has even less concern with those who live in countries other than his own. "An American leaves his country with a heart swollen with pride; on arriving in Europe, he at once finds out that we are not so engrossed by the United States and the great people who inhabit it as he had supposed; and this begins to annoy him."[13]

De Tocqueville detects "a strange melancholy" among the Americans.§§ This he attributes to the fact that though they attain an equality of condition, they always want more. "It perpetually retires before them, yet without hiding itself from sight, and in retiring draws them on.... They are near enough to see its charms, but too far off to enjoy them; and before they have tasted its delights, they die."[14] In a similar vein, de Tocqueville observes that the American "clutches everything ... [but] holds nothing."[15] He is at once "independent but powerless."[16] He is near people but not connected to them. "He is close to them, but does not see them; he touches them, but he does not feel them; he exists only in himself and for himself alone."[17]

## The Lonely American

It is enlightening to compare de Tocqueville's critique of the American character with the thoughts of the American transcendental philosopher Ralph Waldo Emerson (1803–1882). Writing at the same time as de Tocqueville, Emerson echoes de Tocqueville's thoughts, but with approval, not condemnation. In Emerson's writings, the individual is portrayed as being detached and isolated from others. What, in fact, has its locus outside the head, in the world of human interaction and public affairs, is internalized. The individual becomes "self-possessed." He becomes his own private property. He is his own self-contained nation-state, wanting nothing from the external world.¶¶

Emerson was a loner and an isolate and developed a philosophy of life that consecrated the individual's separateness and lack of com-

---

‡‡ Says the aristocratic de Tocqueville, "I have often noticed in the United States, that it is not easy to make a man understand that his presence may be dispensed with; hints will not suffice to shake him off.... This man will never understand that he wearies me to death unless I tell him so, and the only way to get rid of him is to make him my enemy for life." *Democracy in America*, Vol. 2, p. 182.

§§ De Tocqueville was writing in the 1830s. How much more unhappy and insecure is the American today? Consider how many millions are taking some form of psychotropic medication, how many others abuse alcohol and other drugs. Consider how many self-help books are sold each year, as Americans continue their desperate search for something that will make them feel better.

¶¶ "The wise man," writes Emerson, "is the state." *Emerson's Essays*, p. 206.

munity involvement. "Let man stand erect, go alone, and possess the universe."[18] "Build therefore your own world."[19] "Do not seek yourself outside yourself" ["*Ne te quaesiveris extra*"].[20] "Man," we learn, "is insular and cannot be touched ... and holds his individual being on that condition."[21] These are the words of a man unto himself, for himself, by himself, who believes that by extension that is where we all belong. This, as de Tocqueville would see it, describes the typical American.

Writing in 1970, Philip E. Slater, in *The Pursuit of Loneliness*, offers a description of the American character that resonates with the thoughts of de Tocqueville and Emerson, thoughts that were penned some one hundred forty years earlier. Basically, as Slater sees it, Americans are lonely, isolated, and bereft of emotion. "Re-entering America, one is struck first of all by the grim monotony of American facial expressions—hard, surly and bitter—and the aura of deprivation that informs them."[22] Here we have another witness.

Anaïs Nin (1903–1977) is the author of published journals that span more than sixty years, beginning when she was eleven years old and ending shortly before her death. Nin was born in France and immigrated to the United States with her mother and two brothers in 1914, at the age of eleven. About a decade later, after marrying, she returned to France. Subsequently, she made return trips to the United States, where she ultimately spent the last part of her life. Nin is an astute observer with extensive experience in both Europe and the United States. She draws a contrast between Paris and New York:

> In Paris, when entering a room, everyone pays attention, seeks to make you feel welcome, to enter into conversation, is curious, responsive. Here it seems everyone is pretending not to see, hear or look too intently. The faces reveal no interest, no responsiveness.
>
> Overtones are missing. Relationships seem impersonal and everyone conceals his secret life, whereas in Paris it was the exciting substance of our talks, intimate revelations and sharing of experience.[23]

Nin expresses her concern over the American "cult of toughness, its hatred of sensitivity" and issues a warning: "Someday [America] may have to pay a terrible price for this, because atrophy of feeling creates criminals."[24] Here is another vignette, written in 1940:

> No place to sit and talk. You are rushed by the waitress. The radios blare so loudly one is deafened. The lights stun you. Noise and light amplified until the senses become dulled....
>
> In Europe the machines are killing people. Here the machines seem to have dehumanized people. There are few amenities, the softening use of courtesy to palliate the cruelties of life. Under the guise of honesty people are brutal to each other.[25]

This lonely, empty, harsh feeling is a consequence of the pursuit of a separate, private life of self-sufficiency, from which community and collective needs are excluded. "We seek more and more privacy and feel more and more alienated and lonely when we get it."[26] The suburban ideal, which so many Americans pursue, Slater describes as follows:

> The suburban dweller seeks peace, privacy, nature, community, and a child-rearing environment which is healthy and culturally optimal. Instead he finds neither the beauty and serenity of the countryside, the stimulation of the city, nor the stability and sense of community of the small town, and his children are exposed to a cultural deprivation equaling that of any slum child with a television set.[27]***

The pursuit of the American dream has its roots in the need to escape, evade, and avoid.[28] As a consequence, the capacities to enjoy and attain fulfillment are stunted. Americans have a craving to belong but "have a profound tendency to feel like outsiders—they wonder where the action is and wander about in search of it."[29] The isolation and passivity lead to feelings of powerlessness, which the American devotes himself to denying and escaping.†††

Americans are insecure, constantly in pursuit of a feeling of security, which they never attain. There is an underlying anxiety that leans toward paranoia. According to Slater, "Americans devote more of their collective resources to security than any other need."[30] The unrelenting anti-Communism of the 1950s could be offered as one example of this phenomenon. The ease with which Americans commit themselves to a course of war and killing is another illustration of their continual attempts to achieve safety and security.

An inner sense of vague foreboding leads Americans to acquiesce to just about any government action that makes them feel better. Torture—which had been consigned to a time of primitive barbarism—is currently openly acknowledged, debated, and accepted by many. Americans are even willing to see their basic civil rights abrogated, all in the hope of squelching the ever-present anxiety. The Patriot Act, signed into

---

*** Here is de Tocqueville's version: "In the United States a man builds a house in which to spend his old age, and he sells it before the roof is on; he plants a garden and lets it just as the trees are coming into bearing; he brings a field into tillage and leaves other men to gather the crops; he embraces a profession and gives it up; ... [he gets a few days vacation and he travels] fifteen hundred miles in a few days to shake off his happiness ... [in] his bootless chase of that complete felicity which forever escapes him." *Democracy in America*, Vol. 2, pp. 144–145.

††† "The oppressed," says Brazilian educator Paolo Freire, "are not only powerless, but reconciled to their powerlessness, perceiving it fatalistically, as a consequence of personal inadequacy or failure. The ultimate product of highly unequal power relationships is a class unable to articulate its own interests or perceive the existence of social conflict." Max Weber takes the argument a step further and actually speaks of "the will to powerlessness." Freire quoted in Roy Madron and John Jopling, *Gaian Democracies*, p. 115; Weber, *Political Writings*, p. 270.

law on October 26, 2001, allows for the indefinite detention of immigrants; searches of homes or businesses without warrant; and searches
of telephone, e-mail, medical, financial, and library records. ‡‡‡

Americans are fearful and they are angry. Deep down they are angry
with government/parent for lying to them and betraying them. But the
anger rarely, if ever, is outwardly directed at the government. Instead, it
is taken out on immigrants, foreigners, racial minorities, and enemies
real or imagined. For years, the American government has indefinitely
held foreign nationals deemed to be "terrorists," without charges and
without trials, subjecting them to torture and other inhumane treatment.

The United States spends more on its military than the other countries
of the world combined. It has about a quarter million troops stationed
in one hundred thirty countries. By 1990, Pentagon property was valued
at $1 trillion. The U.S. military controls 18 million acres of land world-
wide. With 5.1 million employees, it is the nation's largest employer.[31]

## The Credulous American

Here is another portrait of the American character, this one even more
recent. With a book bearing the foreboding title *Dark Ages America:
The Final Phase of Empire* (2006), Morris Berman, like Philip Slater,
continues with the same motifs initially identified by de Tocqueville.§§§

Americans are lost and alone, clinging to what eludes them. Speaking for Americans, Berman declares, "We are desperate today for
community because we have been lonely and alienated for so long."[32]
He paraphrases Mother Teresa's view on America's spiritual poverty:
"America's poverty ... is worse than that of India's, for it is that of
a terrible loneliness that comes from wanting the wrong things."[33] As
but one example, Berman cites an incident in Orange City, Florida. On
November 28, 2003, Walmart had a sale. A woman was trampled to
a state of unconsciousness by the stampede of eager shoppers. They
wouldn't even move aside for rescue workers, who found the victim

---

‡‡‡ On December 31, 2011, President Barack Obama signed the controversial
National Defense Authorization Act (NDAA) into law. The bill allows the government
to hand over suspected terrorists to the military for indefinite detention—including
U.S. citizens. Suspects are also subjected to potentially being held on foreign soil in
facilities like Guantanamo Bay. People under scrutiny by the NDAA are tried under
a military tribunal instead of a judicial court, violating their Fourth Amendment
rights. In other words, what the Patriot Act did for immigrants, the NDAA does for
American citizens.
§§§ Walter A. McDougall, in *Freedom Just Around the Corner: A New American History, 1585–1828*, has a different take. The American is a con-man, he says. He makes
his point with a lengthy discussion of Herman Melville's *The Confidence-Man*. He then
quotes from M. G. Jean de Crèvecoeur's 1782 *Letters from an American Farmer*. Americans, says Crèvecoeur, are "litigious, overbearing, purse-proud," their society "a general
mass of keenness and sagacious acting against another mass of equal sagacity. Happy when
it does not degenerate into fraud against fraud." "Who is this new man, this American?"
asks McDougall. "As Melville would certainly have it, he or she is a hustler" (p. 4).

slumped over, clutching her DVD player—an apt expression of the self-ish individualism of the average American. When it gets down to basics, says Berman, "America is about as diverse as a one string guitar."[34]

For many Americans, the isolation, the loneliness, brings out a craving for something bigger, an all-encompassing belief to hold on to and bring meaning to their lives. This is where the myth of America comes into play, erected on a foundation of rhetorical democracy. Thus, though Americans are denied the opportunity to govern themselves and are cut loose from meaningful connections to community and one another, they *believe* that they are living in a democratic nation and that their democratic values are what set them apart from the rest of humanity and endow them with the holy mission of saving the world. "Americanism, in short: that is our religion," says Berman.[35]

Religion does not admit of analysis or critique, which is why Americans are incapable of taking an objective, analytic look at their culture and government. One does not question religion. One does not question the beneficence of one's government and its leaders. As Berman points out, only in America is it possible to be "un-American" by disagreeing with one's government. There is no such thing as being "un-Italian" or "un-Danish."[36]

Americans, as a rule, are very gullible and hence easy to manipulate. They believe what their government, via the media, tells them to believe. Anyone who thinks otherwise is a "conspiracy nut." Berman puts it bluntly: "in other countries grown-ups know there is no truth teat to suck on."[37] Like small children, Americans trust their parents—that is, their government and the people who speak for it—and like small children they have a desperate need to be taken care of, to be "okay." They believe what the commercials tell them about various drugs and foods, usually unquestioningly, frequently with dire consequences for their mental and physical health. Bombarded with endless amounts of "information," Americans are notoriously ignorant about the world they live in, including and especially their own country.

Berman, like other writers, makes reference to "the endless restlessness that is so characteristic of America"[38] and observes that though they are always on the move, Americans are "extremely nervous about real change."[39] He offers this quote from the American poet W. H. Auden, from "The Age of Anxiety": "We would rather be ruined than changed."[40] Berman also quotes Nicholas von Hoffman, who describes Americans as living in a glass dome, a sort of terrarium, cut off from reality and the outside world. "Bobbleheads in Bubbleland," Hoffman calls them. "They shop in bubbled malls, they live in gated communities, and they move from place to place breathing their own, private air, in the bubble-mobiles known as SUVs."[41]

It is not surprising that, living in isolation, in "Bubbleland," Americans are anxious, insecure, and fearful. From such a condition—in which one is detached from community both national and international, ignorant of the various political forces at play, subject to manipulation by the media on behalf of a government that wishes to intimidate as a means of exercising control—it is not surprising that Americans should be prone to violence. The detachment, the separation from and misunderstanding of the root causes of power dynamics, results in chronic insecurity and the need to defend oneself against unseen enemies. The homicide rate in the European Union between 1979–1999 was 1.7 per one hundred thousand. In the United States, it was 6.26. In Europe, there is deep-seated opposition to the death penalty. Two-thirds of Americans are in favor of it. The United States routinely engages in ruthless repressions and violent wars on a sustained basis, for the most part unchallenged by the populace whose taxes fund them.

## The Depleted American

Reluctantly, I must agree with three thoughtful writers who have reached the same conclusion over a span of close to one hundred fifty years. Americans are isolated, anxious, insecure, and lonely. One might also argue that the culture that has developed has become what it is so as to provide escape from these very unpleasant conditions. So, if one were to query the average American, putting aside for a moment the economic hardships that persist in 2012, that American might describe himself as the happiest person on earth. Such a response has its basis in denial and the perpetual distraction that contemporary culture provides. The American doesn't know his true feelings and doesn't want to.

One might also reasonably argue that Americans are the way they are because their form of government excludes them from the possibility of the participation that would bring them back to the community in an active way, expanding their emotional and intellectual horizons. After all, as de Tocqueville observes, "Feelings and opinions are recruited, the heart is enlarged, and the human mind is developed only by the reciprocal influence of men upon one another."[42]

Using the United States as his point of reference, and once again misapplying the word "democracy," de Tocqueville makes some thoughtful observations on the relationship between the individual and the state. He says, "In a democratic community individuals are very weak, but the state, which represents them all and contains them all in its grasp, is very powerful.... In democratic communities the imagination is compressed when men think of themselves; it expands indefinitely when they think of the state."[43] One could revise what de Tocqueville has said as follows: 'In a constitutional oligarchy, spread across a vast land mass, where power and control are highly centralized, individuals are very weak.' I think this is an important observation and helps to explain a lot of what has been said about the insecurity, loneliness, and sense of isolation that seem to characterize the average American.

He is made to feel small and powerless by the very existence of a large, powerful central government over which he has no control. He becomes weak and enervated, for "extreme centralization of government ultimately enervates society."[44]

Where there is a big, powerful central government, run by a small oligarchy sharing common interests, and a vast mass of undifferentiated individuals with no valid means for exercising political power, the political situation can easily slide into despotism. De Tocqueville sees a self-enhancing process:

> Thus the vices which despotism produces are precisely those which equality fosters. These two things perniciously complete and assist each other. Equality places men side by side, unconnected by any common tie; despotism raises barriers to keep them asunder; the former disposes them not to consider their fellow creatures, the latter makes general indifference a sort of public virtue.[45]

The equality de Tocqueville refers to—equality of condition—probably never existed to the degree he thinks it did. Even in colonial days, there was gross disparity in wealth, a condition that became more pronounced with the passing of the years. But, more importantly, there is nothing about equality of condition that should keep men asunder. Rather, it is the *political* condition de Tocqueville aptly describes that creates a situation favorable to the emergence of despotism: strong, central government and a mass of individuals with no significant political means at their disposal.

Lacking a true political life, people focus instead on success in business and the pursuit of personal pleasure in their private lives. "They lose sight of the close connection that exists between the private fortune of each and the prosperity of all." Under such circumstances, one would not have to do violence to deprive them of the rights they enjoy: "they themselves willingly loosen their hold."[46]

Having the freedom to pursue one's private interests undisturbed leads to a dread of anarchy, a fear that is sparked by the slightest public commotion. As de Tocqueville puts it, men are willing "to fling away their freedom at the first disturbance." A nation that asks nothing of its government but public tranquility and order "is already a slave at heart, the slave of its own well-being, awaiting only the hand that will bind it." The universal pursuit of private interest leaves an open path to "the smallest parties" who seek to get the upper hand:

> A multitude represented by a few players, who alone speak the name of an absent or inattentive crowd: they alone are in action, while all others are stationary; they regulate everything by their own caprice; they change the laws and tyrannize at will over the manners of the country; and then men wonder to see into how small a number of weak and worthless hands a great people may fall.[47]

Is this not the current condition in the United States? A handful of oligarchs have squandered trillions of dollars on banking interests and foreign wars. Legislation is passed that more and more limits the opportunity to enjoy one's civil rights and engage in meaningful political activity. Americans are cowed by the latest threats of terrorism and pandemic. All of this is the consequence not of democracy, which was explicitly eliminated from consideration by the clique of men who engineered the writing and ratification of the U.S. Constitution. Instead, it is the consequence of a small oligarchy, ruling a vast nation, in which the citizenry has atrophied into a mass of passive, frightened men and women, in the absence of a viable political alternative to the despotism they are living under and don't even understand.

As de Tocqueville points out, there are two kinds of tyranny. Under the Roman emperors, tyranny was odious and obvious. It "was extremely onerous to the few, but it did not reach the many." Of a different nature is tyranny under a constitutional oligarchy, such as exists in the United States. This tyranny "would be more extensive and more mild; it would degrade men without tormenting them."[48] It would be something like living under the tutelage of a parent. However, this is not the parent who seeks to prepare his children for adulthood and then liberate them. This is the parent who seeks to keep the child perpetually passive and dependent. Living in this setting—in which the government ostensibly ministers to the children's needs, controls and oversees their actions—"what remains, but to spare them all the care of thinking and all the trouble of living"? Such a tyranny "every day renders the exercise of the free agency of man less useful and less frequent; it circumscribes the will within a narrower range and gradually robs a man of all uses of himself."[49]

The persistent sense of a lurking presence, the need to conform and acquiesce so as not to trouble the parent who watches over and protects him, the possibility of action leading to independence and adulthood having been eliminated, man is reduced to a state of flabby self-indulgence, which he labels "freedom." In the grips of such a presence, de Tocqueville tells us:

> The will of man is not shattered, but softened, bent, and guided; men are seldom forced by it to act, but they are constantly restrained from acting. Such a power does not destroy, but it prevents existence; it does not tyrannize, but it compresses, enervates, extinguishes, and stupefies a people, till [the] nation is reduced to nothing better than a flock of timid and industrious animals, of which the government is the shepherd.[50] ¶¶¶

The power to bend an entire nation to such tutelage requires deception. The population submits so gently because it believes it is doing so

---

¶¶¶ Gore Vidal has referred to Americans as "sheeple."

voluntarily. This is where the notion of "popular sovereignty" comes in. Always remember, the voice of government tells us, that you, the people, rule and that you, the people, choose your rulers. Thus, de Tocqueville explains, "Every man allows himself to be put in leading-strings, because he sees [that is, he *believes*] that it is not a person or a class of persons, but the people at large who hold the end of his chain." By such a system as this—through elections—"the people shake off their state of dependence just long enough to select their master and then relapse into it again."[51]

Writing more than one hundred fifty years ago, when the electorate was probably more cognizant of its political potential and less thoroughly lulled into a state of quiescence than it is today, de Tocqueville could nonetheless declare, without hesitation:

> It is in vain to summon a people who have been rendered so dependent on the central power to choose from time to time the representatives of that power; this rare and brief exercise of their free choice, however important it may be, will not prevent them from gradually losing the faculties of thinking, feeling and acting for themselves, and thus gradually falling below the level of humanity.[52]

It is folly to believe that those who have been deprived of self-government "should succeed in making a proper choice of those by whom they are to be governed." It is folly to assume that a subservient people will choose to be led by "a liberal, wise, and energetic government."[53]

## The Trivialization of Public Life

De Tocqueville set out all of this in the 1830s. C. Wright Mills, in *The Power Elite* (published in 1956), more than a century later, described in detail the same process de Tocqueville had alluded to. The individual loses his substance by voluntarily bowing to an overpowering and distant oligarchy, while simultaneously "participating" in sham democracy.

Mills speaks of the "grim trivialization of public life." He describes the election of 1954, where national issues of substance were ignored in favor of slander and personal attack, which initially entertained and then alienated prospective voters. "Slogans and personal attacks on character, personal defects, and counter-charges and suspicions were all that the electorate could see or hear, and, as usual, many paid no attention at all."[54]****

---

**** What Mills neglects to mention is that the tawdry nature of electoral campaigns was characteristic of national politics from the beginning. The oligarchy created under the U.S. Constitution in 1787 spawned a vicious competition for personal power that has continued unabated ever since. The Federalists and Alexander Hamilton were spoken for by *The Gazette of the United States*. Thomas Jefferson and the Republicans could count on Philip Freneau's *The National Gazette*. The virulence of the personal attacks makes today's campaigns seem gentlemanly by comparison.

Mills hypothesizes the existence of various local publics, or community discussion groups/parties that represent a specific set of opinions and viewpoints. Such publics are scattered throughout the country, interact with each other, and in some way or another bring their beliefs to the attention of those in power. Public opinion in this version of government has a means of bearing down on elected officials and gaining their cooperation. The discussions themselves, these local interactions, are the mechanism by which the individual educates himself and articulates his viewpoints.

This version, says Mills, is "a fairy tale." In fact, this "community of publics" has been transformed into a "society of masses."[55] Belonging to this mass serves to annihilate the individual and his capacity for honest self-expression. Politically, he becomes a phantom, a shadow on the wall, and nothing more. The political process Mills describes is more like a ballet or a silent movie than an active polity shaping its own destiny. Everyone has a role to play in convincing himself and the next person that democracy exists and that he is actively participating in an act of self-government. "What the public stands for, accordingly, is often a vagueness of policy (called open-mindedness), a lack of involvement in public affairs (known as reasonableness), and a professional disinterest (known as tolerance)."[56]

When a man is part of the masses, says Mills, he lacks "any sense of political belonging." He lacks the political community, where there is shared belief in the purposes of the organization and trust in its leadership. To have political belonging is "to make the human association a psychological center of one's self, to take into our conscience, deliberately and freely, its rules of conduct and its purposes, which we thus shape and which in turn shape us." This kind of political association is a place "in which reasonable opinions can be formulated." It is "an agency by which reasonable activities may be undertaken." And it is powerful enough "to make a difference."[57] Thus, our psychological existence is determined, as adults in the world, by the opportunity we are given to partake in the process of determining those policies and acts of legislation that shape the content and context of our social living. In the absence of such an opportunity, we cease to exist.

As Mills saw it, the political power dynamics of the 1950s were such that there was no opportunity for the individual to engage in political struggle and thus develop into a full adult with political beliefs and a sense of empowerment. What he describes of the political culture he knew is even truer today than it was fifty years ago. On the one hand, there is "the huge corporation, the inaccessible government, the grim military establishment." On the other, we find "the family and the small community." There is nothing in between, "no intermediate associations in which men feel secure and with which they feel powerful." As a consequence, there is "little live political struggle."[58]

In such a context, where political reality has been flattened into a two-dimensional, cardboard cutout, there really is no such thing as "public opinion," because there is no genuine public, just the anonymous mass. As Mills observes, "Public opinion exists when people who are not in the government of a country claim the right to express political opinions freely and publicly, and the right that these opinions should influence or determine the policies, personnel, and actions of their government."[59]

As Mills makes clear, public opinion is not what some polling organization reports to the news media after knocking on a few doors. Public opinion has efficacy, or it is nothing. For example, in February of 2003, millions of people demonstrated in the United States and around the world against an invasion of Iraq. As subsequent events have come to prove, public opinion counted for nothing. In 2008–2009, trillions of dollars were given away to a handful of bankers as the world economy crumbled. There is a hardly a man or woman standing, anywhere in the world—other than the aforementioned handful of bankers—who supported such a policy. Yet the plunder of the public treasury continues. Public opinion counts for nothing. The crowds disperse, "atomized and submissive masses."[60] As these examples demonstrate, public opinion is not something to be honored and respected, it is something to be shaped, manipulated, and controlled, just as Edward Bernays predicted in the 1920s.[††††]

Although the conditions Mills outlines have existed since the days of de Tocqueville and even earlier, there is at least one factor that deserves special mention: the media. Mills uses the term "psychological illiteracy" to refer to the fact that our knowledge of what is real in the world of politics and power is shaped for us by the media. We have little or no first-hand knowledge. A reality is created for us, which we come to believe in. "Our standards of credulity, our standards of reality, tend to be set by these media rather than by our own fragmentary experience."[61]

To resist the media—to see behind one reality to the other—we need a context of meaning, which of course the media do not supply. But if we allow ourselves to delve deeper into meanings, if we leave the realm of stereotypes to enter the realm of real beings and real events, we separate ourselves from those around us and raise our level of anxiety and sense of isolation.

If we want to free ourselves, we have to accept the fact that there are two different realities—one that is pleasant and comforting and the other that is devious and sinister. We have to accept the fact that we are being lied to and manipulated. Yet, if we are willing "to accept opinions in their terms," we "gain the good solid feeling of being correct without having to think."[62]

The media, says Mills—especially television—not only affect how we see external reality, they affect how we see ourselves. They give us our sense of self. They give us our identity. Thus, if we attempt to see

---

†††† Bernays' view is discussed in Chapter 2.

deeper and further, we raise fundamental issues about who we are and how we fit in. Not a very reassuring prospect.

And, most critically, even when the media supply simple, accurate information about the state of the world, they present it in such a way as to make it difficult if not impossible for the individual "to connect his daily life with these larger realities. They do not connect the information they provide on public issues with the troubles felt by the individual. They do not increase rational insight into tensions, either those in the individual or those of the society which are reflected in the individual."[63] In other words, though Americans typically feel cut off from the world around them, in fact, they are deeply affected by what occurs in that world. There is a connection between the tension and suffering in the world and the tensions they feel on a daily basis, but they have been trained to ignore the connection and to believe that they are blissfully content in their private universe. The American does not understand that his personal troubles are shared by others, that they have political implications, that personal troubles often need to be translated into public issues for them to be properly resolved. "They lose sight of the close connection that exists between the private fortune of each and the prosperity of all."[64]

As Mills points out, it is not only the media that fail us in our attempts to stay connected to social reality and be effective in shaping our destinies. Education has a large role to play, as well. It trains us vocationally. It inculcates the values and national loyalties required to maintain the status quo. We are not trained to think critically, to analyze. We are trained to get ahead. We mistake job advancement for self-development, which it is not. "Mass education ... has become—another mass medium."[65] Our schools and colleges fail us. They should train us for "the struggle for individual and public transcendence."[66] Instead, they school us in acquiescence, stereotypes, and blind loyalties.

Americans lead narrow and fragmented lives. Confined by their routines to a repetitive existence, they are denied the opportunity for genuine discussion, debate, and conflict of opinion—which could redirect their energies from the immediate task at hand to the grander issues. They lack a sense of the larger structure and their place in it. "In every major area of life, the loss of a sense of structure and the submergence into powerless milieux is the cardinal fact."[67] Unable to see the whole or his place in it, the American submits to vague inevitability that he can neither comprehend nor avoid. There is no outer dialogue, nor is there an inner dialogue, which we refer to as "thinking."

Unable to transcend his daily existence, the mass man "drifts, he fulfills habits, his behavior is a result of a planless mixture of the confused standards and the uncriticized expectations that he has taken over from others."[68] He loses is self-confidence as a human being. He loses his independence. As de Tocqueville puts it, he "allows himself to be put in leading-strings, because he sees that it is not a person or a class of persons, but the people at large who hold the end of his chain."[69]

It is striking the degree to which de Tocqueville and Mills, with more than a century separating them, reach the same conclusions about the nature and quality of American life. Both identify power—power that is hidden and subtle, power that denies itself as power—as the key ingredient in fragmenting the population, creating a mass of "sheeple" who lack the capacity of self-understanding both individually and collectively.

Mills differentiates between authority—power that is visible and explicitly obeyed—and manipulation, where there is "the 'secret' exercise of power, unknown to those who are influenced."[70] When men want to rule without seeming to do so, probably because they cannot lay claim to the required legitimacy, they will rule invisibly and "benignly," shielding themselves behind the rhetoric of popular rule. Although "authority *formally* resides 'in the people,' ... the power of initiation is in fact held by small circles of men." This is not to be known. There is the risk that power becomes identified by its true colors. "That is why the standard strategy of manipulation is to make it appear that the people ... 'really made the decision.'"[71]

Mills identifies "liberal rhetoric which requires a continual flattery of the citizens" as a key ingredient in keeping the masses quiet.[72] Such a rhetoric becomes a mask for all political positions, a means of exercising political power without appearing to do so. This is consistent with my earlier use of the term "rhetorical democracy." It is not that "the people" are in charge, but that they are led to *believe* that they are. As de Tocqueville points out, since the people are submitting to their own will, why should they in any way object?

Thus, the people are their own oppressors and, of course, they don't know it. They don't know they are being tyrannized. They think they are free. "Instead of justifying the power of an elite by portraying it favorably, one denies that any set of men, any class, any organization has any really consequential power."[73] To reiterate what de Tocqueville said, "Such a power does not destroy, but it prevents existence; it does not tyrannize, but it compresses, enervates, extinguishes, and stupefies a people, till [the] nation is reduced to nothing better than a flock of timid and industrious animals, of which the government is the shepherd."[74‡‡‡‡]

---

‡‡‡‡   Such an outcome is consistent with what Wolin has called "inverted totalitarianism," a form of government whose genius "lies in wielding total power without appearing to, without establishing concentration camps, or enforcing ideological uniformity or forcibly suppressing dissident elements so long as they remain ineffectual." *Democracy Incorporated*, p. 57. See the Introduction for a fuller discussion of Wolin's ideas.

# Democracy as Myth

*With high words, that bore*
*Semblance of worth, not substance.*

I T WASN'T UNTIL the twentieth century that the word "democracy" took on its mythic proportions.* Suddenly, governments
everywhere claimed to be "democratic." Populations from around
the world embraced the word and longed for its liberating benefits. What
they were longing for would probably fall under the heading "liberal
democracy." Liberal democracy (L.D.) is, for the most part, a confusing
amalgam of rhetorical democracy (R.D.) and civic democracy (C.D.).
Application of the term vacillates between reference to a form of government and to an ideology.

This version of democracy is largely the handiwork of a small number of academics who see it as their job to promote seemingly rational
discussion on matters of import without saying anything too unsettling.
It is in this context that the expression "liberal democracy" is most likely
to appear.† The United States will be referred to as a liberal democracy. Western democracies will be understood to be liberal democracies.
Problems arise, however, when one attempts to use the phrase in a way
that defines its meaning.

---

* In Chapter 13, I distinguished four types of democracy and used shorthand notation
for referring to them. A fifth type is introduced in this chapter. Here is a quick recap of
the notation being used: Abbreviations are used to refer to civic democracy (C.D.), liberal democracy (L.D.), political democracy (P.D.), rhetorical democracy (R.D.), and social
democracy (S.D.). Presence of a type is indicated by a plus sign (+) attached to the abbrevia-
tion, absence by a minus sign (–).
† Benjamin Barber offers a concise overview of the objectives of liberal democracy: "It
is concerned more to promote individual liberty than to secure public justice, to advance
interests than to discover good, and to keep men safely apart rather than to bring them
fruitfully together." Barber, *Strong Democracy*, p. 4. See pages 3–25 for an excellent analysis and critique of liberal democracy.

## The Liberal Quagmire

Political scientist Michael Margolis, in *Viable Democracy*, expresses this characteristic thought: "Basically liberal democracy emphasizes facilitation of individual development and self-expression as the primary goals of governments."[1] These are noble sentiments, to which many of us might subscribe, but this sentence expresses an ideology, a set of values, that citizens and governors might subscribe to. It does not define or describe a form of government (person or persons in power).

Margolis then goes on to make the following assertions: "Liberal democracy, however, is not synonymous with democracy itself; it is rather a special type of democracy. Governments can be democratic without being liberal. Conversely they can be liberal without being democratic."[2] The problem with this kind of writing is that it makes no sense. The author is mixing apples and elephants. When he says that liberal democracy is "a special type of democracy," he seems to be using the word to refer to a form of government. When he says, "Governments can be democratic without being liberal," he seems to be using the word "liberal" as an adjective to describe an ideology.

Using the USSR as an example of democracy, which clearly it never was,‡ in the political sense, Margolis aptly describes Great Britain and the United States as "examples of liberalism without democracy," that is, countries with civic democracy (C.D.+) but without political democracy (P.D.–). Thus, I cannot for the life of me understand why Margolis insists on joining together the two words "liberal" and "democracy." I find this is all the more confusing because the title of the book—*Viable Democracy*—seems to be referring to democracy as a form of government.

When describing the thoughts of John Locke and Thomas Jefferson, Margolis states that "Government is the servant of the people."[3] Here he is using "government" in its political context. He then goes on to refer to governmental structures and checks and balances. He begins to offer a critique of liberal democracy, observing that his critique "is not limited to the questioning of the adequacy of the governmental structures which have been used to implement it."[4] In this statement, he clearly differentiates between government and liberal democracy as an ideology.

In discussing the difference between fascism and liberal democracy, Margolis writes, "Instead of following his own inclinations, as he does under a liberal democracy, [under fascism] the citizen subjects his will to a higher one."[5] Is liberal democracy here an ideology or a form of government? What about the following? "The equation of modern democracy with pluralistic competition among groups gained widespread acceptance among the emerging generation of political sci-

---

‡ The former USSR would be an example of social democracy (S.D.+) in the absence of political democracy (P.D.–) and civic democracy (C.D.–).

entists."[6] Here there seems to be confusion between government and the competing groups who agitate in favor of their particular interests. Democracy as competition among rival groups is neither an ideology nor a form of government. It is a sideshow that occurs while people in power make decisions with an occasional nod in the direction of one of the rival groups. Once again, the word "democracy" is being used in a way that ignores its core meaning.

And here is yet another example of Margolis using language imprecisely: "Indeed studies of public opinion and voting behavior show that most citizens do not possess the competence to govern directly."[7] Voting is not governing.§ Voting decides who governs. Margolis speaks of "the traditional liberal concern for individual self-improvement, particularly that achieved through political participation."[8] What he means by "participation" is voting once every few years, writing a letter to one's congressman, or carrying a placard in favor of one's cause. Such activity is not governing and will result in little in the way of "self-improvement." The governors are those who propose legislation, debate it, and vote on it.

When Margolis says, "The popularly elected legislature has long been cited as the cornerstone of liberal-democratic polities," he seems to be talking about government. But remember that in the United States today there is a popularly elected legislature of five hundred thirty-five men and women speaking for more than three hundred million souls. That is oligarchy. The only way to make any sense out of this is to assume that when Margolis says "liberal democracy," he means "democratic oligarchy," which, of course, is oxymoronic. And when he says, "The problem arises from our attempt to incorporate democracy and liberalism into our theory of viable democracy,"[9] I am dumbfounded. I can no longer find a way to talk about what he seems to be saying. I can only ask, yet again, what does he mean by "democracy"? What does he mean by "liberalism"? What does he mean by joining the two words into one expression?

At the end of his book, Margolis outlines a few modest proposals— "major reforms"—for making "democracy" more viable, proposals such as "employing modern data-processing technology in service of the ordinary citizens," encouraging whistle-blowing, and improving accounting methods. He then concludes with this jaw-dropping statement: "Regarding government itself [apparently, then, Margolis has not been talking about government], no radical changes are needed."[10] No comment.

This kind of muddled thinking is typical when a writer feels compelled to pay lip service to democracy without having a clear sense of what the word actually means. Any honest discussion of the topic would reveal that democracy, as a form of government, is nowhere to be found in the Western world, or for that matter anywhere else, and that

---

§ Except when there is a referendum.

for more than two hundred years, we in the United States have been ruled by a clique of oligarchs whose personal interests consistently override the common good.

## The Myth of Republicanism

So, if "democracy" is not an accurate descriptor for the American form of government, what about "republic"? This is a word that has been in circulation for more than two thousand years. But is it a word whose meaning can be trusted? Is it a word we can use with confidence in describing government? Unfortunately, "republic" is probably as confusing and diverse in its meaning and applications as its sister word "democracy." This is the word substituted for "democracy" by the Quids as a means of advancing their economic program while simultaneously placating advocates of democracy.¶ Americans have gone along with the Quids, routinely pledging allegiance to a flag, and the republic for which it stands, without really understanding what any of that means.**

Writers like Thomas Jefferson and James Madison used the term "republic" frequently. In the *Federalist Papers*, No. 10, Madison describes the republican form of government as "a government in which the scheme of representation takes place," in which there is "the delegation of the government ... to a small number of citizens elected by the rest."[11]†† Is this any different from oligarchy?

In *De l'Esprit des Lois*, written in 1748, Montesquieu‡‡ defines republican government as one in which "the people as a body, or some part of the people, holds sovereign power."§§ When, in a republic, the power is in the hands of the people as a whole, says Montesquieu, that republic is known as a democracy. When the sovereign power is in the hands of a part of the people, that republic is known as an aristocracy.[12]

---

¶ The maneuverings of the Quids are discussed in Chapter 12.

** The story of the Pledge of Allegiance is quintessentially American. The Pledge was written for the popular children's magazine *The Youth's Companion* by socialist author and Baptist minister Francis Bellamy and was first published on September 8, 1892. The owners of *The Youth's Companion* were selling flags to schools, and they approached Bellamy to write the Pledge for their advertising campaign. The Pledge (along with a new flag, of course) was marketed as a way to celebrate the four hundredth anniversary of Columbus arriving in the Americas. After a proclamation by President Benjamin Harrison, the Pledge was first used in public schools on October 12, 1892, during Columbus Day observances. Thus, this "patriotic" pledge was nothing more than a marketing gimmick.

†† But Jean-Jacques Rousseau argues that the people are sovereign and that sovereignty, the general will, cannot be represented. He opines, "The deputies of the people therefore are not and cannot be its representatives, they are merely its agents; they cannot conclude anything definitively. Any law which the People has not ratified in person is null; it is not a law. The English people thinks it is free; it is greatly mistaken, it is free only during the election of Members of Parliament; as soon as they are elected, it is enslaved, it is nothing." *Du Contrat Social*, pp. 301–302.

‡‡ Charles-Louis de Secondat, Baron de La Brède et de Montesquieu (1689–1755), more commonly known as Montesquieu, was a French social commentator and political thinker who lived during the Enlightenment. He is best known for *De l'Esprit des Lois* (*The Spirit of the Laws*).

§§ Author's translation.

I find this confusing. Why do we need the word "republic" at all if what we mean is "democracy" or "aristocracy"?

Turning to Plato's *Republic* in search of clarification only adds to the confusion. First of all, Plato never wrote a book entitled *The Republic*. He did write a book entitled *Politeia*, as did Aristotle, whose work has come to us as *Politics*. Why are things different for Plato's work? Cicero (106 B.C.–43 B.C.), Roman statesman, lawyer, political theorist, philosopher, widely considered one of Rome's greatest orators and prose stylists, wrote a book entitled *De republica* between 54 and 51 B.C. Using the Socratic dialogue format—as did Plato—Cicero offered his views on government as the Roman Republic was nearing its end. Though Cicero claimed that a free state was the most desirable form of government and that the worst calamity would be "for a people to permanently renounce this ideal and to substitute for it the slave's ideal of a good master," it is his title *De republica* that has been applied to Plato's work, which advocates the very enslavement Cicero opposed.

In Plato's *Republic*, the highest good is a unified state under the rule of a highly trained and carefully selected aristocracy. The state is built around the needs and education of the Guardians, those who protect the state from foreign enemies, maintain order at home, and enforce the decisions of the Rulers. Anything that will undermine the austerity and "virtue" of the Guardians is to be banned from the state. This results in the careful selection of artistic expression that is acceptable and the banning of everything else. The flute is outlawed. Poets and craftsmen who do not create art of noble character are expelled.

The censorship and control begin in the earliest years. Children will be exposed to certain stories and not others. Children are to be seen and not heard. They are to be trained in obedience from an early age. The musical modes—Mixed Lydian and Hyperlydian—that are used in the composition of dirges and laments are disallowed because they encourage a certain kind of emotion that would have a weakening effect on the Guardians, the warrior class. Passion and emotion of all kind are discouraged, as is violent laughter, for the same reason. There is no room for sexual frenzy. Only pleasure of a moderate and disciplined nature is acceptable.

The creation of the warrior class—the Guardians—from which the Rulers are drawn, requires that those of good stock and robust nature are well attended to while the weak are allowed to die. Those who are corrupt in mind will be put to death. Breeding of the Guardian class will be controlled by the state. There will be mating festivals. Offspring will remain anonymous. Parents will not know their child. The child will not know his parents. The state will assume responsibility for those who are of superior quality. From these, the Rulers will be drawn.

The Guardians are not to own property. They are to discourage either extreme wealth or poverty. Their numbers are to be drawn from women as well as men. Both sexes are given equal opportunity, based on merit. Those of inferior quality will be ruled. It is the job of the ruled to obey without questioning. Everyone is to know his place in society and not to diverge. Truth is a virtue. But government will sometimes deceive when it believes it is to the benefit of the governed.

The government described in Plato's *Republic* is designed specifically to exclude any involvement of the governed in the affairs of government (P.D.–). Civic democracy is excluded as well. Thought and expression are the provenance of state control (C.D.–). However, there are strong elements of social democracy. Wealth and poverty are not tolerated (S.D.+). Women are the equal of men (S.D.+).

Fascism has been defined as "an authoritarian political ideology (generally tied to a mass movement) that considers individual and other societal interests inferior to the needs of the state, and seeks to forge a type of national unity, usually based on ethnic, religious, cultural, or racial attributes."[¶¶] If there is a significant difference between fascism thus defined and the society enunciated in Plato's *Republic*,[***] in which the state is supreme and submission to a warrior class is the highest virtue, I fail to detect it.[†††] What is noteworthy is that Plato's *Republic* is probably the most widely known and widely read of political texts, certainly in the United States, and that the word "republic" has come to be associated with democracy and a wholesome and free way of life in which individual self-expression is a centerpiece.

To further appreciate the difficulty that exists in trying to attach specific meaning to the word "republic," one need only consult the online encyclopedia Wikipedia.[‡‡‡] There one will find a long list of republics divided by period and type. As of this writing (late November 2011),

---

[¶¶]   This particular definition is widely cited online. Any number of definitions, differing in certain particulars and coming from an array of scholarly and popular sources, could be provided, but this one covers the basics nicely for the current purpose.

[***]   The Viennese philosopher Karl Popper warned that teaching students Plato would turn them into "little fascists" (quoted in David Edmonds and John Eidinow, *Wittgenstein's Poker: The Story of a Ten-Minute Argument Between Two Great Philosophers*, p. 179). Cambridge University Press refused to publish Popper's book *The Open Society and Its Enemies* because of its disrespectful treatment of Plato, a common practice in "liberal democracy," where a self-censoring middle class will do anything to protect its status and stifle original thought.

[†††]   One can also detect parallels between the *Republic* and the former USSR. The expressed goal of the Soviet Union was to eliminate wealth and poverty (S.D.+). Men and women were to be treated as equals (S.D.+). The country was ruled by an oligarchy (P.D.–). There was strict control over artistic expression (C.D.–).

[‡‡‡]   In its own words, "Wikipedia is a multilingual, web-based, free-content encyclopedia project." Wikipedia accounts are written collaboratively by volunteers from all around the world. In this sense, it is a democratic project. All can contribute. There is minimal editorial control. Of late, there has been some controversy concerning Wikipedia's reliability on controversial matters. Individuals and government organizations who disapprove of certain content are changing it at will. One could say this is how democracy works. But why not retain the original and all the variations? That way we could see what was changed and why. I have confined my usage of Wikipedia to routine, noncontroversial information.

there are five listings by period (Antiquity, Middle Ages and Renaissance, Early Modern, 19th Century, and 20th Century and Later), encompassing 90 separate republics covered in Wikipedia. The list of republic types is broken down into eight categories (Unitary Republics, Federal Republics, Confederal Republics, Arab Republics, Islamic Republics, Democratic Republics, Socialist Republics, and People's Republics), with a total of 226 entries. There is some overlap between the lists, but one is still left with roughly 300 republics—and roughly 300 ideas of what, exactly, constitutes a republic.

One might reasonably wonder what useful meaning the word "republic" can possibly have when applied in such diverse political contexts. The word—from "*res publica*," an expression of Roman (i.e., Latin) origin—might indeed apply to the Roman Republic, but how can it have any meaning when applied to ancient Athens, which had a radically different form of government existing in roughly the same time frame, and where *res publica* would have no meaning whatsoever?

Let us recall what was going on in Rome in the time of the Republic. Defined as the period from the expulsion of the Etruscan kings (509 B.C.) until Julius Caesar's elevation to dictator for life (44 B.C.),§§§ the Roman Republic covered a span of close to five hundred years in which Rome was free of despotism. The title *rex* was forbidden. Anyone taking on kingly airs might be killed on sight. The state of affairs that prevailed during this period reflects the essence of the word "republic": a *condition*—freedom from the tyranny of one-man rule—and not a form of government. In fact, *The American Heritage College Dictionary* offers the following as its first definition for republic: "A political order not headed by a monarch."[13]

The history of France over the past two centuries offers another example of the absence-of-monarch application of the word "republic." In this space of time, France has had five distinct republics, with interspersed periods of autocratic rule. The First French Republic lasted from 1792 to 1804, beginning with the National Convention (1792–1795) and including the period 1799–1804, when Napoleon Bonaparte ruled the country as First Consul. The First Republic ended with the crowning of Napoleon I as emperor in 1804. After the 1814 downfall of Napoleon I,¶¶¶ rule by a monarch continued with the restoration of the Bourbon Dynasty and the reigns of Louis XVIII (1814–1824), Charles X (1824–1830), and Louis Philippe, "the Citizen King" (1830–1848). A revolution ushered in the Second Republic, which lasted only four years (1848–1852), ending when Louis-Napoléon Bonaparte (nephew of Napoleon I) declared himself emperor. He ruled as Napoleon III

---

§§§ And a short life it was after that. Caesar was assassinated just a month later, on March 15, the Ides of March.

¶¶¶ After the Battle of Waterloo, Napoleon I abdicated, making his son the titular Emperor of France. Napoleon II never ruled, however.

until 1870, when he was captured during the Franco-Prussian War and subsequently deposed by the French, thus initiating the Third Republic (1870–1940), which ended when the Germans invaded France. The Fourth Republic was instituted in 1946 and lasted until 1958, when the Fifth Republic was founded with the adoption of a new constitution drafted under the leadership of Charles de Gaulle. The Fifth Republic continues today. What one notices in this brief overview of French history is that when there is a republic, there is no monarchy, and when there is a monarchy, there is no republic.

John Adams (1735–1826), second President of the United States and one of the prime movers behind the U.S. Constitution, wrote a three-volume study of government entitled *Defence of the Constitutions of Government of the United States of America* (published in 1787), in which he relies on the writings of Cicero as his guide in applying Roman principles to American government.**** From Cicero he learned the importance of mixed governments,†††† that is, governments formed from a mixture of monarchy, aristocracy, and democracy. According to this line of reasoning, a republic is a non-monarchy in which there are monarchic, aristocratic, and democratic elements. For me, this is confusing. Why, if one had just shed blood in unburdening oneself of monarchy, with a full understanding of just how pernicious such a form of government can be, would one then think it wise or desirable to voluntarily incorporate some form of monarchy into one's new "republican" government? If the word "republic" has any meaning at all, it means freedom from monarchy.

The problem with establishing a republic in the United States was that the word had no fixed meaning to the very people who were attempting to apply it. In *Federalist* No. 6, Alexander Hamilton says that "Sparta, Athens, Rome and Carthage were all republics."[14] Of the four mentioned, Rome is probably the only one that even partially qualifies according to Madison's definition from *Federalist* No. 10 (noted earlier): "a government in which the scheme of representation takes place," in which government is delegated "to a small number of citizens elected by the rest."[15]

Madison himself acknowledges that there is a "confounding of a republic with a democracy" and that people apply "to the former reasons

---

**** Cicero may not have been the best role model, however. In addition to being a senator and an orator, he was a slaveholder and slumlord, described by one contemporary as "the greatest boaster alive," a man of great wealth with nothing but contempt for the needs of the common man, or as Cicero would say, "the common herd." See Chapter 5, "Cicero's Witch-Hunt," in Michael Parenti's *The Assassination of Julius Caesar: A People's History of Ancient Rome.*

†††† The notion that the ideal government is a mix of the three basic forms of government—monarchy, aristocracy, and democracy—goes all the way back to Aristotle. According to Michael Parenti, "In actual practice, the diversity of form ... has been a subterfuge, allowing an appearance of popular participation in order to lend legitimacy to oligarchic dominance." *The Assassination of Julius Caesar,* p. 57.

drawn from the nature of the latter."[16] He later points out that were one trying to define "republic" based on existing examples, one would be at a loss to determine the common elements. He then goes on to contrast the governments of Holland, Venice, Poland, and England, all allegedly republics, concluding that "These examples ... are nearly as dissimilar to each other as to a genuine republic" and show "the extreme inaccuracy with which the term has been used in political disquisitions."[17]

Thomas Paine offers a different viewpoint: "What is now called a *republic*, is not any *particular form* of government. It is wholly characteristical [*sic*] of the purport, matter, or object for which government ought to be instituted, and on which it is to be employed, *res-publica*, the public affairs or the public good"[18] (italics in the original). In other words, as Paine sees it, "*res-publica*" describes the subject matter of government, not its form.

Given all the confusion about the most basic issues relating to the meaning of "republic," what is one to do? Perhaps the wisest course would be to abandon the term altogether in discussions of government. Let us grant the word has important historical meaning and some rhetorical appeal. "Vive la Republique!" can certainly mean thank God we are free of the tyranny of one-man, hereditary rule. That surely is the sense the word had in early Rome, in the early days of the United States, and in some if not all of the French and Italian republics. Thus understood, "republic" refers to a condition—freedom from monarchy—not a form of government.

But if one does away with the word "republic," and America under the Constitution was not intended to be a democracy, as Madison repeatedly made clear, then how *do* we describe America's form of government?

In his *Politics*, Aristotle makes the choices simple. "The true forms of government," he says, "are those in which the one or the few, or the many govern." When one rules, it is called "kingship or royalty." Today we might say monarchy, or perhaps autocracy. The rule of the few, he refers to as "aristocracy." When the citizens at large "administer the state for the common interest, the government is called by the generic name—a constitution."‡‡‡‡ These are the terms applied when those who rule—the one, the few, or the many—serve the common interest. These same forms become "perversions" when those in charge serve themselves but not the common good. When the monarch serves his own interests, the government is known as a tyranny. When the few serve their own interests, the government is an oligarchy. When the citizens at large take care of the needy at the expense of the common good, that government is known as a democracy.[19]§§§§

---

‡‡‡‡   Aristotle also uses the word "polity" when speaking of government of the many.
§§§§ Remember, Aristotle was born into the aristocracy. He lived and wrote in fourth-century B.C. Athens as democracy was fading. He was no friend of democracy. However, his denigration of the word "democracy" does not prevent us from using his work to get a grasp

Armed with our insights from Aristotle, let's consider the government of the United States again. We now know it is neither a republic nor a democracy, but just what is it? It is an oligarchy—government by "a small number of citizens." The word "aristocracy" also applies to rule by the few, but, in Aristotle's political vocabulary, this term is reserved for governors who are both wise and virtuous, a characterization that hardly seems apt in the Western world these days. But it matters little which of the two options one chooses—oligarchy or aristocracy—so long as it is made clear that it is the *few*, not the *many*, who govern. The governments currently known as the "Western democracies" should thus more accurately be known as the "Western oligarchies." Each one of these countries has a representative form of government in which a small number—many of them wealthy and self-interested—speak for the rest.

One might legitimately argue that such a simplified classification does not do justice to the fact that there are wide variations from one oligarchic government to the next. There is a remedy. Earlier I differentiated among political democracy (P.D.), social democracy (S.D.), and civic democracy (C.D.). This framework can be applied to differentiate one government from another. For example, the United States is an oligarchy (P.D.–) with a Bill of Rights and a tradition of allowing political dissent (C.D.+), but with a wide disparity in income and wealth (S.D.–).

## The Electoral Myth

"But," you may object, "we all vote in elections. Isn't that what democracy is all about?" Well, let us see. The governors—the one, the few, or the many—must be selected. I can think of at least four ways this can come about. Selection can be by heredity. You are born into the royal family and become Louis XIV. You accede to the throne on May 14, 1643, a few months before your fifth birthday, assume actual personal control of the government eighteen years later, and remain on the throne for the next fifty-four years.

Or else you can take the government by force. That is what the Frenchman known to us as William the Conqueror did. He invaded England with his Norman army, was victorious in the battle of Hastings in 1066, and thereby became the first in a line of English monarchs that continues unbroken to this day.

Or else you can choose your governors by lot, as was done in ancient Athens and in fifteenth-century Florence.

Or you can vote in an election and thereby choose your governors.

Choosing by lot is the most democratic procedure of all. It establishes political equality by allowing anyone to govern, based on a chance event. There is no opportunity to buy the election or manipulate votes. However, the pool of candidates itself can be open-ended, as it was in

---

on certain fundamental concepts in our attempt to understand government and how it works.

Athens, or, for the most part, confined to the upper elements of society, as it tended to be in Florence. The same applies to elections. The pool of candidates can be open to anyone or it can be restricted by membership in a particular party, by property qualification, or by wealth. Voting itself can be restricted—by race, sex, social status, wealth, and so on—or suffrage can be universal. But, no matter, because the means of selecting the governors is independent of the form of government. A society can elect an aristocracy or an oligarchy or even a monarch.

At the height of his career, Napoleon Bonaparte was probably the most powerful person in Western Europe. He enjoyed great popularity at home, if not elsewhere. In 1804, he had himself crowned emperor. He held a plebiscite to confirm his authority and received the enthusiastic support he was seeking. In other words, Napoleon held an election to determine if he would be supreme ruler. Let us imagine that there was universal suffrage and that the election was scrupulously fair. Let us also imagine, just for the sake of argument, that the choice was unanimous, that not a single vote was cast to deny Napoleon the title of emperor. Thus we have a completely democratic, honest election with a unanimous outcome. What kind of government do we have the day after this democratic election? Clearly, an autocracy.

Charles V—who made his home in Spain—presided over an empire that was ten times the size of the Roman Empire. He ruled over the Burgundian Netherlands. He was King of Naples and Sicily, Archduke of Austria, King of the Romans (or German King), and Holy Roman Emperor. It was his empire upon which "the sun never set." "Spain" was not the Spain of today, but many separate "Spains," something like the city-states of northern Italy. Charles needed to be declared King in Navarre, Valencia, Aragon, Castile, and Catalonia. In 1516, at the age of sixteen, he was elected King of Aragon, a "republic" with an elective king. The assembly gave notice that "we who are as good as you, make you, who are no better than we, our king. And we will bear true allegiance if you observe our laws and customs; if not, not."[20] Despite these noble sentiments and stipulations, the day after the election the people of Aragon lived under a monarchy.

Thus, there is no causal relation whatsoever between the means of selecting one's governors and the form of government that results from the selection process. In fact, for obvious reasons, any time you have an election as a means of selecting the governor(s), you automatically will have an oligarchy/aristocracy or an autocracy. Why? Because the many select the few or the one. Thus, voting in which *elections* are fully democratic and fair is in fact *anti*-democratic. One cannot have voting and have a democracy at the same time.¶¶¶¶ Remember, it's a numbers

---

¶¶¶¶ Says Aristotle, "the appointment of magistrates by lot is democratic, and the election of them oligarchical." *Politics*, p. 165.

game. The many choose the few. It is the few who govern, even if we choose them at election time.

"But," you may say, "we *choose* them. They are beholden to us." Neither one of these propositions is necessarily true. In his book *The Ruling Class*, Gaetano Mosca observes:

> The fact that a people participates in electoral assemblies does not mean that it directs the government or that the class that is governed chooses its governors.***** It means merely that when the electoral function operates under favorable social conditions it is a tool by which certain political forces are enabled to control and limit the activity of other political forces.[21]

In other words, it *seems* as if we choose and control, but we don't.

As Mosca points out, the deck is always stacked. "When we say that the voters 'choose' their representative, we are using a language that is very inexact. The truth is that the representative *has himself elected* by the voters ... that *his friends have him elected*" (italics in the original). We end up voting for those who are preselected by virtue of their "moral, intellectual and material *means* to force their will upon others, take the lead over the others and command them"[22] (italics in the original).

Thus, in practice, in popular elections, freedom of choice, "though complete theoretically, necessarily becomes null, not to say ludicrous." The voter, for his vote to have meaning, ends up having to choose from among a very small number of contenders, the two or three who have a chance of succeeding, "and the only ones who have any chance of succeeding are those whose candidacies are championed by groups, by committees, by *organized minorities*"[23] (italics in the original).†††††

The relative handful who are selected to speak for the citizenry are rarely, if ever, a random selection. They are rarely, if ever, demographically representative of the population at large. And they are rarely, if ever, open to the wishes of their constituency. Instead, those selected to represent speak not for their constituency but for the organized minorities who put them in power, minorities with certain values in common, "based on considerations of property and taxation, on common material interests, on ties of family, class, religion, sect or political party."[24] Thus, the preselected minority speaks for an even narrower minority

---

***** As Emma Goldman once tersely observed, "If voting changed anything, they'd make it illegal." Goldman (1869–1940) was a writer and lecturer on anarchist philosophy, women's rights, and social issues. She was imprisoned several times for "inciting to riot" and illegally distributing information about birth control.
††††† Here is one more quote to the same effect: "People who argue for their positions in a town meeting are acting like citizens. People who simply drop scraps of paper in a box or pull a lever are not acting like citizens; they are acting like consumers, picking between prepackaged political items. They had nothing to do with the items. All they can do is pick what is. They cannot actively participate in making what should be." Karl Hess, *Community Technology*, p. 10.

who sponsored their candidacy based on a specific set of goals at odds with the needs and wishes of the vast majority. Mosca was writing in the 1930s. What would he say if he knew that it now takes millions of dollars to get elected to the House of Representatives, tens of millions to be elected senator or governor, and close to a billion to be elected president? He would probably say, "I told you so."

"But," you may argue, "we in the United States have a Constitution and a Bill of Rights that protects our civil liberties." Yes, true. However, the Constitution simply guarantees that we live under an oligarchy,‡‡‡‡‡ one that seems to be drifting toward monarchy. As for the first ten amendments, the Bill of Rights, they are critical to our civic democracy (C.D.+)—our rights to self-expression and freedom of movement—but, as important as they are, they do not determine the form of political government we live under.

"Yes, but," you may ask, "didn't Madison say that the people had the last word, that they were sovereign?" Yes, he did *say* that. On several occasions he said that power is *derived* from the people.[25] He also said that the "ultimate authority ... resides in the people alone,"[26] that the people are "the only legitimate fountain of power,"[27] and that they are "the fountain of authority."[28] These are examples of what I call rhetorical democracy (R.D.+, P.D.−)—democracy of words, not deeds, the most frequently encountered kind of democracy in a world dominated by those who oppose true popular government.§§§§§

Once we clear away the mist of myth and rhetoric, we discover that the American government was established by men who needed to placate the people while setting themselves up as arbiters of the new nation's destiny. In a 1991 book entitled *The Rise and Fall of Democracy in Early America, 1630–1789*, Joshua Miller speaks of "the ghostly body politic" and declares that "despite the explicit anti-democratic statements of the Federalists, Americans persist in describing the government they designed as a democracy."[29] This confusion, he maintains, was deliberately created by the Federalists, who used "pseudodemocratic rhetoric"[30] to make it appear as if "popular sovereignty" was the same thing as "popular government." "The Federalists ascribed all power to a mythical entity that could never meet, never deliberate, never take action. The body politic became a ghost."[31] By ascribing all power to "the people"—an empty abstraction—and transferring that power to a strong central government, the Federalists were able to assume power for themselves while appearing to do just the opposite.

‡‡‡‡‡ Lauro Martines, in the context of the Italian city-states of the Renaissance, speaks of "constitutional oligarchies." *Power and Imagination*, p. 148.

§§§§§ "The true philosophy knows a great and dangerous truth, that society is founded on and held together by myths, that is, untruths." Sheldon S. Wolin, *Democracy Incorporated*, p. 169.

"Popular sovereignty would give the new government the support of the people and, at the same time, insulate the national government from the actual activity of the *people*"[32] (italics added).

Democracy is a form of government in which political power is equally distributed among the citizen population. The people are sovereign not just in principle, but in fact. Aristotle declares, "Private rights do not make a citizen. He is ordinarily one who possesses political power."[33] In other words, our civic rights (C.D.+) do not make us citizens. Our direct participation in government (P.D.+) makes us citizens. "A citizen is one who shares in governing and being governed," according to Aristotle.[34] "What, then, is democracy?" asks Max Weber. "In itself it means simply that no formal inequality of political rights exists between the classes of the population."[35] In a democracy, political equality prevails.

I believe that for those of us living in the Western "democracies" the concept of political equality, as opposed to social equality, has simply disappeared from our lexicon, from our thoughts, from our utterances, from our struggles. We want a better deal for ourselves and our neighbors. Perhaps we even want social justice. But it never occurs to us that without political equality, our wishes cannot be fulfilled.

This was not always true. Once independence had been declared and fought for in the United States, just about everyone was aware of the issue of power and its distribution. Political equality represented a conscious choice for many. This was the case, as well, in the early Italian city-states, to a degree in the Roman Republic, and, of course, in ancient Athens.

# PART III

# THE QUEST FOR UNBRIDLED POWER

*Democracy Crushed*

# The Battlefield after the Battle

*All the ground*
*With shiver'd armour strown, and on a heap*
*Chariot and charioteer lay overturn'd.*

E ARLIER I SUGGESTED that history is nothing but a vast battlefield after the battle is over—a mountain of the corpses of men,
women, and children from around the world and across time who
have been slaughtered to satisfy the warriors in their quest for blood and
glory. If this is the case, then it behooves us to get to know these warriors personally. For it is by understanding their role in history that we
might come to see that the violence is avoidable and that it is an obstacle
to the formation of governments designed to serve the common good. If
we dig beneath the rubble, often we will find that what has been lost is
not just human life but a democratic way of living.

Finding the true meaning of war beneath the rubble is a difficult challenge, because that meaning is too often obscured by those who write
about it. Instead, we are offered endless volumes extolling the "heroes"
who did the killing. We are taught to look up to these "great men" and
to embrace a history drenched in blood.* Very little is written about the
dead or about the connection between the "glory" of conquest and its
consequences for those who did survive—about its effects on civil society. That is, very little is written about the battlefield after the battle is
over. There are, however, a few examples. We are indebted to the playwright Aeschylus, who, in *The Persians*, described the aftermath of the
battle of Salamis in 480 B.C.:

---

* It is not just the dead—those with no voice—who are to be accounted for. There are also
the living whose lives have been devastated. Husbands and fathers are gone for good. Crops
are destroyed. Livelihoods disappear overnight. How are the surviving families to be fed?
Community living, politics, and the distribution of power are permanently altered.

The hulls of our ships rolled over, and it was no longer possible to glimpse the sea, strewn as it was with the wrecks of warships and the debris of what had been men. The shores and the reefs were full of our dead, and every ship that had once been part of the fleet now tried to row its way to safety through flight. But just as if our men were tunny-fish or some sort of netted catch, the enemy kept pounding them and hacking them with broken oars and the flotsam from the wrecked ships. And so shrieks together with sobbing echoed over the open sea until the face of black night ended the scene.[†]

Here is another example, in which Thucydides, writing in the fifth century B.C., portrays the physical suffering and the pathos of war. He is describing the decimation of the Athenians during the course of their invasion of Sicily:

The dead lay unburied, and each man as he recognized a friend among them shuddered with grief and horror; while the living whom they were leaving behind, wounded or sick, were to the living far more shocking than the dead, and more to be pitied than those who had perished. These fell to entreating and bewailing until their friends knew not what to do, begging them to take them and loudly calling to each individual comrade or relative whom they could see, hanging upon the neck of their tent-fellows in the act of departure, and following as far as they could, and when their bodily strength failed them, calling again and again upon heaven and shrieking aloud as they were left behind.[1]

The Athenians are thirsty, desperate, and in retreat, fleeing for their lives:

The Athenians pushed on for the Assinarus, impelled by the attacks made upon them from every side by a numerous cavalry and the swarm of other arms, fancying they should breathe more freely if once across the river, and driven on also by their exhaustion and craving for water. Once there they rushed in, and all order was at an end, each man wanting to cross first, and the attacks of the enemy making it difficult to cross at all; forced to huddle together, they fell against and trod down one another, some dying immediately upon the javelins, others getting entangled together and stumbling over the articles of baggage, without being able to rise again. Meanwhile, the opposite bank, which was steep, was lined by the Syracusans, who showered missiles down upon the Athenians, most of them drinking greedily and heaped together in disorder in the hollow bed of the river. The Peloponnesians also came down and butchered them, especially those in the water, which was thus immediately spoiled, but which they went on drinking just the same, mud and all, bloody as it was, most even fighting to have it.[2]

The living have been taken prisoner by the enemy. Here is Thucydides' description of their fate:

---

† This passage is quoted in Victor Davis Hanson's *Carnage and Culture: Landmark Battles in the Rise of Western Power*, pp. 30–31. Unfortunately, Hanson himself seems to come down on the side of carnage. The legacy of Western civilization, he says, "is a weighty and sometimes ominous heritage that we must neither deny nor feel ashamed about—but insist that our deadly manner of war serves, rather than buries, our civilization" (p. 455).

Crowded in a narrow hole, without any roof to cover them, the heat of the sun and the stifling closeness of the air tormented them during the day, and then the nights, which came on autumnal and chilly, made them ill by the violence of the change; besides, as they had to do everything in the same place for want of room, and the bodies of those who died of their wounds or from the variation in the temperature, or from similar causes, were left heaped together one upon the other, intolerable stenches arose; while hunger and thirst never cease to afflict them, each man during eight months having only half a pint of water and a pint of grain given him daily. In short, no single suffering to be apprehended by men thrust into such a place was spared them.[3]

Early in the sixteenth century, Spanish conquistadores, led by Hernán Cortés, decided they wanted gold that wasn't theirs. To get it, they proceeded to destroy the Aztec culture and annihilate the native population. The capital of Mexico at that time was Tenochtitlan, and therein lay the Aztec treasure and Montezuma, the emperor of the Aztecs. Pedro de Alvarado, second in command, in Cortés' absence massacred 8,000 unarmed Aztec nobility and was about to get to work on the women and children when Cortés appeared. Here is how a witness described the event:

They attacked all the celebrants, stabbing them, spearing them from behind, and these fell instantly to the ground with their entrails hanging out. Others they beheaded: they cut off their heads, or split their head to pieces. They struck others in the shoulders, and their arms were torn from the bodies. They wounded some in the thigh and some in the calf. They slashed others in the abdomen, and their entrails all spilled to the ground. Some attempted to run away, but their intestines dragged as they ran; they seemed to tangle their feet in their own entrails.[4]

Tenochtitlan was under siege from May through August 1521. Cortés described the carnage in a letter to his king, Charles V:

The people of the city had to walk upon their dead while others swam or drowned in the waters of that wide lake where they had their canoes; indeed, so great was their suffering that it was beyond our understanding how they could endure it. Countless numbers of men, women and children came toward us, and in their eagerness to escape many were pushed into the water where they drowned amid the multitude of corpses; and it seemed that more than fifty thousand had perished from the salt water they had drunk, their hunger and the vile stench.[5]

About 100,000 Aztecs perished in the fighting. The tally from the two-year struggle for Tenochtitlan was close to a million. Fifty years later, as a consequence of war and disease—the Europeans had brought with them measles, bubonic plague, flu, whooping cough, and mumps—the population of central Mexico had been reduced from 8 million to less than 1 million. The riches seized by the Spaniards were considerable. Between 1500 and 1650, 150 tons of gold and 16,000 tons of silver were shipped from Mexico and Peru to Spain.

Unfortunately, contemporary civilization continues to offer such horrors, though rarely are we afforded documentary evidence of what the suffering is really like. There are exceptions, however. In 1991, President George H. W. Bush ordered the bombing of Iraqi forces that had invaded Kuwait. The journal of an Iraqi soldier who endured the bombing for thirty-nine days serves as testimony to the consequences of this action. The enemy, it turns out, has a face, a soul, a heart, and a set of lungs. Here are some excerpts from the field journal of a young Iraqi lieutenant:

Tuesday 17 January 1991
    I am very worried. Rather I am very worried for my relatives. They are alone out there. And I know how afraid they are.
    O God! Protect.
    O God! Patience.
    O God! Save us all.

Tuesday 22 January 1991
    What an awful sight: one of the soldiers [disturbed] one of the bombs and suddenly it exploded and the soldier disappeared and I saw [two pieces] of his flesh on the second story of the bunker. Allah aqbar. What a horrible thing to see. I went back to the regiment and found the first section at another place. They had moved to safety.

Thursday 24 January 1991
    The raids began early. They began at about 2:30 a.m. today and have continued heavily without a let-up. I heard news that Bassorah has been bombed heavily. May God have come to help my relatives; I am very worried about them. How I want to see them and find out how they are! God is beneficent. Where are they now? God only knows.
    Ahhhhhhhhh!

Saturday 26 January 1991
    Enemy air strikes continue, and I'm very worried, depressed and bored. I think about my children.

Monday 28 January 1991
    After sunset, a flock of sheep came up to us. Apparently the owner of the flock had been killed in the air raids. The enemy with his modern planes has launched air strikes on a shepherd. Maybe the enemy took the sheep for nuclear or chemical or petroleum sheep. For shame.

Wednesday 30 January 1991
    The air strikes began heavily today and I am still alive. I could be killed at any moment. I am more afraid for my relatives than I am afraid to die. The air raids are nothing new to me, but I am very worried.

2 February 1991
    I was almost killed. Death was a yard away from me. The missiles, machine guns and rockets didn't let up.... Time passed and we waited to

die.... I read chapters in the Qur'an. How hard it is to be killed by some-one you don't know, you've never seen and can't confront. He is in the sky and you're on the ground.

3 February 1991

The pain I've been having all the past 6 months has returned. I am sad. In the last 5 days I've eaten only a few dates and boiled lentils. What have we done to God to endure that? I have no news of my rela-tives. How can I, since I don't know what is happening to me.

What will become of me? What is happening to them? I don't know. I don't know. God protect them. How I miss my children. I know that [Editor's note: woman's first name] is very, very frightened. What hap-pens to her when she hears the planes and missiles? I don't know.

Saturday 16 February 1991

I feel so fatigued that I can't breathe, and I think I am going to faint at any moment from my illness. The only thing that you can find every-where in the world is air, and yet I can't breathe it. I can't breathe, eat, drink or talk. I have been here for 39 days and have not yet gone on leave. The planes came and bombed Battalion headquarters. Most of the positions were destroyed and three soldiers were killed. When the planes came to bomb us, I remained standing because I can't go into the trench.

Sunday 17 February 1991

My illness is getting worse. I am short of breath. I hurt. The air raids have started up again.[6]

I offer these first-hand accounts as graphic reminders of what war is like. They are exceptional because they tell the story we usually don't hear. Most of what we read in histories is not about the gore but about the "glory." The historian's enthusiasm for his subject matter can easily blind us to the fact that the killing is senseless and the misery it engenders is gratuitous.

## Alexander of Macedon: The Gory Glory

*Alexander: The Ambiguity of Greatness*, by Guy MacLean Rogers, is one example of the skewed picture painted by some historians. This book is devoted almost entirely to the description and analysis of bat-tles, battlefield tactics, and battlefield strategies, and it is replete with diagrams and detailed descriptions of arms and armaments. The dia-grams and the enthusiastic tone of the writing are reminiscent of the sports stories that appear the day after a big game:

Alexander commenced the attack with an assault by 1,000 mounted archers against Porus' left wing. This assault was followed by a charge of the Companion cavalry led by Alexander against the Indian left, before their cavalry could mass.

The Indians meanwhile were removing all of their cavalry from their line to meet Alexander's charge. These cavalrymen were followed by Coenus and his men, who began to appear at the rear of the Indian cavalry as it followed Alexander out to the right. The Indians therefore split their forces to deal with Alexander and Coenus.

In that instant, when the Indian cavalry split, and part of it changed direction to meet Coenus, Alexander charged into the Indian line facing him. The Indians immediately fell back into their screen of elephants.[7]

Or:

Once the battle began, the combat was furious and the issue decided relatively quickly. As soon as Alexander was within missile range, he rode at a gallop into the stream at the head of his own troops on the right wing. The left of the Persian line collapsed the moment Alexander was upon them.... The Persians had never before faced such a ferocious attack.[8]

One can easily get caught up in the excitement of such narration. One can easily forget that such engagements are about killing, with 12,000 dead on the Indian side, in this particular battle. But these accounts are not about death. They are about weaponry, strategy, and victory.

For example, we learn that Philip II, Alexander's father, established the first truly professional army in Greek history and that he reorganized the infantry and expanded the cavalry. We learn that while the Athenian hoplites[‡] wielded seven-foot spears with one hand, their conquerors from the north, the Macedonians, wielded, with two hands, sixteen-foot-long pikes known as sarissas, whose sole purpose was to pierce flesh, muscle, and sinew and to fracture bone. It is thanks to these "advances" that Alexander was able to achieve what he did, that is, kill a lot of people.

Something like 100,000 were killed on the Persian side in the battle of Issos. Alexander became enraged when armies in his path had the audacity to resist his advances onto their territory. The people of Tyre, a town on the Mediterranean, not far from Damascus, were particularly stubborn—and they paid for it. Alexander laid siege for seven months. When the Macedonians were finally able to enter the city, they killed at least 8,000 Tyrians. Another 30,000 woman and children were sold into slavery. Two thousand were crucified along the beach as a reminder to anyone who got it in his head to stand in Alexander's way.

At the battle of Guagamela, in Persia, the Macedonians, under Alexander's leadership, took the lives of some 90,000 Persians. In the city of Maracanda, in India, only about 8,000 out of 30,000 survived Alexander's onslaught. At Cyropolis, 8,000 perished. At Cathei, some 17,000 Indians lost their lives; 70,000 were taken prisoner. The Indians did all they could to escape Alexander's savagery. His orders were to stay put. If they did, he assured them, they would not be harmed. Those who fled

---

‡  A hoplite was a citizen-soldier of the ancient Greek city-states.

and were captured were killed, including some 500 who were too sick or to infirm to get out of his way. Some 5,000 Indians were killed while defending their homes. Farther down the road, another 80,000 Indians were killed. In the battle of Oreitae, 6,000 defenders were killed. This is just a sampling.

What are we to make of all this? Who and what was Alexander? What was he up to and why? Allegedly, in 330 B.C., Alexander was avenging the Persian attacks on Greece that began in 499 B.C. and lasted until 448 B.C., when the Persians were finally defeated. Athens was destroyed. Temples were burned. More than a hundred years after the fact, Alexander set out to kill hundreds of thousands of Persians who weren't even alive at the time of the Persian invasion of Greece. And, of course, in no way can this argument be used to justify the slaughter of tens of thousands of Indians whose ancestors never set foot in Greece.

Justification by vengeance is an early example—and there are many to follow—in which gratuitous killing finds its vindication in some kind of rationalized argument. In the times of the Crusades, there was religious justification, to be followed by reasons of state. There is always "good" reason to kill when people want to kill.

One could argue that Alexander was a homicidal maniac, a blood-thirsty butcher, but this is not the path chosen by historian Rogers. He makes passing reference to those who compare Alexander to Hitler or Stalin. But such writers, we are told, have not used their sources well and have failed to place Alexander's achievements in the proper context. "Throughout history," we learn, "the great have often been possessed of godlike abilities, and all-too-mortal flaws and weaknesses. Indeed, it is the flaws and mistakes of the great that allow us to appreciate their gifts, and it is by their missteps and failures that the great are ultimately redeemed as human beings."[9]

As Rogers tells it, on the one hand, Alexander is godlike and we should be in awe. Sure, he killed a lot of people, but that's what gods do. On the other hand, he is human like the rest of us and we should accept him as one of our own, "missteps"§ and all. "Greatness," which sounds like something good, has been equated with slaughter, though we are not to see it as such. Exactly what the difference is between the "achievements" and the "flaws" remains unclear.

Between battles, Alexander and his soldiers would engage in week-long drinking bouts. During one of these drunken revelries, a commander of Alexander's named Cleitus spoke plainly about the way in which the Macedonians were being humiliated by Alexander's courting of the Persians he had conquered. Alexander flew into a rage and ran through Cleitus with a pike he had grabbed from one of the guards. Thus did Alexander slay a loyal commander and good friend, in one of his mis-

---

§ Exactly what is a "misstep" when you are a career killer? You miss your target?

takes.¶ But, we learn, he admitted to it, and therefore he is a decent guy after all. "Alexander's admission of wrongdoing is indeed a historically rare example of a man in a powerful position admitting to making a grave mistake.... To his credit, Alexander made no excuses for his crime."[10]

On another occasion when Alexander's beloved Thessalian horse, Bucephalus, disappeared, Alexander threatened to lay waste the countryside and slaughter the inhabitants, to a man. As he began his mission, locals returned the horse with gifts of peace. Another mistake?

Alexander was slightly wounded in the shoulder when crossing the Choes River. In revenge, the inhabitants of the local settlement were massacred.

When Hephaestion, Alexander's close friend and lover, died of a fever while under the care of his physician Glaucius, Alexander had Glaucius crucified. He also saw fit to massacre the tribe of the Cossaeans, "as a sacrifice to the spirit of Hephaestion."[11] Thus we learn that Alexander was "endearingly loyal"[12] to his boyhood friends.

When Alexander decided to slaughter the Branchidae and sell the women and children into slavery, we learn that he did so not "out of frustration" but after reasoned debate. But this harsh treatment, we learn, is not typical of the "man who treated many war captives with exemplary mercy,"[13] in keeping with "his natural kindness."[14]

Repeatedly, Alexander used torture on his own men when he thought they were conspiring against him, or on enemies when he wanted information. But he was a pious man, consulting the gods before battle and rewarding them after every victory. His piety and feeling of connection to the gods were "powerful motives."[15]

After a battle was over, Alexander would see to it that the Macedonian dead were buried with honor. He visited the wounded and listened to their stories. "He had a precocious understanding of the need of men who have experienced the trauma of combat to release their emotions by sharing them."[16]

When Alexander and his men reached the Persian capital of Persepolis, the city that had been home to the army that had invaded Greece five generations earlier, he decided that the city was to be blotted out. Private homes were sacked. The men were slaughtered. The women were enslaved. But "rape was explicitly forbidden."[17]

When we read the narratives of Alexander's conquests, we can easily forget that we are talking about massive loss of human life. These accounts can sound like a board game, or a series of household chores, or a forestry operation. We learn of "pawn sacrifices,"[18] that is, the deliberate sacrifice of advance infantry as a means of getting leverage for the cavalry behind them. Speaking of the Persian infantry, we learn

¶ One can only assume that killing more than 200,000 Persians was not a mistake but an achievement.

that Alexander's cavalry "was soon cutting them to pieces."[19] That is what I do to carrots on a cutting board. After a decisive victory, we learn that Alexander "was engaged with mopping up the remaining rebels in the area."[20] When I spill some milk on the floor, I mop it up. "The inhabitants of Massaga were cut down."[21] We thin a forest by cutting down some trees. Yes, Alexander killed hundreds of thousands, but we can rest assured that what he did "was not genocide by any definition of that modern word."[22]

This kind of reasoning is common in some histories written by academics and other elitists who have allied themselves with the engines of power. They ask us to embrace the bloody britches of history rather than to be appalled at the savagery. We are asked to engage in a calculus of death in which one mass murderer is to be exonerated by virtue of the excesses of another.

Alexander did not engage in a reign of terror like Stalin's. Unlike Genghis Kahn, Alexander "never made it a *policy* to wipe out the civilian populations of the cities or territories he conquered"[23] (italics in the original). In other words, indeed Alexander did "wipe out" civilian populations. But, he didn't do it routinely. It wasn't his "*policy*."

Alexander did not gather "defenseless civilians into concentration camps and then starve, torture, or gas them to death. Alexander never attempted or committed genocide against any of his enemies.... Nor was Alexander an ethnic fundamentalist, let alone an ethnic cleanser."[24] Well, all right. Let us say that Alexander killed for the fun of it. Does that make him any better or more desirable as a human being than someone whose killing is based in religious hatred? After all, dead is dead.

On July 31, 1945, Harry S. Truman signed away the lives of 130,000 Japanese civilians. We consider him to be a "great" American, don't we? So why shouldn't we accord the same consideration to Alexander? "Many great historical figures have made mistakes and caused great suffering without thereby becoming monsters." Sure, the great "have made terrible mistakes because, in the end, the great, just like the rest of us, finally are human beings," we are told. "If we are able to live with the ambiguity of the great, perhaps we may live better with our own."[25] In other words, "Judge not lest ye be judged." Here we have a paean to nihilism and savagery under the guise of relativism and "objectivity." As to whether Alexander's response to the Persian invasions is justified, Rogers tells us that "is not a question that can be answered objectively,"[26] implying that he remains neutral on the subject, when everything in the tone and tenor of his work says just the opposite.

Rogers is quite ecstatic about Alexander's achievements and does his best to relieve his hero of the moral opprobrium his bloody deeds would seem to call out for. Alexander is held up for admiration alongside creative geniuses such as Mozart, who "also disturbs our rest and reminds us that individual greatness often comes at a high price."[27] Like

Mozart, Alexander is "a prodigy," not of music but of warfare. He is "a virtuoso of violence." He is in charge of a "finely tempered instrument of organized violence."[28] He is "a military genius, indeed a great creative artist of warfare,"[29] "a visionary genius of warfare."[30]

Speaking of Alexander's organized killing, Rogers reminds us of "the daring originality of its conception, leaving aside consideration of the brilliance of its execution."[31] We are in the presence of a "superbly talented professional[s]."[32] If battles can be compared to symphonies, the battle of the Hysdaspes River, in which no fewer than 12,000 Indians were killed, "was his *Jupiter*; his masterpiece."[33]

Alexander not only killed, he plundered. In the Persian capital of Persepolis, he took possession of the "absolutely staggering sum of 120,000 talents."[34] "Alexander was not just 'rich rich,' he was madly rich, the wealthiest man in Greek history."[35] Alexander held court in an enormous pavilion supported by fifty golden uprights and containing a hundred couches. In the center was a chair of pure gold upon which Alexander would sit, with his bodyguards standing close by on all sides. He had a harem of three hundred sixty-five women.

Alexander literally believed himself to be a god, descendant of gods, and he required that all prostrate themselves before him as they would before a god. He ordered that the Greeks vote on whether or not to consider him divine. In response, the Spartans passed a decree stating, "Since Alexander wishes to be a god, let him be a god."[36]

Alexander died of a mysterious fever at the age of thirty-three. No one seems to know exactly what caused it. Was he assassinated? Did he drink himself to death? Was he taken by some infectious disease? These questions remain unanswered. Doggedly defended by his biographer to the end, we are asked to ponder what more Alexander could have accomplished had he lived longer. He could have conquered Arabia and the western Mediterranean. And killed how many more? But let us not dismiss this virtuoso of violence for his dark deeds. "We should ... keep in mind that we often disparage such men—until the next time they are needed."[37]

It is certainly true that Alexander led his men into battle and knew no fear. He was wounded eight times. We are encouraged to value such bravery and ignore the fact that it was driven by violent rage and a desperate need to conquer, kill, and plunder. And one should bear in mind that when extolling the military virtues of Philip II of Macedon and his son, Alexander, one is giving praise to two men who, through violence and conquest, oversaw the demise of the Athenian citizen-state.

Athens had formed an alliance with Thebes in the hope of keeping Philip at bay. In 338 B.C., Philip accepted the challenge of engaging them both. The battle took place on the plain of Chaeroneia. The Macedonians found an opening, and the infantry, supported by a devastating cavalry charge under the leadership of the eighteen-year-old Alexander, emerged victorious. A thousand Athenians lay dead. Another 2,000 were made prisoners. The era of the independent citizen-state was over.

Of all Athenians, it was the great orator Demosthenes (384 B.C.–322 B.C.) who was the first to fully understand the threat represented by Philip and his son. Yet, despite his brilliance, he was unsuccessful in his attempts to rally the Athenians in time. There were those in the Assembly who wanted to mollify Philip. Demosthenes vehemently opposed such a strategy. It would be "better to die a thousand times than pay court to Philip":

> Philip knows that even with complete control of all the rest he can have no security while democracy remains in Athens, that in the event of a single setback every element under the sway of force will come to Athens for refuge. You who are her people are not a people naturally given to the selfish pursuit of power, but strong to prevent it in others or wrest it from them, a thorn in the flesh of despotism, and willing champions for the liberation of mankind.[38]

Even after the Athenian defeat, Demosthenes was unrelenting in his opposition to Philip. He celebrated Philip's assassination and played a leading part in his city's uprising. After Alexander's death in 323 B.C., Demosthenes again urged the Athenians to seek independence from Macedonia in what became known as the Lamian War. However, Antipater, Alexander's successor, quelled all opposition and demanded that the Athenians turn over Demosthenes, among others. Following this request, the Athenian Assembly adopted a decree condemning the most prominent anti-Macedonian agitators to death. Demosthenes, the last voice of a proud and independent Athenian democracy, chose suicide.

## Genghis Kahn: Icon or Savage?

If we jump ahead about a thousand years, we find ourselves in the presence of the man who many consider to be the "greatest" man in history, Genghis Kahn. The numbers he and his descendants killed would put Alexander to shame. They reach into the millions.

The Mongol army conquered more land and people in the first half of the thirteenth century than the Romans did in four hundred years. At its zenith, Genghis' empire—the empire that he and his descendants created—covered an area about the size of the African continent, twenty-two percent of the earth's total land area, comprising some thirty countries, and held sway over a population of over 100 million people.

The Golden Horde shaped the map of Asia and the Middle East as we know it today. A dozen Slavic principalities and cities were united into one large Russian state. Various Asian dynasties were united to create the modern nation of China. The Mongols brought together countries such as Korea and India. The impact on Russian history was especially powerful. Like Alexander, Genghis Kahn "fashioned an almost unbeatable war machine, capable of coordinated operations on an immense scale."[39]

In *Russia and the Golden Horde: The Mongol Impact on Russian History*, by Charles J. Halperin, we see another example of hero worship. Acknowledging that "the Mongols destroyed much of the Russian economy and severely depleted the population" (i.e., killed a lot of people), Halperin devotes his study not to that destruction but to the many benefits the Mongols brought to the lands they conquered.

Like Rogers, historian-defender of Alexander, Halperin leaps to the defense of his own blood-soaked hero:

> Chingis Kahn's military and political genius and charismatic leadership cannot be questioned; neither can the number of lives lost during his pursuit of glory. The same is true of Alexander the Great, Julius Caesar, and Napoleon. Chingis was no more cruel, and no less, than empire-builders before and since. Moral judgments are of little help in understanding his importance, and none is advanced here.[40]

The disclaimer of moral bias is false. The subtitle of Halperin's book is only half true. There is no examination of the destructive impact the Mongols had on Russia. By focusing on what he sees as the positive side of the ledger, Halperin is implicitly taking the moral position that the end justifies the means. In essence, his position is, "Sure, Genghis killed a few people along the way, but look at all the good he did."

Making passing reference to documents that chronicle in detail the Mongol conquests and their devastating effect on the Russian people, Halperin steadfastly refuses to grant us direct access. What he does instead is give us a subtle semantic analysis of these writings to demonstrate that the Russian chroniclers chose words that tended to conceal from themselves and their readers that, in fact, they had been defeated and occupied. We learn that "Russia's intellectual reaction to Mongol rule was both complex and ambiguous. Writers usually showed no reluctance to discuss the Tartars, but tended to restrict themselves to graphic descriptions of Mongol atrocities."[41]

Halperin seems annoyed with the fact that writers got caught up in describing the violence and failed to give due weight to the political implications of the invasion. "The medieval Russian bookmen avoided the intellectual implications of the Mongol conquest."[42] Exactly what the intellectual implications were or should be and why their absence justifies a chapter-length discussion remains to be seen. It would appear that this focus serves as an alternative to facing the gruesome facts and distracting Halperin from the positive side of the ledger, which seems to be rather skimpy.

What exactly did Genghis and the Mongols achieve that was of such benefit as to justify the death that went with it? They brought a very efficient administration—in the person of officials called *baskaki*—

which prevailed in Russia from the thirteenth through the fifteenth centuries. The function of these *baskaki* was to oversee "the collection of tribute, the conscript[ion of] troops, and [maintenance of] order, that is, suppress[ion of] opposition to Mongol rule."[43] Though efficient, it is hard to see what benefit such an administration had for the Russians, who were its helpless victims. The Mongols did put in place a postal system, "the fastest communications system ... the Eurasian continent ... had ever ... known."[44] They also introduced capital punishment and beatings on the shins for failure to pay debt.

In a chapter entitled "Economic and Demographic Consequences," there is not a single mention of the number of people killed and displaced by the Mongols. We do learn that prior to the Mongol attack in 1240, led by Genghis' grandson Batu, the region known as Kievan Rus' had been prosperous, engaged in artisanal activities, and produced enough food to feed itself. We also learn that "The Mongol campaigns of 1237–1240 shattered this economy. Many cities lay in ruins, their populations largely slaughtered." Certain artisanal productions such as cloisonné enameling ceased altogether. Crops were burned. Livestock was run off. There was a precipitous decline in population. It took a hundred years for political activity to resume in this region.[45]

The costs to the Russian economy were not limited to the initial decimation. There was the required tribute. There were the costs of administration. There were other direct and indirect levies. Kidnapped victims were returned only upon payment of ransom. Entire cities were put up for ransom. The great economic toll resulted in the abandonment of many small villages. The peasantry had an especially heavy burden to bear. The nobility—by joining the Tartars in some of their military campaigns against the Russian neighbors—were able to share in the loot.

The Mongol rulers deliberately shaped the society they had conquered by obliterating some cities while favoring others. There was a resultant population shift (i.e., forced migrations) to the north in the direction of Moscow, the principality that became the long-term benefactor of the Mongol policies. When Mongol power withered, "Moscow's hereditary grand princes became autocratic rulers."[46] After 1547, the ruler became known as tsar, or emperor.

But, Halperin explains, Russian autocratic rule, with its home in Moscow, cannot be blamed on the Mongols. The removal by the Mongols of the *veche* (the institution of democratic town meetings), the Mongols' inculcating in their subjects the use of "naked power and utter subservience,"[47] the focused violence that was necessary for the ultimate overthrow of the Mongols—all of these contributing factors in the rise and persistence of Russian autocracy—are blithely dismissed by Halperin.

Although "devastation, extermination, and extortion" took their toll, there was a brighter side. If only for self-serving purposes—the collection of customs taxes—the Mongols developed trade, which had a benefit for the Russian economy as a whole. Trade routes were shifted north to Moscow's benefit.

After about a hundred years of occupation, urban development and economic activity reappeared, thanks to the international commerce fostered by the Mongols. Moscow built a new wall and new churches. "By promoting trade for their own benefit, the Mongols, who had ravaged Russia and plunged it into economic depression, made possible Russia's recovery and new growth."[48]

While addressing the fact that "there is widespread belief that the barbarian Mongols were responsible for Russia's subsequent 'backwardness' and inability to 'keep up' with Europe," Halperin maintains, without supporting argument, that yes, "the conquest was a catastrophe, but a catastrophe need not have permanent effects."[49] The devastation wasn't so terrible after all. Quit the whining.

Halperin concludes his chapter on the economic consequences of conquest with the upbeat observation that "the Golden Horde fostered the resurgence of the Russian economy and subsequent growth of Russian power."[50] In other words, if the Mongols hadn't obliterated the Russian people and their cities, culture, farms, and civic life, then Russia never would have had the opportunity to recover. And don't forget the postal system and those trade routes.

Another book on the subject of Genghis Kahn further demonstrates this fawning view of conquerers. *Genghis Kahn and the Making of the Modern World,* by Jack Weatherford, was a *New York Times* bestseller. I can understand why. It tells its story well. It reads with the voice of authority. It is great adventure. Like Halperin, Weatherford is passionately devoted to the nobility of his hero and the Mongol cause. He studied his subject thoroughly, lived in Mongolia where Genghis lived, rode on horseback across the same countryside Genghis did. Weatherford dedicates his book "To the Young Mongols: Never forget the Mongolian scholars who were willing to sacrifice their lives to preserve your history." He quotes this laudatory passage from Chaucer's *Canterbury Tales*: "This noble king was called Genghis Kahn / Who in his time was of so great renown / That there was nowhere in no region / So excellent a lord in all things."

Here is what Weatherford has to say about Genghis Kahn in his introduction:

As he smashed the feudal system of aristocratic birth and privilege, he built a new and unique system based on individual merit, loyalty, and achievement. He took the disjointed and languorous trading towns along the Silk Route and organized them into history's largest free-trade zone. He lowered taxes for everyone, and abolished them altogether for doctors, teachers, priests, and educational institutions. He established a regular census and created the first international postal system. His was not an empire that hoarded wealth and treasure, instead, he widely distributed the goods acquired in combat so that they could make their way back into commercial circulation. He created an international law and recognized the ultimate supreme law of the Eternal Blue Sky over all people. At a time when most rulers considered themselves to be above the law, Genghis Kahn insisted on laws holding rulers as equally accountable as the lowest herder. He granted religious freedom within his realms, though he demanded total loyalty from conquered subjects of all religions. He insisted on the rule of law and abolished torture, but he mounted major campaigns to seek out and kill raiding bandits and terrorist assassins. He refused to hold hostages and, instead, instituted the novel practice of granting diplomatic immunity for all ambassadors and envoys, including those from hostile nations with whom he was at war.[51]

I quote at length from this piece of propaganda because this is what passes for history and beguiles us into bowing before unbridled power. One can imagine how the many readers of this book have come to see Genghis Kahn with this as their only source of information on the subject. They would think that he was indeed a noble figure and wouldn't have an inkling as to the devastation he wrought.**

In 1241, the Mongols "smashed the feudal system." †† More specifically, in Germany they killed something like 25,000 knights. This feat was repeated in Hungary and Poland to even grander effect, where a combined total of approximately 100,000 of the knighthood and aristocracy were sent to early graves. Writes one chronicler, "The dead fell to the right and to left; like leaves in winter, the slain bodies of these miserable men were strewn along the whole route; blood flowed like torrents of rain."[52]

Once again, there is mention of the trade routes and postal system but no mention of the millions of lives taken to put them in place. Genghis instituted a census so he could collect tribute. His system of taxation and tributes was as heavy an economic burden on the people as the conquest itself.

Genghis did not keep all the wealth—that is, the loot acquired in sacking towns and cities—for himself. Instead, he distributed it among his troops as a means of maintaining their loyalty. Further, this loot was so extensive that even after generous distribution among an army of 100,000 or so, there were great quantities of goods remaining. Vast warehouses had to be built to house them. "For five years, a steady flow of camel caravans lumbered out of the Muslim lands carrying packs of

---

**Here is a different perspective: "The Mongols contributed almost nothing of cultural value—they were, as Pushkin later described them, 'Arabs without Aristotle or algebra,' and they were in no way to be compared with the brilliant Moors who occupied Spain. Indeed the Mongols actively retarded the growth of Russian culture by blocking the stimulus from Byzantium and the West." Robert Wallace, *Rise of Russia*, p. 60.

†† When Weatherford says Genghis "smashed the feudal system" and replaced it with a "new and unique system based on individual merit," he is referring not to civic society at large but to the fighting force that has come to be known as the Golden Horde. Those who were efficient killers and loyal to the Mongol cause were duly recognized.

looted goods to Mongolia, where the population eagerly awaited each load of exotic luxuries."[53]

The "international law" Genghis created is known as totalitarianism, complete submission to the emperor's dictates. As for the "Eternal Blue Sky," it is hard to see how such a belief benefited the tens of millions whose lives were taken. Like Alexander, Genghis prayed to his god before battle and offered thanks after victory. He allowed all religions, so as to not have his power challenged by any religion in particular. The religions canceled each other out. The "bandits and terrorist assassins" he killed were his adversaries, a threat to his hegemony.

Genghis "abolished torture," we learn. However, he was quite comfortable herding masses of the conquered into a moat and using them as a bridge to ride over with his engines of war. One can imagine that there might have been some discomfort as one's bones were broken, eyes gouged out, skull crushed, beneath the weight of other bodies and heavy equipment, as victims were left gasping for air and finding none. One can imagine as well that death might not have been instant. It might have taken hours, perhaps days, before a victim would expire. But there was no torture.[‡‡]

Genghis wreaked havoc throughout the East and the Middle East. As Weatherford points out, the people of the Middle East had the farthest to fall, because they were the most advanced. What he fails to mention is that the people of the Middle East were never able to recover:

> Compared with Europe and India, where only priests could read, or China, where only government bureaucrats could, nearly every village in the Muslim world had at least some men who could read the Koran and interpret Muslim law. While, Europe, China and India had only attained the level of regional civilizations, the Muslims came closest to having a world-class civilization with more sophisticated commerce, technology, and general learning.... The Mongol invasion caused more damage here than anywhere else their horses would tread.[54]

Weatherford says, "Genghis Kahn epitomized ruthlessness in the eyes of the Muslims," implying that Genghis wasn't really ruthless but that he just *appeared* to be "in the eyes of the Muslims."

In the Middle Ages, Baghdad was a city of magnificence, of almost mythic beauty, wealth, and luxury. It was a religious center for Muslims, Christians, and Jews. Then the Mongols took the city. The looting lasted for seventeen days. The city was set afire.

Weatherford cites the following quote, attributed to Genghis Kahn

---

‡‡   Guyuk Kahn, grandson of Genghis, found that Fatima, his mother's advisor, had gained too much power. He accused her of being a witch, subjected her to the most vile torture, rolled her up in a blanket, and had her tossed into a river. But such treatment, we are assured by Weatherford, was exceptional. However, in a similar spirit, Guyuk had the mouths of two of suspected conspirators filled with stone and dirt until they died. *Genghis Kahn and the Making of the Modern World*, pp. 164–165, 167.

by Muslim chroniclers, and dismisses it as apocryphal. Even if Genghis did not utter these words, they certainly do nothing to violate the spirit of his personal ideology as witnessed by his actions:

> The greatest joy a man can know is to conquer his enemies and drive them before him. To ride their horses and take away their possessions. To see the faces of those who were dear to them bedewed with tears, and to clasp their wives and daughters in his arms.[55]

As the Mongol empire grew, so did the need for skilled workers, who were acquired with each new conquest. Those without skills did not fare so well. They

> were collected to help in the attack on the next city by carrying loads, digging fortifications, serving as human shields, being pushed into moats at will, or otherwise giving their lives in the Mongol war effort. Those who did not qualify even for these tasks, the Mongol warriors slaughtered and left behind.[56]

While acknowledging that Genghis Kahn and the Golden Horde destroyed cities and "depopulated expansive areas of land by the laborious destruction of the irrigation system," Weatherford objects to what he calls preposterously high estimates of the death toll resulting from their exploits. The number of dead in central Asia accumulated over a period of five years could not possibly have been as high as 15 million, according to Weatherford.

Determining the number of deaths caused by the Mongol conquests around the world—both from direct causalities and from famine and disease resulting from the destruction of irrigation systems and farms— is a complicated, if not impossible, task. Eyewitness accounts are few. Availability of census records is spotty. And there is the complicating factor of the Black Death that swept Europe and Asia (how much of its spread might have been a consequence of Mongol actions?). Nevertheless, estimates range from 30 million to as high as 60 million deaths in some way attributable to the Mongol conquests. Chinese census estimates suggest the possibility of a population decline from as many as 120 million inhabitants before the Mongol conquest to perhaps 60 million afterward. Could China have lost half of its population, or 60 million people?[57] Although the exact numbers will never be known, few (Weatherford being one of the exceptions) would dispute that Genghis and his descendants took the lives of tens of millions. On a list of "(Possibly) the Twenty (or So) Worst Things People Have Done to Each Other," Genghis Kahn and Mao Zedong are tied for second place, each responsible for some 40 million deaths.[58]

In his closing pages, Weatherford discusses the treatment Genghis Kahn has received at the hands of his critics. He mentions writers such as Montesquieu, who charges the Mongols with having "destroyed

Asia, from India even to the Mediterranean; and all the country which forms the east of Persia they have rendered a desert,"[59] and Voltaire, who describes the Mongols as "wild sons of rapine."[60] Such history, written by those who condemn Genghis and his horde, is referred to as "revisionist" by Weatherford. People who write such history, he tells us, are racists who vilify those from the East out of fear and hostility.[§§] Rather than condemn Genghis, Westerners should appreciate what they have learned from him, "how to fight in the modern era of tank warfare"[61]—the idea of *blitzkrieg*—for example. Let us not forget that Genghis "worked to create something new and better for his people" or that the Mongol armies shattered "the protective walls that isolated one civilization from another" and knotted "the cultures together."[62]

If we turn to history out of a need to understand our past as a means of charting our future, using such writing as a resource can only lead us down the path to violence and the endless sacrifice of human life to no apparent purpose. If, on the other hand, it is our goal to create a civilization that honors the value of human life and democratic values, then we need to look elsewhere. Rather than extol the conqueror, let us pause for a moment and consider an early civilization that existed in that part of southern Russia that today is known as the Ukraine, before it was demolished by the Mongols.

## An Emerging Democracy Is Crushed

Kievan Rus'[¶¶] was a medieval state dominated by the city of Kiev and, to a lesser degree, Novgorod to the north. In the shape of an oval, it comprised about a million square miles of forest land, with a population of about 5 million. Only the Holy Roman Empire was larger. Kiev itself had a population of about 80,000, on par with Paris, Europe's largest city at the time.

Kievan Rus' was founded around 880 by Scandinavian traders (Varangians) called "Rus'." Primarily inhabited by Slavs, a peaceful people who were neither militarily organized nor well armed, the region was ruled by a Scandinavian warrior-elite until at least the mideleventh century. The reigns of Vladimir the Great (980–1015) and his son Yaroslav I the Wise (1019–1054) constitute the Golden Age of Kiev, which saw the acceptance of Christianity and the creation of the first Eastern Slavic written legal code, the Russkaya Pravda.

Promulgated in the eleventh century, foreshadowing in its tone and concerns the Magna Carta issued in England almost two hundred years later (in 1215), the Russkaya Pravda was advanced for its time in attempting to address specific issues that affected both the ruling elite

---

§§ Apparently, Weatherford, who condones the slaughter of tens of millions, is of the purest moral fiber.

¶¶   For a loving portrait of Kievan Rus', see *Rise of Russia* by Robert Wallace.

and its subjects. The Pravda required serious punishment (mostly fines) for arson, deliberate cattle mutilation, collective encroachment on rich people's property, and deliberate damage to forests, hunting grounds, or lands. Noteworthy by its absence is the death penalty.

After the 1113 riot in Kiev, a law was introduced that set limits on the operations of moneylenders. In trying to abolish blood feud, which was quite common at that time, the Russkaya Pravda narrowed its usage and limited the number of avengers to the closest relatives of the dead. It also regulated debt relations between individuals and contained articles of liability and hereditary law. Certain inalienable rights were accorded to women, such as property and inheritance rights.

Prince Vladimir (Vladimir the Great, 958–1015) reigned from 980 until his death. Beginning in 988, he brought Eastern Christianity to Kievan Rus', with long-term political, cultural, and religious consequences. Vladimir's conversion brought with it a favorable change in his character. He abandoned his sexual excesses and military adventures in favor of a peaceful and charitable outlook on life. Early Russian Christianity was infected with his newfound warmth and joyfulness. It was a time of hope and optimism.

Early missionaries had devised two alphabets, derived from the Greek alphabet, to be used in making the scriptures available to the Slavs. One of these missionaries was a monk by the name of Cyril. A modified version of his alphabet—Cyrillic—is the alphabet used in Russia to this day. A body of translations from Greek was thus expressly produced for the Slavic peoples. The existence of this literature facilitated the conversion to Christianity of the Eastern Slavs and introduced them to rudimentary Greek philosophy, science, and historiography without the necessity of learning Greek. Literacy was high. There are surviving love letters and cheat sheets for school, written on birch bark. Kievan Rus' was seen as cultured and enlightened by Europeans.

Enjoying independence from Roman authority and free from the tenets of Latin learning, the Eastern Slavs developed their own literature and fine arts, quite distinct from those of other Eastern Orthodox countries. Vladimir's son, Yaroslav I the Wise (978–1054), who reigned from 1019 until his death, oversaw the construction of Saint Sophia Cathedral in Kiev, which still stands as the city's proudest monument.

Kievan society lacked the class institutions that were typical of Western European feudalism. There was a free peasantry not bound to the land. Farmland could be bought, sold, and bequeathed with little restriction. There was no hierarchical system of fealty like the one that existed in Europe.

In Kiev, autocratic, aristocratic, and democratic institutions existed side by side. Overall rule was in the hands of the prince. There was a council of aristocrats called the *duma* that advised the prince. Members of the *duma* were known as *boyars* and over the years played an increasingly important role in Russian government.

The democratic element of society was represented by the *veche*, or town assembly, which all freemen could attend. Matters ranging from petty quarrels to the acceptance or expulsion of a prince were decided by unanimous vote. In principle, any freeman could summon the *veche* by simply ringing the municipal bell. The *veche* was especially strong in Novgorod. Its princes were hired by contract and expelled if they failed in their duties.

Around 1200, the city of Kiev had a population of approximately 80,000 people, and Novgorod and Chernihiv both had around 30,000 people. On the eve of the Mongol invasion, Kievan Rus' had around 300 urban centers.

Rivalry for power among the Scandinavian princes, the establishment of other regional centers to the north, the decline of Constantinople (which was a major trading partner for Kievan Rus'), and the shifting of trade routes to the north and east—in combination—resulted in the decline of Kievan Rus' in general and of Kiev in particular. However, Kiev remained a vital (if less influential) principality until its culture and people were decimated by Batu Kahn, grandson of Genghis, and his Mongol army.

For their first skirmish with the Mongols, in 1223, the Russians mounted an army of between 40 and 80 thousand. If, as reported, only one in ten returned from that conflict alive, that would have made for a death toll of at least 30 thousand. The Mongols departed and returned to complete the job about fourteen years later. Batu and his Mongol horde descended on the cities of Kievan Rus' from 1237 to 1240, wreaking devastation wherever they went. Speaking of the sacking of the city of Riazan, one chronicler writes, "And they burned this holy city with all its beauty and wealth ... and not one man remained alive.... All were dead. All had drunk the same bitter cup to the dregs. And there was not even anyone to mourn for the dead."[63]

On December 6, 1240, Batu attacked Kiev. The city was looted and burned to the ground. Tens of thousands lost their lives. Bones littered the landscape for miles around. The religious, cultural, and political center of one of the most important and civilized of early cultures had been obliterated.

In 1240, a Benedictine monk by the name of Matthew Paris described what he knew of the devastation of Kievan Rus' wrought by the Mongols:

> They razed cities to the ground, burnt woods, pulled down castles, tore up the vine-trees, destroyed gardens, and massacred the citizens and husbandmen; if by chance they did spare any who begged their lives, they compelled them, as slaves of the lowest condition, to fight in front of them against their own kindred. And if they merely pretended to fight, or perhaps warned their countrymen to flee, the Tartars following in their rear, slew them; and if they fought bravely and conquered, they gained

no thanks by way of recompense, and thus these savages ill-treated their captives as though they were horses.[64]

Giovanni de Plano Carpini, the Pope's envoy to the Mongol Khan, passed through Kiev in February 1246. He wrote:

> They [the Mongols] attacked Russia, where they made great havoc, destroying cities and fortresses and slaughtering men; and they laid siege to Kiev, the capital of Russia; after they had besieged the city for a long time, they took it and put the inhabitants to death. When we were journeying through that land we came across countless skulls and bones of dead men lying about on the ground. Kiev had been a very large and thickly populated town, but now it has been reduced almost to nothing, for there are at the present time scarce two hundred houses there and the inhabitants are kept in complete slavery.[65]

But it was not only the loss of life*** and a burgeoning democratic culture that must be weighed. There are broader consequences that need to be considered as well. The forced immigration to the north, and the opening of new trade routes, brought Moscow to the political center of Russian culture. The most corrupt and violent elements in Muscovy rose to the top to cope with the Mongol oppressors:

> The gropings toward freedom and democracy and the fairness and mildness of the legal code that had marked the Kievan state were wiped out. Russian rulers gradually came to resemble the khans in their harshness and despotism, either through imitation or through the necessity of paying them tribute. Despotism and enserfment, the two key facts of all subsequent Russian history, began under Mongol rule.[66]

Thus, one need wonder no longer, "Why is it that Russian society was so backward in its treatment of its own people? Why were they so submissive? Where did those tsars come from and why were they so cruel?"

Violence was injected into Russian society in heavy doses by the Mongol horde. A burgeoning social structure was crushed. Russia never recovered. What might Russia have become had Kievan values been allowed to mature and flourish? What might the world have become with this gentler influence from the East? Such questions are worth pondering. One begins to appreciate history at a deeper level. One begins to understand that death and destruction leave a legacy that haunts civilization into the indefinite future.

---

*** The Mongols destroyed a dozen or more cities in Kievan Rus'. At a minimum, there was a loss of hundreds of thousands of lives. The death toll could have reached into the millions.

# Power Concealed

*And was the first*
*That practiced falsehood under saintly show,*
*Deep malice to conceal, couch'd with revenge.*

MONARCHY ENGENDERS WAR. Oligarchy engenders war. The monarch leads his troops into battle. Oligarchs let others do the fighting for them. No longer is there a Genghis Kahn leading his troops into battle on horseback. Now there are meetings and discussions, held in private, in which a plan of conquest is laid out, a plan that serves the power interests of those who have envisioned it. This plan is then translated into symbolic language that can be used to motivate those who actually engage in battle, as well as those on the sidelines who provide for its moral and financial support. History offers many examples of this kind of violence at a distance.*

In an oligarchy, a three-tiered structure supports collective violence on a large scale. At the top, Level I, are the hidden powerbrokers. Level II is made up of those in government who craft the laws and policies and raise the funds to satisfy the wishes of those driving the action. And at the bottom, Level III, are those who do the actual killing: the soldiers and the secret agents.

The structure is designed to confound attempts at establishing accountability. Events just seem to happen, as the population at large is left to watch helplessly from the sidelines. Who is one to blame—the soldiers, the legislators, the invisible oligarchs?

## The Corporation, Hidden Power, and the Catholic Church

Matters became this complicated when, beginning in the Middle Ages,

---

* The latest, most up-to-date violence at a distance is executed via drones, or remotely operated aircraft. Seated in the den of his house, operating a computer, an employee of the U.S. government can track and gun down humans in far-off lands. He can then wash his hands and join the family for Sunday dinner.

the corporation was introduced into the mix. A corporation is not a person, it is a concept. How can it "do" anything? It can't. Its membership can. But we never see the membership. All we see is the image that the corporation projects into the public space. So when the corporation "does" something, it is not clear that something is even being done, or who is doing it. The chain of cause and effect remains hidden. And so we remain forever mystified. That is the way it's supposed to be.

Basically, a corporation is a small group of people who organize to acquire power and wealth, anonymously and without accountability. It has been defined thusly: "1. A body that has been granted a charter legally recognizing it as a separate legal entity having its own rights, privileges and liabilities distinct from those of its members. 2. Such a body created for purposes of government. 3. A group of people combined into one body."[1]

The first definition makes clear that the liabilities of the corporation and those who make up its membership are different. In essence, the entity of the corporation is to a degree (less and less so these days) liable for its actions. Its *individual members* are not. And that is the chief advantage to the membership. Membership need not fear the consequences of the corporation's collective action, nor is that action or the deliberations behind it routinely manifest to the curious public.

The longest-lived, wealthiest, and most powerful corporation in the world is neither Goldman Sachs nor Exxon-Mobil nor Pfizer. It is the Catholic Church, an organization that came into being two millennia ago, can claim a following in excess of a billion, and is in control of wealth—stocks and bonds, real estate, works of art, gold, and rare gems—that has been estimated to be in the trillions.

In 313, Constantine I (Constantine the Great) issued the Edict of Milan. By proclaiming religious toleration throughout the empire and legalizing Catholicism, Constantine made himself the first Christian emperor. Thus were the corporate Church and the corporate State briefly united.

Constantine decided that he should move his capital from Rome, which had been the seat of power for about a thousand years, to the Greek city of Byzantium, which he rebuilt on a grand scale and consecrated in 330. Tensions arose as the two seats of power—Rome and Constantinople—vied for control. Continued rivalry with the Eastern Church led, in 1054, to a permanent schism in which the Eastern Church, with its seat in Constantinople, and the Western Church, with its seat in Rome, became two separate entities.

With the collapse of the Roman Empire in the West, the Catholic Church emerged as the dominant power. It succeeded in expanding its power by attaching itself to and co-mingling with the various nation-states as they began to organize themselves around prominent leaders. In 496, the pagan king Clovis I, of the Franks, converted to Catholicism. On Christmas Eve, in the year 800, Charlemagne, King of the

Franks, was crowned Holy Roman Emperor by Pope Leo III. This peaceful merging of Church and State ultimately led to persistent wrangling for dominance and control by one or the other.

This uneasy alliance lasted for about a thousand years. The Church's corporate power was undermined in 1534, when King Henry VIII made himself Supreme Head of the Church of England after Pope Clement VII refused to annul his marriage to Catherine of Aragon. The power of the church suffered another important setback at the time of the French Revolution, when, in August 1789, the French canceled the Church's power of taxation. Declaring that all church property in France belonged to the nation, confiscations were ordered and Church properties were sold at public auction. Anti-Church laws were passed by the Legislative Assembly and its successor, the National Convention. In 1809, when Pope Pius VII pressured Napoleon to reestablish Catholicism in France, Napoleon countered by insisting that the Pope resign his office. When the Pope refused, Napoleon had him arrested.

The Church owes much of its early power to its bloody deeds. Fought over a period of nearly two hundred years, between 1095 and 1291, the Crusades were a series of religiously sanctioned military campaigns waged by much of Latin Christian Europe, particularly the Franks of France and the Holy Roman Empire, against the Muslims in the East.

It is estimated that 3 million were killed.[†] In 1098, when Antioch fell, 100,000 Muslims were massacred. The fall of Jerusalem in 1099 led to the massacre of another 70,000. The pools of blood were so deep as to come up to the knees of the horses. Richard the Lionhearted executed 3,000 Muslim prisoners all by himself. The Crusaders lost hundreds of thousands from among their own ranks, mostly from disease and starvation. But what was this all about? How did it happen that hundreds of thousands of Europeans, over a period of two hundred years, traveled thousands of miles to foreign lands to kill people of a different religion? Were these just random events? Was there a locus of power? If so, where was it? How were these people organized? Where did they get their motivation?

As a means of consolidating its power and establishing its universal legitimacy, the Catholic Church organized pilgrimages to distant lands. Hitherto, pilgrimages had been nonviolent. That changed in 1095, when Pope Urban II addressed the Council of Clermont and called on the knights of Europe to stop fighting one another and to band together against the heathens in the East. His goal was to control the knights, expand the power of the Roman Church, and ultimately bring the Eastern Church in Constantinople to heel. "By giving these 'pilgrims' to Jerusalem a sword," says Karen Armstrong in *Holy War: The Crusades*

---

† Here and elsewhere I am using "Selected Death Tolls for Wars, Massacres and Atrocities Before the 20th Century," at http://users.erols.com/mwhite28/warstat0.htm, as a source for fatality figures.

*and Their Impact on Today's World*,‡ "Urban made violence central to the religious experience of the Christian layman and Western Christianity had acquired an aggression that it never entirely lost."[2]

The next Crusade was organized by Bernard, Abbot of Clairvaux, at the bidding of Pope Eugenius. Bernard's eloquence, charisma, and political skills made him one of the most powerful men in Europe. On March 31, 1146, he addressed a large assembly of French barons. When his speech was over he knelt down and embraced the cross. Soon the entire assembly was on its knees embracing the crosses that had been prepared for the occasion. In the weeks that followed, Bernard toured France, preaching the new Crusade. Towns and villages were abandoned to wives and children as the men rushed to answer Bernard's summons.

In 1187, Saladin, Sultan of Egypt, conquered Jerusalem after nearly a century of Christian rule. After the Christians surrendered the city, Saladin spared the civilians and for the most part left churches and shrines untouched. Saladin is remembered respectfully in both European and Islamic sources as a man who "always stuck to his promise and was loyal." The reports of Saladin's victories shocked Europe. Pope Gregory VIII called for the Third Crusade (there were at least nine, all told), which was led by several of Europe's most important leaders: Philip II of France, Richard I of England (aka Richard the Lionhearted), and Frederick I, Holy Roman Emperor.

The Fourth Crusade (1202–1204) was originally intended to conquer Muslim-controlled Jerusalem by means of an invasion through Egypt. Instead, in April 1204, the Crusaders of Western Europe invaded and conquered the Christian (Eastern Orthodox) city of Constantinople, capital of the Byzantine Empire. The city was set afire, leaving 15,000 people homeless. For three days, the crusaders ravaged the city. Many ancient and medieval Roman and Greek works were either stolen or destroyed. The magnificent Library of Constantinople was destroyed. The Crusaders systematically violated the city's holy sanctuaries, destroying, defiling, or stealing all they could lay hands on. It was said that the total amount looted from Constantinople was about 900,000 silver marks, or 50,000 pounds of gold. As described by Speros Vryonis in *Byzantium and Europe*, "The Latin soldiery subjected the greatest city in Europe to an indescribable sack. For three days they murdered, raped, looted and destroyed on a scale which even the ancient Vandals and Goths would have found unbelievable."[3] This is seen as one of the final acts in the Great Schism between the Eastern Orthodox Church and Roman Catholic Church, in essence eliminating any threat to Roman dominance.

Catholic popes were not content to kill only heathens in far-off lands. When the faithful wandered from strict orthodoxy, when there

---

‡ I recommend this book highly. Armstrong writes with compassion and courage about a critical period in Western history. The book leaves the reader with a deepened understanding of these critical events and their relevance to Western identity and current events in the Middle East.

were competing ideologies with competing loyalties, it was expedient to use these same crusader fighting forces, under papal command, to slaughter those nearer to home.

In the south of France, there was a religious community known as the Cathari or Albigensians. There were a peaceful people who worshipped a god of love and peace. They believed that power and love cannot co-exist and specifically renounced the principle of power. When they persisted in living out their beliefs, Pope Innocent III (though innocent he certainly was not) saw to it that they were slaughtered, with a loss of life estimated to be as high as a million.[§]

The Crusades brought the Catholic Church an enormous increase in power, prestige, and wealth. Feudalism was undermined in favor of strong centralized power. Churches and monasteries were able to purchase the estates of those leaving for a Crusade at a mere fraction of their real value. Sometimes lands were donated in exchange for prayers and pious benedictions. Returning crusaders, broken in health and spirit, sought refuge in monasteries, which they endowed with their remaining worldly goods.

Thus is history made. People are organized and motivated to kill by individuals who have the requisite authority, charisma, and lust for blood. The Crusades are one of the earliest examples of corporate violence—in which we see the separation between the organizers of the violence and those who execute it. The Pope does not ride out on his steed, leading his men into battle. He has others do that for him. In a literal sense, there is no blood on his hands. He remains above the fray, though in essence he is at the center of it. This style of conquest is characteristic of the modern era. India offers another example.

## The British in India[¶]

So that the oligarchs in London, Paris, and Amsterdam could accumulate the wealth they coveted, the economy of India was taken over and destroyed. Indians were starved to death by the millions.

Many of us from the "civilized" West would undoubtedly point to India with a mixture of resignation, concern, and disdain. "Those poor Indians, they breed like rabbits and can't even feed and clothe themselves." Matters were not always this way. In fact, looking back just a few hundred years, an entirely different picture emerges:

> In the middle of the seventeenth century, Asia still had a far more important place in the world than Europe. The riches of Asia were incomparably greater than those of the European states. Her industrial techniques

---

§ Simon de Montfort, leader of the crusaders, ordered his troops to gouge out the eyes of one hundred Albigensian prisoners, cut off their noses and lips, then send them back to the towers led by a prisoner who had one remaining eye.
¶ See Henry George, *Progress and Poverty*, pp. 117-119.

showed a subtlety and a tradition that the European handicrafts did not possess. And there was nothing in the more modern methods used by the traders of the Western countries that Asian trade had to envy. In matters of credit, transfer of funds, insurance, and cartels, neither India, Persia, nor China had anything to learn from Europe.[4]

Under the name "Governor and Company of Merchants of London Trading into the East Indies," the oldest of the European East India Companies was granted an English Royal Charter by Elizabeth I on December 31, 1600. This action united government and business in common pursuit for the first (but not the last) time. At least one-fifth of the company's nominal capital of 3.2 million pounds was in Dutch hands, and a large proportion of that capital came from financiers in Amsterdam, Paris, Copenhagen, and Lisbon who were also directly concerned in the company's affairs.

Expecting to find an outlet for British broadcloth, the governors of the East India Company were disappointed to learn that there was no market for it, but they did find Indian-made items that could be sold at considerable profit back home. For a time, these trade relations were satisfactory to both parties. Commerce was active. The British adjusted to Indian culture. Indians worked under British employ. There were even intermarriages. The one sticking point was that Indian merchants would accept only silver or gold in payment for their goods.

By the end of the seventeenth century, British and French wool merchants were no longer willing to put up with competition from Indian textiles, which had become the rage among the rising bourgeoisie. These merchants sought and won restrictions on trading activities with India. The British were going to have to change their strategies.

But, even before trade restrictions, the British were getting restive. It was not possible to maintain indefinitely a high level of profits when faced with competition from other sources. There was opposition to the drain on European silver that was going to pay for the Indian goods. In 1669, Gerald Ungier, manager of a factory in Bombay, wrote to his directors, "The time now requires you to manage your general commerce with the sword in your hands." A similar sentiment had been expressed earlier in the century by a Dutchman named Jan Pieterzoon Coen. "Trade in India," he declared, "must be conducted and maintained under the protection and favour of your weapons, and the weapons must be supplied from the profits enjoyed by the trade, so that trade cannot be maintained without war or war without trade."[5]

All of this was finally settled in 1757. On June 23, the forces of the East India Company under Robert Clive** met the army of Siraj-ud-

---

** Major-General Robert Clive (1725–1774), First Baron Clive, also known as Clive of India, was a British soldier who established the military and political supremacy of the East India Company in southern India and Bengal. He is credited with securing India, and the wealth that followed, for the British crown.

Doula, the Nawab of Bengal, at the small village of Plassey, between Calcutta and Murshidabad. Outnumbered but ever resourceful, the British bribed key members of the opposing forces and managed to prevail over the Nawab of Bengal and his French allies.

The battle of Plassey is considered to be one of the pivotal events leading to the eventual expansion of the British Empire into today's South Asia. The enormous wealth gained from the Bengal treasury, as well as access to a massive source of food grains and taxes, allowed the Company to significantly strengthen its military might and opened the way for eventual British colonial rule, mass economic exploitation, and cultural domination.

Britain could now tax its new subjects to finance its commercial and military activities. It was in a position to force the cultivation of opium and use the profits from the sale of the drug for the purchase of teas to be sold in Europe. Sepoys, Indian soldiers under British command, were sent to destroy textile factories run by Indian manufacturers. Independent weavers who refused to work for the pitiful wages the East India Company offered had their thumbs cut off.[††] In a matter of three decades after the battle of Plassey, the East India Company achieved a virtual stranglehold on the economic and political life of eastern India. "Textile exports from India were subject to 80 percent tariffs while imports to India had 2.5 percent tariffs."[6] The British had destroyed the Indian textile industry and replaced it with their own.

In 1857, Indian soldiers rebelled against their British overlords. The British reprisals were savage. Rebels and suspected rebels were set before the mouths of cannons and blown to pieces:

> To the steady beat of drums, the captured rebels were first stripped of their uniforms and then tied to cannons, their bellies pushed hard against the gaping mouths of the big guns. The order to fire was given. With an enormous roar, all the cannons burst into life at once, generating a cloud of black smoke that snaked into the summer sky. When the smoke cleared, there was nothing left of the rebels' bodies except their arms, still tied to the cannons, and their blackened heads, which landed with a soft thud on the baking parade ground. It was a terrible way to die and a terrible sight to witness.[7]

One enthusiastic supporter of this butchery offered the following account in a letter that appeared in some Indian and English newspapers:

> All the city people found within the walls [of the city of Delhi] when our troops entered were bayoneted on the spot; and the number was consider-

---

[††]  British smuggling of opium from British India into China in defiance of China's drug laws erupted into open warfare between Britain and China in 1839 (the Opium Wars). There is a negligible difference, if any at all, between the tactics of the British oligarchy— destruction of factories owned by Indian rivals to the East India Company, the cutting off of thumbs, drug running, and smuggling—and those employed in the organized crime activities of the Mafia.

able, as you may suppose, when I tell you that in some houses forty and fifty persons were hiding. These were not mutineers, but residents of the city, who trusted to our well-known mild rule for pardon. I am glad to say they were disappointed.[8]

The numbers of deaths from these actions are not known with certainty, but they range from the hundreds of thousands to the millions.[‡‡]

The numbers of deaths resulting from famine, taxation, and land policies are better known, however. The British devastation of India was initially achieved by the simple means of taxing the people into destitution. Between 1765 and 1772, revenues leaving Bengal for London rose from 817,000 pounds sterling to more than 2.3 million pounds sterling. During the same period, 10 million Bengalis died from starvation, reducing the population by one-third.[9]

During British rule in India, there were approximately twenty-five major famines that spread through states such as Tamil Nadu in the south, Bihar in the north, and Bengal in the east. Altogether, between 30 and 40 million Indians were the victims of famine in the latter half of the nineteenth century alone.[10][§§]

That is not the end of it. In 1943, there was another great famine in Bengal. This was wartime. Although Bengal had enough rice and other grains to feed itself, millions of people were suddenly too poor to buy it. The Bengal government refused to stop the export of food from the region. The Viceroy of India, Archibald Wavell, made an urgent request for release of food stocks for India. Prime Minister Winston Churchill responded with a telegram asking, if food was so scarce, "why Gandhi hadn't died yet." An estimated 4 million Indians lost their lives to starvation.[11]

And the suffering continues still. In the twenty-first century, the era of globalization, a great "leap forward" in India has been hailed. What "leaping" there is, however, benefits a small segment of middle-class entrepreneurs. Small farmers and villagers, on the other hand, are being forced to plant crops for export. As a result, they can't feed themselves. As reported in the Huffington Post (December 7, 2011), since 1997, 200,000 Indian farmers have chosen suicide.

This is history, the killing field. And economic warfare is even more devastating than the old-fashioned kind. Battle-torn cities and country-

---

‡‡   Appalling as the British actions were, the events of 1857 had an even greater impact, which continues to this day. In the Indian uprising, Hindus and Muslims had joined forces to oppose their British masters. Their valiant effort did not succeed, but the British learned an important lesson. They realized they had to create a divide between Hindu and Muslim if they were to remain in power. This they did with a new policy that favored Hindus over Muslims. Muslims "were denied opportunities of employment in the government as well as modern education to ensure that they remained backward compared to the Hindus and thus forever in contention with them." *Insight Guide: India*, p. 48.

§§ During the Great Famine of 1876–1878, 1.5 million died in Madras. Women and children who stole from gardens or gleaned in fields were "branded, tortured, had their noses cut off, and were sometimes killed" (Peter Linebaugh, *The Magna Carta Manifesto*, p. 147). Life expectancy doubled once India gained its independence from Britain in 1947.

sides can reconstitute themselves. An impoverished nation—one whose infrastructure has been gutted, that has been denied the means of even feeding itself—is without hope.¶¶

In India, Latin America, and elsewhere around the world, specific individuals, hiding behind a corporate shield and with government protection, have taken over lands and peoples for private exploitation, with consequences that remain unremediated to this date. We who look on from the sidelines are left powerless and misinformed as to what is really happening and what it means. In this way, hidden power is able operate with impunity and without limits.

## Democracy in the Middle Ages: The Commons

As I suggested earlier, if one digs beneath the rubble one often finds that what is lost when a society is crushed is not just human life but a democratic way of living. This was the case in Kievan Rus'. One could say that the same applies to the destruction of medieval society in the West.

The Crusades are often celebrated for doing away with feudalism.*** Discussions of the subject rely on three assumptions: (1) feudalism was not a good thing; (2) slaughter was the only means of eliminating it; and (3) what replaced it was far superior. I would like for a moment to speak to the first assumption.

Feudalism has been defined as "a type of government in which political power was treated as a private possession and was divided among a large number of lords."[12]††† Even under Charlemagne's reign, it was the local count who was in charge in any particular region, not the emperor. The count had full judicial, financial, and military power over his small domain. Feudalism was a form of government with a strong leader at its head, but one in which power over day-to-day life was widely dispersed and fragmented, thus making effective centralization of control almost impossible. Society was composed of small, cohesive communities in which members counted on the support of fellow community members.

---

¶¶   A similar situation developed in Latin America. In this instance, it was the United States, not Britain, that provided the government assistance, and it was the United Fruit Company, not the East India Company, that provided the corporate structure. Behind the corporate anonymity, however, one finds a face. In Latin American history, the face belongs to Sam "The Banana Man" Zemurray. In *Bananas: How the United Fruit Company Shaped the World*, Peter Chapman reports that the United Fruit Company was "more powerful than many nation states ... a law unto itself and accustomed to regarding the republics [i.e., the banana republics] as its private fiefdom" (pp. 1–2). Chapman claims that more regime changes have probably been undertaken in the name of bananas than oil. Chapman's book was reviewed in the *New York Times Book Review* on March 2, 2008. Additional information on United Fruit Company can be found at http://mayaparadise. com and at http://www.unitedfruit.org/chron.htm.
***   Genghis Kahn and Napoleon Bonaparte have also been credited with this achievement, at an even greater cost in human life.
†††   Two excellent resources on the subject of feudalism are Joseph R. Strayer, "The Two Levels of Feudalism," in *Life and Thought in the Early Middle Ages*, edited by Robert S. Hoyt, and Joseph R. Strayer, *Western Europe in the Middle Ages*.

Feudalism existed in an agrarian society built around sustenance farming, and in which the common good prevailed over private interests. Each
peasant had a share of the land in his village and access to commons for
pasture and woodcutting. There was a sharing of plows and draft animals,
a pooling of labor. Government, as such, was reduced to the barest minimum. "The effective units of cooperation were pitifully small—the agricultural community of a few hundred inhabitants, the military community
of the lord and a few score followers."[13] The feudal system produced small,
local governments that emerged from the interests of the governed. Consequently, these structures were flexible and open to experimentation.

Such a society, with its strong democratic elements, was clearly an
obstacle to papal wishes to dominate Western Europe with a Church
presence. But it is worth speculating what the Western world might look
like today had this kind of society with this form of government been
allowed to evolve to its natural limits. It is easy to argue that our industrial age with its highly centralized governments is far superior to the
primitive medieval agrarian society.[‡‡‡] Such arguments were employed
to justify replacing the emerging agrarian democracy that existed in
the United States prior to the signing of the U.S. Constitution with a
central oligarchy. Yet is it necessarily true that an alienated society that
produces bombers and cell phones in abundance is superior to one that
is community based and involved in the production of food that is good
for the belly and good for the ecology?

The way in which we organize our society with regard to our agricultural needs has a significant impact on government and community
life. Sharing some land in common brings us together. Eliminating the
commons divides us. The notion that there are public lands—open fields
for public use (usually grazing) and public forests for the gathering of
fruits and firewood—goes back to the Middle Ages and was officially
recognized in the Magna Carta,[§§§] which was promulgated in 1215 and
1217 by King John of England. The owner of a single cow had a place
to graze it. Nuts, fruits, herbs, and mushrooms could be gathered at
will. Commoning "provided subsistence, a safety net against unemployment or low wages, and social security for the old."[14]

The concept and existence of the commons, with its origins in the
Middle Ages, continued well into the modern era. It is as viable today as
it was when it first emerged. If it has disappeared from our civilization, it
is because it was willfully excised by hidden powers who saw fit to take
what was owned in common and make it their own private property.

As has happened so often throughout history, when the powerful see
something of value, they want to seize it. And seize it they will, if given

---

‡‡‡  We forget, at our own peril, that all societies at their core are agrarian. This is true for
the obvious reason that without food to eat we will all starve to death.
§§§  See Peter Linebaugh, *The Magna Carta Manifesto: Liberty and Commons for All*, for
an eloquent exposition of and impassioned plea for the commons.

half a chance. The Enclosure Movement, as it is euphemistically known, is the process through which the system of the commons of Britain was dismantled. The act of "enclosure" has been described as follows:

> The process whereby open land or common land was parceled up into privately owned blocks or fields. In Britain this started in the 16th century AD, gathering pace during the 17th and 18th centuries, and is known as the *Enclosure Movement*. This mainly meant re-allocating the rights that people had to cultivation plots and common grazing so that compact farms were created. From the early 18th century this required a private Act of Parliament.[15]

A definition can be a sterile thing. In an attempt at neutrality, it can be completely depersonalized. So let us look deeper. How and why was the commons undone? What was the locus of power behind the actions? Even use of the word "enclosure" suggests an attempt at a whitewash. For me, the word has benign associations—a corral where a horse frolics of a summer's morning, a picket fence around the vegetable garden in a backyard. Would you guess that the word "enclose" in this context is synonymous with the word "steal"?

Members of the aristocracy—a loosely formed corporate entity—out of greed and indebtedness simply took what wasn't theirs and got Parliament to pass a law making it legal. Between 1814 and 1820, the Duchess of Sutherland dispossessed 15,000 tenants from 794,000 acres of land in northern Scotland and replaced them with 131,000 sheep of her own.[16]¶¶¶ Here is the voice of John Sinclair, first president of the English Board of Agriculture and lobbyist for enclosure, speaking of the commons: "Let us not," he said, "be satisfied with the liberation of Egypt, or the subjugation of Malta, but let us subdue Finchley Common; let us conquer Hounslow Heath, let us compel Epping Forest to submit to the yoke of improvement."[17]

Losing access to open public land, the subsistence farmer lost his independence and was obliged to work on someone else's land for marginal wages or else was driven to the industrialized cities to join the masses of the starving and unemployed that resided there. Beginning in 1549 with Kett's Rebellion,**** there was rioting, bloodshed, and death. In 1607, an uprising in Rockingham Forest protested enclosures by the Tresham family. Fifty people defending their right to the commons were massacred.[18] Thousands more were killed elsewhere under similar circumstances. In the Peasants War in Germany (1524–1525), 100,000

---

¶¶¶ As Vandana Shiva points out, while one acre of arable land could produce six hundred seventy pounds of bread, it could support only a few sheep. *Earth Democracy*, p. 19.
**** Rebels—tradesmen, yeomen, and commoners—in the tens of thousands set up campsites throughout lowland England. They established an alternative government under the Oak of Reformation and "prayed" (i.e., demanded) that "henceforth no man shall enclose any more." Linebaugh, *Magna Carta Manifesto*, p. 54.

German peasants lost their lives, demanding, among other things, the restoration of their right to the forest commons.

Here, again, we can recognize the modern style of conquest—the powerful rising above it all, keeping their hands clean of the consequences of their actions. In the good old days, the conquering "hero" would ride into the fray with his army, slaughtering at will. The reward was "glory" and booty. The booty for the "heroes" of the Enclosure Movement was land.

As civilization has "progressed," the means of conquest have become more genteel. Still, where necessary, the most brutal and ruthless devastation of a country and its people will be effectuated.[††††] However, if like the Duchess of Sutherland, one has friends in high places, one simply takes land and has a law passed legitimizing it. Eventually an entire economy is changed. Society develops a new bottom rung of the displaced and desperately poor. This is what is known as economic warfare.[‡‡‡‡] With such tactics, it is possible to impoverish countries and continents and bring about death in the millions, from starvation and disease, without firing a single shot.

Vandana Shiva has brought the issue of "enclosure" up to date. She speaks of the "atmospheric commons."[19] Food and water, resources vital to sustenance, "must stay in the commons,"[20] she says. Here she has in mind globalization and its effect on access to water and ownership of seeds. "Globalization," she declares, "is, in fact, the ultimate enclosure—of our minds, our hearts, our imaginations, and our resources."[21] Modern enclosures include the privatization of water[§§§§] through the building of dams and canals, groundwater mining, patents on life forms and biodiversity (in the guise of intellectual property rights), all in the service of corporate profits. As Shiva points out, we are forced to pay the corporations for what they have stolen from us. The corporations "elevate property created through theft of the commons into a sacred category, defining all attempts to protect the common good as a taking for which the original 'takee' must be compensated."[22]

Shiva reminds us that there is a direct connection between democ-

---

[††††] The Iraq invasion of 2009 is an excellent recent example.

[‡‡‡‡] In *Confessions of an Economic Hit Man*, John Perkins explains how it is done in modern times: "Today we do not carry swords. We do not wear armor or clothes that set us apart.... We seldom resort to anything illegal because the system itself is built on subterfuge, and the system is by definition legitimate" (pp. xx–xxi). Perkins worked for a private company whose business was to go to Third World countries and convince them to take out enormous loans they could not afford, to build an infrastructure—electrical grid, systems of transportation—they did not need. Construction companies like Halliburton, Bechtel, and Brown & Root made huge profits. The banks had an endless source of revenue from loans these impoverished countries would never be able to repay. Starting in 1970, based on the "modernization" of its economy (i.e., theft of its resources), Ecuador entered a state of steady decline. "The official poverty level grew from 50 to 70 percent, under- or unemployment increased from 15 to 70 percent, and public debt increased from $240 million to $16 billion" (p. xviii).

[§§§§] In Bolivia, collecting rainwater was forbidden.

racy and the commons:

> The very notion of the commons implies a resource is owned, managed, and used by the community.... Decisions about what crops to sow, how many cattle will graze, which trees will be cut, which streams will irrigate which field at what time, are made jointly and democratically by the members of the community. A democratic form of governance is what made, and makes, a commons a commons.[23]

As Shiva sees it, the commons are a real-life example that in fact democracy is possible, that it can and does work. "Functioning commons demonstrate that people can govern themselves, that democratic self-organization and self-governance work, and that people can cooperate, share, and jointly make democratic decisions for the common good."[24] To usurp the commons is to crush democracy. It is a political act, an assault on self-governance.

But there is always a face behind the assault, if we look hard enough—the Duchess of Sutherland, who stole 794,000 acres of land; the directors of the East India Company, who destroyed a thriving Indian economy and created famine; Winston Churchill, who appears to have overseen the starvation of millions; or Dan Amstutz, former Cargill vice president, who drafted the World Trade Organization's Agreement on Agriculture, leading to the imposition of cash crops at the expense of sustenance farming and the death by suicide of tens of thousands of Indian peasant farmers. In each instance, local self-determination is sacrificed to the needs of hidden, centralized power. There is no mystery to history. It is not about "imperialism," "colonialism," "capitalism," "communism," or "globalization." Such abstractions do nothing. They cannot act. Only human beings can.¶¶¶¶

---

¶¶¶¶ Crane Brinton, author of *A Decade of Revolution, 1789–1799*, puts it this way: "Modern historiography, with its pseudo-scientific bias, has emphasized the material circumstances, the economic motive, anything but the deliberate volition of men" (p. 162).

# 18 ❧

# Power Revealed

## Napoleon in Myth and Reality

*Towards him they bend*
*With awful reverence prone; and as a god*
*Extol him equal to the Highest in heaven.*

L ET US NOT forget, in speaking of gratuitous violence, the little man from Corsica, Napoleon Bonaparte (1769–1821).* Perhaps one of the first modern psychopaths, Napoleon dreamt of ruling the world from his throne in Paris. He got closer than most in making his dream come true.†

Napoleon's first public recognition as a military man occurred on 13 Vendémiaire (October 5),‡ 1795, when he used his artillery to fire point-

---

* I recommend J. Christopher Herold's *The Age of Napoleon* for a comprehensive overview of Napoleon and his era. The book is a highly readable and honest appraisal of the man. My only reservation is that the volume includes no footnotes, endnotes, or bibliography. For those who would like a more worshipful approach to our hero, there is Robert Asprey, *The Reign Of Napoleon Bonaparte*. On the other hand, in *Napoleon Bonaparte: A Life*, Alan Schom describes Napoleon as a cold-hearted manipulator. Alfred Cobban's two-volume *A History of France* makes this difficult period in modern history quite comprehensible. Volume 1 covers the period from 1715 – 1799, Volume 2, the period from 1799 - 1871. Crane Brinton's *A Decade of Revolution, 1789 - 1799* provides a useful overview of the revolutionary period and offers some interesting insights.
† There is not enough space in this book to discuss all of history's warriors. Certainly, however, Xerxes of Persia deserves at least a brief mention. According to Herodotus, Xerxes transported an army of 5.3 million from Persia to the shores of Attica. Xerxes described his grandiose ambitions as he prepared for war: "The sun will then shine on no land beyond our borders, for I will pass through Europe from one end to the other, and with your aid make of all the lands which it contains one country.... By this course then we shall bring all mankind under our yoke, alike those who are guilty and those who are innocent of doing us wrong." Quoted in M. I. Finley, *The Portable Greek Historians*, p. 86.
‡ In 1793, the revolutionary government of France established a new calendar—one that was more "natural," less religious—which remained in effect until 1805. According to that calendar, the month of Vendémiaire corresponded to September 22–October 21.

blank on hundreds of his countrymen, royalists who were marching in opposition to a new constitution. Five or six hundred were killed or wounded. From this modest beginning, Napoleon developed his skills as a military technician and propagandist, and ultimately conquered most of Western Europe. At its peak, his empire held sway over some 44 million souls. His wars led to the death of some 6.5 million people, close to fifteen percent of that population.

It is instructive to compare Napoleon with two other "heroes": Alexander and Genghis Khan. All three are responsible for many deaths. But Napoleon differed from the others in emotional make-up and motivation. Both Alexander and Genghis cared about human life—in the way the fox hunter cares about the life of the fox. The fox hunter wants a living fox so he can hunt it down and kill it. Alexander and Genghis were driven by a similar mentality. They wanted to kill for the sport of it, for the physical thrill of it. Each one of them entered into the heart of the battle, risking life and limb. Each was in the thick of it, flailing away, cutting through flesh and sinew until reaching a point of exhaustion.

For Napoleon, the life of his foe had even less meaning than it did for Alexander or Genghis. Napoleon wanted just one thing: power. He would take it any way he could get it. If he had to kill, he would. If he had to lie, he would. If he had to negotiate, manipulate, or betray, he would. He was probably the first warrior for whom the world was a chessboard—sacrifice a pawn here, a bishop there, end up with a rook or two. In the process, hundreds of thousands of lives would be consumed, cultures demolished. Like Alexander and Genghis, Napoleon had many admirers in his time and does to this day.§ The contradiction between Napoleon's conduct and the image he created of himself with the help of his admirers has been aptly summed up by his biographer. Speaking of Napoleon's early success in Italy against the Austrians, J. Christopher Herold observes, "Already he acted by instinct as if he owned the world. Already he viewed mankind with contempt; already mankind looked up to him as the hero of centuries."[1]

Napoleon had little or no sense of honor. In contrast to Alexander and Genghis, who were loyal to their troops, Napoleon showed not a shred of devotion to his comrades in battle, nor a mote of concern for their well-being. He would use up their lives like kindling to start a fire. When that kindling was gone, he would get more and use it up with the same abandon. French General Jean Baptiste Kléber, who served under Napoleon, once observed that Napoleon was the kind of general who needed a monthly income of ten thousand men.[2]

---

§ The great literary figures of the nineteenth century—writers such as Stendhal, Goethe, Heine, and Hegel—were all smitten with Napoleon and his achievements. Others were more circumspect. For example, Beethoven, who had originally dedicated the Eroica Symphony to Napoleon, changed his mind once Napoleon had himself crowned emperor.

## The Cost of Victory

We usually overlook the fact that when conquering heroes conquer, they are not only killing off hundreds of thousands of "the enemy"— that is, the army composed of the humble folk who live on the land the conqueror chooses to take—but they are also offering up hundreds of thousands of their own. These, too, are real people with real lives, though to read history one would not think so.

Initially, conscripts for Napoleon's armies were chosen by lot. Between 1801 and 1804, the goal was 60,000 per year. In 1805, the number jumped to 210,000. For the period 1805–1813, an estimated 2.3 million men were called up. The actual number reporting for duty was probably less. Married men were exempt, which helps explain the dramatic rise in marriages in France—from 203,000 in 1811 to 387,000 in 1813. Thousands of others mutilated themselves to avoid conscription.¶

Press gangs would patrol the streets and sweep up young people to serve against their will. When necessary, they would be flogged into submission. Napoleon drove his men—often little more than boys— beyond what was endurable. Regardless of how they started, they ended up desperate savages. After victory in Milan in 1796, Napoleon commented, "The ill-fed soldiers let themselves go to excesses of cruelty that make one blush for being a man."[3] By the time of his defeat in Russia, toward the end of his career, Napoleon had used up an army of at least a million men, about which he had this to say: "A man like me troubles himself little about a million men."[4] As for the enemy dead, he quipped, "Remember, gentlemen, what a Roman emperor said: 'The corpse of an enemy always smells sweet.'"[5]

The piles of corpses grew at an astounding rate, even for modern times. The victory over the combined Austro-Russian army at Austerlitz, on December 2, 1805, was considered to be one of Napoleon's most important achievements. Napoleon lost 9,000 men to the enemies' 26,000. Speaking of Napoleon's campaign in Poland in the winter of 1806–1807, Herold observes, "The sufferings of the troops were incredible, and the sufferings they inflicted on the population, with official sanction, in order to keep themselves fed and warm, were scarcely less appalling."[6] In the battle that took place at Eylau, in East Prussia, in February 1807, "the carnage was the worst thus far seen in modern history."[7] Of their 75,000 troops, the Russians lost more than a third, or 25,000, killed and wounded, while Napoleon, "the victor," with an army of 50,000, lost the same number or more—more than half his army, which was in a shambles. "Filthy, in rags, hungry and cursing their emperor, the troops turned into so many marauders. Nothing edible, combustible or furry was safe from them."[8]

---

¶ Apparently the English treated their recruits even worse than Napoleon did. Flogging was common. According to Herold, "English generals were more lavish with their soldiers' lives than were their French and German colleagues." *The Age of Napoleon*, p. 249.

Napoleon's presence in Saragossa, Spain, sparked valiant resistance on the part of the local population. It took thirty-eight days to penetrate their outer defenses. "Every house was a fortress and had to be blown up; every street was a battlefield."[9] The siege took the lives of 20,000 Spanish soldiers. An additional 30,000 civilians died in combat or of disease and hunger.

In May 1809, Napoleon bombarded the city of Vienna.** On May 21, he entered the city. A vicious battle with the Austrians ensued, just across the Danube. Napoleon got away with 19,000 in casualties, the Austrians with 24,000. In a subsequent battle on July 6, the Austrians lost 40,000, against 34,000 for the French. Thus, within a period of just six weeks, well over 100,000 men had been killed or wounded. Napoleon's disastrous Russian adventure of 1812 resulted in almost a million casualties. The battle of Borodino, alone, cost some 30,000 Frenchmen killed or wounded, some 45,000 Russians killed or wounded.

Inspecting the battlefield at Eylau, after what Napoleon counted as a victory, he wrote:

> To visualize the scene one must imagine, within the space of three square miles, nine or ten thousand corpses; four of five thousand dead horses; rows upon rows of Russian field packs; the remnants of muskets and swords; the ground covered with cannon balls, shells, and other ammunition; and twenty-four artillery pieces, near which could be seen the corpses of the drivers who were killed while trying to move them—all this sharply outlined against a background of snow.[10]

And here is the battlefield at Borodino, six weeks after the battle, as described by Count Phillipe-Paul de Ségur:

> We all stared around us and saw a field, trampled, devastated, with every tree shorn off a few feet above the earth.... Everywhere the earth was littered with battered helmets and breastplates, broken drums, fragments of weapons, shreds of uniforms, and blood-stained flags. Lying amid this desolation were thirty thousand half-devoured corpses. The scene was dominated by a number of skeletons lying on the crumbled slope of one of the hills; death seemed to have established its throne up there.[11]

The same Ségur described the French troops in retreat across a frozen Russian landscape, during the first heavy snowfall:

> Everything in sight became vague, unrecognizable. Objects changed their shape; we walked without knowing where we were or what lay ahead, and anything became an obstacle.... Yet the poor wretches [the soldiers] dragged themselves along, shivering, with chattering teeth, until the snow packed under the soles of their boots, a bit of debris, a

---

** The composer Joseph Haydn, in his seventy-seventh year, died of the shock three weeks after the bombardment.

branch, or the body of a fallen comrade tripped them and threw them down. Then their moans for help went unheeded. The snow soon covered them up and only low white mounds showed where they lay. Our road was strewn with these hummocks, like a cemetery.[12]

To warm themselves, the troops would set a whole house afire. Ségur's description continues:

The light of these conflagrations attracted some poor wretches whom the intensity of the cold and suffering had made delirious. They dashed forward in a fury, and with gnashing teeth and demoniacal laughter threw themselves into those raging furnaces, where they perished in dreadful convulsions. Their starving companions watched them die without apparent horror. There were even some who laid hold of the bodies disfigured and roasted by the flames, and—incredible as it may seem—ventured to carry this loathsome food to their mouths.[13]

## The Egyptian Campaign: Defeat and Denial

Bizarre as it might seem, all of this death and devastation were a diversion for Napoleon, an indirect means of trying to defeat his arch enemy—the one he never fully engaged in battle, the one who ultimately oversaw his decisive defeat—England. Napoleon had dreams of amassing a vast armada and sailing across the Channel and taking Britain directly, by force. Reluctantly, he had to admit that such an adventure would most likely end in humiliating defeat. He would just have to settle for getting them elsewhere. He would deplete their empire in India, starting with Egypt. In a letter to the French Directory and his Foreign Minister, Talleyrand, Napoleon wrote, "the day is not far off when we shall appreciate the necessity of seizing Egypt, in order really to destroy England."[14] And so began the Egyptian campaign. Though much of his effort and success was in Europe, for Napoleon, "this tiny Europe" was a "molehill." "We must go to the Orient," he proclaimed. "All great glory has been acquired there."[15] Much can be learned about Napoleon's character and about his skill as both general and politician from a study of this one operation—which ultimately ended in total defeat.

The Egyptian expedition began with a convoy of four hundred ships covering between two and four square miles at open sea. Aboard were 34,000 land troops, 16,000 sailors and marines, 1,000 civilian personnel, and a treasury of 4.6 million francs, enough to meet the payroll for about four months. On July 1, 1798, after taking Malta along the way, Napoleon's fleet was in sight of Alexandria. An Arab chronicler reported that when the people on shore looked at the horizon, they "could no longer see water but only sky and ships; they were seized by unimaginable terror."[16]

Egypt was ruled by a caste of warriors known as the Mameluke. Says Herold of the Mameluke, "Nothing exceeded his courage except his arrogance, ignorance, cruelty and greed."[17] On July 21, Napoleon's army defeated the Mameluke at Embaba, on the west bank of the Nile, across from Cairo. Napoleon decided to give his victory the grand title "Battle of the Pyramids." He claimed the enemy's strength at 78,000, or three times his, when in fact the numbers were roughly equal. Napoleon is alleged to have addressed his entire army with the words, "Soldiers, forty centuries look down upon you." As Herold points out, however, there is no way such an event could have taken place. Perhaps Napoleon simply made such a remark to some officers standing nearby.

The British had been tracking the French activity with an armada of their own. Admiral Horatio Nelson was in command. He found the French anchored in Aboukir Bay on Egypt's Mediterranean coast and ordered an immediate attack. One-third of the French crew was on shore. Despite the overwhelming firepower of the French fleet, Nelson was able to maneuver some of his ships behind the French, putting them under attack from both sides. The battle was intense. The French commander was killed, and Nelson received a severe head wound. The French flagship *l'Orient* caught fire and blew up, in an explosion felt fifteen miles away. In the end, eleven French battleships had been captured or destroyed, and one admiral and three captains killed. This was a victory for the English, who blockaded the harbor. The French army was trapped in Egypt.

Napoleon's response to this devastating turn of events was to pretend it hadn't happened:

> He made believe that he controlled Egypt, when in fact he never controlled more than Cairo and a few other key cities.... He made believe he was in Egypt with the approval of the [Turkish] sultan for three months after the sultan had declared war and vowed his destruction.... He encouraged the sheiks of the Divan [governing council] of Cairo to believe that he and his army were about to embrace Islam and that his coming had been predicted in the Koran; the sheiks did not believe a word of it, but they dutifully passed on the good word in their proclamations to the populace, which did not believe it either.[18][††]

Napoleon stayed in Egypt for another year after Nelson's victory. Over the course of that year, matters deteriorated considerably. The Egyptian populace became more and more hostile. Napoleon ran out of money and had to resort to various ruses and taxes to find something to pay his troops. But there was never enough. By the time he left in 1799, Napoleon had accumulated a debt of 12 million francs. The troops longed to return home. Morale was at its lowest point. One-third of the troops suffered from an Egyptian eye disease. Syphilis and gonorrhea were rampant. In December, the bubonic plague made an appearance. Yet to his government back in France, Napoleon wrote, "We lack nothing here. We are bursting with strength, good health,

---

†† It is not hard to see the parallels between Napoleon's make-believe in Egypt in 1798 and America's make-believe in Iraq in 2012.

and high spirits." His biographer comments, "To maintain such fictions in the teeth of such realities borders either on true heroism or on sheer madness."[19] I would offer another explanation. It was Napoleon, not Edward Bernays,‡‡ who was the true founder of the field of public relations (i.e., public deception). He had no regard for the truth and would use any distortion he could come up with to create a reality favorable to his own advancement. In fact, such a facility, as much as or more than his battlefield tactics, explains Napoleon's rise to power.

Napoleon managed to sneak through Nelson's blockade at Aboukir Bay and made it back to Paris by October 1799. Quick to switch gears from general in the field to backroom schemer, Napoleon sensed an opportunity to steer the country away from its democratic leanings and turn it into a dictatorship under his control.

## Revolutionary Government

It is unfortunate that the mere mention of the French Revolution evokes thoughts of the Reign of Terror, a period of violence lasting from September 5, 1793, to July 27, 1794, in which as many as 40,000 lives were lost. §§ But as horrible as it was, the terror is not the whole story. Over the ten-year period from 1789 to 1799, France experimented with three different kinds of government, each with its own merits, all of which were shunted aside and forgotten once Napoleon made himself emperor.

The Revolution began in a relatively peaceful, reasonable fashion. It was Maximilien Robespierre who unleashed mass hysteria by calling for the execution of the king in a country where the king was considered to be God's voice on earth. After Louis XVI was executed, some of the citizens who had witnessed the beheading ran to have their clothes soaked in the king's blood, still dripping from his head. Others in the crowd went mad, slit their throats, or jumped into the River Seine.¶¶

Robespierre, of course, did not strike the fatal blow himself. And many might be inclined to believe that the Reign of Terror that followed the king's execution just seemed to happen. Yet it was Robespierre who argued, "Louis must die, so that the country may live." By a close vote (361 in favor, 288 opposed), the National Convention voted to execute the king. On January 21, 1793, Louis XVI was sent to the guillotine.***

Prior to the Revolution, the legislative body was known as the *États*

---

‡‡   See Chapter 2.

§§ The Terror which might seem to be an example of collective madness, was for the most part orchestrated by a handful of men hungry for personal ascendancy. In *A History of Modern France*, Alfred Cobban makes repeated reference to various agitators playing on the discontent of the people, stirring up passions by spreading false rumors for the purpose of gaining personal power (Vol. 1, p. 184).

¶¶   See Adam Zamoyski, *Holy Madness: Romantics, Patriots and Revolutionaries*, p. 1.

***   See Alfred Cobban, *A History of Modern France*, Vol. 1, *Old Regime and Revolution, 1715–1799*, p. 210. A timeline of the French Revolution is available at http://en.wikipedia.org/wiki/Timeline_of_the_French_Revolution.

*Généraux.* It was made up of three *états* (estates, or classes). The clergy constituted the first estate, the nobility the second. Everybody else, principally the middle class, was part of the third estate. In gatherings of the legislative body, each of the estates had one vote. If the first two estates joined ranks, they could override the third estate and thus frustrate the wishes of the vast majority of Frenchmen.

Under pressure from the nobility (the second estate), who wished to separate itself from the monarchy's financial crisis, Louis XVI summoned the *Etats Généraux* for the first time since 1614. On May 5, 1789, the delegates gathered. After a wrangling for power, the middle class (third estate) emerged victorious.

The third estate separated itself from the *Etats Généraux*, held its own meeting, and called for elections in the spring of 1789. All male citizens who paid taxes were granted the franchise. Six hundred ten delegates of the third estate were selected and declared themselves the National Assembly, an assembly not of the estates but of "the People." They invited the other estates to join them, but made it clear they intended to conduct the nation's affairs with or without them. As they might in a true democracy, citizens were able to give expression to their grievances. Delegates brought with them *cahiers de doléances*, or lists of grievances representing the expressed concerns of their constituencies. The Assembly directed its attention to such critical issues as debt, taxation, and food shortages.

After July 9, 1789, the Assembly became known as the National[†††] Constituent Assembly and continued in its deliberations despite opposition from the king. As of July 14, 1789, it became the effective government of France. On September 3, 1791, after two years of deliberation, the Assembly adopted France's first written constitution.

The Constitution of 1791 was a mixture of moderation and innovation. Although it established a constitutional monarchy and granted the king veto power over the legislature, it was doing so as an assembly of citizens with equal rights and equal voting power. To further assert its power, the middle class created a unicameral legislature. There was to be no upper house to overpower those representing the more popular interests. A system of recurring elections was established. The Declaration of the Rights of Man, adopted on August 26, 1789, became the preamble of the constitution. All men had the same rights. These rights were to be respected by the government. There was to be freedom of speech and assembly. Popular sovereignty as opposed to the divine right of kings was to be the law of the land.

This new government, though a monarchy, represented a significant step in the direction of democracy. This moderate state of affairs lasted about a year. The king's use of his veto power and the rising discontent throughout the nation resulted in crisis and the overthrow of the monarchy. Not to be overlooked is the conflict within the assembly and the role played by Robespierre.

---

††† As in Pennsylvania, in 1776, this was a peaceful change in government before the Revolution.

Once the constitution had been drafted, the Constituent Assembly was to be dissolved. It was Robespierre who proposed that all members of the Constituent Assembly be denied a place in the new legislative body. These were level-headed, serious-minded legislators who probably would have acted as a stabilizing force. By denying them participation in the new assembly, Robespierre was making room for the factionalism and personal power struggles that would ultimately lead to his rising to the role of dictator over a war-torn and divided country. None of this was necessary, and it might not have occurred had it not been for the personal ambition of men like Robespierre. ‡‡‡

The Constitution of 1793§§§ replaced the Constitution of 1791. Under the new constitution, France was no longer a monarchy. It was a republic. There were to be no property requirements for voting or holding office. The government was to ensure "a right to subsistence." Citizenship was liberally defined. There were provisions for direct elections, with one delegate per 40,000 citizens.¶¶¶ There were to be run-off elections when there was no absolute majority, and in some cases (when there was a tie), selection by lottery. Elections were to be held annually. Provision was made for an executive council composed of twenty-four members, serving for a year only.

Annual elections, an executive council of twenty-four, unicameral legislature—such provisions made this constitution one of the most democratic in modern times. And along with it went a liberal, democratic approach to modifying the constitution:

> If, in one-half of the departments plus one, one-tenth of the regularly constituted primary assemblies requests the revision of a Constitutional Act or the amendment of some of its articles, the Legislative Body shall be required to convoke all the primary assemblies of the Republic to ascertain if there are grounds for a National Convention.[20]

In reaction against the terror and the militarization of a society in a state of constant warfare, a third, more conservative constitution was adopted in 1795. Under this constitution, only qualified property holders could vote. Instead of one house speaking for everyone, there was a bicameral legislature: a Council of Five Hundred and a Council of Ancients (made up of 250 members). Each council was to have one-third of its membership renewed annually. The Ancients had veto power but could not initiate legislation. There was to be an executive made up of five directors, chosen by the Ancients out of a list sent to them by the Five Hundred, one director facing retirement each year.****

---

‡‡‡ One is reminded of the destructive role played by Alcibiades in ancient Athens (see Chapter 3)

§§§ The text of this constitution is available at http://chnm.gmu.edu/revolution/d/430/.

¶¶¶ This rate of representation was more generous than James Madison's offer of one per 50,000 for the U.S. Constitution.

**** Even this conservative constitution is in some ways progressive when compared with

When Napoleon appeared on the scene in October 1799, this third constitution—with its five-member Directory—was in place. There were serious economic and political issues to be addressed. But in the view of at least one historian,†††† France did not need to be rescued from itself by a savior in the person of Napoleon Bonaparte. There is every indication that without Napoleon's intervention, a stable oligarchy with democratic leanings would have survived and evolved. So that here again we see, as in the case of Philip II and Alexander,‡‡‡‡ how warriors, consecrated as heroes, can undo years of patient work and experimentation in government and set civilization back dramatically.

On 18 Brumaire (November 9), 1799, Napoleon's coup replaced the Directory of five with a Consulate of three. On February 7, 1800, a public referendum confirmed Napoleon as First Consul, a position that would give him executive powers above the other two consuls. In 1802, another plebiscite was held confirming Napoleon as First Consul for Life. In 1804, he had himself crowned Emperor and found the support he was looking for in yet another plebiscite.

Like Alexander and Genghis Khan, Napoleon's chief weapon was terror.§§§§ Faced with armed opposition early in January 1800, he commented, referring to himself, "The First Consul believes that it would serve as a salutary example to burn down two or three large communes.... Experience has taught him that a spectacularly severe act is ... the most humane method. Only weakness is inhuman."[21] "At home as abroad," he said, "I reign only through the fear I inspire."[22] In a similar vein, and at an earlier period in his life, in the midst of the the Reign of Terror—he was twenty-four at the time—Napoleon expressed himself as follows:

> Among so many conflicting ideas and so many different perspectives, the honest man is confused and distressed and the skeptic becomes wicked.... Since one must take sides, one might as well choose the side that is victorious, the side which devastates, loots, and burns. Considering the alternative, it is better to eat than to be eaten.[23]

---

the current situation in United States, where there are 535 representatives speaking for a population of more 300 million people, as opposed to 750 representatives for a population of about 25 million under the French Constitution of 1795. In other words, this French government was seventeen times more representative than the current U.S. government. Further, the French constitution provided for a plural executive, each director serving for a maximum of five years. No one executive was all-powerful, as is the case in the United States.

†††† Crane Brinton, in *A Decade of Revolution, 1789–1799*, provides an even-handed discussion of the Directory (pp. 212–221).

‡‡‡‡ See Chapter 16.

§§§§ Madame Germaine de Staël (1766–1817) described Napoleon's power succinctly: "The terror he inspires is inconceivable." Madame de Staël was an essayist and writer of letters whose opinions traveled the Continent. Her salon was host to some of the most outstanding men of letters and politics of the time. She was independent and outspoken and even took on the likes of Napoleon himself. In her salon, which she referred to as a "hospital for defeated parties," she united a wide array of those who opposed Napoleon's totalitarian rule. Herold, *The Age of Napoleon*, pp. 122, 155.

Second only to terror in Napoleon's arsenal was propaganda, written and directed by the man himself. He composed his own epic poem, glorifying war and conquest and his indomitable determination to crush his adversary wherever he found him. In June 1799, Napoleon defeated the Austrians at Marengo in a surprise counterattack. This victory cost Napoleon 6,000 men to the Austrians' 9,000. Afterward, he issued an account of the battle, celebrating the loss of only 600 men. This "victory bulletin" was just one of many hundreds that were to follow over the next thirteen years, each one a minor masterpiece of rhetoric and deception designed to elevate himself and his cause in the eyes of his readers. It was this unbroken narrative of grandiloquence and hubris that won over many of Napoleon's admirers.¶¶¶¶

## Myth vs. Reality

As it was with Alexander and Genghis Khan, so it was with Napoleon. His many admirers set aside his endless butchery and built a memorial to what they believed to be his many achievements. The most often mentioned is the Civil Code. With the assistance of a commission he appointed, Napoleon himself ultimately reorganized and established a new a uniform code of law for an entire society, based solidly on Roman law. This undertaking, initiated once he had established himself as supreme leader, and vaunted as an important step in the modernization of Western society, was the cornerstone in Napoleon's attempt to exercise total control over the population.

As was the practice in ancient Rome, Napoleon's Civil Code granted the father despotic control over the family. He had the right to imprison his own child for one month. On getting married, the wife passed from the control of her father to that of her husband. Wives had no rights and could not own property, placing them under a level of control even more strict than that which prevailed under the *Ancien Régime*. "Women should stick to knitting," Napoleon once said.[24] He also declared, "The husband must possess the absolute power and right to say to his wife: 'Madam, you shall not go out, you shall not go to the theatre, you shall not receive such and such a person; for the children you shall bear shall be mine.'"[25] These are hardly words one would expect from the author of what has been alleged to be a most advanced codification of law.

Napoleon also created a system of public education whose ultimate aim was the same as that of the Civil Code: total control. All schools were placed under the direct supervision of the state. Higher, special-

---

¶¶¶¶ Where necessary, Napoleon would make up events to outrage and motivate his followers. During his Russian campaign, he alleged that "sixty-year-old women and young girls of twelve [were] raped by groups of thirty to forty [Russian] soldiers" (Herold, *The Age of Napoleon*, p. 360). Things haven't changed much. In October 1990, the fifteen-year-old daughter of the Kuwaiti Ambassador to the United States claimed that Iraqi soldiers came into a maternity ward, took babies out of incubators, and left them on the floor to die.

ized schools were well funded. The education of the masses was generally neglected. "It was Napoleon's conviction that too much instruction
for the lower classes was dangerous to the social order."[26] Here is an
example of the catechism devised by Napoleon to be repeated by French
schoolchildren: "*Question:* What should one think of those who fail in
their duties to our emperor? *Answer:* According to the Apostle Saint
Paul, they would resist the order established by God Himself and would
make themselves deserving of eternal damnation."[27]

Napoleon's regime produced an impressive list of public works.
The penal code had prescribed forced labor for an amazing number of
offenses. By virtue of this convenience, Napoleon had a limitless supply
of cheap labor to build his roads, canals, and bridges. Hitler achieved
similar goals with similar strategies.

As Genghis had done for the East, Napoleon succeeded in recon-
figuring the map of Europe. Certainly not by intention, his wars ultimately led to the unification of Germany. Where his troops trod, it has
been said, feudal society crumbled. "He was the unwitting midwife of
the modern world."[28]

Assumed but not expressed in the undying admiration for Napoleon and his achievements are the beliefs that (1) the achievements were
beneficial and desirable, and (2) they could not have been realized without the deaths of millions. In practical terms, despite staggering costs
in lives and property inflicted as Napoleon built his empire, after his
defeat, France emerged reduced to her borders of 1790, saddled with
a bill of almost a billion francs in reparations, and with several of her
provinces under occupation by the forces that had defeated him.

By virtue of Napoleon's many writings and of the writings of those
who interviewed him, we have been provided with an unusual glimpse
into the emotional make-up of the psychopathic "hero." In essence,
Napoleon was an emotional void.[29] He was suicidally depressed
throughout most of his life, beginning in adolescence. The other side of
suicide is homicide, hence the decades of savagery. At the age of seventeen, Napoleon wrote:

> Always alone in the midst of men, I come to my room to dream by myself,
> to abandon myself to my melancholy in all its sharpness. In which direc-
> tion does it lead today? Toward death.... What fury drives me to my own
> destruction? Indeed what am I to do in this world? Since die I must, is
> it not just as well to kill myself?... Since nothing is pleasure to me, why
> should I bear days that nothing turns to profit?... Life is a burden to me
> because I taste no pleasure and all is pain to me.[30]

One can dismiss these thoughts as the romantic meanderings of ado-
lescent self-pity. But I think that would be a mistake. It makes perfect
sense to understand Napoleon's drive to conquer the world as nothing
more and nothing less than his desperate attempt to escape the inner

void described in this passage. He was lacking in human emotion, which is why he could kill with such alacrity and convincingly distort reality to suit his purposes.

Like any bully, Napoleon was a coward. His behavior at one of his lowest points paints a most revealing picture. Napoleon had been defeated. He had surrendered his throne and was being escorted into exile on the island of Elba. Although he still thought of himself as the conquering hero, admired by his people, as he progressed along his journey he discovered that was not completely true. He saw himself hanged in effigy. Screaming women converged on his carriage, haranguing him for the deaths of their sons and husbands, ready to tear him to pieces. Napoleon cowered in terror behind his grand marshal of the palace. In fear for his life, he disguised himself as a postilion and rode in front of his own carriage. Later he posed as Colonel Neil Campbell, the British commissioner. With any army of 500,000 behind him, Napoleon could be pretty tough. On his own, confronted with an infuriated mob, he was a frightened little boy.

In *The Insanity of Normality: Toward Understanding Human Destructiveness*, Arno Gruen identifies self-pity as one of the traits typical of the psychopath. Napoleon, in defeat, could have been transported to the guillotine or consigned to a dungeon. Instead, he was exiled to the island of Saint Helena***** and resided at a sprawling residence known as Longwood. He was surrounded by servants and admirers and was referred to as "Your Majesty." He and his entourage consumed seventeen bottles of wine, eighty-eight pounds of meat, and nine chickens a day, as well as champagne and liquor. Nonetheless, Napoleon's "sufferings" became known to Pope Pius VII, the very same man who had been arrested and imprisoned by Napoleon. Pius VII pleaded that the prince regent "lighten the sufferings of so hard an exile."[31] Napoleon himself sent a message to Sir Hudson Lowe, who was responsible for overseeing his confinement on the island. Speaking of himself in the third person, Napoleon wrote, "You have miscalculated the height to which misfortune, the injustice and persecution of your government, and your own conduct have raised the emperor. His head wears more than an imperial crown—it wears a crown of thorns."[32] Here we see Napoleon comparing his "sufferings" at Longwood to those of Christ. One can dismiss such words as ludicrous self-indulgence, yet they are revealing of just who and what Napoleon really was. He believed those words as uttered.

---

***** Napoleon lived in exile on two separate occasions. The first time, in 1814, he was exiled to the Italian island of Elba. After three hundred days, he escaped with the small army that had been allotted to him and attempted to reestablish his ascendancy in Europe. He returned to Paris to a hero's welcome and raised an army of 200,000. One hundred days later, he was defeated in the Battle of Waterloo. This time, he was exiled to Saint Helena, an island in the Atlantic about a thousand miles from the nearest land mass.

The Napoleonic legend was created during Napoleon's lifetime, and with his enthusiastic support. It was developed and established at a leisurely pace during his five and a half years of exile on Saint Helena. As Herold points out, "Nothing could be more ironic than the contrast between the atmosphere of pettiness that pervaded his little court and the lofty image that was manufactured there."[33] Napoleon's greatest asset in this regard was an admirer by the name of Comte Emmanuel de Las Cases (1766–1842), a French historian who accompanied him into exile. His *Mémorial de Sainte-Hélène* (1822–1823) records his master's life in exile and his recollections of past events. Here is Napoleon on camera, speaking of himself without a blush:

> I have closed the gaping abyss of anarchy, and I have unscrambled chaos. I have cleansed the Revolution, ennobled the common people, and restored the authority of kings. I have stirred all men to competition, I have rewarded merit wherever I found it, I have pushed back the boundaries of greatness. All this, you must admit is something. Is there any point on which I could be attacked and on which a historian could not take up my defense? My intentions, perhaps? He has evidence enough to clear me. My despotism? He can prove that dictatorship was absolutely necessary. Will it be said that I restricted freedom? He will be able to prove that license, anarchy, and general disorder were still on our doorstep. Shall I be accused of having loved war too much? He will show that I was always on the defensive. That I wanted to set up a universal monarchy? He will explain that it was merely the fortuitous result of circumstances and that I was led to it step by step by our very enemies. My ambition? Ah, no doubt he will find that I had ambition, a great deal of it—but that grandest and noblest, perhaps, that ever was: the ambition of establishing and consecrating at last the kingdom of reason and the full exercise, the complete enjoyment of all capabilities! And in this respect the historian will perhaps find himself forced to regret that such an ambition has not been fulfilled.[34]

The power of such panegyric is irresistible. It has as much basis in reality as the "crown of thorns" Napoleon was forced to wear during his exile. There is not a hint of remorse at the millions of lives lost, or the gratuitousness of it all.

This capacity to create an alternate reality, with conviction, was perhaps Napoleon's greatest asset. It was this ability that enabled him to resort to totalitarian dictatorship while simultaneously convincing the French that he was a friend of the people and supported the ideals of the French Revolution. It is also the primary reason men like him are so dangerous to civilized living. The reality of their destructive power is buried beneath a snowstorm of rhetoric and self-glorification. We enter the reality they create for us because it is so captivating. We lose track of who such men really are. We lose control of our collective destiny.

Here is another vision of the man. Here is Napoleon off camera. Gaspar, Baron Gourgaud (1783–1852) was a soldier in Napoleon's army who accompanied him into exile. His *Journal de Ste-Hélène* was not published until 1899, long after his death. Here we find Napoleon the tyrannical egotist and brutal cynic. Speaking to Gourgaud of his own worries, Napoleon says, "Bah! The main thing is oneself.... Isn't it true Gourgaud, that it's a lucky thing to be selfish, unfeeling? If you were, you wouldn't worry about the fate of your mother or your sister, would you?" As to Napoleon's attitude toward those who surround him, he explains, "What do I care how people feel about me, so long as they show me a friendly face!... I pay attention only to what people say, not to what they think.... All being said, I like only people who are useful to me, and only so long as they are useful."[35] Spoken like a true psychopath.

Recall how Napoleon claimed to have "ennobled the people." Here we learn his technique: "there is nothing like summary courts-martial to keep the lower classes and the rabble in line.... Hang, exile, prosecute—that's what they [the Bourbons] must do.... The French nation has no character."[36]

François-René, vicomte de Chateaubriand (1768–1848), French writer, politician, and diplomat, had this to say about the glorification of Napoleon:

Gone are the sufferers, and the victims' curses, their cries of pain, their howls of anguish are heard no more. Exhausted France no longer offers the spectacle of women plowing the soil. No more are parents imprisoned as hostages for their sons, nor a whole village punished for the desertion of a conscript.... It is forgotten that everyone used to lament those victories, forgotten that the people, the court, the generals, the intimates of Napoleon were all weary of his oppression and his conquests, that they had had enough of a game which, when won, had to be played all over again.[37]

# Darkness Visible

## Hidden Power Comes to Light

*Yet from those flames*
*No light; but rather darkness visible . . . where peace*
*And rest can never dwell.*

W HEN THE ALCOHOLIC loses control, he starts hiding bottles. The drug abuser who shoots up tries to hide the track marks. The compulsive gambler lies about where the money is going. Each is an addict. And the addict always wants new highs, better highs, higher highs. More and more he lies to himself and to those around him. The lying, the cover-up, the self-deception get grander and grander. The deception becomes almost an end in itself. The addict lives in constant fear of being found out and feels a desperate need to hide his actions. But at some point, no matter how resourceful the addict, what is hidden begins to overtake his attempts at cover-up. Soon, what was hidden becomes visible. The wife knows, friends and relatives know, the boss knows, the medical profession knows, possibly even law enforcement knows.

The story is no different for modern-day, power-addicted oligarchs. They engage in the same constant search for new highs, but this time the highs are limitless wealth and unquestioned power—and if the stepping stones to achieving those highs are depredation, starvation, and slaughter, so be it. And as with any other addiction, at some point, the enormity and the consequences of the enterprise overtake all attempts to cover them up. This is what happened in the global financial crisis of 2008, when the fallout of the addictive behavior of power-brokers worldwide left bankers in the United States alone needing a handout of something like $23 trillion while modest, middle-class homeowners were being dispossessed and forced to live in tents.* For the banks that were too big to fail, the secret had finally grown too big to keep.

Americans live under a rhetorical democracy that has, for two centuries, provided ample cover for America's oligarchic underpinnings. It is unclear just how much longer the democratic myth can be sustained, however, and the risk of discovery in some sense might help to explain the recent frenzy in the arenas of politics and finance. Time is running out for the power addicts.

## Political Deception and Its Consequences

The democratic myth breeds the lie. The professional politician owes his loyalty to his paymasters, those who supplied the millions that got him into office.† Yet the democratic myth requires that the politician pay verbal homage to the voters, hence the lie.

When listening to campaign speeches, when entering the voting booth, we must willingly, subconsciously, suspend disbelief—as we would do when setting out to enjoy an evening of theater. We must choose to believe in something that we know has no basis in reality. We must believe the lie. Here are a few witticisms that express this widely accepted truth:[1]

> Since a politician never believes what he says, he is always astonished when others do. —*Charles De Gaulle*

---

* The role of bankers in depleting government treasuries is nothing new. In part as a consequence of French support for the American Revolution, the French government found itself on the verge of bankruptcy in the late eighteenth century. French officials turned to Swiss banker and speculator Jacques Necker to solve their problem. Magically, he managed to raise money without raising taxes. How? By borrowing. The French government's interest on debt in 1774 was 93 million francs. By 1789, thanks to Necker's borrowing, that interest had grown to 300 million francs (Cobban, *A History of Modern France*, Vol. 1, p. 124). Even earlier, in the sixteenth century, Charles V, Holy Roman Emperor and King of Spain, had serious debt problems of his own. His royal life style and his wars cost him dearly, and he was constantly in need of money. He also resorted to borrowing and, as a result, was "never ... entirely out of the clutches of the international bankers" (William Thomas Walsh, *Philip II*, p. 170).

† This a well-recognized and long-standing tradition of American politics. After the election of 1884, Jay Gould (1836–1892)—wealthy American financier, railroad developer, speculator, robber baron—wired President-Elect Grover Cleveland to express his satisfaction with the outcome of the vote. "I feel ... that the vast business interests of the country will be entirely safe in your hands," Gould said. Quoted in Howard Zinn, *A People's History of the United States*, p. 252.
    There is an excellent website called OpenSecrets.org. Go there to find a detailed account of everyone in federal government (the House of Representatives, the Senate, the Presidency) listing how much money they have received and from whom. See also MapLight. org, which traces the votes on a particular bill to the donors whose money helped shape the outcome. Three books to consult on the subject of money and government are *The Best President Money Can Buy* by Greg Palast and *The Buying of the President 2000* by Charles Lewis. David Cay Johnston, in *Free Lunch: How the Wealthiest Americans Enrich Themselves at Government Expense and Stick You with the Bill*, gives many salient examples of how businessmen thrive on government handouts.

Politicians are the same the world over; they promise to build a bridge even where there is no water. —*Nikita Khrushchev*

A politician spends half his time making promises, and the other half making excuses. —*Anon.*

Give a politician a free hand, and he'll put it in your pocket. —*Anon.*

It's unfortunate that a mere ninety percent of the politicians give the other ten percent a bad name. —*Anon.*

A politician listens to the people in order to know, not what to do, but what to say. —*Anon.*

Politicians are bought, not made. —*Anon.*

There are two sides to every question, and a good politician takes both. —*Anon.*

Politics is the conduct of public affairs for private advantage. —*Ambrose Bierce*

The drawback in voting for the man of your choice is that he is seldom a candidate. —*Anon.*

Amusing as such observations might be, they contain more than a grain of truth and should be taken seriously. The combination of lying and self-deception that is the basis of our political system is pathological. We are choosing to believe in non-reality.

Writers such as Plato, Rousseau, and Machiavelli believed that deception is an essential element of government, that only the wise are wise enough to understand the virtues of submitting to the system, that only a select elite are capable of understanding the necessities of various governmental policies and actions. Without secrecy and deception, governors cannot govern. For the many to submit and obey, it is necessary to conceal the engines of government from public scrutiny. Writing close to a hundred years ago, Max Weber observed that "officialdom's most important *instrument of power* is the transformation of official information into *secret information* by means of the infamous concept of 'official secrecy,' which ultimately is merely a device to *protect* the administration *from control*"[2] (italics in the original).

The secret creates two classes of men—those who know and those who don't. It is godlike to be among those who know, to be able to create a reality that the vast majority assume to be authentic, while concealing critical information that contradicts that constructed reality. To be in a position of power, to be a guarder of secrets, is to render oneself superior:[‡]

> He that would reason with another, and honestly explain to him the motives of the action he recommends, descends to a footing of equality. But he who undertakes to delude us, and fashion us to his purpose by a specious appearance, has a feeling that he is our master.... At every turn he admires his own dexterity; he triumphs in the success of his artifices, and delights to remark how completely mankind are his dupes.[3]

And what exactly are some of the consequences of being a victim of such deception and manipulation? We feel inferior. We feel powerless. We feel childlike. We feel anxious, because the deception is never complete and absolute—for the moment or over time. "The bubble is hourly in danger of bursting, and the delusion of coming to an end."[4] It is submission to the lie, as much as anything else, that makes us feel insecure. We need to create an imaginary interior world where we feel empowered and safe. Sheldon S. Wolin points out that "it is only mildly hyperbolic to characterize lying as a crime against reality."[5]

We sense that something else is going on. But we don't really want to know that we are being betrayed. We are afraid to discover the truth that is being concealed. It is too disturbing. We want to believe in the beneficence of those who govern. Thus, we are "kept in perpetual vibration, between rebellious discontent, and infatuated credulity,"[6] and in the process we are denied the opportunity to expand our powers of reasoning and probe into the essence of things.

The lie creates two realities—one visible and one hidden, one desirable and reassuring, the other menacing. Power is both dispersed and hidden, making it more difficult to identify the parties responsible for any given action. Things seem to just happen spontaneously, outside the purview of any particular set of interests.

For example, in 1951, Mohammad Mosaddeq came to power as Prime Minister of Iran. [§]He was committed to democratizing his country and nationalizing the oil industry, which was under British control at the time. Mosaddeq came into political conflict with the Shah and resigned in protest. There was agitation in the streets and Mosaddeq was reinstated with increased authority. Under two separate grants of emergency powers, Mosaddeq set out to strengthen democratic institutions and limit the power of the monarchy. He cut the Shah's personal budget, restricted the Shah's ability to communicate with foreign diplomats, and transferred ownership of royal lands to the state. Further, Mosaddeq instituted land reforms that established village councils,

---

‡ "At bottom, lying is the expression of a will to power." Sheldon S. Wolin, *Democracy Incorporated*, p. 263.

§ The narrative presented here is based primarily on information from http://en.wikipedia.org/wiki/Mohammad_Mosaddegh and http://en.wikipedia.org/wiki/1953_Iranian_coup_d'état and on Morris Berman's account in *Dark Ages America: The Final Phase Empire*.

implemented collective farming, and increased the share of agricultural production that went to the peasants. These land reforms weakened aristocratic landowners, earning Mosaddeq more enemies.

In August 1953, the Shah signed a decree dismissing Mosaddeq as Prime Minister. Violent clashes broke out in the streets of Tehran between supporters of the Shah and supporters of Mosaddeq. Shops were looted and mosques were burned; nearly three hundred died. Pro-Shah tank regiments bombarded the Prime Minister's official residence. Mosaddeq escaped the attack, but the next day he surrendered to the Shah's forces. The Shah—who had fled the violence for the safety of Rome—returned and was restored to full power. Mosaddeq was convicted of treason, imprisoned for three years, and held under house arrest for the remainder of his life.

As told in the newspapers, the story was a simple one. There was popular dissatisfaction with Mosaddeq and his policies and massive support for the Shah and his policies, resulting in Mosaddeq's removal from office. Justice was done. Yet this is not the true story.

The string of events was carefully orchestrated and paid for, in secrecy, by the CIA, under the direction of Donald Wilber.¶ Kermit Roosevelt Jr. (grandson of President Theodore Roosevelt) coordinated events on the street:

> Thugs were hired to attack religious leaders, throw rocks at mosques, and then make it appear as though this had been on Mossadegh's orders; army officers and members of the Majlis [the Iranian parliament] were bribed; and the heavily funded Kermit Roosevelt hired a mob to stage a pro-shah march through the streets of Tehran.[7]

Iranian underworld figures local strongmen were recruited to join the effort to discredit Mosaddeq. The Shah's forces were led by Fazlollah Zahedi, a retired general and former Interior Minister in Mosaddeq's cabinet. Upon Mosaddeq's fall, Zahedi declared himself to be the new Prime Minister. The Zahedi government promptly negotiated fresh agreements with foreign oil interests, much to the benefit of the United States and Britain. Mission accomplished.

Here we have an example of darkness made visible. The hidden oligarchic machinations have been revealed for public scrutiny.** We have been given the opportunity to see both realities, to understand that the

---

¶ Wilber's official report on the action was published in 2000 and is now available at http://web.payk.net/politics/cia-docs/published/one-main/main.html.
** A detailed timeline of clandestine CIA activities since World War II is available at http://www.serendipity.li/cia/cia_time.htm. The timeline, compiled by Steve Kangas, is based on William Blum's *Killing Hope: U.S. Military and CIA Interventions since World War II* (published in 1995) and Jonathan Vankin and John Whalen's *The 60 Greatest Conspiracies of All Time* (published in 1997). The site also reports that, according to an estimate by the Association for Responsible Dissent, as of 1987, CIA covert operations had taken as many as six million lives (Coleman McCarthy, "The Consequences of Covert Tactics").

reality we were fed was false, that the hidden reality was nefarious and out of our control. And we can now see that the values we are led to believe we are supporting when we vote in elections, and that we read about in the morning papers, are sometimes in fact the opposite of the values being embraced by those who rule in darkness.

## Visible vs. Invisible Oligarchs

In the early years of the twenty-first century, political and financial power has become concentrated into the hands of fewer and fewer individuals, and their reach has grown ever more expansive. Modern technology makes it possible to earn tens of millions of dollars at the click of a mouse. Modern media make it possible for a few oligarchs to manipulate the masses to suit hidden purposes on a scale that was never before conceivable.

As a consequence, hidden powers have been able, in the United States, to exert growing influence in the legislature, the executive, the judiciary, and the media. With this degree of control, these power-brokers have little motivation to cover their actions. Their greed and their desire to manipulate the mechanisms of government to suit their personal agendas—and, too often, the absence of even token opposition—have led them to engage in brazen, even reckless, conduct. The oligarchs now have the luxury of being less concerned with deception and more concerned with getting what they want when they want it, and then getting some more. The powers behind the "throne" of American government are becoming visible. The distinctions between the visible and the invisible oligarchs are beginning to dissolve.

In the past, someone like Donald Rumsfeld, Secretary of Defense under George W. Bush, would have hidden in the shadows and let someone in government send business his way. Instead, he chose to assume a government post and do the job himself. Rumsfeld's last major role in the private sector before moving into George W. Bush's Defense Department was as Chairman of Gilead Sciences—a biopharmaceutical company that discovers, develops, and commercializes drugs, primarily anti-viral agents such as the flu vaccine Tamiflu. When he took office, Rumsfeld's shares in Gilead were estimated to be worth between $5 million and $28 million. In 2005, an avian flu scare was partially sparked by a warning from President Bush's top health adviser, Mike Leavitt, that a pandemic could cause nearly 2 million deaths in the United States alone. Though Rumsfeld recused himself in the event of possible Pentagon involvement in the case of a flu epidemic, one can imagine that he profited handsomely when the government ordered 20 million doses of Tamiflu at a price of $100 per dose.††

More recently, in 2009, another wave of concern erupted over swine

––––––––––––––––––––––

†† See http://www.globalresearch.ca/index.php?context=va&aid=1148.

flu, which some have argued is a man-made form of the virus whose virulence has been grossly exaggerated. Nonetheless, once again Gilead Sciences was in a position to profit from sales of its Tamiflu vaccine. With his government and media connections, Rumsfeld certainly had the motive and the opportunity to encourage the panic that resulted in governments around the world stockpiling the drug to combat the threatened pandemic. And this time, there was even talk of forced inoculations. This is darkness almost visible.

The case with Dick Cheney[‡‡]—former Vice President of the United States—is even more clear cut. In 1978, Cheney was elected congressman from Wyoming. In 1981, he became Chairman of the Republican Policy Committee, a position he held until 1987. In 1988, Cheney was elected House Minority Whip. A year later, he became Secretary of Defense under President George H. W. Bush.

In September 1990, the Pentagon asserted that 250,000 Iraqi troops with 1,500 tanks were massed on the border with Saudi Arabia, but photos of these forces were never made public. However, Soviet satellite images taken the same day showed no troops near the border. Journalist Jean Heller learned about the Soviet imagery and presented the information to Dick Cheney's office at the Pentagon. The story was ignored. In January 1991, Operation Desert Storm began. The United States, along with allied forces, invaded Kuwait, ostensibly for the purpose of expelling Iraqi troops. In the wake of this operation, Cheney hired Halliburton (a USA-based oilfield services, engineering, and construction corporation with international operations in more than 70 countries and close to 300 subsidiaries, affiliates, branches, brands, and divisions worldwide) to put out more than 700 wellhead fires and engaged Halliburton subsidiary Brown & Root to rebuild public buildings and restore computer systems in Kuwait. On July 3 of the same year, Secretary Cheney was awarded the Presidential Medal of Freedom by President George H. W. Bush for his work on the Gulf War.

In 1992, Cheney, as Secretary of Defense, paid Halliburton and Brown & Root $8.9 million for two studies on how to downsize the military. In August, Halliburton was selected by the U.S. Army Corps of Engineers to provide support services for the military for five years, based on a plan that Halliburton itself had drawn up. Cheney left government service at the end of George H. W. Bush's term in January 1993.

In October 1995, Cheney became Chairman and CEO of Halliburton. During his five years with Halliburton, the company was awarded $2.3 billion in federal contracts, almost twice the total from the previous five years, as well as taxpayer-insured loans of $1.5 billion.

---

‡‡  Primary sources for the discussion of the actions of Dick Cheney and Halliburton include the following websites: http://www.halliburtonwatch.org, http://www.cbc.ca/fifth/dickcheney/halliburton.html,  http://www.corpwatch.org/article.php?list=type&type=15, and http://en.wikipedia.org/wiki/Dick_cheney.

In 1998, Cheney negotiated Halliburton's purchase of Dresser Industries for $7.7 billion. After the merger, the company faced numerous asbestos-related lawsuits. The claims drove several Halliburton divisions into bankruptcy, and Halliburton's stock fell in value 80 percent in one year. In August 2000, Cheney left Halliburton to run as George W. Bush's Vice President. He retired with a generous settlement of Halliburton stock, which he promptly sold for $30 million. By November, Halliburton stock had lost between $3 and $4 billion of its total market value. Many questioned whether Cheney had taken advantage of insider information when he sold his stock two months earlier.

In January 2001, President Bush announced the formation of the National Energy Policy Development Group, with Cheney as chair. This was an opportunity for Mr. Cheney to use his influence to promote policies that could ultimately increase the value of his Halliburton holdings. After the attacks of September 11, 2001, Cheney was an outspoken proponent of war with Iraq. In August 2002, he told an audience of veterans, "There's no doubt that Saddam Hussein now has weapons of mass destruction [and that he will use them] against our friends, against our allies and against us." In 2003, after the U.S. invasion of Iraq, Halliburton subsidiary Kellogg Brown & Root (KBR)§§ was awarded a no-bid contract to extinguish oil well fires in Iraq. The contract had no time limit and no dollar limit. At the time, Cheney was earning hundreds of thousands of dollars per year in deferred compensation from Halliburton and was in possession of 433,333 shares of unexercised Halliburton stock options.

In 2008, Halliburton celebrated $4 billion in operating profits, producing an impressive 22 percent return for investors at a time when many companies were reporting record losses. Simple overcharges and incompetence were contributing to these profits, however. For example, the company was charging the government $2.64 per gallon to transport gasoline into Iraq while its competitors were transporting gasoline for less than half that price. Halliburton's profit numbers were impressive, but so too were the numbers of claims from Pentagon investigators of overcharges and waste, not to speak of spiraling claims of negligence in the workmanship of services provided. The problems included faulty electrical wiring that led to deaths and injuries on bases KBR built, and a failure to provide adequately clean water supplies to the troops.

It is easy to get bogged down in the details of war profiteering, exploitation of labor, and neglect for the wellbeing of the troops being inadequately served by companies like Halliburton and KBR. It is really the bigger picture that matters if any of these practices are to be reversed.

---

§§   KBR was formed after Halliburton's 1998 acquisition of Dresser Industries, when Dresser's engineering subsidiary M. W. Kellogg merged with Halliburton's construction subsidiary Brown & Root. This made KBR the perfect all-purpose contractor for wartime support and post-war reconstruction services.

The names and the faces change, but the destruction of vital economic and social resources—and the senseless taking of life—continue. If we are to be informed and effective citizens, it is essential for us to understand the ways in which the government is run for and by men like Dick Cheney. He is a prime example of someone who blithely slips from visible to invisible oligarchy and back again, along the way acquiring enormous wealth and power. Cheney is not an extraordinary man, and his abuses are not extraordinary abuses. There were many before him and there will be many to follow. It is the *system* that must be changed.

The formula for the aspiring oligarch is simple. Start modestly. Get yourself elected to a government position (in Cheney's instance, the House of Representatives), a modest enough beginning. Then make yourself prominent and powerful in your party's operation. Then get yourself appointed to a high government position, such as Secretary of Defense. Then make war and pass along hundreds of millions of dollars in government contracts to a major corporate contact. They will do very well—and they will remember you. They will take you on as CEO or Board member once you leave your government position. And you will do extremely well. And if you're really lucky, you can go back into government and make more war. And pass on more contracts. Etc. And so forth. And so on.

## The Business of Government Is Business

The Rumsfeld and Cheney stories are not anomalies or distortions. They demonstrate the American oligarchy at work. But perhaps the best example of all time comes from the men of Goldman Sachs.¶¶ As a result of the financial crisis of 2008, and in the light of day, Goldman executives past and present were able to take something like $63 billion of taxpayers' money and put it into the pockets of the bankers so they could get back to the tables and continue their gambling. As Matt Taibbi points out in his article "The Great American Bubble Machine," Goldman, in essence, became the government at a critical moment and hence was able to redirect funds to its own benefit while the rest of us watched our assets vaporize. The bubbles that burst were the same kinds of bubbles that Goldman routinely creates and benefits from. Comparing "the world's most powerful investment bank" to a "great vampire squid ... relentlessly jamming its blood funnel into anything

---

¶¶ Sources for this discussion of America's 2008 financial meltdown include Matt Taibbi, "The Great American Bubble Machine," http://www.rollingstone.com/politics/news/the-great-american-bubble-machine-20100405; Marina Litvinsky, "Corruption-US: How Wall Street Paid for Its Own Funeral," http://www.informationclearinghouse.info/article22146.htm; and http://en.wikipedia.org/wiki/Goldman_Sachs. An excellent overview is provided by Tanya Cariina Hsu, "Death of the American Empire: America Is Self-Destructing & Bringing the Rest of the World Down with It," http://www.globalresearch.ca/index.php?context=va&aid=10651.

that smells like money," Taibbi describes the bank's strategy as follows:

> The formula is relatively simple: Goldman positions itself in the middle of a speculative bubble, selling investments they know are crap. Then they hoover up vast sums from the middle and lower floors of society with the aid of a crippled and corrupt state that allows it to rewrite the rules in exchange for the relative pennies the bank throws at political patronage. Finally, when it all goes bust, leaving millions of ordinary citizens broke and starving, they begin the entire process over again, riding in to rescue us all by lending us back our own money at interest.[8]

The proof that Goldman knew their housing market bets were at risk of going sour comes from the fact that they bought a form of insurance (known as credit default swaps) from American International Group (AIG) to cover their potential losses. AIG itself was sucked into the speculative bubble, went broke, and couldn't make good on its IOUs, which is where the American taxpayers came in. We took up the slack so AIG could pay Goldman, to save Goldman from having to take a haircut, as they say on the street. Bear in mind that when you and I go to the table and lose, we are compelled to live with the consequences. There is no way out for us.

Most of the Goldman names are familiar. Former Goldman CEO Henry Paulson was George W. Bush's Secretary of the Treasury at the time when when "bailout" (read "handout") was introduced into our socioeconomic lexicon. Robert Rubin was Bill Clinton's Secretary of the Treasury. He had spent twenty-six years at Goldman, where he became Co-Chairman of the board, before becoming Chairman of Citigroup, which in turn got a $300 billion taxpayer handout from Paulson. John Thain,[***] a former Goldman banker, Chairman at Merrill Lynch, got his billions from Paulson via Bank of America. Former Goldmanite Robert K. Steel headed up Wachovia and got himself and fellow executives $225 million in payments as his bank was headed for demise.

Mark A. Patterson became Treasury chief of staff in early 2009, despite having served as a Goldman lobbyist as recently as 2008. Edward M. Liddy is a former Goldman director whom Paulson put in charge of AIG. Liddy was the one who took government bailout money for AIG and passed it along to Goldman. The heads of the Canadian and Italian

---

[***]  After a little more than a year with Merrill, Thain could see that his job was in jeopardy. So he did the only sensible thing. He doled out executive bonuses a month ahead of schedule, in the amount of between $3 and $4 billion. He had already spent $1.2 million to lavishly decorate his Merrill Lynch office while the firm was fighting to survive, with costs as follows: decorator Michael Smith ($800,000), two area rugs ($131,000), two guest chairs ($87,000), a nineteenth-century credenza ($68,000), four sets of curtains ($28,000), a mahogany pedestal table ($25,000), six dining room chairs ($37,000), a George IV desk ($18,000), a custom coffee table ($16,000), a sofa ($15,000), a chandelier ($13,000), a mirror ($5,000), six wall sconces ($2,700), and a trash can ($1,400). See http://www.huffingtonpost.com/2009/01/22/john-thains-12-million-re_n_160024.html.

national banks[†††] are Goldman alumni, as are the head of the World Bank, the head of the New York Stock Exchange, and the last two heads of the Federal Reserve Bank of New York (which, as Taibbi points out, is in charge of overseeing Goldman). Neel Kashkari, former Goldman Vice President, was named Assistant Secretary of the Treasury under Paulson and moved on to head the Office of Financial Stability, which was set up to manage administration of the $700 billion bailout plan.[‡‡‡]

The government (person or persons in power) was discriminating in how it directed its handouts. Certainly, considering the Goldman ties of the participants, it can be no accident that Goldman's two chief competitors— Lehman Brothers and Bear Stearns—received no funds and were allowed to fail, leaving Goldman as one of the only major players still standing.

Nor did Paulson as Secretary of the Treasury keep his former employer, Goldman Sachs, at arm's length. According to a story that appeared in the *New York Times*,[9] from September 16 to 21, 2008— when Goldman, like Lehman and Bear Stearns, was at risk of failure— Paulson and Lloyd C. Blankfein, Chairman of Goldman Sachs, spoke twenty-four times. On the morning of September 16, it was announced that AIG would receive an $85 billion handout, a substantial portion of which would be passed along to Goldman.

Much of the current climate of boom and bust is a consequence of a carefully worked-out strategy that has involved the purchase of visible oligarchs (i.e., elected representatives and appointed government officials) by invisible oligarchs (i.e., bankers) over a period of more than a decade. These governmental players have worked to ensure that legislation and regulation have been structured to allow the speculative frenzy that is so profitable for the bankers. From 1998 to 2008, Wall Street investment firms, commercial banks, hedge funds, real estate companies, and insurance conglomerates made political contributions in excess of $1.7 billion and spent another $3.4 billion on lobbyists.[§§§] These investments have paid off. For example, in 1999, under President Bill Clinton, the Glass-Steagall Act of 1933 was repealed. Glass-Steagall had been put in place in response to the Depression of 1929 and

---

††† The head of the Italian national bank, Mario Draghi, went on to become governor of the European Central Bank. Mario Monti, Italy's new Prime Minister, is also a former Goldman employee.

‡‡‡ Lawrence Summers, formerly Director of the White House National Economic Council, might have been a beneficiary of Goldman largesse. In 2009, it was disclosed that Summers had been paid millions of dollars the previous year by companies that he would subsequently have influence over as a public servant. He earned $5 million from the hedge fund D. E. Shaw and collected $2.7 million in speaking fees from Wall Street companies that received government bailout money. The case of Revolution Money is even more suspicious. Summers served on the board of directors of this small startup company, which in 2009 received $42 million from a group of investors that included Goldman Sachs, Citigroup, and Morgan Stanley. These banks had received billions in bailout money from Summers and were undergoing government "stress testing" at the time of their investment. Mark Ames, "Is Larry Summers Taking Kickbacks from the Banks He's Bailing Out?"

§§§ Goldman's contribution was $46 million. See www.wallstreetwatch.org/reports/part2.pdf.

was designed to prevent commercial banks—the ones that take deposits and give out loans and mortgages—from making the kinds of risky investments that began to catch up with them in 2008 and tipped many banks, major and minor, into insolvency.

## A System in Need of Repair, or the Past Revisited?

You might say, "This is terrible. The system is broken. We have to fix it." To which I might respond, "Exactly what system are you referring to?" If you go back two hundred years, to the American government at its point of origin, at the end of the eighteenth century, you will discover that the system is functioning exactly as designed. The constitutional oligarchy was established as a means to empower bankers and speculators at the expense of the common good.

Recall that at the end of the Revolution, the holders of state and Continental war bonds, who had bought them at a fraction of their face value, wanted and got interest paid on the full value. The true patriots, those who had risked their lives and their livelihood for the young nation, were seeing their welfare sacrificed to the whims of the speculators who had stayed on the sidelines the entire time. In order to feed the speculators the revenues they demanded, the farmers had to be taxed at intolerable rates, leading to bankruptcy and loss of farms and livestock. The result was Shays' Rebellion and others events like it.

Thus, the underlying domestic conflict—one of the oldest known to man—that followed the war with Britain was the conflict between debtor and creditor.¶¶¶ This conflict entailed opposition between two political forces, one that favored democracy and one that wanted to put an end to democracy and install an oligarchy. More often than not, the state legislatures were responsive to the demands of their small farmer constituents. For men like James Madison, that was the problem—too much democracy at the state level.

It becomes apparent that the Constitution was conceived as a means of stifling democracy and empowering the wealthy few. Madison is explicit on this matter. In a letter to Jefferson, he speaks of the tyranny of "the major number of constituents,"[10] a curious turn of phrase. When the vast majority of the populace simply seeks, by legal means, to secure its own survival, can this honestly be construed as tyranny? Apparently so, for Madison was not alone among those attending the Constitutional Convention to fear "the extremes of democracy," as Hamilton put it. Others were "tired of an excess of democracy," leery of "a headstrong democracy" and the "prevailing rage of excessive democracy," and concerned about "democratized tyranny" and "democratic licentiousness."[11]

---

¶¶¶ It has been alleged that the British printed counterfeit bills in large quantities, leading to a hyper-inflated currency, as a means of undermining the economy.

Over the years, the Constitution has meant different things to different people. It has been open to various interpretations. There is an entire discipline known as constitutional law whose sole purpose is to determine what the Constitution actually means. Many Americans consider elections and civil liberties to be the very soul of democracy and hence emphasize this aspect of the Constitution. Others speak of checks and balances. Some think the executive, that is, the president, has too much power. Others think he has not enough. But at the time of the final ratification of the Constitution in 1789, its supporters had much narrower concerns, and they all related to the wishes of the speculators, that is to say the bondholders and creditors.

Basically, there were two specific items in the Constitution, usually overlooked in contemporary discussion, that mattered most to the most ardent supporters of the Constitution. The first sentence of Article I, Section 10, reads as follows:

> No State shall enter into any Treaty, Alliance, or Confederation; grant Letters of Marque and Reprisal; coin Money; emit Bills of Credit; make any Thing but gold and silver Coin a Tender in Payment of Debts; pass any Bill of Attainder, ex post facto Law, or Law impairing the Obligation of Contracts, or grant any Title of Nobility.

I will repeat the section, passing over what is archaic or not relevant to the current discussion. Now we have an abbreviated version that contains the two key elements:

> No State shall ... coin Money; emit Bills of Credit; make any Thing but gold and silver Coin a Tender in Payment of Debts; pass any ... Law impairing the Obligation of Contracts.

These words were aimed directly at the state legislatures that had successfully undermined bond speculators in their efforts to collect the full face value and the full interest on the bonds they had purchased for pennies on the dollar. States had been issuing paper money to ease the farmers' burden. That option was outlawed by the new federal Constitution.

At the time the Constitution was written, "Obligation of Contracts" had a specific meaning. The contracts being referenced were the bonds held by speculators. State legislatures had used various stratagems to interfere with the execution of these contracts. Any such actions, by virtue of the Constitution, were now illegal.

As far as the speculators were concerned, these few phrases were the core of the legal document they had created. These few phrases alone justified the entire endeavor. "As a result of the protection that Section 10 afforded creditors, more people proclaimed that clause 'the best in the Constitution' than any other in the document." The governor of Virginia declared Section 10, "a great favorite of mine." A New Jersey Federalist claimed that "Nothing, in the whole Federal Constitution, is more necessary than this very section." Even if the Constitution had done nothing more than ban paper money, that would have been enough "to recommend it to honest men."[12]

At the end of the eighteenth century, when the Constitution was conceived and the speculators were enthroned, the vast majority of the population, eighty percent or more, was farmers eking out a living. Their needs and wishes were ignored and overridden by a small elite at odds with the common good. William Whiting of Berkshire Country, Massachusetts, wondered:

> what more ready method can be devised to enrich and aggrandize a numbers [sic] of individuals at the expence [sic] of the community at large and thereby put it in their power to introduce that odious state of Aristocracy, to the utter subversion of our present republican constitution, than by permitting them to draw from the people near fifty p[er] Cent interest [on their war bonds every year].[13]

In the fall of 1786, in the state of Rhode Island, nearly half of the bonds were owned by just sixteen people. In 1789, a Pennsylvania newspaper reported that of the £111,000 that the state government had collected in taxes and handed over to bondholders, £70,000 had gone to a mere twelve investors. By 1790, only about two percent of Americans owned bonds.[14]

Bondholders argued that the American credit rating suffered at the hands of state legislatures that allowed debts to go unpaid, resulting in a low credit rating that discouraged foreign investors. One essayist declared, "To hear a speculator, in this country, declaim on [the] importance" of the government's credit rating, "is really a great act of barefacedness." After all, it was the speculator who—by refusing to pay face value for the bonds, waiting until they had "already depreciated 500 *per cent* and who by his cheapening; and haggling, would, were it then in his power; have reduced [them] still lower!"—was undermining the credit market. [15]

According to the speculators, the economy would be depleted by going easy on taxpayers. Not so, argued Pelatiah Webster, a Philadelphia merchant. Instead, it is the speculators who deplete the economy with their wasteful and lavish practices. "There are," he said, "5,000 people in Pennsylvania, who live by broking and speculating, who would otherwise be employed in lawful trades, or in agriculture. They are infinitely more harmful to our country than the Hessian fly."[16] ****

The heavy taxes required to pay the speculators "cast a damp and deadening languour on the very *first springs*, the *original principle* and *source* of our national wealth,"[17] that is to say the hard work of ordinary citizens such

---

**** The Hessian fly, or barley midge, is a species of fly that is a significant pest of cereal crops, including wheat, barley, and rye. A native of Asia, it was transported into Europe and later into North America, supposedly in the straw bedding of Hessian troops during the American Revolution (1775–1783).

as the farmers and artisans who comprised the vast majority of the population. Those who favored taxing to pay bondholders argued that the burden of necessity was a good motivator for farmers and would make them more productive. Webster replied that instead of being *"goaded on* by dire necessity and the dreadful spurs of pinching want," farmers and artisans should be *"animated* by an increase of happiness and hope of reward."[18]

Another writer argued that domestic debt was the problem. "Reducing our domestick [*sic*] debt within the bounds of justice, reason and common sense would enable us to do justice to our foreign creditors, and so to keep our faith, and maintain our reputation abroad." In other words, instead of raising taxes to pay speculators, use tax money to pay off foreign debt and the country would be on solid ground. Writing in the year 2012, would anyone argue otherwise?

The Constitution was written and a centralized federal government was established so that speculators would get paid in 1789. In the year 2009, the system worked as planned and they got paid once again. Bank speculators, significantly less than one percent of the population, who lost hundreds of billions of dollars on bad bets, in collaboration with key members of government and in violation of the needs of the vast majority of the population, captured trillions of dollars of public money.

In the 1780s, debtors, most of them hard-working farmers, saw their life's earnings and everything they owned—livestock, farms, even pots and pans and precious heirlooms—pass from their hands into the hands of their creditors. When even that was not enough, they were thrown into jail, where they sometimes resorted to taking their own lives. In 1785, Philip Peeble, who had fallen on hard times, killed his entire family before turning his weapon, an axe, on himself.[19] Similar stories are being repeated with increasing frequency in the current financial crisis. There has been a spate of homicidal sprees in recent years that could well be driven by economic hardship.

In the 1780s, it was the farmers and artisans who were being passed over in favor of the speculators. The scenario is not much different today. A handful of Wall Street speculators were bailed out in the trillions. General Motors, which indirectly and directly provides a living wage for hundreds of thousands of workers, was allowed to fall into bankruptcy.[††††] In the 1780s, it was the farmers and artisans who lost their homes. In 2009, it was the same class of people, the small homeowners, who were denied assistance as the payments on their mortgages exceeded their ability to pay them.

After all, the worldwide economic crisis was preventable. If the government had stepped in as defaults started rising in 2008 and subsi-

---

†††† On June 8, 2009, General Motors filed for bankruptcy. On July 10, 2009, after receiving government money, General Motors was back in business. The bankruptcy enabled GM to renegotiate labor contracts. As part of the deal, labor was compelled to forgo its right to strike.

dized the homeowners the way they eventually subsidized Wall Street, homeowners would be living in their homes, not in tents, and the value of mortgages would have held. Banks would not have been burdened with toxic assets. The stock market would not have gone into a tail-spin. Such action on the part of the government would have been called socialism. But when the visible oligarchs do the bidding of the invisible oligarchs and the same money is passed along to speculators, that is called responsible action and good government.‡‡‡‡

To a degree, the invisible and the visible oligarchies have merged. We no longer have to search the darkened recesses§§§§ to learn how government works. It is right before us, bright as day. The bankers who used to control things from behind the scenes are operating on the world stage for everyone to see. As Henry George so eloquently phrased it, "in high places sit those who do not pay to civic virtue even the compliment of hypocrisy."[20]¶¶¶¶

Sir Josiah Stamp, former head of the Bank of England, had an interesting take on banking.***** In 1927, he was the second richest man in England. He observed:

> Banking was conceived in iniquity and was born in sin. The bankers own the earth. Take it away from them, but leave them the power to create money, and with the flick of the pen they will create enough deposits to buy it back again. However, take it away from them, and all the great fortunes like mine will disappear and they ought to disappear, for this would be a happier and better world to live in. But, if you wish to remain the slaves of bankers and pay the cost of your own slavery, let them continue to create money.[21]††††††

---

‡‡‡‡   On the island of Manhattan, banks, like birds of prey, hover on just about every street corner, eager to swoop down and grab the next dollar in their talons. They have appeared by the hundreds since the crisis in 2008. Curiously, Chase Bank didn't wait until 2008. In the spring of 2006, Chase purchased Bank of New York's retail operations and began a pre-meltdown expansion. Did they have advance knowledge?

§§§§ Obviously, there is a fair amount that is still hidden, or partially hidden. For example, Bilderberg is a meeting (known to the public but held in secret at various sites in Europe) of powerful elites from around the world who gather to set the course of the world economy and to preside from afar over governmental affairs, especially those of the United States. The Mount Pelerin Society, founded in 1947 by Austrian economist Frederick von Hayek, serves a similar function. The British American Project (BAP) was founded in 1985 to perpetuate the close relationship between the United States and Britain. A maximum of twenty-four candidates are invited to join annually: twelve from the USA and twelve from the UK. BAP's purpose is to enlist young leaders in the service of conservative, elitist military and economic objectives. Candidates are aged between 28 and 40 and are drawn from the brightest young leaders in business, government, the media, voluntary and nonprofit organizations, medicine, sport, and the armed forces.

¶¶¶¶   George's *Progress and Poverty* (1879) should be required reading for every college graduate. George writes eloquently and with passion. His ideas on government and social progress are as relevant today as the day they were written.

*****   For a discussion of the system Stamp laments, see "The Shadow Money Lenders: The Real Significance of The Fed's Zero-Interest-Rate Policy (ZIRP)," by Matthias Chang, http://www.globalresearch.ca/index.php?context=va&aid=11491.

†††††† As discussed in Chapter 10, Amschel Rothschild, founder of the Rothschild dynasty, made the same point when he said, "Give me control of the economics of a country; and I care not who makes her laws."

The list of those who have warned about the power of the bankers is long indeed. Some of their more memorable comments are presented below. I begin with Napoleon Bonaparte, who knew a thing or two about power:

When a government is dependent upon bankers for money, they and not the leaders of the government control the situation, since the hand that gives is above the hand that takes. Money has no motherland; financiers are without patriotism and without decency; their sole object is gain." —*Napoleon Bonaparte*

History records that the money changers have used every form of abuse, intrigue, deceit, and violent means possible to maintain their control of governments by controlling money and its issuance. —*President James Madison*

The money power preys upon the nation in times of peace and conspires against it in times of adversity. It is more despotic than monarchy, more insolent than autocracy, more selfish than bureaucracy. —*President Abraham Lincoln*

Whoever controls the volume of money in any country is absolute master of all industry and commerce. —*President James A. Garfield*

And they who control the credit of a nation direct the policy of governments, and hold in the hollow of their hands the destiny of the people. —*The Rt. Hon. Reginald McKenna, Chancellor of the Exchequer*

A great industrial nation is controlled by its system of credit. Our system of credit is privately concentrated. The growth of the nation, therefore, and all our activities are in the hands of a few men.... We have come to be one of the worst ruled, one of the most completely controlled and dominated, governments in the civilized world—no longer a government by free opinion, no longer a government by conviction and the vote of the majority, but a government by the opinion and the duress of small groups of dominant men. —*Woodrow Wilson, while campaigning for president, 1912*‡‡‡‡‡

The truth is the Federal Reserve Board has usurped the Government of the United States. It controls everything here and it controls all our foreign relations. It makes and breaks government at will. —*Louis T. McFadden, Chairman of Banking & Currency Committee, 1932*

It is well enough that people of the nation do not understand our banking and monetary system, for if they did, I believe there would be a revolution before tomorrow morning. —*Henry Ford*

---

‡‡‡‡‡ A volume compiling "the more suggestive portions" of Woodrow Wilson's campaign speeches, *The New Freedom: A Call for the Emancipation of the Generous Energies of a People*, was published in 1913. The full text is available at http://www.gutenberg.org/ebooks/14811.

Well, Henry, the cat is out of the bag. It used to be a secret that the United States was run for the benefit of the bankers. It no longer is. Too often, however, we overlook the fact that the problem can be traced back to those in government—those who have it within their power to influence events but who too often fail to uphold the public trust. Our attention is diverted instead onto the Wall Street scoundrels. AIG has had to change its name and logo to protect its employees from physical assault. But the real culprits—the legislators and government officials without whose connivance none of this ever could have happened—escape unharmed. It is typical, especially in the United States, that the citizenry, even as it is being robbed and driven to destitution, never challenges and holds accountable its own government, the people in power who determine its individual and collective destinies. Thus, it is true that "Those in power maintain their power because those without power do not understand the power dynamics operant in the world in which they live."[22]

# The Pathology of Power

*So stretch'd out in length the arch-fiend lay*
*Chain'd on the burning lake.*

ISTORY IS A vast killing field. The ever-growing mountain of corpses is the handiwork of conventional warriors who use spears, war axes, arrows, gunshot, as well as a newer breed of economic warriors whose never-ending quest for profit leads to mass starvation. By either path—one more immediate, one delayed—tens of millions are sacrificed to the whims of individuals in power—individuals such as Alexander, Genghis Khan, Napoleon, Pope Urban II, the Duchess of Sutherland, the Directors of the East India Company, Sam "The Banana Man" Zemurray. Of course, the list of culprits is many times longer. I have deliberately left out the familiar cast of modern villains—Hitler, Stalin, Mao, Pol Pot, to name just a few. But the theme is the same—gratuitous killing organized by power-hungry mass murderers. Does it have to be this way?* Are the mass killings and endless suffering inevitable? Does the form of government play a role in determining history's outcome? Who are these people who exercise deadly power without remorse? Are they like us? Are they different?

## Power or Corruption: Which Comes First?

It is customary at this point to quote John Emerich Edward Dalberg-Acton, First Baron Acton (1834–1902), commonly known as simply Lord Acton. Lord Acton was an English historian, the only son of Sir Ferdinand Dalberg-Acton, Seventh Baronet, and grandson of Admiral Sir John Acton, Sixth Baronet. Born in Naples, Italy, Lord Acton was a liberal thinker for his time. He was also a Roman Catholic, but one who did not take kindly to the doctrine of papal infallibility. He

---

* George Orwell gets right to the point: "The central problem [is] how to prevent power from being abused." *A Collection of Essays*, p. 65.

expressed his objections in a letter dated April 1887, in which he made this bold declaration:

> I cannot accept your canon that we are to judge Pope and King unlike other men, with a favourable presumption that they did no wrong. If there is any presumption it is the other way, against the holders of power, increasing as the power increases. Historic responsibility has to make up for the want of legal responsibility. *Power tends to corrupt, and absolute power corrupts absolutely.* Great men are almost always bad men, even when they exercise influence and not authority, still more when you superadd the tendency or the certainty of corruption by authority. There is no worse heresy than that the office sanctifies the holder of it.[1] (italics added)

This is the famous dictum: "Power tends to corrupt, and absolute power corrupts absolutely." I'm not sure I agree with it, however. I believe that one could argue, with equal justification, just the opposite—not that power corrupts people but that people corrupt power.[†]

Imagine an individual from a wholesome family background, someone who was treated with respect by his parents, who received genuine love and support during his formative years, who was validated for his abilities and encouraged in his strivings for independence and self-expression. I doubt strongly that such a person would abuse power, given the opportunity. I also doubt that such a person would seek power in the first place.

What is confusing about Lord Acton's remarks is that he would seem to be in agreement with me on one thing: "Great men are almost always bad men." That is my point exactly. It is the *men* who are bad. They bring their badness to the situation in which power is to be exercised. The men themselves are the corrupting factor. Thus, I think Acton has contradicted himself. But in so doing, he has raised an important issue. Are "great men" different from us in their psychological and moral makeup?

Enter Sigmund Freud, who in 1914 had this to say on the subject of war and death:

> Psychological—or, more strictly speaking, psycho-analytic—investigation shows … that the deepest essence of human nature consists of instinctual impulses which are of the elementary nature, which are similar in all men and which aim at the satisfaction of certain primal needs. These impulses in themselves are neither good nor bad.... A human being is seldom altogether good or bad; he is usually "good" in one relation and "bad" in another, or "good" in certain external circumstances and in others decidedly "bad."[2]

---

† In *The Insanity of Normality: Toward an Understanding of Human Destructiveness,* Arno Gruen makes the point that "power need not corrupt, provided that the preconditions for corruption are not present in the person" (p. 140). De Tocqueville makes a similar observation: "Men are not corrupted by the exercise of power," he says, "but by the exercise of a power which they believe to be illegitimate" (*Democracy in America,* Vol. 1, p. 9).

Freud is saying we are all made from the same stuff. We all have the same basic destructive impulses. No one is fundamentally good or bad. Once again, I beg to differ. I do not believe that adult human behavior in a social setting is determined by instincts that are basically biological in nature and animal in origin. We are different from the animals. Animals kill for a meal. Humans kill for the fun of it.

I *do* agree with Alice Miller,[‡] who, speaking of the source of hatred in adult life, says, "Nobody comes to the world with the wish to destroy.... If he is maltreated by a cruel upbringing he will develop the very strong wish to take revenge. He will be driven to destroy others or himself but only by his history and never by inborn genes."[3] Further, "The so-called bad child becomes a bad adult and eventually creates a bad world."[4] In other words, the way in which children are treated will determine the role they play in adult life. "Modern psychology has shown us," explains Alfred Adler,[§] "that the traits of craving for power, ambition, and striving for power over others, with their numerous ugly concomitants, are not innate and unalterable. Rather they are inoculated into the child at an early age."[5]

## The Child Makes the Man

Sociologist Philip E. Slater wrote a book entitled *The Glory of Hera: Greek Mythology and the Greek Family*.[¶] He set out to explore the attitude of men toward women in ancient Greece and found himself up against an apparent paradox. In Greek society, the women were virtual nonentities. They had no legal rights—a man could sell his daughter or even his sister into concubinage—and no political or social standing. They were confined to the household and domestic responsibilities and were essentially abandoned by their husbands, who enjoyed life outside the home and sexual encounters with other males.

However, in Greek mythology and literature, women occupy a place that in many ways equals and at times even overshadows that of their male counterparts. How is it that Greek women on the one hand are derogated and dismissed and on the other are deified, worshiped, admired, and even feared? They seem simultaneously to be disempowered and empowered within very same culture.

As Slater points out, in Greek culture one sees juxtaposed the child's attitude toward his mother and the adult male's attitude toward his wife. As a conscious adult male, the Greek disdains and subjugates the

---

‡ Alice Miller (1923–2010) was a Swiss psychoanalyst who was one of the first modern writers to raise the issue of childhood abuse and its consequences for adult living.
§ Alfred Adler (1870–1937) was an Austrian medical doctor, psychologist, and founder of the school of individual psychology. He was one of Freud's early collaborators, but eventually they parted ways. Adler abandoned Freud's theory of instincts and instead focused on the importance of community and social relations in forming the personality.
¶ Hera was the Greek goddess of women and marriage.

women in his life, who are compared to "sows, vixen, bitches, donkeys, weasels and monkeys."[6] But within the adult male psyche is the little boy who, based on early experiences with his mother, is in thrall to an overpowering matriarch whom he both fears and worships. "The social position of women and the psychological influence of women are thus quite separate matters."[7]

While denied a public life or political authority, within the home the women were dominant figures, a circumstance that was reinforced by the male's abandonment of this domain to their almost exclusive control.[**] In Greek drama, women are active and aggressive—in some ways more so than men. Jocasta and Antigone are good examples.[††] These are not the women of men's adult life, says Slater, but the mothers of their childhood.

If the man needs to prove himself or find an outlet for his rage, battles and competitions provide ready opportunity. For the woman, her children are the primary outlet for aggression. Hera takes out her jealous feelings on her stepchildren. There are several instances in Greek mythology—Medea kills her son in a jealous rage against Jason; Procne kills her son and serves him up to her husband in a stew—in which a mother kills her own children out of spite against a husband who has betrayed her. Might not this same emotional dynamic be played out in the real Greek households of the time? "If the wife resents her husband's superiority, she can punish arrogance (or even masculinity) in her son."[8] The frustrated, disempowered, humiliated mother takes out her anger on her children. "Destructive unconscious impulses toward male children must have been strong."[9] This, according to Slater, would certainly explain the menacing aspect of women in Greek mythology.

Furthermore, he asks, is it not possible that the widespread homosexuality in ancient Greek culture was the adult male's response to being used by his mother as a substitute for her absentee husband, thereby establishing her dominance over the male and visiting upon her child the humiliation that was visited upon her? "The male child was hers—under her control and subject to her whims, and it was here that her feelings could be given full expression."[10] This idea seems reinforced by the fact that the fearsome women of Greek mythology are fully mature women, while men preferred to marry barely pubescent girls and encouraged depilation of body hair, thus making the wife less like the childhood mother.

----

** Until relatively recently, this aspect of Greek life was replicated in contemporary American culture. In the many homes where the man was the sole support, worked longed hours, and ended the day with a long commute, women were the sole arbiters of their children's fate, especially in the earliest years.

†† In Greek mythology, Jocasta was the wife of Laius and both mother and wife of their son Oedipus, from whence Freud derived his "Oedipus complex." Antigone was a daughter of the accidentally incestuous marriage between Oedipus and his mother Jocasta. Sophocles wrote three tragedies on the subject of Oedipus: "Oedipus the King," "Oedipus at Colonus," and "Antigone."

On the one hand, the mother glorifies the son, is ambitious on his behalf, and sees him as an extension of herself, someone she can use to make her presence felt in the male world and seek vengeance. On the other hand, the son is the object of her contempt and hatred, because he represents to her all the harm she suffers at the hands of the men in her life. She must cut him down the way she is cut down. First she gives him his manhood and then she must take it away. "Her need for self-expression and vindication requires her both to exalt and to belittle her son, to feed on and to destroy him."[11]

Slater reasons that since the mother both exalts and demeans her son, as an adult he will have an extremely unstable self-concept. "He will feel that if he is not a great hero he is nothing, and pride and prestige become more important than love."[12] The mother's focus on her son's body and maleness makes physicality and appearance a concern for the male adult, who is in constant need of having his body validated as worthy and masculine.

Slater characterizes the Greek male as grandiose and boastful, hell-bent on glory at any cost, seeming to have a knack for turning even routine events—singing, riddle solving, drinking, staying awake—into occasions for him to excel in the face of male competition. This excessive need to excel results in envy, vindictiveness, and revenge in the face of the success of others—all of which might be explainable by the mother's fomenting a grandiose self-definition in her son and then puncturing it. I believe Slater's observations are insightful, but I think he is speaking of the aristocracy, not the male population in general.

Drawing on Plutarch's *Lives*, Slater points out how Alexander exemplifies all that is typical of the Greek male,‡‡ including an incestuous relationship with his mother. Alexander was obsessed with his own glory and exquisitely sensitive to the smallest slight; he demanded adulation from his followers. His mother, Olympias, has been described as a jealous and vindictive woman who seemed to have deliberately poisoned the relationship between Alexander and his father, Philip II, and generated ambitions in her son for the purpose of satisfying her own needs. Slater quotes another scholar to the effect that Alexander "received not only maternal love from his mother but conjugal love as well."[13] As Slater observes,

> It is easy to see how this combination of overdetermined love, exploitation, and aggrandizement, laced with a bit of antagonism toward men and maleness ... would produce a man who is generally confident, even reckless, but with his self-regard always problematic, his sensitivity to criticism acute, and his need for respect, honor, and glory exaggerated to insatiability.[14]

I think this psychological analysis provides an interesting insight into the circumstances that might have produced an Alexander. The same

---

‡‡   Once again, I believe he is speaking of the aristocracy.

kind of reasoning could apply to any one of history's "heroes." Childhood humiliation leads to rage, and an attendant lust for blood and conquest, in adulthood. The lust for power is unquenchable because its origins are subconscious.

In the modern world, things have changed. The blood lust is there, but the physical courage and sense of honor that accompanied the mass killing in ancient and medieval times have died off. What is left is the modern cold-blooded armchair killer—while the visible oligarch poses as head of state, the invisible oligarch hides in the shadows, wielding deadly power from behind the scenes.

## The Nosology of Destructiveness

Killing does not earn the same social respect it once did. In the good old days, the conquistador could glory in his gory acts, but in today's culture, the killer has to offer a benign, well-mannered, civilized veneer in order to gain the power he needs to satisfy his wish to destroy. It is in this context that terms like "narcissistic personality" and "psychopath" enter the discussion.§§

The narcissist is one who has a grandiose sense of who he is. He is preoccupied with fantasies of unlimited power. He is arrogant and exploitative. He lacks empathy. The description of the psychopath is similar. He is glib, superficially charming, cunning, and manipulative; he can be charismatic. He is emotionally empty and callous, and he lacks empathy. He shows no remorse and refuses to or cannot accept responsibility for his actions. He craves power over others. He is grandiose. He is a pathological liar, that is, he is a habitual or compulsive liar. He has no allegiance to the truth and will happily say whatever needs to be said to gain the power he seeks. People are the means to an end. They have no value in and of themselves. He is given to sexual promiscuity.

Psychoanalyst Otto F. Kernberg described malignant narcissism as a syndrome characterized by a narcissistic personality disorder with antisocial features, paranoid traits, and aggressive behavior. According to George H. Pollock, the malignant narcissist is someone who is "pathologically grandiose, lacking in conscience and behavioral regulation with characteristic demonstrations of joyful cruelty and sadism."[15] Kernberg claimed that malignant narcissism should be regarded as part of a spectrum of pathological narcissism ranging from the antisocial character described by Cleckley¶¶ (what we now call a "psychopath")

---

§§   Erich Fromm, in *The Anatomy of Human Destructiveness* (originally published in 1973), introduced the term "necrophiles." These are people who "want to destroy everything and everybody, often even themselves; their enemy is life itself" (p. 387).
¶¶   Hervey Milton Cleckley (1903–1984) was an American psychiatrist who pioneered the field of psychopathy. His book *The Mask of Sanity* (originally published in 1941), which provided a clinical description of psychopathy, is regarded as a landmark study. He coined the term "mask of sanity" to describe his observations that the psychopath can appear to be normal and engaging, in contrast to people with major mental disorders, who may experience overt hallucinations or delusions.

at the high end of severity, to malignant narcissism in the mid-range, to narcissistic personality disorder at the low end.[16]

In today's world, the accumulation of vast wealth has become synonymous with the acquisition of unlimited power. James Duffy speaks of "oligarchic kakistocrats." He says,

> The wealthy continue to get more and more obscene in the extent to which they aggregate ever more wealth. Such a concentration of wealth entails the sacrifice of more and more persons who must be assigned to less and less prosperity or to ever more misery in poverty.... This is about greed-envy-malice expressed as obscene wealth accumulation for the sake of expressing malice toward those whom one makes poorer.[17]

Duffy also uses the term "psychopathic sadist" to describe someone who "feels compelled to destroy goodness in order to disparage that which he envies." His greed is "caused by a profound subjective sense of emptiness due to massive self-loathing" brought on by "having one's self-development tragically and severely aborted very early in life."[18] The psychopathic sadist delights in fantasizing about the human misery and death brought on by the acquisition of ever-increasing wealth and power. This taking of delight, with sexual overtones, in the suffering of others, Duffy refers to as "lustmord."

Sir Winston Leonard Spencer-Churchill (1874–1965), KG (The Most Noble Order of the Garter), OM (Order of Merit ), CH (Order of the Companions of Honour), TD (Territorial Decoration), FRS (Royal Fellow of the Royal Society), PC (Her Majesty's Privy Council for Canada), was Prime Minister of England, once from 1940 to 1945 and then again from 1951 to 1955. He is considered by many to be one of Britain's greatest twentieth-century "heroes." Affectionately called "old bull dog," Churchill is particularly remembered for his indomitable spirit while leading Great Britain to victory in World War II. He was personally responsible for ordering the firebombing of Dresden, the baroque capital of the German state of Saxony. Thirteen hundred heavy bombers dropped more than thirty-nine hundred tons of high-explosive bombs and incendiary devices in four raids, destroying thirteen square miles of the city and causing a firestorm that consumed the city center, resulting in some forty thousand deaths among the civilian population. Churchill also had a plan for blanketing Germany with forty thousand anthrax bombs, but this scheme was never realized. Earlier, in 1919, he had called for an airborne chemical assault against Kurds and Afghans. "I do not understand the squeamishness about the use of gas," he said. "I am strongly in favor of using poison gas against uncivilized tribes."[19] This is the voice of lustmord.

Here it is again, with an American accent. Theodore—"Teddy"—Roosevelt (1858–1919) was the twenty-sixth President of the United States. Prior to becoming president, Roosevelt personally led his Rough Riders up San Juan Hill during the Spanish-American War, in which

Cuba was to be "liberated." Roosevelt was assistant secretary of the Navy at the time the war broke out, and he claimed that war stimulated "spiritual renewal." His only regret on returning from Cuba was that "there was not enough war to go around."[20]

When the Philippines were annexed by President William McKinley (1843–1901), seventy thousand American troops were sent to pacify the islands. General Jack Smith promised to turn the Philippines into a "howling wilderness." He told his soldiers, "I want no prisoners. I wish you to kill and burn; the more you kill and burn the better it will please me."[21] This too is the voice of lustmord. And yet again we have it coming from Teddy Roosevelt. As president, Roosevelt continued McKinley's policy in the Philippines. Two hundred fifty thousand were killed, perhaps more, mostly civilians. Roosevelt referred to the decimation of the native population as "the most glorious war in our nation's history."[22]***

In an article entitled "The Usurpation of Identity," psychoanalyst Stanley Rosenman speaks of the "predator," he who "has lived a life of unacknowledged mortification," leading to "fury and the desire to escape, transform, and exchange his identity."[23] This need for escape leads to projective identification, in which the hated elements of his own identity are magically, in the predator's imagination, projected onto and transferred into the enemy, who then must be mortified and destroyed, thus relieving the predator of inner stress and self-hatred.

The predator is driven by hunger for acknowledgment, as well as unbearable envy and greed. "He catastrophically crashes into the enemy to emblazon himself into the latter's psyche," thereby "suck[ing] up the victim's vitality." The predator has an overwhelming need to escape the void within. "By devouring the scapegoat's vivacity, he undoes his own vapidness."[24] Each time he kills a victim, he is left with a feeling of being alive. Thus, for the predator, death is life.

Arno Gruen, in his article "An Unrecognized Pathology: The Mask of Humaneness," makes a similar point. He speaks of those extremists for whom violence provides a necessary feeling of being alive. It is their own humaneness that they seek to escape. It fills them with a sense of dread and vulnerability. They must kill it in others and in themselves:

> Out of revenge towards life itself, they are compelled to kill the humaneness in themselves that has become their inner enemy. They do this by

---

*** Here is what Mark Twain had to say on the subject of the Philippines: "We have pacified some thousands of the islanders and buried them; destroyed their fields; burned their villages; and turned their widows and orphans out-of-doors; furnished heartbreak by exile to some dozens of disagreeable patriots; subjugated the remaining ten millions by Benevolent Assimilation, which is the pious new name of the musket; we have acquired property in the three hundred concubines and other slaves of our business partner, the Sultan of Sulu, and hoisted our protecting flag over that swag.... And so by these Providences of God—and the phrase is the government's, not mine—we are a World Power." Quoted in Howard Zinn, *A People's History of the United States*, p. 309.

projecting their inner alienated part ... onto others who are seen as harboring their own hated humaneness.... Under the guise of a heroic pose, they must destroy the dignity in others around them, the dignity which they do not possess.[25]

People kill to escape an inner emptiness. They kill to feel alive. They kill because they are ill, not out of loyalty to an ideology. Outwardly, these people seem to be just like us. They can "represent friendliness personified." "They wear a mask of seeming emotional health: they are automatons who are merely mimicking a personality with human feeling but are without empathy."[26] We are taken in because "we misinterpret this role-playing as an expression of genuine humanity."[27]

In *The Mask of Sanity*, Hervey Cleckley portrays the ineffable "normality" of the psychopath:

> The observer is confronted with a convincing mask of sanity.[†††] ... [He] finds verbal and facial expressions, tones of voice, and all the other signs we have come to regard as implying conviction and emotion and the normal experiencing of life.... Only very slowly ... does the conviction come upon us that, despite these intact rational processes ... we are dealing here not with a complete man at all but with something that suggests a subtly constructed reflex machine which can mimic the human personality perfectly.... So perfect is this reproduction of a whole and normal man that no one who examines him in a clinical setting can put in scientific or objective terms why, or how, he is not real.[28]

In referring to Cleckley's work, Gruen underscores the political risks we all face by failing to see beyond the mask of normality to what lies behind it. We are impressed with the power of the psychopath. He makes us feel safe. We think we can trust him. He seems to know so much. He sees farther, or at least he so impresses us. These men who are in charge have the ability to determine for us what reality is, and it is that power which enables them to hoodwink us into believing them. Often they speak to us in the tone of everyday conversation. They seem to be neutral. They offer not a hint that there is something sinister about them. Says Gruen, "psychopaths simulate feelings to confuse us, so that we doubt our own feelings and perceptions and start to feel guilty."[29]

---

††† Here is an interesting example of such a "mask of sanity." In May 1950, India's ambassador to China—K. M. Pannikar—met with Chairman Mao, who was responsible for the death of at least forty million of his countrymen. Pannikar described Mao thusly: his face is "pleasant and benevolent and the look in his eyes is kindly"; there is "no cruelty or hardness in his eyes or in the expression of his mouth." He compared Mao favorably with Nehru. Both men were "men of action with dreamy idealistic temperaments." Both "may be considered humanists." Pannikar's reaction to Mao is an illustration of behavior that Thucydides observed two thousand years earlier: "it is generally the case that men are readier to call rogues clever than simpletons honest, and are as ashamed of being the second as they are proud of being the first." Pannikar quoted in Ramachandra Guha, *India after Gandhi: The History of the World's Largest Democracy*, p. 176; Thucydides quoted in M. I. Finley, *The Portable Greek Historians*.

In *The Insanity of Normality*, Gruen speaks of those who "want to convince others that they act, think and feel appropriately. These," he says," are the people whom I want to expose as the truly insane among us." The "feelings" they show are displayed for effect, not because they are genuinely felt. Charismatic psychopaths are excellent performers. They endanger us because "they cannot face the chaos, the rage, and the emptiness inside them." As an antidote, they seek power—"the only way to stave off the threat of inner chaos and dissolution."[30]

In modern culture, Gruen sees a pattern that parallels what Slater found in ancient Greece. Gruen points to the role of frustrated and demeaned mothers who both resent and overvalue their sons as a means to boost their own self-esteem. "By means of her admiration, she seduces her son into believing that he has an extraordinary importance to her, thereby evoking and continually reinforcing in him a dream of greatness and fame."[31]

Gruen distinguishes between a man who is content to gain power by joining a group and submitting to someone else's power, and the individual who must have the power for himself. The former is probably someone who was crushed and dominated by his father. The latter—he who must have all the power for himself—had a mother "who made her son the sole love object," nourishing his ambition and grandiosity.[32] Through her son, such a mother will realize her own dreams of glory. From time to time, it appears as if some of these powerful men engage in acts that are in fact designed to bring down the structure around them as well as themselves. According to Gruen, "they are taking revenge on their mother: they are deliberately negating what she tried to achieve through them."[33]

## Power as Addiction

When someone wants something desperately, can never get enough of it, and becomes obsessive in his desire and destructive in his pursuit of it, we call him an addict. Gruen speaks of "power-obsessed men."[34] Adler speaks of "power intoxication" and the "craving for power." He describes personal power as "a disastrous delusion" that "poisons man's living together."[35] Said John Adams, "The love of power is insatiable and uncontrollable."[36]

Let us return briefly to one of the Anti-Federalists (democrats), whose writings were quoted earlier. Consider what "The Impartial Examiner," from Virginia, has to say about men given power:

> It requires no great degree of knowledge in history to learn what dangerous consequences generally result from large and extensive powers. Every man has a natural propensity to power; and when one degree of it is obtained, *that* seldom fails to excite a thirst for more:—an higher point being gained, still the soul is impelled to a farther pursuit. Thus

step by step, in regular progression, she proceeds onward, until the lust of domination becomes the ruling passion, and absorbs all other desires.... Hence, should it not be a *maxim*, never to be forgotten—that a free people ought to entrust no set of powers, that may be abused without controul (sic), or afford opportunities to designing men to carry dangerous measures into execution, without being responsible for their conduct.[37]

I think it can be argued that not "every man" lusts for power—but only some men, a special subset of men. Such men are to be understood as one would understand any addict, and this is exactly what "The Impartial Examiner" has done. "Step by step," he tells us, the lust for power progresses until it becomes "the ruling passion, and absorbs all other desires." This is the language of addiction. The power addict progresses in his addiction just the way the alcoholic does. Addiction to power is an addiction like any other. The desire is blinding and all-consuming, which is why power should never be surrendered to those who seek it. The Anti-Federalists (democrats) seem to have understood this better than any who were writing on the subject at the time—or have since.

Addicts are not open to reason or persuasion. All they can think about is their next fix. This applies to power addicts as well. Don't they realize that they could destroy the planet for themselves, their children, and their grandchildren, or that they themselves could die by the reckless abuse of power? The answer is no. All they know is that they need the next fix, the next million dollars, the next war, the next deception. They are desperate to fill the void within. They have to calm the rage, control the chaos. Nothing else exists. Nothing else matters. That is what addiction is all about.

There are people who abuse power on a local level—a father, a priest, a judge, a school teacher, a police officer. They abuse power when given power. They do not pursue power beyond what is made readily available to them. And there are others who are devoted to the pursuit of power at the highest levels. They crave it, lust for it, are addicted to it. They can never have enough. These are the men who rule the world. It is not unheard of for a drug addict to kill to get the money he needs for a fix. For someone who is addicted to power, killing *is* the fix.

If we stay with this line of reasoning, we are compelled to accept that "they"—history's "heroes"—*are* different from "us"—those who care about human life—and that thus one can divide the world into two kinds of people. There are those who are kind and those who are cruel. Some people are deeply troubled by human suffering. Others are not.

Those who are untroubled by human suffering are usually the ones in power. This is why history is what it is—an endless battlefield stretching in all directions as far as the eye can see, a field strewn with corpses in various stages of decomposition. It is this way because for the past five thousand years, power addicts have been in charge of government. Their need for death and destruction is insatiable. Government is structured in such a way as to supply them with the levers of power they need to satisfy their lustmord.

Organized killing has been justified in terms of "reasons of state," "reasons of religion," "national interests," "national security," "oil," "*lebensraum*." But behind every one of these justifications is the blood lust of a particular individual in power.

# The Pathology of
# Political Disengagement

*Vain wisdom all, and false philosophy:*
*Yet with a pleasing sorcery, could ... excite*
*Fallacious hope, or arm the obdured breast*
*With stubborn patience.*

POLITICAL SCIENTIST JOHN Wikse wrote a book entitled *About Possession: The Self as Private Property* (published in 1977). In it, he confesses, he speaks the language of political psychology in an attempt to understand the psychology of the typical American in political terms. He takes certain words of Greek origin—such as "idiocy" and "ecstasy"—traces them back to their original meaning, and then uses them in that sense to describe and explain the American political mentality. Wikse maintains that the modern American has made himself his own private property, to be possessed personally, separate and apart from the community (i.e., the polis). To the ancient Greeks, this was *idiotic*. A man who took no interest in politics was an idiot* and was frowned upon. According to Wikse, in the original Greek sense, "Idiotic freedom ... is the freedom of the solitary, private man."[1] Idiocy is "the internalization of human identity."[2]

Wikse quotes Oscar Wilde to the effect that in ancient times the motto was to "know thyself." In modern times, it is to "be thyself," to be authentically who you *really* are. To be who you really are is to avoid commingling yourself with others. To be yourself, you must be separate. To find yourself, you must look inward. The Greeks lacked the concept of subjectivity. For them, to know oneself was to look out-

---

* The Greek root of "idiot" is *"idios,"* meaning "one's own" or "private." The Greek *"idiotes"* referred to a "private person" one not taking part in public affairs.

ward—to find oneself in one's participation in the polis, the world of political action.

To live without a context, to live outside of rather than within the community, is to live in a state of *ekstasis*, to be out of place, to be without a place. To be without a context, to be out of place, without genuine connections to the life of the polis, is, as Aristotle put it, to be either a beast or a God.

In Plato's allegory of the cave, people are in chains and unable to see each other. All they can see are the images, shadows, that pass before them on the wall. They do not know the origins of these images nor can they understand the true meaning of the events that lie behind the images. Those who can use the images like pieces in a puzzle—predicting the pattern of events or guessing which image will come next—are awarded prizes.

Such an allegory certainly applies to a life lived in *ekstasis* in the year 2012, in which the individual is disengaged from and powerless to have an impact on the critical events that occur around him. The passive observer is denied access to important information and never fully understands the power dynamics that govern his destiny. Events thus seem accidental and without cause. The "reality" that flashes by on a TV screen is no different from the shadows on the walls of Plato's cave. It is not surprising that, under such circumstances, the individual has no sense of history and no firm grasp of future alternatives. Time is compressed into a fleeting present. Internalized political "activity" is mythic in nature. Inner hope is equated with reality.† Belief in one's government takes on a religious nature. One does not question the government any more than one questions God. One simply prays harder.

## Identity and Politics

Most modern Americans would probably argue that involvement in political life is incidental and peripheral to their existence as *Homo sapiens*. They would define their identity in terms of the job they hold, their love life, their social life, their family life. Yet we have political urges‡ just as we have sexual urges. These political urges are grounded in a fundamental need to exercise control over our destinies, to be connected to fellow human beings in a friendly and cooperative manner, to be identified to ourselves and others as being present and existing.

The American—who has a shaky sense of his own identity stemming from his detachment from political reality—fears his loss of identity, fears that others will take it from him. He must hold on to that identity, as he would hold on to money. He has to prove that he has it,

---

† In his essay "Inside the Whale," George Orwell refers to George Bernard Shaw and H. G. Wells as progressives: "the yea-sayers ..., always leaping forward to embrace the ego-projections which they mistake for the future." *A Collection of Essays by George Orwell*, p. 243.
‡ Max Weber says, "in normal times [the] political instinct sinks below consciousness." *Political Writings*, p. 21.

put it on display, by performing for others and himself so as to convince himself that he exists.

Society, an abstraction, is construed as the enemy. We must hold onto ourselves over and against society, which will, given the opportunity, take control of us and make us disappear. We must be cautious in our interactions with others, because they might want to possess us, denying us the opportunity to possess ourselves. These are the conditions of *idiocy.*

Because we hold onto ourselves—our identity—as property, as something fixed and objectified, as something separate from meaningful action, our only sense of self-worth comes from what others think of us. So we are beholden to others for establishing our existence by their response to us. We passively await the judgment of others because we feel powerless to create ourselves in the world.§ Under such circumstances, as Jean-Jacques Rousseau observed, "a really happy man is a hermit."[3]

Living beyond and without genuine community interaction, gathered up unto ourselves, we have internalized a sense of powerlessness that we never truly identify or call by its proper name. We live lives that are empty, lives that we must continually fill up with distractions. When we allow ourselves to reach a resting state, we are profoundly bored. It is the boredom from which we seek escape via perpetual motion, action without purpose.

Wikse uses as examples American transcendental writers such as Emerson and Whitman. For essayist Ralph Waldo Emerson (1803–1882), impotence, in the sense of lack of efficacy in the world, is a virtue. According to Emerson, feeling powerless, being unable to take action, being in a state of separateness and alienation from the world, are desirable conditions. "My very impotency," says Emerson, "shall become a greater excellency than all skill and toil."[4] For poet Walt Whitman (1819–1892), freedom is "completeness in separation."[5] As Wikse sees it, this is the essence of transcendentalism—a retreat from the external material world of contingency to an inner, self-contained world of pure self-sufficiency. This is the psychology of political indifference. Because I believe that I am, in fact, powerless to affect the world of political affairs, I create a philosophical position that justifies and ennobles my political defeat, thus making a virtue of necessity.¶

---

§ Jean-Paul Sartre (1905–1980) was a one of the leading figures in twentieth-century French philosophy—an existentialist philosopher, playwright, novelist, screenwriter, political activist, biographer, and literary critic. The theme of self-validation and freedom from the eyes of others is at the core of his play "*Huis Clos*" ("No Exit"). "*Huis Clos*" is a story about *l'enfer* (hell), and in it we learn, "*L'enfer, c'est les autres.*" Hell is the Others, those who devour me with their looks—"*ces regardent qui me mangent,*" these looks that eat me up. If only there were a mirror, I could see for myself who I am. But in hell there are no mirrors. I am dependent on others to reflect back to me who I am. The hero struggles to free himself from the social nature of identity but eventually must succumb. As Sartre sees it, being connected, observed, and judged, these are the ultimate defeat. This is hell. To hold one's own image in a mirror, to be self-possessed, is victory.

¶ In his essay on the American novelist Henry Miller (1891–1980), who is best known for *Tropic of Cancer*, George Orwell speaks of Miller's political quietism, his escape into

Wikse speaks of the "inward migration of the polis." Instead of seeing the polis as being "out there" in external, material reality, we convince ourselves that this too we own and possess. This version of the polis is one that we create in our imagination. We then project it onto the outside world and believe that we understand political reality. In this world we have created, we believe ourselves omnipotent. Thus, are we protected from the crushing feeling of powerlessness.

Alexis de Tocqueville observed these same tendencies during his travels in America in the 1830s. A quote from *Democracy in America* illustrates Wikse's notion of *ekstasis*. In these comments, de Tocqueville's frame of reference is Europe. Because he focuses his interest on local American government, rather than the centralized national government, de Tocqueville fails to realize that his observation applies to America as well. He is describing a situation in which "the source of public virtue is dried up."[6]

> The greatest changes are effected there [in Europe] without [the citizen's] concurrence, and ... without his knowledge; nay, more, the condition of his village, the police of his street, the repairs of the church or the parsonage, do not concern him; for he looks upon all these things as unconnected with himself and as the property of a powerful stranger who he calls the government.[7]

De Tocqueville also aptly portrays Wikse's sense of *idiocy*. Those who enjoy equality of condition, he says,

> owe nothing to any man, ... expect nothing from any man; they acquire the habit of always considering themselves as standing alone, and they are apt to imagine that their whole destiny is in their own hands.... [Democracy] throws [every man] back forever upon himself alone and threatens in the end to confine him entirely within the solitude of his own heart.[8]

Recall that when de Tocqueville uses the word "democracy," he is speaking not of political equality but of "equality of condition," social equality. But is it the equality of condition that throws man back upon himself, that necessitates the inner migration of the polis and a political life lived out in the imagination? Or is it the "powerful stranger," the government, that denies him any honest form of political activity? Elsewhere, de Tocqueville suggests that it is the government itself that produces the isolation, not equality of condition.

---

individualism and sensualism, his "passive, non-cooperative attitude" (p. 249). Miller, says Orwell, embraces the viewpoint "of a man who believes the world-process to be outside his control and who in any case hardly wishes to control it" (p. 242). "Inside the Whale," in *A Collection of Essays by George Orwell*.

## Politics and Sanity

In Greek, the word "*stasis*" refers both to the stability of balanced forces (or equilibrium) and to the presence of such forces (or factionalism). "*Ekstasis*" is the condition of being beyond, without, or separate from factionalism or civic strife. It is also the condition of "withdrawal of the soul into a mythic or prophetic trance," which leads to insanity and bewilderment.[9] In medieval times, "*ekstasis*" became "*alienatio mentis*," which is the basis for the English "alienation." "*Lien*" is the French word for "tie." The insane person is known as an "*aliené*," "he who is without ties." Thus, our terms for insanity and for separation from the political process have a common origin.

"What ancient Athenian," asks Benjamin R. Barber in *Strong Democracy*, "what Christian, what feudal freeman or feudal serf, what Spartan mother or Theban sister, what soldier, what patriot, what clansman or tribesman or townsman could imagine that to be uprooted, unclaimed, and alone was to be free?"[10] He then offers a quote from Ayn Rand's *The Fountainhead*, in which the protagonist, Howard Roark, speaks as follows:

> I came here to say that I do not recognize anyone's right to one minute of my life. Nor to any part of my energy. Nor to an achievement of mine. No matter who makes the claim, how large their number or how great their need. I wish to come here and say that I am a man who does not exist for others.[11]

Here we see expressed, without reserve, and to the extreme, the arrogant self-centeredness of the individualist. Here is the loner who is of, for, and by himself.

Like Roark, we are taught to believe that participation in political process is incidental to our emotional well-being or intellectual development or, equally as deceptive, that by voting in elections we are satisfying that need. Yet, it is by virtue of one's participation in the affairs of the nation that the process of identity transformation from adolescence into adulthood is brought to completion and a person "capable of independent judgment and aware of others as autonomous persons in their own right" comes into being.[12]

How are we to know what is real and what is not about the world we live in? We can know only by coming together and talking with each other about what we see and know. This is what political existence is all about, says Hannah Arendt.** It is not about making laws. "Without trusting in action and speech as a mode of being together, neither the reality of one's self, of one's own identity, nor the reality of the surround-

---

**Hannah Arendt (1906–1975) was an influential German political theorist. Arendt's work deals with the nature of power and the subjects of politics, authority, and totalitarianism. Much of her work focuses on affirming a conception of freedom that is synonymous with collective political action among equals.

ing world can be established beyond doubt."[13] Thus, political life has epistemological significance. What we know to be true does not precede political existence. It is an outcome of that existence. "Politics," says Barber, "is not the application of Truth to the problem of human existence but the application of human relations to the problem of truth."[14]

Etymologically speaking, as suggested earlier, political detachment and insanity have common origins. With this connection in mind, it might be instructive to compare the adult living in a state of *ekstasis* with the adult whose emotional makeup has been skewed by a traumatic childhood.

We can translate the experience of early family life into the language of adult political existence. If government is understood to be the exercise of power in a group setting where vital interests are at stake, then the family can be seen as a political unit in which parents are the government (rulers) and children are the subjects. When the child is old enough to speak, a power dynamic emerges over who is in charge of the child's mind and body. It is at this point that household government begins to take on a certain color. The initial choice is between democracy, a family government based on respect for individual needs, wishes, and thoughts, or tyranny, in which the child is an extension of the parent, individuality disappears, and the child's mental and bodily integrity is disregarded.

The abuse of one's child is a political act, an extreme form of tyranny in which the power urges of the parents-rulers predominate and the rights of the child-subject are obliterated. The child has no resources to fall back upon, no allies to come to his defense. His body is broken. His soul is crushed. And through all of this the child is denied even the status of victim. The parents manipulate the facts so as to make the child believe that the fate he lives out is the fate he deserves, the inevitable and necessary outcome of his own behavior.

Experience that is too overwhelming for the child to absorb consciously is dissociated and stored in a separate consciousness. Thus, the child experiences amnesia for traumatic events. This magical disappearance of a dreaded reality is reinforced by parental indoctrination. The child is taught to deny the reality of what he senses and feels. He is taught to honor and trust those who betray him. He is taught to keep secrets and to lie to the outside world about what takes place at home. He is coerced into abandoning what he knows to be true in favor of what he knows to be false. His life depends upon it. This is what is known as brainwashing.

As the child from such a household evolves into adolescence and early adulthood, he may well develop what Erik H. Erikson has called "identity diffusion."[††] He will experience a

---

†† Erik H. Erikson (1902–1994) was a developmental psychologist and psychoanalyst. In the context of identity diffusion, he speaks of "a loss of centrality, a sense of dispersion and confusion, and a fear of dissolution" (pp. 122–123) and describes "an inability to

painfully heightened sense of isolation; disintegration of the inner continuity and sameness; an overall sense of being ashamed; an inability to derive a sense of accomplishment from any kind of activity; a feeling that life is happening to the individual rather than being lived by his initiative; a radically shortened time perspective and, finally, a basic mistrust.[15]

Such a person, though living among others, will feel alone, detached, and powerless. He will go through life looking at the world from without. It is as if he were passing through his own neighborhood at night, and through a lighted window observing his family seated around the dinner table, himself included. He is a stranger in his own home, a stranger in his own neighborhood. He is the Outsider. The trauma has created a void where emotion should be. The secrecy has created a barrier to interaction. The tentative sense of his own identity and right to exist, the lack of emotion, the secrecy, compel him to adopt a position of distance and detachment with regard to the life process, a distance and detachment that are necessary for the preservation of a shattered personality.

The Outsider clings to his identity as it continually slips from his grasp. Identity is something that "I present to others, and that others present to me."[16] The term can have meaning only as long as I reside among others. The Outsider is he who seeks to disregard this meaning. To abide among others, for the Outsider, is to risk falling apart, disintegrating. Holding himself together is what life is all about for the Outsider. But what exactly is he holding on to? His nonphysical "thingness," the structural totality of disparate parts that constitutes his psychological being.

The Outsider feels at risk when entering the realm of social interaction. He is incapable of bringing the "I" of today into the world of tomorrow. That is why, when he is called upon to make choices, he falters and fails, ultimately sinking into a state of paralysis. The person who cannot bring himself into tomorrow is in a constant battle with time, struggling to race past it or postpone it. This state of being resembles what Erikson has described as "time diffusion," in which "Every delay appears to be a deceit, every want an experience of impotence, every hope a danger, every plan a catastrophe, every potential provider a traitor. Therefore time must be made to stand still, if necessary, by the magic means of catatonic immobility—or by death."[17]

The imminent, though subconscious, sense of dispersing into nonexistence, of fragmenting into nonorganization, is the fundamental concern of the person with identity diffusion. He is in a constant struggle to maintain a subjective, personal connection to himself over time. This is the basis for his sanity. It is what he is holding on to. It is this sense of connectedness to himself that is threatened by his insertion into the world. He cannot both hold on to himself and hold on to the world. The

---

concentrate [and] an excessive awareness as well as an abhorrence of competitiveness" (p. 128). "Ego Development and Historical Change."

competitive demands of social life, political life, and career, the necessity of choice and responsibility, are distractions from the primordial concern of sheer existence and hence are shunted aside and minimized. Choices are left to chance and the influence of external conditions. The focus is on existence per se rather than on existing this way or that.

Thus, the Outsider leads a life in *ekstasis*, outside of and beyond the reach of the marketplace of push and pull, demand and counterdemand. He struggles through life on a day-to-day basis, seeming to the uninformed observer to be okay. Although appearing to be part of life, he is alienated from his surroundings, frightened, alone, cut off, dead inside.

Exactly how does such a person fit into the system? He doesn't. He might be in the middle of it, by force of circumstances, but he is not connected to it. The world of government and public affairs takes place around him. He sees it as external to him, existing in a remote and untouchable way, providing opportunities or taking them away at whim, generating a civic context that may go from bad to worse but that functions independently of his thoughts, dreams, or wants. In fact, this state of "ecstasy" replicates the experience of his childhood. At home, events were uncontrollable, unpredictable, impoverishing, and violent. In the public arena, as an adult he is no more powerful than the child.

## The Freedom to Not Exist

But there is, for the Outsider, an irresolvable paradox. To truly exist—to be powerful—is to be an active participant in the world of human affairs. For the Outsider, such engagement entails disappearance. He is thus in the paradoxical position of having to deny his existence in order to hold on to it. Gathered unto himself, in a state of self-annihilation, he feels safe from annihilation by outside forces. He finds his existence in a state of nonexistence.

To be a polis unto oneself is an obvious impossibility, yet this was Emerson's ideal, as it was that of the Greek Cynics, who saw the wise man as he who "was sufficient to himself, and independent of everything outside of himself."[18] It was also Plato's goal in the *Republic*. He speaks to the man "who wants to see and found a city within himself ... [and who] would mind the things of this city alone, and of no other."[19]

The person who is a polis unto himself feels powerless to change things, feels isolated from the processes that control the outcome of human events, feels trapped in his body with little or no means for release based on freedom and mutuality, withdraws further into himself, and ends up believing that this is where he belongs. Thrown back upon himself, longing deep down for connectedness but believing it is both dangerous and impossible, he develops an ideology that justifies and rationalizes as fixed and desirable the isolation and alienation that are self-imposed. He will convince himself that trapped inside his body is where he belongs, that involvement in community affairs is a distraction and a waste of time.

A traumatic childhood can lead to contempt for community life in adulthood, a contempt that finds its expression in the lying and villainy of the political leader or the passivity and disengagement of the Outsider. Emerson is an example of the latter. His writings are an eloquent and impassioned plea for nonexistence, a rationalization for a pathological fear of being in the world. His withdrawal from political life reproduces many of the childhood symptoms—fear, isolation, powerlessness—from which he seeks relief. It is the cure that is killing him.

Erikson speaks of "identity diffusion." Durkheim[‡‡] speaks of "anomie." One describes the psychological consequences of a traumatic childhood, the other the psychological consequences of political disengagement. Yet they both use the same language. In the words of one interpreter of Durkheim, anomie results in "a painful uneasiness or anxiety, a feeling of separation from the group or of isolation from group standards, a feeling of pointlessness or that no certain goals exist."[20] This is no different from what Erikson has had to say about identity diffusion.

When a civilization fragments and becomes undone, its politics dies. The sense of connectedness to the larger whole disappears. The individual, in a state of *ekstasis*, becomes fragmented as well. He becomes the Outsider, not for psychological reasons but for political reasons. Arnold Toynbee[§§] has described what it is like to undergo such an experience. There is

> a painful consciousness of being "on the run" from forces of evil which have taken the offensive and established their ascendancy. The passive expression of this consciousness of continual and progressive moral defeat is a sense of drift. The routed soul is prostrated by a perception of its failure to control its environment; it comes to believe that the Universe including the soul itself, is at the mercy of a power that is as irrational as it is invincible.[21]

Toynbee could be describing the mental life of an adult survivor of childhood trauma or that of a man without a country. In either case—whether living out a traumatic childhood or the demise of a civilization—the outcome is the same: a small, frightened, isolated, out-of-control child-citizen.

The child-citizen will go to great lengths to feel that he is accepted and cared for by his parents-rulers. He will do whatever he must to win security, and he experiences anxiety anytime he senses its potential loss. This explains the child-citizen's tacit agreement to belief in a just

---

‡‡  David Émile Durkheim (1858–1917) was a French sociologist and pioneer in the development of modern sociology and anthropology.

§§  Arnold Joseph Toynbee (1889–1975) was a British historian whose twelve-volume analysis of the rise and fall of civilizations, *A Study of History* (published between 1934 and 1961), was a synthesis of world history—a metahistory based on universal rhythms of rise, flowering, and decline—that examined history from a global perspective.

and caring government. By substitution, government is mother. She will watch over and take care of him, just as long as he cooperates.

National life becomes family life. "The nation ... becomes an expanded home,"[22] a homeland, "a place of protection where the dangers of the world outside cannot enter."[23] "By behaving properly and affectionately toward [religious and political rulers], the child can become a member of a bigger family, the larger community; he knows that he will always be provided for; he need no longer be anxious."[24] Mother-government is expected to give the child-citizen what the child never got when living at home with his parents. Just as the child coming from an abusive household must deny the reality of who his parents are and how they treat him, so the child-citizen denies the reality of what his government is and how it treats him. To disobey mother-government—to be one's own person, to engage in the exercise of self-government, the true meaning of democratic living—is to risk the parent's wrath:

> Parents first direct the child in the name of their own authority; and later, using words like "law," "duty," and "sin," they demand similar behavior in the name of political and religious rulers. Violations of these injunctions become associated with immediate and terrible punishment, with the withdrawal of parental affection and support, and with the dreaded anxiety of separation.[25]

Mother-government does not in fact live up to the child-citizen's expectations. Her lack of control, her hidden motives, the meanness behind her apparent generosity, her lying and hypocrisy, all of these frighten the child-citizen. As a means of masking what he sees and protecting himself from the dread of punishment and abandonment, he develops an ideology, a set of beliefs that are a reincarnation of the beliefs that got him through childhood. The nation is glorified and idealized.

The traumatized child was trained in denial and self-deception by his own parents. He lived out in person the brutality of family life on a daily basis. He knows who his parents really are and what they are capable of. He also knows what they tell him to believe and how they present themselves to the outside world. Thus, he is at the juncture of two realities¶¶—one that is based in power, dominance, and cruelty, another that is based in a myth of love and kindness—one that is true, another that is false. With this training, he feels quite at home in the world of government and human affairs in the year 2012. He once again finds himself at the juncture of two realities, one transparent and benign, another hidden and mean-spirited.

---

¶¶   Karl Marx speaks of a double life of twin illusions: (1) the illusion of a separate, "inner-most actuality," that is, a separate, self contained self, and (2) the "imaginary" membership in the sovereignty of the state, where there is illusory selfhood and imaginary citizenship. *Writings of the Young Marx on Philosophy and Society*, p. 226, cited in Wikse, *About Possession*, p. 148.

The American today is expected to bow to authority unquestioningly, even as he is told he has the freedom to do otherwise. He is told to trust those in power at the very moment they betray him. He is encouraged to participate in the affairs of public life while simultaneously being denied access to the necessary means and knowledge. He is living in a world that preaches openness and honesty while simultaneously insisting on the necessity of secrecy in matters of state. He is living in a nation that preaches peace and democracy while sustaining an ever-increasing war budget, a nation that in the name of democracy supports the decimation of weaker countries for purposes of private gain. He is told—as he was as a child—that it is dangerous "out there," where the enemy lurks, but safe "in here," when in fact—as it was when he was a child—the enemy lies within. He is living in a world based on power, fear, deception, exploitation, and hypocrisy. For the traumatized child, that is the world he grew up in. His natural response to such a situation is the response he learned as a child—to believe in the good intentions of those who abuse him while retreating to a position of acquiescence, numbness, and indifference toward the outcome of events that dramatically impinge upon his well-being and his very existence.

To a greater or lesser degree, we are all denied the benefits of true citizenship. For the Outsider, this betrayal is a replication of the childhood experience of being crushed, terrorized, and lied to. For the Outsider, political life in the nation-state and political life in the home are one and the same. The dynamics of the one recapitulate and feed off of the other. Powerlessness, fear, identification with the aggressor, denial, and evasion are typical responses of an abused child living at home with his family. These same responses are brought into play in the life of the polis in adulthood. The victim of childhood abuse recreates the psychological conditions of his earlier trauma by projecting them onto political life and then responding as he did when he was a child. According to Wilhelm Reich,***

> We see in patriarchal society ... how the authoritarian oppression of the child promotes the genesis of a structure of subordination, which conforms to the organization of the society at large, which for its part continually reproduces itself in the patterning of childhood. The parents act as executors of the dominant order, while the family instills its ideology.[26]

Thus, self-discovery and full recovery from childhood trauma entail

***  Wilhelm Reich (1897–1957) was an Austrian American psychiatrist and psychoanalyst who published prolifically in European journals on psychoanalysis. Reich's "character analysis" was a major step in the development of what today would be called "ego psychology." In Reich's view, a person's entire character, not just individual symptoms, could be looked at and treated as a neurotic phenomenon. He argued that unreleased psychosexual energy could produce actual physical blocks within muscles and organs, and that these would act as a "body armor," preventing release of the energy.

critical insight into the workings of nation-state and family—an under-standing of their interconnectedness and interdependency. The same applies to the adult living in a state of *ekstasis*. He must come to terms with the fact that the propaganda he has been fed conceals a reality that is just the opposite of the one portrayed. His recovery from a state of *ekstasis* entails a transformation of political consciousness from that of a child to that of an adult. Denial and subversion of intellect are preconditions for the survival of family myth. Shattering the family-government myth frees the intellect. The liberated adult is able to think critically about political realities and the nature of state power. For the first time, he understands and is in a position to live out the true mean-ing of his adult identity. He no longer sees himself as an island unto himself. He recognizes that he is part of the main.

# PART IV

# PARADISE REGAINED

*Democracy in
the Modern Age*

# Empowerment and the Process of Change

*Celestial light,*
*Shine inward, and the mind, through all her powers,*
*Irradiate; there plant eyes, all mist from thence*
*Purge and disperse, that I may see and tell*
*Of things invisible to mortal sight.*

ALTHOUGH WE HAVE been made to feel powerless, in fact we are not. We discover our power once we begin to penetrate the fog of mystification that passes for truth. To get a fresh look at things as they are, we must first get past things as they appear to be.

We are living in a man-made world, yet we act as if we were subject to an alien force beyond our ken or control. We consciously hope for the best while subconsciously waiting for the worst. We fail to realize that our way of understanding and thinking about the world—our private lives, the organizations we work for, the public realm of civic responsibility—determines the degree to which we are helpless victims of circumstance or masters of our own destiny.

In our films and fiction and TV, we seem fascinated with transcending time and space, exploring new worlds in our imagination, conceiving of super-real forces that invade the world we know in ways that are mystifying and terrifying. We have a compelling interest in otherworldliness and the implicit belief that somewhere there is a thread tying us to fantastic forces. Eventually the unthinkable will occur.

## Seeing beyond Appearances

The fanciful speculation we allow ourselves via our cultural experiences stands in sharp contrast to the perspective we apply to our government and political life. In that realm, we assume that things will go on forever, just as they are, an assumption that reflects not so·much conviction as it does an intense wish that things stay the same. Sheldon S. Wolin describes the contradiction thusly: "The same society that enthuses over economic, technological, and scientific advances, and devours novelty in its popular culture and consumer goods, also includes an extraordinary number of citizens who, when it comes to politics and religion, passionately reject the idea that experiment or novelty is welcome."[1]

However, let us assume that for many there *is* a genuine wish to bring about change for the better, change that renders our government responsive to the common will. The kind of change required can be called "transformative change." To participate in such change calls for an attitude that takes nothing for granted.* Yet it is most common, in our day-to-day living, to operate on the assumption that what we see at first glance is in fact real. According to Arno Gruen, "We all desperately want the appearance of things to correspond to the truth."[2] This seems to have been the case throughout the history of civilization. Plato's allegory of the cave suggests that the philosophers of his age were dealing with the same problem. What is shadow? What is reality? The method of systematic doubt formulated by Descartes, as well as the tradition of scientific thinking represented by the accomplishments of people like Galileo, Freud, and Marx, operates on the assumptions that what we see is not necessarily real and that the reality behind appearance must be discovered with the aid of historical investigation and critical thinking.

Lines from Gilbert and Sullivan's *H.M.S. Pinafore*—"Things are seldom what they seem, / Skim milk masquerades as cream"—echo the theme of counterfeit reality, a theme that transcends all disciplines. We are beginning to understand its application to human psychology even as we joke about it. One psychiatrist says "Good morning" to the other. The second wonders what the first meant by that.

We also understand that the physical reality we see—the table in front of us, for instance—conceals an atomic structure that we can only infer but that is real nonetheless. However, the process of learning to see through to hidden reality is a slow one. We are especially laggard in applying this kind of understanding to our personal lives and to political structures and processes, where the costs of mistaking shadow for substance are so high.

We have become accustomed to confounding myth with reality. We believe so strongly in the ideals we associate with our form of government that we have trained ourselves to ignore the discrepancy that exists between our beliefs about our government and the reality of what that government actually is. We fail to recognize that those in power have a vested interest in our not seeing the truth. "It can only be by blind-

---

* Vandana Shiva says, "In order to effect change we need to adopt a structural and transformative analysis that addresses the underlying forces that form society." *Earth Democracy*, pp. 131–132.

ing the understanding of man," warns Thomas Paine, "and making him believe that government is some wonderful mysterious thing, that excessive revenues are obtained."[3] We have been taught that to question one's government is to be "un-American." Our early writers, however, were steeped in a different tradition. According to Paine, "The defects of every government and constitution, both as to principle and form must ... be as open to discussion as the defects of a law, and it is a duty which every man owes to society to point them out."[4]

Americans, in particular, are victims of self-inflicted naiveté. We have nurtured the belief that everything is okay and that we can trust our leaders to work things out to our benefit. This persistent belief in a benign world, regardless of the accumulating evidence that contradicts it, has been given a name. It is called "metanoia," which James Duffy defines as the "naïve ... faith in the innocence and benevolence of others who are actually a danger to oneself."[5] Many of us suffer from metanoia. While a paranoid person will think he is in danger when he isn't, a metanoid person will think he is safe when he isn't. A metanoid is liable to call someone who sees hidden dangers "a paranoid conspiracy nut." Metanoia insulates us from the disturbing reality around us and thus renders us powerless to do anything about it.

In this context, it is relevant to consider the term "American exceptionalism," the belief that the United States occupies a special place among the nations of the world. By virtue of its national credo, historical evolution, and political and religious institutions, America is unique. It is not to be judged by the same standards that are applied to other peoples. In fact, it is not to be judged or critiqued in any way. It represents the incarnation of the highest ideal that any government can aspire to. In this light, the United States occupies a quasi-religious niche in the pantheon of gods who reign on earth. Any "true" American would no more criticize or scrutinize the United States than one would criticize God himself, or herself.

A satirical essay written by an Anti-Federalist (democrat) at the time the Constitution was being debated demonstrates that the concept of American exceptionalism goes back to the earliest days of the nation. In this piece, the author has assumed, in the first person, the voice of an oligarch who is agitating for the new government:

> I believe in the infallibility, all-sufficient wisdom, and infinite goodness of the late convention; or in other words, I believe that some men are of so perfect a nature that it is absolutely impossible for them to commit errors or design villainy.... I believe that to speak, write, read, think, or hear any thing against the proposed government is damnable heresy, execrable rebellion, and high treason against the sovereign majesty of the convention.[6]

Thus, the term "metanoia" has special relevance to understanding what makes an American an American. Americans believe unquestioningly in the benign intentions of their government. Such a belief is a fundamental element of their ethos. Unfortunately, it prevents them from seeing accurately and acting responsibly. It is like an anesthetic to their political sensibilities.

John Quincy Adams, Secretary of State, addressing the House of Representatives on July 4, 1821, gave voice to the American ideal. He also issued a warning:

> [America] has, in the lapse of nearly half a century, without a single exception, respected the independence of other nations while asserting and maintaining her own. She has abstained from interference in the concerns of others, even when conflict has been for principles to which she clings, as to the last vital drop that visits the heart. She has seen that probably for centuries to come, all the contests of that Aceldama[†] the European world, will be contests of inveterate power, and emerging right.
>
> Wherever the standard of freedom and Independence has been or shall be unfurled, there will her heart, her benedictions and her prayers be. But she goes not abroad, in search of monsters to destroy. She is the well-wisher to the freedom and independence of all. She is the champion and vindicator only of her own. She will commend the general cause by the countenance of her voice, and the benignant sympathy of her example.
>
> She well knows that by once enlisting under other banners than her own, were they even the banners of foreign independence, she would involve herself beyond the power of extrication, in all the wars of interest and intrigue, of individual avarice, envy, and ambition, which assume the colors and usurp the standard of freedom. The fundamental maxims of her policy would insensibly change from liberty to force.... She might become the dictatress of the world. She would be no longer the ruler of her own spirit....
>
> [America's] glory is not dominion, but liberty. Her march is the march of the mind. She has a spear and a shield: but the motto upon her shield is, Freedom, Independence, Peace. This has been her Declaration: this has been, as far as her necessary intercourse with the rest of mankind would permit, her practice.[7]

We can respect the ideal articulated by Adams. Yet we must also acknowledge that this ideal was abandoned some time ago and that Adams' worst fears about what would happen to America once she became involved in foreign wars have been realized: "She might become the dictatress of the world. She would be no longer the ruler of her own spirit."

*All Quiet on the Western Front* is a novel by Erich Maria Remarque, a German veteran of World War I. The book, published in 1928, describes the German soldiers' extreme physical and mental duress during the war, and the detachment from civilian life felt by many of these soldiers upon returning home from the front. One of the characters wonders, "What would become of us if everything out there were quite clear to us?" That is the key question, the one we should all be ponder-

---

† "Aceldama" is a Biblical reference that means "field of blood."

ing. What would the world become if we all saw clearly? Seeing clearly, unflinchingly, that is the challenge.

If we wish to escape the harmful effects of metanoia, we must find the courage and self-discipline necessary to see clearly and critically. We must think first and then act. As Henry George said:

> Social reform is not to be secured by noise and shouting; by complaints and denunciation; by the formation of parties, or the making of revolutions; but by the awakening of thought and the progress of ideas. Until there be correct thought, there cannot be right action; and when there is correct thought, right action *will* follow.[8] (italics in the original)

We take action after we have studied the conditions that need to be changed and have come to understand what caused them to be the way they are. Once we understand the cause, we can consider an alternative that will produce a different outcome. Thus, thinking critically—seeing the truth at the deepest level—is empowering. It is liberating.

We must train ourselves in healthy skepticism when it comes to our government. We must train ourselves to not automatically believe in official pronouncements and reports. By no means should we assume the good intentions of those who govern. Nor should we assume that they are like us. We do not all share the same emotional makeup. There are those who have compassion for human suffering. And there are those who don't.

## Cyclical vs. Transformative Change

We are living through a period of rapid change at every level—social, economic, cultural, technological, political. We are left with feelings of uprootedness and insecurity, and so we superimpose a structure of permanence on a changing world, blocking out all that doesn't fit. In the process, we end up mistaking shadow for substance. Like the people in Plato's cave, we sit in a darkened room, watching shadows cast upon the wall, choosing to take those shadows for reality.

The sun rises and sets, the tides come in and go out, the seasons change. We go to sleep, wake up, spend five days a week working and two days recovering. For most us, this cyclical reversal of complementary states is what we mean when we say "change." This recurring, repetitive, cyclical change, however, when viewed within a larger context, is not change so much as sameness. It has none of the characteristics of transformative change—novelty, unpredictability, irreversibility—which are of the greatest significance in the world of human affairs. Rather, it is the background, the *basso continuo*, against which transformative change takes place.‡

---

‡ Sheldon S. Wolin offers this contrast: "Change suggests a modification that retains a prior 'deeper' identity. Transformation implies supersession, or submergence, of an old identity and the acquisition of a new one." *Democracy Incorporated*, p. 96.

Transformative change is different from cyclical change. It is nonrepetitive and irreversible. It represents the development of something new and it occurs within a context of temporality, emerging from the flow of past events and movements, extending itself into an indeterminate future with consequences, not all of which can be foreseen. It has direction.

Transformative change in the social setting takes two different forms. When it is, or appears to be, beyond the control of the person or persons it affects, it is "natural change." This is a process that takes place over an extended period. The transformation is gradual. It is experienced passively. Because we rarely consciously experience such change, we fail to anticipate it or understand the directing forces behind it. It seems unpredictable and uncontrollable. In the social setting, this is the change we fear most. It can come from anywhere, at any time, and it can do anything—like some of the mysterious forces depicted in science fiction. It is intransitive. It has no object and, in a sense, no subject, or at least it appears to be lacking in both.

Transformation that occurs as a consequence of forethought, foreknowledge, foresight, and initiative is, with regard to the person or persons who initiate it, "artificial change." It takes the form of action and reaction. It is transitive. It has subject and object. It has purpose. It has direction and a degree of predictability. This is the change that permits us to take charge of our lives and the world we live in, change that enhances our sense of competency, self-worth, and inner security.

Most of the transformative change known to man, taken individually or collectively, is of the natural sort. It occurs without our understanding or our initiative. The helpless infant—lacking in language, ideas, beliefs, political preferences, the ability to hold a job and get married—over the course of time acquires all of these. The movement from city-state to nation-state, from spinning wheel to textile mill, from thirteen colonies to fifty states—these are all examples of natural transformation across broad sectors of civilization. In none of these cases were the ultimate outcomes and consequences the result of planning, foresight, or initiative, individual or collective, on the part of the party or parties involved.

We seem to be quite comfortable with such change. However, we tend to be uneasy with the prospect of artificial change, change that we bring about. We usually expect the worst from gaining foreknowledge and taking initiative, assuming, without good reason, that it is best to leave things as they are. If we meddle, matters might get worse. Such an assumption reflects an underlying pessimism and an unreasoning trust in "fate," letting things take their "natural" course.

And yet the degree to which natural or artificial change prevails in our individual or collective lives is potentially self-determined to a much greater degree than any one of us realizes. Much of what passes for natural transformation is open to human intervention. By means of critical thinking followed by thoughtful action we can create something new that serves the common good.

## Temporality: The Future Is Real

We miss many opportunities in life because a distorted sense of time obliterates historical perspective and truncates the future by forcing us to view it in terms of short-term cycles, mere transposition of present circumstances to a future date. We look for cyclical repetition, which we dub change, and then falsely conclude that things stay roughly the same.

Most of us like to think of ourselves as living in the present, coming from a past that is vague in its meaning though rich in emotional content and heading into a future that is structureless, remote, and ill-defined. Such a notion of time denies temporality and anchors us in an indefinite present that doesn't really exist. The present is an artifact, a contrivance, a convention we use to superimpose structure on our lives and stretch out the duration of time, perhaps insulating ourselves against thoughts of our own decline and demise. Paulo Freire observed, "As men emerge from time, discover temporality, and free themselves from 'today,' their relations with the world become impregnated with consequence."[9] We need to do away with the here and now. Seen from a larger perspective, it doesn't exist.

There is no "is." There is only "was" and "will be." Notice how I couldn't avoid the "is" in the last sentence. The "is" is the necessary platform from which we can look backward to what was and forward to what isn't yet. But it is a floating platform with no piers or piles to sustain it, a weightless anchor we throw overboard into the flow of time, an imaginary magic carpet, at one moment no larger than the head of a pin, at another large enough to blanket the universe.

When I say "the here and now," this very moment, what do I mean? However I define it, the here and now, like quicksilver, eludes my grasp. Is the present the moment I have the thought, "Is the present the moment I have the thought"? Is it the moment I hit the first letter of the sentence, "I"? We could go on refining the question into infinity, because the present is the infinitely small gap between the future and the past. But for convention's sake, it can be "While I am sitting at the computer," "Today," "This week," "This year," or "The next fifty years," depending on our perspective.

We live with the disturbing paradox that the part of time in which we exist disappears before our eyes. Like light-sensitive film the moment we open the box to take a look at it, the present moment loses the very properties we wanted to examine in it. That aspect of temporal reality that we can most readily examine and reflect upon—the past—is no longer with us and open to our influence. That part of reality—the future—that will have the greatest impact on our lives cannot be known with certainty. The present doesn't exist. That past cannot be acted upon. The future cannot be known. We are in a terrible predicament.

Yet, in many ways, we are what we have been. We are the accumulation of what we have lived through. We tend to appreciate this when we think of ourselves, but when we loose our gaze upon the world, we take the world, our nation, as it is and forget where it came from. This is a mistake. For if it is true that I am what I was, it is also true that this country is what it was. Consequently, we should be treating the past with a great deal more respect than we do, and we should come to understand that to know ourselves as a people we must know our past, objectively and accurately, because that past defines who and what we are. By discarding our past and its meaning—as Americans in particular are wont to do—we are discarding ourselves and our sense of identity, our rootedness to ourselves and to each other. This is one important source of insecurity in our culture. It is not possible to deny an identity and simultaneously have one.

In a similar fashion, I am what I will be. The world is what it will be. It makes sense to pay attention to the future in a way that is creative and productive, with the understanding that the future is not a mere repetition of what is or what has been, but a coming into being of what isn't yet. [§]

Thus, the reality we see is not "real" reality. What "is" is not what *really* is. What "is" is what is in the process of becoming. This is the sense in which the future is always with us. The future is not an unreal or arbitrary abstraction but rather a concrete attribute of things as they exist in what we call the "present."

It is not that difficult to conceptualize the "will be" in the "is." In fact, in a limited way, such thinking is a part of our daily living. When I say, "I am going to plant some dahlias in the backyard," what I really mean is that I am going to bury a small woody growth in the ground that bears no resemblance at all to the lusty green leaves and coral petals I have in mind when I plant it. I am planting something that isn't yet. Likewise, one can incorporate into the "who I am now" some future goal toward which one takes initiative long before it is realized. In other words, potential is real.

Joe decides to lose weight. In order to do so, he has to become a thin person in his imagination before he becomes a thin person in reality. Otherwise, he will never lose weight. The future is in the present.

Our relation to the future is hampered by the fact that transformative change is a slow, gradual process. It happens, but we don't *see* it happening. We have to reconstruct it retroactively to see it. We see it after it happens. This is where history comes in. To initiate transformative change, on the other hand, we have to "see" it before it happens. This is where imagination comes in.

If I take a seat on a bench along the esplanade that borders the Hudson River near the 79th Street marina in New York City, I can watch the setting sun dip behind the New Jersey palisades across the way. Yet

---

§ In the following paragraphs I am speaking the language of Friedrich Hegel. My understanding of Hegel's dialectics, is based on a reading of Herbert Marcuse's *Reason and Revolution: Hegel and the Rise of Social Theory.*

something strange occurs. I see the sun as it hovers, already partially hidden by the cliff-top, and know that within fifteen minutes it will have completely disappeared. I give myself the assignment of "watching" its movement, the way I can watch the young boy on his bicycle as he rides across my line of vision. Without fail, the sun sets at the assigned time. Without question, it has moved from one position to another, in a relatively short period. And yet I can detect no movement. This is a lesson in humility concerning my ability to detect a change that takes place in front of me and that I have devoted myself to observing.

## Discontinuity

Irreversible, man-made change takes place at an even slower rate and hence is even more difficult to detect. And yet it does take place, just as surely as the sun sets. To see it, it is necessary to adopt the proper time perspective. It is necessary to make use of the analytic techniques of contrast and comparison—to engage in the discipline of historical study.

I can remember a time many years ago when, as a teenager, I could ride safely on the subways alone in almost any area of the city, day or night. I can compare that reconstructed memory to the present situation and draw some conclusions about the change that has taken place.

Thus, if our time span is long enough, we can actually see a discontinuity in development. What once was has become something quite different. This raises the issue of identity. When there is continuing transformation, over a substantial span of time, does the individual or societal element under study change into someone/something different from what he/it started as? And if someone/something different has emerged, do we need a different perspective and different concepts to make sense of this newly emergent entity?

For example, at the age of thirty, is Joe the same person he was at the age of three days? If we could look at his DNA in both instances, we would probably say yes. But on just about any other level of analysis, the person of thirty is not the same as the person of three days. Even in terms of simple appearance, if Joe had a photograph of himself at three days and asked a friend to detect the resemblance, in most cases that friend would have a tough time, so dramatically has Joe evolved from what he was then. Every cell in his body has changed many times over. Of course, at thirty, Joe can speak, walk, run in a marathon, read, write, and do arithmetic. Joe at three days could do none of those things. It is really a question of two different beings, though by convention we assign them the same identity.

Consider the United States of America. When we think of the country we are pledging allegiance to, we are probably thinking of the continental USA, a vast connecting system of highways and power lines, cityscapes, oil wells, factories, a population of more than 300 million, an elaborate and highly structured governmental bureaucracy, a TV set in every living room.

On June 21, 1788, the United States was born, that is to say, the Constitution had been ratified by nine out of the thirteen states. The population was about 3 million, only a hundredth of what it is today. There was no President. Currency as we know it did not exist. The land mass was one-third of what it is today. There was no USA west of the Mississippi River. In 1800, Washington, D.C., became the nation's capital. The White House, which stood on a desolate bog, had no bathrooms, and water had to be carried by hand a distance of five city blocks. Are we, in the year 2012, pledging allegiance to one and the same country that came into existence in 1788? Or, once again, is it a question of convention based on social and legal necessity rather than ontological reality?

Thus, things are not what they seem. They *seem* to be fixed and unchanging, when the opposite is the case. The "present," the "is," *seems* tangible, real, and extended in time, when in fact it is so small and fleeting as to have no meaningful existence, while the future— which we relegate to some position of distant remoteness—has been alive, well, and living within the "present" all along. Thus, to find reality, we must first destroy appearances, what "obviously seems to be the case." We must begin with the negation of the given.

## Critical Thinking

If we are deliberately, consciously, going to undertake to change something about ourselves or the world we live in, the first step is to acknowledge that something is wrong. For some, this is the most difficult step of all. It means "being critical," making negative statements, "being judgmental." It means recognizing and accepting the fact that thought has an important "negative" role to play. Otherwise, it is not possible to advance in a self-determined way.

Negativity and critical thinking have gotten bad press in American culture. "If you can't find something good to say, don't say anything at all" is a common admonition. We have heard it since childhood. Such an attitude has become an intrinsic part of our etiquette and thought processes. We are expected to speak and think deferentially of someone else's ideas, whether we agree or not. It is considered poor manners to do otherwise. We are inundated with appeals to the power of positive thinking. What about the power of negative thinking? Learning, growth, and implementation of new ideas can only occur once we have seen what is wrong with things as they are.

It is unfortunate but true that negativity is frequently confused with "negativism." The person who looks to see what is wrong is seen as a "boat rocker," a "poor sport," a "poor loser," a "pessimist." There are indeed people who are negativistic, those who are always complaining and critical in a way that is self-defeating and undermining, people whose response to negativity is passivity and retreat.

But negativity—as opposed to negativism—is a universal attribute of reality, not of people. In other words, things are wrong with us and with the world around us, whether we choose to see them or not. Thus, the true meaning of negativity involves using critical thinking to penetrate surface appearances and release inner potential. Paradoxically, the negative is more positive than the positive, because the negative holds out the possibility that there is a way to makes things better.

What "is" must pass away before something new can come into being. Things cannot develop their potentialities except by perishing. This is the "destructive" aspect of the process of transformative change. Everything "is" only in the sense that the process of its becoming something else is not yet manifest. Being is continual becoming. Every state of existence has to be surpassed. The real field of knowledge is thus not the given facts about things as they are, but rather the critical evaluation of those facts as a prelude to their passing beyond their given, manifest form.

All of this can be very unsettling to contemplate. Change is everywhere. What we seek is something fixed to hold on to. And so we cling to any branch we can find as the river surges forward.

There is a law in physics that says, "for every action there is an equal and opposite reaction." In a sense, this applies to human beings as well. Where there is change or the possibility of change, we humans resist. We are especially resistant to change that reaches deep into the essence of our psychological and social being.

Resistance can have positive as well as negative consequences. Change that hasn't been subject to resistance is not real change. Thus, resistance is a necessary reaction to what is new. It is both an emotional reaction against and an intellectual means of assimilating something new, integrating it into existing frameworks and setting up new ones where necessary. However, sometimes people resist adamantly, without self-examination or struggle, and refuse to budge. Such resistance is morbid and inhibits new growth. A person should be open to considering new ideas and then perhaps rejecting them after fair consideration.

Developing and implementing new ideas will be less discouraging and more successful to the degree to which the resistance factor is taken into account from the outset, recognizing that it is both human and necessary. Innovators must become skillful in helping others work through their resistance. What this means is having enough self-confidence, patience, and insight into human behavior to allow someone to differ; to help him explore and fully express the nature, meaning, and significance of this difference; and to help, through argument and persuasion, move him from one position to another.

Innovative thinking requires living with doubt, incompleteness, and incertitude and feeling comfortable with others who do the same. Allowing oneself to see past the illusion to what it conceals can be threatening, and might be especially so for someone for whom being in control is of critical importance. The psychological consequences of moving from one perceived reality to another were explored by Helen Merrell Lynd in a little-known book published more than fifty years ago.

## Change and the Loss of Self

Lynd's *On Shame and the Search for Identity* is a sustained discussion of what happens to a person when he sees something suddenly, for the first time, that contradicts some basic assumption he has about life. He is taken by surprise and made to seem foolish in his own eyes for being so mistaken for so long about such an important matter. He feels violated in some fundamental way. It is not so much what others might think about this deficit but what he himself thinks. "The deepest shame," says Lynd, "is not shame in the eyes of others but weakness in one's own eyes."[10]

Shame is not so much an emotion as it is a state of being, a state that arises without any warning when "patterns of events ... of which we are not conscious come unexpectedly into relation with those of which we are aware."[11] Even if one sees it coming, one cannot fend it off. Once it arrives, it is haunting and inescapable. One is left with a feeling of powerlessness. What we thought to be true about ourselves and our environment turns out to be invalid. And most importantly, our belief in our own ability to know what is true is brought into question. This is fundamentally the most threatening part of the whole process. It is not what one discovers about what one didn't know that is most troubling but what one discovers about one's own *capacity* to know. This question of our capacity to know strikes at the core of our sense of self, our identity, our psychological being.

As Lynd points out, unlike joy, sadness, or anger, shame is such an isolating experience because "there is no readily expressive language"[12] with which to communicate it. Going through such an experience in partnership with one or more other people who have had or are having similar experiences will help to facilitate the transition from one state to another. What is required and not easily achieved is a readjustment in one's perception of who one is, of the world one lives in. Lynd quotes Tolstoy's *Anna Karenina*, where the profoundly disorienting effect of shame is aptly portrayed. Anna, a proper married woman, has found that she has feelings for another man, fundamentally betraying who she thinks she is. While riding on a train from Moscow to Petersburg,

> something seemed to choke her, and all objects and sounds in the wavering semi-darkness surprised her by their exaggerated proportions. She kept having doubts as to whether the train were going backwards or forwards, or were standing still altogether; was it Annuska there, sitting next her, or was it a stranger?

"What is that on the hook?—my fur shuba or an animal? And what am I doing here? Am I myself, or someone else?"[13]

As new reality replaces old reality, a person begins to lose his sense of connectedness to himself and to the world. He experiences a loss of identity. He is no longer at home in the world or in his own body. He loses known landmarks. His ability to trust has been undermined. He can no longer trust in himself, in his world, or in his ability to know.

This penetrating experience of shame when one begins to discover that one has been fundamentally wrong about something explains, as much as anything, the reluctance to explore an alternative reality. One had placed one's confidence with enthusiasm in a reality that never existed. In desperation, one clings to familiar details as a source of security:

> As trust in oneself and in the outer world develop together, so doubt of oneself and of the world are also intermeshed. We have relied on the assumption of one perspective ... and found a totally different one.... We have become strangers in a world where we thought we were at home.[14]

> The overall quality of shame involves the whole life of a person, all that he is, including the parents who have created and nurtured that life.... Loss of trust, exposure, failure, the feeling of homelessness—these experiences of shame—become still more unbearable if they lead to the feeling that there is no home for anyone, anywhere.... Experience of shame may call into question, not only one's own adequacy and the validity of the codes of one's immediate society but the meaning of the universe itself.[15]

Lynd once again quotes from *Anna Karenina*. This time it is Anna's husband whose universe has been shattered. Alexy Karenin is an aristocrat and civil servant who lives life by the spoonful. He is in control, unfeeling, unruffled. He is predictable. His life is predictable and so is everyone in it—until his wife, Anna, falls in love with another man. Karenin wants to believe that his wife has been true to him and tries to convince himself that she has. But

> he could not help feeling that he was confronted with something illogical and absurd, and he did not know what to do. Karenin was face to face with life; he was confronted with the possibility that she might be in love with some other person besides himself, and that seemed quite absurd and incomprehensible to him because it was life itself. All his life he had lived and worked in official spheres, dealing with the reflection of life. And every time he had come up against life itself, he had kept aloof from it. Now he experienced a sensation such as a man might experience who, having calmly crossed a bridge over a chasm, suddenly discovers that the bridge has been demolished and that there is a yawning abyss in its place. The yawning abyss was life itself and the bridge that artificial life Karenin had been leading.16

In order to bring about change in the form of government, as individuals working alone and in small groups, we need to find the courage to experiment with our ideas. We might have to go through a mild version of the disorientation Lynd describes. Such an experience, though unsettling, is neither devastating nor debilitating. It is something like awakening from a disturbing dream.

Here is an exercise to try. It should take just a few moments. Keep track of your physical and emotional responses as you first consider the project and then actually struggle through to some kind of conclusion. I have chosen something that is difficult and unsettling to envision. That is the whole idea. It will give you an idea of what it means to let go of the fixity of things as given. Momentarily lift your eyes from this page and, in your imagination, try to construct a society with no police force and no prisons.

I can imagine that such an exercise might produce a tightening in the gut, maybe a queasy feeling, maybe a dryness in the mouth—in other words, fear. Then comes the sense that it is absolutely inconceivable and impossible to construct such a society, even in one's imagination. But bear in mind that in ancient Athens there was no police force. There were no prisons. It could be that you can come up with no solution that seems viable. Perhaps there is none in contemporary society. The attempt, however, to conceive of such a possibility should enable you to understand what it means to let go of perceived reality and to struggle to think about social change.

23 ❧

# The Democratic Process

*This must be our task*
*In heaven, this our delight.*

A S WE BEGIN to think about what it would be like to head down the road to democracy, we should not have in mind a superhighway with four lanes in each direction, traffic speeding along at seventy-five miles an hour, endless stretches of concrete with a blinding sun reflecting off the polished surfaces of the cars in front of us.

The road to democracy is a different kind of road—a beautiful, winding country road. Traffic moves at a leisurely pace. Trees line the roadway. Around each turn is a new vista. Only one lane runs in each direction. Drivers take their time. But we don't mind. We're not in a hurry anyway. We are enjoying the scenery and the leisurely pace of the ride. This is what a democratic society is like.

We might feel the need to make things better right away. This is certainly an understandable response based on conditions locally and globally. However, transformative change doesn't happen overnight. It cannot be forced under pressure of time, even though time is of the essence.

The sense of urgency must be transcended. We should be looking for ways to make long-term differences rather than quick fixes. Quick fixes might be quick, but they tend to leave things unchanged in the long run. Social problems *are* soluble. But they can seem insoluble and overwhelming if the time frame is too short. Considering all the societal and environmental ills we face, it could be that time is running out. We have to act as if it weren't. Taking this "as if" stance requires an act of faith. We are allowed such indulgences once we become committed to fundamental change.

It will be easier to overcome the sense of urgency if we are able to distance ourselves from the immediacy of current reality as, in fact, we seek to transform it. Here is where the Archimedean lever comes in handy. It is the means by which we can lift ourselves up into the heavens even as we try to change things down here on earth.

## The Archimedean Lever

Suppose instead of thinking of Americans, or Canadians, or Russians, or Chinese, or Ugandans, we think of all of these peoples taken collectively. Suppose instead of thinking of all these peoples in political, social, or geographic terms, we take a step backward and start thinking in biological terms. What do all of these peoples taken collectively have in common? They are members of the species *Homo sapiens.* Looking at it this way puts matters into a different perspective. There are no longer people of different skin colors, stature, and bone structure. There are no longer turf battles, saber rattling, and slaughter. None of that. Just a species, in Philip E. Slater's words, "an awkward species in an unpredictable world."[1]

As we seek the Archimedean lever, moving farther and farther away from our subject matter, into layers of atmosphere surrounding the earth, we come to realize that not only are we just a species, we are but one species among millions of species. That is a humbling thought. And further, we realize that all of these species, millions of them, are part of an ecosystem composed of air, water, and earth. And that all species are in constant interaction with each other and their environment. And that distortions and imbalances in the ecosystem affect all members of the system, directly or indirectly. And that for one species to thrive, all must thrive. So, when we speak of the common good, we are really speaking of the good of the ecosystem. If we can create a government that serves the common good—a government that equates the common good with the health of the ecosystem—then we will have a good government, a government that embraces the well-being of all species, not just the "awkward" one known as *Homo sapiens.*[*]

In *Gaian Democracies:*[†] *Redefining Globalisation and People-Power,* Roy Madron and John Jopling report that all is not well with our ecosystem. In the past thirty-two years,[‡] "forest cover has shrunk by 12%, the ocean's biodiversity by a third and freshwater ecosystems by 55%." Many species have seen their numbers cut in half. Since 1970, "North Atlantic cod stocks have collapsed from an estimated 264,000 tons to under 60,000." In the United States and United Kingdom combined, damage to the ecosystem has resulted in $250 billion loss in one year. "Thanks to industrial farming methods, 24 billion tons of topsoil ... washes off the land into the sea every year."[2]

Community is withering at a similar pace. "Through the unrelenting destruction of local cultures, lifestyles, knowledge and communities, we are witnessing the steady erosion of humanity's cultural diversity, flexibility and capacity for self-sufficiency."[3] The Union of Concerned

---

* In *Earth Democracy,* Vanadana Shiva speaks of "a planetary consciousness that connects the individual to the earth and all life" (p. 11). She says we are "earth citizens and earth children" (p. 7).
† Gaia is the Greek goddess of the earth.
‡ The authors' point of reference is 2003, the year their book was published.

Scientists warns, "A great change in our stewardship of the Earth and the life on it is required if vast human misery is to be avoided and our global home on this planet is not to be irretrievably mutilated."[4]

In forming our political groups, Madron and Jopling suggest that we follow the rules of nature. We have been using physics as our model for abstract thought. What would happen if we started using biology as our model instead? Physics teaches us that matter can be neither destroyed nor created. Yet, in the United States alone, the population increases by eight new arrivals every minute. That is biology. Biology deals with coming into being—the emergence[§] of something that did not exist before. This is the kind of thinking we should be applying to our thoughts about government.

Biology deals with small occurrences, taking place in complex and subtle interactions, from which emerges something that is more complex and different from the sum of its parts. When people get together with a common purpose to discuss matters of common concern, there are many interactions. Subtle and modest changes occur during the various exchanges, with the result that no participant is exactly the same at the end of the experience and that the thoughts themselves have evolved in interesting and unpredictable ways.

Madron and Jopling believe that if "we can think of 'democracy' as meaning a system through which members of communities organize themselves, rather than a system for controlling them,[¶] our democratic systems would be getting closer to being complex, adaptive and self-organizing," something like the tissues of our body.[5]

In *A Dream Deferred: America's Discontent and the Search for a New Democratic Ideal*, Slater uses similar language:

> Democracy is created anew every day or it is not really democracy. Democracy is not laid down like a blueprint; it grows like a forest. Democracy is self-creating. It is a permanent state of self-reinvention. Thinking and doing are not separate steps but part of the same self-correcting process.[6]

> Living in a truly democratic environment requires a comfort with constant motion and flux, an ability to accept permanent imperfection, chronic development.... Democracy is a process, not a product.[7]

Before democracy can put down roots, it needs to germinate. People who share a common interest meet in small groups. That shared interest

---

§ Jeffrey Goldstein has defined emergence as "the arising of novel and coherent structures, patterns, and properties during the process of self-organization in complex systems" ("Emergence as a Construct: History and Issues," *Emergence: Complexity and Organization*, vol. 1, no. 1, p. 49). An overview of the concept of emergence as applied to nature and human society can be found at http://en.wikipedia.org/wiki/Emergence.

¶ In *Love's Body*, Norman O. Brown differentiates governments that are fraternal from governments that are paternal. One chooses between the "fraternal principle of equality" and the "paternal principle of domination" (p. 18).

is democracy—its meaning, its purpose, its possibilities. They engage in an unstructured exchange of ideas. They have no particular expected outcome. The discussions are exploratory and expressive. The group is tolerant of different personalities and accepting of different ideas. Respect for person and thought breeds trust and mutual growth. A meeting of Alcoholics Anonymous (AA) offers a good example of this kind of interaction.

In AA, there are no mailing lists and no bureaucracy. There is no outside financial support. AA advocates no causes, no political candidates. It takes no public stands. Its only source of funds is the money dropped into the basket that is passed around at the end of each meeting. Meetings take place every week at the same time and location. Anyone who wishes to attend does so, provided he or she has an interest in no longer drinking. Participants experience a great deal of acceptance, a feeling of fellowship and mutual support.

## Civic Gatherings

Working off the AA model, how could we set about transforming society? Our organizational mechanism could be "civic gatherings," which could be set up like AA meetings. The structure could be similar, but the content would be different. Instead of discussing struggles in dealing with drinking, we could use the meetings as a forum for those who want to express their thoughts on the subject of democracy. The civic gathering would not be about activism, sectarianism, or the advancement of special interests. Its ultimate goal would be to find the vocabulary for addressing the common good on a national level, using as its resources the ideas, energy, and spirit of those in attendance. The participants would have the opportunity to talk about democracy and to decide if it is something that appeals to them or not. Democracy as a practice would emerge from such discussions. The word itself would take on new meaning as new ways of talking about it would evolve.**

At the beginning of each gathering, participants could draw straws for who would serve as moderator for the day. That person's purpose would be to keep the conversation flowing and to make sure that everyone has an opportunity to speak, that differences of opinion are respected, that participants are treated with kindness and respect, and that the discussion stays on topic. The moderator could read a mission statement, such as this one:

> The civic gathering is a forum for discussing government and democracy. It is a means for becoming engaged in civic life. It is not about activism, sectarianism, or the advancement of special interests. It is about the identification and articulation of common beliefs and com-

---

** The democratic societies that emerged in the United States around 1790 are discussed in Chapter 12. See also Eugene Perry Link, *Democratic-Republican Societies, 1790–1800.*

mon interests. It is about collective self-possession and transformation. The dialogue is the action.

By means of dialogue we gain awareness of the political reality we live in and our role in perpetuating it. We begin to understand how government works, what democracy means, and how democracy can be a means for establishing a government that embraces the common good.

By means of dialogue we transform ourselves from passive observers to active participants. By means of dialogue we establish connections with our fellow citizens. We learn to listen. We learn to articulate our views. We learn to declare our differences in a respectful manner.

Civic gatherings are nonviolent. They show respect for the individual, regardless of race, color, gender, or religion. They are conducted in a manner that combines spontaneity with self-discipline in an atmosphere of peace and acceptance.

Gatherings could be completely open-ended and unstructured, or they could be fueled by broadly framed questions. What is government? Where is the money going? Where should the money go? What is freedom? Are we free? What is good government? What is political change and how does it come about? What is power? Who has it? For what purpose? What is the common good? What is civic virtue? What is democracy? Is democracy feasible? Is democracy desirable? What are my hopes for democracy? What is the connection between elections and democracy? Who should govern? Are we wise enough to govern?

Civic gatherings would not be part of any particular political movement. There would be no true believers. Instead, the gatherings could serve as a catalyst for political transformation, both individual and collective. They would be a place of comfort and security, a place for intellectual and emotional development. Debate and friendly disagreement would be encouraged. Angry dissent and personal attack would be out of place.

Such gatherings are based on the assumption that positive social change has its roots in critical self-awareness and that action without critical self-awareness will miss its mark and lead to a sense of defeat and powerlessness. The way we relate to each other in the process of transforming *ourselves* will determine the nature of the government that grows out of our efforts. Civic gatherings are a microcosm of the new world we strive to create. Friendship is the basic form of social connection, one based in trust, hope, and respect for differences. True friendship is noncompetitive and can develop only in an atmosphere where egotism and the need for ascendancy and self-promotion are absent.

We connect to each other as part of a group as a consequence of our commonly held beliefs and visions. Yet we may not fully comprehend these beliefs and visions until we talk to one another about them. As we formulate our thoughts and hear ourselves talk, we learn for the first time just how important our beliefs and visions are to ourselves and to others. In the process of talking to each other and discovering that we are listened to with deference, we begin to develop trust. Our confidence in ourselves, in our beliefs, and in our neighbors increases. Beliefs and hopes shared in common, trust in others—these are what create a community.[††]

The "Great Community" is the national community, the community of communities. But it does not yet exist. Although as Americans we share common boundaries and a common heritage, we are not bound to each other through common goals and mutual allegiance. One important purpose of civic gatherings would be to provide a means for a sense of community to spread throughout the nation. First one civic gathering would be established, and then another somewhere else. These early gatherings would start a correspondence to keep each other up to date on their latest experiences. They would help others start up. Soon there would be a whole network of gatherings across the country.

In this way, civic gatherings can become a catalyst for a national transformation. The establishment of community, participation in community life, the bonding of individual to individual, community to community—these are the outcomes civic gatherings are conceived to engender. They are based in mutual respect. They are peaceful. They are out in the open. They are democracy in its true form—a form that does not know violence, that does not know secrecy.

At some point, gatherings might wish to coalesce to conduct local assemblies to debate national issues. These would be larger, more formal meetings, perhaps with set agendas. An issue would be debated and voted upon. The results would be posted on a community bulletin board and communicated to other assemblies around the nation. As these assemblies became more and more numerous, they would occupy more and more political space. They would become the focus of national attention. Gradually a shadow government would emerge. Eventually, the shadow government would become the functioning government, and the earlier government would move into the shadows. Political transformation would be realized.

## Action vs. Activism

Paulo Freire (1921–1997) was a Brazilian educator who undertook to bring literacy to adult illiterates and succeeded remarkably well in his enterprise. Freire took his teaching out of the classroom and into the community, basing his pedagogy on local practices and language. His

---

†† In *Gaian Democracies*, Madron and Jopling argue for the need for "liberating leadership" (p. 22). It is my belief that in a true democracy, there are no leaders. There is no one who, by virtue of charisma or speaking ability, takes charge, thus developing a following whom he can then "lead" in a direction of his own choosing. In a democracy, everyone leads and everyone follows. Or, better yet, everyone participates. Leadership infantilizes those who follow. Those who lead too often lust for power. Looking back to ancient Athens (see Chapter 3), one might point to the positive roles of Cleisthenes and Pericles in shaping Athenian democracy. Conversely, however, one would also have to recall Alcibiades, who did his best to destroy it. And one could reasonably argue that had there been no leaders of this stature (positive or negative), Athens would have been an even stronger democracy.

goal was to establish an active dialogue among participants, because he believed that dialogue liberates and monologue oppresses. At the end of thirty hours of participation in these "culture circles," adults were reading and writing. Quite an achievement! In these integrated group experiences, everyone made good progress, not just a few star pupils. The concept of participatory change can apply to any group setting and is especially useful in the context of democracy discussion groups, where the goal is not to instruct but rather to actively engage members in exchanges that are transformative for everyone who participates.

Freire differentiates between "action" and "activism." Activism proceeds in the absence of dialogue.[‡‡] It is narrow in its goals and operates in isolation. In contrast, action emerges from dialogue and is imbued with a deep understanding of the issues at stake. It operates within a broad temporal framework. It is based in interaction with other human beings and the world, which is experienced as knowable, objective reality.

Activism arises out of reactivity. Government advocates a policy or takes an action. As a consequence, I am angry, anxious, outraged, despondent, desperate. I feel driven to do *something*, on my own or in collaboration with others. I write a letter to my congressman. I join a protest in opposition. These emotions and these responses are both wholesome and appropriate. Yet they change nothing. They are simply reactive.

Reactivity is a form of denial. It enables us to deceive ourselves into thinking we are empowered when, in fact, we aren't. When I react, I am playing by someone else's rules. I am playing on his turf. Though I might, acting alone or with others, bring about some short-term beneficial result, government structures and power dynamics remain intact.

To have lasting impact, we need to create a new playing field, to attack the problem at its cause, to have a vision of something different that is creative and innovative, to be moved to action with feelings of hope and celebration, as opposed to feelings of despair, frustration, or hatred. Our goal should be to act in a way that is independent of the conditions that motivate us to take action. Action under these circumstances is truly free, unfettered by our responses to what someone else has said or done. We are joined together in community with our fellow citizens.

Thus, our first critical step is to accept, rather than deny, our own individual powerlessness.[§§] At any moment, there is great and unnecessary suffering at home and abroad. There is nothing we can do to stop it now, as it is happening. Paradoxical as it may seem, accepting our powerlessness frees us from reactivity and in fact leads to empow-

---

‡‡   As Freire puts it, "Without dialogue, self-government cannot exist." *Education for Critical Consciousness*, p. 24.
§§Powerlessness is a primary tenet of Alcoholics Anonymous. The alcoholic's very first step is to admit that he is powerless over alcohol. Once he truly accepts his powerlessness in this area of his life—where he has no real power—he is freed up to exercise power where he really does have it. The same applies to our political lives. We can become truly empowered once we accept our powerlessness over current events.

erment. This has to be a conscious choice, leading at first to a brief period of resignation and hopelessness, then to a feeling of inner peace. We are aware of the reality that surrounds us, but we are no longer enchained by our emotional response to events. In our imagination, we have discovered a new world and a new playing field. This vision is our inspiration. It is the world we are working to create. It is a vision of government that embraces the common good.

The lack of genuine community and critical insight results in a lack of groundedness. Lacking a deep understanding of what ails the community, people look for outside solutions and fluctuate between baseless optimism and baseless despair. "Tragically frightened, men fear authentic relationships, and even doubt the possibility of their existence. On the other hand, fearing solitude, they gather in groups lacking in any critical and loving ties which might transform them into a cooperating unit, into a true community."[8]

Freire believes genuine hope is born "with an increasingly critical perception of the concrete conditions of reality. Society now reveals itself as something unfinished, not as something inexorably given. It has become a challenge rather than a hopeless limitation."[9] By participating in critical dialogue—dialogue that is "nourished by love, humility, faith and trust"[10]—we develop a critical consciousness that enables us to transform the world rather than simply adjust to it. In the process, we escape our isolation and connect ourselves to our fellow man.

Slater makes a similar observation: "Democracy means participation—it is a matter not of sacrifice, but of contribution, which is a form of self-assertion. Democracy requires maintaining one's point of view 'until it has found its place in the group thought.' For it is the joining of differences ... that is creative."[11]

It is often argued—usually by those who have power to lose—that people are not ready for democracy. But, says Slater, "there are no preliminary steps to democracy any more than there are preliminary steps to riding a bicycle. You get on, you fall off, you keep trying until you get the hang of it."[12] We are made ready for democracy by becoming involved in the process of creating democracy. "Democracy is on-the-job training. There is no preparation, no way to avoid mistakes."[13] The outcome is self-created coherence.[14]

## Political Ideals

We associate our civic life with words like "freedom," "justice," and "equality." We assume that these ideals exist as options for us to exercise or not, that they exist independently of our connection to them. In *Strong Democracy: Participatory Politics for a New Age*, Benjamin R. Barber argues otherwise. These values, he says, do not exist in the abstract. They are a creation—the outcome of our interaction with each other in the democratic process. Without that critical interaction, they do not exist. They cannot be simply claimed and enjoyed. "To be free," he says, "we must be self-governing; to have rights we must be citizens."[15] Our rights disappear as soon as we stop participating, and that participation has to be something more than just voting in elections.

Some writers would have us believe that freedom and power are separate and perhaps conflicting ideas. They would have us believe that politics is "the art of power" and freedom "the art of anti-politics."[16] Not so, says Barber: "Freedom and power are not opposites."[17] The purpose of freedom is to enable us to take charge of our lives, collectively, not simply to be "free" to mind our own business in seeking our own private fulfillment. Politics should not be, as it has become in a society governed by liberal politics, "a kind of human zookeeping."[18] It is "the art of planning, coordinating, and executing the collective futures of human communities. It is the art of inventing a common destiny for women and men in conflict."[19]

The quest for certainty has led to the belief that becoming politically involved requires some a priori knowledge that legitimizes our political endeavors. But the democratic process is not about prior knowledge. It is about open-ended interaction, for which there can be no prior knowledge. The outcome is not predetermined and hence cannot be predicted since there is no exclusive pathway to a goal that one must "know" in advance. Thinkers who base their theory of action on prior knowledge are compelled to advocate a course of inaction. "Privacy and passivity are celebrated not because they maximize individual liberty ... but because privacy and passivity alone guarantee that no delusive certainty will come to dominate a world in which truth has no warrant."[20] Thus, the lack of the possibility of certain knowledge is translated into "the impossibility of affirmative politics."[21]

Americans have unknowingly become victims of Cartesian solipsism. They believe only in private knowledge. They believe that everything they need to know, they can know by searching their own minds—something they can do in the absence of any dialogue with the outside world. Such knowledge is fixed and rigid. It has little bearing on the changing world of give and take in the marketplace of ideas.

Americans are traditionally highly moral and authoritarian in their religious beliefs. Yet, for the most part, these private moral virtues do not have a significant impact in the realm of community living. "We lace our laws with moral strictures that affect to enforce morality by fiat (Prohibition once, the school-prayer and anti-abortion movements today), yet we eviscerate the public institutions and neglect the public services (parks, schools, libraries, cultural institutions) that promote public morality and civic pride."[22] Our convictions—religious and political—are personal and private. They do not allow for doubt or flexibility. But when we think of acting on our beliefs in the outside world, we are riddled with doubt and hesitancy and so we do nothing.

Knowledge that emerges when one exchanges views in the community is different from knowledge that is personal and private. This new kind of knowledge is neither absolute nor certain. It changes somewhat with each interaction. It addresses, in fact, issues that can never be satisfactorily resolved in the abstract, that is to say, privately. What is "truth"? What is "justice"? We begin to answer these questions when we explore the needs and dreams we share with others in the community as we attempt to improve the human condition in the real world. "Politics does not rest on justice and freedom; it is what makes them possible.... Politics is not the application of Truth to the problem of human relations but the application of human relations to the problem of truth.... [Politics is] the form of interaction for people who cannot agree on absolutes."[23] Before there can be common truth, there must be citizens.

Common truth is the outcome of civic exchange. The process is based on constructive conflict and disagreement. The contradiction between means and ends is eliminated. One does not have to ask, does the end justify the means? The end *is* the means. They are one and the same. The outcome one seeks is in the process one helps to create.

Conflict, like community, is not incidental to politics.¶¶ It is its defining essence. Politics is conflict resolution. Where there are no differences, there is nothing to debate and resolve. If everyone agrees at the outset, then politics and the democratic process are obviated. There is no active participation. There is no opportunity for growth and transformation.

Politics begins in discord and ends in agreement. As Barber points out, conflict is what prevents participatory democracy from degenerating into totalitarianism. For where there is monolithic community, all "in agreement," the individual loses his individuality. He merges with the community. There is no choice. There is simply submission to an abstraction known as "the popular will," "race," "nation." Barber refers to this as "unitary democracy." It is this kind of popular movement that can lose its anchor and become as tyrannical as the most bloodthirsty of monarchs, as happened during the French Revolution. It is this kind of popular movement, based in an abstract collectivity, that has given true democracy, based in concrete reality where there is conflict and debate, a bad name.

Democracy is inclusive—of ideas *and* people. And so there are as many solutions as there are voices. There are voices that sing in harmony and there are some that, by our standards, are out of tune. Yet, in a true democracy, all voices must be heard.

---

¶¶   "The collision of opposite opinions produces the spark which lights the torch of truth." Quoted in Link, *Democratic-Republican Societies, 1790–1800*, p. 156.

## Living with Uncertainty

Resolution comes not through compromise but through creative redefinition of the problem. "This requires flexible participants, people able to look beyond the personal agenda they enter the group with, able to develop along with the group."[24] The process is based on the "conviction that there are extraordinary possibilities in ordinary people."[25] Democracy is open-ended. The outcome is uncertain. Living with uncertainty can be unsettling, on one's own. But living it out within the context of the group process can be exciting and invigorating.

Many of us fear conflict based on experiences we had growing up at home, or experiences we are exposed to via the media. We associate conflict with trauma, stress, and mental or physical harm. Yet conflict can be salutary in a community setting where respect for differences is embraced. We learn how to disagree in a friendly, deferential manner. To do so requires that we have confidence in our own point of view and at the same time a willingness to accept that we might become inspired to modify our ideas based on our conversations in the community.

We tend to grow up imbued with a concern that our efforts at communication will be thwarted, that we as individuals will be demeaned for our thoughts. We have developed a deep distrust of our fellow man. Very little, if any, of this distrust, however, is based on actually having participated in something like a civic gathering where there are shared values and a common purpose. We have so little opportunity for an honest exchange of views that it is difficult if not impossible to imagine a friendly setting in which such an exchange might occur. Attend an AA meeting and you will see that in fact it *is* possible.

There is no question that, initially, where there are differences—and where good will has not yet been established through experience in community conversation—there may be a lack of sensitivity. Things may be stressful at first. Enduring this minor and temporary discomfort, however, will seem a small sacrifice when we begin to understand the benefit for ourselves and for the community of becoming actively involved in the democratic process. As Barber states, strong democracy envisions politics as a way of living, "the way that human beings with variable but malleable natures and with competing but overlapping interests can contrive to live together communally ... to their mutual advantage."[26]

"Malleable" is a key word. Most of us see ourselves as fixed and immutable. Most of us are threatened if we are challenged to defend our position, if we are challenged to modify our position. Yet when we lack physical flexibility we are willing to engage in stretching exercises to loosen ourselves up. Habitual participation in community dialogue will have the same effect on our thought processes. Initially, we will be rigid and defensive. But gradually we will become more flexible and open to new possibilities.

"Competing but overlapping interests" is another key component of Barber's political thought. He reminds us that in most instances, even where there are strong differences, there probably exists some common-ality that can serve as a bridge to a mutually satisfactory solution. It is not important that any one individual or faction be "right." The only expectation should be that we contribute our thoughts in a nonaggres-sive and constructive manner. Anyone who does that is doing some-thing very important for the democratic process. And it is this kind of process that will create a future that we can all collectively embrace.

The word "consensus" usually makes an appearance in discussions of conflict and conflict resolution. Once consensus has been reached, by definition, the goal has been achieved and the democratic ideal has been realized. Yet consensus as a concept has its roots in constitutional oligarchy. It has the odor of backroom dealings. Often it involves decep-tion, manipulation, secrecy, horse trading. "I'll give some of this, if you give some of that." Where there is consensus, the participants walk out as they walked in. They have selected a solution. They have not invented a solution. They have not reconstrued the problem, its solution, or their perception of the problem and its solution. The experience has not been personally transformative, as it would have been had the process been a truly democratic one. Democratic process is not about suppressing, tol-erating, or resolving conflict. It is about transforming conflict into some-thing that is different from the constituent givens. As Barber observes,

> The basic difference between the politics of bargaining and exchange and the politics of transformation is that in the former, choice is a matter of selecting among options and giving the winner the legitimacy of con-sent, whereas in the latter, choice is superseded by judgment and leads men and women to modify and enlarge options as a consequence of see-ing them in new, public ways. For this reason, decision without common talk always falls short of judgment and cannot be the basis of strong democratic politics.[27]

Politics has as its starting point a common awareness that something needs to be done. There is a political question that needs to be resolved, which Barber formulates as follows: "What shall we do when something has to be done that affects us all, we wish to be reasonable, yet we dis-agree on means and ends and are without independent grounds for mak-ing the choice?"[28] As this question makes clear, politics is about doing something. It is about taking action, making a choice. Says Barber, "To be political is to *have* to choose"[29] (italics in the original). In choosing, we must try to find a responsible answer, even when there is no abstract way of warranting the validity, justice, or truth of the action we propose to take. All preconceptions fly out the window except those that pertain to the nature of the process itself. The process is not neat, clean, orderly, or predictable. It is a "grimy ... muddled activity of reluctant doers who must nonetheless do as best they can."[30] In the words of Montaigne,*** it is "mixed and artificial, not straight, clean, constant, or purely innocent."[31]

Barber lists seven key concepts that, taken collectively, constitute the arena for the democratic process. They are action, publicness, necessity, choice, reasonableness, conflict, and the absence of an independent ground.[32]

## Political Action

"Action" is a most common, everyday word. It takes on special meaning, however, when embedded in the context of democratic process. By equating politics with action, Barber makes it clear that politics is not a spectator sport. Nor is it somehow passively securing our private rights. Politics as action entails changing something in the real world of common living, such as building a hospital, making peace, levying taxes. Politics is not a thing, a place, a set of institutions, or an attitude. Politics is about doing something. If it isn't about doing something, then it isn't politics.

Politics involves not just any action, but public action—the domain of the "we," in the largest sense of the word. There are other kinds of actions that are either marginal to the great community of the common good or explicitly private. These are not political actions. Actions are political and democratic when we are all actively engaged in taking those actions and they have consequences for all of us. The notion of what is private versus what is public can change over time and from one context to another. Barber uses smoking to illustrate such a change. Smoking was once a private matter. When it was discovered that smoking was harmful to all of us, even to those not smoking, then smoking became a public matter. Political action was taken, and smoking was banned from most public spaces.

Political action is driven by necessity. It has a logic of cause and effect that plays itself out in the public realm. A law is passed when people, living in public spaces, are dying from secondary smoke. Political action—democratic political action—is exercised in response to a common need and has as its goal the resolution of that common need. Where there is a known social necessity, inaction is as fraught with consequence as is action. Thus, we are responsible for the conditions of our society whether we act or whether we remain passive.

Political action involves choice, deliberate choice. In the democratic context, the choice will be made after there has been public deliberation among those who will live out the consequences of the action. Choice that is impulsive, whimsical, or arbitrary is not democratic choice. It is not invested with the necessary participatory, deliberative energy that the democratic process requires. As Barber points out, "If action is to be political, it must issue from forethought and deliberation, from free

---

*** Michel Eyquem de Montaigne (1533–1592) was an influential French philosopher and essayist.

and conscious choice. Anyone can be an actor. Only a citizen can be a *political* actor"[33] (italics in the original).

Choices should be reasonable. They should take into account the expressed concerns and interests of the other participants in the political debate. They should be responsive, not coercive. They will emerge from conflict and difference of opinion but will be offered in the spirit of fair play. More often than not they will be made after participants have reformulated their views on the nature of a required outcome and hence have transformed their way of seeing and thinking. They will involve "the reformulation of private interests in the setting of potential public goals."[34]

Barber notes that, too often, fragmentary efforts at engaging people in the decision-making process in the absence of a true democratic community produce results that are then used to support the contention that people cannot govern themselves. Social scientists and political elites "throw referenda at the people without providing adequate information, full debate, or prudent insulation from money and media pressures and then pillory them for their lack of judgment."[35] True democracy, he says, "is not government by 'the people' or government by 'the masses,' because a people are not yet a citizenry.... Masses make noise, citizens deliberate; masses behave, citizens act; masses collide and intersect, citizens engage, share, and contribute."[36]

One could legitimately argue that democratic process requires community and that there is little or none of that commodity to be found in our current society. Therefore, democracy is not possible. My reply to that assertion is that community is not a preexisting entity but rather the outcome of the democratic process, the creation of democratic living. Bring people together, get them to start discussing matters of common concern, and community is the outcome. Under the current system, the individual's civic life is made up of his ties to his government. There are no civic ties that bind him to his fellow citizens. The democratic process remedies that deficiency.

"Community" is not simply all of the people who live on the same block or in the same town. It is not based in geographic identity. True community comes into being once there is public necessity, resulting in conflict, debate, and choice. Participation creates community. It creates citizens. "Community without participation first breeds unreflected consensus and uniformity, then nourishes coercive conformity, and finally engenders unitary collectivism of a kind that stifles citizenship and the autonomy on which political activity depends."[37]

When we enter community discussion in response to a community need, to the degree possible we should do so without any ideologies to fetter our interactions. Where there is true democratic process, Barber says, there is an "absence of an independent ground."[38] What this means is that for the political process to be democratic, it must not be driven by any preexisting ideology or beliefs that are used to shape and determine the outcome. There are no preexisting abstractions that must be honored and conformed to, no theory of truth or of justice. The debate must be free, spontaneous, and creative. Concrete circumstances and the give and take of verbal exchange provide the only source of direction.

## Talk vs. Speech

Barber attaches special importance to the word "talk," a word from common, everyday usage that takes on enriched meaning when applied to the democratic process. He differentiates between "talk" and "speech." Rightly, he observes that speech is a weapon in adversarial exchanges, while talk, in Barber's lexicon, entails listening with interest and empathy. He speaks of the "mutualistic art of listening," in which the listener strives to understand the speaker's position and identify points of commonality, rather than seek weaknesses to be attacked.

"Good listeners," says Barber, "may turn out to be bad lawyers, but they make adept citizens and excellent neighbors."[39] Where there is listening, there is silence, the time it takes to reflect upon the other person's words and try to find a means for empathizing with his position. When words are simply being hurled back and forth, I can barely wait for you to finish so I can express my view and explain to you why your view is in error. These kinds of exchanges are the opposite of what Barber has in mind when he speaks of "talk." At a Quaker meeting, there is no endowed voice running the service. Everyone sits equally in silence until someone has a thought. That thought is expressed, and then there is more silence until the next is expressed. Compare this to the staged "political debate" at election time, where the goal is to score points against an adversary rather than reflect upon his thoughts and find points of agreement.

Talk, as Barber sees it, is made up of words laden with emotional as well as cognitive import. The emotional component of the human exchange needs to have its place, but always in a manner that shows respect for both listener and speaker. Words that have been purged of their emotional weight and neutralized can create artificial and sterile exchanges. True meaning and intent remain concealed. Talk is an opportunity for expressing empathy and affection, as well as passion, provided it is not laced with hostility or animosity.

Where there is talk, there is "conversation." There was a time when the word "conversation" carried with it rich associations of connectedness, thoughtfulness, and personal fulfillment founded in mutuality, with topics of consequence as the subject matter. Such occurrences—"unrehearsed intellectual adventure[s]"[40]—are rarities in our current society, where exchanges are devoted to factual updates, gossip, and "venting." Yet political conversations are an essential element of a true democracy. And they are not confined to moments of debate and decision making. They are an integral component of daily living. They once were, to a much greater degree than they are today.

Talk is a vital means for keeping our beliefs and values alive. It also provides an opportunity for us to reexamine our ideas in the light of what others have to say. It is a necessary immunization against the ossification of our ideas. We can easily slip into smug self-satisfaction within our own thoughts, just as easily as we can accept received truths without examining them. When we have to explain and defend our beliefs, we are more likely to appreciate their true value. And if we are humble enough, we are more likely to realize that they might need to be modified.

Barber makes the interesting point that talk is important even after the vote has been taken and the decision has been made. Dissenters need the opportunity to express their dissent and their disappointment. Stifling these voices is harmful to the individuals who must swallow their frustration. It might lead to their withdrawal from the democratic process. Stifling the voices of dissent might deprive the other group members of an important reminder of why an alternative opportunity might have been desirable. Court opinions routinely include the dissenting views. Frequently they are the most interesting and relevant parts of the documentation.

Language is the medium of conversation. Language is made up of words and phrases that have particular meanings and connotations. Language has the power to shape reaction to what is being expressed. The Pentagon needs money for a "police action." It turns out, what they really mean is "war." But using the word "war" will certainly make participants more cautious in authorizing the funds. The Pentagon seeks money for "pacification." Pacification sounds like a good thing. It leads to peace. However, it turns out that pacification entails killing people, often civilians. A conversation about killing people is likely to produce an outcome that is different from one on the topic of pacification. "Banks need a 'bailout,'" says Treasury. Don't you mean "handout"? we might ask. Why should banks get a handout? Thus, where there is democratic process, not only do the citizens frame the debate, they also frame the terms of the debate. Barber reminds us that "what we call things affects how we do things."[41] If we are not careful, we lose control of our future by losing control of our language. "Left to the media, the bureaucrats, the professors and the managers, language quickly degenerates into one more weapon in the armory of elite rule."[42]

Conversation, based in a language that is honest and alive, is a means of establishing commonality and community. It is broad and open-ended in its format. It "achieves a rich ambiguity rather than a narrow clarity."[43] Conversation takes effort. It requires taking the trouble to find the right word, to speak in a way that is both meaningful and deferential. It is an opportunity not only for self-expression but also for getting to know the other person. It is this "getting to know the other person" that establishes the basis for commonality, which is the platform through which the democratic process fulfills its purpose. This purpose includes more than simply getting business done. It includes the enjoyment and celebration of community life. Politics as currently conceived and enacted is based in adversarialism and breeds enemies. Democratic politics when it is functioning as intended creates friendships. In the words of Jean-Jacques Rousseau, the democratic process "produces a remarkable change in man." Through participation, man's "faculties are exercised and developed, his ideas broadened, his feelings ennobled, and his whole soul elevated."[44]

## Mutualism vs. Majoritarianism

One of the most frequent charges against a hypothesized democracy is that it entails "majoritarianism," "the tyranny of the majority." The mentality that conceives of this outcome sees a room filled with competing private interests in which a cohort of superior numbers overpowers a less well-organized or numerically inferior minority. In this situation, there are "winners" and "losers." But this version of "democracy" is not democracy at all.

"Majoritarianism," says Barber, "is a tribute to the failure of democracy: to our inability to create a politics of mutualism that can overcome private interests."[45] It is the mentality that prevails at election time and within the various congressional caucuses, where politics is adversarial, where power interests collide and bargain their way to some kind of compromise. This version of "democracy" in fact describes the situation that prevails in the sham democracy promoted by the ruling oligarchy. What is missing from this version is the role of conversation and deliberation. Democracy is not about selecting from a menu of preestablished options. It is about creating choices in an atmosphere of mutuality. In Barber's words, it is "an autonomous and self-regulating domain of common talk and common action."[46]

Democracy prevails where private interests are transcended in the name of the common good. It entails judgment rather than preference. It is the domain of amateurs, not experts. In the language of sham democracy, the starting point is "I want such and such." True democracy speaks a different language, saying "Such and such would be good for us."

A practical example of mutualism versus majoritarianism would be a private versus a public choice in purchasing an automobile. As a private person, I might choose a gas-guzzling sport utility vehicle. Were I to have a mechanism for reconstituting myself through the democratic process, I might come to realize that such a private choice violates the common good by polluting the air, depleting natural resources, and causing an unfavorable change in climate. Thus, within a forum in which I am able to see the public consequences of my private choice, I might choose to act contrary to my initial private preference. This would be an example of democracy at work. The question "What kind of car do I want?" becomes "What kind of world do I want?"

In sharp contrast to the true democratic process is the act of vot-ing, which to many Americans is equivalent to democracy and political participation. Barber takes a different tack. He contrasts the conversa-tional, communitarian, celebratory elements of the democratic process with the act of voting, which he compares to using a public toilet. "We wait in line with a crowd in order to close ourselves up in a compartment where we can relieve ourselves in solitude and privacy of our burden, pull a lever, and then, yielding to the next in line, go silently home."[47]

# Democratizing the Oligarchy

*We may chance*
*Re-enter heaven; or else in some mild zone*
*Dwell, not unvisited of heaven's fair light,*
*Secure.*

POWER IS THE lifeblood of government. One could say that the individuals in power are like the red blood cells that carry oxygen throughout the human body. For a person to be in good health, new cells must be constantly added to the blood. In the human body, bone marrow supplies those new cells. In the governmental body, elections are the source of new cells (new government officials). For government to be healthy, its blood/power must circulate freely and without obstruction.

The heart pumps blood through the human body. Over time and with age, the arteries become narrowed due to accumulating deposits of cholesterol and thickening of the arterial walls. As a consequence, the heart must work harder to force the blood through the body. Organs and extremities receive less blood than they need and begin to malfunction.

In government, new ideas, new perceptions, new energy, and new motivation enter the circulation with the election of new officials. But when the same officials remain in power for extended periods, they begin to fall victim to destructive forces, money chief among them. Money narrows the arteries of the governmental body just as cholesterol narrows the arteries of the human body, eventually impeding the flow of fresh blood and, with it, the flow of new ideas, vision, and motivation. The governmental body becomes lethargic and develops an obsessive urge to consume more of the very substance that is producing the debility—money.

## The Power Clot

Power clots occur in government, just as blood clots occur in the human body, and with the same potentially devastating effect.* Where power is stagnant, where it gathers in one place and doesn't move, it can form an embolism, threatening the very life of government. The United States today is a good example of stagnant power and its consequences. Congress has become enfeebled due to a lack of new blood. Power has shifted to the President, the only remaining vital element.

Although America has long been considered the torchbearer of democracy, it is, in fact, the least democratic of the constitutional oligarchies that call themselves democracies in today's world. One could easily argue that the U.S. government has devolved into an elected monarchy. The power once exercised by the Congress has been repackaged and transferred in toto to the executive branch. The excitement and lavish display associated with a presidential election, the astounding sums involved in getting elected and celebrating the victory, the applause and genuflection attendant upon the president's entrance are not significantly different from such honors offered up to a reigning monarch.†

By just about any measure other than its military adventures, the U.S. government, as a government, is either dead or dying. No one, not even the oligarchs who founded the country, would consider a government that shows so little self-respect, so little integrity, so little allegiance to its purposes and the spirit of its founding—a government that only grudgingly offers its citizens even the bare minimum—to be a viable, healthy entity.

What has happened to produce such an outcome? One has but to consider the concentration, distribution, and flow of power to answer that question. On paper, most of the power in the U.S. government lies with Congress. Congress controls the purse. Congress declares war. Congress can impeach. Congress can amend the Constitution. The president's greatest power is his power to veto, a power the Congress can override. The president's military powers are only as great as Congress allows. So, what has happened to all that congressional power?

The corporate money that returns the same House and Senate members to their seats year after year is the cholesterol clogging the arteries of government.‡ Power no longer flows freely. It coagulates and clots.

---

* Power, says Philip E. Slater, "is healthy when evenly distributed, and highly toxic in heavy concentrations." Further, he notes, "Power is like alcohol—if everybody gets a little, a good time can be had by all, but if a few people consume the whole supply you can count on a bad night." *A Dream Deferred*, pp. 15, 56.

† Gore Vidal, writing in 1983, put it bluntly: "The President is a dictator." *The Second American Revolution and Other Essays (1976–1982)*, p. 263.

‡ David Cay Johnston, *Free Lunch: How the Wealthiest Americans Enrich Themselves at Government Expense and Stick You with the Bill* (2007), uses a different image. "To those who lust for power," he asks, "of what use is acquiring power unless they can abuse it? In this, the philosophy of the power monger is no different from that of the cancer cell, which mindlessly seeks growth until it overwhelms the host" (p. 14).

Embolisms form. They get bigger and bigger. And the governmental body gets weaker and weaker. Aging and debilitated, Congress becomes powerless. Practically the only new blood is in the presidency, and so that is where the power flows. With campaigns paid for by the corporate interests that they then must serve, senators and congressmen have grown weak with apathy and self-satisfaction, quite contentedly watching their responsibility to govern passed along to the executive.

Here is an example of a power clot. Bill Thomas of California was elected to the House of Representatives for the first time in 1978. He retired from Congress in 2007, after serving for twenty-nine years. During that period, no one but this one man had the opportunity to speak for the citizens who happened to live in the 22nd Electoral District of California. Thomas' power over the electoral process in his district was so great that in 2004 no one even took the trouble to challenge his re-election.

Thomas ruled the House Ways and Means Committee from 2001 until he left Congress in 2007. Ways and Means is the chief tax-writing committee of the U.S. House of Representatives. The committee has jurisdiction over all taxation, tariffs, and other revenue-raising measures, as well as other government programs including Social Security, unemployment insurance, Medicare, enforcement of child support laws, Temporary Assistance for Needy Families, foster care, and adoption programs. It is one of the most powerful committees in the House of Representatives. Its chairman is one of the most powerful people in the House, indeed one of the most powerful people in the country.

Thomas was a key proponent of several of President George W. Bush's agenda items, including three major tax cuts and the Medicare Prescription Drug, Improvement and Modernization Act of 2003 (P.L. 108-173). On signing the Medicare drug bill, President Bush said,

> With the Medicare Act of 2003, our government is finally bringing prescription drug coverage to the seniors of America. With this law, we're giving older Americans better choices and more control over their health care, so they can receive the modern medical care they deserve.... Our nation has the best health care system in the world. And we want our seniors to share in the benefits of that system. Our nation has made a promise, a solemn promise to America's seniors. We have pledged to help our citizens find affordable medical care in the later years of life. Lyndon Johnson established that commitment by signing the Medicare Act of 1965. And today, by reforming and modernizing this vital program, we are honoring the commitments of Medicare to all our seniors.

Here is what President Bush *did not* mention: The bill contained a provision that prohibited the government from negotiating the best price possible for the available drugs. Such negotiations characterize the dealings of just about any health plan in the world. Another governmental bureau, the U.S. Department of Veterans Affairs, negotiates for the lowest drug prices it can get. But, in the Medicare program, such nego-

tiation was actually prohibited. This provision had two consequences:
(1) Elderly people on fixed incomes, in ill health, were compelled to
pay enormous sums for their medication,§ and (2) drug companies were
guaranteed enormous profits. This is where Bill Thomas comes in.

As the Medicare drug legislation was being crafted, there was considerable opposition to its non-negotiation provision. But Chairman
Thomas was wily and ruthless in undermining any attempts to give the
bill a fair hearing. Among his tactics was holding informal meetings at
a time and place known only to supporters of the bill. In *Free Lunch:
How the Wealthiest Americans Enrich Themselves at Government
Expense and Stick You with the Bill*, David Cay Johnston sets the scene:

> On the ground floor of the capitol, near a bust of Raoul Wallenberg, lies an
> unmarked corridor. A guard stands watch, making sure no tourists enter.
> Beyond the guard the drab, eerily silent hallway meanders through the
> building until it ends at a set of cream-colored, saloon-style swinging doors.
>      Not just tourists were unwelcome. So were some members of Con-
> gress. This is a room for those whom the man who controlled it for five
> years called "the coalition of the willing." The willing, in this case, meant
> a willingness to engage in a particularly underhanded scheme to take from
> the many to benefit the few while appearing to do the opposite.[1]

In this drab, saloon-like setting, Thomas conducted his secret business
and succeeded in passing a bizarre piece of lopsided legislation. Surely it is
no coincidence that of the $1.2 million he raised for his 2005–2006 cam-
paign, the top five contributors came from the health care and pharma-
ceuticals industries. Nor is it surprising that on retiring from Congress,
Thomas was hired by the lobbying firm of Buchanan Ingersoll & Rooney,
which lobbies on behalf of health and drug companies. This is how the
American government works. This is what a power clot looks like.

## The Cure

What can be done to bring government back to health?¶ The pages that
follow outline one person's answer—mine—as they describe an exercise
in experimental government. My goal is to reconceive government as
something malleable and evolving, not something sculpted in marble,
inert and unchanging. You may agree with some of these proposals or
with none of them. I encourage you to develop your own alternatives.
In the process, it will become more evident that real change is possible.

At the foundation of the U.S. government is a bicameral legisla-

---

§ This provision explains why those who can afford to do so go to Canada or Mexico,
where they can get the same medication at discounts up to 70 percent of the American price.
¶ Way back in 1786, it was proposed that local assemblies meet twice a year: "once to
instruct their Senators, and once ... to examine their conduct, that they might be able to
judge whether they are safe persons to be trusted in [the] future." Holton, *Unruly Americans and the Origins of the Constitution*, p. 129.

ture—a House of Representatives and a Senate. Members of the House are chosen based on population, whereas two Senators are allotted to each state regardless of population. There is a judiciary with a Supreme Court as the court of final appeal. And there is an executive branch (which I address in the chapter that follows). My plan for democratizing the oligarchy retains this structural integrity while modifying the process to ensure that power is more widely dispersed and circulates more freely, thus creating a polity that is more likely to respond to the wishes and needs of the governed.

The first step is to set limits on the terms of those who serve in Congress. The more people who serve, the more democratic the government. The more people who serve, the more widely dispersed the power and the healthier the government.** It is longevity in office that breeds the self-indulgence and short-sightedness that plague our current government. A congressman who knows he will be elected term after term, that re-election will be virtually assured as long as he has the continued support of his special-interest patrons, will listen to those paymasters and no one else.

Under the Articles of Confederation, delegates to Congress were appointed for only one year at a time and were not allowed to serve more than three years in any six. Most state legislatures had similar provisions. Recall that under the original Pennsylvania Constitution, elections were to occur annually. A representative could serve no more than four years in any seven.

The length of tenure in office was one of the deepest concerns of the Anti-Federalists (democrats). As discussed earlier, the "Centinel" of Philadelphia warned the American citizenry to watch out or they would end up with a *"permanent* ARISTOCRACY" (italics and capital letters in the original).[2] On the same subject, "Brutus" said,

> It is probable that senators once chosen for a state will ... continue in office for life. The office will be honorable if not lucrative. The persons who occupy it will probably wish to continue in it, and therefore use all their influence and that of their friends to continue office. Their friends will be numerous and powerful, for they will have it in their power to confer great favors; besides it will before long be considered as disgraceful not to be re-elected. It will therefore be considered as a matter of delicacy to the character to the senator not to return him again.

How prescient!

In the early Renaissance, executives could serve for one year only in the communes and city-states in northern Italy. In Florence, in the same time frame, the term of office was even shorter: governing officials chosen by lot were rotated out of office every two months and had to wait two years before they could serve again.

---

** In the next several paragraphs the attentive reader will notice some repetition. I am recycling material used earlier and bringing it together at this point for purposes of emphasis and focus.

There were similar precautions in ancient Athens. No citizen could serve on the council of 500, the *boule,* for two consecutive annual terms or for more than two terms in his lifetime, nor could he be head of the *boule* more than once. In the Roman Republic, a law was passed imposing a limit of a single term on the office of censor.†† The magistrates—tribune of the plebeians, aedile, quaestor, praetor, and consul—served one-year terms and were forbidden re-election until a number of years had passed.

As R. K. Sinclair points out in his discussion of Athenian democracy, "The related notions of limited tenure and rotation and the principle of collegiality‡‡ severely curtailed the opportunities for individuals ... to use office to acquire a position of leadership."[3] Aristotle makes repeated reference to tenure in office. "Where there is natural equality of the citizens," he writes, "and it would be unjust that anyone should be excluded from the government ... then it is better, instead of all holding power, they adopt a principle of rotation."[4] As one of the principles of democracy Aristotle lists "restriction of the tenure of office to six months, that all of those that are of equal rank may share in them." In other words, where there is political equality, justice requires that everyone be given a chance to serve.

In addition to upholding the principles of serving and sharing in office, rotation serves to limit the concentration of power. Aristotle's writing is instructive here again: "The short tenure of office prevents oligarchies and aristocracies from falling into the hands of families.... It is not easy for a person to do any great harm when his tenure of office is short, whereas long possession begets tyranny in oligarchies and democracies."[5] Finally, he writes that "no one should hold the same office twice, or not often, except in the case of military offices; ... the tenure of all offices ... should be brief."[6] The more people who rotate through a given office, the less likely it is that someone wishing to extend an offer of bribery will find a willing recipient. It is easier to corrupt the few than the many.

In Volume 1 of *Democracy in America*, de Tocqueville raises the issue of whether the president should be allowed to serve more than one term. "Intrigue and corruption are the natural vices of elective government," he writes, "but when the head of state can be re-elected, these evils rise to a great height and compromise the very existence of the country." The principle of re-electability "tends to degrade the political morality of the people and to substitute management and intrigue for patriotism."[7]

Article I, Section 1 of the U.S. Constitution establishes the legislative branch of government. It reads, "All legislative Powers herein granted shall be vested in a Congress of the United States, which shall consist of a Senate and House of Representatives."

---

†† The censor was an officer in ancient Rome who was responsible for maintaining the census, supervising public morality, and overseeing certain aspects of the government's finances.

‡‡ Collegiality in this context is defined as "the sharing of power among colleagues within the field of their competence." R. K. Sinclair, *Democracy and Participation in Athens,* p. 80.

Article I, Section 2 establishes the House: "The House of Representatives shall be composed of Members chosen every second Year by the People of the several States, and the Electors in each State shall have the Qualifications requisite for Electors of the most numerous Branch of the State Legislature."§§ This clause could be amended with an addition of just a few words, as follows: "No Member shall serve more than once in any four-year period and twice in a lifetime."

Article I, Section 3 reads as follows: "The Senate of the United States shall be composed of two Senators from each State, chosen by the Legislature thereof [modified by Amendment XVII], for six Years; and each Senator shall have one Vote."

Term-limiting modifications could also be applied to the Senate. In addition to providing for rotation in office, shortening the length of each Senate term to four years would allow for more varied participation. Four years is certainly enough time to do whatever harm or good a person is apt to do in office. Therefore Article I, Section 3 could be amended as follows: "The Senate of the United States shall be composed of two Senators from each State, chosen for four Years; and each Senator shall have one Vote. No Senator shall serve more than once in any six-year period and twice in a lifetime."

There is precedent for thus amending the Constitution to limit the length of tenure in office. The Twenty-Second Amendment reads as follows: "No person shall be elected to the office of the President more than twice, and no person who has held the office of President, or acted as President, for more than two years of a term to which some other person was elected President shall be elected to the office of the President more than once."

Congress passed the Twenty-Second Amendment in 1947 in response to Franklin D. Roosevelt's election to a fourth term as president. It was felt that continuation in office for an unlimited period invested a single person with too much power. The same reasoning should apply to members of the House and Senate. Power needs to circulate. Tenure in office needs to be limited.

It is easy to imagine that, under these new restrictions, a different kind of person would seek office, with different expectations and motivations. He might be more responsive to the public weal because he would owe little or nothing to corporate interests. He would be more likely to act responsibly with regard to the common good and less likely to acquiesce to imperatives from the executive branch. Such a person—and everyone else—would understand that service in office was not a lifetime sinecure. Thus, he would be less appealing to corporate interests. Election to office of any particular

---

§§I believe the confusing language in the second half of the sentence refers to the facts that many states had property qualifications and other restrictions denying the vote to potential members of the electorate and that the qualifications to vote for the "most numerous Branch" of the legislature—preseumably the state Assembly, as opposed to the state Senate—were less restrictive.

individual would buy a lobbyist very little, because at the end of a two- or four-year period, the congressman or senator would step down.[¶¶]

## Elections

Another critical issue for those who wish to move the constitutional oligarchy in the direction of more responsiveness and greater access is that of elections. Ask an American, "What makes the United States a democracy?" and he would probably answer without hesitation, "Elections, of course." However, elections are not a form of government, but instead are a means of choosing those who govern. When the many select the few on Election Day, they wake up to an oligarchy the following morning.

Yet, the average American would argue that even in an oligarchy it is more democratic to choose one's governors than to have them chosen by others. An oligarch could inherit his office by virtue of birth or be appointed by a monarch or be elected. One could reasonably assume that the elected oligarch would be more responsive to the common good. If one looks around in the United States these days, however, that would be a hard argument to sustain.

Would it be possible with a degree of inventiveness to make elections more democratic and hence end up with representatives who are more responsive to the common good? As it stands now, it takes about a billion dollars to become president, $100 million to become mayor of New York, $60 million to become governor of New Jersey, and millions to become a member of the House of Representatives. This hardly sounds democratic.

The candidates we vote for in primaries or on Election Day are chosen for us by a cabal of power brokers, both visible and invisible. And then, of course, Election Day voting itself is ripe for abuse or accident. In many elections, most polling hours are during the workday. Workers must rush to the polls before or after work, then stand in line for hours only to find that they are not properly registered, or the ballots have run out, or the machines don't work. As has been demonstrated in the state of Ohio,[***] even in today's computerized voting, it is easy enough to steal an election if you have access to the software. As Stalin pointed out, it is not who votes that counts but who counts the votes.

Suppose we set things up differently. Let us say that we established a pool of candidates, and that from this pool candidates were selected by lottery[†††] to appear on the ballot. That would completely eliminate the back-

---

[¶¶]   Another way to limit the influence of lobbyists is to institute the "rights of instruction and recall." Under this restriction, a representative's constituency gives him specific instructions on how he is to vote on designated issues. Should he fail to vote as instructed, he can be recalled from office and replaced.

[***]   If you visit this website, http://whatreallyhappened.com/WRHARTICLES/2004votefraud_ ohio.html, you will learn something about what happened in Ohio during the presidential election of 2004.

[†††]   Said Montesquieu, "Suffrage by lot is natural to democracy." Quoted in Barber, *Strong Democracy*, p. 290.

room dealing and would ensure a larger and more representative sampling.

Let's use as an example an election for a representative in Michigan's Fourth Congressional District. Anyone who wanted to run could submit his or her name or the name of a friend or relative. There might end up being hundreds or even thousands of submissions. Each would be numbered and standardized, with the same information: the individual's name, address, date of birth, passport photo, and contact information, as well as a brief biography, a brief statement of policy positions, and party affiliation, if any. All this information would be required to fit on one side of a single piece of paper. If there were more than five hundred submissions, the pool would be narrowed down to five hundred by lottery.

The next phase would be to call—from the electorate—a jury of fifty, who would review the submissions and reject those they found unfit or undesirable. Notice how democratic this process is—there are no experts, no secrets, or no party loyalists. Instead, the same people who vote in the elections determine whom they will be able to vote for. Potentially, their selections could be as prejudiced and arbitrary as those of the power brokers, but there would be many more viewpoints, and certainly some would be speaking for the common good.

There could be separate pools set up for each party and one for independent candidates (those without a party affiliation). In addition, there could be a pool of unaffiliated candidates made up of applicants across the nation who wished to serve at large; that is, these candidates would be chosen irrespective of their geographic location.

The citizens would now have several pools of vetted candidates to draw on for membership in the House of Representatives in Michigan's Fourth District. Let us say five weeks before Election Day another lottery was held. From the fifty names still remaining in each pool after the jury winnowed down the submissions, one candidate would be selected by lot to appear on the ballot. A maximum number of pools of candidates would be set so the ballot would not be too cumbersome.

After the candidates had been selected, their resumes would be mailed out along with the ballot.[‡‡‡] The voters would then have the time to read about each of the candidates and to make thoughtful choices. Three government-sponsored debates with all the candidates participating would give the voters the chance to see the candidates in action. After voters made their final decision, they would sign and date their ballots[§§§] and then mail or hand deliver them to their local polling place, where the votes would be counted.[¶¶¶]

---

[‡‡‡] Barber objects to home voting, which he sees as "privatistic voting" (*Strong Democracy*, p. 290). I think his concerns are legitimate, but I believe the benefits of home voting outweigh its disadvantages, especially if other forms of participation, such as civic gatherings, offer the opportunity for face-to-face exchanges.

[§§§] Stockholders vote their proxies by such a procedure. Many organizations select their officers in a similar fashion.

[¶¶¶] A further streamlining of the process is a system known as "instant-runoff voting"

Such a procedure could be used to fill vacancies in the House and the Senate.**** There would be no dog and pony shows leading up to the election. It would be a peaceful and thoughtful process. Wealthy individuals or corporations would have little to no opportunity to buy candidates in advance of the election.

## Amending the Constitution

Democratizing our oligarchic form of government will require amending the Constitution, so let us look at the amending process itself. Article V describes this process:

> The Congress, whenever two-thirds of both houses shall deem it necessary, shall propose amendments to this constitution, or on the application of the legislatures of two-thirds of the several states, shall call a convention for proposing amendments,†††† which, in either case, shall be valid to all intents and purposes, as part of this constitution, when ratified by the legislatures of three-fourths of the several states, or by conventions in three-fourths thereof, as the one or the other mode of ratification may be proposed by the Congress.

Until now, only Congress has initiated the amendment process. The states have never exercised their option to do so.

The amendment process would be even more spontaneous and democratic if voters themselves were in the position to initiate it. There could be an amendment to the Constitution specifying that, if 5 percent of registered voters in a state appeal for an amendment by petition, the state is obliged to submit it to Congress, and then if twenty-six states concur, the amendment would be submitted to a national referendum. Passage of the amendment would require a simple majority of all registered voters. If the amendment did not garner that number of votes, then it would not be adopted.

---

(IRV), in which voters rank candidates in order of preference. If no candidate is the first preference of a majority of voters, the candidate with the fewest number of first-preference rankings is eliminated and his votes are redistributed at full value to the remaining candidates according to the next ranking on each ballot. This process is repeated until one candidate obtains a majority of votes among candidates not eliminated. The advantage to the voter who selected a minority candidate is that if his first-choice candidate does not win, his second-choice candidate might. IRV is used to elect members of the Australian House of Representatives and the president of Ireland. It is also employed by several jurisdictions in the United States, including San Francisco, Minneapolis, and Pierce County, Washington.
**** Maybe the reader has some thoughts on how to choose the President.
†††† In the effort to democratize the oligarchy by amending the Constitution, a state-initiated Constitutional Convention is one option. However, there is a risk that such a gathering would be hijacked by the very power brokers whose influence it seeks to curtail. Gerald Gunther of Stanford Law School offers a rosier picture: "The convention delegates would gather after popular elections—elections where the platforms and debates would be outside congressional control, where interest groups would seek to raise issues other than the budget, and where some successful candidates would no doubt respond to those pressures. Those convention delegates could claim to be legitimate representatives of the people. And they could make a plausible—and I believe correct—argument that a convention is entitled to set its own agenda." Quoted in Gore Vidal, *The Second American Revolution*, p. 270.

In outlining these ideas for democratizing the oligarchy—involving more people in government, getting power circulating and more dispersed—I am aware that there are many other possibilities. In fact, each reader should come up with his or her own ideas. Doing so is a liberating and empowering experience.‡‡‡‡

Initially one might feel overwhelmed by the daunting prospect of bringing about change. Yet, as Gandhi observed, "It is necessary for us to emphasize the fact that no one need wait for anyone else in order to adopt a right course. Men generally hesitate to make a beginning, if they feel the objective cannot be had in its entirety. Such an attitude of mind is in reality a bar to progress."[8] In other words, think long term and the prospects will seem brighter. Have a five-year plan and a ten-year plan.

The process of change starts as soon as someone begins to understand political structures at a deeper level, speaks to a friend or relative about what he or she is thinking, puts those thoughts on paper, when a few people get together to exchange some thoughts on the subject of democracy. It keeps multiplying in ways that are mostly invisible, because people you don't know are engaged in experimental thinking as well. Thoughtful people around the country will begin to identify themselves to each other and form small groups. This IS the long-awaited change, and all of it is transformative change. Yet, the change is in the process, not the outcome. By the time you reach the goal of democratic reform that you have set, the transformative change that got you there has been realized.

One practical way to initiate and guide this change is to form a new political party whose primary purpose is constitutional reform.§§§§ It could be called the Party for Constitutional Reform (PCR), and it should be separate from and independent of the civic gatherings discussed earlier. Those civic gatherings should be open-ended, ongoing discussion groups with no particular goals in mind. In contrast, the Party for Constitutional Reform would have a very specific agenda.

Topping its agenda would be setting term limits for members of the House of Representatives and the Senate. To achieve this goal, the PCR would first need to secure enough signatures on petitions to get its candidates on the ballot and then, one by one, get members elected to both

---

‡‡‡‡ Barber proposes a "National Initiative and Referendum Act" that "would permit Americans to petition for a legislative referendum either on popular initiatives or on laws passed by Congress." *Strong Democracy*, p. 285. Thanks to the work of Ed and Joyce Koupal (see Dwayne Hunn, and Doris Ober, *Ordinary People Doing the Extraordinary. The Story of Ed and Joyce Koupal and the Initiative Process*, 2001) and the support of Senator Mike Gravel, there is a "National Initiative for Democracy" consisting of the "Democracy Amendment" and the "Democracy Act." The National Initiative for Democracy (NI4D) is a meta-legislative proposal that would allow citizens, independently of Congress and the executive, to propose and vote on laws. See the website, www.ni4d.org.

§§§§ Interestingly, in the state of New York, there is a movement afoot to hold a constitutional convention that would introduce some amendments to the state constitution that are similar to those I am proposing on the national level. See letter to the *CPA Journal*, December 2009, from Brian M. Kolb, New York State Assembly, Minority Leader.

houses of Congress¶¶¶¶ and to state legislatures as well, who support PCR's initiatives to set term limits. If enough people around the country are in agreement, this goal could be achieved in five years and maybe even sooner, depending on how massive is the groundswell of enthusiasm for change. It would be best not to bundle together various amendments in one package and attempt to get them enacted in toto. A better strategy, especially at the outset, is to proceed one step, one amendment, at a time, beginning with the term-limit amendment.

In the early years of the republic, just about anything was possible in the United States, largely because of what seemed to be a limitless supply of unclaimed land. Every American had the notion—the dream— that there was no limit to what he could accomplish in material terms and that proper legislation would facilitate his climb up the ladder of success. Government was there to help one make one's way and then stay out of one's path. At the outset, government was a private, personal affair. There was little sense of its role in advancing the common good.***** This became the guiding American ethos.

This ethos continues to this day, yet there are no longer land and resources without limit. And it could well be that we are sated on material acquisition, that we crave something more substantial and longer lasting, and that good government could be a significant element in helping us attain that deeper fulfillment. In this regard, Americans could learn a few lessons from the Swiss.†††††

## Democracy in Switzerland

Broadly speaking Switzerland is run by a parliamentary government loosely modeled on the U.S. Constitution. There are two houses: the Council of States (an equivalent of the U.S. Senate) that has 46 representatives (two from each canton [a political division like a state] and one from each half-canton) and a National Council (similar to the U.S. House of Representatives) made up of 200 members elected under a system of proportional representation. Like the United States, Switzerland is an oligarchy. Up until 1971 when women were granted the vote, it was an all-male oligarchy. However, the Swiss have incorporated many democratizing elements that Americans would do well to emulate.

For example, in the lower house there are forty representatives for every million Swiss. This compares to only two representatives for every

---

¶¶¶¶   There is also the state convention option. See earlier.
*****   In the year 2012, if someone in the nation's capital speaks of raising taxes there will be an uproar of opposition from Mr. Joe Taxpayer himself. He perceives it as a question of money being taken out of his pocket. Once that money leaves his pocket, however, and enters government coffers, Joe loses interest. Rarely, if ever, does Joe know or care about how government spends his money. For this is a question involving the common good, a matter of little interest to Joe.
†††††  See Gregory A. Fossedal's, *Direct Democracy in Switzerland*, for a most readable study of Swiss government.

million citizens in the United States. In other words the Swiss have twenty times the amount of representation. Combining both houses, 240 men and women speak for a population of 7.5 million Swiss. For the United States to reach an equivalent level of representation, Congress would have to expand from its current size of 535 members to 18,000. The effect of that expansion would be to diminish the importance and power of any particular member of Congress. Observes Fossedal, "the sheer numerousness of the [Swiss Parliament's] representatives ... helps keep the body from degenerating into arrogance.... By diffusing power, it renders the legislature less vulnerable to manipulation, whether by wealth, particular interests in the press, or by other pressures."[9]

Among developed countries, Swiss legislators are the lowest paid legislators. Serving in government for them is thus an act of sacrifice, an act of citizenship. The legislature meets for four three-week periods annually. Most legislators return to their regular job for the forty weeks a year when parliament is not in session. As a consequence, the parliament includes a broad spectrum of Swiss economic and social interests. In addition to lawyers, there are small businessmen and housewives. They work as legislators under modest, egalitarian circumstances. There are no special perks, special entrances, or numerous staffers as one finds in the halls of the U.S. Congress. One could say that it is an "amateur" legislature. From the point of view of a true democrat, that is its greatest asset.

Likewise, the executive branch nurtures modesty and humility. There is no one all-powerful executive. Instead the executive comprises a committee of seven made up of the head of each ministry (cabinet posts in the United States), each of whom will serve as president for a period of one year. This committee of seven, which meets once a week, debates and then votes on policies. There is no executive veto power. When visiting dignitaries come to Switzerland, they meet with all seven. There is no strong charismatic personality in charge.

The judiciary in Switzerland has none of the pomp and self-importance associated with the federal judiciary in the United States. In the United States, nine members serve on the Supreme Court for life. The Swiss equivalent has 54 judges who serve for six years. Once again there is a broader spectrum of participation than in the U.S. judiciary. Fewer than 80 percent of Swiss judges are lawyers. In the United States, 100 percent of the justices on the Supreme Court are attorneys. The Swiss judiciary does not legislate. It does not rule on what is or isn't constitutional. It decides cases within their jurisdiction and nothing more.

Referenda and initiatives are built into the Swiss governmental process. There are three types of referenda. All proposals for constitutional amendments or international treaties are subject to an obligatory referendum. The citizenry must express its approval both via a majority vote on the national level and a separate majority vote on the cantonal level. Second, any Swiss law can be challenged within 90 days of passage if 50,000 citizens demand that a popular vote be held.‡‡‡‡‡ Finally, there is a popular initiative. With 100,000 signatures on a formal petition citizens can demand a constitutional amendment or the removal or modification of an existing provision. For this initiative to pass, there must also be a double majority: one on the national level and the other on the cantonal or state level.

The initiative and referendum process has served to create an actively engaged, informed, and empowered citizenry. One of its most powerful effects has been on legislators. Knowing that whatever they propose may ultimately be defeated by referendum, legislators are more likely to act in accordance with the wishes of their constituency.

For the most part this referendum process has not produced anything startling or destabilizing. The Swiss citizens have used their power with discretion. In 1897, they voted against the establishment of a National Bank. In 1918, they voted in favor of proportional representation. In 1919, they voted in favor of joining the League of Nations. In 1923, they voted against new customs duties. In more recent times the Swiss have voted on such issues as consumer protections laws, the 44-hour work week, voting rights for women, liquor and tobacco taxes, and entry into the European economic community. More than half of the constitutional provisions were voted on by the citizens themselves.

As in ancient Athens, Switzerland has no standing professional army: the Swiss Army is a citizen militia. Also as in ancient Athens, generals are elected to lead in times of crisis. Once the crisis is over, the general loses his position of power.

Swiss democracy has been strengthened and reinforced by demographic diversity§§§§§ and the strong role played by local governments at the cantonal and community level for hundreds of years. Swiss topography, with its mountains, valleys, and gorges, produced numerous local communities thriving in isolation, one from the other, each developing strong local traditions, allegiances, and governance. This decentralized, centripetal force has fostered the democratizing spirit that characterizes the Swiss government. To this day, citizenship is established not at the national level by an elaborate, impersonal, and intricate government bureaucracy but by a vote of citizens at the local level. An individual becomes a Swiss citizen by appeal to the local canton government.

## Democratic Murmurings in the United States

There are some hints of this democratizing spirit in the United States as of this writing. As the central government, the centrifugal force, has become less and less responsive to the needs to its citizens, the centrip-

---

‡‡‡‡‡  This would be the equivalent of approximately 1.8 million in the United States.
§§§§§  There are three languages accepted at the national level: French, German, and Italian.

etal force—the local governments—is becoming more and more asser-
tive. There is a spontaneous movement toward democracy.

As the wars in Iraq and Afghanistan became increasingly brutal and
the central oligarchy continued to ignore the many voices in opposition,
local governments took action. City councils and state legislatures passed
resolutions condemning the wars and calling for the immediate withdrawal
of troops. On June 26, 2011, mayors from around the world met in Baltimore and approved a resolution that the federal government stop funding
the wars and bring home the troops and the funds supporting them.

In 2009 Congress passed and the President signed a "healthcare
reform" bill. Ostensibly it was designed to rescue millions of Americans
from the abuses of healthcare insurers. However, the bill, as it stands,
actually delivers these same Americans into the talons of these same
predators, this time in shackles.¶¶¶¶¶ By federal law, Americans are being
required to purchase health insurance from private insurance companies.
Says Virginia Attorney General, Ken Cuccinelli, "There has never been
a point in our history where the federal government has been given the
authority to require citizens to buy goods or services."****** There is growing opposition to the healthcare reform bill at the state level. Attorneys
general in fourteen states have prepared lawsuits challenging the bill.

In response to the financial crisis of 2008, the central government
has passed along trillions of dollars to private banking interests. This
provoked much outrage accompanied by a sense of powerlessness. Yet
here again, local governments are beginning to assert themselves. If
the central government and the central bank, known as the Federal
Reserve, cannot be counted on to act responsibly, well then maybe the
states should start their own banks and use the funds to serve the needs
of the local citizenry. North Dakota started its own state bank in 1919,
and of all the states—some of which are experiencing financial crises
that match those of the Great Depression—it is doing just fine. Here is a
status report on North Dakota from the *Huffington Post*:

'It's the worst situation states have faced in decades, perhaps going as far
back as the Great Depression in some states.'

Unless you're North Dakota—a state with a sizable budget surplus,
and the only state that is adding jobs when other states are losing them.
A poll reported on February 13 ranked that weather-challenged state
first in the country for citizen satisfaction with their standard of living.
North Dakota's affluence has been attributed to oil, but other states
with oil are in deep financial trouble. The big drop in oil and natural
gas prices propelled Oklahoma into a budget gap that is 18.5% of its
general-fund budget. California is also resource-rich, with a $2 trillion
economy; yet it has a worse credit rating than Greece. So what is so

---

¶¶¶¶¶ See Jerry Mazza, "Thanks for Nothing, Mr. 'Health Care Reform' President,"
*Online Journal*, March 26, 2010.
****** See "14 US States Challenge Health Care Reform," www.yahoo.com, March 23, 2010.

special about North Dakota? The answer seems to be that it is the only state in the union that owns its own bank. It doesn't have to rely on a recalcitrant Wall Street for credit. It makes its own.[10]

Candidates for office in Florida, Illinois, Oregon, Massachusetts, Idaho, and California are all running on platforms that include proposals for state banks.

On Saturday, September 25, 2010, a "People's Assembly" was held at Hostos College, in the Bronx, New York. This local assembly of citizens addressed issues of national concern. On the agenda were immigration, jobs, and education.

Some citizens of Vermont have taken matters one step further. They are seeking to secede from the union altogether:

> On Jan. 15, in the state capital of Montpelier, nine candidates for statewide office gathered in a tiny room at the Capitol Plaza Hotel, to announce they wanted a divorce from the United States of America. "For the first time in over 150 years, secession and political independence from the U.S. will be front and center in a statewide New England political campaign," said Thomas Naylor, 73, one of the leaders of the campaign.[††††††]

According to a poll conducted in 2007, the organizers have the support of at least 13 percent of the voters.[‡‡‡‡‡‡]

---

††††††   Christopher Ketcha, "The Secessionist Campaign for the Republic of Vermont," www.Informationclearinghouse.info, January 31, 2010.

‡‡‡‡‡‡   As I write these words on a sunny winter's morning in early February, in the year 2012, there is much more to be said on the subject of "democratic murmurings," which are now more aptly described as a "democratic movement," a subject to be explored more fully in the conclusion.

# 25

# The Executive

*"Thus far these beyond*
*Compare of mortal prowess, yet observed*
*Their dread commander; he, above the rest*
*In shape and gesturer proudly eminent,*
*Stood like a tower"*

ALTHOUGH IT WAS Alexander Hamilton's dream to have an executive for life (that is, a king), and a hereditary one at that, he never lived to see his dream come true. However, were he alive today he might exult to see the president of the United States wield power that indeed would be the envy of many a monarch. Yet, one could argue that, though currently the president has great power *in reality*, in fact that power is *circumscribed on paper* by constitutional limitations.

## Congressional Powers

According to Article I, Section 1 of the Constitution, the Congress legislates:

> All legislative powers herein granted shall be vested in a Congress of the United States, which shall consist of a Senate and House of Representatives.

Although the president's signature is required for an act of legislation to become law, Article I, Section 7 states that the Congress can have its way if it can muster a two-thirds majority:

> Every order, resolution, or vote to which the concurrence of the Senate and House of Representatives may be necessary (except on a question of adjournment) shall be presented to the President of the United States; and before the same shall take effect, shall be approved by him, or being disapproved by him, shall be repassed by two thirds of the Senate and House of Representatives, according to the rules and limitations prescribed in the case of a bill.

Article I, Section 8 outlines the scope of congressional power in some detail:

> The Congress shall have power to lay and collect taxes;...To borrow money on the credit of the United States; ...To regulate commerce with foreign nations, and among the several states, and with the Indian tribes; ...To coin money, regulate the value thereof, and of foreign coin, and fix the standard of weights and measures; ...To establish post offices and post roads; ...To define and punish piracies and felonies committed on the high seas, and offenses against the law of nations; ...To declare war; ..To raise and support armies, ...To provide and maintain a navy; ...To make rules for the government and regulation of the land and naval forces; ...To make all laws which shall be necessary and proper for carrying into execution the foregoing powers, and all other powers vested by this Constitution in the government of the United States, or in any department or officer thereof.

In other words, the Congress has a lot of power.

## Presidential Powers

The presidential powers are outlined in Article II, Section 2:

> The President shall be commander in chief of the Army and Navy of the United States...; he may require the opinion, in writing, of the principal officer in each of the executive departments, upon any subject relating to the duties of their respective offices, and he shall have power to grant reprieves and pardons for offenses against the United States, except in cases of impeachment.
>
> He shall have power, by and with the advice and consent of the Senate, to make treaties, provided two thirds of the Senators present concur; and he shall nominate, and by and with the advice and consent of the Senate, shall appoint ambassadors, other public ministers and consuls, judges of the Supreme Court, and all other officers of the United States, whose appointments are not herein otherwise provided for, and which shall be established by law.

In Section 3, we learn that the president

> shall from time to time give to the Congress information of the state of the union, and recommend to their consideration such measures as he shall judge necessary and expedient; he may, on extraordinary occasions, convene both houses, or either of them, and in case of disagreement between them, with respect to the time of adjournment, he may adjourn them to such time as he shall think proper; he shall receive ambassadors and other public ministers; he shall take care that the laws be faithfully executed, and shall commission all the officers of the United States.

It says in Section 4 that the president is impeachable; he

shall be removed from office on impeachment for, and conviction of, treason, bribery, or other high crimes and misdemeanors.

Thus, according to the Constitution, the Congress makes all the laws; it makes all the rules. It raises taxes, controls finances, raises armies, and declares war. It can fire the president when it deems he has committed impeachable offenses.

So what power is left to the president? He does have command of the army, but can only exercise that command if Congress declares war. He can veto legislation, but Congress can override his veto. He can make treaties, but they must be ratified by the Senate. He can appoint "ambassadors, other public ministers and consuls, judges of the Supreme Court, and all other officers of the United States," but only with the approval of the Senate. In other words, on paper the president's powers are curtailed and relatively modest.

What powers does the U.S. Constitution grant the president outright?

- "He may require the opinion, in writing, of the principal officer in each of the executive departments, upon any subject relating to the duties of their respective offices"; that is, he can command his cabinet officers to send him some reports.
- "He shall have power to grant reprieves and pardons for offenses against the United States, except in cases of impeachment"; that is, he can get his buddies out of jail. Gerald Ford pardoned Richard Nixon for his impeachable offenses. Bill Clinton pardoned Marc Rich, who was indicted in 1983 on charges of racketeering and mail and wire fraud, arising out of his oil business; Glen Braswell, who had served three years for a 1983 mail fraud conviction; and Carlos Vignali, who had served six years of a fifteen-year sentence for cocaine trafficking in Los Angeles.
- He can make recommendations to Congress.
- He shall receive ambassadors, a tame, passive responsibility.
- "He shall take care that the laws be faithfully executed"—laws that Congress has passed.
- "[He]shall commission all the officers of the United States." And just what does it mean to commission an "officer," here referring to civil officials? According to an opinion delivered by Chief Justice Marshall in 1803 in the case of *William Marbury v. James Madison*, then-Secretary of State of the United States, this responsibility merely means signing the commission for the officer nominated by him and approved by the Senate.

Thus, according to the U.S. Constitution, the president is basically a figurehead whose most important functions are to receive and appoint officials, to collect and issue reports. This is not by accident. The Constitution was written at a time when kings ruled the western world. Adams, Madison, and Jefferson did not put up with the hardships of colonial life and the bloody separation from King George III just to set up another kingship. They wanted oligarchy, not monarchy. In fact, under the system devised by the Continental Congress—the Articles of Confederation—the president of the United States was known as the "President of the United States in Congress Assembled" and held office for only one year.

## The Executive Order

So why then is there all this fuss about who serves as president? He has no real power, not according to the United States Constitution. But you might ask, "Well, what about executive orders?"

In 1917, when the "War to End All Wars"—that is, World War I—was in full swing, Congress gave President Woodrow Wilson temporary powers to immediately enact laws regulating trade, economy, and other policies as they pertained to enemies of America. In so doing Congress passed along to the executive the power to legislate, in clear violation of the Constitution.

A key section of the War Powers Act contained language specifically excluding American citizens from its effects. Franklin Delano Roosevelt wanted to change that.

In the midst of the Great Depression, on March 5, 1933, FDR convened a special session of Congress in which he introduced a bill amending the War Powers Act to remove the clause excluding American citizens from being bound by its effects. Removing this clause would allow the president to declare national emergencies and unilaterally enact laws to deal with them. Both Houses of Congress approved this far-reaching amendment in less than 40 minutes with no debate. Hours later, FDR officially declared the Depression a national emergency and started issuing a string of executive orders that effectively were the New Deal.

Four days later, on March 9, FDR issued Proclamation 2040, which is excerpted here:

> Now, therefore, I, Franklin D. Roosevelt, President of the United States of America, in view of such continuing national emergency and by virtue of the authority vested in me by Section 5 (b) of the Act of October 6, 1917 (40 Stat. L. 411) as amended by the Act of March 9, 1933, do hereby proclaim, order, direct and declare that all the terms and provisions of said Proclamation of March 6, 1933, and the regulations and orders issued thereunder are hereby continued in full force and effect until further proclamation by the President.

What this provision means is that any order or proclamation issued by any president is automatically law once published in the *Federal Register*. What it also means is that, without interruption, we have been living in a state of national emergency since March 9, 1933. For nearly the past eight decades we have been living in a country in which the Constitution is in a state of suspension and the legislative function is in the hands of the president—a condition specifically proscribed by the Constitution. That is, any president at any time can declare a state of emergency and accrue to himself any and all powers he so chooses.

Consider this quote from the Senate Report, 93rd Congress, November 19, 1973, Special Committee on the Termination of the National Emergency, United States Senate:

> Since March 9, 1933, the United States has been in a state of declared national emergency....Under the powers delegated by these statutes, the President may: seize property; organize and control the means of production; seize commodities; assign military forces abroad; institute martial law; seize and control all transportation and communication; regulate the operation of private enterprise; restrict travel; and, in a plethora of particular ways, control the lives of all American citizens.
>
> A majority of the people of the United States have lived all of their lives under emergency rule. For 40 years, freedoms and governmental procedures guaranteed by the Constitution have, in varying degrees, been abridged by laws brought into force by states of national emergency.

During his twelve-year tenure, FDR issued 3,766 executive orders. Truman issued 893 as president. In his brief tenure in office JFK issued 213.*

Here are some examples of executive orders issued by JFK, cited in *The Executive Order: A Presidential Power Not Designated by the Constitution,* by Harry V. Martin.[1] Bear in mind that executive orders are repeatedly modified, overruled, or eliminated within the same administration or subsequent ones, so that the following examples are probably not still in effect exactly as written, if at all.

10995: Right to seize all communications media in the United States

10997: Right to seize all electric power, fuels, and minerals, both public and private

10999: Right to seize all means of transportation, including personal vehicles of any kind and total control of highways, seaports and waterways

11000: Right to seize any and all American people and divide up families in order to create workforces to be transferred to any place the government sees fit

11001: Right to seize all health, education, and welfare facilities, both public and private

11002: Right to force registration of all men, women, and children in the United States

11003: Right to seize all air space, airports, and aircraft

11004: Right to seize all housing and finance authorities in order to establish "Relocation Designated Areas" and to force abandonment of areas classified as "unsafe"

---

* If readers go to www.archives.gov/federal_register/executive_orders/disposition_tables. html#top they can do some research themselves, though some of the more controversial orders seem to have a way of disappearing from the *Federal Register.*

11005: Right to seize all railroads, inland waterways, and storage facilities, both public and private

Writes Martin,

> A series of Executive Orders, internal governmental departmental laws, unpassed by Congress, the Anti-Drug Abuse Act of 1988 and the Violent Crime Control Act of 1991, has whittled down Constitutional law substantially. These new Executive Orders and Congressional Acts allow for the construction of concentration camps, suspension of rights and the ability of the President to declare Martial Law in the event of a drug crisis. Congress will have no power to prevent the Martial Law declaration and can only review the process six months after Martial Law has been declared. The most critical Executive Order was issued on August 1, 1971. Nixon signed both a proclamation and Executive Order 11615. Proclamation No. 4074 states, "I hereby declare a national emergency," thus establishing an economic crisis. That national emergency order has not been rescinded.
>
> The crisis that changed the direction of governmental thinking was the anti-Vietnam protests. Fear[ing] that such demonstrations might explode into civil unrest, Executive Orders began to be created to allow extreme measures to be implemented to curtail the demonstrations. The recent Los Angeles riots after the Rodney King jury verdict only reinforced the government's concern about potential civil unrest and the need to have an effective mechanism to curtail such demonstrations.

It is not even clear if Congress has the power to rescind the War Powers Act because all authority is vested in the president. A president could so act, but such an occurrence is not likely.[†]

Does it seem extraordinary and absurd that this could be the case? It sure does to me. Why then is no one making a fuss about it? There is a conspiracy of silence surrounding the state of our government. This state of affairs is very comfortable for the ruling clique, which can exercise its power through the acts of one man, the president. Well, doesn't Congress still pass laws that have effect? Yes, it does. The facade of democracy must be maintained.

Indeed we are living through a constitutional crisis. Under the circumstances, the real issue is not the president but the presidency. If we are to begin the process of constituting a democracy, we must begin by setting limits to presidential power.

## Democratizing the Presidency

As it now stands, a person can serve as president, and usually does serve, for two consecutive terms of four years. The disadvantage of this system is that for his first term the president's primary concern is getting reelected. He cannot afford to offend anyone. Then in his second term, as the focus shifts to

---

† However, since the War Powers Act is blatantly unconstitutional it is *ipso facto* null and void.

his successor, the president is already considered a lame duck. Wouldn't one four-year term be a reasonably long enough period of time to achieve something of merit? If the president was only allowed to serve one term, his political clout would not be tempered by concerns with reelection: he could act as freely and forcefully as he chose. Should a president overstep his powers the electorate would have to endure such conditions for no longer than four years.

Article II, Section 1, The Executive Branch, of the Constitution begins as follows, "The executive power shall be vested in a President of the United States of America. He shall hold his office during the term of four years." It could be amended to read, "He shall hold his office for one four-year term during his lifetime."

Although the word "veto" does not appear in the United States Constitution, in effect the president has veto power. As per Article I, Section 7 all legislation passed by both Houses of Congress must be presented to the president. If he approves of the legislation, he signs it into law. If he does not approve, he must return the bill, unsigned, within ten days, excluding Sundays, to the House of the United States Congress in which it originated, while Congress is in session. In effect, this is a veto, because if the president does not sign the bill, it does not become law. Only if both Houses of Congress agree, by a two-thirds margin, to override the veto does that bill become law.

Such arbitrary power invested in a single executive harkens back to the days of monarchy. One could reduce the odium of such a procedure by requiring a simple majority of votes in both Houses instead of a two-thirds majority. The relevant clause in Article I, Section 7 reads as follows, "If after such reconsideration *two thirds* of that House shall agree to pass the bill, it shall be sent, together with the objections, to the other House, by which it shall likewise be reconsidered, and if approved by *two thirds* of that House, it shall become a law" [italics added]. It would be simple to modify the clause to read as follows: "If after such reconsideration a *simple majority* of that House shall agree to pass the bill, it shall be sent, together with the objections, to the other House, by which it shall likewise be reconsidered, and if approved by a *simple majority* of that House, it shall become a law."

A great deal of power accrues to the president by virtue of his license to distribute jobs—in the thousands—ranging from minor administrators to ambassadors. The patronage system, also known as the spoils system, is an informal practice in which a political party, after winning an election, gives government jobs to its supporters as a reward for working toward victory and as an incentive to keep working for the party: it is *not* a system of awarding offices on the basis of some measure of merit independent of political activity.

When the president makes appointments, job tenure is contingent on pleasing him. Under such circumstances, political loyalty often trumps independent, objective judgment and undermines individual integrity. If there were a lottery system, on taking office the president could choose to work with those administrators in place or else could take his chances and fill one or all of the positions by vetted lottery.‡

Significant power accrues to the president by his right to appoint Supreme Court Justices, who serve for life and whose decisions can have a dramatic impact on the entire nation. Currently, Supreme Court nominations are an opportunity for the most blatant political infighting and calumny. The only way to remove such important decisions from politics is by eliminating the presidential appointment power altogether. Under this new system there could be a vetted pool of candidates on hand. When vacancies occur there would be a lottery, and so the vacancy would be filled without attempts to stack and control the Court one way or the other.

## War Powers

The most widely abused presidential power stems from the president's role as Commander in Chief. Not only may the president, with or without constitutional authority, bring the United States into open warfare around the world but also the pretext of war or a context of hostilities has resulted in a tradition of issuing executive orders in which the president has assumed dictatorial powers. Any attempt to establish some form of accountability on the part of the government to the people would thus have to curtail the presidential power to engage in war.

The relevant clause from Article II, Section 2 reads as follows, "The President shall be Commander in Chief of the Army and Navy of the United States, and of the militia of the several states, when called into the actual service of the United States." This wording does not sound especially ominous, particularly when one takes into account that among the congressional powers listed in Article I, Section 8 are the powers

> to declare war...; to raise and support armies, but no appropriation of money to that use shall be for a longer term than two years; to provide and maintain a navy; to make rules for the government and regulation of the land and naval forces; to provide for calling forth the militia to execute the laws of the union, suppress insurrections and repel invasions; to provide for organizing, arming, and disciplining the militia, and for governing such part of them as may be employed in the service of the United States, reserving to the states respectively, the appointment of the officers, and the authority of training the militia according to the discipline prescribed by Congress.

Add to these powers Congress's powers over the purse, which are as follows:

> The Congress shall have power to lay and collect taxes, duties, imposts and excises, to pay the debts and provide for the common defense and

---

‡ In a lottery there is a pool of names. A name is selected randomly and that person becomes the office holder. In a vetted lottery, there is first a procedure in which certain criteria are applied to the pool of candidates. Only those who meet the criteria are included in the vetted lottery.

general welfare of the united states; to borrow money on the credit of
the United States;... To coin money, regulate the value thereof, and of
foreign coin, and fix the standard of weights and measures.

The president cannot raise an army on his own nor can he fund the
army. Yet, consider the following: for many years the United States was
involved in intense, violent conflict in both Korea and Vietnam, without a declaration of war.

On June 25, 1950, North Korean troops crossed the 38th parallel
and began an invasion of South Korea. The very next day President
Harry Truman responded by extending the Truman Doctrine to the
Pacific, announcing military support for the French in Indochina as
well as the Philippine government fighting the Huks, and preparing a
swift American response in Korea.

The Korean War finally ended in July 1953. Half of Korea's industry had been destroyed and a third of all homes. The disruption of
civilian life was almost complete. The numbers of casualties for the
United States, South Korea, North Korea, and China were as follows: South Korea, 137,899 deaths; the United States, 36,516; North
Korea, 215,000; and China, 150,000—for a total (the armies of other
countries were involved in smaller numbers) of 539,415. Though dead
is dead, this war never happened because war was never declared. It
was a "police action"—also known as the "Forgotten War" and the
"Unknown War"—initiated by the president. It ended in a stalemate,
and no armistice was ever signed.

The Tonkin Gulf Resolution (officially known as the Southeast Asia
Resolution, Public Law 88-408) was a joint resolution of both Houses
of Congress passed on August 7, 1964, in response to two alleged
minor naval skirmishes off the coast of North Vietnam between U.S.
destroyers and North Vietnamese torpedo ships, known collectively as
the Gulf of Tonkin Incident. The Tonkin Gulf Resolution is of historical significance because it gave President Lyndon B. Johnson authorization, without a formal declaration of war by Congress, for the use of
military force in Southeast Asia. Specifically, it authorized the president
to do whatever necessary to assist "any member or protocol state of the
Southeast Asia Collective Defense Treaty."

The Johnson administration subsequently relied on the resolution
to engage in a rapid escalation of U.S. military involvement in the Vietnam conflict. In 1968 Johnson failed to secure the Democratic nomina-
tion for a second term when he was defeated by Eugene McCarthy, a
steadfast opponent of the war, in the primaries. Richard Nixon won the
1968 election; he and Henry Kissinger then intensified and extended
the war effort.

This war, which was not a war, began in 1959 and officially ended
sixteen years later, in 1975, in a humiliating defeat for the most power-

ful nation on earth. In the interim, some 220,000 South Vietnamese, 58,000 Americans, 30,000 Laotians, and 1,760,000 North Vietnamese were killed, for a total of 2,680,000 casualties, not counting the dead among those nations with lesser involvement.

The next war that didn't happen—this one under the leadership of President George Herbert Walker Bush—was brief. Known alternatively as the "Persian Gulf War," the "First Gulf War," the "Second Gulf War," or "Desert Storm," it lasted only about six months, from August 1990 through February 1991. Some 35,000 Iraqi soldiers were killed. The Iraqi infrastructure was pummeled. The civilian death toll was more than 100,000.

Beginning in 2003, under the leadership of President George W. Bush, Iraq was crushed again. The final tallies are not yet in, but we know that Iraqi infrastructure has been decimated, the culture destroyed, and there are millions of refugees and millions killed.

## The War Powers Resolution

In the midst of the war in Vietnam, faced with increasing political pressure to bring it to an end, Congress passed the War Powers Resolution (P.L. 93-148)—over President Nixon's veto—on November 7, 1973. It was an attempt by Congress to set limits on the presidential war-making powers, yet did not directly speak to the connection between "declaring war" and "making war." The question never asked and never answered is, "Is it an impeachable offense for a president to make war without a declaration of war from Congress?" Nor was any reference made to the fact that, without the congressional authorization of funds, no war could even take place.

According to the text of the War Powers Resolution, its purpose is as follows:

> It is the purpose of this joint resolution to fulfill the intent of the framers of the Constitution of the United States and insure that the collective judgment of both the Congress and the President will apply to the introduction of United States Armed Forces into hostilities, or into situations where imminent involvement in hostilities is clearly indicated by the circumstances, and to the continued use of such forces in hostilities or in such situations.

The resolution spells out the constitutional constraints on military engagements. As it reminds the president,

> The constitutional powers of the President as Commander-in-Chief to introduce United States Armed Forces into hostilities, or into situations where imminent involvement in hostilities is clearly indicated by the circumstances, are exercised only pursuant to (1) a declaration of war, (2) specific statutory authorization, or (3) a national emergency created by attack upon the United States, its territories or possessions, or its armed forces.

Absent these conditions, no president has any business making war. So says Congress.

The resolution then goes on to specify exactly what it expects the president to do when war is imminent or ongoing:

> The President in every possible instance shall consult with Congress before introducing United States Armed Forces into hostilities or into situation[s] where imminent involvement in hostilities is clearly indicated by the circumstances, and after every such introduction shall consult regularly with the Congress until United States Armed Forces are no longer engaged in hostilities or have been removed from such situations.

Furthermore, when military engagement is in the offing,

> the President shall submit within 48 hours to the Speaker of the House of Representatives and to the President pro tempore of the Senate a report, in writing, setting forth (A) the circumstances necessitating the introduction of United States Armed Forces; (B) the constitutional and legislative authority under which such introduction took place; and (C) the estimated scope and duration of the hostilities or involvement.

In situations of continuing warfare,

> the President shall, so long as such armed forces continue to be engaged in such hostilities or situation, report to the Congress periodically on the status of such hostilities or situation as well as on the scope and duration of such hostilities or situation, but in no event shall he report to the Congress less often than once every six months.

Basically, the president shall consult and report, which is not the same as saying no war shall occur without the *joint agreement* of Congress and the president.

However, in addition, Congress gave itself the power to end hostilities and have the troops brought home:

> Within sixty calendar days after a report is submitted or is required to be submitted pursuant to section 4(a)(1), whichever is earlier, the President shall terminate any use of United States Armed Forces with respect to which such report was submitted (or required to be submitted), unless the Congress (1) has declared war or has enacted a specific authorization for such use of United States Armed Forces, (2) has extended by law such sixty-day period, or (3) is physically unable to meet as a result of an armed attack upon the United States. Such sixty-day period shall be extended for not more than an additional thirty days if the President determines and certifies to the Congress in writing that unavoidable military necessity respecting the safety of United States Armed Forces requires the continued use of such armed forces in the course of bringing about a prompt removal of such forces.

Later, in the same resolution, this same idea is spelled out even more clearly and succinctly:

> At any time that United States Armed Forces are engaged in hostilities outside the territory of the United States, its possessions and territories without a declaration of war or specific statutory authorization, such forces shall be removed by the President if the Congress so directs by concurrent resolution.

Thus, Congress has actually given itself the power to end war, although I am not aware that it has ever succeeded in exercising that power or even tried to exercise it. Further, some have argued that the resolution itself is unconstitutional. Certainly it has been treated as such by any president who has held office since its passage. In other words, it has been ignored.

## Modified War Powers

War is a serious matter. Millions are killed and maimed; economies are destroyed, both abroad and at home. The decision to wage war should not be made at the whim of one powerful individual. Responsibility for making that decision should be shared.

The obvious solution is an amendment to the Constitution. It could be simply entitled "War Powers," and it might read like this:

(1) There shall be a War Council, comprised of the President; a Senator, serving for one year and once in a lifetime; and a Member of the House of Representatives, serving for one year and once in a lifetime, with the Members of Congress selected by lottery.

(2) There shall be no movement of troops, weaponry, or machines of war, by land, sea, or air, either covertly or overtly, including guided missiles, remotely operated drones, and similar equipment, either for hostile purposes, for purposes of advisement in hostile situations, or for purposes of intimidation, nor shall any agent of the United States government, overtly or covertly, act so as to undermine the government of, sabotage, or cause violence to occur in, a foreign nation without the express, unanimous approval of the War Council. The War Council shall oversee the continuance of all such activities.

(3) Should any presence on foreign soil, of personnel or equipment, as outlined above in Section 2, continue longer than a two-week period, there shall be a joint resolution of Congress, recurring every three months, sustained by a roll-call vote of a two-thirds majority, approving such foreign engagement. Failure to obtain said approval shall result in the immediate disengagement of American personnel and equipment and their return to their base of origin.

(4) The use of chemical, biological, or nuclear weapons is expressly forbidden.

(5) At no time, and under no circumstances, shall agents of the United States government, or agents designated by the United States government, apply torture, which is to say psychological or physical stress,

as defined by national and international protocols, to captives under its control nor shall it authorize others to apply torture to captives who have been expressly transferred to second or third parties for the purpose of torturing at arm's length, as a means of escaping account-ability for its acts.

(6) Under no circumstances shall military personnel or weaponry be directed against, used to coerce or intimidate, American civilians or civilians of any other country.

The government's power to kill is its greatest and most awesome power. Its armaments and armies, its militant posturing, all serve to intimidate and cower not only "the enemy" but also those who live under its shadow, namely American citizens. A country constantly at war or continually on the verge of war is a country in which civil rights, rule by law, and access to the truth have all become extinct. That is why any attempt to democratize the oligarchy must address the war power as a means of creating a space where democracy might take root.

# 26

# Diversity in the East

*"But now, at last, the sacred influence*
*Of light appears, and from the walls of heaven*
*Shoots far into the bosom of dim Night*
*A glimmering dawn"*

W E ARE NOW in the third millennium A.D., and what we see are mostly either oligarchies or monarchies. However, there are signs of democracy here and there, for example in Estonia, one of the smallest countries in the world, and in India, one of the largest.

## Democratic Trends in Estonia

Estonia is a Northern European country of about 17,000 square miles on the Baltic Sea. It has a population of 1.4 million. Its largest city and capital is Tallinn, with a population of 403,500.

Estonia was settled around 8,500 years ago, immediately after the Ice Age, and for most of its history has lived under the heel of its powerful neighbors: the Danish, Swedish, and Russians. Starting in 1918, Estonia fought for and won its independence after a war lasting two years. During World War II, Estonia was occupied and annexed first by the Soviet Union and subsequently by the Third Reich, only to be reoccupied by the Soviet Union in 1944. Estonia regained its independence on August 20, 1991.

Its form of government is parliamentary as opposed to presidential.* In a presidential government, there is a strong independent executive, put in place by direct election. In a parliamentary system the ministers of the executive branch are drawn from the legislature and are accountable to that body. The head of government is both the de facto chief executive and chief legislator; in contrast, in a presidential system, the legislative and

---

* The United States and all of Latin America have presidential governments.

executive branches are separate. In the American presidential system, the president holds power regardless of his conduct and his popular support, except in extreme cases where impeachment comes into play. However, in a parliamentary system, the prime minister holds office only as long as he retains the parliament's confidence. If he loses that confidence, a new parliament is elected, which then chooses a new prime minister.

The parliament of Estonia has 101 members. With a population of 1.4 million, that is an approximate ratio of one representative per 10,000 people. In the United States that ratio is about one to 600,000. In Estonian elections there is proportional representation. Each party posts a list of candidates, and after all the votes are counted, the party with the most votes gets the most seats in parliament. The party with the second highest vote total gets the second highest number of seats, and so on. This kind of voting is more democratic than the plurality voting that prevails in the United States, where if a candidate wins a majority in his electoral district, he wins the election. Under this winner-takes-all plurality system the party that controls Congress is not necessarily the party that won the most votes.[†]

In Estonia, the Riigikogu (parliament) elects the President of the Republic. The president then asks the party leader who has collected the most votes to form the new government. Before assuming office the new prime minister must gain the approval of parliament. He then proceeds to form his cabinet. The president proposes and the Riigikogu appoints the Chairman of the National Court, the Chairman of the Board of the Bank of Estonia, the Auditor General, the Legal Chancellor and the Commander-in-Chief of the Defense Forces. Notice how the Commander-in-Chief and the Chief Executive are not one and the same as they are in the United States. Note also how the ultimate power resides with the legislative body.

A member of the Riigikogu has the right to compel government officials to account for their actions. This enables members of the parliament to monitor closely the activities of the executive branch and the earlier mentioned high state officials. Note how much more accountability there is in this parliamentary system as opposed to the system in the United States, where the president has independent powers that the Congress has difficulty controlling.

Supreme judicial power is vested in the Supreme Court or Riigikohus, on which nineteen justices serve. Nominated by the president and then approved by the Riigikogu, the Chief Justice serves a nine-year

---

† Proportional representation has been implemented at times in the United States. Many cities, including New York City, once used this system to elect city councilmen as a way to break up the Democratic Party's monopoly on elective office. In Cincinnati, Ohio, proportional representation was adopted in 1925 to get rid of a Republican Party machine, but the Republicans successfully overturned this system in 1957. With proportional representation, otherwise marginalized social, political, and racial minorities have been able to attain elected office. Proportional representation is still used in Cambridge, Massachusetts, and Peoria, Illinois.

term on the bench. Compare this to the U.S. Supreme Court in which nine justices have life appointments.

In contrast to the United States, where voters can only vote before or after work, often have to wait in the cold outside polling places, and are frequently disenfranchised, Estonia has been using Internet voting (e-voting) in local elections since 2005. In 2007, 30,275 individuals voted in the parliamentary election over the Internet.

In 2007, of 169 countries, the Estonian press was ranked the third freest in the world. In 2009, the United States received a ranking of twentieth.

"Well, of course," you say, "Estonia is a tiny country. It is not surprising that it is more democratic than the United States. Democracy works best in small areas and with small populations."

In response I suggest, "Let us take the case of India and see if your argument holds up."‡

## Democratic Trends in India

India has a land mass of 1,269,368 square miles, about one hundred times that of Estonia. It has a population of 1.17 billion people, about one thousand times that of Estonia and about four times that of the United States, which has more than three hundred million residents.

It is important for us in the West to understand India, its way of life, and its way of governing. Despite its ancient civilization, it is a recent arrival (1947) to the world of constitutional oligarchies. To understand India is to understand how a government can bend to the demands of its local constituencies while simultaneously struggling to remain faithful to a vision of national unity and democratic ideals of inclusion and justice. By studying India, I hope to debunk once and for all the myth that democracy can only work on a small scale.

Of all the world's oligarchies, India has the strongest democratic tendencies. Its approach to government has been both enthusiastic and experimental. Thus we can learn something about democratic processes, democratic forms of government, and the social structure that might support such a government by examining events in India.

The Indian government I am referring to is the government as it exists on paper and to some degree in the present. Unfortunately, much of what was remarkable about the Indian experiment was short-circuited in 1975 when Indira Gandhi assumed dictatorial powers and tried to pack the government with her followers, inaugurating a period of government corruption and the abandonment of democratic ideals

‡ For a broad overview of Ancient India and Hinduism, see Lucille Shulberg, *Historic India*, New York: Time-Life Books, 1967/1973. Fareed Zakaria has a chapter on modern India in *The Post-American World*, New York: W.W. Norton & Company, 2008, pp. 129–166. For an excellent and comprehensive history of modern India, see Ramachandra Guha, *India After Gandhi. The History of the World's Largest Democracy*, New York: Harper Perennial, 2007.

from which India has never fully recovered.

## Hinduism in India

To understand anything about India, one must begin with Hinduism. Although it is considered a religion, Hinduism is much more subtle, complex, and pervasive than what we Westerners consider a religion to be. It is more a way of life, a spiritual orientation, than it is a religion in the narrow sense of the word. It includes a philosophy as well as a social structure. It permeates every aspect of Indian civilization, private as well as public. It is a form of worship, a guide to right living, and a formula for structuring society.

Hinduism is often called the oldest living religion. Among its roots is the historical Vedic religion of Iron Age India. Although it is formed from diverse traditions it has no single founder. It is the world's third largest religion after Christianity and Islam, with approximately one billion adherents, of whom about 905 million live in India.

Hinduism as a religion is based in oral tradition and written texts. These scriptures discuss theology, philosophy, and mythology and provide information on the practice of *Dharma* (religious living). Among these texts, the Vedas and the Upanishads are the oldest and most authoritative.

Contemporary Hinduism is predominantly monotheistic, although perhaps it can be characterized more appropriately as monistic. It also includes traditions that can be interpreted as pantheistic, polytheistic, and even atheistic. The gods number in the millions. In fact, two important characteristics of Hinduism are its diversity and inclusiveness, which defy any definition that attempts to set its boundaries. It has no single belief system or creed, but is held together by a common origin and a unifying spirit. One might say that its defining essence is openness and acceptance. A contemporary theologian claims that Hinduism cannot be defined, but is only to be experienced.

Prominent themes in Hindu beliefs include *Dharma,* ethics/duties; *Samsāra,* reincarnation, the continuing cycle of birth, life, death, and rebirth; *Moksha,* liberation from *Samsāra,* the cycle of birth, life, death, and rebirth; and *Yogas,* the various paths or practices that lead to a life of spiritual fulfillment.

The word *karma* is commonly used in the Western world. Its literal translation is action, work, or deed, and it can be described as the "moral law of cause and effect."[§] Good actions bring a positive response; bad actions bring a negative response. In other words, it is another form of the Golden Rule: "do unto others as you would have them do unto you." Good karma will get you into a better life on your next go-round; bad karma will earn you a bad life. Another feature of Hinduism that is commonly known in the Western world is the man-

---

§ http://en.wikipedia.org/wiki/Hinduism.

tra—an invocation, praise, or prayer that through its meaning, sound, and chanting style helps a devotee focus the mind on holy thoughts or express devotion to God or the deities.

Yet focusing on some of Hinduism's fundamentals probably detracts from an appreciation of this religion's deeper significance. In its broadest sense, Hinduism claims that we are all connected, that all humans, animals, and plants are part of the same universal spirit. To harm any part of the whole, even the smallest part, is to harm the whole. Hindus revere nature in all of its manifestations.

Hinduism is a non-individualistic, non-controlling way of looking at life. As such, it exists in sharp contrast to Western religions like Christianity and Judaism. Jehovah, the Jewish God of the Old Testament, is an angry, controlling, demanding figure. He issues commandments and, like a strict, unyielding father, must be obeyed. The world of the Hebrew Bible is competitive and violent. There is "an eye for an eye and a tooth for a tooth."¶

In the Catholic religion there is one voice on earth, the Pope. He too must be obeyed; he enforces a creed from which there must be no deviation. Heterodoxy can lead to excommunication and persecution.

Hinduism knows none of this. There is no single creed. There is no all-powerful father. Hindus can believe what they will and practice how they will. They create modest family shrines in their own homes. They meditate and chant, worshiping and honoring those beliefs, icons, symbols, and traditions that have personal meaning to them. There are as many versions of Hinduism as there are people who practice it.

Western religions preach that each of us is a separate being. We must separately find our way in a hostile world ruled by one powerful God. This mentality has the tendency to massify believers, to stifle thought and independence, to crush the life force. In Hinduism, "there is no heresy or apostasy, because there is no core set of beliefs, no doctrine, and commandments. Nothing is required, nothing is forbidden."[1] Hinduism is a peaceful, nonviolent religion, and "the Hindu mind-set is to live and let live."[2]

In contrast with Western religion, Hinduism is at one with the life force that is everywhere and in everything. Humans are not superior to animals, are not separate from nature. They are at one with it.

The Hindu scriptures refer to celestial entities called *Devas,* "the shining ones," which may be translated into English as "gods" or "heavenly beings." *Devas* are an integral part of Hindu culture and are depicted in art, architecture, and icons. Mythological stories about them are related in the scriptures, in Indian epic poetry, and in the Puranas.** They are often distinguished from *Ishvara,* a supreme per-

---

¶ To which Mahatma Gandhi once famously replied, "Soon the whole world will be blind and toothless."

** The Puranas are a group of important religious texts consisting of narratives of the history of the universe from creation to destruction; they include genealogies of the kings, heroes,

sonal god, with many Hindus worshiping *Ishvara* in a particular form as their chosen ideal. Which form of *Ishvara* to worship is a matter of individual preference and of regional and family traditions.

The ultimate goal of life—referred to as *moksha, nirvana, or samadhi*—can be understood in several ways: as the realization of one's union with God or of one's eternal relationship with God; as the realization of the unity of all existence; as the attainment of perfect unselfishness, knowledge of the self, and perfect mental peace; and as detachment from worldly desires. Attaining this goal liberates one from *Samsāra* and ends the cycle of rebirth.

Yoga is another word that has entered the English language and is in common usage, as many Americans have embraced the various forms of physical discipline collectively known as "Yoga." In the Hindu religion, based on how one defines the goal of life, there are several methods, or *yogas,* for attaining it. There is *Bhakti Yoga,* the path of love and devotion; *Karma Yoga,* the path of right action; *Rāja Yoga,* the path of meditation; and *Jñāna Yoga,* the path of wisdom. One's life goal and the path or paths for attaining the life goal are all individual choices. Practicing one yoga does not exclude practicing others. Many schools believe that the different yogas naturally blend into and aid other yogas.

Status is intrinsic to Hinduism. Hindu society has traditionally been categorized into four classes, called *Varnas,* which in Sanskrit means "color, form, appearance." The group, rather than the individual, is the fundamental social unit.

There are four *Varnas.* The *Brahmins* are teachers and priests. The *Kshatriya* are the class of warriors, nobles, and kings. The *Vaishyas* include farmers, merchants, and businessmen. At the bottom are the *Shudras,* the servants and laborers. Hindus and scholars do not agree on whether the *caste system* is an integral part of Hinduism sanctioned by the scriptures or an outdated social custom. Many social reformers, especially men like Mahatma Gandhi,†† were opposed to the caste system and sought to overturn it by appealing to nobler traditions in the Hindu belief system.

Hindus advocate the practice of *ahimsā* (nonviolence) and respect for all life, because divinity is believed to permeate all beings, including plants and non-human animals. Out of respect for higher forms of life, many Hindus (between 20% and 40% of the population) embrace vegetarianism. Observant Hindus who do eat meat almost always abstain from beef. The cow in Hindu society is traditionally identified as a caretaker and a maternal figure. Hindu society honors the cow as a sym-

---

sages, and demigods and descriptions of Hindu cosmology, philosophy, and geography.

†† Mohandas Karamchand Gandhi (1869–1948), known around the world as Mahatma ("Great Soul") Gandhi, was the pre-eminent political and spiritual leader of India during the movement toward independence. He was the pioneer of *satyagraha*—resistance to tyranny through mass civil disobedience, firmly founded on *ahimsā* or complete nonviolence—which led India to independence and inspired movements for civil rights and freedom across the world.

bol of unselfish giving, and the slaughter of cows is legally banned in almost all states of India.

India's religious diversity is matched by its social and political diversity, brought about by influences from the many different peoples who settled its land. Similarly, in the West, tribes of invaders shaped the cultures of France, England, and Germany. One tribe merged with another and then was subsumed by and integrated with the next. The Angles and the Saxons became the Anglo-Saxons. In the fifth century A.D., they migrated to the land that became known as England. Half a millennium later, in 1066, the Normans—themselves descended from Viking conquerors and of mostly Frankish and Gallo-Roman stock—invaded that land. They overpowered and subsumed the Anglo-Saxons to create what we consider to be the English people, an integrated amalgam of these different tribes.

India, like Europe, was subject to multiple invasions over thousands of years, which originated in the northern passes and then spread throughout the subcontinent. There was a major difference, however. In India the various tribes and peoples never merged as they did in Europe. They ended up living side by side, maintaining their native cultures, languages, and forms of worship. This unusual phenomenon helps explain a great deal about Indian culture and religion.

In the absence of a homogeneous people, religion in India needed to be flexible, adaptable, and diverse if it was to appeal to large numbers of different peoples. And so we have Hinduism. Society needed to be highly structured to contain inter-tribal warfare and to provide a specific place for each new arrival. Thus we have the caste system, in which generation after generation passes on, from father to son, the same social function—potter, shepherd, merchant, warrior, lord, Brahman—shaped by the same traditions and techniques as prescribed in the Hindu texts. Everything is in its place. Everything is well ordered.

For centuries India was a collection of hundreds of separate principalities, kingdoms, and states. When the British left India in 1947, they had to cajole, bribe, and threaten more than five hundred rulers into relinquishing their power in favor of a unified India. Thus, it is not surprising to learn that India has had a difficult time setting up a strong center. There is a constant struggle among well-organized and vocal local governments with party lines of their own. In addition, India is a country of 17 languages and 22,000 dialects.

## Indian Governance

The Indian National Congress (also known as the Congress Party and abbreviated as INC) is India's major political party. Founded in 1885, it became the leader of the Indian independence movement. Yet, its power has waned, and no other major political party has taken its place. Thus India is led by a coalition government made up of the INC and other parties. But even though the coalition has led the country through a period of economic growth, it can still lose an election, as it did in 2004. The local and regional constituencies found no good reason to remain loyal to the coalition. They expressed their dissatisfaction by jumping ship. This occurred because "India's elections are not really national elections at all. They are rather simultaneous regional and local elections that have no common theme."[3]

Central power is weak. As a consequence, and in contrast to countries like the United States that have a strong central government, India rarely engages in warlike activities. The first thing Nehru[‡‡] did on gaining independence was to make peace. In the last week of March in 1947, he held an Asia Relations Conference in New Delhi to which twenty-eight countries sent representatives. The opening and closing sessions, open to the public, attracted audiences of 20,000. Nehru gave the opening address. For the following two days, in alphabetic order, a representative of each of the countries spoke on the broad issues and common concerns of the gathering. These speeches were followed by round-table discussions on themes like national movements for freedom, racial problems, economic development, and women's movements. A Western observer reported that the city of Delhi was filled with the most intricate variety of people, strange in costume and countenance—brocades from South-East Asia, bell-bottoms from the Eastern Soviet Republics, braided hair and quilted robes from Tibet, ... dozens of curious languages and polysyllabic titles... [representing] nearly half the population of the world.[4]

At this conference Nehru advocated for a strong united India that would make a place for itself in the world of nation-states. His mentor, Mahatma Gandhi, whose moral leadership has probably done more than any other to lend a peaceful dimension to international relations, spoke with a different voice. Like Nehru, he advocated for India, but a different India—not the India of the new capital in New Delhi, but the "real India," the India of the villages and local governments, the communal India that Nehru sought to overcome and transcend by means of a strong central government.

Embodied in these two statesmen—both driven by passion, integrity, and intellect—we see two diametrically opposed positions on the subject of government and its organization. One speaks for a strong center, the other for a weak center and a multitude of strong local voices. This tension, which the Greeks would refer to as a state of *stasis*, is the principal dynamic of all government, no matter how construed; it is the tension between the centrifugal forces pulling toward the center and the centripetal forces pulling away from the center and toward the local constituencies. It is the tension between unity and diversity.

---

‡‡   Jawaharlal Nehru (1889–1964) was India's first and longest serving minister, serving from 1947 until 1964. He was a leading figure in the Indian independence movement. Respected for his intellect, integrity, and statesmanship throughout the world, Nehru played an important role in the international politics of the postwar era.

Nowhere was the force of diversity stronger than in the framing of India's Constitution. After India achieved independence from Britain in August 1947, it was faced with the task of constituting itself as a government. The deliberative process continued over a period of three years and produced a document of 395 articles, deemed to be the longest constitution in the world. The proceedings were published in eleven bulky volumes, some of them one thousand pages long.

Submissions were solicited from the public at large.§§ There were hundreds of responses, reflecting the diversity of India's population. One group asked that the Constitution be based on Hindu principles, and another argued for a prohibition against the slaughter of cattle. Low-caste people demanded an end to "ill treatment by upper caste people" and "reservation of separate seats on the basis of their population in legislature." Linguistic minorities asked for "freedom of speech in [the] mother tongue" and the "redistribution of provinces on linguistic basis." Religious minorities spoke to their individual needs. The District Teachers Guild of Vizianagaram and the Central Jewish Board of Bombay requested "adequate representation" of their kind "on all public bodies including legislatures etc."[5] There were thousands of competing claims and demands.

When India achieved its independence it was an agrarian economy. Nearly three-fourths of the workforce were in agriculture, which accounted for 60% of the gross domestic product: "The peasant was the backbone of the Indian nation and of the Indian economy."[6] The farming techniques used were those passed down from one generation to the next. The water, fuel, fodder, and fertilizer were all drawn from local resources. In essence, agriculture then embodied the caste system at work, providing the framework for a very localized and traditional endeavor with specific applications that never changed. And alongside the peasants were artisans who performed their functions in an equally ritualized fashion:

> Everywhere, those who worked on the land lived side by side with those who didn't. The agriculturalists who made up perhaps two-thirds of the rural population depended crucially on the service and artisanal castes: blacksmiths, barbers, scavengers, and the like. In many parts there were vibrant communities of weavers. In some parts, there were large populations of nomadic pastoralists.
>
> On the social side, too, there were similarities in the way life was lived across the subcontinent. Levels of literacy were very low. Caste feelings were very strong, with villages divided into half a dozen or more endogamous [intra-marrying] *jatis* [communities]. And religious sentiment ran deep.
>
> Rural India was pervaded by an air of timelessness. Peasants, shep-

---

§§ Compare these proceedings to those in the United States in 1787. The American deliberations were completed in four months, not three years. They took place in complete secrecy and in complete isolation from the rest of the country. No public input was allowed. There is no official record of these proceedings. There were fifty-five delegates to the American convention, compared to three hundred in India.

herds, carpenters, and weavers all lived and worked as their forefathers had done. As a survey in the 1940's put it, "there is the same plainness of life, the same wrestling with uncertainties of climate ... the same love of simple games, sport and songs, the same neighbourly helpfulness, and the same financial indebtedness."[7]

This way of life that Nehru condemned and Gandhi exalted was the foundation of India. I believe it still is. And I believe that the strength of these rural communities that evolved over hundreds of years is the key to understanding the evolution of India's unique form of government. These small villages constitute the centripetal force that prevents the center from exercising the authority that founders like Nehru wish it could.

India is referred to as the "Republic of India." It comprises twenty-eight states and seven union territories, with its capital in New Delhi. The Indian Parliament, or legislative branch, consists of an upper house called the *Rajya Sabha* and a lower house called the *Lok Sabha*. The *Rajya Sabha* is limited to 250 members, 12 of whom are chosen by the president of India for their expertise in specific fields of art, literature, science, and social services. These members are known as nominated members. The remainder of the body is elected by state and territorial legislatures. Terms of office are for six years, with one-third of the members facing re-election every two years.

The *Lok Sabha* (called the House of the People in the Constitution) is the directly elected lower house of Parliament. The Constitution limits the *Lok Sabha* to a maximum of 552 members. It currently has 545 members including the Speaker and two appointed members.

Each *Lok Sabha* is formed for a five-year term, after which it is automatically dissolved unless extended by a Proclamation of Emergency, which may extend the term in one-year increments. As of 2012 there have been fifteen *Lok Sabhas* elected by the people of India; the current *Lok Sabha* was formed in May 2009.

The *Lok Sabha* shares legislative power with the *Rajya Sabha*, except in the area of money bills, which can be only be introduced in the *Lok Sabha*. If conflicting legislation is enacted by the two houses, a joint conference is held to resolve the differences. In such a session, the *Lok Sabha* generally prevails, because it includes more than twice as many members as the *Rajya Sabha*.

Motions of no confidence against the government can only be introduced and passed in the *Lok Sabha*. If the no-confidence motion passes by a majority vote, the prime minister and the Council of Ministers resign collectively. However, the prime minister may threaten the dissolution of the *Lok Sabha* and recommend this to the president, forcing an untimely general election.

The executive branch is headed by the president who is the Head of State and Supreme Commander of the Indian Armed Forces. He is elected by the elected members of Parliament (*Lok Sabha* and *Rajya*

*Sabha*) and by the members of the state legislatures (*Vidhan Sabhas*).¶¶ The president appoints the prime minister, the recognized leader of the majority party, who heads the government and Council of Ministers.***

## Division and Conflict

Indian leadership has been sensitive to the destructive effects and injustice of the caste system. Provisions were written into the Constitution to open the doors to those who had been excluded from equal opportunity in Indian society. The Indian word for this program is "reservation."††† The Constitution refers to marginalized groups as "Scheduled Castes" (SC) and "Scheduled Tribes" (ST). It mandates that seats be reserved for SCs and STs in local and national governments, in institutions of higher education, and in the civil service. The same policy has been extended to women. Village councils must reserve 33% of their seats for women.‡‡‡ Seventy-six seats in Parliament are reserved for SCs. When combined with the STs, nearly one-quarter of the seats in Parliament are reserved for under-represented minorities.

The Indian Constitution provides for a independent election commission to oversee elections.§§§ In the first general election in 1951, fifty-five political parties participated.¶¶¶ The electorate comprised 176 million Indians, 85% of whom could neither read nor write. The first step was to identify and register these 176 million voters. Then came the logistics of voting. Some 224,000 polling booths were constructed and equipped with two million steel ballot boxes, requiring 8,200 tons of steel; 16,500 clerks were employed on sixteen-month contracts to type and collate the electoral rolls. About 380,000 reams of paper were used for printing the rolls. The elections and the electorate were spread over a million square miles. In remote hill villages, bridges had to be specially

---

¶¶   A formula is used to allocate votes so that the number of votes cast by each state's assembly members is proportional to the population of each state; in addition, the vote from the state assembly is given equal weight to that from Parliament.

***   In parliamentary government there is a distinction between the Head of State, the president, the Queen, largely a ceremonial position, and the Head of Government, the prime minister, the executive in charge of government on a day-to-day basis.

†††   Americans use the word "quota" in this context.

‡‡‡   Most Americans, I assume, are appalled at the existence of a caste system, which is basically a system of segregation. Yet what might an Indian think who came to study American society over the past one hundred years or so? He would probably see little difference between the role played by blacks in the United States and that of the "untouchables" in India. In the South, for example, blacks were systematically denied the vote, had to sit in the back of the bus, use separate bathrooms and separate water fountains, and eat at separate restaurants. For a black to cohabit with a white was to risk his life. In the North, in the twentieth century, if you are a white policeman you can pump an unarmed black full of lead without consequence. Women would probably be seen as a caste as well. Before passage of the Nineteenth Amendment to the Constitution in 1920, women were denied the vote and were excluded from many occupations, which only recently have been opened to them.

§§§   The U.S. Constitution has no such provision.

¶¶¶   In the United States there are only two major parties.

constructed to enable voters to cross rivers to reach the polling places.

Ultimately, about 60% of registered voters actually voted, impressive considering the high level of illiteracy. One polling place in the jungle reported more than 70% voting. A 110-year-old man made it to the voting booth propped up by a great-grandson on either side. A 95-year-old woman, deaf and hunchback, cast her vote. Many reached the voting booths by walking for days through perilous jungles, camping along the way, enjoying song and community dance in the evening.[8]

As expected, there were many skeptics about the value of an election in which so many illiterate people voted. One academic observed, "A future and more enlightened age will view with astonishment the absurd farce of recording the votes of millions of illiterate people." In fact, the results give the lie to such views: voters made intelligent choices. The outcome impressed even the most elitist skeptics. One did not need to prepare for an electoral form of government by having a transitional, less participatory, more exclusive form of government. The commonest among the common are capable of making intelligent choices in choosing their representatives.

The emergence of India as a nation-state was marked by struggle, stress, conflict, dissatisfaction, compromise, and antagonism. The most divisive issue was religion. Starting in the sixteenth century and continuing into the middle of the nineteenth century, Islamic (Persian) forces invaded and ruled most of India. At its height in the seventeenth century, the Mughal Empire, a blend of Persian and Indian religions and traditions, produced a culture rich in literature, art, and architecture with such achievements as the Taj Mahal, considered one of the seven wonders of the world. However, the Mughal rule also succeeded in dividing the country along religious lines, resulting in violent conflict that has never fully been resolved.

The intention had been to create a united Indian nation-state with Indians and Muslims living side by side. Had the British left sooner, that might have been the outcome. However, by the time independence was achieved, compromise was impossible. The outcome is two nation-states: Pakistan, a Muslim state, and India, mostly Hindu.

A related source of conflict has been the state of Kashmir, a highly desirable plot of land lying between both countries, which has strong local traditions and is populated principally but not exclusively by Muslims. As issues of nationhood emerged in Kashmir, both Muslims and Hindus sought advantages for themselves at the expense of their counterparts. Vigorous local factions vied to keep Kashmir independent as a separate entity, or to become part of Pakistan, or to become an Indian state, or even to be split in two. The outcome is a disputed territory ruled by three countries: Pakistan, India, and China.

The fate of Kashmir is simply one among many of the divisions, diversions, and conflicts encountered in bringing India together as a united state. Another is language. As mentioned earlier there are seventeen national languages in India, each with its own form of writing, literary traditions, and dialects. When India was divided up into states, the intention was to partition the country along linguistic lines. However, because of the overwhelming reality of organizing a nation from scratch and the intense conflict generated by religious differences, language did not play a part in the state boundaries. The intended solution then was to make Hindustani the national language. However, although spoken in most of northern India, Hindustani, a combination of Hindi and Urdu, was virtually unknown in eastern and southern India.

The agitation for linguistic autonomy would not go away. By far, the most adamant were speakers of Telugu, who inhabited an area on the southeast coast. This language, with a rich literary tradition, was spoken by more people than any other, except for Hindi. There were petitions, representations, marches, and fasts in favor of creating a state for Telugu speakers, to be named Andhra Pradesh. On October 19, 1952, a man named Potti Sriramulu began a fast unto death[****] for that cause. Support for his cause was increasing, and it became harder and harder for Nehru to ignore the demand for linguistic autonomy. On December 15, fifty-eight days into his fast, Potti Sriramulu died. His death led to rioting, destruction of property, and loss of life. Two days after his death, Nehru agreed to the creation of a Telugu-speaking state, to be named Andhra Pradesh.

As was to be expected, granting linguistic autonomy to speakers of Telugu only intensified similar demands made by other peoples speaking other languages. A States Reorganization Commission (SRC) was established to conduct a linguistic survey of all of India and make recommendations on state reorganization to the national government. Through 1954 and 1955, the commissioners visited 104 towns and cities, interviewed more than 9,000 people, and received 152,250 written submissions.

On November 1, 1956, Indian states were reorganized along linguistic lines, with the city of Bombay, over violent protests, remaining bilingual. This achievement was an expression of the real India, as Gandhi saw it, not the artificial and arbitrary India that Nehru sought to superimpose. "The creation of linguistic states was ... a victory of the

---

[****] In India, there is a long tradition of asceticism and self-denial, rooted in religion and the search for enlightenment. The fast became a means of moral suasion. Gandhi personified this aspect of Indian religious philosophy. He lived a spiritual and ascetic life of prayer, fasting, and meditation and advocated nonviolence. As independence approached there was bloody conflict between Hindus and Muslims. On August 24, 1946, Gandhi held a twenty-four-hour fast. The violence continued. On September 2, Gandhi began another fast. By the next day, Hindus and Muslims were coming to him and laying down their arms. On January 13, 1947, Gandhi fasted yet again. This fast was addressed to the people of India, the people of Pakistan, and the government of India, which he wanted to release funds owed to Pakistan. On the night of January 15, the government agreed to release the funds. Gandhi's health was failing. On January 17, Gandhi received the guarantees of peace that he was looking for and ended his fast.

popular will," revealing "an extraordinary depth of popular feelings."[9] The great fear that further subdividing and atomizing India would fragment the country into isolated elements proved unjustified. In fact, the outcome has been just the opposite. The strong sense of linguistic and provincial pride has had a unifying effect on the local level and has done nothing to undermine national cohesion.

## American and Indian Governance Compared

Comparing Indian and American governance should have a humbling effect on any American who thinks he lives in a democracy. For example, take the *Lok Sabha* and compare it to its counterpart in the United States, the House of Representatives. Rotation in office is a means of preventing the concentration of power and its attendant abuses. It is a democratizing element in government. In India, the house that speaks for the people is automatically dissolved every five years, resulting in new elections. There is a completely fresh slate of representatives. Compare that to the House of Representatives where some members serve continuously for as long as thirty, forty, or even fifty years.

In 1971, Indira Gandhi won the parliamentary election. Her opponent challenged the election results in court. She and her party were accused of corrupt electoral practices such as spending more money than allowed and using the offices of government for her campaign machinery. The case dragged on for years. In 1975, Mrs. Gandhi was called to testify in court. She was in the witness box for five hours. In October 1977, she was arrested. Can one imagine an American president being summoned to court for corrupt election practices, submitting to examination and agreeing to testify for five hours, and then subsequently being arrested on orders from the legislative branch? Yet accountability is what democracy is about. It was one of the most notable features of government in ancient Athens where any citizen could hold an official to account in court.

Consider the fact that in India parliamentary seats are reserved for disadvantaged minorities, as a means of giving them a voice. There is no such practice in the United States. Look at the trouble that was taken in India to make voting easy and accessible and to give everyone a chance to vote without any discrimination whatsoever. In the United States voting is still a tangle of local regulations. It was not until 1975 that the Federal Election Commission was established. Its job is to try and exercise some control over campaign financing, but it has no mandate to oversee elections. In some U.S. states, minorities are routinely excised from the election rolls, voting machines do not work, there is voting fraud, and absentee ballots go uncounted. For example in Clay County, Kentucky, the circuit court judge, the county clerk, and election officers were charged with changing votes on the voting machine.

Consider how in the United States the executive acquires more and more power and is unfettered by constraints of constitutional law or congressional interference. Compare this to the situation in India where the *Lok Sabha* can, with a simple majority, cast a vote of no confidence, compelling the prime minister and his cabinet to resign at once. Obviously the equivalent legislative body in the United States has no such option at its disposal. The continued responsiveness by the Indian national government to local needs has no parallel in the United States.††††

In his book on India, Guha differentiates between a "melting pot" and a "salad bowl."[10] The United States is a melting pot. Various ethnic, racial, and religious groups arrive on American shores and are gradually "melted"—that is, assimilated—into the larger whole. The outcome is a soft, undifferentiated, viscous substance known as "the American." In contrast, India is a salad bowl in which various ingredients mix together to become an identifiable whole while simultaneously retaining their individual identities. This creates a society with a characteristic richness and diversity. There are strong local cultures and political allegiances that compete with each other for recognition from the center. The result is a constant pull and tug, which is what a vibrant political life is all about.‡‡‡‡

Says one observer, "Democracy is India's destiny. A country so diverse and complex cannot really be governed any other way."[11],§§§§ In fact, one might argue that India is a true democracy, masquerading as an oligarchy. It is ungovernable as an oligarchy and would probably do remarkably well as a democracy. Right now it is getting the benefits of neither form of government. As Zakaria points out, too often critical issues are determined by "organized minorities—landowners, powerful castes, rich farmers, government unions, local thugs. Nearly a fifth of the members of the Indian parliament," he adds, "have been accused of crimes, including embezzlement, rape, and murder."[12] This is what happens when power is centralized and stagnant.

Democracy is an expression of unity in diversity. It is a steady state of tension between centrifugal forces, drawing toward the center, and centripetal forces, drawing away from the center toward the local.

---

†††† Having said this, it is important to remember that in the United States, in the years immediately after the signing of the Declaration of Independence, there were these same strong local constituencies, which were expressed in thirteen different state constitutions; they offered the pull and tug of different economic and social interests. This was an honest beginning to democracy, a heterogeneous amalgam of competing local governments, which was ultimately overpowered by the constitutional oligarchy installed in 1787.

‡‡‡‡ Interestingly, what makes Manhattan appealing to tourists is the "salad bowl effect." There are Chinatown, Little Italy, and Curry Hill where one finds an abundance of Indian specialty shops and restaurants. There are Ukrainian and Polish enclaves on First Avenue, below 14th Street. In some local grocery stores, one is as likely to hear Spanish as English. It is the diversity that enthralls both natives and tourists.

§§§§ I believe in this particular instance that the word "democracy" actually does apply, although I suspect the writer is as confused as are most on the subject, because on paper India is a constitutional oligarchy.

When democracy is working, the center will be weak, and the local elements will be strong and diverse. Separate local sovereignties will give expression to the national sovereignty. This is the case in India, to the degree that it is allowed. Indian society is democratic by virtue of its religious, linguistic, and cultural diversity and its loyalty to these local cultures that exist at the level of the largest state down to the smallest local village. India loses itself when it tries to imitate the ways of Western oligarchies.

Zakaria notes, "India is a strong society with a weak state. It cannot harness its national power for national purpose."[13] Yet India's strength *is* its weak state. It is a strength that has yet to be exploited. In the Western sense India is "weak." It is not a war-mongering state that seeks to dominate other states. Yet India "is a strong society." Indian government should be built on that strength without trying to override it with a strong center. This Gandhi understood better than anyone.

Referring to India, Zakaria observes, "It is bottom up development, with society pushing the state."[14] This is what democracy is like. In a true democracy, society is the state. The theme of local sovereignties expressing their will at the expense of the central, national will is a repeated theme.

> India's elections are not really national elections at all. They are rather simultaneous regional and local elections that have no common theme.... Every government formed for the last two decades has been a coalition, comprising an accumulation of regional parties with little in common.... A majority of the country's twenty-eight states have voted for a dominant regional party at the expense of a so-called national party.[15]

Thus India is a democracy posing as an oligarchy. It gives the lie to the oft-repeated argument that democracy is suited only for a small country with a homogeneous people. India has much to teach the Western world about the potential for living under a democratic form of government.

Yet since independence in 1947, India has been plagued with recurrences of fratricidal violence. Hindus have committed atrocities against Muslims, Muslims against Hindus. Ethnic and tribal minorities have engaged in guerilla warfare against civilian populations and government authorities. Thousands have lost their lives.

A fair amount of the violence has been generated by eager politicians who seek to establish a power base by inflaming one group against another. Their goal is to gain visibility for themselves and their party at election time, enabling them to win some seats in Parliament and garner the benefits that gaining power entails.

In addition, corruption is pervasive in India. Government, at all levels, has become one enormous feeding trough. Those who lust for power and wealth are able to use elections to advance their private interests at the cost of the common good.

Fratricidal violence and corruption are two corrosive forces eating away at the civic body. I believe there is a very simple solution to these problems. Because it is principally the elections that are the occasion for violence and corruption, why not do away with them altogether? Instead, why not set up a system of lotteries? One could start at the local village level and work all the way up to the top. Anyone could nominate himself, a friend, or a relative. Every six months or so, probably no longer than a year, a lottery would be held. Whoever won would then serve in office for the prescribed time period. The chosen candidate would be vetted by a sufficiently large jury, also chosen by lot. If a simple majority does not vote in favor of the candidate, based on pre-determined criteria, then another lottery is held, until the jury can agree on a candidate. Every three months a jury is called, sufficiently large, to review the office holder's performance. If a simple majority does not approve it, then another lottery is held and the office holder is replaced.

This is how democracy should work. It worked this way in Athens. It could work this way in India.

# Democracy Come True

*"Wherein the just shall dwell,*
*And, after all their tribulations long,*
*See golden days, fruitful of golden deeds,*
*With joy and love triumphing, and fair truth."*

CURRENTLY, IN LATIN America the word "democracy" has taken on a new meaning, as political movements of various stripes are declaring themselves "democratic" in nature. Of international significance is the movement known as "Bolivarian democracy," which has its roots in Venezuela under the leadership of Hugo Chávez.[*]

## The Bolivarian Republic of Venezuela

On July 25, 1999, 131 deputies were elected to the Venezuelan Constituent Assembly.[†] In December of that year, the Constitution of the

---

[*] Simón Bolívar (1783–1830) was a South American political leader. Together with José de San Martín, he played a key role in Latin America's successful struggle for independence from Spain.
[†] Here are some reading suggestions for anyone interested in learning more about Latin America in general and Venezuela and Brazil in particular. Each one of these books has something important to say on the subject of democracy. Howard J. Wiarda and Harvey F. Kline in *A Concise Introduction to Latin American Politics and Development* offer a broad overview of Latin American politics and government. It has a chapter on democracy. *Readings in Latin American Politics: Challenges to Democratization* edited by Peter R. Kingstone is a collection of essays. There are sections devoted to six countries and their struggles to claim democracy. Curiously there is no section on Venezuela. The contributors' use of the word "democracy" is often at odds with its usage in this book.In addition, there are two important books, one on Brazil and one on Venezuela, that offer important insights into what democracy is and how it can be implemented. *Participatory Institutions in Democracy Brazil* by Leonardo Avritzer examines participatory institutions in four Brazilian cities, comparing and contrasting what works where and why. Gregory Wilpert, in *Changing Venezuela by Taking Power: The History and Policies of the Chavez Government* offers a well-balanced discussion of the Venezuelan constitution and governmental policies. It provides a close examination of particular programs and the level and nature

Bolivarian Republic of Venezuela was approved by popular referendum.‡ With 350 articles, it is one of the world's longest, most complicated, and most comprehensive constitutions.§

Instead of the usual three branches of government, the Bolivarian Republic of Venezuela has five:

1. The executive branch (the presidency)
2. The legislative branch (the National Assembly)
3. The judicial branch (the judiciary)
4. The electoral branch (*poder electoral*, or electoral power)
5. The citizens' branch (*poder ciudadano*, or citizens' power)

The electoral branch is headed by the National Electoral Council (CNE) and is responsible for the independent oversight of all elections in the country: municipal, state, and federal. The citizens' branch comprises the *defensor del pueblo* (ombudsman or "defender of the people"), the Chief Public Prosecutor (fiscal general), and the *contralor general* (comptroller general). It is responsible for representing and defending the citizens in their dealings with the organs of the Venezuelan state.

The 1999 Constitution gives added strength to the office of the president. It extends his term from five to six years, with a two-term limit. Under certain conditions, the president has the power to dissolve the National Assembly. Venezuelan voters have the right to remove their president from office before the expiration of his term.

The Constitution converts the formerly bicameral National Assembly into a unicameral legislature; it also substantially reduces and transfers many of the legislative branch's powers to the president. There are 32 justices appointed to the Supreme Tribunal of Justice by the National Assembly. Each judge serves a 12-year term. The 1999 Constitution also guarantees free, quality healthcare to all Venezuelan citizens and explicitly proscribes, under any circumstance, its privatization.

The president appoints the vice president who decides the size and composition of the cabinet and makes appointments to it with the involvement of the National Assembly. Legislation can be initiated by the executive branch, the legislative branch, the judicial branch, the citizen branch (ombudsman, public prosecutor, and controller general) or a public petition signed by no fewer than 0.1% of registered voters. The president can ask the National Assembly to reconsider portions of laws he finds objectionable, but a simple majority of the Assembly can override these objections. Deputies to the National Assembly serve 5-year

---

of participation in each. We get a clear sense of where the government has succeeded and where it has not. The title does not do justice to the book; it is not about taking power.
‡ Recall how the U.S. Constitution was adopted by state legislatures. Approval by only nine out of thirteen was required to make it the law of the land. There was no popular referendum.
§ There is a copy of the Venezuelan Constitution, in English, at http://en.wikisource.org/wiki/Constitution_of_the_Bolivarian_Republic_of_Venezuela.

terms, and may be re-elected for a maximum of two additional terms. ¶

Thus the Constitution establishes a constitutional oligarchy, with a mix of democratic and monarchic leanings. This is a presidential oligarchy, in contrast to the Indian oligarchy, which is parliamentary, a more democratic form. Eliminating the upper house of the legislature, as a "check" on the popular branch, is a step in the direction of democracy. However, transferring powers from the legislature to the presidency is monarchic, as are the longer terms and the provision allowing the president to dissolve the legislature. Providing for a presidential recall referendum is democratic, as is the manner of selecting judges. Yet in 2009, an amendment was passed abolishing term limits for the president and other office holders, a step in the direction of monarchy.**

From a democratic perspective, there is much that is positive about the Venezuelan Constitution. It might be the most democratic constitution ever written. Although it looks better on paper than it does in practice and the application of its letter and spirit may be uneven, the document itself has merit simply as an expression of democratic will.

For example, the Constitution is written in gender-neutral language. Every time it refers to an officer holder or government actor, both feminine and masculine titles are applied ("presidente" and "presidenta"). It holds that the government is not only subject to the law but also is obligated to satisfy the demands of social justice. Not only are civil rights recognized but so are the rights to employment, housing, and healthcare. The Constitution also specifically acknowledges the value of the mother and homemaker: "The state recognizes work at home as an economic activity that creates added value and produces social welfare and wealth. Homemakers are entitled to Social Security in accordance with law."

In addition, the Constitution itemizes four kinds of referenda: consultative, recall, approving, and rescinding. Each has its own particular requirements for implementation. The Constitution also makes indirect reference to the limitations of representative government: "Participation is not limited to electoral policies, since the need for the intervention of the people is recognized in the processes of formation, formulation and execution of public policy."

The Venezuelan Constitution is up to date in acknowledging the state's ecological responsibilities. The state is mandated to protect the environment, biological diversity, genetic resources, ecological processes, and national parks.

The Bolivarian Revolution seeks to build in Venezuela a mass move-

---

¶  http://venezuelanalysis.com/ is an indepenbdent web site devoted to discussion and analysis of Venezuealan society and government.

** As Wilpert observes, "While the Chávez government has embarked on an important project of increasing citizen participation in a wide variety of state institutions, it has also increased the importance and strength of the presidency, which tends to undermine the participatory policies" (op. cit., p.6)

ment to implement Bolivarianism based on concepts of economic and political sovereignty (anti-imperialism); grassroots political participation via popular votes and referenda (participatory democracy); economic self-sufficiency; a national ethic of patriotic service; equitable distribution of Venezuela's vast oil revenues; and the elimination of corruption.[††]

Chavez has implemented various social welfare programs (Bolivarian *misiónes* or "missions"), funded by oil profits that are being harnessed in what he calls "a new socialist revolution." The Bolivarian missions have launched government antipoverty initiatives, constructed thousands of free medical clinics for the poor, instituted educational campaigns that have reportedly made more than one million adult Venezuelans literate, and enacted food and housing subsidies. During the Chávez presidency, the infant mortality rate has fallen by 18.2%, poverty has declined, and the illiteracy rate has fallen to 4.8%, one of the lowest in Latin America.[‡‡]

Each mission focuses on a particular area that requires the investment of government time and effort; to date, Educational, Electoral, Environmental, Food and Nutrition, Healthcare, Housing, Identification, Indigenous Rights, Land Reform, Rural Development, Science, Socioeconomic Transformation, Civilian Militia, and Culture Missions have been implemented. They serve as the basis for organizing local constituencies in identifying their local needs and assuming active responsibility in seeing that those needs are met. Under the banner of Bolivarism, Chávez has established Bolivarian schools, Bolivarian circles,[§§] and the Universidad Bolivariana de Venezuela.

In 2005, at the World Social Forum in Porto Alegre, Brazil, Chávez referred to his program as democratic socialism, a form of socialism that emphasizes grassroots democratic participation in neighborhood committees. He offered himself as an advocate for "a new type of socialism, a humanist one, which puts humans, and not machines or the state, ahead of everything."

In June 2002, the Local Public Planning Council Law (CLLP) was approved.[¶¶] The goal was to provide for community development based on direct citizen participation. Under the original law, councils were formed at the municipal level with significant government control. The government could override council decisions. In the case of Caracas, "local" could mean a population of two million people.

Gradually these citizen-based organizations have gained more and more autonomy and authority. What started as "local," defined at the munici-

---

[††] As Wilpert points out, corruption has by no means been eliminated, and when it comes to the rule of law, Venezuelans rank themselves at 5.8 on a scale of 1–10. The average for Latin America is 5.1 (ibid., pp.42–43).

[‡‡] Internationally, Venezuela is ranked seventy-first for literacy. The United States is in twentieth place. Cuba and Estonia are tied for second place.

[§§] These workers councils were replaced by Community Planning Councils (see later discussion) in 2002.

[¶¶] This law was updated and modified in March 2006 and November 2009.

pal level, has evolved into "communal" at the neighborhood level. In April 2006 the Venezuelan government passed the Law of Communal Councils.

Each communal council is limited to a self-defined area encompassing less than 400 families. Once given official state recognition, the communal council has access to federal funds and loans for community projects. All key council decisions are made via discussion and majority vote within a Citizens' Assembly (described below), with a quorum of at least 10% of the adult community present.*** Although autonomous, councils are required to coordinate with municipal administrations so they can receive funds from various levels of government.

The local councils are under the governance of a Citizens' Assembly, in which every individual living within the defined area above the age of fifteen can participate. The assemblies have the power to elect and recall community spokespeople, as well as approve projects and development plans for the community.

Assembly meetings are two- to six-hour public events that are often held outdoors in the streets, basketball courts, empty lots, or other public spaces. Typically attendance ranges from 50 to 150 citizens. The frequency of assemblies varies from weekly to less than once a month.

Each Citizens' Assembly has an executive body made up of one elected spokesperson from each work committee or community organization, one elected spokesperson from each defined micro-neighborhood, and one elected spokesperson from any government oversight committee.

Under the auspices of the Citizens' Assembly there is a local financial management unit made up of five community members elected by the assembly. This group registers local cooperatives that can open individual bank accounts, which drives efforts toward participatory budgeting and prioritizing of community needs. These cooperatives support local economies and micro-financing and provide social welfare resources.

Another group of five community members elected by the Citizens' Assembly is the "Unit of Social Control." This independent group monitors and reports on the use of council resources and the activities undertaken toward the community development plan.

As Wilpert points out,††† there are several reasons why the local public planning councils, modeled after those in Porto Alegre, Brazil, (described in detail in a later section) were not as successful as they might have been. The councils were formed by the mayor and other government officials. This is an example of top-down participation, participation initiated and structured by the government. In addition, there was resistance from elected officials. Financial resources were not commensurate with the size of the population. Too often there were not enough citizens at the local level who were qualified to do the required work.

---

*** In the interest of increasing participation, the CLPP reform law of 2009 increased the required quorum to 30%.

††† Wilpert's book was published in 2006, prior to the reform of 2009.

Nonetheless, thousands of community councils have been formed throughout the country; they in turn have established more than 100,000 cooperatives in all areas of business and nearly 300 communal banks, which have received $70 million in micro-loans. In 2006, the councils received $1.5 billion of a national community development budget of $53 billion. In 2007 that amount was increased to $5 billion. These monies have funded many community projects, including street paving, sports fields, medical centers, and sewage and water systems. In addition to undertaking initiatives on their own, the local councils also audit government performance. Citizens have the right to demand an accounting, both financial and non-financial, of any governmental institution.‡‡‡

The Chávez government, starting in 2001, has instituted significant land reform programs both in rural and urban areas. In the countryside, by the end of 2005 a total of 3 million hectares of state-owned land had been distributed to more than 200,000 families.§§§

There has been a marked population shift from rural areas to the cities. Currently only 12% of the population is rural, compared with 35% in 1960. Legislation providing for the redistribution of urban land was drafted in conjunction with local communities and with community participation in mind. Many of the poor have occupied abandoned land and built their own housing. The goal of the land reform is to go into the poorest *barrios* to provide title to existing occupants, renovate dilapidated buildings, and develop community amenities and open space—all with the active participation of those who will be directly affected. By mid-2005, there were 5,600 active land committees representing 800,000 families and close to 4 million individuals.

Chávez's efforts to empower local communities, to provide them with the structures they need to organize themselves and with the funds to take care of themselves, as well as his initiatives in healthcare and literacy, have all borne fruit and have benefited the population at large. They represent social democracy (SD+) at work. However, they are overseen by a national government that is veering toward monarchy (PD -).¶¶¶

If one compares Venezuela and India, one finds an important difference. In India, local power is claimed by local communities. In Venezuela, local power is granted by a strong center. As long as there is a strong center, citizens cannot be fully empowered. They cannot develop to their fullest adult potential. They are in many ways being infantilized by a powerful father, whose shadow they live under.****

---

‡‡‡ The empowerment of the citizenry to hold its officials accountable for their conduct was a key ingredient in the democracy of ancient Athens.
§§§ Each family was allotted 11.5 hectares, or about 28 acres.
¶¶¶ One writer claims that "the transition from political democracy to economic democracy is possible, but the transition from economic democracy to political democracy is impossible." Jean-François Revel, *Without Marx or Jesus*, New York: Doubleday, 1971, p. 95.
**** I recently (February, 2011) met with a young Colombian businessman who had been living in Venezuela for the past two years. He said that Chávez had been true to his word in

## Governance in Brazil

Brazil, officially the Federative Republic of Brazil, is the only Portuguese-speaking country in South America. It occupies nearly half of that continent. By land area, it is the fifth largest country in the world and, with a population of 183,886,761, the fifth most populous country.[††††]

The current Brazilian Constitution was promulgated on October 5, 1988.[‡‡‡‡] During a two-year process, it was written from scratch by a Constitutional Congress elected in 1986. It is referred to as the "Citizen Constitution" and has been amended fifty-seven times. There are a Consumers' Defense Code (1990), a Children's and Youth Code (1995), and a new Civil Code (2002).

The form of government is a constitutional oligarchy, of the presidential variety,[§§§§] with a bicameral legislature. Brazil is a federation of one federal district, 26 states, and 5,564 municipalities. Both the states and the municipalities can be split or joined together into new states and municipalities if their citizens express a desire to do so in a plebiscite. States have autonomous administrations, collect their own taxes, and receive a share of taxes collected by the federal government. Each has a governor and a unicameral legislative body.

Title II of the Constitution enumerates "Fundamental Rights and Guarantees" and has five chapters. Chapter I is devoted to "Individual and Collective Rights and Duties." Chapter II outlines "Social Rights," and Chapter IV presents "Political Rights."[¶¶¶¶]

Chapter 1, Article 5 guarantees "the secrecy of correspondence and of telegraphic data and telephone communications ... except, in the latter case, by court order, in the cases and in the manner prescribed by law for the purposes of criminal investigation or criminal procedural finding of facts."[*****] In Chapter 2, Article 6, the "Social Rights" read as follows: "Education, health, work, habitation, leisure, security, social security, protection of motherhood and childhood, and assistance to the destitute."

The Civil Code issues strict penalties for violation of civil rights and of the rights of minorities and women. Brazil has approved a law prohibiting bail for people arrested for committing acts of prejudice against any minority or ethnic group. The law empowers the government to act against those who spread hate speech (like Neo-Nazis) or those who practice discrimination against certain groups. It also reserves a certain percentage of jobs in government and in large companies for disabled people. Finally, it

---

the early years, but that in recent years there have been cronyism, corruption, gangs in the streets, and loss of citizen loyalty.

[††††]  I am using Wikipedia as my resource.

[‡‡‡‡]  The Brazilian Constitution of 1988 precedes the Venezuelan Constitution by more than a decade.

[§§§§] There is a two-term limit.

[¶¶¶¶]  An English translation of the Brazilian Constitution can be found at http://www.v-brazil.com/government/laws/.

[*****]  In the United States, the "Patriot Act" of 2001 expressly denies these guarantees of privacy.

empowers Black people to seek reparations for prejudice against them.

In an effort at true democracy, the Constitution provides avenues for direct popular participation, in addition to voting in regularly scheduled elections. It provides for plebiscites and referenda, as well as the possibility of ordinary citizens proposing new laws. In 1993 a plebiscite concerning the form of government confirmed the presidential system. In 2005 there was a referendum concerning prohibition of the sale of firearms and ammunition; citizens voted against the ban.

Title I, Article 4 establishes Brazil's position in the international community:

> The international relations of the Federative Republic of Brazil are governed by the following principles: national independence; prevalence of human rights; self-determination of the peoples; non-intervention; equality among the states; defense of peace; peaceful settlement of conflicts; repudiation of terrorism and racism; cooperation among peoples for the progress of mankind; granting of political asylum.

Title II, Chapter 1, Article 5 proscribes the death penalty: "There shall be no punishment: a) of death, save in case of declared war under the terms of article 84, XIX; b) of life imprisonment; c) of hard labor; d) of banishment; e) which is cruel."†††††

Title II, Chapter 2, Article 7 addresses the issue of workers' rights, both urban and rural. These rights include job protection, wage guarantees, guaranteed yearly bonus, participation in profits, a family allowance for low-income workers, 120-day maternity leave, paternity leave, and free day care and preschool education.

Article 8 specifically addresses the issue of unions and prohibits

> the dismissal of a unionized employee ... from the moment of the registration of his candidacy to a position of union direction or representation and, if elected, even if as a substitute, up to one year after the end of his term in office, unless he commits a serious fault as established by law.

According to Article 9, "The right to strike is guaranteed," and Article 10 guarantees the right of government employees to organize.

Unlike Venezuela in which the executive has been strengthened at the expense of the legislature, in Brazil, the legislature has the power to set limits on the president and hold him accountable. In Title IV, Chapter 1, Section II, Article 49, the legislature is empowered

> to stop the normative acts of the Executive Power which exceed their regimental authority or the limits of legislative delegation; ... to supervise and control directly or through either of its Houses, the acts of the Executive Power, including those of the indirect administration.

---

††††† In the United States, in 2009, there were fifty-two executions.

The Brazilian Constitution is an unusual founding document in several respects. It assigns to the national government responsibility for the well-being of its citizens by specifically outlining civil guarantees and social rights. It contains the unusual constitutional provisions of the right to strike and the guarantee of minority employment. It empowers the legislature to set limits on the executive to a noteworthy degree. It is also unusual in that municipalities are considered elements in the federation, thus empowering them within the nation, not just at the local level.

I wonder if there is any other constitution that gives states the right to redraw their own boundaries. Also unusual is the provision for plebiscites and referenda in a nation of close to two hundred million people, as well as specific guarantees for the fair treatment of workers. The explicit rejection of violence in favor of the peaceful resolution of international conflict is refreshing.

In the United States, people view government as unwelcome or as a dangerous nuisance at best. In turn, the government has accepted very little specific responsibility for the advancement of the common good. The Brazilian Constitution demonstrates that government can be a force for the good of all. Having said this, one must bear in mind that, as in the case of Venezuela, the application of this document has produced uneven results. Some areas in Brazil are among the most lawless in the Western hemisphere. However, there are also examples of highly civilized experiments in democratic living.

Considering the degree of respect and autonomy granted municipalities, it is not surprising to discover that there have been interesting experiments in self-government at the local level. Porto Alegre (literally "Joyous Port") is the eleventh most populous municipality in Brazil and the capital city of the southernmost Brazilian state of Rio Grande do Sul. It has a population of 1,436,123, which is just slightly more than that of the entire nation of Estonia.

## Participatory Budgeting

In 1989, the government of Porto Alegre initiated a form of self-government known as participatory budgeting that is being imitated throughout Brazil and around the world. Participatory budgeting turns the budgeting process into an opportunity for democratic deliberation and decision making, in which residents decide how to allocate part of the municipal budget. Ordinary citizens are given the opportunity to present their demands and priorities for improvement. Through discussions and negotiations they influence budget allocations made by their municipalities. About 50,000 residents participate annually, with the number increasing each year.

The city is divided into sixteen administrative districts, and there are five city-wide themes or areas of focus: public transport and traffic;

education, culture, and leisure; healthcare and social security; economic development and taxation; and city management and urban development. There is about $200 million per year to allocate to construction and services in these areas.

The nine-month participatory budgeting cycle starts in January. The first round of meetings review the previous years' budget. Then local neighborhood meetings are held to identify local needs. In the third round of meetings investment proposals are finalized that are then presented to city officials. Each February there is instruction from city specialists in technical aspects of city budgeting.

In March plenary assemblies are held in each of the city's sixteen districts as well as assemblies dealing with the specific themes listed earlier. These large meetings—with participation that can reach over 1,000 people—elect delegates to represent specific neighborhoods. The mayor and staff attend these assemblies to respond to citizen concerns.

In the following months delegates meet weekly or biweekly in each district to review technical project criteria and district needs. City department staff may participate according to their area of expertise. At the second regional plenary, delegates prioritize the districts' demands and elect forty-two councilors representing all districts and thematic areas to serve on the Municipal Council of the Budget. The main functions of the Municipal Council of the Budget are to reconcile the demands of each district with available resources and to propose and approve an overall municipal budget.

Since participatory budgeting has been instituted, there has been a dramatic improvement in the quality of life for residents. For example, the percentage of households connected to the sewer and water system increased from 75% in 1988 to 98% in 1997. The number of schools quadrupled since 1986. Porto Alegre's health and education budget increased from 13% (1985) to almost 40% (1996) of the total municipal budget.

Various studies have suggested that participatory budgeting results in more equitable public spending, a higher quality of life, increased satisfaction of basic needs, greater government transparency and accountability, increased levels of public participation (especially by marginalized or poorer residents), and learning norms of democracy and citizenship. Based on the success in Porto Alegre, it is estimated that more than 1,200 municipalities around the world have initiated participatory budgeting.‡‡‡‡‡

Leonardo Avritzer has undertaken a very thoughtful study on par-

---

‡‡‡‡‡ Earlier in this chapter there was a brief comparison between democratic trends in India and Venezuela. The same difference applies when one compares the Venezuelan councils and the participatory budget process in Porto Alegre. In Venezuela, local independence emanates from the central power, and local power is under central control and is contingent. In Porto Alegre, local power is claimed by local communities, and the local initiative is indigenous and autonomous.

ticipation in Brazil. In *Participatory Institutions in Democratic Brazil* he compares the experiences of four cities—São Paolo, Belo Horizonte, Porto Alegre, and Salvador—with three different forms of participation: participatory budgeting, health councils, and city master plans. He assesses three variables: civil society strength, political society composition, and institutional design. He found that the most important variable in effectively instituting participatory budgeting was civil society strength. In Porto Alegre, there were many neighborhood associations, with a significant level of participation by a large segment of the population. These neighborhood associations pre-dated the initiation of participatory budgeting and constituted the foundation for the active involvement of the community. Institutional design was also a significant factor. The programs most likely to succeed were those where the initial dynamic and design emanated from within the community, as opposed to being handed down by the top; that is, government officialdom.

## Nationalizing the Porto Alegre Model

One can learn a great deal about the potential for democracy by studying these examples of participatory democracy in place in Brazil and around the world. One can also imagine what it might be like if one applied the Porto Alegre model to an entire country. Wouldn't that indeed produce a national democracy? Here is how it might work.

The goal would be to review and deliberate national issues on the local level. Local assemblies would make specific proposals that would then be reviewed by a central council that would finalize national policies and legislation. Barber speaks of a "national system of neighborhood assemblies,"[1] each made up of 1,000 to 5,000 citizens. In Barber's version, these assemblies would be discussion groups and forums in which the citizenry cross-examines its representatives and holds them accountable for their choices. The assemblies could create initiatives involving local land use and neighborhood cleanup and might eventually be involved in devising legislation.

Yet Barber does not hold out the possibility that the citizenry of New York, broken down into local assemblies, could then set the budget for the city, as is done in Porto Alegre. He wants to keep things very local and is cautious about redistributing power even on the local level, and especially not on the national level. He fears "encroach[ing] on the present delegation of governmental responsibility."[2] But if the power dynamics at the center—the national level—remain as they are, nothing changes. Citizens will remain cowed by forces over which they have no control. They will have no say in matters of war and peace. They will not be involved in deciding how money is spent. They will remain despondent and passive. They would probably only show mild interest, at best, in local assemblies that fundamentally lacked the power necessary to truly transform themselves and the condition of society.

Barber admits that "almost all of the proposals examined in this chapter focus on local citizenship and therefore have the defects of parochialism."[3] He seems to share the fears of the liberal democrats he so aptly criticizes that tampering with existing government institutions could unleash a mob-like movement that would undo government altogether and replace it with some form of "unitary democracy"; that is, totalitarianism. He advocates "prudent democratic reforms" that add "participatory ingredients to the constitutional formula" without "removing representative ingredients." "The objective," he says, "is to reorient liberal democracy toward civic engagement and political community, not to raze it." He warns that "to call for a constitutional convention is to invite disaster."[4]

I share Barber's concern about hasty, impulsive actions. I am also aware that any change involves risks, some of which are predictable, some of which are not. However, as I argued earlier, leaving the power dynamics intact also entails risk. The notion that we can trust to the current power structure has no basis in reality.

I think Barber would profit from reading his own book in which he convincingly argues that the democratic process itself is transformative and civilizing. People who participate in civic gatherings where they have the opportunity to meet and discuss the meaning of words like "government" and "democracy," and who jointly come up with some ideas of how to redirect national policies, hardly seem to be a menace to humankind. I firmly believe that such people, when working together in thousands of assemblies across the country, would govern wisely.[§§§§§]

In Porto Alegre there are sixteen districts for a population of about 1.5 million. If we were to maintain that ratio for the United States with its population of more than 300 million, the result would be 3,200 districts around the country. Meetings from each district could be housed in high school auditoriums that can accommodate 500 or more attendees or in town halls, like the one in New York City,[¶¶¶¶¶] with a seating capacity of 1,495.

---

§§§§§ There is legitimate concern about the state of affairs when one form of government is replaced by another. There is an in-between time when there is "no" government. In fact, however, there are many layers of government and bureaucracy that would guarantee a stable transition. Such a transition was begun in 1776. As Thomas Paine points out, "For upward of two years from the commencement of the American War, and to a longer period in several of the American states, there were no established forms of government.... Yet during this interval, order and harmony were preserved as inviolate as in any country in Europe." Paine, *The Complete Writings of Thomas Paine*, p. 358.

¶¶¶¶¶ New York City's Town Hall opened its doors in 1921. It was built by the League for Political Education as a space where people of every rank could meet to discuss the issues of the day. The Town Hall was designed by the renowned architectural firm of McKim, Mead & White to reflect the democratic principles of the League. To this end, box seats were not included in the theater's design, and every effort was made to ensure that there were no seats with an obstructed view. This design principle gave birth to the Town Hall's long-standing mantra: "Not a bad seat in the house."

In 1935, Town Hall began broadcasting "America's Town Meetings of the Air." This

In Porto Alegre the local councils addressed five themes. On the national level in the United States, I can imagine sixteen: War and Peace; Justice; Budget; Natural Resources, Conservation, and Ecology; Utilities; Commerce; Immigration; Education; Culture; Parks; Healthcare; Transportation; Urban Planning; Agriculture; Government******; and Foreign Affairs.

Because the object of democracy is the involvement in government of as many people as possible, these sixteen themes, spread over 3,200 districts, create 51,200 assemblies devoted to debating national issues. If one imagines a minimum of five hundred participants in each local assembly, then 25,600,000 citizens could be involved in government on a rotating basis. Over a ten-year period the entire adult population would have participated in the democratic process at least once.

Participants would be chosen by lot, just as they are in selecting juries.†††††† Agendas would be compiled by drawing on various resources. Imagine that the Pentagon wants to build a new bomber. It would submit a detailed request that appears on the agenda at each of the 3,200 "War Assemblies" around the country. In addition, district members with fifty signatures on a petition could get their item on the agenda. During the meeting itself, members chosen by lot would be able to submit items for consideration.

To use Barber's language, assemblies would provide the opportunity for both "talk" and "speech." A chairman for the day would be chosen by lot. For example, the Pentagon proposal would be argued for by one proponent and opposed by one opponent, both of whom would be knowledgeable on the subject matter. This exercise of "speech" would last perhaps thirty minutes.‡‡‡‡‡‡

After the debate, held on stage before the assembly, a committee made up of a dozen or so citizens, chosen by lot from the members of the assembly, would gather around a conference table on stage. This same committee would have already set the agenda for the assembly after considering the various submissions. They now engage in a conversation about all the proposals before the assembly, a discussion that is

---

radio program was on the air for more than twenty years, ultimately carried by seventy-eight stations with a listening audience of 2.5 million. The series was launched on NBC's Blue Network on Memorial Day, 1935; the topic of discussion was the coexistence of communism, fascism, socialism, and democracy. On March 2, 1944, there was a debate on the subject, "Can Our Foreign Policy Be Democratic in Wartime?" On April 4, 1947, the topic for discussion was "Do We Really Elect Our Own President?"

****** The theme of "government" would oversee, critique, and modify government and the bureaucracy. Should there be an executive? Should it be singular or plural? What would be the qualifications of the person serving as the executive? How would the executive be chosen? Should there be more, fewer, or different themes? Are the assemblies functioning as intended?

†††††† As when serving on a jury, each assembly member is assigned a number. That number would then be used to make selections by lot.

‡‡‡‡‡‡ This could be achieved with one expert presenting his position via closed-circuit TV to multiple assemblies at once.

overheard by the entire assembly. Once this experience reaches its natural conclusion, six or so members of the assembly, chosen by lot, address the assembly expressing their views. After all views have been heard, the committee drafts a proposal that is read aloud to the assembly and then posted on a bulletin board for the entire community to read.

Each item on the agenda is discussed and debated, using the same format. For example, the assembly focusing on "War" would debate such issues as raising an army, disbanding an army, making war, ending war, opening a military base, or closing one. The assembly proceeds through the agenda until all items have been addressed and then adjourns. At a subsequent meeting of this assembly the various proposals receive a final reading and discussion by another committee chosen by lot. Each of the finalized proposals is then submitted to a vote of the assembly. Items that are approved by a majority of votes of those present are accepted.

The next step is for a representative of the district assembly, chosen by lot, to argue for these approved proposals before a central committee.§§§§§§ The central committee, comprising representatives of 3,200 districts, follows the same procedure, this time arriving at decisions that are binding on the national level.¶¶¶¶¶¶

Most but not all proposals will require funding. After each of the sixteen themes have been legislated, the 3,200 budget assemblies review the monetary requests, using the same procedures that generated the legislation before them. They then prepare several different budgets, emphasizing different priorities. These budget proposals are mailed out in a national referendum.

Let us say there are five budget proposals. One budget might allocate the majority of funds to war, another to education, and yet another to transportation. The allotments will vary, giving voters meaningful choices. Among the choices are "none of the above." If no budget proposal receives the votes of a majority of registered voters or if a majority vote "none of the above," then the budget process is revisited and another vote taken until a budget is accepted. Voters who reject the budget have the option of expressing their preferences by checking these boxes: "I would like to see more of this." "I would like to see less of that."

Making war, like agreeing on a budget, requires a national referendum. Considering its great social and economic costs, the decision to wage war should require approval by a two-thirds majority of registered voters.

---

§§§§§§ Should this member decline to serve in this capacity, another member is chosen by lot.
¶¶¶¶¶¶    Barber (op. cit., pp.273–278) proposes the use of modern technology to set up "electronic town meetings," a form of "teledemocracy" using cable television and video capabilities for connecting people across the country.

## Council Democracy

Toward the end of his life, when he was no longer serving in government, Thomas Jefferson became convinced of the importance of small-scale, local governance units of about one hundred souls each, which he referred to as "wards." The wards he had in mind were modeled on the New England township. Jefferson believed that the salvation of the new American government depended on the creation of these local wards as the primary unit of governance: they would be "elementary republics" where "the voice of the whole people would be fairly, fully, and peaceably expressed, discussed, and decided by the common reason" of all citizens.[5] Here is a lengthy quote from a letter to Samuel Kercheval, dated July 12, 1816:

> Divide the counties into wards on such size as that every citizen can attend, when called on, and act in person. Ascribe to them the government of their wards in all things relating to themselves exclusively. A justice, chosen by themselves, in each, a constable, a military company, a patrol, a school, the care of their own poor, their own portion of the public roads, the choice of one or more jurors to serve in some court, and the delivery, within their own wards, of their own votes for all elective officers of higher sphere, will relieve the county administration of nearly all its business, and will have it better done, and by making every citizen an active member of government, and in the offices nearest and most interesting to him, will attach him by his strongest feelings to the independence of his country, and its republican Constitution....
>
> We should thus marshal our government into, 1, the general federal republic, for all concerns foreign and federal; 2, that of the State, for what relates to our own citizens exclusively; 3, the county republics, for the duties and concerns of the county; 4, the ward republics, for the small, and yet numerous and interesting concerns of the neighborhood.[6]

Although one might disagree about the content or work of these little republics, it is significant that Jefferson believed that they "would be the main strength of the great one."[7] This is government from the bottom up. The strength and stability of the government lie in its foundation of local governments, not in the top or central government. It was his wish that everybody feel that "he is a participator in the government of affairs, not merely at an election one day in the year, but every day."[8]

The philosopher Hannah Arendt [*******] conceived of modern government as taking one of two forms: as based either on the two-party system or on what she calls the "council system." [††††††] In her argument, she referred in some detail to Jefferson's notion of wards and gave other examples as well.

---

[*******] Hannah Arendt (1906–1975) was a German American political theorist. Her work deals with the nature of power, and the subjects of politics, authority, and totalitarianism. Some of her better known works are *The Origins of Totalitarianism* (1951), *The Human Condition* (1958), *On Revolution* (1963), *Men in Dark Times* (1968), *The Life of the Mind* (1978).
[††††††] See *On Revolution*.

At times of dramatic change in government, local citizens spontaneously gather, forming themselves into councils or perhaps neighborhood associations. The "section" or Paris neighborhood association
was an important organizing force during the French Revolution. In
Russia in 1905, a time of popular uprising, there emerged local *soviets*,
or councils, as the principal organizing force. In 1919, in Germany,
returning soldiers and workers seeking government changes spontaneously formed themselves into *räte* or councils.

A similar phenomenon occurred in Hungary in 1956. Councils of
writers and artists were born out of coffee-house discussions. In addition, councils of workers and soldiers, student councils, and councils
of civil servants all appeared spontaneously in response to the turn of
political events. Arendt draws parallels as well between councils and
the medieval townships and the Swiss cantons.‡‡‡‡‡‡‡ As noted earlier, it
was the existence of neighborhood associations that provided the foundation for participatory budgeting in Porto Alegre. It is noteworthy that
at the very time when some theorists would predict anarchy or lack of
structure because of a breakdown of official rule, there appear instead
locally grown associations that provide a means for structuring a political response and establishing a new form of government.

Arendt was definitely on the side of the council system as opposed to
the party system. Nonetheless, she was an elitist and without apologies.
It was her belief that those who would constitute the backbone of the
councils, people of integrity and courage, are not necessarily the ones
to manage or administer the government, "in a sphere of life whose
principle is necessity."[9] The elites she had in mind are neither elite by
birth or wealth. They are elites "sprung from the people."[10] These are
bottom-up elites, not top-down elites—people who emerge from the
councils and stand out by their administrative abilities. This conception
is no different from Jefferson's belief in rule of a "natural aristocracy."

I do not think Arendt fully worked out the distinction between those
who are politically gifted but unfit to govern because of a lack of administrative abilities and those who are fit to govern. In ancient Athens there
were magistrates, selected by lot, who administered, and there were
large juries who oversaw their performance. If one believes that modern
society is too complex to be administered by persons chosen by lot, then
these individuals could be chosen from among a pool of those who have
been trained for the purpose. However, it is my belief that those who
administer should not govern. Instead, governance, deliberation, and
legislation should be the provenance of all of us. We may not have the
knowledge to design a bridge from New York to Paris, but we are com-

---

‡‡‡‡‡‡‡ She could have also mentioned local governance in villages in India and the
local associations in Pennsylvania that responded to the events of the Revolution. Recall
how after the Constitution was signed, forty-two democratic societies—local discussion
groups—emerged around the country in the newly formed United States.

petent to decide whether such an undertaking is a wise use of resources.

I like Jefferson's concept of "wards." I like Arendt's concept of the "council system." However, I do not believe in leaders or elites, especially in the area of politics. There are at least two good arguments against having leaders to guide us. First, when we have leaders, they take over. We become small-minded and passive. Second, how do we know which leaders to trust? Who are the "true believers?" The early Puritans faced this very problem. They were Calvinists who believed that those who should rule are those who had received God's grace. But how could these people be recognized? The Puritans had to acknowledge that there was no way to differentiate between those who were true believers and those who were faking it. So they had to open the Church to those whose "appearance" and conduct would seem to qualify them for membership, in the process making way for hypocrisy.

Determining which leaders are "democratic" raises the same issue. Assuming it is desirable to have leaders, how can we differentiate between those who truly have the common good at heart and those who are faking it, who are out for personal power and are simply good impersonators? The answer is we cannot. And in fact, those who appear to be most devoted to the common good might simply be good actors. We follow them only to end up where we started, being taken over by self-serving oligarchs.

In his essay "Popular Sovereignty as Procedure," the German philosopher Jürgen Habermas§§§§§§ holds out the possibility that regular folk, through a process of deliberative interaction, can reasonably and responsibly take charge of their collective destiny. He refers to the French Revolution as ushering in a modern age that has the following characteristics: "the understanding of political practice in terms of self-determination and self-realization; and the trust in rational discourse, through which all political authority was supposed to legitimate itself."[11] The French Revolution established a new kind of historical consciousness, one that believed that "a new beginning could be made."[12] It created a generation of emancipated individuals who decided for themselves "the rules and manner of their living together"[13]; they gave themselves the laws they wanted to obey. He also speaks of "cooperative practice centered in conscious political will-formation."[14] Habermas refers to nineteenth-century German philosopher Julius Fröbel, who said,

---

§§§§§§ Jürgen Habermas (born 1929) is a German sociologist and philosopher in the tradition of critical theory and pragmatism. He is perhaps best known for his theory on the concepts of 'communicative rationality' and the 'public sphere'.

Habermas's theoretical system is devoted to revealing the possibility of reason, emancipation, and rational-critical communication latent in modern institutions and in the human capacity to deliberate and pursue rational interests. Among his works are *The Structural Transformation of the Public Sphere* (1962) and *Between Facts and Norms: Contributions to a Discourse Theory of Law and Democracy* (1992).

> We seek the social republic, that is, the state in which the happiness, free-
> dom and dignity of each individual are recognized as the common goal of all
> and the perfection of the law and power of society springs from the *mutual
> understanding* and agreement of *all its members*.[15] [italics in original]

Fröbel offers a thoughtful response to the concern about majority rule,
the so-called "tyranny of the majority." By "resigning their will" the
minority are not "declar[ing] their opinion to be incorrect," nor are they
being called on to abandon their aims. Rather, there are postponing "the
application of their convictions until they succeed in better establishing
their reasons and procuring the necessary number of affirmative votes."[16]

Like Arendt, Habermas speaks of council democracy and the "spontaneously emergent voluntary association" as the building block of a democratic government. A society "integrated through associations instead of
through markets would be a political ... order."[17] Habermas makes the
distinction, as Arendt did, between *communicatively generated* power
and *administratively employed* power" [italics in original].[18] Yet like
Arendt he seems to have identified the conflict without resolving it.

One of the most lucid, straightforward proposals for political democracy comes from Stephen Shalom, professor of political science at William Paterson University in New Jersey. He addresses all the obstacles
and objections and seems to come up with reasonable solutions.¶¶¶¶¶¶¶

Rejecting the Leninist notion that there are a set of people who know
our interests better than we do, he sees peoples' attitudes and interests
not as something given or fixed, "but as a work in progress, improving
as people function in a humane society."[19] His critique of representative democracy (a term I believe is oxymoronic) is that it undervalues
the importance of citizen participation and that representatives do not
in fact honestly represent the interests of their constituency. Shalom's
objection to referendum democracy is that it denies citizens access to
the deliberative process. A referendum "encourages people to express
their pre-existing views on polarized positions."[20] There are winners
and losers, but no one is the wiser.

Shalom thus rejects both the referendum and the "autonomous
community," or commune, as solutions to the problems of democracy.
He believes that many large-scale problems, such as ecology, require
a larger context for a satisfactory resolution. Shalom's solution is to
return to the concept of councils, in his case, "nested councils." Issues
that can be satisfactorily addressed at the lowest, most local, face-to-
face level will go no farther than a local-level council. Issues that are
more far reaching get bumped up to the next higher level council, to
which each lower council sends a delegate.

Shalom argues that these delegates should not be mandated to vote

---

¶¶¶¶¶¶¶ Stephen Shalom, *A Political System for a Good Society*, http://www.zcommuni-
cations.org/a-political-system-for-a-good-society-by-stephen1-shalom.

as they did in their local council when they serve in this higher level council, but that they should be free to deliberate and debate anew in this new setting. Their value stems from the fact that they have participated in the lower level deliberation and hence can honestly represent the local viewpoint, while perhaps modifying their position in the higher level deliberation based on new input. Whenever the higher level discussion became contentious and might potentially violate the spirit of the lower council's wishes, the issue would be returned to the lower level council for a decision.

The connection between the delegate and the lower council would be an organic one. Delegates would return to the lower level council on a regular basis. They would serve brief terms on a rotating basis. The lower council would have the right of recall.

Shalom has a well-balanced view on the subject of consensus vs. majority decisions by voting. Consensus, the outcome of sustained discussion in which all viewpoints are considered and individuals are required to increase their level of understanding and empathy for differing positions, is the desired procedure. However, there are issues where an unyielding minority stands in the way of resolution, no matter how much discussion there is. Under these circumstances, says Shalom, there should be a vote that empowers the majority view. As he observes, "If majorities oppress minorities, that is not democracy. Yet if minorities can block majorities, that too is undemocratic."[21]

Shalom provides a very intelligent solution to this dilemma. Juries would be randomly selected from the population at large. Serving over a period of six months to a year, these juries would provide oversight of council decisions. They would be a court of appeal of sorts whose job would be to make sure that the Constitution and individual rights have been respected.[********]

It is easy to argue that proposing such a form of government is naïve, utopian, and impractical. Yet to me such a proposal seems almost prosaic in that it is solidly grounded and involves many people debating the same issues around the country. It is difficult to imagine that anything wild or impulsive could occur as a result. It is easier to imagine that initially, at any rate, the process would be slow, plodding, and unimaginative.

Let us not forget that one of the chief benefits of this form of government, and to me this seems incontrovertible, will be the energizing effect of citizen participation around the country on issues of concern that affect everyone. A society that practiced such a form of government on a national level would be a dynamic society, a civilized society, perhaps even a humane society.

--------

[********] See also *The Democracy Collaborative* whose mission is "to advance a new understanding of democracy for the 21st century and to promote new strategies and innovations in community development that enhance democratic life." *http://www.Community-Wealth.org/about/about-us.htm*. In this context see the work of Gar Alperovitz, especially *America Beyond Capitalism: Reclaiming Our Wealth, Our Liberty and Our Democracy.*

## Politics vs. Economics: Which Comes First?

Some will say that economic issues need to be considered before we can work toward establishing a political democracy. Globalization has made wage slaves of all of us. Economic disparities both within and between countries need to be addressed before civilization can set itself aright. Barber disagrees. He argues that the political reordering must come first: "Democracy proclaims the priority of the political over the economic."[22] "Politics precedes economics," he says, because it "creates the central values of economy and society."[23] "It remains the sovereign realm in which the ordering of human priorities takes place."[24] I agree.

Max Weber, writing in the early twentieth century, devoted considerable space to a discussion of politics and its priority in civic affairs. Unlike Marx, he sought to understand political behavior in political—not economic—terms. He believed that politics is autonomous with regards to economics. It is not economic life but the form of government that determines character.

Weber emphasized the importance of political education. A nation becomes politically educated, he said, when it shares "responsibility ... for its own political fate, which is the only way a nation can possibly be trained in the exercise of political judgment."[25] When "a nation is well informed about how its officials are conducting *their affairs,* so that it constantly controls and influences their work,"[26] it is politically educated. Weber underscored this point: "No *economic* factor can substitute for such education" [emphasis in original].[27]Political maturity requires *"parliamentary supervision and control,"* especially where there are misdeeds to be accounted for [italics in original].[28, ††††††††]

Weber was an old-fashioned "statist"; that is, he believed that the nation-state is and should be the highest expression of the political community. He spoke of the "nation's enduring economic and political *power* interests" [italics in original],[29] of the need "to preserve and raise the quality of our national species"[30] as determined by the "commitment to the historical obligations imposed on one's own nation by fate." In other words, he spoke the language of German nationalism at the same time Germany was being defeated in war.

Yet, Weber seemed to have the soul of a democrat. He repeatedly expressed his concern for the returning soldiers and that they be granted political standing in any new system of government. "The returning

†††††††† Thus it is that Americans of a certain generation achieved a degree of political maturity when, in fact, government officials were held accountable for their conduct before the court of public opinion. In 1972, the Senate Watergate Committee, under the leadership of Sam Ervin, set about holding the President of the United States accountable for his complicity in illegal activity surrounding his re-election. The investigation and the public hearings aired over television led to his eventual resignation. That was the last time a president was held accountable for his conduct. The exposure of lies and deception, as a result of the actions of responsible legislators, undoubtedly had a tonic effect on those of us who were there to witness it.

soldiers," he wrote, "must not be faced with the need to fight sterile domestic battles for electoral rights before they can acquire the instruments of power which will give them a decisive say in the running of the state they have defended."[31]

Weber believed that the open discussion of political issues should never be stifled, even in the midst of war. Against the claim "that any criticism of our political arrangements simply puts weapons into the hands of our enemies," he replied, "For twenty years we were gagged with this argument, until it was too late."[32]

Mobocracy, the menace of the "street," Weber attributed to the "*layabouts* and coffee-house intellectuals ... who have manufactured the bellicose politics of the 'street,' and who have done so ... entirely in the service of the government and *only* to the extent desired or permitted by the government" [italics in original].[33]

Wistfully, Weber looked toward Switzerland where a pacifist, democratic-leaning government was in control. It is only such "communities which renounce political power [that] are able to provide the soil on which other virtues may flourish."[34]

Writing in the midst of war and the collapse of government, Weber seemed to have held out some hope for democracy. One hundred years later, we are in a similar situation. The rights and well-being of returning soldiers are in question. Open debate is being stifled. We are being defeated on the battlefield, whether we admit it or not. The question is, Are we ready for democracy yet?

# CONCLUSION ❧

## The Citizen State

*"For who can yet believe, though after loss,*
*That all these puissant legions, whose exile*
*Hath emptied heaven, shall fail to re-ascend,*
*Self-raised, and re-possess their native seat?"*

"L'ETAT C'EST MOI," said Louis XIV. "*I* am the state." "L'Etat c'est nous," say I. "*We* are the state." We have been the state all along. We just have not realized it. The state is the Great Community. It is the community of communities. It is *our* community. We make it and shape it by what we do and do not do. No government would long endure without the support of its citizens.

Yet there is a difference between passive support and active involvement. Ancient Athens was a citizen-state: the citizenry and the government were one and the same. The citizens set policy, passed laws, controlled the treasury, received ambassadors, made war, and sued for peace. They did everything that a government does. They were the government. I believe that, as the American oligarchy withers, the government that replaces it will be closer to a citizen-state than anything we have seen in a long time.

We have been trained to believe that our role as citizens is to vote every so often in national elections and then to go about our business; thus voting and citizenship are one and the same. We have also been trained to believe that to not vote is to violate our birthright. Not only must we vote but we are also to take the election seriously, no matter how unworthy the candidates, how shoddy, comical, and corrupt the campaign. When we vote in violation of our deeper beliefs and sense of dignity, we are engaging in an act of self-denigration. We wither as humans. We begin to disappear.

The political lie is ever present. It corrupts those who lie and those who believe the lie. We know we are being lied to, and yet we consistently pretend to believe and then are deflated when our belief, once again, proves unjustified. When we go to vote the next time, we believe all over again. We choose not to make the connection between the politician's words at election time and his deeds the day after. We want to believe in the beneficence of those who govern. We become more and more disengaged, more and more disillusioned, more and more anxious about what is happening around us that we cannot direct in any way. We lack the words to describe what has occurred and what has become of us as individuals, as a national community.

## To Vote or Not to Vote: That Is the Question

There is no question that allowing citizens to choose their national leaders by voting, represented a step forward for humankind. Instead of submitting to a pre-determined leadership, citizens were granted the right to select those who would speak for them.* It is also true that there was a time in the United States when the lead-up to a national election was a time for impassioned debate among the citizenry and serious thought about some grander vision, about how the country should be run and for whose benefit. I believe that intelligent and committed political discussion came to an end some forty years ago. Since then we have been living in a "managed democracy," to use Wolin's term,† "a political form in which governments are legitimated by elections that they have learned to control." This is a form of government that attempts to keep alive the appearance of democracy while simultaneously defeating its primary purpose: self-government. Democratic myths persist in the absence of true democratic practice.

Though sacrosanct for just about all of us, the election as a means of choosing representation might have outlived its usefulness. Earlier I proposed to replace it by a lottery, sometimes referred to as sortition. As its name implies, the lottery is the equivalent of dropping a bunch of names in a hat and then randomly choosing one. A vetted lottery is one in which the names in the hat have been reviewed for eligibility.

Under this system, for example, anyone could run for the U.S. Senate. A person could submit his name or that of a friend or relative on a standardized form. A jury of randomly chosen citizens, numbering in the hundreds, would then vet the applicants. Those applicants who were not citizens, who were not of sufficient age, or whose opinions and records were not appealing to a particular juror would be rejected. A vote would be taken, and let's say that only those candidates who received a majority of 55% would remain in the lottery.

There are then two options: (1) a random selection of some of those

---

* Though even at the outset, there were restrictions, such as property qualifications, and a vying for power by those in a position to do so.
† See the Introduction for a discussion of Sheldon Wolin's *Democracy Inc: Managed Democracy and the Specter of Inverted Totalitarianism.*

who remain in the lottery pool would become candidates in a traditional election, or (2) the senator would be chosen by lottery. That is, a name would be randomly pulled from the vetted pool and that person would become senator. In ancient Athens where these procedures were followed, there was an additional precaution. Every six months a jury was assembled, again with hundreds of members, to review the performance of the office holder. In our case, we could say that if 55% of the jurors were unhappy with the senator's performance, he would be dismissed from office and a new senator chosen by lottery.

Obviously, this is an extreme alternative to what is in place, but it has certain clear advantages. Without an election, the opportunities for deception and manipulation would disappear altogether. A lottery would also minimize the opportunities for candidates to be bought by powerful corporate interests. There would be no $60 million senator or $1 billion president. The senator chosen by lottery would be free to act according to his beliefs because he would owe nothing to anyone. Because no promises were made, there would be no promises to break.

Or we could make more modest innovations to our current system, ones more in keeping with the traditions of American governance, Earlier I compared government to the human body. In the human body when blood circulates freely, the individual is healthy. When there are blockages, he is in trouble. The same applies to government. Power is the lifeblood. Where it circulates freely the government is in good health. When power coagulates—that is, when the same person is re-elected repeatedly over a period of years and decades—the health of the government, and hence of its citizen population, declines. The solution is rotation in office. In 1947, the Congress passed the Twenty-Second Amendment to the Constitution in response to FDR's being elected to serve four terms in office. It was the belief at the time that excessive tenure resulted in a concentration of power that represented a threat to good government. The belief is as sound today as it was then.

The practice of rotation in office was initiated early in American history. More than two hundred years ago, in 1807, Jefferson summed it up as follows: "If some termination to the services of the chief Magistrate be not fixed by the Constitution, or supplied by practice, his office, nominally four years, will in fact become for life."[1] Jefferson's immediate successors, James Madison and James Monroe, also adhered to the two-term principle.

The same principle could be applied to the Senate and House of Representatives today. An amendment to the Constitution could be passed preventing a senator or representative from serving more than two terms in a lifetime. As a further precaution it could call for two non-consecutive terms, thus preventing even slight coagulations (i.e., concentrations of power) from forming. Not only would such an amendment lessen the concentration and potential abuse of power but it would also open the opportunity for more people to serve in office, injecting new blood into the system on a more regular basis.

Furthermore, those who would seek office under these term limits would be less likely to lust for power and more likely to be those who seek service in the common good. By comparison to those who govern today, they would be amateurs, not experts or professional politicians. In a democracy, it is the amateurs, not the experts, who should govern. Where there is frequent rotation in office, government takes on a different aspect: it is fluid, changing, evolving, organic, alive, experimental, and responsive—not fixed, immutable, unyielding, or impenetrable.‡

## Envisioning Change

Earlier, I differentiated between cyclical change and transformative change. Examples of cyclical change are the rising and setting of the sun or the change in seasons. Cyclical change is repetitive. In contrast, where there is transformative change, something new appears. For example, an acorn grows into a tall oak tree. What emerges is radically different from the original cause, an acorn. Such change is irreversible. The oak tree cannot return to its origins and become an acorn. This is an example of transformative change.

However, when social or psychological transformative change occurs, cognitive and emotional issues arise. We have a certain image of what our government is and how we relate to it. Our government has an identity; it is seen as a certain kind of government, behaving in a certain way. We as individual citizens become subsumed within this identity, whether we choose to be or not. What happens to us when our government changes? In some measure our universe has been tampered with. That is an unsettling feeling, which is one reason why transformative change is resisted so rigorously.

There was a time when being identified as being American would bring a smile of gratitude and a handshake from a foreigner. Now it is just as likely to bring a snub. Do we like our government and how it is seen around the world? Do we like the way it feels to be associated with such a government? Would we like to be associated with a different kind of government? Are we pleased with the way in which our government addresses the needs of its citizens? These are questions we should be asking ourselves.

Perhaps some readers would like to live under a government that is less feared and more respected, a government that is kinder and gentler, a gov-

---

‡ In a CNBC interview Warren Buffet suggested that it would be a easy matter to reduce the budget deficit. Simply pass an amendment to the Constitution stating that "anytime there is a deficit of more than 3% of GDP all sitting members of Congress are ineligible for re-election." This is an example of creative government.

ernment that embraces the common good. "But," you say in quiet despair, "how can our government possibly be changed? It is simply not possible."

Although such a belief is certainly understandable, I do not believe it is justified. I believe that change is possible, provided it is introduced in a thoughtful and gradual way. First we change our attitude, our outlook on life. To repeat the thoughts of Henry George, right reason precedes right action. We become thoughtful, rather than reactive. We take nothing for granted. We become more analytical, more skeptical, and less credulous about the government we live under; we become more imaginative and hopeful about the government we intend to replace it with. We allow our imagination free rein as we think up new possibilities. For it is only through imagination and creativity that change comes about.

Let us imagine that our responses to national and international occurrences of political consequence can be contained in a water pitcher. When the pitcher is full that condition equals 100% of our possible political responses. There can be no more. Now let us imagine that when the pitcher is full it contains two different components: one component is reactivity, and the other is creativity. At any moment the pitcher contains various proportions of one or the other component. Potentially, it could be all reactivity, or it could be all creativity. When you increase one component, you decrease the other.

Speaking for myself and, I suspect, for many people in the United States and around the world, most of our political responses are reactive. We have feelings of anguish, outrage, despondency, melancholy, and powerlessness, all of which are understandable responses to conditions that disturb us. The problem with these responses is that they are debilitating. More importantly, they change nothing.

"Well," you say, "when we are outraged we take to the streets and protest." Protests are a good thing. They bring us together. They are uplifting. They allow us to give expression to our political concerns. When we protest, we make ourselves visible to the larger body politic who are also uplifted. All of this is good, but it changes nothing. In February 2003, I was a proud participant in a demonstration opposing the war in Iraq. It was a wonderful experience. It was empowering; it was exhilarating. I established bonds of friendship with people I had never seen before and will never see again. Yet it changed nothing.§ The war followed its inexorable destiny despite our best efforts to deter its course.

Let us imagine—and certainly it is conceivable though doubtful— that such a demonstration would stop the war. That would be a good thing. What the demonstration would not do, however, is change the government, the people in power who want to wage war. Therefore, one could, with reasonable confidence, predict that war would still occur,

---

§ Demonstrations directed at the government, qua government, as opposed to a specific government policy, are more likely to meet with success.

because the government is structured so as to ensure its occurrence.

Reactivity is a normal human response. For most of us, I believe, it fills the pitcher. There is no room left over for creativity. Change begins when reactivity diminishes and creativity increases. We need to take a step backward and become more objective, more thoughtful and philosophical, and less reactive. When we do this, the pitcher starts to fill up with creative ideas about how government can be changed for the better.

We change the world by changing ourselves and each other by means of political dialogue. Political dialogue is an exchange among equals in which listening is as important as speaking, if not more so. When our neighbor speaks we listen with empathy and interest, trying to understand how he reached his position, probing to see if there is some small way in which we might actually agree with him. We are not waiting for him to finish so we can spout our thoughts. There is no hurry; our thoughts can wait. It is not about speechifying: "Listen to me. I know what I am talking about. If you don't agree with what I have to say, you are an idiot." That kind of behavior too often passes for political talk and discourages us from exploring our thoughts with our neighbor. This is why I encourage civic gatherings—neutral, friendly gatherings of people who want to explore their political ideas and learn by listening to what others have to say.

## Democracy at Work

Although we might dismiss some of the ideas outlined in this book as one dreamer's folly, in fact, there are more examples of democracy around us than we realize. For instance, Iceland, like many countries throughout Europe, recently experienced an economic crisis when its financial markets collapsed. For a brief period, starting in 2003, Iceland was home to unbridled speculation and unrivaled wealth. The country's banks were privatized. They offered online banking whose minimal costs allowed them to offer relatively high rates of return. The accounts, called IceSave, attracted many English and Dutch small investors. But as investments grew, so did the banks' foreign debt. By 2007 the bank debt was 900 times Iceland's GDP. The world financial crisis of 2008 resulted in the failure of Iceland's three main banks. The Krone lost 85% against the Euro. At the end of the year Iceland declared bankruptcy.

In response, the International Monetary Fund (IMF) and the European Union wanted to take over the debt and impose drastic measures on the people of Iceland to enable the private banks to honor their loans. In addition to their usual taxes, Icelanders were being asked to pay an additional $130 per month for fifteen years. There were protests. And here is where matters get interesting.

Olafur Ragnar Grimsson, the head of state, refused to ratify the law that would have made Iceland's citizens responsible for its bankers' debts and instead accepted calls for a referendum. The international community exerted great pressure and offered many and sundry threats. The Icelanders persisted.

In the March 2010 referendum, 93% voted against repayment of the debt. The IMF immediately froze its loan to Iceland. But with the support of a determined citizenry, the government launched civil and penal investigations into those responsible for the financial crisis. Interpol put out an international arrest warrant for the former president of the Kaupthing bank, Sigurdur Einarsson, as the other bankers implicated in the crash fled the country.

Icelanders did not stop there. They decided to draft a new constitution that would free the country from the exaggerated power of international finance and virtual money. To write the new constitution, the people of Iceland elected 25 citizens from among 522 adults not belonging to any political party, but each recommended by at least 30 citizens. This document was not the work of a handful of politicians in a closed gathering, but was written on the Internet. The meetings were streamed online, and citizens were able to send their comments and suggestions, witnessing the document as it took shape. The constitution that eventually emerged from this participatory democratic process will be submitted to parliament for approval after the next elections. This is democracy at work.

Here is another example. In this case, there is an imaginative use of the jury to counteract electoral irregularities.

In 2003, the government of British Columbia (BC) signed into law the creation of a Citizens' Assembly to examine the BC voting system. It was made up of two randomly selected citizens from each of BC's 79 electoral districts as well as two Aboriginals and a chairperson, for a total of 161 jurors.

The work of the Citizens' Assembly proceeded in three stages: a learning period, public hearings, and a period of deliberation. The learning period was under the direction of the University of British Columbia, with an advisory board made up of other interested groups. Public hearings were held throughout BC and attended by more than 3,000 citizens. Each hearing was also attended by between four and sixteen assembly members from local, bordering, and distant electoral wards to ensure that the Citizens' Assembly had the chance to hear the concerns of other districts. The public was free to apply to make presentations to the hearings and submit written statements.

Finally, in the deliberation process the Citizens' Assembly synthesized everything its members had heard and considered the alternative electoral systems available. It decided on which system it believed was in the best interests of BC: a majority of 146 to 7 voted to recommend the adoption of a single transferable vote system over the current first-past-the-post system.

Then a referendum was held to approve the Citizen's Assembly recommendation. It garnered majority support in 77 of BC's 79 districts and 58% of the popular vote, just short of the 60% target required to enact the proposal. In 2009, there was another referendum in which the electoral proposal was again defeated.

A similar procedure was followed in the state of Minnesota. In response to the contested results in the 2009 Senate election, two nonprofit organizations formed the group, the Citizens' Jury on Election Recounts.

To serve on the Citizen's Jury, twenty-four jurors were selected from the electoral rolls using an anonymous and random method that ensured demographic balance. Over three 3-day sessions in June 2009 the jury convened to hear presentations on possible changes to the electoral system. To ensure impartiality, presenters were chosen to represent all sides of the argument; they included political party representatives, academics, election officials, and others. The jury had the opportunity to ask questions, study evidence, and discuss and deliberate in small or large groups, eventually compiling a list of recommendations for changes to the election procedure. Many of the proposals were later passed by both Minnesotan houses and signed into law in 2010.

Undoubtedly there are other examples like these.¶ Undoubtedly, there are more such examples to come. For when the failure of the government to respond to the needs of its citizens becomes extreme, acquiescence is no longer an option. There is ample evidence in the year 2012 that we have reached such a moment. People from around the world are demanding that their voices be heard. What started in Tunisia in December 2010 spread to Egypt, Libya, Bahrain, Syria, and Yemen and came to be known as the "Arab Spring." It was followed by "Autumn in America," better known as "Occupy Wall Street," which started on Wall Street and spread to cities throughout the United States and then to Western Europe. The energy generated by these voices of dissent has spread throughout society and has become incorporated into the social consciousness. "These are the times that try men's souls," wrote Thomas Paine in 1776, as one government was dissolving, soon to be replaced by another. Were he alive today, he might be expressing similar sentiments.

What is interesting about periods of crisis is that they are times ripe for change. For a full decade after Paine's words were penned, the United States was in a period of constant flux. There were thirteen different governments loosely united by the Articles of Confederation. Yet, these were spirited and productive times. Although a war was being fought with Britain, the new American society was relatively stable. Men and women stood proud and thought deeply about how they should be governed and whom they should trust.

---

¶ In response to a Supreme Court decision granting corporations the rights of persons, there has emerged an organization called "Move to Amend"(movetoamend.org). Its goal is to have the Constitution amended by gathering signatures on a petition that reads, "We, the People of the United States of America, reject the U.S. Supreme Court's ruling in Citizens United, and move to amend our Constitution to firmly establish that money is not speech, and that human beings, not corporations, are persons entitled to constitutional rights."

It is in times of transition that we have the opportunity to revisit much of what we have routinely taken for granted. Whom should we believe? Do the old answers still work? These questions, which we ponder today, are the same ones debated by the Anti-Federalists (democrats) in early America. Remember that it was the Anti-Federalists who favored decentralized, local government that provided for the maximum participation of the largest number of citizens. This is the kind of government that is most likely to respond to the current crisis. When local people sit down together and discuss what is wrong and what could be done to fix it, they are establishing the foundation for a government that will be responsive to their needs.

One could reasonably argue that, before the year 1789, monarchy was the prevailing form of government around the world. It was found wanting. It had no eyes with which to look into the future and was grossly unresponsive to the common weal. An emerging world required a new form of government.

Beginning in 1789, in the West principally but not exclusively, monarchy was replaced by oligarchy as the prevailing form of government. For more than two hundred years, oligarchic governments, in which a handful speak for all, have controlled events and outcomes to suit their needs. Like the monarchies that they replaced, oligarchies have been found grossly unresponsive to the common weal. Like the monarchies that they replaced, oligarchies have no eyes to see the future. Once again, an emerging world requires a new form of government.

Citizenship has dwindled to the point of disappearing. War has become a way of life. The global economy based on speculation and on exploitation of resources both human and natural is teetering on the edge of total collapse. The quality of the air, water, and soil has deteriorated. Species are disappearing from the planet on a daily basis.

The oligarchy's way of doing business is to concentrate resources and economic power in one central location so that it can exercise total control. It has created vast industrialized farms at the expense of family farming. It has taken control of seeds and fertilizers. It is in the process of centralizing financial interests in fewer and fewer banks. It has built its empire on the premise of never ending expansion and inflation. This oligarchy that speaks for less than 1% of the population is sucking the economy dry, wreaking havoc in foreign lands, decimating civilizations, snuffing out human life like so many candles on a birthday cake.** A form of government that does not even pretend to address the common good has outlived its legitimacy.

---

** The taking of civilian lives, which used to be referred to as "collateral damage," seems to have become a chosen strategy. In targeted countries, there are lists of civilians who are to be eliminated. A half-million Iraqi children were starved to death. It seems as if there is a return to the total warfare of Genghis Kahn: destroy the farms and the irrigation systems, destroy the infrastructure, destroy the houses, and decimate the entire population so that nothing is left.

If one considers the consequences for the environment, and if one allows for the fact that before the end of the twenty-first century, at the present rates of economic expansion and consumption of fossil fuels, oil might have disappeared as a natural resource, then one realizes that both the economy and society need to undergo a fundamental restructuring based on different premises. Life will become less materialistic. Life will become simpler and richer. Community life will be revitalized. Small and local is where we are headed.

"An exclusive right to form or alter a government is annexed to society in every moment of its existence," said John Taylor, of Carolina, a member of one of the democratic societies that flourished between 1790 and 1800.[2] In other words, government is in a continual state of renewal and evolution. Thomas Paine expressed it this way: "A nation though continually existing, is continually in a state of renewal and succession."[3]

The question to ponder is this: "Assuming that citizens have a vision of what a new world would look like, might they join with kindred spirits in taking their collective destiny into their own hands?" Thomas Paine was optimistic on the subject. "Mankind, it appears to me," he said, "are always ripe enough to understand their true interest."[4] Writing in 1776, as the colonies were about to become states and the government that had been monarchic was in the process of becoming oligarchic, he made a simple observation that applies as well today, as we begin the transition from oligarchy to democracy: "We have it in our power to begin the world over again."[5]

We, the people, the vast majority—that is, more than 99% of us— are not a special interest group. We are the stuff and substance of this society. As such we need a government that speaks for us, a government that is sensitive to the ecosystem and responsive to local needs and small-scale enterprises. We need a government that has a human face to it, a government in which local voices, sensitive to day-to-day realities, exercise power on behalf of the common good. We need a democracy.

# APPENDIX ❧

# Hegel's Philosophy of History

L IKE PLATO BEFORE him, Hegel is an idealist. For Plato, what we think of as the real world is a mere shadow of reality. Instead, "reality" is in the essence of things. The chair I am sitting on has an essence, a design. That essence is the "reality," not the physical chair itself. Atop four legs is a small horizontal plane to which a vertical plane is attached on one side. This is a universal statement about my chair; it describes its essence. It also describes all chairs that ever were, are, or will be. For Plato, this schematic description of the chair—the universal statement about the chair—is the chair. There is a universe of such universals or ideas—a universe that preexists the material world—and it this universe that Plato seeks to explain. The material world that we consider to be reality is thus derived from and determined by the universe of ideas. It is a universe that is fixed in time and static.

Like Plato, Hegel's universe is comprised of ideas—but a different kind of idea from that envisaged by Plato. For Hegel, ideas originate as thought and have no material correlates. Let us imagine that in the material world there is a geologist. He seeks to understand different rock formations. He identifies sedimentary rock and wants to know what materials compose it, where they came from, and what brought them all together in the same place. Hegel asks similar questions about the universe of ideas. What is an idea? Where does it come from? How do ideas relate to each other and to the material world? The ideas that seem to interest him the most are the mental processes that produce the ideas.

One can say that, if there is an idea, somewhere there is a mind that generates it. When we think of mind, we think of a person with a head on his shoulders and a brain in his head. We know he has a mind when we hear him talk and read what he writes. Now imagine that we take that mind out of his head and spread it throughout the universe, so that the universe is a disembodied mind thinking thoughts. Broadly speaking, this is what Hegel has done. For Hegel, universal history is the struggle of that mind to discover itself.

In Hegel's philosophy, God is the philosopher. And the philosopher is God. God is thinking the world into existence. What is that like? How does that come about? Questions like these supply Hegel with his subject matter. In Hegel's words, "It may be said of Universal History, that it is the exhibition of Spirit [Mind]* in the process of working out the knowledge of that which it is potentially." [1] Unlike Plato's universe, Hegel's universe is a universe in a state of constant evolution, in the process of coming into being.

For Hegel, the life of the mind is life in its highest form. The self-conscious mind— the mind thinking thoughts, aware as it thinks thoughts that it is thinking thoughts—is the highest form of being, the union of the subjective and the objective. It is the essence of the divine. Hegel's philosophy of history has its basis in this kind of idealism.

Humans approach the divine as their thought processes evolve to higher levels of abstraction, to a more encompassing consciousness of thought as the ultimate aim of life. The same applies to the various civilizations that comprise universal history. A civilization, like a human individual, can be more or less conscious of its existence and of the nature of its existence. In Hegel's philosophy, progress in the development of civilization entails increasing self-awareness.

Hegel similarly understand the writing of history. Herodotus is an example of an historian writing what Hegel calls "Original History." The subject matter comprises data and events, but not much more. There is no historian meditating on these facts. "Reflective History" is represented by Jacob Burckhardt's *The Civilization of the Renaissance in Italy*. He uses events as a jumping-off point for commentary. This is more thoughtful history, but it is still grounded in the specifics of its subject matter. "Philosophical History" is the kind of history written by Hegel. It is at another remove from concrete reality. The goal for Hegel is to understand the unfolding of societies around the globe and across time, not in their concrete details but in their ideas, the essences behind their existence.

Do societies come and go as the result of chance events and natural circumstances? Or does the succession of societies have a structure? Is it predictable? Does it have direction? Hegel answers the last three questions in the affirmative. History is a rational process, writes Hegel. It is rational because "Reason is the Sovereign of the World." Reason is also the "Substance of the universe"—"that by which and in which all reality has its being and subsistence." [2] Reason supplies its own form, its own content, its own energy. It is both subject and object. It is the unity of all being, both natural and spiritual. It knows no imperfection, containing as it does all form, matter, and power within itself. Other-

---

* In German the word is *geist*, which can mean, "spirit," "mind," or "ghost." Mind seems to apply here because we are talking about ideas.

wise stated, reason is God. And it is God as reason that brings about the unfolding of the history of peoples: "A Providence (that of God) presides over the events of the World." [3]

Does God have a plan? Is there an end state that he has in mind? Apparently he does. The goal of history is the ultimate realization of freedom in its highest, most evolved state. And what is freedom, if not mind thinking its thoughts, conscious that it is doing so? Freedom, then, is a state of mind. Mind is free because it depends on nothing but itself. It is "self-contained existence." [4] And it is self-contained existence that is free.

Writes Hegel, "I am free ... when my existence depends upon myself.† This self-contained existence of Spirit[Mind] is none other than self-consciousness— consciousness of one's own being." [5] Mind is the object of its own study in the form of self-consciousness, the highest form of being. One might characterize this kind of freedom as psychological freedom, as spiritual freedom. It is a subjective experience and is reminiscent of Descartes' *cogito ergo sum*, "I think therefore I am." The process of thinking is self-validating. Reality is in the head. Descartes thought himself into existence. This seems to be what Hegel is doing as well.

Freedom in this special sense is the measure of societal evolution. History is the gradual entering into awareness of the potential for freedom among humankind and then its realization by different societies as they progress through its enactment. In a very Freudian pronouncement, Hegel declares that "the whole process of History ... is directed to rendering this unconscious impulse [towards freedom] a conscious one." [6]

Freedom in the abstract, as an idea, has its realization in the state. "All the worth which the human being possesses ... he possesses only through the State.... The State is the divine Idea as it exists on Earth." [7] True freedom cannot exist without the state. As it was for Plato in *The Republic*, freedom is knowing one's place in the state. And as it was with Plato, there are those who command and those who obey. To act morally is to submit to the universal divine will, [8] which to some of us would seem the opposite of freedom.

Hegel, in keeping with tradition, acknowledges three forms of government: monarchy, aristocracy, and democracy. History begins in monarchy, either patriarchal or military in origin. In the next two phases, individuality asserts itself in the form of aristocracy and democracy. The fourth and final phase culminates in monarchy again, which Hegel refers to as the second phase of royalty, a different kind of monarchy.

History is attached to the state. Without the state there is no history: "The State is the Idea of Spirit [Mind] in the external manifestation of

---

† See Chapter 21 for a discussion of self-contained existence, the self as private property.

human Will and its Freedom. It is to the State, therefore, that change in the aspect of History indissolubly attaches itself." [9] History begins when the state begins to keep its own records. This is the state taking consciousness of itself.

Hegel seems to have a deep appreciation for India's culture, religion, poetry, and philosophy. Yet in Hegel's time, India fell outside the bounds of history because it had no constitution or state that kept records of itself. Hegel attributes this deficiency to the caste system, a system of bondage derived from nature that deprives the nation of a direction in which to develop. India is stagnant in time. It exists in the eternal present.

The state has one thing in common with religion, philosophy, and art: All unite the subjective and the objective and form a hierarchy of values, with the state and religion at the top. Religion shares top billing with the state because it "constitutes the general basis of a people's character." [10]

Each nation has a national spirit, a particular individuality. The individual internalizes this spirit, which becomes the basis for his character and identity, supplying him with a place in the world. An Englishman knows he is an Englishman.

## *Phases of History*

Initially, man is immersed in nature. There is a lack of differentiation. Gradually he separates himself from nature and becomes aware of his capacity for freedom.

Universal history begins in the East, the *childhood* of history, with the awareness that one is free. The despot rules. "The freedom of that one [ the despot] is only caprice; ferocity – brutal recklessness of passion.... That *one* is therefore only a Despot; not a *free man*." [11] In such a setting, subjects follow moral imperatives out of obedience, the way a child obeys a parent. They have no internalized sense of right and wrong.

Ancient Athens represents progress to the next phase, *adolescence*, the "boisterous and turbulent" phase. [12] There is awareness that some are free, but not all: There are slaves. Here we find individuals with a sense of morality and individual volition. However, they do not yet regard morality abstractly, "but immediately bound up with the Real, as in a beautiful work of *Art*." ‡ [13]

Rome represents the *manhood* of history. Rome is manhood because it "acts neither in accordance with the caprice of a despot [the orient], nor in obedience to a graceful caprice of its own [Athens]; but works for a general aim, one in which the individual perishes and realizes his own private object only in that general aim." [14] In other words, a true

---

‡   Hegel uses italics throughout his text.

man is he who chooses to sacrifice his well-being and his will to the will of the state.

In Rome, the "geniality and joy of soul" that characterized Athens have given way to "harsh and rigorous toil." On the one hand, Romans submit to the universal, an abstraction, and lose their individuality; however, by becoming at one with the state, which they embody, "in their individual capacity they become persons with definite rights as such."[15] The state recognizes them as individuals, separate from the state.

The strong Roman state produces strong individuals in opposition to it, leading to a new kind of despotism. In response to the pain inflicted by despotism, spirit withdraws into itself, "leaves the godless world, seeks for a harmony in itself, and begins now an inner life." Individual personality is purified "and elevated into universality," [16] leading to Christianity and the fourth and final phase.

The story of freedom, its unfolding and realization, culminates in *old age*—mind "in its perfect maturity and *strength*" [17]—as realized in the German nations under the influence of Christianity. The ultimate goal has been attained. There is general awareness that man as such is free. "*The final cause of the World at large*, we allege to be the *consciousness* of its own freedom on the part of Spirit [Mind], and *ipso facto*, the *reality* of that freedom."[18] This we learn "is God's purpose with the world." [19]

Living out this evolution from childhood to old age involves the union or interaction of two forces: the idea and passion. That union constitutes "Liberty, under the conditions of morality in a State." [20] The idea is God's contribution. Passion is man's contribution. Thus history is driven forward by reason–mind–God, living out his idea while using humankind as the *means* for doing so.

As the state becomes more and more entrenched, inertia builds up. Yet its idea, its essence seeks forward movement in further development. Forward movement finds its release in history's heroes. These "*World Historical Individuals*" operate on a general principle "of a different order from that on which depends the *permanence* of a people or a State." [21] They see farther and are inspired by a passion that drives them to take civilization to the next level. In driving a people to the next developmental stage, heroes operate outside the bounds of social morality and are not to be judged by the standards of private virtue.

For example, while striving for personal gain, Caesar, without knowing it, was also living out mind's plan for societal evolution. In this living out of mind's idea for the world, the particular, the individual is "too trifling a value as compared with the general: Individuals are sacrificed and abandoned" [22] to the grander ambition that someone like Caesar is able to enact.

Once a people has lived out and realized its national spirit, its idea, and all opposition has disappeared, the soul-spirit languishes. There is no forward movement, no vitality. "The essential, supreme interest has consequently vanished from its life, for interest is present only where there is opposition." [23] A people becomes a poison to itself, leading to death. However, as one phase in development perishes, it reveals itself in its final form. One can see the universal elements in its inherent principle, which "can be grasped in its universality thereby revealing the imminent potential of its next phase of development."[24]

What is left when the soul withers is what Hegel calls *"customary* life (the watch wound up and going on of itself)," which leads to natural death. "Individuals become isolated from each other and from the whole; aggressive selfishness and vanity prevail." [25] This, in fact, was Kitto's observation about ancient Athens in decline [§] and might apply as well to the United States in the twenty-first century. As Hegel observes,

> Thus perish individuals, thus perish peoples by a natural death; and though the latter may continue in being, it is an existence without intellect or vitality; having no need of its institutions, because the need for them is satisfied – a political nullity and tedium. In order that a truly universal interest may arise, the Spirit of a People must advance to the adoption of some new purpose; but when can this new purpose originate? It would be a higher more comprehensive conception of itself – a transcending of its principle – but this very act would involve a principle of anew order, a new National Spirit. [26]

## Commentary

There is something whimsical and arbitrary about Hegel's use of the word "freedom." Freedom in the abstract is nondependence, complete independence, even "self-contained existence." Yet its actualization seems to be the exact opposite: complete dependence on the state for one's place in the world and one's very identity. And it can certainly be no mere coincidence that God's plan for the world just happens to be that embodied by the German nations under Christianity, the very conditions being lived out by Hegel himself and which he clearly seems to favor.

Hegel's philosophy is based on the assumption that essence precedes existence. The idea of the thing precedes and determines the thing itself. This is what idealism is all about. Can one argue the opposite—that existence precedes essence? It is true that, for change to occur, consciousness of the desired change must precede it. There must be some vision of the desired state to be reached before it can be realized. Yet that vision is something that is created in reality in interaction with like-minded individuals. It does not exist in any absolute, a priori, sense.

Hegel's vision of government happens to be the warrior state, a state that is driven forward by the bloody deeds of its heroes who

---

§   See above, p.72.

operate outside the standards of accepted moral conduct. This is to be condoned, writes Hegel, because these heroes take civilization to its next step. I have argued earlier that true progress in society takes place despite its heroes, not because of them. Violence achieves nothing other than misery for its victims. Hegel seems to think this is the way it should be: Individual lives must be sacrificed to the unfolding of the universal ideal.

According to Hegel the only genuine form of government is the nation-state, a form of government that makes war with other nation-states. History is the history of what nation-states do. India presents him with a particular problem. As a civilization, when judged by its religion, philosophy, and poetry, India was obviously one of the most highly developed societies. Its sense of morality, its reverence for nature, and the richness of its culture reflect qualities that Hegel clearly admires. Yet India was not a nation-state. It had no conquests. And in Hegel's terms it had no history. But might not such a form of government be a desirable alternative to the nation-state? This is something to ponder.

Does a country wither and die when it has fulfilled its principle, has lived out its contradiction, and can no longer move ahead? It is Hegel's position that each society must constantly be striving toward a higher form of development, must constantly be in the process of superseding itself. If it does not, it settles into *"customary* life," withers, and dies. Yet what about the Athenians, living in a civilization that was home to "geniality and joy of soul?" Their striving was toward social justice and creative expression through the arts. Could not such a society long endure, if left to its own devices? It was war that brought them down, not an inner contradiction.

Do different nations have different principles or ideas that define their essence? Perhaps. I would say that the defining principle of ancient Athens was its government—democracy. To me, India's defining principle seems to be its religion. One could say that the defining principle of the United States is the accumulation of individual wealth through unending economic expansion. But I argue that these principles evolved over time and then eventually defined the people. They did not precede their existence.

Does history have direction? If so, what is that direction? What determines what the direction is? As I see it, if history has a direction, it is to establish a form of government that sanctifies individual existence and promotes the highest development of each and every citizen, an outcome that is conceived and realized by the citizens themselves. There is no history, as Hegel understands it. The striving he speaks of is the burden that society bears in overcoming the abuse of power by those whom Hegel considers to be its heroes. Such heroes have no place in a democracy.

# ENDNOTES

INTRODUCTION: THE SPECTER OF GOVERNMENT

1   Sheldon S. Wolin, *Democracy Incorporated: Managed Democracy and the Specter of Inverted Totalitarianism*, p. 44.
2   Ibid.
3   Ibid., p. 47.
4   Ibid., p. 57.
5   Ibid., p. 108.

CHAPTER 1: WHAT IS HISTORY AND WHY DOES IT MATTER?

1   Alexis de Tocqueville, *Democracy in America*, Vol. 2, pp. 92–93.
2   Hayden White, *Metahistory: The Historical Imagination in Nineteenth Century Europe*, p. 90.
3   Quoted in ibid., p. 107.
4   Quoted in ibid., p. 308.
5   Leo Tolstoy, *War and Peace*, p. 1101.
6   Ibid., p. 1104.
7   Ibid., p. 1110.
8   William Godwin, *Enquiry Concerning Political Justice and Its Influence on Morals and Happiness*, Book 1, chapter 2. Out of print; quotes cited herein are drawn from the online version cited in the Bibliography.
9   Sheldon Richman, "War Is a Government Program," May 31, 2007. Web; C. Wright Mills, *The Power Elite*, p. 202; Max Weber, *Political Writings*, pp. 310–311.
10  Randolph Bourne, "War Is the Health of the State." Web. This is the first part of Bourne's larger essay "The State," which was left unfinished at his death in 1918.
11  William Godwin, *Enquiry Concerning Political Justice and Its Influence on Morals and Happiness*, Book 1, chapter 2.
12  Anaïs Nin, *The Diary of Anaïs Nin*, Vol. 6, p. 400.

CHAPTER 2: FALSE FRIENDS

1   Quoted in Michael Parenti, *History as Mystery*, p. 23.
2   Quoted in Benjamin R. Barber, *Strong Democracy: Participatory Politics for a New Age*, p. 17.
3   Jean-Jacques Rousseau, *Du Contrat Social*, p. 280 (author's translation).
4   *The Federalist Papers*, No. 10, p. 81.
5   Ibid.
6   Ibid., p. 82.
7   Ibid., No. 55, p. 340.
8   Alexis de Tocqueville, *Democracy in America*, Vol. 1, p. 259.
9   Ibid., p. 209.
10  Ibid., p. 211.
11  Ibid., p. 249.
12  Ibid., p. 234.
13  Ibid., p. 262.
14  Ibid., p. 264.
15  Ibid., p. 269.
16  *The American Heritage College Dictionary*, 3rd Edition.
17  *Webster's New World Dictionary*, 2nd College Edition.
18  Alexis de Tocqueville, *Democracy in America*, Vol. 1, p. 272.
19  Ibid., p. 269.
20  Ibid., p. 267
21  Ibid., p. 273.

22    Ibid.
23    Ibid., p. 277.
24    John Stuart Mill, "On Liberty," in *Utilitarianism; On Liberty; Considerations on Representative Government; Remarks on Bentham's Philosophy*, p. 131.
25    John Stuart Mill, "Considerations on Representative Government," in *Utilitarianism; On Liberty; Considerations on Representative Government; Remarks on Bentham's Philosophy*, p. 223.
26    Ibid., p. 234.
27    Ibid., p. 342.
28    Ibid., p. 344.
29    Ibid., p. 346.
30    Ibid., p. 347.
31    Ibid., p. 348.
32    Ibid., pp. 306–307.
33    Ibid., p. 309.
34    Ibid., p. 310.
35    Ibid., p. 354.
36    Ibid., p. 356.
37    Bertrand Russell, *A History of Western Philosophy*, p. 190.
38    Edward Bernays, *Propaganda*, p. 71.
39    Ibid., p. 37.
40    Quoted in the *New York Times*, March 20, 1994.
41    Plato, *The Republic of Plato*, p. 128.
42    Quoted in M. I. Finley, *Democracy Ancient and Modern*, p. 4.
43    Quoted in Evan Esar, *20,000 Quips and Quotations*, p. 211.
44    Quoted in ibid., p. 212.
45    Quoted in ibid.
46    Even Esar, *20,000 Quips and Quotations*, pp. 211–213.
47    E. M. Forster, *Two Cheers for Democracy*, p. 70.
48    Quoted in Evan Esar, *20,000 Quips and Quotations*, p. 211.

### CHAPTER 3: ANCIENT ATHENS

1    M. I. Finley, *Democracy Ancient and Modern*, p. 59.
2    R. K. Sinclair, *Democracy and Participation in Athens*, p. 80.
3    Aristotle, *Politics*, p. 56.
4    Ibid., p. 209.
5    Ibid., p. 240.
6    Quoted in H. D. F. Kitto, *The Greeks*, pp. 145–146.
7    I. F. Stone, *The Trial of Socrates*, p. 136.
8    Ibid., p. 134.
9    Ibid., p. 29.
10    Quoted in ibid., p. 32.
11    Quoted in ibid., p. 117.

### CHAPTER 4: GOVERNMENT AND CHARACTER

1    John Stuart Mill, "Considerations on Representative Government," pp. 210–211.
2    Ibid., p. 220.
3    Ibid., p. 224.
4    Ibid., p. 227.
5    William Godwin, *Enquiry Concerning Political Justice and Its Influence on Morals and Happiness*, Book 1, chapter 4.
6    Ibid., Book 1, chapter 1.
7    Ibid., Book 1, chapter 4.
8    Max Weber, *Political Writings*, p. 205.
9    Aristotle, *Introduction to Aristotle*. 1947. Ed. Richard McKeon, p. 548.
10    Aristotle, *Politics*, pp. 288, 300.
11    Jean-Jacques Rousseau, *Confessions*, Book 9, quoted in Benjamin R. Barber, *Strong Democracy: Participatory Politics for a New Age*, p. 213, fn. 1.
12    Plato, *The Republic of Plato*, pp. 277–278.
13    Ibid., p. 282.
14    Ibid., p. 283.
15    Ibid., p. 285.
16    Ibid., p. 289.
17    I. F. Stone, *The Trial of Socrates*, p. 146.
18    M. I. Finley, *Democracy Ancient and Modern*, p. 171.
19    Werner Jaeger, *Paideia: The Ideals of Greek Culture*, Vol. 1, p. xxii.
20    Ibid., p. xix.

21  Ibid., p. xxii.
22  Ibid., p. xxvi.
23  Ibid., p. xxiii.
24  Ibid., p. xiii.
25  M. I. Finley, editor, *The Portable Greek Historians: The Essence of Herodotus, Thucydides, Xenophon, Polybius*, p. 254.
26  Quoted in I. F. Stone, *The Trial of Socrates*, p. 50.
27  Quoted in ibid., p. 53.
28  Quoted in ibid., p. 211.
29  Quoted in ibid., p. 48.
30  Charles Freeman, *The Greek Achievement*, p. 89.
31  John Stuart Mill, "Considerations on Representative Government," p. 233.
32  H. D. F. Kitto, *The Greeks*, p. 75.
33  Ibid., p. 28.
34  Ibid., p. 94.
35  Ibid., p. 98.
36  M. I. Finley, editor, *The Portable Greek Historians: The Essence of Herodotus, Thucydides, Xenophon, Polybius*, p. 267.
37  Ibid., p. 268.
38  Ibid., p. 269.
39  Ibid., p. 271.
40  Ibid., p. 273.
41  Kitto, *The Greeks*, pp. 158–159.
42  Ibid., p. 173.
43  Ibid., pp. 158–159.
44  R. K. Sinclair, *Democracy and Participation in Athens*, pp. 42–43.

## CHAPTER 5: THE ROMAN REPUBLIC

1  Harriet I. Flower, editor, *The Cambridge Companion to the Roman Republic*, p. 114.
2  Ibid., p. 124.
3  Ibid., p. 325.
4  *The Federalist Papers*, No. 34, p. 206.
5  Ibid., No. 10, p. 82.
6  Ibid., No. 63, p. 387.
7  *The Federalist Papers*, No. 55, p. 340.

## CHAPTER 6: EXPERIMENTS IN GOVERNMENT

1  Quoted in Daniel Waley, *The Italian City-Republics*, p. 65.
2  Quoted in ibid., p. 36.
3  Ibid., p. 138.
4  Jacob Burckhardt, *The Civilization of the Renaissance in Italy*, p. 95.
5  Quoted in Lauro Martines, *Power and Imagination, City-States in Renaissance Italy*, p. 129.
6  Quoted in ibid., p. 29.
7  See Daniel Waley, *The Italian City-Republics*, pp. 102–103.
8  Quoted in ibid., p. 157.
9  *On Princely Government*, quoted in John Dunn, editor, *Democracy: The Unfinished Journey, 508 B.C. to A.D. 1993*, p. 60.
10  Ibid., p. 61.
11  Jacob Burckhardt, *The Civilization of the Renaissance*, pp. 147–148.
12  Quoted in ibid., p. 174.

## CHAPTER 7: EARLY VOICES IN AMERICA

1  Quoted in Jackson Turner Main, *The Anti-Federalists: Critics of the Constitution 1781–1788*, p. 9.
2  Quoted in ibid.
3  Quoted in ibid.
4  *The Federalist Papers*, No. 1, p. 36.
5  Ibid., No. 55, p. 344.
6  Ibid., No. 64, p. 395.
7  Herbert J. Storing, editor, *The Anti-Federalist: Writings by the Opponents of the Constitution*, p. 351.
8  Ibid., p. 126.
9  Ibid., p. 291.
10  Jackson Turner Main, *The Anti-Federalists: Critics of the Constitution, 1781–1788*, p. 10.
11  Herbert J. Storing, editor, *The Anti-Federalist: Writings by the Opponents of the Constitution*, p. 109.

12  Ibid., p. 132.
13  Ibid., p. 304.
14  *The Federalist Papers*, No. 37, p. 227; No. 39, p. 241; No. 49, p. 314.
15  Ibid., No. 46, p. 294.
16  Ibid., No. 49, p. 313.
17  Ibid., No. 51, p. 321.
18  Ibid., No. 57, p. 353.
19  Ibid., No. 49, p. 313.
20  Ibid., p. 314.
21  Ibid.
22  Ibid., p. 315.
23  Ibid., p. 316.
24  Ibid., No. 11, p. 91.
25  Ibid., No. 23, p. 153.
26  Herbert J. Storing, editor, *The Anti-Federalist: Writings by the Opponents of the Constitution*, p. 305.
27  Ibid., p. 307.
28  Ibid., p. 146.
29  Ibid., p. 67.
30  Ibid., p. 94.
31  Ibid., p. 305.
32  Ibid., p. 267.
33  Ibid., p. 264.
34  Ibid., p. 271.
35  *The Federalist Papers*, No. 35, p. 214.
36  Ibid., p. 216.
37  Ibid., No. 36, p. 217.
38  Ibid., No. 71, p. 432.
39  Herbert J. Storing, editor, *The Anti-Federalist: Writings by the Opponents of the Constitution*, p. 214.
40  Ibid., p. 340.
41  Jackson Turner Main, *The Anti-Federalists: Critics of the Constitution, 1781–1788*, p. 142.
42  Herbert J. Storing, editor, *The Anti-Federalist: Writings by the Opponents of the Constitution*, p. 343.
43  Ibid., p. 126.
44  Ibid., p. 219.
45  Ibid., p. 214.
46  *The Federalist Papers*, No. 63, p. 384.
47  Herbert J. Storing, editor, *The Anti-Federalist: Writings by the Opponents of the Constitution*, p. 119.
48  *The Federalist Papers*, No. 55, p. 342.
49  Ibid., No. 63, p. 384.
50  Ibid., No. 51, p. 324.
51  Herbert J. Storing, editor, *The Anti-Federalist: Writings by the Opponents of the Constitution*, p. 249.
52  Ibid., p. 166.
53  Ibid., p. 122.
54  Ibid., p. 19.
55  Ibid., pp. 189–190.
56  Ibid., p. 289.
57  Ibid., p. 284.
58  Ibid., p. 111.
59  Ibid., p. 161.
60  Quoted in Ryan McMaken, "The 'Founding Fathers.'" Web.
61  Herbert J. Storing, editor, *The Anti-Federalist: Writings by the Opponents of the Constitution*, p. 150.
62  Ibid., p. 111.
63  Ibid., p. 49.
64  Ibid., p. 91.
65  Ibid., p. 138.
66  Ibid., p. 353.
67  Ibid., p. 163.
68  Ibid., pp. 182–183.

CHAPTER 8: DEMOCRACY DENIED

1  Woody Holton, *Unruly Americans and the Origins of the Constitution*, p. 128.
2  Ibid., p. 131.

3    Quoted in Howard Zinn, *A People's History of the United States: 1492–Present*, p. 91.
4    Ibid., p. 95.
5    George Washington, "George Washington to James Madison, 5 November 1786," *The Papers of George Washington*. Web.
6    Quoted in Charles Beard, *An Economic Interpretation of the Constitution*, p. 322.
7    Quoted in ibid., p. 306.
8    Quoted in ibid., p. 321.
9    Quoted in ibid., pp. 304–305.
10   Quoted in Kenneth C. Davis, *America's Hidden History: Untold Tales of the First Pilgrims, Fighting Women, and Forgotten Founders Who Shaped a Nation*, p. 227.
11   Charles Beard, *An Economic Interpretation of the Constitution*, p. 149.
12   Woody Holton, *Unruly Americans and the Origins of the Constitution*, p. 190.
13   Charles Beard, *An Economic Interpretation of the Constitution*, p. 161.
14   Quoted in ibid., p. 315.
15   Quoted in ibid., p. 197.
16   Quoted in ibid., p. 198.
17   Quoted in ibid., p. 199.
18   Quoted in ibid., p. 202.
19   Herbert J. Storing, editor, *The Anti-Federalist: Writings by the Opponents of the Constitution*, p. 234.
20   Quoted in Main, *Anti-Federalists: Critics*, pp. 187–188.
21   Quoted in Charles Beard, *An Economic Interpretation of the Constitution*, pp. 231–232.
22   Ibid., p. 232.
23   Ibid.
24   Quoted in Herbert J. Storing, editor, *The Anti-Federalist: Writings by the Opponents of the Constitution*, p. 204.
25   Quoted in ibid., p. 206.
26   Quoted in Jackson Turner Main, *The Anti-Federalists: Critics of the Constitution, 1781–1788*, p. 202.
27   Quoted in ibid., p. 222.
28   Quoted in ibid., p. 250.
29   Max Weber, *Political Writings*, p. 311.
30   Gore Vidal, *The Second American Revolution and Other Essays (1976–1982)*, p. 250.
31   Quoted in Woody Holton, *Unruly Americans and the Origins of the Constitution*, p. 10.
32   Quoted in ibid., p. 206.
33   See Herman Husband, *Proposals to Amend and Perfect the Policy of the Government of the United States of America*.
34   Quoted in Woody Holton, *Unruly Americans and the Origins of the Constitution*, p. 166.
35   Quoted in ibid., p. 210.
36   Herbert J. Storing, editor, *The Anti-Federalist: Writings by the Opponents of the Constitution*, p. 146.
37   Ibid., p. 67.

## CHAPTER 9: AMERICA'S EARLY OLIGARCHY

1    George Mason, "Objections to the Constitution of Government Formed by the Convention," ca. September 17, 1787. Web.
2    Quoted in Charles Beard, *An Economic Interpretation of the Constitution*, pp. 223–224.
3    Quoted in ibid., pp. 224–225.
4    Herbert J. Storing, editor, *The Anti-Federalist: Writings by the Opponents of the Constitution*, p. 78.
5    Ibid., p. 76.
6    Ibid., p. 232.
7    Ibid., p. 287.
8    Ibid., p. 159.
9    Ibid., p. 203.
10   Quoted in Gore Vidal, *The Second American Revolution and Other Essays (1976–1982)*, p. 255.
11   Quoted in Andrew Shankman, *Crucible of American Democracy: The Struggle to Fuse Egalitarianism and Capitalism in Jeffersonian Pennsylvania*, p. 19.
12   Quoted in Jerry Fresia, *Toward an American Revolution: Exposing the Constitution and Other Illusions*, p. 19.
13   *The Federalist Papers*, No. 10, p. 77.
14   Ibid., p. 78.
15   See Richard Shenkman, *Gaining Power at Any Cost: Presidential Ambition*, chapter 1.
16   Joseph J. Ellis, *His Excellency: George Washington*, p. xiv.
17   Ibid., p. 46.
18   Ibid., p. 260.
19   Ibid., p. 184.

## CHAPTER 10: ALEXANDER HAMILTON AND THE BRITISH CONNECTION

1  Ron Chernow, *Alexander Hamilton*, p. 158.
2  Ibid., p. 156.
3  Quoted in Gore Vidal, *Inventing a Nation: Washington, Adams, Jefferson*, p. 105.
4  Quoted in Thomas Lloyd, *The Congressional Register: Or, History of the Proceedings and Debates of the First House of Representatives of the United States of America*, Vol. 1, p. 185.
5  Gore Vidal, *Inventing a Nation: Washington, Adams, Jefferson*, p. 95.
6  *Journal of the Senate of the United States of America, Being the First Session of the Twenty-Second Congress,* Web. pp. 433–446.
7  Ibid., p. 434.
8  Ibid., p. 437.
9  Ibid., p. 438.
10  Quoted in Alexander James, "The History of Money." Web.
11  See Gore Vidal, *Inventing a Nation: Washington, Adams, Jefferson*, p. 33.
12  See Ron Chernow, *Alexander Hamilton*, p. 237.
13  Quoted in ibid., p. 564.
14  Quoted in ibid., p. 562.
15  Quoted in ibid., p. 568.
16  Quoted in ibid., p. 566.
17  Quoted in ibid., p. 553.
18  Quoted in Garry Wills, *James Madison*, p. 62.

## CHAPTER 11: DEMOCRACY AFFIRMED

1  Alan Taylor, *American Colonies: The Settling of North America*, p. 264.
2  Quoted in ibid., p. 266.
3  Quoted in ibid., pp. 271–272.
4  Quoted in Andrew Shankman, *Crucible of American Democracy: The Struggle to Fuse Egalitarianism and Capitalism in Jeffersonian Pennsylvania*, p. 4.
5  J. Paul Selsam, *The Pennsylvania Constitution of 1776*, p. 53.
6  Ibid., p. 93.
7  Quoted in ibid., p. 113.
8  Quoted in ibid., p. 116.
9  Quoted in ibid., p. 120.
10  Quoted in ibid., p. 121.
11  Quoted in ibid., p. 139.
12  Quoted in ibid., p. 144.
13  Quoted in ibid., p. 145.
14  Quoted in ibid., p. 148.
15  Quoted in ibid., p. 159.
16  Quoted in ibid., p. 190.
17  Quoted in ibid.
18  Quoted in ibid., p. 193.

## CHAPTER 12: THE STRUGGLE CONTINUES

1  Quoted in Andrew Shankman, *Crucible of American Democracy: The Struggle to Fuse Egalitarianism and Capitalism in Jeffersonian Pennsylvania*, p. 67.
2  Quoted in ibid., p. 68.
3  Quoted in ibid., p. 80.
4  Quoted in ibid., p. 86.
5  Ibid., p. 186.
6  Ibid., p. 229.
7  Quoted ibid., p. 225.
8  Quoted in ibid., p. 166.
9  Quoted in ibid., p. 157.

## CHAPTER 13: DEMOCRACY DEFINED

1  John G. Gunnell, *Political Philosophy and Time*, p. 40.
2  Ibid., p. 107.
3  J. Paul Selsam, *The Pennsylvania Constitution of 1776*, p. 148.
4  *The Federalist Papers*, No. 49, p. 314.
5  Vandana Shiva, *Earth Democracy: Justice, Sustainability, and Peace*, p. 8.
6  Ibid., p. 91.
7  Ibid., p. 82.
8  Edward Bernays, *Propaganda*, p. 37.
9  Samuel Noah Kramer, *Cradle of Civilization*, p. 34.

## CHAPTER 14: AMERICAN GOVERNMENT

1  Max Weber, *Political Writings*, pp. 268–269.
2  Alexis de Tocqueville, *Democracy in America*, Vol. 2, p. 4.
3  Ibid., p. 78.
4  Ibid., p. 43.
5  Ibid., p. 44.
6  Ibid., p. 258.
7  Ibid., p. 63.
8  Ibid., p. 64.
9  Ibid., p. 275.
10  Ibid., Vol. 1, pp. 274–275.
11  Ibid., p. 277.
12  Ibid., Vol. 2, p. 83.
13  Ibid., p. 183.
14  Ibid., p. 147.
15  Ibid., p. 144.
16  Ibid., p. 311.
17  Ibid., p. 336.
18  Ralph Waldo Emerson, *The Journals and Miscellaneous Notebooks of Ralph Waldo Emerson*, Vol. 3, *1826–1832*, p. 99.
19  Ralph Waldo Emerson, *Emerson's Essays*, p. 38.
20  Ibid., p. 77.
21  Ralph Waldo Emerson, *Selections from Ralph Waldo Emerson*, p. 61.
22  Philip E. Slater, *The Pursuit of Loneliness*, p. xii.
23  Anaïs Nin, *The Diary of Anaïs Nin*, Vol. 3, *1939–1944*, p. 14.
24  Ibid., p. 28.
25  Ibid., p. 34.
26  Philip E. Slater, *The Pursuit of Loneliness*, p. 7.
27  Ibid., p. 9.
28  Ibid., p. 131.
29  Ibid., p. 110.
30  Ibid., p. 1.
31  See Morris Berman, *Dark Ages America: The Final Phase of Empire*, p. 143.
32  Ibid., p. 239.
33  Ibid., p. 237.
34  Ibid., p. 240.
35  Ibid., p. 249.
36  Ibid., p. 284.
37  Ibid., p. 282.
38  Ibid., p. 252.
39  Ibid., p. 253.
40  Quoted in ibid., p. 236.
41  Quoted in ibid., p. 282.
42  Alexis de Tocqueville, *Democracy in America*, Vol. 2, p. 117.
43  Ibid., p. 56.
44  Ibid., p. 317.
45  Ibid., p. 109.
46  Ibid., p. 149.
47  Ibid., p. 150.
48  Ibid., p. 335.
49  Ibid., pp. 336–337.
50  Ibid., p. 337.
51  Ibid.
52  Ibid., p. 339.
53  Ibid.
54  C. Wright Mills, *The Power Elite*, p. 253.
55  Ibid., p. 300.
56  Ibid., p. 306.
57  Ibid., p. 308.
58  Ibid.
59  Ibid., p. 309.
60  Ibid.
61  Ibid., p. 311.
62  Ibid., p. 312.
63  Ibid., p. 315.
64  Alexis de Tocqueville, *Democracy in America*, Vol. 2, p. 149.
65  C. Wright Mills, *The Power Elite*, p. 317.

66  Ibid., p. 319.
67  Ibid., p. 321.
68  Ibid., p. 322.
69  Alexis de Tocqueville, *Democracy in America*, Vol. 2, p. 337.
70  C. Wright Mills, *The Power Elite*, p. 316.
71  Ibid., p. 317.
72  Ibid., p. 331.
73  Ibid., p. 336.
74  Alexis de Tocqueville, *Democracy in America*, Vol. 2, p. 337.

CHAPTER 15: DEMOCRACY AS MYTH

1   Michael Margolis, *Viable Democracy*, p. 26.
2   Ibid., p. 27.
3   Ibid., p. 30.
4   Ibid., p. 42.
5   Ibid., p. 73.
6   Ibid., p. 99.
7   Ibid., p. 101.
8   Ibid, p. 120.
9   Ibid., p. 165.
10  Ibid., p. 175.
11  *The Federalist Papers*, No. 10, pp. 81–82.
12  Charles-Louis de Secondat, Baron de La Brède et de Montesquieu, *De l'Esprit des Lois*, pp. 11–12.
13  *American Heritage College Dictionary*, 3rd Edition.
14  *The Federalist Papers*, No. 6, p. 57.
15  Ibid., No. 10, pp. 81–82.
16  Ibid., No. 14, p. 100.
17  Ibid., No. 39, p. 241.
18  Thomas Paine, *The Complete Writings of Thomas Paine*, p. 369.
19  Aristotle, *Introduction to Aristotle*. 1947. Ed. Richard McKeon, p. 591.
20  Quoted in Jacques Barzun, *From Dawn to Decadence: 500 Years of Western Cultural Life*, p. 93.
21  Gaetano Mosca, *The Ruling Class*, p. 98.
22  Ibid., p. 154.
23  Ibid.
24  Ibid., p. 155.
25  *The Federalist Papers*, No. 37, p. 227; No. 39, p. 241; No. 49, p. 314.
26  Ibid., No. 46, p. 294.
27  Ibid., No. 49, p. 313.
28  Ibid., No. 51, p. 321.
29  Joshua Miller, *The Rise and Fall of Democracy in Early America, 1630–1789*, p. 105.
30  Ibid., p. 106.
31  Ibid., p. 113.
32  Ibid., p. 121.
33  Quoted in Aristotle, *Introduction to Aristotle*. 1947. Ed. Richard McKeon, p. 550.
34  Quoted in ibid., p. 604.
35  Max Weber, *Political Writings*, p. 275.

CHAPTER 16: THE BATTLEFIELD AFTER THE BATTLE

1   M. I. Finley, *The Portable Greek Historians: The Essence of Herodotus, Thucydides, Xenophon, Polybius*, p. 371.
2   Ibid., p. 377.
3   Ibid., p. 379.
4   Quoted in Victor Davis Hanson, *Carnage and Culture: Landmark Battles in the Rise of Western Power*, p. 174.
5   Quoted in ibid., p. 192.
6   Quoted at "An Iraqi Lieutenant's War Diary." Web.
7   Guy MacLean Rogers, *Alexander: The Ambiguity of Greatness*, p. 198.
8   Ibid., p. 71.
9   Ibid., p. xviii.
10  Ibid., p. 166.
11  Ibid., p. 266.
12  Ibid., p. 240.
13  Ibid., p. 154.
14  Ibid., p. 125.

15    Ibid., pp. 90–91.
16    Ibid., p. 50.
17    Ibid., p. 125.
18    Ibid., p. 54.
19    Ibid., p. 73.
20    Ibid., p. 169.
21    Ibid., p. 187.
22    Ibid., p. 226.
23    Ibid., p. 281.
24    Ibid., p. 282.
25    Ibid., p. 294.
26    Ibid., p. 282.
27    Ibid., p. 293.
28    Ibid., p. 283.
29    Ibid., p. 286.
30    Ibid., p. 115.
31    Ibid., p. 284.
32    Ibid., p. 219.
33    Ibid., p. 200.
34    Ibid., p. 125.
35    Ibid., p. 126.
36    Ibid., p. 271.
37    Ibid., p. 220.
38    Quoted in Charles Freeman, *The Greek Achievement*, p. 320.
39    Charles J. Halperin, *Russia and the Golden Horde: The Mongol Impact on Medieval Russian History*, p. 23.
40    Ibid., p. 22.
41    Ibid., p. 73.
42    Ibid.
43    Ibid., p. 33.
44    Ibid., p. 93.
45    Ibid., pp. 75–76.
46    Ibid., p. 87.
47    Ibid., p. 96.
48    Ibid., p. 83.
49    Ibid., p. 86.
50    Ibid.
51    Jack Weatherford, *Genghis Kahn and the Making of the Modern World*, p. xix.
52    Quoted in ibid., p. 154.
53    Ibid., p. 127.
54    Ibid., p. 109.
55    Quoted in ibid., p. 113.
56    Ibid., p. 112.
57    http://en.wikipedia.org/wiki/Mongol_Empire.
58    http://necrometrics.com/pre1700a.htm.
59    Quoted in Jack Weatherford, *Genghis Kahn and the Making of the Modern World*, p. 254.
60    Quoted in ibid., p. 255.
61    Ibid., p. 262.
62    Ibid., p. 267.
63    Quoted in Robert Wallace, *Rise of Russia*, p. 55.
64    Quoted in Jack Weatherford, *Genghis Kahn and the Making of the Modern World*, pp. 148–149.
65    Quoted at http://schools-wikipedia.org/wp/m/Mongol_Empire.htm.
66    Robert Wallace, *Rise of Russia*, p. 60.

## CHAPTER 17: POWER CONCEALED

1    *American Heritage College Dictionary*, 3rd Edition.
2    Karen Armstrong, *Holy War: The Crusades and Their Impact on Today's World*, p. 67.
3    Quoted at http://en.wikipedia.org/wiki/Fourth_Crusade.
4    J. Pirenne, *History of the Universe*. Quoted from Auguste Toussaint, *History of the Indian Ocean*. Web.
5    Quoted from Toussaint, *History of the Indian Ocean*. Web.
6    Vandana Shiva, *Earth Democracy: Justice, Sustainability, and Peace*, p. 29.
7    Quoted in Lion M. G. Agrawal, *Freedom Fighters of India*, p. 43.
8    Quoted in Christopher Herbert, *War of No Pity: The Indian Mutiny and Victorian Trauma*, p. 180.
9    Alexander Cockburn, "How the British Destroyed India." *See also* Mukerjee,  Madhusree. *Churchill's Secret War: The British Empire and the Ravaging of India during World War II*.
10    http://en.wikipedia.org/wiki/Bengal_famine_of_1943.

11    Ibid.
12    Joseph R. Strayer, "The Two Levels of Feudalism," in *Life and Thought in the Early Middle Ages*, edited by Robert S. Hoyt, pp. 51–52.
13    Joseph R. Strayer, *Western Europe in the Middle Ages*, pp. 74–75.
14    Peter Linebaugh, *The Magna Carta Manifesto: Liberty and Commons for All*, p. 102.
15    http://www.answers.com/topic/enclosure-4.
16    Karl Marx, "The Duchess of Sutherland and Slavery," reproduced at http://www.marxists.org/archive/marx/works/1853/03/12.htm.
17    Quoted in Peter Linebaugh, *The Magna Carta Manifesto: Liberty and Commons for All*, pp. 142–143.
18    Ibid., p. 77.
19    Vandana Shiva, *Earth Democracy: Justice, Sustainability, and Peace*, p. 8.
20    Ibid., p. 9.
21    Ibid., p. 30.
22    Ibid., p. 46.
23    Ibid., p. 21.
24    Ibid., p. 54.

## CHAPTER 18: POWER REVEALED

1     J. Christopher Herold, *The Age of Napoleon*, p. 65.
2     Ibid., p. 78.
3     Ibid., p. 60.
4     Ibid., pp. 365–366.
5     Ibid., p. 342.
6     Ibid., p. 181.
7     Ibid., p. 182.
8     Ibid., p. 183.
9     Ibid., p. 218.
10    Quoted in ibid., p. 182.
11    Quoted in ibid., p. 352.
12    Quoted in ibid., pp. 352–253.
13    Quoted in ibid., p. 356.
14    Ibid., p. 67.
15    Quoted in ibid., p. 68.
16    Quoted in ibid., p. 69.
17    Ibid.
18    Ibid., p. 75.
19    Ibid., p. 76.
20    "French Constitution of 1793." Web.
21    Quoted in J. Christopher Herold, *The Age of Napoleon*, p. 131.
22    Quoted in ibid., p. 287.
23    Quoted in ibid., pp. 18–19.
24    Quoted in ibid., p. 147.
25    Quoted in ibid.
26    Ibid., p. 149.
27    Ibid., pp. 165–166.
28    Ibid., p. 295.
29    J. Christopher Herold, *The Age of Napoleon*, p. 31.
30    Quoted in ibid., p. 412.
31    Quoted in ibid.
32    Ibid., p. 409.
33    Quoted in ibid., pp. 413–414.
34    Quoted in ibid., pp. 416–417.
35    Quoted in ibid., p. 417.
36    Ibid., p. 435.

## CHAPTER 19: DARKNESS VISIBLE

1     Evan Esar, *20,000 Quips and Quotations*. pp. 613–615, 848.
2     Max Weber, *Political Writings*, p. 179.
3     William Godwin, *Enquiry Concerning Political Justice and Its Influence on Morals and Happiness*, Book 5, chapter 15.
4     Ibid.
5     Sheldon S. Wolin, *Democracy Incorporated: Managed Democracy and the Specter of Inverted Totalitarianism*, p. 261.
6     Ibid., p. 6.
7     Morris Berman, *Dark Ages America: The Final Phase of Empire*, p. 166.

8    Matt Taibbi, "The Great American Bubble Machine."
9    Gretchen Morgenson and Don van Natta Jr., "Paulson's Calls to Goldman Tested Ethics."
10   Quoted in Woody Holton, *Unruly Americans and the Origins of the Constitution*, p. 7.
11   Ibid., p. 5.
12   Ibid., p. 9.
13   Ibid., pp. 108–109.
14   Ibid., p. 37.
15   Ibid., p. 95.
16   Ibid., p. 122.
17   Ibid.
18   Ibid., pp. 123.
19   Ibid., p. 44.
20   Henry George, *Progress and Poverty*, p. 546.
21   Quoted by Darryl Schoon, "Davos Debt & Denial." Web.
22   Ibid.

## CHAPTER 20: THE PATHOLOGY OF POWER

1    John Emerich Edward Dalberg-Acton [Lord Acton], *Historical Essays and Studies*, appendix. Web.
2    Sigmund Freud, "Thoughts for the Times on War and Death," pp. 281ff., quoted in Hans-Jürgen Wirth, "9/11 as a Collective Trauma," p. 364.
3    The English translation of this article was transmitted to Lloyd deMause, editor of *The Journal of Psychohistory*, who then distributed it to readers on the Psychohistory list on October 17, 2001. The Psychohistory list discussion group can be found at http://www.psychohistory.com/htm/11_discussion.html.
4    Alice Miller, *Banished Knowledge*, p. 143.
5    From Adler's 1928 article "The Psychology of Power," quoted in the Adlerian Translation Project Archives at the Alfred Adler Institute of San Francisco. Web.
6    Philip E. Slater, *The Glory of Hera: Greek Mythology and the Greek Family*, p. 25.
7    Ibid., p. 8.
8    Ibid., p. 28.
9    Ibid., p. 29.
10   Ibid., p. 30.
11   Ibid., p. 33.
12   Ibid.
13   Quoted in ibid., p. 43.
14   Ibid.
15   George H. Pollock, "Process and Affect: Mourning and Grief." Quoted at http://en.wikipedia.org/wiki/Malignant_narcissism.
16   Otto F. Kernberg, "The Psychotherapeutic Management of Psychopathic, Narcissistic, and Paranoid Transferences."
17   James Duffy, October 23, 2004, personal communication.
18   Ibid.
19   Chris Floyd, "Churchill—Drunk with Thrill of Genocide," http://www.rense.com/general47/thil.htm.
20   Quoted in William Loren Katz, "Iraq, the US and an Old Lesson."
21   Ibid.
22   Ibid.
23   Stanley Rosenman, "The Usurpation of Identity," p. 195.
24   Ibid.
25   Arno Gruen, "An Unrecognized Pathology: The Mask of Humaneness," p. 266.
26   Ibid., p. 268.
27   Ibid., p. 267.
28   Hervey Milton Cleckley, *The Mask of Sanity*, pp. 404–406.
29   Arno Gruen, *The Insanity of Normality: Toward Understanding Human Destructiveness*, p. 163.
30   Ibid., p. 15.
31   Ibid., pp. 94–95.
32   Ibid., p. 149.
33   Ibid., p. 134.
34   Ibid., p. 133.
35   Alfred Adler, "The Psychology of Power," quoted in the Adlerian Translation Project Archives at the Alfred Adler Institute of San Francisco. Web.
36   Quoted in David McCullough, *John Adams*, p. 70.
37   Herbert J. Storing, editor, *The Anti-Federalist: Writings by the Opponents of the Constitution*, p. 290.

## CHAPTER 21: THE PATHOLOGY OF POLITICAL DISENGAGEMENT

1   John Wikse, *About Possession: The Self as Private Property*, p. 6.
2   Ibid., p. 46.
3   Quoted in ibid., p. 96.
4   Ralph Waldo Emerson, *Selections from Ralph Waldo Emerson*, edited by S. Wicher, p. 146.
5   Walt Whitman, *Leaves of Grass*, edited by S. Bradley, p. 499.
6   Alexis de Tocqueville, *Democracy in America*, Vol. 1, p. 97.
7   Ibid., p. 96.
8   Alexis de Tocqueville, *Democracy in America*, Vol. 2, pp. 105–106.
9   John Wikse, *About Possession: The Self as Private Property*, p. 50.
10  Benjamin R. Barber, *Strong Democracy: Participatory Politics for a New Age*, p. 71.
11  Ayn Rand, *The Fountainhead*, quoted in ibid.
12  Robert J. Pranger, *The Eclipse of Citizenship: Power and Participation in Contemporary Politics*, p. 99.
13  Hannah Arendt, *The Human Condition*, p. 208.
14  Benjamin R. Barber, *Strong Democracy: Participatory Politics for a New Age*, pp. 64–65.
15  Erik H. Erikson, "Ego Development and Historical Change," p. 126.
16  Erik H. Erikson, quoted in David J. de Levita, *The Concept of Identity*, p. 6.
17  Erik H. Erikson, "Ego Development and Historical Change," p. 141.
18  Francis Barker, *The Political Thought of Plato and Aristotle*, p. 57, quoted in Wikse, *About Possession*, p. 6.
19  Quoted in John Wikse, *About Possession: The Self as Private Property*, p. 7.
20  Sebastian De Grazia, *The Political Community: A Study of Anomie*, p. 5.
21  Quoted in ibid., p. xiii.
22  Ibid., p. 37.
23  Ibid., p. 95.
24  Ibid., p. 21.
25  Ibid., p. 48.
26  Wilhelm Reich, "The Imposition of Sexual Morality," in *Sex-Pol: Essays 1929–1934*, edited by Lee Baxandall, p. 110.

## CHAPTER 22: EMPOWERMENT AND THE PROCESS OF CHANGE

1   Sheldon S. Wolin, *Democracy Incorporated: Managed Democracy and the Specter of Inverted Totalitarianism*, p. 123.
2   Arno Gruen, *The Insanity of Normality: Toward Understanding Human Destructiveness*, p. 65.
3   Thomas Paine, *The Complete Writings of Thomas Paine*, p. 375.
4   Ibid., p. 351.
5   James Duffy, October 23, 2004, personal communication.
6   Quoted in Charles Beard, *An Economic Interpretation of the Constitution*, p. 295.
7   Quoted at John Quincy Adams, "On U.S. Foreign Policy." Web.
8   Henry George, *Social Problems*, p. 242.
9   Paulo Freire, *Education for Critical Consciousness*, p. 4.
10  Helen Merrell Lynd, *On Shame and the Search for Identity*, p. 31.
11  Ibid., p. 34.
12  Ibid., p. 66.
13  Leo Tolstoy, *Anna Karenina*, p. 120.
14  Helen Merrell Lynd, *On Shame and the Search for Identity*, p. 46.
15  Ibid., pp. 56–57.
16  Leo Tolstoy, *Anna Karenina*, pp. 154–155.

## CHAPTER 23: THE DEMOCRATIC PROCESS

1   Philip E. Slater, *A Dream Deferred: America's Discontent and the Search for a New Democratic Ideal*, p. 148.
2   Roy Madron and John Jopling, *Gaian Democracies: Redefining Globalisation and People-Power*, pp. 54–56.
3   Ibid., pp. 58–59.
4   Ibid., p. 65.
5   Ibid., pp. 54–56.
6   Philip E. Slater, *A Dream Deferred: America's Discontent and the Search for a New Democratic Ideal*, pp. 19–20.
7   Ibid., p. 178.
8   Paulo Freire, *Education for Critical Consciousness*, p. 6.
9   Ibid., p. 13.
10  Ibid., p. 45.
11  Philip E. Slater, *A Dream Deferred: America's Discontent and the Search for a New Democratic Ideal*, p. 154.

12   Ibid., p. 179.
13   Ibid.
14   Ibid., p. 182.
15   Benjamin R. Barber, *Strong Democracy: Participatory Politics for a New Age*, p. xvi.
16   Ibid., p. 35.
17   Ibid., p. 37.
18   Ibid., p. 40.
19   Ibid., p. 53.
20   Ibid., p. 62.
21   Ibid.
22   Ibid., p. 63.
23   Ibid., pp. 64–65.
24   Philip E. Slater, *A Dream Deferred: America's Discontent and the Search for a New Democratic Ideal*, pp. 155.
25   Harry Emerson Fosdick, quoted in ibid., p. 181.
26   Benjamin R. Barber, *Strong Democracy: Participatory Politics for a New Age*, p. 118.
27   Ibid., p. 136.
28   Ibid., pp. 120–121.
29   Ibid., p. 121.
30   Ibid.
31   Quoted in ibid., p. 121.
32   Ibid., p. 122.
33   Ibid., p. 126.
34   Ibid., p. 128.
35   Ibid., p. 154.
36   Ibid., pp. 154–155.
37   Ibid., p. 155.
38   Ibid., p. 129.
39   Ibid., p. 175.
40   Quoted in ibid., p. 184.
41   Ibid., p. 197.
42   Ibid.
43   Ibid., p. 185.
44   Jean-Jacques Rousseau, *Du Contrat Social*, book 1, chapter 8, quoted in ibid., p. 232.
45   Benjamin R. Barber, *Strong Democracy: Participatory Politics for a New Age*, p. 198.
46   Ibid., p. 259.
47   Ibid., p. 188.

## CHAPTER 24: DEMOCRATIZING THE OLIGARCHY

1    David Cay Johnston, *Free Lunch: How the Wealthiest Americans Enrich Themselves at Government Expense and Stick You with the Bill*, p. 235.
2    Herbert J. Storing, editor, *The Anti-Federalist: Writings by the Opponents of the Constitution*, p. 19.
3    R. K. Sinclair, *Democracy and Participation in Athens*, p. 80.
4    Aristotle, *Politics*, p. 56.
5    Ibid., p. 209.
6    Ibid., p. 240.
7    Alexis de Tocqueville, *Democracy in America*, Vol. 1, pp. 141–142.
8    Quoted in Vandana Shiva, *Earth Democracy: Justice, Sustainability, and Peace*, p. 97.
9    Gregory A. Fossedal, *Direct Democracy in Switzerland*, p. 84.
10   Ellen Brown, "Growing Number of Candidates Campaign for State-Owned Banks."

## CHAPTER 25: THE EXECUTIVE

1    Martin, Harry V. "The Executive Order: A Presidential Power Not Designated by the Constitution." *Freeamerica*, 1995. web.

## CHAPTER 26: DIVERSITY IN THE EAST

1    Fareed Zakaria, *The Post-American World*, p.153.
2    Ibid., p. 156.
3    Ibid., p. 162.
4    Ramachandra Guha, *India After Gandhi: The History of the World's Largest Democracy*, p.162.
5    Ibid., pp. 116–117.
6    Ibid., p. 209
7    Ibid., p. 210.
8    Ibid., pp. 143–159.
9    Ibid., p. 206.

10   Ibid., p. 757
11   Fareed Zakaria, *The Post-American World*, p. 144.
12   Ibid., p. 142.
13   Ibid., p. 161.
14   Ibid., p. 145.
15   Ibid., pp. 162–163.

CHAPTER 27: DEMOCRACY COME TRUE

1    Benjamin R. Barber, *Strong Democracy: Participatory Politics for a New Age*, p. 269.
2    Ibid., p. 270
3    Ibid., p. 302.
4    Ibid., p. 308.
5    Quoted in Hannah Arendt, *On Revolution*, p. 250.
6    Thomas Jefferson, *The Portable Thomas Jefferson*, pp. 556–557.
7    Quoted in Hannah Arendt, *On Revolution.*, p. 253.
8    Quoted in ibid., p. 254.
9    Ibid., p. 274.
10   Ibid., p. 277.
11   Jürgen Habermas, "Popular Sovereignty as Procedure," in James Bohman and William Regh, editors, *Deliberative Democracy: Essays on Reason and Politics*, p. 39.
12   Ibid.
13   Ibid., p. 40.
14   Ibid., pp. 40–41.
15   Quoted in ibid., p. 46.
16   Ibid., p. 47.
17   Ibid., p. 53.
18   Ibid., p. 55.
19   Stephen Shalom, "A Political System for a Good Society," p. 1. Web.
20   Ibid., p. 3.
21   Ibid., p. 5.
22   Ibid., p. 257.
23   Ibid., p. 252.
24   Ibid., p. 266.
25   Max Weber, *Political Writings*, p. 144.
26   Ibid., p. 180.
27   Ibid., p. 25.
28   Ibid., p. 182.
29   Ibid. p. 20
30   Ibid., p. 16.
31   Ibid., p. 107.
32   Ibid., p. 132.
33   Ibid., p. 124.

CONCLUSION: THE CITIZEN STATE

1    Quoted in a Wikipedia article on the Twenty-Second Amendment with the following reference, "Thomas Jefferson: Reply to the Legislature of Vermont, 1807. ME 16:293."
2    Quoted in Eugene Perry Link, *Democratic-Republican Societies, 1790–1800*, p. 100.
3    Ibid., p.104.
4    Thomas Paine, *The Complete Writings of Thomas Paine*, p. 347.
5    Ibid., p.45.

APPENDIX: HEGEL'S PHILOSOPHY OF HISTORY

1    George Wilhelm Friedrich Hegel, *The Philosophy of History*, pp. 17–18
2    Ibid, p. 9
3    Ibid., p. 13
4    Ibid., p. 17
5    Ibid.
6    Ibid., p. 25
7    Ibid., p. 39
8    Ibid., p. 48
9    Ibid., p. 47
10   Ibid., p. 50
11   Ibid., p. 18
12   Ibid., p. 106
13   Ibid.
14   Ibid., p. 107

15    Ibid.
16    Ibid., p. 108
17    Ibid., p. 109
18    Ibid., p. 19
19    Ibid., p. 20
20    Ibid., p. 23
21    Ibid., p. 29
22    Ibid., p. 33
23    Ibid., p. 74
24    Ibid., p. 78
25    Ibid., pp. 76–77
26    Ibid., p.75

# BIBLIOGRAPHY

Adams, John. *Defence of the Constitutions of Government of the United States of America....* London, 1787. Reprinted by The Lawbook Exchange, Clark, NJ, 2001. Print.

Adams, John Quincy. 1821. "On U.S. Foreign Policy." Web. <http://www.fff.org/comment/AdamsPolicy.asp>.

Adler, Alfred. "The Psychology of Power," *in* Franz Kobler (ed.), *Gewalt und Gewaltlosogkeit: Handbuch des activen Pazifismus.* Zurich: Rotapfel-Verlag, 1928. Excerpts quoted in the Adlerian Translation Project Archives at the Alfred Adler Institute of San Francisco. Web. <http://pws.cablespeed.com/~htstein/qu-power.htm>.

Agrawal, Lion M. G. *Freedom Fighters of India.* Delhi, India: ISHA Books, 2008. Print.

Alperovitz, Gar. *America Beyond Capitalism: Reclaiming Our Wealth, Our Liberty and Our Democracy.* New York: Wiley, 2011. Print.

*The American Heritage College Dictionary*, 3rd edition. New York: Houghton Mifflin, 1993. Print.

Ames, Mark. "Is Larry Summers Taking Kickbacks from the Banks He's Bailing Out?" *AlterNet*, May 29, 2009. Web. <http://www.alternet.org/economy/140327/is_larry_summers_taking_kickbacks_from_the_banks_he's_bailing_out/>.

"An Iraqi Lieutenant's War Diary." 1991. Web. <http://library.thinkquest.org/18220/gulfwar/diary.html>.

Arendt, Hannah. *The Human Condition.* Chicago: University of Chicago Press, 1958. Print.

—-. *Life of the Mind.* Ed. Mary McCarthy, 2 vols. New York: Harcourt Brace Jovanovich, 1978. Print.

—-. *On Revolution.* 1965. New York: Penguin Books, 1977. Print.

—-. *The Origins of Totalitarianism*, revised edition. 1951. New York: Schocken, 2004. Print.

Aristotle. *Introduction to Aristotle.* 1947. Ed. Richard McKeon. New York: Random House/Modern Library, 1992. Print.

—-. *Politics.* Mineola, NY: Dover, 2000. Print.

Armstrong, Karen. *Holy War: The Crusades and Their Impact on Today's World.* 1988. New York: Anchor Books, 2001. Print.

Asprey, Robert. *The Reign of Napoleon Bonaparte.* New York: Basic Books, 2002. Print.

Avritzer, Leonardo. *Participatory Institutions in Democratic Brazil.* Baltimore: Johns Hopkins University Press, 2009. Print.

Barber, Benjamin R. *Strong Democracy: Participatory Politics for a New Age.* Berkeley: University of California Press, 1984. Print.

Barker, Francis. *The Political Thought of Plato and Aristotle*. New York: Dover, 1959. Print.

Barzun, Jacques. *From Dawn to Decadence: 500 Years of Western Cultural Life*. New York: HarperCollins, 2000. Print.

Beard, Charles. *An Economic Interpretation of the Constitution*. MacMillan, 1913. Mineola, NY: Dover Publications, 2004. Print.

Berman, Morris. *Dark Ages America: The Final Phase of Empire*. New York: W.W. Norton, 2006. Print.

Bernays, Edward. *Propaganda*. New York: H. Liveright, 1928. Reprinted with introduction by Mark Crispin Miller. Brooklyn, NY: Ig Publishing, 2005. Page citations refer to the 2005 edition. Print.

Blum, William. *Killing Hope: U.S. Military and CIA Interventions*. Monroe, ME: Common Courage Press, 1995. Print.

Bourne, Randolph. "War Is the Health of the State." 1918. Web. <http://struggle.ws/hist_texts/warhealth-state1918.html>.

"Brazilian Constitution." n.d. Web. <http://www.v-brazil.com/government/laws/>.

Brinton, Crane. *A Decade of Revolution, 1789–1799*. 1934. New York: Harper and Row, 1963. Print.

Brown, Ellen. "Growing Number of Candidates Campaign for State-Owned Banks." *Huffington Post*, February 22, 2010. Web. <http://www.huffington-post.com/ellen-brown/growing-number-of-candida_b_470411.html>.

Brown, Norman O. *Love's Body*. New York: Random House, 1966. Print.

Burckhardt, Jacob. *The Civilization of the Renaissance in Italy* [translation of *Die Kultur der Renaissance in Italien*]. 1860. New York: Harper and Brothers, 1958. Print.

Burgh, James. *Political Disquisitions: Or, An Enquiry into Public Errors, Defects, and Abuses*, 3 volumes. Philadelphia, 1775. Carlisle, MA: Applewood Books, 2009. Print.

Chang, Matthias. "The Shadow Money Lenders: The Real Significance of the Fed's Zero-Interest-Rate Policy (ZIRP)." *Global Research*, December 26, 2008. Web. <http://www.globalresearch.ca/index.php?context=va&aid=11491>.

Chapman, Peter. *Bananas: How the United Fruit Company Shaped the World*. Edinburgh, Scotland: Canongate Books, 2007. Print.

Chernow, Ron. *Alexander Hamilton*. New York: Penguin Press, 2004. Print.

Cicero. *The Republic and The Laws*. Trans. Niall Rudd, with an introduction and notes by Jonathan Powell and Niall Rudd. 1998. Oxford, UK: Oxford University Press, 2008. Print.

Cleckley, Hervey Milton. *The Mask of Sanity*. 1941. St. Louis: Mosby, 1964. Print.

Cobban, Alfred. *A History of Modern France*, 2 vols. Middlesex, UK: Penguin Books, 1957. Print.

Cockburn, Alexander. "How the British Destroyed India." *CounterPunch*, August 6–8, 2005. Web. <http://www.counterpunch.org/2005/08/06/the-rise-and-fall-of-chandrababu-naidu-western-poster-boy-parrots-that-read-tarot-a-brothel-in-mumbai-how-the-british-destroyed-india/>.

Dalberg-Acton, John Emerich Edward [Lord Acton]. *Historical Essays and Studies*. Eds. John Neville Figgis and Reginald Vere Laurence. London: Macmillan, 1907. Web. <http://oll.libertyfund.org/title/2201/203934>.

Da Padova, Marsiglio. *Defensor pacis*. 1324. Web. <http://www.archive.org/stream/defensorpacisofm08emer/defensorpacisofm08emer_djvu.txt>.

Davis, Kenneth C. *America's Hidden History: Untold Tales of the First Pilgrims,*

*Fighting Women, and Forgotten Founders Who Shaped a Nation.* New York: HarperCollins, 2008. Print.

DeCarolis, Lisa Marie. "A Biography of Alexander Hamilton (1755–1804)." *From Revolution to Reconstruction,* University of Groningen, 1994–2010. Web. <http://odur.let.rug.nl/~usa/B/hamilton/hamilxx.htm>.

De Grazia, Sebastian. *The Political Community: A Study of Anomie.* Chicago: University of Chicago Press, 1948. Print.

de Levita, David J. *The Concept of Identity.* Translated by Ian Finlay. Paris: Mouton, 1965. Print.

Dewey, John. *The Public and Its Problems.* New York: H. Holt, 1929. Print.

Dickens, Charles. *Bleak House.* London, 1852–1853. New York: New American Library, 1964. Print.

Dolbeare, Kenneth M. *Political Change in the United States: A Framework of Analysis.* New York: McGraw-Hill, 1974. Print.

Dunn, John, Editor. *Democracy: The Unfinished Journey, 508 B.C. to A.D. 1993.* 1992. Oxford, UK: Oxford University Press, 2001. Print.

Durkheim, David Émile. *Suicide.* 1897. New York: Free Press, 1997. Print.

Edmonds, David, and John Eidinow. *Wittgenstein's Poker: The Story of a Ten-Minute Argument Between Two Great Philosophers.* New York: HarperCollins, 2001. Print.

Ellis, Joseph J. *His Excellency: George Washington.* New York: Vintage Books, 2005. Print.

Emerson, Ralph Waldo. *Emerson's Essays.* Ed. Arthur Hobson Quinn. New York: Charles Scribner's Sons, 1920. Print.

—-. *The Journals and Miscellaneous Notebooks of Ralph Waldo Emerson,* Vol. III. *1826–1832.* Eds. William H. Gilman et al. Cambridge, MA: Harvard University Press, 1963. Print.

—-. *Selections from Ralph Waldo Emerson.* Ed. S. Wicher. New York: Houghton Mifflin, 1960. Print.

Erikson, Erik H. "Ego Development and Historical Change." In *Identity and the Life Cycle: Selected Papers by Erik H. Erikson.* Monograph 1 of *Psychological Issues,* 1 (1). New York: International Universities Press, 1959. Print.

Esar, Evan. *20,000 Quips and Quotations.* New York: Doubleday, 1968. Print.

Farrand, Max (ed.). *The Records of the Federal Convention of 1787,* 4 vols. New Haven, CT: Yale University Press, 1911. Volumes 1–3. Web. <http://memory.loc.gov/ammem/amlaw/lwfr.html>.

Finley, M. I. *Democracy Ancient and Modern.* 1973. New Brunswick, NJ: Rutgers University Press, 1996. Print.

—-. ed. *The Portable Greek Historians: The Essence of Herodotus, Thucydides, Xenophon, Polybius.* 1959. New York: Penguin Books, 1977. Print.

Flower, Harriet I., ed. *The Cambridge Companion to the Roman Republic.* Cambridge, UK: Cambridge University Press, 2004. Print.

Floyd, Chris. "Churchill—Drunk with Thrill of Genocide." *Moscow Times,* January 9, 2004. Web. <http://www.rense.com/general47/thil.htm>.

Forster, E. M. *Two Cheers for Democracy.* New York: Harcourt, Brace World, 1951. Print.

Fossedal, Gregory A. *Direct Democracy in Switzerland.* 2002. New Brunswick, NJ: Transaction Publishers, 2009. Print.

"14 US States Challenge Health Care Reform." *AFP,* March 23, 2010. Web. <http://www.thefreelibrary.com/14+US+states+challenge+health+care+reform-a01612174938>.

Freeman, Charles. *The Greek Achievement*. New York: Penguin Books, 1999. Print.

Freire, Paulo. *Education for Critical Consciousness*. London: Crossroad, 1974. Print.

"French Constitution of 1793." Web. <http://chnm.gmu.edu/revolution/d/430/>.

Fresia, Jerry. *Toward an American Revolution: Exposing the Constitution and Other Illusions*. Boston: South End Press, 1988. Print.

Freud, Sigmund. "Thoughts for the Times on War and Death," *in* James Strachey (ed.), *The Standard Edition of the Complete Psychological Works of Sigmund Freud*, Vol. XIV. *1914–1916: On the History of the Psycho-Analytic Movement, Papers on Metapsychology and Other Works*, p. 281ff. London: Hogarth Press, 1915. Web. <http://www.pep-web.org/document.php?id=se.014.0000a>.

Fromm, Erich. *The Anatomy of Human Destructiveness*. 1973. New York: Henry Holt, 1992. Print.

Geisst, Charles R. *Wall Street: A History, from Its Beginnings to the Fall of Enron*. New York: Oxford University Press, 1997. Print.

George, Henry. *Progress and Poverty*. 1879. New York: The Robert Schalkenbach Foundation, 1992. Print.

—-. *Social Problems*. 1883. New York: The Robert Schalkenbach Foundation, 1992. Print.

Gilbert, G. M. *Nuremberg Diary*. New York: Farrar, Straus, 1947. Print.

Gladwell, Malcolm. *Outliers*. New York: Little Brown, 2008. Print.

Godwin, William. *Enquiry Concerning Political Justice and Its Influence on Morals and Happiness*, 4th edition. London: J. Watson, 1842. Web. <http://dwardmac.pitzer.edu/Anarchist_Archives/godwin/PJfrontpiece.html>.

Goldstein, Jeffrey. "Emergence as a Construct: History and Issues." *Emergence: Complexity and Organization*, 1 (1, 1999): 49–72. Print.

Gordon, John Steele. "The Great Crash (of 1792)." *American Heritage*, 50 (3, May–June 1999): 20, 24. Web. <http://www.americanheritage.com/content/great-crash-1792>.

Gruen, Arno. *The Insanity of Normality: Toward Understanding Human Destructiveness*. 1963. Berkeley, CA: Human Development Books, 1992. Print.

—-. "An Unrecognized Pathology: The Mask of Humaneness." *Journal of Psychohistory*, 30 (3, Winter 2003): 266–272. Print.

Guha, Ramachandra. *India After Gandhi: The History of the World's Largest Democracy*. New York: Harper Perennial, 2007. Print.

Gunnell, John G. *Political Philosophy and Time*. Middletown, CT: Wesleyan University Press, 1968. Print.

Habermas, Jürgen. *Between Facts and Norms: Contributions to a Discourse Theory of Law and Democracy*. Cambridge, MA: MIT Press, 1998. Print.

—-. "Popular Sovereignty as Procedure," *in* James Bohman and William Regh (eds.), *Deliberative Democracy: Essays on Reason and Politics*. Cambridge, MA: MIT Press, 1997. Print.

—-. *The Structural Transformation of the Public Sphere*. Cambridge, MA: MIT Press, 1991. Print.

Halperin, Charles J. *Russia and the Golden Horde: The Mongol Impact on Medieval Russian History*. Bloomington: Indiana University Press, 1985. Print.

Hamilton, Alexander, James Madison, and John Jay. *The Federalist Papers*. Ed. Clinton Rossiter. New York: New American Library, Penguin Putnam, 1961. Reprinted with replacement introduction and additional notes by Charles R. Kessler. 1999. New York: Signet Classic, Penguin Putnam, 2003. Page citations for individual letters refer to the 2003 edition. Print.

Hanson, Victor Davis. *Carnage and Culture: Landmark Battles in the Rise of Western Power.* New York: Anchor Books, 2001. Print.

Hegel, Georg Wilhelm Friedrich. *The Philosophy of History.* New York: Dover Publications, [1821 – 1831] 1956. Print.

Helvétius, Claude Adrien. *De l'Esprit.* 1758. Paris: Editions Sociales, 1968. Print.

Herbert, Christopher. *War of No Pity: The Indian Mutiny and Victorian Trauma.* Princeton, NJ: Princeton University Press, 2008. Print.

Herold, J. Christopher. *The Age of Napoleon.* New York: American Heritage, 1963. Print.

Hess, Karl. *Community Technology.* 1979. Port Townsend, WA: Loompanics Unlimited, 1995. Print.

Hofstadter, Richard. *Anti-Intellectualism in American Life.* New York: Vintage Books, 1962. Print.

Holton, Woody. *Unruly Americans and the Origins of the Constitution.* New York: Hill and Wang, 2007. Print.

Hsu, Tanya Cariina. "Death of the American Empire: America Is Self-Destructing & Bringing the Rest of the World Down with It." *Global Research,* October 23, 2008. Web. <http://www.globalresearch.ca/index.php?context=va&aid=10651>.

Hunn, Dwayne, and Doris Ober. *Ordinary People Doing the Extraordinary: The Story of Ed and Joyce Koupal and the Initiative Process.* Los Angeles: People's Lobby, 2001. Print.

Husband, Herman. *Proposals to Amend and Perfect the Policy of the Government of the United States of America.* Philadelphia, 1782. Print.

Huxley, Aldous. *Brave New World.* 1932. New York: Harper Perennial Modern Classics, 2006. Print.

Ibn Khaldun. *Prolegomena.* 1370. Abridged edition. Princeton, NJ: Princeton University Press, 2004. Print.

*Insight Guide: India.* London: Apa Publications, 1998. Print.

Jaeger, Werner. *Paideia: The Ideals of Greek Culture,* 3 vols. New York: Oxford University Press, 1939–1944. Print.

James, Alexander. "The History of Money." *Portland Independent Media Center,* June 22, 2003. Web. <http://nesara.insights2.org/MH1.html>.

Johnston, David Cay. *Free Lunch: How the Wealthiest Americans Enrich Themselves at Government Expense and Stick You with the Bill.* New York: Penguin Group, 2007. Print.

Journal of the Senate of the United States of America, Being the First Session of the Twenty-*Second Congress* ..., pp. 433–446. Web. <http://books.google.com/books?id=PZVHAQAAIAAJ&source=gbs_navlinks_s>.

Kangas, Steve. "Timeline of CIA Atrocities." n.d. Web. <http://www.serendipity.li/cia/cia_time.htm>.

Katz, William Loren. "Iraq, the US and an Old Lesson," *CounterPunch,* April 28, 2004. Web. <http://www.counterpunch.org/katz04282004.html>.

Kennedy, Margrit. *Interest and Inflation Free Money: Creating an Exchange Medium that Works for Everybody and Protects the Earth.* 1987. Sydney, Australia: Seva International, 1995. Web. <http://userpage.fu-berlin.de/~roehrigw/kennedy/english/>.

Kernberg, Otto F. "The Psychotherapeutic Management of Psychopathic, Narcissistic, and Paranoid Transferences," *in* Theodore Millon (ed.), *Psychopathy: Antisocial, Criminal and Violent Behavior.* New York: Guilford Press, 2003. Print.

Ketcham, Christopher. "The Secessionist Campaign for the Republic of Vermont."

*Time*, January 31, 2010. Web. <http://www.informationclearinghouse.info/article24541.htm>.

Kitto, H. D. F. *The Greeks.* 1951. New York: Penguin Books, 1979. Print.

Kline, Harvey F. *A Concise Introduction to Latin American Politics and Development.* New York: Westview Press, 2007. Print.

Kramer, Samuel Noah. *Cradle of Civilization.* New York: Time-Life Books, 1967. Print.

Lewis, Charles, and the Center for Public Integrity. *The Buying of the President 2000.* New York: Avon Books, 2000. Print.

Linebaugh, Peter. *The Magna Carta Manifesto: Liberties and Commons for All.* Berkeley: University of California Press, 2008. Print.

Link, Eugene Perry. *Democratic-Republican Societies, 1790–1800.* New York: Columbia University Press, 1942. Print.

Linott, Andrew. *The Roman Republic.* Great Britain: Sutton Publishing, 2000. Print.

Litvinsky, Marina. "Corruption-US: How Wall Street Paid for Its Own Funeral." *IPS*, March 4, 2009. Web. <http://www.informationclearinghouse.info/article22146.htm>.

Lloyd, Thomas. *The Congressional Register: Or, History of the Proceedings and Debates of the First House of Representatives of the United States of America.* New York: Harrison and Purdy, 1789. Print.

Lorenzetti, Ambrogio. "Frescoes of the Good and Bad Government." n.d. Web. <http://www.wga.hu/frames-e.html?/html/l/lorenzet/ambrogio/governme/>.

Lynd, Helen Merrell. *On Shame and the Search for Identity.* London: Routledge & Kegan Paul, 1958. Print.

Madron, Roy, and John Jopling. *Gaian Democracies: Redefining Globalisation and People-Power.* Devon, UK: Green Books, 2003. Print.

Main, Jackson Turner. *The Anti-Federalists: Critics of the Constitution, 1781–1788.* 1961. New York: W. W. Norton, 1974. Print.

Marcuse, Herbert. *Reason and Revolution: Hegel and the Rise of Social Theory.* 1941. Boston: Beacon Press, 1969. Print.

Margolis, Michael. *Viable Democracy.* New York: Penguin Books, 1979. Print.

Martin, Harry V. "The Executive Order: A Presidential Power Not Designated by the Constitution." *FreeAmerica*, 1995. Web. <http://dmc.members.sonic.net/sentinel/gvcon5.html>.

Martines, Lauro. *Power and Imagination: City-States in Renaissance Italy.* New York: Knopf, 1979. Baltimore, MD: Johns Hopkins University Press, 1992. Print.

Marx, Karl. *Capital*, Vol. 1. *A Critique of Political Economy.* 1867. Ed. Friedrich Engels. London: Penguin Classics, 1990.

—-. *Writings of the Young Marx on Philosophy and Society.* Trans. L. D. Easton and K. H. Guddat. New York: Doubleday Anchor Books, 1967.

—-. "The Duchess of Sutherland and Slavery," *The People's Paper,* No 45, March 12, 1853. <http://www.marxists.org/archive/marx/works/1853/03/12.htm>.

Marx, Karl, and Friedrich Engels. *The Communist Manifesto.* 1848. New York: Signet Classic, 1998. Print.

Mason, George. "Objections to the Constitution of Government Formed by the Convention," ca. September 17, 1787 [manuscript document]. George Washington Papers, Manuscript Division, Library of Congress. Web. <http://www.virginiamemory.com/online_classroom/shaping_the_constitution/doc/masons_objections>.

Mazza, Jerry. "Thanks for nothing, Mr. 'Health Care Reform' President." *Online Journal,* March 26, 2010. Web. <http://www.freedomportal.net/index.php?topic=16277.0>.

McCarthy, Coleman. "The Consequences of Covert Tactics." *Washington Post*, December 13, 1987. Print.

McCullough, David. *John Adams*. New York: Simon and Schuster, 2001. Print.

McMaken, Ryan. "The 'Founding Fathers'." October 31, 2005. Web. <http://www.lewrockwell.com/mcmaken/mcmaken110.html>.

Mencken, H. L. *Notes on Democracy*. New York: Knopf, 1926. Reprinted with introduction and annotations by Marion Elizabeth Rodgers. New York: Dissident Books, 2009. Print.

Mill, John Stuart. "Considerations on Representative Government," *in* Geraint Williams (ed.), *Utilitarianism; On Liberty; Considerations on Representative Government; Remarks on Bentham's Philosophy*. 1861. London: Dent, Everyman Library, 1993. Print.

—-. "On Liberty," *in* Geraint Williams (ed.), *Utilitarianism; On Liberty; Considerations on Representative Government; Remarks on Bentham's Philosophy*. 1859. London: Dent, Everyman Library, 1993. Print.

Miller, Alice. *Banished Knowledge*. 1988. New York: Anchor Books, 1990. Print.

Miller, Joshua. *The Rise and Fall of Democracy in Early America, 1630–1789*. University Park: Pennsylvania State University Press, 1991. Print.

Mills, C. Wright. *The Power Elite*. 1956. New York: Oxford University Press, 2000. Print.

Montesquieu, Charles-Louis de Secondat, Baron de La Brède et de. *De l'Esprit des Lois*. 1748. Paris: Editions Garnier Frères, 1961. Print.

Morgenson, Gretchen, and Don van Natta Jr., "Paulson's Calls to Goldman Tested Ethics." *New York Times*, August 8, 2009. Web. <http://www.nytimes.com/2009/08/09/business/09paulson.html?adxnnl=1&pagewanted=all&adxnnlx=1323781605-0/ym3oMnHvFecWlSM9pByQ>.

Mosca, Gaetano. *The Ruling Class (Elimenti di Scienza Politica)*. New York: McGraw Hill, 1939. Print.

Mukerjee, Madhusree. *Churchill's Secret War: The British Empire and theRavaging of India during World War II*. New York: Basic Books, 2010. Print.

Muzzey, David S. *An American History*. Boston: Ginn, 1911. Print.

"National debt." n.d. Web. <http://www.federalbudget.com/>.

Nin, Anaïs. *The Diary of Anaïs Nin*, Vol. 3. *1939–1944*. New York: Harcourt Brace, 1969. Print.

—-. *The Diary of Anaïs Nin*, Vol. 6. New York: Harcourt Brace, 1969. Print.

Orwell, George. "Inside the Whale," in *A Collection of Essays by George Orwell*. 1946. New York: Harcourt, Brace, Jovanovich, 1953. Print.

Paine, Thomas. *The Complete Writings of Thomas Paine*. Edited with an introduction by Philip S. Foner. New York: The Citadel Press, 1945. Print.

Palast, Greg. *The Best Democracy Money Can Buy: An Investigative Reporter Exposes the Truth about Globalization, Corporate Cons, and High-Finance Fraudsters*. 2002. New York: Penguin, 2004. Print.

Parenti, Michael. *The Assassination of Julius Caesar: A People's History of Ancient Rome*. New York: The New Press, 2003. Print.

—-. *History as Mystery*. San Francisco: City Lights Books, 1999. Print.

Parker, Richard D. *Here, the People Rule: A Constitutional Populist Manifesto*. Cambridge, MA: Harvard University Press, 1994. Print.

Parrington, Vernon L. *The Colonial Mind, 1620–1800*. 1927. New York: Harcourt Brace & World, 1954. Print.

Perkins, John. *Confessions of an Economic Hit Man*. San Francisco: Berrett-

Koehler, 2004. Print.

Peterson, Merrill D. *The Portable Jefferson.* New York: Viking Penguin, 1975. Print.

Pirenne, J. *History of the Universe.* Paris, n.p., 1950. Print.

Plato. *The Republic of Plato.* Trans. with an introduction and notes by Francis MacDonald Cornford. New York: Oxford University Press, 1958. Print.

Pollock, George H. "Process and Affect: Mourning and Grief." *International Journal of Psychoanalysis,* 59 (1978): 255–276. Print.

Popper, Karl R. *The Open Society and Its Enemies,* Vol. 1. *The Spell of Plato.* 1962. Princeton, NJ: Princeton University Press, 1971. Print.

Potter, David M. "The Quest for National Character," *in* John Higham (ed.), *The Reconstruction of American History.* New York: Harper Torch Books, 1962. Print.

Pranger, Robert J. *The Eclipse of Citizenship: Power and Participation in Contemporary Politics.* New York: Holt, Rinehart and Winston, 1968. Print.

Reich, Wilhelm. "The Imposition of Sexual Morality," in Lee Baxandall (ed.), *Sex-Pol: Essays, 1929–1934.* New York: Vintage Books, 1972. Print.

Revel, Jean-François. *Without Marx or Jesus.* New York: Doubleday, 1971. Print.

Richman, Sheldon. "War Is a Government Program." *Future of Freedom Foundation,* May 30, 2007. Web. <http://www.informationclearinghouse.info/article17799.htm>.

Rogers, Guy MacLean. *Alexander: The Ambiguity of Greatness.* New York: Random House, 2004. Print.

Rosenman, Stanley. "The Usurpation of Identity." *Journal of Psychohistory,* 30 (2, Fall 2002): 190–208. Print.

Rousseau, Jean-Jacques. *Du Contrat Social.* 1762. Paris: Editions Garnier Frères, 1962. Print.

Rudé, Georges. *The Crowd in History: A Study of Popular Disturbances in France and England 1730–1748.* New York: John Wiley & Sons, 1964. Print.

—-. *The Crowd in the French Revolution.* New York: Oxford University Press, 1959. Print.

"Rules of debate." May 28–29, 1787. Web. <http://avalon.law.yale.edu/18th_century/debates_528.asp> *and* <http://avalon.law.yale.edu/18th_century/debates_528.asp>.

Russell, Bertrand. *A History of Western Philosophy.* 1945. New York: Touchstone, 1972. Print.

Schom, Alan. *Napoleon Bonaparte: A Life.* New York: Harper Perennial, 1998. Print.

Schoon, Darryl. "Davos Debt & Denial." *Financial Sense,* February 13, 2009. Web. <http://www.financialsense.com/fsu/editorials/schoon/2009/0213.html>.

Schumpeter, Joseph A. *Capitalism, Socialism and Democracy.* 1942. Third edition reprinted with an introduction by Thomas K. McCraw. New York: HarperPerennial Modern Classics, 2008. Print.

Selsam, J. Paul. *The Pennsylvania Constitution of 1776.* 1936. New York: Octagon Books, 1971. Print.

Shalom, Stephen. "A Political System for a Good Society." *ZNet,* May 19, 2006. Web. <http://www.zcommunications.org/a-political-system-for-a-good-society-by-stephen1-shalom>.

Shankman, Andrew. *Crucible of American Democracy: The Struggle to Fuse Egalitarianism and Capitalism in Jeffersonian Pennsylvania.* Lawrence: University Press of Kansas, 2004. Print.

Shenkman, Richard. *Gaining Power at Any Cost: Presidential Ambition.* New York: HarperCollins, 1999. Print.

Shiva, Vandana. *Earth Democracy: Justice, Sustainability, and Peace.* Cambridge,

MA: South End Press, 2005. Print.

Shulberg, Lucille. *Historic India*. 1967. New York: Time-Life Books, 1973. Print.

Sinclair, R. K. *Democracy and Participation in Athens*. 1988. New York: Cambridge University Press, 1993. Print.

Slater, Philip E. *A Dream Deferred: America's Discontent and the Search for a New Democratic Ideal*. 1991. Boston: Beacon Press, 2001. Print.

—-. *The Glory of Hera: Greek Mythology and the Greek Family*. Boston: Beacon Press, 1968. Print.

—-. *The Pursuit of Loneliness*. New York: Beacon Press, 1970. Print.

Stone, I. F. *The Trial of Socrates*. Boston: Little, Brown, 1988. Print.

Storing, Herbert J. (ed.). *The Anti-Federalist: Writings by the Opponents of the Constitution*. Chicago: University of Chicago Press, 1985. Print.

Strayer, Joseph R. "The Two Levels of Feudalism," *in* Robert S. Hoyt, *Life and Thought in the Early Middle Ages*. Minneapolis: University of Minnesota Press, 1967. Print.

—-. *Western Europe in the Middle Ages*. New York: Appleton-Century-Crofts, 1955. Print.

Taibbi, Matt. "The Great American Bubble Machine." *Rolling Stone*. Reprinted online April 5, 2010, from July 9, 2009, issue. Web. <http://www.rollingstone. com/politics/news/the-great-american-bubble-machine-20100405>.

Taylor, Alan. *American Colonies: The Settling of North America*. New York: Penguin, 2002. Print.

Tolstoy, Leo. Anna Karenina. 1877. New York: Random House, Modern Library, 2000. Print.

—-. *War and Peace*. 1869. New York: Random House, Modern Library, 2008. Print.

Tocqueville, Alexis de. *Democracy in America*, Vol. I. Paris, 1835. New York: Vintage Books, 1945. Print.

—-. *Democracy in America*, Vol. II. Paris, 1840. New York: Vintage Books, 1958/1945. Print.

Toussaint, Auguste. History of the Indian Ocean. London: Routledge & Kegan Paul, 1966. Print.

Toynbee, Arnold Joseph. *A Study of History*, 10 volumes. Originally published 1934–1961. Abridgment of Volumes 1–6 by D. C. Somervell. New York: Oxford University Press 1987. Print.

Trenchard, John, and Thomas Gordon. *Cato's Letters: Or, Essays on Liberty, Civil and Religious, and Other Important Subjects*. Annotated by Ronald Hamowy (ed.), 2 vols.; updated version of the 4-volume 6th edition published in 1755. Indianapolis, IN: Liberty Fund, 1995.

Vankin, Jonathan, and John Whalen. *The 60 Greatest Conspiracies of All Time*. Secaucus, NJ: Citadel Press, 1997. Print.

"Venezuelan constitution." n.d. Web. <http://en.wikisource.org/wiki/Constitution_of_the_Bolivarian_Republic_of_Venezuela>.

Vidal, Gore. *Inventing a Nation: Washington, Adams, Jefferson*. New Haven, CT: Yale University Press, 2003. Print.

—-. *The Second American Revolution and Other Essays (1976–1982)*. New York: Vintage Books, 1983. Print.

Waley, Daniel. *The Italian City-Republics*. 1979. London: Longman Group UK, 1988. Print.

Wallace, Robert. *Rise of Russia*. New York: Time-Life Books, 1967. Print.

Walsh, William Thomas. *Phillip II*. 1937. Rockford, IL: TAN Books, 1987. Print.

Washington, George. *The Papers of George Washington*. n.d. Web. <http://gwpa-

pers.virginia.edu/index.html>.

—-. "George Washington to James Madison, 5 November 1786." Web. *The Papers of George Washington.* http://gwpapers.virginia.edu/documents/constitution/1784/madison2.html>.

Weatherford, Jack. *Genghis Khan and the Making of the Modern World.* New York: Crown, 2004. Print.

Weber, Max. *Political Writings.* Cambridge, UK: Cambridge University Press, [1895–1919] 2003. Print.

—-. *The Protestant Ethic and the Spirit of Capitalism.* 1905. New York: Routledge, 2001. Print.

*Webster's New World Dictionary*, 2nd college edition. New York: Simon and Schuster, 1982. Print.

White, Hayden. *Metahistory: The Historical Imagination in Nineteenth Century Europe.* Baltimore: Johns Hopkins University Press, 1973. Print.

Whitman, Walt. *Leaves of Grass.* Edited by S. Bradley. New York: Holt, 1949. Print.

Wiarda, Howard J., and Peter R. Kingstone (eds.). *Readings in Latin American Politics: Challenges to Democratization.* New York: Houghton Mifflin, 2006. Print.

Wikse, John. *About Possession: The Self as Private Property.* University Park: Pennsylvania State University Press, 1977. Print.

Wills, Garry. *James Madison.* New York: Time Books, 2002. Print.

Wilpert, Gregory. *Changing Venezuela by Taking Power: The History and Policies of the Chavez Government.* New York: Verso, 2006. Print.

Wirth, Hans-Jürgen. "9/11 as a Collective Trauma." *Journal of Psychohistory*, 30 (4, Spring 2003): 364. Print.

Wolin, Sheldon S. *Democracy Incorporated: Managed Democracy and the Specter of Inverted Totalitarianism.* Princeton, NJ: Princeton University Press, 2008. Print.

Zakaria, Fareed. *The Post-American World.* New York: W. W. Norton, 2008. Print.

Zamoyski, Adam. *Holy Madness: Romantics, Patriots and Revolutionaries.* New York: Penguin, 2001.

Zinn, Howard. *A People's History of the United States: 1492–Present.* 1980. New York: HarperPerennial, 1990. Print.

# INDEX

*Arthur D. Robbins, Ph.D.*

Arthur D. Robbins is a psychologist with a practice in Manhattan. He has a bachelor's degree in English from Queens College, a doctorate in psychology from the New School for Social Research and a doctorate in French and Romance Philology from Columbia University, where he specialized in 18th century political thought. Dr. Robbins spent a year and a half in Paris studying psychopathology at the Sorbonne. His articles on French literature and psychopathology have appeared in scholarly journals.